All in One®

Recommended by Teachers, Trusted by Toppers

BUSINESS STUDIES

Class 11

EVERYTHING YOU NEED TO SCORE

- *Simplified NCERT Theory*
- *Chapter Exercise*
- *All Types of Exam Pattern Questions*
- *CBQs; MCQs, A-R, Case Based*
- *Sample Question Papers*

CBSE Exams 2026

Author
Ishita Agarwal

arihant
SUCCESS AND NOTHING LESS

arihant
SUCCESS AND NOTHING LESS

ARIHANT PRAKASHAN
(School Division Series)

卐 ADMINISTRATIVE & PRODUCTION OFFICES

Regd. Office

'Ramchhaya' 4577/15, Agarwal Road, Darya Ganj, New Delhi -110002
Tele: 011- 47630600, 43518550; Fax: 011- 23280316

卐 *Head Office*

Kalindi, TP Nagar, Meerut (UP) - 250002, Tel: 0121-7156203, 7156204

卐 SALES & SUPPORT OFFICES

Agra, Ahmedabad, Bengaluru, Bareilly, Chennai, Delhi, Guwahati, Hyderabad, Jaipur, Jhansi, Kolkata, Lucknow, Nagpur & Pune.

PO No : TXT-XX-XXXXXXX-X-XX

Published By Arihant Publications (India) Ltd.

For further information about the books published by Arihant, log on to www.arihantbooks.com or e-mail at info@arihantbooks.com

Follow us on

卐 PRICE ₹375.00

PRODUCTION TEAM

Publishing Managers
Mahendra Singh Rawat & Keshav Mohan

Cover Designer
Salman Shaikh

Inner Designer
Ankit Tyagi

Project Head
Saurabh Gupta

Page Layouting
Amit Bansal

Proof Reader
Apoorvi

Index *cum* Study Planner

One Book- Endless Features
to Help you Succeed

01
CHAPTER

Evolution and Fundamentals of Business

Business is an institution organised and operated to provide goods and services to society under the incentive of private gain.
— *BO Wheeler*

YOUR STUDY GOALS
1.1 History of Trade and Commerce in India
1.2 Rise of Intermediaries
1.3 Human Activities
1.4 Concept of Business
1.5 Classification of Business Activities
1.6 Business Risk

YOUR PRACTICE GOAL
- Objective Type Questions (70 Qs ; MCQs, A-R, Statements, Matching)
- Subjective Questions (15 SAs, 9 LAs)
- Case Study Based Questions (Short Case Studies-10, Long Case Studies-1)
- Self Assessment Test (8 MCQs, 7 SAs, 3 LAs)

1.1 History of Trade and Commerce in India

Archaeological evidences have shown that trade and commerce was the mainstay of economy of ancient India, carried out by both water and land routes.

Silk route was an ancient network of trade routes and helped in establishing commercial and political contacts of India with adjoining foreign kingdoms and empires of Asia and the world. Spice route was used for the trade of spices and linked the East and West by sea.

Trade and commerce have helped India play a vital role in the economic world in the following ways
- During ancient times, Indians were the masters of the seaborne trade of Europe, Asia and Africa.
- In the beginning of 18th century, almost every nation on Earth obtained its supplies of fine cotton and silk fabric, spices, indigo, sugar, drugs, precious stones and many curious works of art from India in exchange of gold and silver.

In this Chapter

At the start of each chapter, all the chapter topics have been listed, so that students may know what they are going to study.

Gender Equality in the Joint Hindu Family

According to the **Hindu Succession (Amendment) Act, 2005**, the daughter of a coparcener of a joint hindu family shall by birth, become a coparcener. At the time of partition of such a joint hindu family, the coparcenary property shall be equally divided to all the coparceners irrespective of their gender (male or female). The eldest member (either male or female of joint hindu family shall become *karta*. Married daughter has equal rights in property of a joint hindu family.

Boxed Matter

Information in the boxes is given to focus on important points related to the concepts.

Complete Theory in Each Chapter

Each chapter has Complete, Easy to Understand and Simplified theory covering latest syllabus and latest NCERT Textbook. Theory is developed in such a way that it is suitable for all types of learners.

Flow Chart

To quickly recall the concepts, flow charts are given at many places.

1.5 Classification of Business Activities

Business activities can be classified into two broad categories, which are as follows

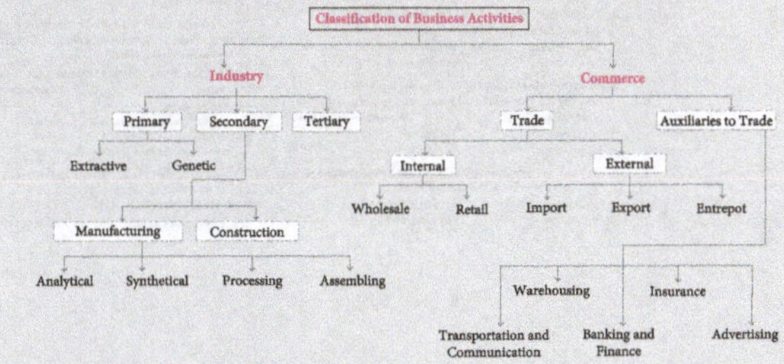

1.2 Rise of Intermediaries

A financial intermediary is an institution or an individual that acts as a middleman to facilitate the channel of funds between lenders and borrowers indirectly. Intermediaries include commission agents, brokers and distributions both for wholesale and retail goods.

Some important **features** of intermediaries are
- Intermediaries provide financial assistance to the business.
- The lenders give funds to these institutions and they extend the funds to borrowers.
- Intermediaries provide financial security to the manufacturers, by taking responsibility for the risks involved, especially in foreign trade.

During the Mughal period and the days of the East India Company, the institution of **Jagat Seths** developed and exercised great influence. Bankers began to act as trustees and executors of endowments (funding). Foreign trade was financed by loans and the rate of interest was kept high for longer voyages. Commercial operations were increased by the emergence of credit transactions and availability of loans and advances.

Transport

It refers to the physical movement of goods from the place of production to the place of consumption. Transport by land and water was popular in the ancient times that helped in maintaining trade. Trade routes were structurally wide and suitable for speed and safety.

Following were the significant regions for maritime trade
- Malabar Coast has a long history of international maritime trade going back to the era of the Roman Empire. Pepper was particularly valued in the Roman Empire and it was known as **Black Gold**.
- An alternate route to India for spices other than Malabar Coast led to the discovery of America by Columbus in 15th century. Spices was also the reason for **Vasco da Gama** visiting the shores of Malabar in 1498.
- Calicut emporium was visited by Chinese ships to acquire items, like frankincense (essential oil) and myrrh (fragrant resin used in perfumes, medicines) from the middle East, as well as pepper, diamonds, pearls and cotton from India.
- On the Coromandel Coast, Pulicat was a major port in the 17th century. Textiles were principally exported from Pulicat to South-East Asia.

One Book- Endless Features

to Help you Succeed

Mind Map

A quick revision visual tool for the complete chapter.

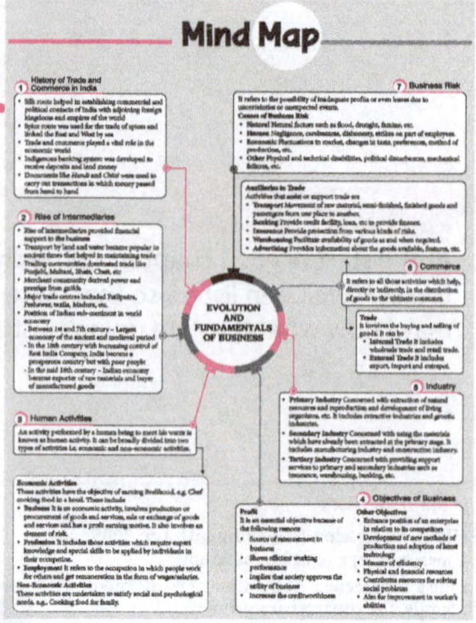

Case Study Based Questions

Short Case Studies

Case Study 1

Rohit is a school teacher who spends his weekdays teaching students at a private school, for which he receives a monthly salary. On weekends, he volunteers at a local animal shelter, where he cares for abandoned pets without any monetary compensation.

Although his teaching job is his primary source of income, he finds immense joy and fulfillment in helping the animals at the shelter.

His weekends provide him with an opportunity to contribute to the community and make a positive impact, even though it doesn't generate any income. This balance between earning and giving back reflects two different types of human activities.

(i) Specify the type of human activities Rohit is involved in during his weekdays and weekends.

(ii) Differentiate between the two activities Rohit engages in on any two basis.

Ans.

(i) The type of human activities Rohit is involved in during his weekdays and weekends are

- Teaching at school – Economic activity
- Volunteering at animal shelter – Non-economic activity

(ii) Following are the differences between economic and non-economic activities

Basis	Economic Activities	Non-economic Activities
Meaning	They are undertaken to earn money or livelihood.	They are undertaken to satisfy social or psychological motives.
Result	They result in production of goods and services.	They result in mental/ psychological satisfaction.

Case Study 2

Charu and Renuka are childhood friends. Charu is a consultant while Renuka is an architect. They contributed equal amounts and purchased a building for ₹ 2 crore. After a year, they sold it for ₹ 3 crore and shared the profits equally.

(i) Are they doing the business? Give reason in support of your answer.

(ii) State the feature of business which is being highlighted in the given example.

Ans.

(i) No, they are not doing business as they are not involved in doing sale and purchase of land/plot on a regular basis. To be a business activity, dealing of goods must be on a regular and recurring basis.

Case Studies

To give the students a practice of applying their knowledge, each chapter has a separate section carrying case studies.

Exam Pattern Questions

To make students completely prepared for examination, Exam Pattern Questions are provided after theory. These questions cover all types of questions, like; MCQs, Case Based Questions, Assertion-Reason, SA & LA Type Questions. All the questions are fully explained helping students to understand, how to write the answers to get full marks in the exam.

EXAM PATTERN QUESTIONS

Objective Type Questions

Multiple Choice Questions (MCQs)

1. .... was an ancient network of trade routes that connected the East and the West.
(a) Spice route (b) Silk route
(c) Sea route (d) None of these

2. Maritime routes that linked the East and the West by sea used for the trade of spices is known as
(a) spice route (b) silk route
(c) sea route (d) ship route

3. "It is payable at sight and is like a demand bill." Identify the type of Hundi mentioned in the given statement. Competency Based Que
(a) Darshani (b) Jokhmi
(c) Sah-jog (d) Dhani-jog

4. .... was the capital of Pandyas who controlled the pearl fisheries of the Gulf of Mannar.
(a) Surat (b) Kanchi
(c) Madura (d) Patliputra

7. Which of the following does not characterise business activity?
(a) Production of goods and services
(b) Presence of risk
(c) Sale or exchange of goods and services
(d) Salary or wages

8. "It emphasises that business activities are conducted to earn money or livelihood, distinguishing it from non-economic activities."
Identify the characteristic of business from the given statement. Competency Based Que
(a) Profit earning
(b) Regular dealings in goods and services
(c) An economic activity
(d) Sale or exchange of goods and services

9. "It highlights that transactions must occur consistently rather than a one time sale or purchase to be considered a part of business."
Identify the characteristic of business from the given

One Book- Endless Features

to Help you Succeed

Self Assessment Test

Complete Test of chapter in Exam format.

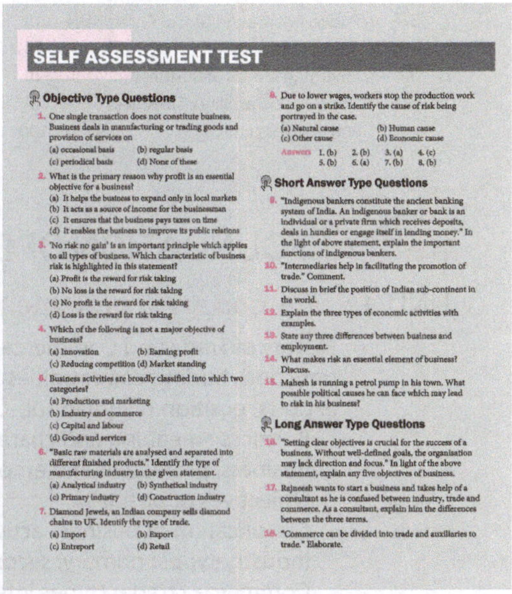

SELF ASSESSMENT TEST

Objective Type Questions

1. One single transaction does not constitute business. Business deals in manufacturing or trading goods and provision of services on
(a) occasional basis (b) regular basis
(c) periodical basis (d) None of these

2. What is the primary reason why profit is an essential objective for a business?
(a) It helps the business to expand only in local markets
(b) It acts as a source of income for the businessman
(c) It ensures that the business pays taxes on time
(d) It enables the business to improve its public relations

3. 'No risk no gain' is an important principle which applies to all types of business. Which characteristic of business risk is highlighted in this statement?
(a) Profit is the reward for risk taking
(b) No loss is the reward for risk taking
(c) No profit is the reward for risk taking
(d) Loss is the reward for risk taking

4. Which of the following is not a major objective of business?
(a) Innovation (b) Earning profit
(c) Reducing competition (d) Market standing

5. Business activities are broadly classified into which two categories?
(a) Production and marketing
(b) Industry and commerce
(c) Capital and labour
(d) Goods and services

6. "Basic raw materials are analysed and separated into different finished products." Identify the type of manufacturing industry in the given statement.
(a) Analytical industry (b) Synthetical industry
(c) Primary industry (d) Construction industry

7. Diamond Jewels, an Indian company sells diamond chains to UK. Identify the type of trade.
(a) Import (b) Export
(c) Entreport (d) Retail

8. Due to lower wages, workers stop the production work and go on a strike. Identify the cause of risk being portrayed in the case.
(a) Natural cause (b) Human cause
(c) Other cause (d) Economic cause

Answers 1. (b) 2. (b) 3. (a) 4. (c) 5. (b) 6. (a) 7. (b) 8. (b)

Short Answer Type Questions

9. "Indigenous bankers constitute the ancient banking system of India. An indigenous banker or bank is an individual or a private firm which receives deposits, deals in hundies or engage itself in lending money." In the light of above statement, explain the important functions of indigenous bankers.

10. "Intermediaries help in facilitating the promotion of trade." Comment.

11. Discuss in brief the position of Indian sub-continent in the world.

12. Explain the three types of economic activities with examples.

13. State any three differences between business and employment.

14. What makes risk an essential element of business? Discuss.

15. Mahesh is running a petrol pump in his town. What possible political causes he can face which may lead to risk in his business?

Long Answer Type Questions

16. "Setting clear objectives is crucial for the success of a business. Without well-defined goals, the organisation may lack direction and focus." In light of the above statement, explain any five objectives of business.

17. Rajneesh wants to start a business and takes help of a consultant as he is confused between industry, trade and commerce. As a consultant, explain him the differences between the three terms.

18. "Commerce can be divided into trade and auxiliaries to trade." Elaborate.

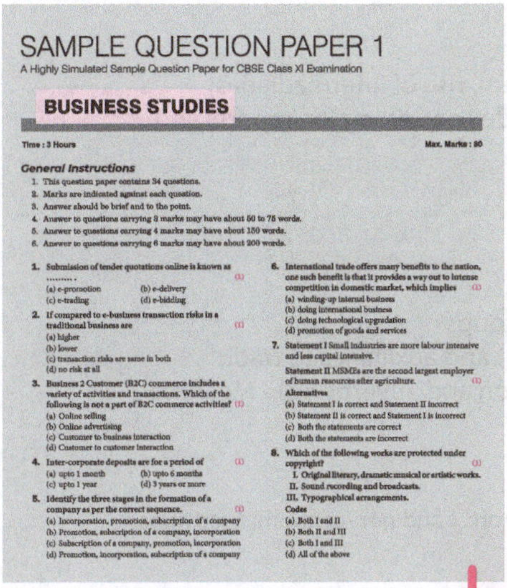

SAMPLE QUESTION PAPER 1

A Highly Simulated Sample Question Paper for CBSE Class XI Examination

BUSINESS STUDIES

Time : 3 Hours Max. Marks : 80

General Instructions

1. This question paper contains 34 questions.
2. Marks are indicated against each question.
3. Answer should be brief and to the point.
4. Answer to questions carrying 3 marks may have about 50 to 75 words.
5. Answer to questions carrying 4 marks may have about 150 words.
6. Answer to questions carrying 6 marks may have about 200 words.

1. Submission of tender quotations online is known as .... (1)
(a) e-promotion (b) e-delivery
(c) e-trading (d) e-bidding

2. If compared to e-business transaction risks in a traditional business are (1)
(a) higher
(b) lower
(c) transaction risks are same in both
(d) no risk at all

3. Business 2 Customer (B2C) commerce includes a variety of activities and transactions. Which of the following is not a part of B2C commerce activities? (1)
(a) Online selling
(b) Online advertising
(c) Customer to business interaction
(d) Customer to customer interaction

4. Inter-corporate deposits are for a period of (1)
(a) upto 1 month (b) upto 6 months
(c) upto 1 year (d) 3 years or more

5. Identify the three stages in the formation of a company as per the correct sequence. (1)
(a) Incorporation, promotion, subscription of a company
(b) Promotion, subscription of a company, incorporation
(c) Subscription of a company, promotion, incorporation
(d) Promotion, incorporation, subscription of a company

6. International trade offers many benefits to the nation, one such benefit is that it provides a way out to intense competition in domestic market, which implies (1)
(a) winding-up internal business
(b) doing international business
(c) doing technological upgradation
(d) promotion of goods and services

7. Statement I Small industries are more labour intensive and less capital intensive.
Statement II MSMEs are the second largest employer of human resources after agriculture. (1)
Alternatives
(a) Statement I is correct and Statement II incorrect
(b) Statement II is correct and Statement I is incorrect
(c) Both the statements are correct
(d) Both the statements are incorrect

8. Which of the following works are protected under copyright? (1)
I. Original literary, dramatic musical or artistic works.
II. Sound recording and broadcasts.
III. Typographical arrangements.
Codes
(a) Both I and II
(b) Both II and III
(c) Both I and III
(d) All of the above

Sample Question Papers

To make students practice of examination in real sense, there are 3 Sample Question Papers at the end. All these Sample Questions Papers are exactly prepared on the latest syllabus & pattern of examination.

Latest Course Structure

Total Marks : 100

Units		Periods	Marks
PART A	**Foundation of Business**		
1.	Nature and Purpose of Business	18	
2.	Forms of Business Organisations	24	16
3.	Public, Private and Global Enterprises	18	
4.	Business Services	18	14
5.	Emerging Modes of Business	10	
6.	Social Responsibility of Business	12	10
	and Business Ethics	**100**	**40**

Units		Periods	Marks
PART B	**Finance and Trade**		
7.	Source of Business Finance	30	
8.	Small Business	16	20
9.	Internal Trade	30	20
10.	International Trade	14	
11.	Project Work	30	20
Total		**120**	**60**

PART A FOUNDATION OF BUSINESS

UNIT 1 Evolution and Fundamentals of Business

History of Trade and Commerce in India : Indigenous banking system, rise of intermediaries, transport, trading communities : merchant corporations, major trade centres, major imports and exports, position of Indian sub-continent in the world economy.

- Business : meaning and characteristics
- Business, profession and employment: Concept
- Objectives of business
- Classification of business activities-Industry and Commerce
- Industry-types: primary, secondary, tertiary-Meaning and sub-groups
- Commerce - trade: (types internal, external, wholesale and retail) and auxiliaries to trade (banking, insurance, transportation, warehousing, communication and advertising) - Meaning
- Business risks - Concept

- To acquaint the history of Trade and Commerce in India.
- Understand the meaning of business with special reference to economic and non-economic activities.
- Discuss the characteristics of business.
- Understand the concept of business, profession and employment.
- Differentiate between business, profession and employment.
- Appreciate the economic and social objectives of business.
- Examine the role of profit in business.
- Understand the broad categories of business activities-industry and commerce.
- Describe the various types of industries.
- Discuss the meaning of commerce, trade and auxiliaries to trade.
- Discuss the meaning of different types of trade and auxiliaries to trade.
- Examine the role of commerce- trade and auxiliaries to trade.
- Understand the concept of risk as a special characteristic of business.
- Examine the nature and causes of business risks.

UNIT 2 Forms of Business Organisations

- Sole Proprietorship-Concept, merits and limitations.
- Partnership-Concept, types, merits and limitations of partnership, registration of a partnership firm, partnership deed. Types of partners
- Hindu Undivided Family Business: Concept
- Cooperative Societies-Concept, merits, and limitations
- Company-Concept, merits and limitations; Types: Private, Public and One Person Company Concept
- Formation of company-stages, important documents to be used in formation of a company.
- Choice of form of business organisation

- List the different forms of business organisations and understand their meaning.
- Identify and explain the concept, merits and limitations of Sole Proprietorship.
- Identify and explain the concept, merits and limitations of a Partnership firm.
- Understand the types of partnership on the basis of duration and on the basis of liability.
- State the need for registration of a partnership firm.
- Discuss types of partners - active, sleeping, secret, nominal and partner by estoppel.
- Understand the concept of Hindu Undivided Family Business.
- Identify and explain the concept, merits and limitations of Cooperative Societies.
- Understand the concept of consumers, producers, marketing, farmers, credit and housing co-operatives.
- Identify and explain the concept, merits and limitations of private and public companies.
- Understand the meaning of one person company.
- Distinguish between a private company and a public company.
- Highlight the stages in the formation of a company.
- Discuss the important documents used at various stages in the formation of a company.
- Distinguish between the various forms of business organisations.
- Explain the factors that influence the choice of a suitable form of business organisation.

UNIT 3 Public, Private and Global Enterprises

- Public sector and private sector enterprises : Concept
- Forms of public sector enterprises : Departmental Undertakings, Statutory Corporations and Government Company.
- Global Enterprises-Features.
- Joint Venture
- Public Private Partnership : Concept

- Develop an understanding of public sector and private sector enterprises
- Identify and explain the features, merits and limitations of different forms of public sector enterprises.
- Develop an understanding of global Enterprises, Public Private Partnership by studying their meaning and features.

UNIT 4 Business Services

- Business services : Meaning and types.
- Banking-Types of Bank accounts-savings, current, recurring, fixed deposit and the multiple option deposit account.
- Banking services with particular reference to Bank Draft, Bank Overdraft, Cash Credit and e-banking : Meaning, Types of digital payments
- Insurance-Principles, Types-life, Health, Fire and marine insurance : Concept
- Postal services-Mail Registered Post, Parcel, Speed post, Courier : Meaning.

- Understand the meaning and types of business services.
- Discuss the meaning and types of business services, banking.
- Develop an understanding of different types of bank account.
- Develop an understanding of the different services provided by banks.
- Recall the concept of insurance.
- Understand Utmost Good Faith, Insurable Interest, Indemnity, Contribution, Doctrine of Subrogation and Causa Proxima as principles of insurance
- Discuss the meaning of different types of insurance-life, health, fire, marine insurance.
- Understand the utility of different telecom services.

UNIT 5 Emerging Modes of Business

- E-business-concept, scope and benefits.

- Give the meaning of e-business.
- Discuss the scope of e-business.
- Appreciate the benefits of e-business
- Distinguish e-business from traditional business.

UNIT 6 Social Responsibility of Business and Business Ethics

- Concept of social responsibility
- Case of social responsibility
- Responsibility towards owners, investors, consumers, employees, government and community
- Role of business in Environment protection
- Business ethics-Concept and Elements

- State the concept of social responsibility.
- Examine the case for social responsibility
- Identify the social responsibility towards different interest groups.
- Appreciate the role of business in environment protection.
- State the concept of business ethics.
- Describe the elements of business ethics.

PART B FINANCE AND TRADE

UNIT 7 Sources of Business Finance

- Concept of business finance
- Owners' funds-equity shares, preference shares, retained earnings
- Borrowed funds: debentures and bonds, loans from financial institution and commercial banks, public deposits, trade credit, Inter Corporate Deposits (ICD).

> - State the meaning, nature and importance of business finance.
> - Classify the various sources of funds into owners' funds.
> - State the meaning of owners' funds.
> - State the meaning of borrowed funds.
> - Discuss the concept of debentures, bonds, loans from financial institutions and Commercial Banks, trade credit and Inter Corporate Deposits.
> - Distinguish between owners' funds and borrowed funds.

UNIT 8 Small Business and Enterprises

- Entrepreneurship Development (ED) : Concept, characteristics and need. Process of Entrepreneurship Development : Start-up India scheme, ways to fund Start-up.
- Intellectual Property Rights and Entrepreneurship.
- Small scale enterprise as defined by MSMED Act 2006 (Micro, Small and Medium Enterprise Development Act).
- Role of small business in India with special reference to rural areas.
- Government schemes and agencies for small scale industries: National Small Industries Corporation (NSIC) and District Industrial Centre (Dic) with special reference to rural, backward areas.

> - Understand the concept of Entrepreneurship Development (ED), IPRs.
> - Understand the meaning of small business
> - Discuss the role of small business in India
> - Appreciate the various government schemes and agencies for development of small scale industries. NSIC and DIC with special reference to rural, backward area.

UNIT 9 Internal Trade

- Internal trade - meaning and types
- Services rendered by a wholesaler and a retailer
- Types of retail - trade - Itinerant and small scale fixed shop retailers
- Large scale retailers - Departmental stores, chain stores concept
- GST (Goods and Services Tax) : Concept and Key Features

- State the meaning and types of internal trade.
- Appreciate the services of wholesalers and retailers.
- Explain the different types of retail trade.
- Highlight the distinctive features of departmental stores, chain stores and mail order business.
- Understand the concept of GST.

UNIT 10 International Trade

- International Trade - concept and benefits
- Export trade- meaning and procedure
- Import trade- meaning and procedure
- Documents involved in International Trade. Indent, letter of credit, shipping order, shipping bills, mate's receipt (DA/DP)
- World Trade Organisation (WTO) meaning and objectives

- Understand the concept of international trade.
- Describe the scope of international trade to the nation and business firms.
- State the meaning and objectives of export trade.
- Explain the important steps involved in executing export trade.
- State the meaning and objectives of import trade.
- Discuss the important steps involved in executing import trade.
- Develop an understanding of the various documents used in international trade.
- Identify the specimen of the various documents used in international trade.
- Highlight the importance of the documents needed in connection with international trade transactions.
- State the meaning of World Trade Organisation.
- Discuss the objectives of World Trade Organisation in promoting international trade.

UNIT 11 Project Work

- As per CBSE guidelines

Question Paper Design

SN	Typology of Questions	Marks	Percentage
1.	**Remembering and Understanding:** Exhibit memory of previously learned material by recalling facts, terms, basic concepts, and answers. Demonstrate understanding of facts and ideas by organizing, comparing, translating, interpreting, giving descriptions, and stating main ideas	44	55%
2.	**Applying:** Solve problems to new situations by applying acquired knowledge, facts, techniques and rules in a different way	19	23.75%
3.	**Analysing, Evaluating and Creating:** Examine and break information into parts by identifying motives or causes. Make inferences and find evidence to support generalizations. Present and defend opinions by making judgments about information, validity of ideas, or quality of work based on a set of criteria. Compile information together in a different way by combining elements in a new pattern or proposing alternative solutions.	17	21.25%
	Total	**80**	**100%**

01 CHAPTER

Evolution and Fundamentals of Business

Business is an institution organised and operated to provide goods and services to society under the incentive of private gain.
— BO Wheeler

YOUR STUDY GOALS

- 1.1 History of Trade and Commerce in India
- 1.2 Rise of Intermediaries
- 1.3 Human Activities
- 1.4 Concept of Business
- 1.5 Classification of Business Activities
- 1.6 Business Risk

YOUR PRACTICE GOAL

- Objective Type Questions (70 Qs ; MCQs, A-R, Statements, Matching)
- Subjective Questions (15 SAs, 9 LAs)
- Case Study Based Questions (Short Case Studies-10, Long Case Studies-5)
- Self Assessment Test (8 MCQs, 7 SAs, 3 LAs)

1.1 History of Trade and Commerce in India

Archaeological evidences have shown that trade and commerce was the mainstay of economy of ancient India, carried out by both water and land routes.

Silk route was an ancient network of trade routes and helped in establishing commercial and political contacts of India with adjoining foreign kingdoms and empires of Asia and the world. Spice route was used for the trade of spices and linked the East and West by sea.

Trade and commerce have helped India play a vital role in the economic world in the following ways

- During ancient times, Indians were the masters of the seaborne trade of Europe, Asia and Africa.
- In the beginning of 18th century, almost every nation on Earth obtained its supplies of fine cotton and silk fabric, spices, indigo, sugar, drugs, precious stones and many curious works of art from India in exchange of gold and silver.
- The period of 18th century was marked by substantial commercial activities and urban development. There were diverse types of coins and weighing practices.

Indigenous Banking System

Indigenous bankers constitute the ancient banking system of India. An indigenous banker or bank is defined as an individual or private firm which receives deposits and engages itself in lending money.

Initially, the metals were used as money due to high durability and divisibility.

Documents such as *Hundi* and *Chitti* were used to carry out transactions in which money passed from hand to hand.

Hundi means an unconditional order made by a person which directs another person to pay a certain sum of money to the person whose name is mentioned on the order.

Hundi as Practiced by Indian Merchant Communities

Hundi	Functions
Darshani	It is payable at sight. It is like a demand bill. Moreover, it is negotiable.
Muddati or Miadi	It is payable after a certain time period, like a 'time bill'. Banks generally provide loans for the security of such hundis.
Dhani-jog (Darshani)	It is payable to the bearer or owner.
Sah-jog (Darshani)	It is made payable only to a respectable person. It is freely transferrable, but it is not payable to bearer.
Firman-jog (Darshani)	It is payable to the order. It is opposite of Dhani-jog hundi.
Dekhan-har (Darshani)	It is payable to the presenter or bearer.
Dhani-jog (Muddati)	It is payable to any person and there is no liability over who received payment but payment is made after a fixed period of time.
Firman-jog (Muddati)	It is made on demand or order and after a fixed term.
Jokhmi (Muddati)	It is made against dispatched goods. If goods lost in transit, then the holder of the hundi has to bear the cost and drawee carries no liability.

Economic Activities by Ancient People

- Agriculture and domestication of animals.
- Weaving cotton, dyeing fabrics, making clay pots, utensils and handicrafts, sculpting, cottage industries, masonry, manufacturing, transports (i.e. carts, boats and ships), etc.
- Workshops (Karkhana) for their skilled artisans who worked and converted raw material into finished goods.
- Family based apprenticeship system duly followed in acquiring trade specific skills.
- Artisans, craftsmen and skilled labourers of various kinds learnt and develop skills and knowledge, which were passed on from one generation to another.

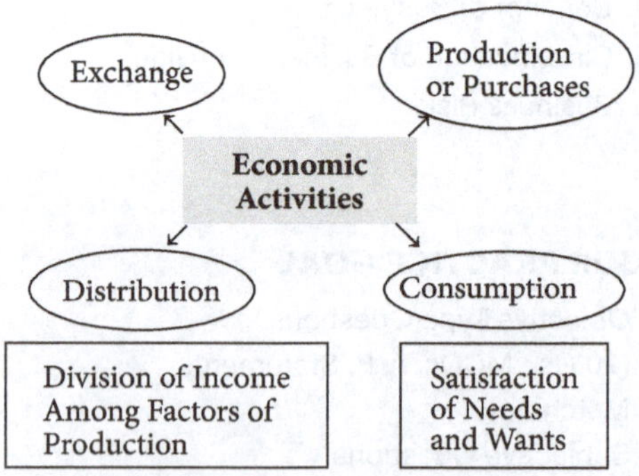

Transfer of Goods and Services
(Monetary Vs Barter)

1.2 Rise of Intermediaries

A financial intermediary is an institution or an individual that acts as a middleman to facilitate the channel of funds between lenders and borrowers indirectly. Intermediaries include commission agents, brokers and distributions both for wholesale and retail goods.

Some important **features** of intermediaries are

- Intermediaries provide financial assistance to the business.
- The lenders give funds to these institutions and they extend the funds to borrowers.
- Intermediaries provide financial security to the manufacturers, by taking responsibility for the risks involved, especially in foreign trade.

During the Mughal period and the days of the East India Company, the institution of **Jagat Seths** developed and exercised great influence. Bankers began to act as trustees and executors of endowments (funding). Foreign trade was financed by loans and the rate of interest was kept high for longer voyages. Commercial operations were increased by the emergence of credit transactions and availability of loans and advances.

Transport

It refers to the physical movement of goods from the place of production to the place of consumption. Transport by land and water was popular in the ancient times that helped in maintaining trade. Trade routes were structurally wide and suitable for speed and safety.

Following were the significant regions for maritime trade

- Malabar Coast has a long history of international maritime trade going back to the era of the Roman Empire. Pepper was particularly valued in the Roman Empire and it was known as **Black Gold**.
- An alternate route to India for spices other than Malabar Coast led to the discovery of America by Columbus in 15th century. Spices was also the reason for **Vasco da Gama** visiting the shores of Malabar in 1498.
- Calicut emporium was visited by Chinese ships to acquire items, like frankincense (essential oil) and myrrh (fragrant resin used in perfumes, medicines) from the middle East, as well as pepper, diamonds, pearls and cotton from India.
- On the Coromandel Coast, Pulicat was a major port in the 17th century. Textiles were principally exported from Pulicat to South-East Asia.

Trading Communities

In ancient times, different communities dominated trade in different parts of the country.

- **Punjabi** and **Multani** merchants managed the business in Northern region.
- **Bhats** managed the business in the States of Gujarat and Rajasthan.
- **Mahajans** managed the business in Western India.
- **Chatt** community was important in South India.
- In urban centres such as Ahmedabad, the Mahajan community collectively represented by their chief called *Nagarseth*. Community such as *Hakim* and *Vaid* (physician), *Wakil* (lawyer), *Pandit* or *Mulla* (teachers), Painters, Musicians, Calligraphers, etc. were active.

Merchant Corporations

Merchant corporations were established on formal basis. They formulated their own rules of membership and professional code of conduct. The merchant community derived power and prestige from guilds (federations). Guilds were autonomous corporations formed to protect the interests of the traders.

Some major sources of revenue for merchant corporations were

- **Trade and industry taxes** like traders had to pay octroi duties (either in cash or in kind) that were levied on most of the important articles at varying rates.
- **Custom duties and tariffs**, varied according to commodities and province to province, respectively.
- **Ferry tax**, which had to be paid for passengers, goods, cattle and carts.
- The local bodies had the right to receive **labour tax**.
- The guild merchants acted as custodians of religious interests, constructed temples and levied **corporate tax** on their members. The guild chief directly dealt with the king or tax collectors and settled the market toll on behalf of its fellow merchants, at a fixed sum of money.

Major Trade Centres

- **Patliputra** It is known as Patna today. It was a commercial town which was a major centre for exports of stones.
- **Peshawar** It was a major exporting centre for wood and for the import of horses.
- **Taxila** It served as a major centre on the important land route between India and Central Asia.
- **Indraprastha** It was the commercial junction on the royal road where most routes leading to the East, West, South and North converged.
- **Mathura** It was an emporium of trade where people depended on commerce. Many routes from South India touched Mathura and Broach.
- **Varanasi** It grew as a major centre of textile industry and become famous for beautiful gold silk cloth and sandalwood workmanship.
- **Mithila** The traders of Mithila traded at the ports on the islands of Java, Sumatra and Borneo. Mithila established trading colonies in South, China, especially in Yunnan.
- **Ujjain** Various types of clothes such as agate, carnelian, muslin and mallow were exported from Ujjain to different centres. It also had trade relations with Taxila and Peshawar.
- **Surat** It was the emporium of Western trade during the Mughal period. Textiles of Surat were famous for their gold borders (Zari).
- **Kanchi** It is known as Kanchipuram today. In Kanchi, Chinese used to come to purchase pearls, glass and rare stones and in return they sold gold and silk.
- **Madura** It was the capital of Pandayas who controlled the pearl fisheries of the Gulf of Mannar. It attracted foreign traders, particularly Romans, for carrying out overseas trade.
- **Broach or Bharuch** It was the greatest seat of commerce in Western India. It was situated on the banks of river Narmada and was linked with all important marts by roadways.
- **Kaveripatta** It is known as Kaveripatnam today. It was a convenient place for trade with Malaysia, Indonesia, China and the Far East. It was the centre of trade for perfumes, cosmetics, scents, silk, wool, cotton, corals, pearls, gold and precious stones and also for ship building.
- **Tamralipti** It was one of the greatest ports connected both by sea and land with the West and Far East. It was linked by road to Banaras and Taxila.

Major Exports and Imports

Exports	Imports
Spices, wheat, sugar, indigo, opium, sesame oil, cotton, parrot, live animals and animal products like hides, skin, furs, horns, tortoise shells, pearls, sapphires, quartz, crystal, lapis lazuli, granites, turquoise and copper, etc. were the major exports.	Horses, animal products, Chinese silk, flax and linen, wine, gold, silver, tin, copper, lead, rubies coral, glass, amber, etc. were the major imports.

Re-industralisation: A New Beginning of India

After independence, India went for centralised planning and the process of rebuilding the economy started in the following ways

- The first Five Year Plan was implemented in India in 1952 under which importance was given to the establishment of modern technological and scientific institutes, space and nuclear programmes. However, Indian economy failed to develop at a rapid pace due to lack of capital formation, rise in population, huge expenditure on defence, etc. Thus, India agreed to economic liberalisation in 1991.
- At present, India is one of the fastest growing economies in the world and a preferred FDI destination.
- The Government of India has taken many initiatives such as 'Make in India', 'Skill India', 'Digital India' and roll out of the Foreign Trade Policy (FTP 2015-2020), etc. which are expected to help the economy in terms of exports and imports and trade balance.

Position of Indian Sub-continent in World Economy

- Between 1st and 7th centuries, India is estimated to have the largest economy of the ancient and medieval world. It controlled about one-third and one-fourth of the world's wealth. Many travellers such as Megasthenes, Xuanzang (Huen Tsang), Faxian (Fa Hien), Al Beruni (11th century), IbnBatuta (11th century), Frenchman Francois (17th century), etc. referred India as ***Swarna Bhumi*** and ***Swarndweep***.
- In 18th century, with the increasing control of East India Company, India became a country which was prosperous but with people who were poor.
- In the mid-18th century, the British empire began to establish in India and used revenues generated by the provinces under its rule for purchasing raw materials, spices and goods. This changed Indian economy from being an exporter of processed goods to the exporter of raw materials and buyer of manufactured goods.

1.3 Human Activities

An activity performed by a human being to meet his wants is known as human activity. It can be broadly divided into two types of activities i.e. economic and non-economic activities.

1. Economic Activities

Activities which are undertaken by people with an objective of earning livelihood are known as economic activities.

Types of Economic Activities

- **Business** It is an economic activity which is concerned with the purchase or production and sale of goods or provision of services, with a view to earn income in the form of profit by satisfying the needs of the people.
- **Profession** It includes those activities which require expert knowledge and special skills to be applied by individuals in their occupation. Those engaged in profession are called **professionals** and earn income by charging professional fee.
- **Employment** It refers to the occupation in which people work for others and get remuneration in the form of wages/salaries. Those who are employed by others are called **employees** and the one who employs is called **employer**.

Economic Activity
Chef Cooking in a Restaurant

Difference between Business, Profession and Employment

Basis	Business	Profession	Employment
Mode of Establishment	Its establishment depends on entrepreneur's decision and other legal formalities.	It is established on getting membership of a professional body and certificate of practice.	It is established on getting appointment letter and entering into service agreement.
Nature of Work	It involves providing goods and services to the public.	It involves rendering of personalised and expert services.	It involves performing work as per service contract or rules of service.
Qualification	No minimum qualification is necessary in business.	Qualifications, expertise and training in specific field as prescribed by the professional body is a must in profession.	Qualification and training as prescribed by the employer is must in employment.
Reward or Return	Profit earned is a reward in business.	Professional fee is a reward in profession.	Salary or wages is a reward in employment.
Capital Investment	Capital investment is required as per size and nature of business.	Limited capital is needed for establishment of profession.	No capital is required in employment.
Risk	Profits are uncertain and irregular risk is present in business.	Fee is generally regular and certain but some risk is present in profession.	Fixed and regular pay and no or little risk is present in employment.
Transfer of Interest	Transfer of interest is possible in business with some formalities.	Transfer of interest is not possible.	Transfer of interest is not possible.
Code of Conduct	No code of conduct is prescribed in business.	Professional code of conduct is to be followed in profession.	Norms of behaviour laid down by the employer are to be followed in employment.
Example	Shop, factory, etc. are examples of business.	Legal, medical profession, chartered accountancy, etc. are examples of profession.	Jobs in banks, insurance companies, government departments, etc. are examples of employment.

2. Non-economic Activities

Activities which are undertaken to satisfy social and psychological needs are called non-economic activities. These are concerned with love, sympathy, patriotism, sentiments, etc. e.g. Mother cooking for family members, mother teaching her child at home.

Non-economic Activities: Mother cooking for Family Members

1.4 Concept of Business

Business includes all activities and enterprises that aim to make a profit by offering goods and services needed by society. It acts as the driving force for a country's economy, helping improve people's quality of life. Profits encourage businesses to keep providing the essential goods and services.

Characteristics of Business

Characteristics of Business
- An economic activity
- Production or procurement of goods and services
- Sale or exchange of goods and services
- Dealing in goods and services on a regular basis
- Profit earning
- Uncertainty in return
- Element of risk

1. **An Economic Activity** Business is an economic activity as it includes exchange of goods and services with the purpose of earning money or livelihood. It can be undertaken either on small and individual level or on large-scale in a more organised and formal level.
2. **Production or Procurement of Goods and Services** Every business enterprise produces the goods or acquires them from producers to sell them to consumers and earn profit in the process.
3. **Sale or Exchange of Goods and Services** Business involves transfer or exchange of goods and services for value. If goods are produced not for purpose of sale, it cannot be called as business activity.

4. **Dealing in Goods and Services on a Regular Basis** Business deals in goods and services on regular basis. One single transaction of sale or purchase does not constitute business.
5. **Profit Earning** The primary objective of business is to earn profit. For this, businessmen make all possible efforts to increase the volume of sales and reduce cost.
6. **Uncertainty in Return** It refers to the lack of knowledge relating to the amount of money that the business is going to earn in a given period. In business, there is always a possibility of loss.
7. **Element of Risk** Business involves an element of risk. The factors associated with risks include changes in consumer taste and fashion, changes in method of production, increased competition in market, natural calamities, fire, theft, accidents, etc.

Dealing of Goods and Services on Regular Basis

Mohan sells his mobile at a profit. It does not constitute business as it is not on a regular basis. On the other hand, Rohan keeps a stock of mobile phones and regularly sell them. This will constitute business.

Objectives of Business

One of the major objectives of business is profit. It is an essential objective because of the following reasons

- It is a source of income for the businessman.
- It can be reinvested in business.
- It is an indicator of efficient working, performance and success of a business.
- If a business is earning profits then it implies that the society approves the utility of business.
- A business earning profits is able to honour its liabilities on time. This increases the credit worthiness of business and builds up its reputation.

Multiple Objectives of Business

Only one objective can not lead business towards excellence. Objectives are needed in every area. Some of them are

Objective	Explanation
Market Standing	A business enterprise must try to enhance its market share as it can earn more only when large number of customers are recognising and purchasing its products.
Innovation	It refers to development of new methods of production and adoption of new and latest technologies. There are two kinds of innovation, i.e. innovation in products or services and innovation in various skills and activities needed to supply products and services.
Productivity	It is a measure of efficiency. Every enterprise must aim at greater productivity through the best possible use of resources, to ensure continuous survival and progress.
Physical and Financial Resources	An enterprise should aim to acquire physical and financial resources according to its need and use them efficiently.
Earning Profit	Every businessman seeks to earn profit by satisfying the consumers want.
Social Responsibility	It refers to the obligation of business firms to contribute resources for solving social problems and work in a socially desirable manner.

1.5 Classification of Business Activities

Business activities can be classified into two broad categories, which are as follows

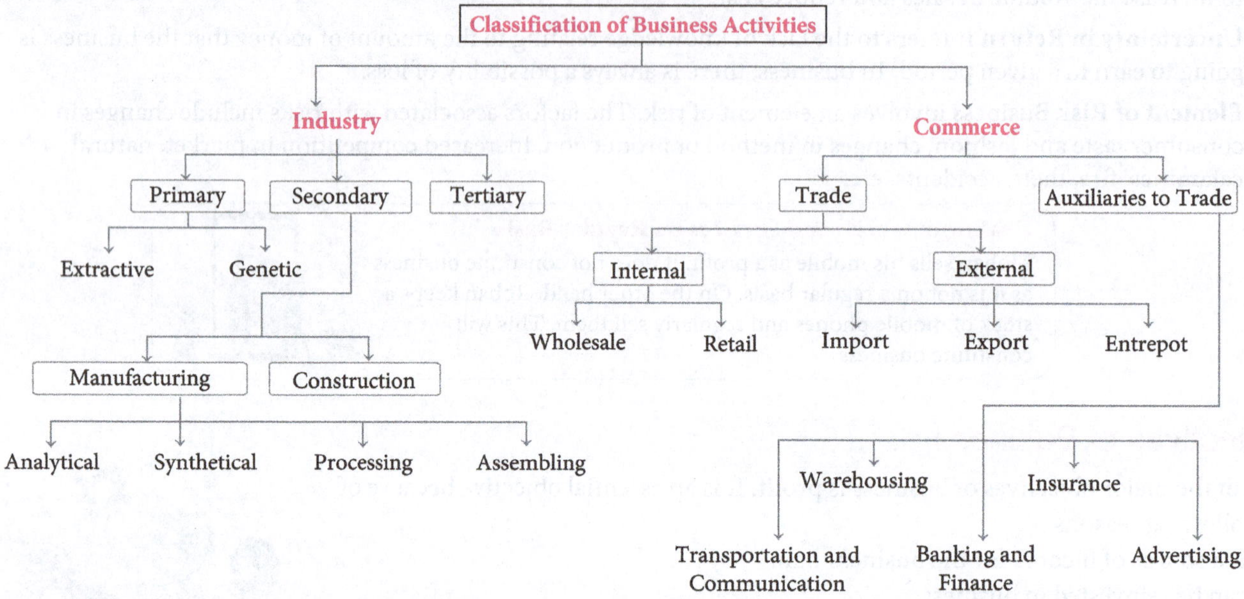

Industry

Industry includes all those business activities that are concerned with the production of goods and services by converting raw material into useful products. e.g. Cotton textile industry refers to all manufacturing units producing textile goods from cotton.

Classification of Industries

Industries can be divided into three categories

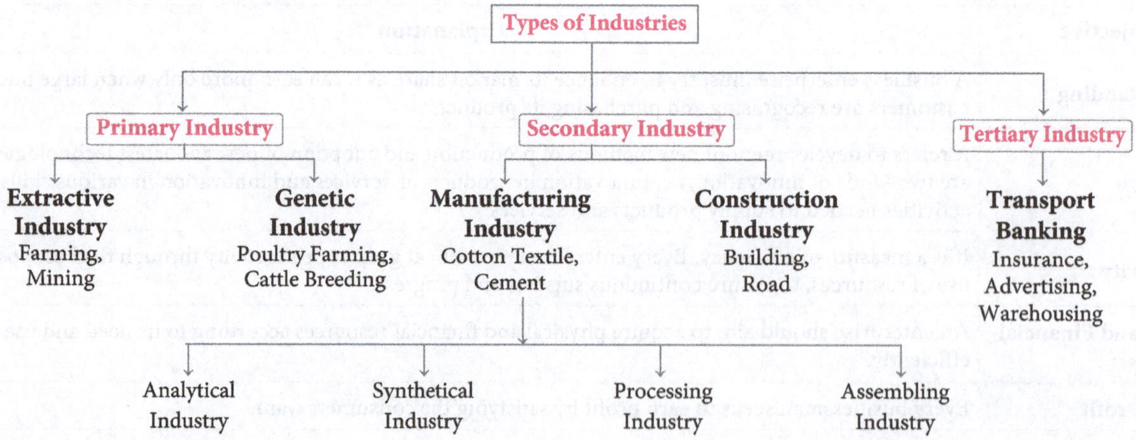

I. Primary Industries

These industries include all those activities which are concerned with extraction of natural resources and reproduction and development of living organisms, plants, etc. They are further sub-divided into two categories

Type	Explanation
Extractive Industry	It includes all those activities which extract or draw out various products from natural resources like the earth, soil, water, air, etc. Important extractive industries include farming, mining, lumbering, hunting and fishing operations.
Genetic Industry	It involves activities like breeding and reproduction of plants and animals. It include seeds and nursery companies. In addition, activities of cattle breeding farms, poultry farms and fish hatchery come under genetic industries.

II. Secondary Industries

These industries are concerned with using the materials which have already been extracted at the primary stage, to produce the finished goods. They are further sub-divided into two categories

Type	Explanation
Manufacturing Industry	It convert raw materials or semi-finished products into finished products. These industries can be further divided into four categories • **Analytical Industry** A basic raw material is analysed and separated into different finished products. • **Synthetical Industry** Two or more raw materials are combined together to make a new product. • **Processing Industry** Involves successive stages for manufacturing a product. • **Assembling Industry** Different components are assembled to make a finished product.
Construction Industry	It includes all those industries which are engaged in construction of buildings, roads, dams, bridges, etc. Engineering and architectural skills are an important part in construction industry.

III. Tertiary Industries

These industries are concerned with providing support services to primary and secondary industries. Various types of service providing industries are insurance, warehousing, banking, transportation and communication, packaging and advertising.

Commerce

It refers to all those activities which help, directly or indirectly, in the distribution of goods to the ultimate consumer. It provides the necessary link between producers and consumers. There are certain activities which help in removing hindrances in the process of exchange for maintaining free flow of goods and services. The hindrance may be in respect of persons, place, time, risk, finance and information. Commerce includes two types of activities i.e. trade and auxiliaries to trade.

Trade

It involves the buying and selling of goods. Trade removes the hindrance of person as it serves as a connecting link between the producer and the consumer. It can be classified into two types

Internal or Home Trade	External or Foreign Trade
It means buying and selling of goods and services within the geographical boundaries of a country. It can be further classified as • **Wholesale Trade** Refers to buying and selling of goods in large quantities. • **Retail Trade** Refers to buying and selling of goods and services in small quantities.	It refers to buying and selling of goods and services between two or more countries. It is of following three types • **Export** Refers to the sale of goods to a foreign country. • **Import** Refers to the purchase of goods from foreign countries. • **Entrepot** Refers to import of goods for the purpose of export.

Auxiliaries to Trade

Activities which assist or support trade are known as auxiliaries to trade. These activities help in removing various hindrances which arise in connection with production and distribution of goods.

The main auxiliaries to trade are

1. **Transport and Communication** Transport refers to the movement of raw material, semi-finished and finished goods and passengers from one place to another. It removes the hindrance of place by moving good from place of production to the markets for sale.
   Communication facilities such as postal services, telephone, etc. help producers, traders and consumers to exchange information with one another.
2. **Banking and Finance** Banks and financial institutions provide credit facility, loan, etc. to provide finance for smooth flow of business activities. Banks eliminate the hindrance of finance.
   In foreign trade, commercial banks help exporters in collecting money from importers. They also help promoters of companies to raise capital from the public.

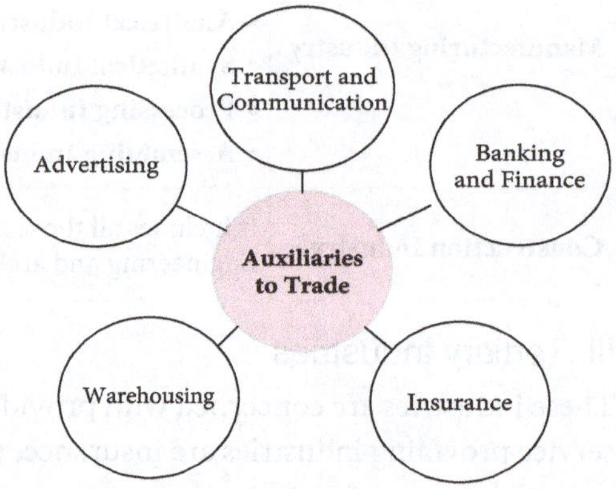

3. **Insurance** It provides protection to businessman from some kinds of risks such as risk of loss due to fire, theft, accident, etc. Businessmen have to pay a nominal amount of premium to get compensated for the loss incurred, from the insurance company. Thus, insurance removes the hindrance of risk.
4. **Warehousing** Warehouses help the businessmen to overcome the problem of storage. They facilitate the availability of goods whenever required, eliminate the hindrance of time and helps in stabilising prices.
5. **Advertising** It helps producers and traders to promote the goods and services available in the market. Thus, it removes the hindrance of information.

1.6 Business Risk

It refers to the possibility of inadequate profits or even losses due to uncertainties or unexpected events. Generally, an enterprise faces two types of risks

1. **Speculative Risk** It involves both the possibility of gain as well as possibility of loss. It arises due to changes in market conditions including fluctuations in demand and supply.
2. **Pure Risk** It involves only the possibility of loss or no loss. Fire, theft, strike are the examples of pure risk.

Nature of Business Risks

- Risk is an essential part of every business. No business can escape from or avoid risk as it can be minimised but cannot be eliminated.
- Business risks arise due to uncertainties like natural calamities, changes in government policy, improvement in technology, etc.
- The degree of risk depends mainly upon the nature (types or goods and services produced and sold) and size (volume of production and sale) of business.
- Profit is the reward for risk taking. An entrepreneur undertakes risks under the expectation of higher profit.

Causes of Business Risks

Business risks arise due to a variety of causes which are

Cause	Explanation
Natural Causes	Natural calamities such as flood, drought, famine, hailstorm, etc. result in heavy loss of life, property and income.
Human Causes	Negligence, carelessness, dishonesty, strikes, riots, etc. on the part of employees are the most important factors of this cause.
Economic Causes	These are related to a chance of loss due to changes in the market conditions. There can be fluctuations in the market, change in taste, preferences, method of production, competition, etc.
Other Causes	It includes physical and technical disabilities, political disturbances, mechanical failures, fluctuations in exchange rates, etc.

Causes of Business Risks

The demonetisation of ₹ 500 and ₹ 1,000 notes in 2016 had a great impact on business enterprises. It is an example of economic cause.

The damage of machine by employees or the strikes carried out by workers affect the productivity. It is an example of human cause.

Mind Map

EVOLUTION AND FUNDAMENTALS OF BUSINESS

1 History of Trade and Commerce in India

- Silk route helped in establishing commercial and political contacts of India with adjoining foreign kingdoms and empires of the world
- Spice route was used for the trade of spices and linked the East and West by sea
- Trade and commerce played a vital role in the economic world
- Indigenous banking system was developed to receive deposits and lend money
- Documents like *Hundi* and *Chitti* were used to carry out transactions in which money passed from hand to hand

2 Rise of Intermediaries

- Rise of intermediaries provided financial support to the business
- Transport by land and water became popular in ancient times that helped in maintaining trade
- Trading communities dominated trade like Punjabi, Multani, Bhats, Chatt, etc
- Merchant community derived power and prestige from guilds
- Major trade centres included Patliputra, Peshawar, taxila, Madura, etc.
- Position of Indian sub-continent in world economy
  - Between 1st and 7th century – Largest economy of the ancient and medieval period
  - In the 18th century with increasing control of East India Company, India become a prosperous country but with poor people
  - In the mid 18th century – Indian economy became exporter of raw materials and buyer of manufactured goods

3 Human Activities

An activity performed by a human being to meet his wants is known as human activity. It can be broadly divided into two types of activities i.e. economic and non-economic activities.

Economic Activities
These activities have the objective of earning livelihood. e.g. Chef cooking food in a hotel. These include

- **Business** It is an economic activity, involves production or procurement of goods and services, sale or exchange of goods and services and has a profit earning motive. It also involves an element of risk.
- **Profession** It includes those activities which require expert knowledge and special skills to be applied by individuals in their occupation.
- **Employment** It refers to the occupation in which people work for others and get remuneration in the form of wages/salaries.

Non-Economic Activities
These activities are undertaken to satisfy social and psychological needs, e.g., Cooking food for family.

4 Objectives of Business

Profit
It is an essential objective because of the following reasons

- Source of reinvestment in business
- Shows efficient working performance
- Implies that society approves the utility of business
- Increases the creditworthiness

Other Objectives

- Enhance position of an enterprise in relation to its competitors
- Development of new methods of production and adoption of latest technology
- Measure of efficiency
- Physical and financial resources
- Contributes resources for solving social problems
- Aim for improvement in worker's abilities

5 Industry

- **Primary Industry** Concerned with extraction of natural resources and reproduction and development of living organisms, etc. It includes extractive industries and genetic industries.
- **Secondary Industry** Concerned with using the materials which have already been extracted at the primary stage. It includes manufacturing industry and construction industry.
- **Tertiary Industry** Concerned with providing support services to primary and secondary industries such as insurance, warehousing, banking, etc.

6 Commerce

It refers to all those activities which help, directly or indirectly, in the distribution of goods to the ultimate consumer.

Trade
It involves the buying and selling of goods. It can be

- **Internal Trade** It includes wholesale trade and retail trade.
- **External Trade** It includes export, import and entrepot.

Auxiliaries to Trade
Activities that assist or support trade are

- **Transport** Movement of raw material, semi-finished, finished goods and passengers from one place to another.
- **Banking** Provide credit facility, loan, etc to provide finance.
- **Insurance** Provide protection from various kinds of risks.
- **Warehousing** Facilitate availability of goods as and when required.
- **Advertising** Provides information about the goods available, features, etc.

7 Business Risk

It refers to the possibility of inadequate profits or even losses due to uncertainties or unexpected events.

Causes of Business Risk

- **Natural** Natural factors such as flood, drought, famine, etc.
- **Human** Negligence, carelessness, dishonesty, strikes on part of employees.
- **Economic** Fluctuations in market, changes in taste, preferences, method of production, etc.
- **Other** Physical and technical disabilities, political disturbances, mechanical failures, etc.

EXAM PATTERN QUESTIONS

Objective Type Questions

Multiple Choice Questions (MCQs)

1. ………… was an ancient network of trade routes that connected the East and the West.

(a) Spice route (b) Silk route
(c) Sea route (d) None of these

2. Maritime routes that linked the East and the West by sea used for the trade of spices is known as

(a) spice route (b) silk route
(c) sea route (d) ship route

3. "It is payable at sight and is like a demand bill." Identify the type of Hundi mentioned in the given statement. Competency Based Que

(a) Darshani (b) Jokhmi
(c) Sah-jog (d) Dhani-jog

4. ………….. was the capital of Pandyas who controlled the pearl fisheries of the Gulf of Mannar.

(a) Surat (b) Kanchi
(c) Madura (d) Patliputra

5. Nimru is an NGO operating in the district of Seelampur since 2006. It deals in providing medicines and other medical facilities to the rural, backward and below poverty line people in the district. In case of need, arrangements are made by the NGO to shift critical patients to referred hospitals. Name the type of human activities performed by the NGO 'Nimru'. Competency Based Que

(a) Economic activities (b) Non-economic activities
(c) Spiritual activities (d) None of these

6. Identify the type of activity illustrated in the below picture where mother is teaching her own child.

(a) Economic activity (b) Non-economic activity
(c) Spiritual activity (d) None of these

7. Which of the following does not characterise business activity?

(a) Production of goods and services
(b) Presence of risk
(c) Sale or exchange of goods and services
(d) Salary or wages

8. "It emphasises that business activities are conducted to earn money or livelihood, distinguishing it from non-economic activities."
Identify the characteristic of business from the given statement. Competency Based Que

(a) Profit earning
(b) Regular dealings in goods and services
(c) An economic activity
(d) Sale or exchange of goods and services

9. "It highlights that transactions must occur consistently rather than a one time sale or purchase to be considered a part of business."
Identify the characteristic of business from the given statement. Competency Based Que

(a) Profit earning
(b) Regular dealings in goods and services
(c) Production or procurement of goods and services
(d) Sale or exchange of goods and services

10. Ruchika is a practicing Chartered Accountant. She has her CA Firm in Gujarat. She deals in providing income tax and GST related services to her clients against very reasonable consultancy fees. She follows a systematic code of conduct and adheres to professional ethics as laid down by the Institute of Chartered Accountants of India (ICAI).
Identify the type of economic activity performed by Ruchika as referred to in the above case. Competency Based Que

(a) Business (b) Profession
(c) Employment (d) None of these

11. "It emphasises the business's responsibility to act in a way that benefits society."
Identify the type of business objective mentioned in the given statement. Competency Based Que

(a) Social responsibility
(b) Market standing
(c) Workers' performance and attitude
(d) Physical and financial resources

12. **An enterprise's goal to acquire and efficiently use physical and financial resources is known as**
(a) market standing
(b) productivity
(c) physical and financial resources
(d) social responsibility

13. **Automobile and computer industry are the example of ....**
(a) processing industry (b) assembling industry
(c) synthetic industry (d) None of these

14. **.............. industry provides service to primary and secondary industry**
(a) Tertiary (b) Analytical
(c) Extractive (d) Synthetical

15. **Which of the following statements is incorrect?**
(a) Analytical industries separate a basic raw material into different finished products, such as crude oil being processed into products like kerosene, petrol and diesel
(b) Synthetical industries use a single raw material to create a final product, for example, in the cement industry
(c) Processing industries involve successive stages in production, such as sugar industry
(d) Assembling industries involve combining different components to create a finished product, as seen in the automobile industry

16. **Raj, Rohan, Ramesh and Rajesh pursued their Master's Degrees in Business Management from a reputed institute in Delhi. After completion of their studies, all of them got engaged in different fields. Raj got a job at an oil refinery industry as a junior executive in finance.**

Rohan joined his family business in sugar industry in Jalandhar, Punjab. Ramesh opened his own dairy firm and Rajesh join the construction business. Identify the type of industry Mr. Rohan worked with as highlighted in the above case. **Competency Based Que**
(a) Analytical industry
(b) Synthetical industry
(c) Processing industry
(d) Assembly industry

17. **Intest is a company involved in the manufacturing of computers and related items. It's a very popular name among the computer-savvy youth in India. There are different models of Desktop, Laptop, Tabs, Gaming and Workstations manufactured and sold by the company in the Indian market. Which type of Industry is highlighted in the above case?** **Competency Based Que**
(a) Genetic industry
(b) Extractive industry
(c) Processing industry
(d) Assembly industry

18. **"This industry involves activities such as breeding and reproduction of plants and animals. Activities like cattle breeding farms and poultry farms fall under this type." Identify the type of industry from the given statement.** **Competency Based Que**
(a) Extractive industry
(b) Genetic industry
(c) Manufacturing industry
(d) Analytical industry

19. **"In this industry, raw materials are combined to create a new product, such as mixing lime, clay and mortar to make cement."** **Competency Based Que**
Identify the type of industry from the given statement.
(a) Analytical industry (b) Synthetical industry
(c) Genetic industry (d) Extractive industry

20. **Which of the broad categories of industries covers oil refineries and sugar mills?**
(a) Primary (b) Secondary
(c) Tertiary (d) None of these

21. **Identify the type of industry shown in the below picture.**

(a) Extractive industry (b) Assembling industry
(c) Processing industry (d) None of these

22. **ABC Industries is a diversified manufacturing company specialising in various types of production processes. Recently, the company expanded into multiple sectors. In one division, ABC processes crude oil and separates it into products like kerosene, petrol and diesel. Another division combines different raw materials to produce sugar.**

In a third division, chemicals are added step-by-step to produce cement. Lastly, ABC's automobile division assembles components to create finished cars. The company has also ventured into construction, taking on projects like building roads and bridges, requiring skilled engineers and architects.

Which type of industry is ABC Industries involved in when they assemble components to manufacture cars? **Competency Based Que**
(a) Analytical industry (b) Synthetical industry
(c) Processing industry (d) Assembling industry

23. Akash Textile Ltd. is involved in manufacturing textile products such as shirts, trousers, kurtas, pajamas, etc. In which industry is the company involved? Competency Based Que

(a) Processing industry (b) Synthetical industry
(c) Analytical industry (d) Extractive industry

24. Identify the type of industry shown in the below picture.

(a) Extractive industry (b) Assembling industry
(c) Processing industry (d) None of these

25. Mahesh is a successful entrepreneur dealing in the automobile sector, especially with two wheelers in Ahmedabad. He has been constantly earning good profits from his business and investing surplus towards the expansion of his business. All the latest two wheeler models are available at his showroom.

His marketing and sales teams are managed to create new customers from time to time. His unique style of business management has brought him success. Name the type of business activity in which Mahesh is involved. Competency Based Que

(a) Tertiary industries (b) Secondary industries
(c) Trade (d) Auxiliaries to trade

26. After completing the graduation, three close friends (Govind, Satish and Vinod) decided to start trading of goods and services. Govind started purchasing mobile accessories from China to be sold in India.

Satish established his Tea business and started purchasing tea from Assam and selling it to America. Vinod deals in purchase of Chocolates from Switzerland and sell them to Bangladesh and Nepal. Identify the types of external trade in which Vinod is involved. Competency Based Que

(a) Entrepot trade (b) Export trade
(c) Import trade (d) Both (a) and (b)

27. Briju is a big businessman who deals in selling Nestle products in his locality. He purchased products of Nestle directly from the state distributor in bulk quantities and sold them in the market to small shopkeepers from different corners of the city. Identify the type of trade followed by Briju general store. Competency Based Que

(a) Wholesale trade (b) Retail trade
(c) International trade (d) Entrepot trade

28. India imports goods from China to export them in Bangladesh. Identify the type of trade mentioned in the case. Competency Based Que

(a) Import (b) Entreport
(c) Export (d) None of these

29. Which of the following is/are treated as auxiliaries to trade?

(a) Banking industry (b) Insurance industry
(c) Transportation industry (d) All of these

30. Identify the hindrance of commerce illustrated in the below picture.

(a) Hindrance of finance (b) Hindrance of risk
(c) Hindrance of information
(d) Hindrance of time

31. Identify the hindrance of commerce highlighted in the below picture.

(a) Hindrance of information
(b) Hindrance of risk
(c) Hindrance of time (d) Hindrance of finance

32. Advertising helps in removing the hindrance of ……………

(a) information (b) risk
(c) time (d) finance

33. XYZ Pvt. Ltd. is a company that produces consumer electronics. To expand its market reach, the company relies on various support services to ensure smooth operations. XYZ transports raw materials and finished products between manufacturing units and retail outlets, using road and rail transport. The company also relies on communication facilities like email and phone to stay in touch with suppliers and customers.

To manage finances, XYZ frequently uses banking services to secure loans and handle payments for international transactions, especially when exporting goods. To protect against potential losses from incidents like theft or damage, the company has insurance coverage.

Additionally, XYZ uses warehouses to store its products, allowing it to manage inventory levels effectively and ensure products are available when needed. Finally, the company invests in advertising campaigns to inform potential customers about its products and attract new buyers.

Which auxiliary to trade primarily helps XYZ Pvt. Ltd. eliminate the hindrance of time in their operations?

Competency Based Que

(a) Transport and communication
(b) Banking and finance
(c) Warehousing (d) Advertising

34. Which of the following statements is incorrect?

(a) Transport and communication are essential auxiliaries to trade as they remove the hindrance of place by moving goods from production sites to markets and providing communication channels for information exchange
(b) Banks and financial institutions only provide loans and credit to businesses for domestic trade and do not play any role in facilitating foreign trade
(c) Insurance protects businesses against various risks, such as loss due to fire or theft, by compensating them in exchange for a premium, removing the hindrance of risk
(d) Warehousing assists businesses in overcoming storage challenges, ensuring goods are available when needed and stabilising prices, removing the hindrance of time

35. The possibility of inadequate profits or even losses due to uncertainties are known as ....

(a) business risks (b) business contingencies
(c) business ventures (d) None of these

36. .... is the reward for risk taking.

(a) Profit (b) Loss
(c) Trade (d) Activity

37. Which of the following statements is incorrect?

(a) Business risks are inevitable and arise due to uncertainties like natural disasters, changes in government policy and technological advancements
(b) Business risks can be entirely eliminated if the business takes appropriate preventive measures
(c) The degree of risk a business faces depends largely on the nature and size of the business, such as the type of goods produced and the volume of sales
(d) Profit is considered the reward for taking risks, with higher risks offering a higher chance of profit to the entrepreneur

38. Business risk is not likely to arise due to

(a) strikes (b) employee dishonesty
(c) defect in machine (d) profit earning

39. "Negligence, dishonesty, carelessness are the most important factors of this cause." Identify the cause of business risk highlighted in the above statement.

Competency Based Que

(a) Natural cause (b) Human cause
(c) Other cause (d) Economic cause

40. 'Strikes' come under which type of risk?

(a) Natural causes
(b) Human causes
(c) Economic causes
(d) None of the above

41. ABC Industries, a large manufacturer of consumer goods, recently faced a series of challenges. During the summer, a severe drought affected one of their major production locations, causing a delay in raw material supply and resulting in significant financial losses. Additionally, some employees went on strike due to dissatisfaction with working conditions, disrupting the production process.

Meanwhile, ABC noticed that consumer preferences were shifting toward more sustainable products, creating increased competition in the market. To make matters worse, a recent political disturbance in one of their overseas markets caused fluctuations in exchange rates, impacting their international profits.

Which of the following represents an economic cause of business risk faced by ABC Industries?

Competency Based Que

(a) The severe drought that caused delays in raw material supply
(b) The strike by employees that disrupted production
(c) The shift in consumer preferences towards sustainable products
(d) The political disturbance causing exchange rate fluctuations

Direction *Read the case study and answer the questions 42 to 45 on the basis of the same*

Four friends, Neha, Amit, Rohan and Priya, decided to venture into different areas of trade and industry after completing their studies. Neha began importing electronic gadgets from Japan to sell in India. Amit started a textile business where he purchased fabrics from Mumbai and exported them to Germany. Rohan purchased perfumes from France and sold them to neighbouring countries like Bhutan and Bangladesh. Priya joined her family's cattle breeding business and managed the day-to-day operations on the farm.

42. "Neha began importing electronic gadgets from Japan to sell in India." Identify the type of external trade highlighted in the above statement.

(a) Import (b) Export
(c) Entreport (d) None of these

43. "Amit started a textile business where he purchased fabrics from Mumbai and exported them to Germany." Identify the type of external trade highlighted in the above statement.

(a) Import (b) Export
(c) Entreport (d) None of these

44. "Rohan purchased perfumes from France and sold them to neighbouring countries like Bhutan and Bangladesh." Identify the type of external trade highlighted in the above statement.

(a) Import (b) Export
(c) Entreport (d) None of these

45. "Priya joined her family's cattle breeding business and managed the day-to-day operations on the farm." Identify the type of industry being discussed in the above statement.

(a) Extractive industry (b) Genetic industry
(c) Manufacturing industry (d) Construction industry

Assertion-Reason

Direction (Q.No. 46 to 55) *Read the following Assertion (A) and Reason (R) and choose the correct alternative from the following*

Alternatives

(a) Both Assertion (A) and Reason (R) are true and Reason (R) is the correct explanation of Assertion (A)
(b) Both Assertion (A) and Reason (R) are true, but Reason (R) is not the correct explanation of Assertion (A)
(c) Assertion (A) is true, but Reason (R) is false
(d) Assertion (A) is false, but Reason (R) is true

46. Assertion (A) The barter system was commonly used in ancient India for the exchange of goods and services.

Reason (R) The barter system allowed people to exchange goods directly in the absence of a standardised currency.

47. Assertion (A) In ancient India, Hundis were used as a negotiable financial instrument for transactions.

Reason (R) Hundis served as a written order for payment, guaranteeing the transfer of money from one person to another.

48. Assertion (A) Earning livelihood is the main aim of economic activities.

Reason (R) It helps people in earning their bread and butter by performing several activities.

49. Assertion (A) Business represents the exchange of goods and services.

Reason (R) Risk and uncertainties are always there in any form of business.

50. Assertion (A) Acquiring physical and financial resources according to the business's needs is essential for efficient operations.

Reason (R) Resources should be used efficiently to ensure the smooth functioning and growth of the enterprise.

51. Assertion (A) Profit earning is essential for the survival, growth and expansion of any business.

Reason (R) It is the sole objective of all business firms.

52. Assertion (A) Secondary industries involve the transformation of raw materials into finished products, such as manufacturing furniture from wood or producing machinery from metal.

Reason (R) Secondary industries include activities like mining and agriculture, where raw materials are directly obtained from the environment.

53. Assertion (A) Auxilliaries to trade are also known as services.

Reason (R) Auxilliaries to trade help in carrying out activities related to industry and trade.

54. Assertion (A) Warehousing facilitates the availability of goods as and when required.

Reason (R) Warehousing removes this hindrance of place by providing facility of storage of goods.

55. Assertion (A) Business risks can arise due to natural calamities like floods, droughts and hailstorms.

Reason (R) These are examples of economic causes of business risk.

Two Statements Based MCQs

Direction (Q.No. 56 to 65) *Read the following statements carefully and choose the correct alternative*

Alternatives

(a) Statement I is correct and Statement II is incorrect
(b) Statement II is correct and Statement I is incorrect
(c) Both the statements are correct
(d) Both the statements are incorrect

56. Statement I The silk route was mainly used for transporting spices from India to the West.

Statement II The spice route was a network of sea routes that linked the East and West primarily for spice trade.

57. Statement I The barter system was an efficient method of trade, with no need for alternative forms of currency.

Statement II The Hundi system in ancient India served as an early form of credit and financial transactions.

58. Statement I The indigenous banking system in ancient India included barter exchange and lending money by private firms.

Statement II Indigenous bankers provided financial support through instruments like Hundi and Chitti.

59. Statement I Transport during ancient India was mainly restricted to land routes due to the lack of maritime technology.

Statement II India's Malabar Coast was a significant region for international maritime trade, even attracting Roman interest in pepper.

60. Statement I Business means a state of being busy in non-economic activities.

Statement II A mother cooking for her son is a non-economic activity.

61. Statement I Business, as an economic activity, includes the exchange of goods or services for the purpose of earning money or livelihood.

Statement II A single transaction of sale or purchase constitutes a business.

62. Statement I Profit earning is an essential objective of business and all efforts aim to increase sales and reduce costs.

Statement II Businesses always guarantee profits, as they minimise the risk of losses.

63. Statement I The main aim of every business is to earn profit.

Statement II Customer satisfaction is also required with profit motives.

64. Statement I A business is required to add to its prospects in the long-run.

Statement II Social objectives are desired to be achieved for the benefit of the society.

65. Statement I Primary industries includes manufacturing industry and construction industry.

Statement II Tertiary industry tries to remove various hindrances which arises during production and distribution of goods and services.

Matching

66. Match the following

Column I	Column II
A. Business	(i) Providing personalised services to earn fees
B. Profession	(ii) Performing work as per service contract to earn salary
C. Employment	(iii) Provision of goods and services to earn profit

Codes

	A	B	C
(a)	(i)	(ii)	(iii)
(b)	(iii)	(ii)	(i)
(c)	(ii)	(iii)	(i)
(d)	(iii)	(i)	(ii)

67. Match the following

Column I	Column II
A. Extractive industry	(i) Mixing of chemicals to manufacture cement
B. Genetic industry	(ii) Processing of crude oil
C. Analytical industry	(iii) Rearing of cattle for milk
D. Synthetical industry	(iv) Extracting minerals from earth

Codes

	A	B	C	D
(a)	(i)	(ii)	(iii)	(iv)
(b)	(iv)	(iii)	(ii)	(i)
(c)	(ii)	(iii)	(i)	(iv)
(d)	(iii)	(ii)	(iv)	(i)

68. Match the following

Column I	Column II
A. Import	(i) Sale of tea from India to Japan
B. Export	(ii) Export of commodities from European countries to export them to Nepal
C. Entrepot	(iii) Purchase of toys from China into India

Codes

	A	B	C
(a)	(i)	(ii)	(iii)
(b)	(iii)	(ii)	(i)
(c)	(ii)	(iii)	(i)
(d)	(iii)	(i)	(ii)

69. Match the following

Column I	Column II
A. Advertising	(i) Hindrance of place
B. Warehousing	(ii) Hindrance of risk
C. Insurance	(iii) Hindrance of time
D. Transport	(iv) Hindrance of information

Codes

	A	B	C	D		A	B	C	D
(a)	(i)	(ii)	(iii)	(iv)	(b)	(iv)	(iii)	(ii)	(i)
(c)	(ii)	(iii)	(i)	(iv)	(d)	(iii)	(ii)	(iv)	(i)

70. Match the following

Column I	Column II
A. Natural causes	(i) Mechanical failure, fluctuation in exchange rate
B. Human causes	(ii) Rise in interest rate, change in fashion
C. Economic causes	(iii) Strikes, riots
D. Other causes	(iv) Flood, earthquake

Codes

	A	B	C	D		A	B	C	D
(a)	(i)	(ii)	(iii)	(iv)	(b)	(iv)	(iii)	(ii)	(i)
(c)	(ii)	(iii)	(i)	(iv)	(d)	(iii)	(ii)	(iv)	(i)

Answers

1. (b) Silk route
2. (a) spice route
3. (a) Darshani
4. (c) Madura
5. (b) Non-economic activities
6. (b) Non-economic activity
7. (d) Salary or wages
8. (c) An economic activity
9. (b) Regular dealings in goods and services
10. (b) Profession
11. (a) Social responsibility
12. (c) physical and financial resources
13. (b) assembling industry
14. (a) Tertiary
15. (b) Synthetical industries combine two or more raw materials to create a final product.
16. (c) Processing industry
17. (d) Assembly industry
18. (b) Genetic industry
19. (b) Synthetical industry
20. (b) Secondary
21. (b) Assembling industry
22. (d) Assembling industry
23. (a) Processing industry
24. (a) Extractive industry
25. (c) Trade
26. (a) Entrepot trade
27. (a) Wholesale trade
28. (b) Entrepot
29. (d) All of these
30. (b) Hindrance of risk
31. (c) Hindrance of time
32. (a) information
33. (c) Warehousing
34. (b) Banks and financial institutions play a significant role in facilitating foreign trade by offering services such as issuing letters of credit, foreign exchange transactions.
35. (a) business risks
36. (a) Profit
37. (b) Risks are an unavoidable part of business, they can be minimised but not completely removed.
38. (d) profit earning
39. (b) Human cause
40. (b) Human causes
41. (c) The shift in consumer preferences towards sustainable product
42. (a) Import
43. (b) Export
44. (c) Entreport
45. (b) Genetic industry
46. (a) Both Assertion (A) and Reason (R) are true and Reason (R) is the correct explanation of Assertion (A)
47. (a) Both Assertion (A) and Reason (R) are true and Reason (R) is the correct explanation of Assertion (A)
48. (a) Both Assertion (A) and Reason (R) are true and Reason (R) is the correct explanation of Assertion (A)
49. (b) Risk and uncertainty are not the primary aspects of what constitutes business, which is centered around the exchange of goods and services.
50. (a) Both Assertion (A) and Reason (R) are true and Reason (R) is the correct explanation of Assertion (A)
51. (c) Businesses may have multiple objectives, such as providing quality products, achieving customer satisfaction, or fulfilling social responsibilities.
52. (c) Mining and agriculture are primary industries.
53. (a) Both Assertion (A) and Reason (R) are true and Reason (R) is the correct explanation of Assertion (A)
54. (b) Warehousing removes the hindrance of time by providing facility of storage of goods.
55. (c) These are examples of natural causes of business risk.
56. (b) Silk route helped India in establishing commercial and political contacts with neighbouring foreign countries.
57. (b) The barter system, while used in ancient trade, had significant limitations, such as the lack of a common measure of value and the need for a double coincidence of wants. This inefficiency eventually led to the development of currency.

58. (c) Both the statements are correct

59. (b) Ancient India had well-developed maritime trade routes, particularly along the Malabar coast, which was known for trading pepper (also called 'Black Gold') with foreign nations, including the Roman Empire.

60. (b) Business involves economic activity.

61. (a) A single transaction does not constitute business, as business requires regular dealings.

62. (a) While profit is a primary objective of business, it is not guaranteed, as businesses inherently face uncertainties and risks that can lead to losses due to factors like market changes, competition or natural calamities.

63. (c) Both the statements are correct

64. (c) Both the statements are correct

65. (d) Manufacturing and construction industries are part of secondary industries. Auxilliaries to trade help in removing various hindrances.

66. (d) (iii) (i) (ii)

67. (b) (iv) (iii) (ii) (i)

68. (d) (iii) (i) (ii)

69. (b) (iv) (iii) (ii) (i)

70. (b) (iv) (iii) (ii) (i)

Subjective Questions

Short Answer Type Questions

1. Discuss the significant regions for maritime trade.

Ans. Following were the significant regions for maritime trade

(i) Malabar Coast has a long history of international maritime trade going back to the era of the Roman Empire. Pepper was particularly valued in the Roman Empire and it was known as Black Gold.

(ii) An alternate route to India for spices other than Malabar Coast led to the discovery of America by Columbus in 15th century. Spices was also the reason for Vasco da Gama visiting the shores of Malabar in 1498.

(iii) Calicut emporium was visited by Chinese ships to acquire items, like frankincense (essential oil) and myrrh (fragrant resin used in perfumes, medicines) from the middle East, as well as pepper, diamonds, pearls and cotton from India.

(iv) On the Coromandel Coast, Pulicat was a major port in the 17th century. Textiles were principally exported from Pulicat to South-East Asia.

2. State any four major sources of revenue for merchant corporations.

Ans. Following are the four major sources of revenue for merchant corporations

(i) Trade and industry taxes were a major source of revenue. Traders had to pay octroi duties (either in cash or in kind) that were levied on most of the important articles at varying rates.

(ii) Custom duties and tariffs were another sources that varied according to commodities and province to province, respectively.

(iii) The ferry tax was another source of income generation which had to be paid for passengers, goods, cattle and carts.

(iv) The guild merchants acted as custodians of religious interests, constructed temples and levied corporate tax on their members. The guild chief directly dealt with the king or tax collectors and settled the market toll on behalf of its fellow merchants, at a fixed sum of money.

3. Discuss the following trade centers

(i) Kanchi **(ii) Kaveripatta**

Ans. Following are the two trade cemters

(i) **Kanchi**

Today known as Kanchipuram, it was here that the Chinese used to come in foreign ships to purchase pearls, glass and rare stones and in return they sold gold and silk.

(ii) **Kaveripatta**

Also known as Kaveripatnam, it was scientific in its construction as a city and provided loading, unloading and strong facilities of merchandise. Foreign traders had their headquarters in this city. It was a convenient place for trade with Malaysia, Indonesia, China and the Far East. It was the centre of trade for perfumes, cosmetics, scents, silk, wool, cotton, corals, pearls, gold and precious stones and also for ship building.

4. Briefly describe the position of Indian sub-continent in the world economy.

Ans. Following is the position of Indian sub-continent in the world economy

(i) Between 1st and 7th centuries, India is estimated to have the largest economy of the ancient and medieval world. It controlled about one-third and one-fourth of the world's wealth.

Many travellers such as Megasthenes, Xuanzang, Faxian, Al Beruni (11th century), IbnBatuta (11th century), Frenchman Francois (17th century), etc. referred India as Swarna bhumi and Swarndweep.

(ii) With the increasing control of East India Company, India became a country which was prosperous but with people who were poor.

(iii) In the mid-18th century, the British empire began to establish in India and used revenues generated by the provinces under its rule for purchasing raw materials, spices and goods. This changed Indian economy from being an exporter of processed goods to the exporter of raw materials and buyer of manufactured goods.

5. "An activity can be economic activity in one situation and non-economic in another situation." Do you agree? Give an example to justify your answer. Competency Based Que

Ans. Yes, I agree with the statement. Human activities are classified into economic and non-economic activities. Economic activities are those which are performed for some economic consideration, whereas non-economic activities are performed for psychological satisfaction or out of love, affection, etc.

e.g. When a doctor treats a patient in a hospital or a clinic, he charges fee for that, thus it becomes an economic activity. However, when the same doctor treats his son/daughter at home, it becomes a non-economic activity.

6. State any four objectives of business.

Ans. Following are the four objectives of business

(i) **Market Standing**

A business enterprise must try to enhance its market share as it can earn more only when large number of customers are recognising and purchasing its products.

(ii) **Innovation**

It refers to development of new methods of production and adoption of new and latest technologies. There are two kinds of innovation i.e. innovation in products or services and innovation in various skills and activities needed to supply products and services.

(iii) **Productivity**

It is a measure of efficiency. Every enterprise must aim at greater productivity through the best possible use of resources, to ensure continuous survival and progress.

(iv) **Physical and Financial Resources**

An enterprise should aim to acquire physical and financial resources according to its need and use them efficiently.

7. "Profit is a crucial goal for any business." Discuss.

***Or* What is the role of profit in a business?** NCERT

Ans. Profit is an essential objective because of the following reasons

(i) Profit is a source of income for the businessman, as it is the excess of revenue over cost.

(ii) Profit can be reinvested in business. It is a good source of finance for expansion and growth of business.

(iii) Profit is an indicator of efficient working, performance and success of a business. If a business is managed efficiently, it will earn profit.

(iv) If a business is earning profits then it implies that the society approves the utility of business.

(v) A business earning profits is able to honour its liabilities on time. This increases the credit worthiness of the business and builds up its reputation.

8. How does business contribute to economic development of a country? NCERT

Ans. The business helps to stabilise, stimulate and contribute to the growth of economics in the following ways

(i) **Investing in People's Demand**

Business allow people to have access to the commodities and services they need to be productive. When it comes to encouraging economic growth in a region, new business owners who respond to market demands are crucial participants. It contributes to economic expansion.

(ii) **Bringing Employment Opportunities to Economy**

Business requires more people for the production activities, hence more people are employed.

(iii) **Increase Technology Development**

Business acquiring new technology such as machinery or labour incentives methods from a foreign nation brings technological development. Thus, the advanced productivity increases the income of a region and are directly impacted when new businesses export goods and services to neighbouring regions.

9. "Different types of industries contribute to the economic development." In the light of the given statement, explain the various types of industries. Competency Based Que

***Or* What are the various types of industries?** NCERT

Ans. Following are the various types of industries

(i) **Primary Industries**

These include all those activities which are concerned with the extraction and production of natural resources. These industries can further be classified into extractive industries and genetic industries.

(ii) **Secondary Industries**

These are concerned with using the materials which have already been extracted at the primary stage. These industries can further be classified into manufacturing industries (analytical, synthetical, processing and assembling indstries) and construction industries.

(iii) **Tertiary Industries**

These are concerned with providing support services to primary and secondary industries as well as activities relating to trade such as transport, banking, insurance, warehousing, communication, packaging and advertising.

10. "Differentiating between extractive and genetic industries is crucial for understanding their roles in the economy." Discuss the key differences between extractive and genetic industries with the help of suitable examples. Competency Based Que

Ans. Following are the differences between extractive and genetic industries

Basis	Extractive	Genetic Industries
Meaning	Extractive industries are concerned with drawing out products from natural sources such as soil, sea and air. The products of such industries are generally used for producing finished goods.	Genetic industries are concerned with activities like reproduction, breeding and multiplication of animals and plants.
Source	These industries extract or draw out products from natural sources.	These industries remain engaged in breeding plants and animals for their use in further reproduction.
Examples	Farming, mining and fishing are some of the examples of extractive industries.	The examples of genetic industries are agricultural activities for the production of crops, animal husbandry, dairy farming and poultry farming.

11. "Secondary industries play a vital role in the economic development of a country." Discuss the types of secondary industries in reference to the context of the statement. Competency Based Que

Ans. Secondary industries are concerned with using the materials which have already been extracted at the primary stage, to produce the finished goods. They are further sub-divided into two categories

(i) **Manufacturing Industry**

It convert raw materials or semi-finished products into finished products. These industries can be further divided into four categories

- **Analytical Industry** In such industries, a basic raw material is analysed and separated into different finished products.
- **Synthetical Industry** In this industry, two or more raw materials are combined together to make a new product.
- **Processing Industry** It involves successive stages for manufacturing a product.
- **Assembling Industry** In this industry, different components are assembled to make a finished product.

(ii) **Construction Industry**

It includes all those industries which are engaged in construction of buildings, roads, dams, bridges, etc. Engineering and architectural skills are an important part in construction industry.

12. "Trade helps in making the goods produced available to ultimate consumers or users." In the light of the given statement, discuss the various types of trade. Competency Based Que

Ans. Trade can be classified into two types

(i) **Internal, Domestic or Home Trade**

It means buying and selling within the geographical boundaries of a country. Internal trade can further be classified as

- **Wholesale Trade** It implies buying and selling of goods in large quantities.
- **Retail Trade** It refers to buying and selling at goods in small quantities.

(ii) **External Trade/Foreign**

Trade It refers to buying and selling of goods and services between two or more countries. External trade is of following three types

- **Export** It refers to the sale of goods to a foreign country.
- **Import** It refers to the purchase of goods from foreign countries.
- **Entreport** It refers to import of goods for the purpose of export.

13. How does commerce help in the removal of hindrance of person, place and time?

Ans. Commerce embraces all those activities which help to break the barriers between producers and consumers. It is the sum total of all those processes which are engaged in the removal of hindrance of person, place and time.

Following is the description of how these hindrances get removed

(i) Hindrance of person refers to the problem of contact between producers and consumers. This hindrance is removed by trade.

(ii) Hindrance of place refers to the problem of distribution of goods at distant places without loss. Auxiliaries to trade removes this hindrance by transportation.

(iii) Hindrance of time refers to the problem of existence of time gap between production and consumption of goods. This hindrance is removed by warehousing or storage.

14. Explain how industry, trade and commerce are interrelated.

Ans. Industry, trade and commerce are closely related to each other. Industry produces goods which are distributed through commerce. No commercial activity is possible in the absence of industry. At the same time, industrial production is meaningless without the distribution of goods through commerce.

If industry is the backbone of commerce, commerce serves as the lifeline of industry. Trade provides the necessary support to industry and maintains a smooth flow of commerce. Thus, there is a high degree of interdependence between industry, trade and commerce.

15. State the nature of business risk.

Ans. Nature of business risk can be described with the help of the following points

(i) Business risks arise due to uncertainties. Natural calamities, changes in government policy, improvement in technology, etc. are some of the examples of uncertainty.

(ii) Risk is an essential part of every business. No business can escape from or avoid risk. Risk can be minimised but cannot be eliminated.

(iii) The degree of risk depends mainly upon the nature (types or goods and services produced and sold) and size (volume of production and sale) of business.

(iv) Profit is the reward for risk taking. Greater the risk involved in a business, higher is the chance of profit. An entrepreneur undertakes risks under the expectation of higher profit.

Long Answer Type Questions

16. Discuss the development of indigenous banking system in Indian sub-continent. NCERT

Ans. Indigenous banking system played a prominent role in lending money and financing domestic and foreign trade with currency and letter of credit. It developed in the following ways

(i) With the development of banking, people began to deposit precious metals with lending individuals functioning as bankers or Seths and money became an instrument for supplying the manufacturers with a means of producing more goods.

(ii) Intermediaries or institutions were developed which provided considerable financial security to the manufacturers by assuming responsibility for the risks involved, especially in foreign trade.

The institution of Jagat Seths also developed and exercised great influence during the Mughal period and the days of the East India Company.

(iii) Bankers began to act as trustees and executors of endowments. The emergence of credit transactions and availability of loans and advances enhanced commercial operations.

(iv) The indigenous banking system benefitted the manufacturers, traders and merchants with additional capital funds for expansion and development.

17. "Hundi is an unconditional order in writing directing another to pay a certain sum of money to a person named in the order". In the light of the given statement, explain the various types of 'Hundis' that became popular in ancient times. Competency Based Que

Ans. Following are the various types of 'Hundis' that became popular in ancient times

(i) **Darshani**
It is a hundi which is payable at sight. It is like a demand bill. Moreover, it is negotiable.

(ii) **Muddati**
It is a hundi which is payable after a Miadi certain time period, like a time bill. Banks generally provide loans for the security of such hundis.

(iii) **Dhani-jog**
'Mani' in local terms means owner. It is (Darshani) generally payable to the bearer or owner.

(iv) **Sah-jog** (Darshani)
This is a hundi made payable only to a respectable person. It is freely transferrable. But it is not payable to bearer.

(v) **Finnan-jog**
This type of hundi is payable to the (Darshani) order. It is opposite of Dhani-jog hundi.

(vi) **Dekhan-har**
This type of hundi is always payable to (Darshani) the presenter or bearer.

(vii) **Dhani-jog** (Muddati)
This type of hundi is payable to any person and there is no liability over who received payment but payment is made after a fixed period of time.

(viii) **Firman-jog**
This type of hundi is made on demand or (Muddati) order and after a fixed term.

(ix) **Jokhmi** (Muddati)
This is a hundi which is made against dispatched goods. If goods lost in transit, then the holder of the hundi has to bear the cost and drawee carriers no liability.

18. Discuss any six major trade centers in ancient India.

Ans. Following are the major trade centers in ancient India

(i) **Pataliputra**

Known as Patna today. It was not only a commercial town, but also a major centre for export of stones.

(ii) **Peshawar**

It was an important exporting centre for wool and for the import of horses. It had a huge share in commercial transactions between India, China and Rome in the first century AD.

(iii) **Taxila**

It served as a major centre on the important land route between India and Central Asia. It was also a city of financial and commercial banks. The city occupied an important place as a Buddhist centre of learning. The famous Taxila University flourished here.

(iv) **Indraprastha**

It was the commercial junction on the royal road where most routes leading to the East, West, South and North converged.

(v) **Mathura**

It was an emporium of trade and people here subsisted on commerce. Many routes from South India touched Mathura and Broach.

(vi) **Varanasi**

It was well placed as it lay both on the Gangetic route and on the highway that linked North with the East.

It grew as a major centre of textile industry and became famous for beautiful gold silk cloth and sandalwood workmanship. It had links with Taxila and Bharuch.

19. State the meaning of economic activities. Discuss the key differences between economic and non-economic activities.

Ans. Economic activities are undertaken by people with the objective of earning money. For example, production, exchange and distribution of product.

Following are the differences between economic and non-economic activities

Basis	Economic Activities	Non-economic Activities
Meaning	They are undertaken to earn money or livelihood.	They are undertaken to satisfy social or psychological motives.
Result	They result in production of goods and services.	They result in mental/ psychological satisfaction.
Types	Business, profession and employment are types of economic activities.	Charity, social service, patriotism, etc. are types of non-economic activities.
Purpose/ Motive	Their purpose is to earn money and to create wealth.	Their purpose is to provide psychological satisfaction.
Contribution to GDP	They contribute towards GDP of a country.	They do not contribute towards a country's GDP.
Example	Labourer constructing a house on contract basis is an example of economic activities.	Labourer constructing his own hut is an example of non-economic activities.

20. Compare business with profession and employment. NCERT

Ans. Following are the differences between business, profession and employment

Basis	Business	Profession	Employment
Mode of Establishment	Its establishment depends on entrepreneur's decision and other legal formalities.	It is established on getting membership of a professional body and certificate of practice.	It is established on getting appointment letter and service agreement.
Nature of Work	It involves providing goods and services to the public.	It involves rendering of personalised and expert services.	It involves performing work as per service contract or rules of service.
Qualification	No minimum qualification is necessary in business.	Qualifications, expertise and training in specific field as prescribed by the professional body is a must in profession.	Qualification and training as prescribed by the employer is must in employment.
Reward or Return	Profit earned is a reward in business.	Professional fee is a reward in profession.	Salary or wages is a reward in employment.
Capital Investment	Capital investment is required as per size and nature of business.	Limited capital is needed for establishment of profession.	No capital is required in employment.
Risk	Profits are uncertain and irregular risk is present in business.	Fee is generally regular and certain but some risk is present in profession.	Fixed and regular pay and no or little risk is present in employment.

21. "Business involves the production and exchange of goods and services to earn profits." List and explain its characteristics. **Competency Based Que**

Ans. Following are the characteristics of business

(i) **An Economic Activity**

Business is an economic activity as it includes exchange of goods and services with the purpose of earning money or livelihood. It can be undertaken either on small and individual level or on large-scale in a more organised and formal level.

(ii) **Production or Procurement of Goods and Services**

Every business enterprise produces the goods or acquires them from producers to sell them to consumers and earn profit in the process. Goods may include daily use items such as sugar, pen, etc. or capital goods like machinery, furniture, etc. Services may include facilities like transportation, banking, electricity, etc which are offered to consumers, business firms and organisations.

(iii) **Sale or Exchange of Goods and Services**

Business involves transfer or exchange of goods and services for value. If goods are produced not for purpose of sale, it cannot be called as business activity.

(iv) **Dealing of Goods and Services on a Regular Basis**

Business deals in goods and services on regular basis. One single transaction of sale or purchase does not constitute business.

(v) **Profit Earning**

The primary objective of business is to earn profit. For this, businessmen make all possible efforts to increase the volume of sales and reduce cost.

22. Explain the key differences between industry, trade and commerce.

Ans. Following are the key differences between industry, trade and commerce

Basis	Industry	Commerce	Trade
Meaning	It means production of goods and services.	It means distribution of output of goods and services produced by industry.	It means sale, transfer or exchange of goods and services.
Nature	It represents the supply side of goods and services.	It represents demand side of goods and services.	It represents exchange of goods and services i.e. both supply and demand.
Creation of Utility	It creates utility by changing the form of materials.	It creates place and time utility by movement of goods and services from one place to another.	It creates possession utility through the process of exchange.
Scope	It includes all productive activities i.e. extractive, genetic, manufact-uring and construction industries.	It includes trade as well as auxiliaries to trade.	It includes home and foreign trade.

23. Discuss the following auxillairies to trade

(i) Transport and communication **(ii) Warehousing** **(iii) Banking and finance**

Ans.

(i) **Transport and Communication**

Transport refers to the movement of raw material, semi-finished and finished goods and passengers from one place to another. Transport removes the hindrance of place by moving good from the place of production to the markets for sale, through road, rail or coastal shipping. Communication facilities such as postal services, telephone, etc. are also necessary so that producers, traders and consumers may exchange information with one another.

(ii) **Warehousing**

Warehouses help the businessmen to overcome the problem of storage. They facilitate the availability of goods whenever required, eliminate the hindrance of time and helps in stabilising prices.

(iii) **Banking and Finance**

Banks and financial institutions provide credit facility, loan, etc. to provide finance for smooth flow of business activities.

Banks help businessmen to overcome the problem of funds and eliminate the hindrance of finance. In foreign trade, commercial banks help exporters in collecting money from importers.

Commercial banks also help promoters of companies to raise capital from the public.

24. "Business risk refers to the possibility of a business experiencing losses due to various factors." In the light of the given statement, explain business risk and its causes. Competency Based Que

Or

Explain the concept of business risk and its causes. NCERT

Ans. A business risk may be defined as the possibility of loss due to some unforeseeable, unpredictable and unfavourable event in future.

Business risks arise due to a variety of causes which are

(i) **Natural Causes**

Natural calamities like flood, earthquake, lightning, heavy rains, famine, etc. are beyond human control. They result in heavy loss of life, property and income.

(ii) **Human Causes**

These include such events like carelessness, negligence or dishonesty of employees, stoppage of work due to power failure, strikes, riots, management inefficiency, etc.

(iii) **Economic Causes**

These include uncertainties caused due to economic fluctuations such as changes in demand for goods, competition, price, collection of dues from customers, change of technology or method of production, etc. Financial problems like rise in interest rate and higher taxation, etc also come under economic causes as they raise the cost of operation of business unexpectedly.

(iv) **Other Causes**

Other unforeseen events like political disturbances, mechanical failures, fluctuations in exchange rates, etc. also lead to the possibility of business risks.

Case Study Based Questions

Short Case Studies

Case Study 1

Rohit is a school teacher who spends his weekdays teaching students at a private school, for which he receives a monthly salary. On weekends, he volunteers at a local animal shelter, where he cares for abandoned pets without any monetary compensation.

Although his teaching job is his primary source of income, he finds immense joy and fulfillment in helping the animals at the shelter.

His weekends provide him with an opportunity to contribute to the community and make a positive impact, even though it doesn't generate any income. This balance between earning and giving back reflects two different types of human activities.

(i) Specify the type of human activities Rohit is involved in during his weekdays and weekends.

(ii) Differentiate between the two activities Rohit engages in on any two basis.

Ans.

(i) The type of human activities Rohit is involved in during his weekdays and weekends are

- Teaching at school – Economic activity
- Volunteering at animal shelter – Non-economic activity

(ii) Following are the differences between economic and non-economic activities

Basis	Economic Activities	Non-economic Activities
Meaning	They are undertaken to earn money or livelihood.	They are undertaken to satisfy social or psychological motives.
Result	They result in production of goods and services.	They result in mental/ psychological satisfaction.

Case Study 2

Charu and Renuka are childhood friends. Charu is a consultant while Renuka is an architect. They contributed equal amounts and purchased a building for ₹ 2 crore. After a year, they sold it for ₹ 3 crore and shared the profits equally.

(i) Are they doing the business? Give reason in support of your answer.

(ii) State the feature of business which is being highlighted in the given example.

Ans.

(i) No, they are not doing business as they are not involved in doing sale and purchase of land/plot on a regular basis. To be a business activity, dealing of goods must be on a regular and recurring basis.

(ii) The feature highlighted in the given example is 'dealings in goods and services on a regular basis. Business deals in goods and services on regular basis. One single transaction of sale or purchase does not constitute business.

Case Study 3

Raj sells his play station to his friend at a profit of ₹ 2000, which is a one time transaction. On the other hand, Rajesh owns a shop that specialises in selling electronic toys, including play stations. Rajesh also buys second hand play stations, refurbishes them, and sells them to earn a consistent profit. While Raj's activity is more of a personal sale, Rajesh's activity involves regular transactions aimed at earning a profit.

(i) Identify whether activities carried out by Raj and Rajesh are business activities or not.

(ii) State any three charactersitics of business.

Ans.

(i) Raj's activity is not a business activity as it involves a one-time sale of personal property. Rajesh's activity, however, is a business activity as it involves regular buying and selling with the aim of earning profit.

(ii) Following are the characteristics of business

- **Dealing of Goods and Services on a Regular Basis**
  Business deals in goods and services on regular basis. One single transaction of sale or purchase does not constitute business.
- **Profit Earning**
  The primary objective of business is to earn profit. For this, businessmen make all possible efforts to increase the volume of sales and reduce cost.
- **Uncertainty of Return**
  It refers to the lack of knowledge relating to the amount of money that the business is going to earn in a given period. In business, there is always a possibility of loss.

Case Study 4

Imran, Manpreet, Joseph and Priyanka have been classmates in Class X. After their exams are over, they happen to meet at a common friend Ruchika's house. Just when they are sharing their experiences of examination days, Ruchika's father, Mr. Raghuraj Chaudhury intervenes and asks about their well-being.

He also enquires from each one of them about their career plans. But none of them has a definite reply. Mr. Raghuraj, who himself is a businessman, suggests to them that they can opt for business as a promising and challenging career.

Joseph gets excited by the idea and says, "Yes, business is really good for making lots of money even more than is possible by becoming an engineer or a doctor."

Mr. Raghuraj opines, "Let me tell you, young man, there is a lot more to business than merely money." He then gets busy with some other guests. On the basis of above case, answer the following questions **NCERT Modified**

(i) Is Mr. Raghuraj correct in his assertion? On the basis of your understanding of the chapter, state the features of business.

(ii) Joseph thinks that the only objective of business is to earn money. Is he correct?

Ans.

(i) Yes, Mr. Raghuraj is correct in his assertion. Business is much more than merely earning money. As per my understanding of the chapter, business possesses the following features
- It is an economic activity.
- It involves sale or exchange of goods and services for value.

(ii) No, Joseph is not correct. Profit earning is not the only objective of business. The objectives of business can be classified as economic objectives and social objectives. Earning profit, survival, optimum use of resources, creating market standing, growth, innovation, productivity and manager's development are economic objectives of business.
On the other hand, supply of good quality products, avoiding unfair trade practices, employee welfare, generation of employment and protection of environment are the social objectives of business.

Case Study 5

Dr. Reena has earned a reputation as one of the top cardiologists. After years of dedicated study and practice, she has developed expertise in treating heart conditions and providing life-saving interventions for her patients. Beyond her medical skills, Dr. Reena is highly regarded for her compassionate care, treating each patient with personal attention and empathy.

Her services are highly sought after, and she's known for going beyond standard treatment by educating her patients on maintaining a healthy heart through lifestyle choices.

As a specialist, Dr. Reena not only contributes to the health and well-being of her community but also demonstrates the important role of skilled professionals in society. Her work is primarily motivated by the desire to serve others and improve lives, although it also provides her with financial stability and recognition.

(i) Identify the type of economic activity highlighted in this case.

(ii) State its characteristics.

Ans.

(i) The type of economic activity highlighted in the case is an example of profession which is an economic activity.

(ii) The characteristics of profession as an economic activity are
- Professionals render a specialised service based upon advanced and specialised knowledge and skill.
- It involves a confidential relationship between a practitioner and a client.
- It is bound by a distinctive ethical code.
- Professionals earn income by charging professional fees.

Case Study 6

Arnav is employed as a Sales Executive at XYZ Limited Company, where he plays a key role in boosting the company's sales performance. With a monthly salary of ₹ 40,000, his responsibilities involve reaching out to potential clients, building relationships and strategically promoting the company's products to drive revenue.

Arnav's job requires him to meet set sales targets and he is evaluated based on his performance in achieving these goals. His daily work activities include client meetings, product demonstrations and strategising ways to increase market share for XYZ Limited.

This job provides Arnav with a stable income and career growth opportunities, aligning his personal goals with the company's objectives. In return, he is expected to deliver results that contribute directly to the company's financial success.

(i) Identify the type of economic activity highlighted in this case.

(ii) State some characteristics of economic activity identified in (i).

Ans.

(i) The economic activity highlighted in the case is employment.

(ii) The characteristics of employment as an economic activity are
- There is a contract existing between the employer and employee.
- Employee performs according to the assigned task.
- Remuneration is given to employees for delivering value services.

Case Study 7

Identify and state the type of economic activity in the following cases

(i) Harish sells mobile phones on behalf of his employer.

(ii) It requires minimum academic and other qualifications.

(iii) A hawker sells toys for children outside a function.

Ans.

(i) Selling mobile phones on behalf of employer is employment. It refers to the occupation in which people work for others and get remuneration in the form of wages/ salaries. Those who are employed by others are called employees and the one who employs is called employer.

(ii) Profession requires minimum academic and other qualifications. It includes those activities which require expert knowledge and special skills to be applied by individuals in their occupation. Those engaged in profession are called professionals and they earn income by charging professional fee.

(iii) Sale of toys by hawker outside function is business. It is an economic activity which is concerned with the purchase or production and sale of goods or provision of services, with a view to earn income in the form of profit by satisfying the needs of the people.

Case Study 8

GMR Industries entered the airports space in early 2005 and is today counted amongst the top 5 airport private airport developer and operators globally. GMR Industries presently owns and operates Delhi International Airport and Hyderabad International Airports. Apart from being the largest private airport company in India, GMR Industries is the only Indian airport developer to have developed and operated airports outside India.

(i) Identify and state the types of industry discussed in the case.

(ii) Identify and state the category of industry being discussed in above case.

Ans.

(i) GMR Industries is a secondary industry. These industries are concerned with using the materials which have already been extracted at the primary stage, to produce the finished goods.

(ii) The category of industry discussed in the case is construction industry. It includes all those industries which are engaged in construction of buildings, roads, dams, bridges etc. Engineering and architectural skills are an important part in construction industry.

Case Study 9

Shiela after graduating from college went back to her home town in Meghalaya. It was small town with very few job opportunities. The karbi tribal women in that area were uneducated but still practiced the method of obtaining traditional colours from natural wild herbs. Their most popular dye was indigo obtained from the leave called 'Sibu'. Using these colours they added variety to their textiles. The women were mainly confined to their homes and they did not know how to make a living out their talent. Shiela went from door to door and analysed the problem that existed.

She thought of setting-up the business of buying textiles from them and converting them to suits in her factory in Noida. Her business turns out to be a great success.

(i) State the types of business activity Shiela is engaged in.

(ii) Specify the category of the type of business activity performed by Shiela.

(iii) Which type of business activity is undertaken by Karbi tribal women by getting indigo obtained from the leave called 'Sibu'?

Ans.

(i) The type of business activity Shiela is engaged in industry. Industry includes all those business activities that are concerned with the production of goods and services by converting raw material into useful products.

(ii) The category of the type of business activity performed by Shiela is secondary industry (manufacturing industry). These industries are concerned with using the materials which have already been extracted at the primary stage to produce the finished goods.

(iii) The type of business activity undertaken by karbi tribal women is primary activity.

Case Study 10

Mohan was running a trading business in India now he extended its operations to UAE and USA by establishing places of business in these countries. In order to increase sales in UAE the company adopted selling strategies like sales promotion and advertising. As the company had an excellent credibility in the capital market, it was able to meet all its financial requirements by borrowing from CNO Bank.

(i) Identify and explain the auxiliaries to trade used by Mohan for running his business.

(ii) Identify the type of trade carried by Mohan earlier and now.

Ans.

(i) The auxiliaries to trade used by Mohan for running his business are

- **Advertising**

  It makes possible for producers and traders to promote the goods and services available in the market. Thus, it removes the hindrance of information. Advertising helps in providing information about the goods available, its features, price, etc. and inducing customers to buy particular items.

- **Banking and Finance**

  Banks and financial institutions provide credit facility, loan, etc. to provide finance for smooth flow of business activities. Banks help businessmen to overcome the problem of funds and eliminate the hindrance of finance.

  In foreign trade, commercial banks help exporters in collecting money from importers. Commercial banks also help promoters of companies to raise capital from the public.

(ii) The type of trade carried by Mohan earlier was internal trade. It means buying and selling of goods and services within the geographical boundaries of a country.

The type of trade carried by Mohan now is external trade. It refers to buying and selling of goods and services between two or more countries.

Long Case Studies

Case Study 11

In ancient India, the Greeks sailed from Eqypt in the month of July and arrived at Muziri in about 40 days. They stayed on the Malabar Coast for about three months and commenced their return journey from Muziri in December or January.

As the Indian seas were infested by pirates. The Greek merchants brought with them cohorts of archers on board their ships.

Egypt being at this period subject to Rome, the archers who accompanied the Greek merchants were Roman soliders. The Pandyan kings sent embassies to Rome and had employed Roman soldiers as guards. There was a colony of Yavana merchants at Kaveri pattanam, whose existence in an index of properity of merchant communities and professional classes.

That Roman gold pound largely into Tamil country at this period is attested by the numerous Roman coins dating from the region of Augustus to that of Zeno which have been found buried in different parts of Tamil Nadu. On the basis of the given information about ancient India, answer the following questions

(i) State the concept used in ancient India whose existence is an index of prosperity of merchant communities and professional classes.

(ii) Enlist the important kinds of concept whose existence is an index of prosperity of merchant communities and professional classes.

(iii) Enlist a few examples of the concept used in ancient India whose existence is an index of prosperity of merchant communities and professional classes.

Ans.

(i) The existence of trade centre is an index of prosperity of merchant communities and professional classes.

(ii) Trade centre were all kinds of towns like port towns, manufacturing towns, mercantile towns, the sacred centres and pilgrimage towns.

(iii) The following were the leading trade centres in ancient India

- **Pataliputra**

  Known as Patna today. It was not only a commercial town, but also a major centre for export of stones.
- **Peshawar**

  It was an important exporting centre for wool and for the import of horses. It had a huge share in commercial transactions between India, China and Rome in the first century AD.
- **Taxila**

  It served as a major centre on the important land route between India and Central Asia. It was also a city of financial and commercial banks. The city occupied an important place as a Buddhist centre of learning. The famous Taxila University flourished here.
- **Indraprastha**

  It was the commercial junction on the royal road where most routes leading to the East, West, South and North converged.

Case Study 12

XYZ Enterprises is a growing manufacturing company that has been steadily expanding its operations over the years. The company has been focusing on enhancing its market share by introducing innovative products and improving production efficiency through the adoption of modern technologies.

With a dedicated workforce, the company strives to improve the workers' performance and attitude to contribute positively to productivity. XYZ Enterprises also emphasises the importance of acquiring the right physical and financial resources to support its growing needs. The company believes in fulfilling its social responsibility by contributing to community development and addressing environmental issues.

Additionally, the company ensures consistent profitability to reinvest in its business and provide better returns to its shareholders.

(i) Identify and state the three objectives of business mentioned in the case.

(ii) Why is earning profit essential for a business?

Ans.

(i) The three objectives of business mentioned in the case are

- **Physical and Financial Resources**

  An enterprise should aim to acquire physical and financial resources according to its need and use them efficiently.
- **Workers' Performance and Attitude**

  A business should aim at improving workers' performance, to ensure a positive attitude on the part of workers.

  Workers' performance and attitude determine their contribution towards productivity and profitability of any enterprise.
- **Social Responsibility**

  It refers to the obligation of business firms to contribute resources for solving social problems and work in a socially desirable manner.

(ii) Earning profit is an essential objective because of the following reasons

- Profit is a source of income for the businessman, as it is the excess of revenue over cost.
- Profit can be reinvested in business. It is a good source of finance for expansion and growth of business.
- Profit is an indicator of efficient working, performance and success of a business. If a business is managed efficiently, it will earn profit.
- If a business is earning profits then it implies that the society approves the utility of business.
- A business earning profits is able to honour its liabilities on time. This increases the credit worthiness of the business and builds up its reputation.

Case Study 13

Rajiv owns a growing furniture manufacturing business called 'Comfort Creations,' known for its eco-friendly and modern designs. He started the company in a small workshop, focusing on sustainable furniture crafted from reclaimed wood. Over the years, his business has expanded, attracting a large customer base interested in both style and sustainability.

However, as the business grew, Rajiv encountered new challenges related to distribution, financing and marketing, which he needed to address to sustain his company's growth and meet the increasing demand.

To tackle these issues, Rajiv partnered with a reputable logistics company, 'Swift Movers,' that specialises in handling delicate and oversized items. Swift Movers transports Rajiv's furniture pieces from his workshop to retail outlets and customers across the country, allowing Comfort Creations to overcome geographic limitations and reach customers in distant markets.

Whether it's a single chair or a full set of living room furniture, Swift Movers ensures safe and timely delivery, which has helped Rajiv build a reputation for reliability and customer satisfaction.

Rajiv also relies heavily on banking and finance services. He established a relationship with Greenline Bank, which provides him with flexible loans and credit facilities to purchase raw materials in bulk and maintain smooth cash flow throughout the production process.

These banking services help Rajiv overcome financial constraints that would otherwise limit his production capacity. Recently, Greenline Bank even assisted him in setting up a system for international transactions, enabling Rajiv to import high quality, sustainable materials from overseas suppliers at competitive rates, giving Comfort Creations an edge in the eco-friendly furniture market.

In addition, Rajiv has invested in advertising to raise brand awareness and promote his products. Recognising the importance of reaching a broader audience, he runs targeted social media campaigns that highlight the eco-friendly aspects and unique craftsmanship of his furniture. These ads provide potential customers with information about 'Comfort Creations' products, showcasing their features, prices and sustainable origins.

Rajiv's advertising efforts not only attract environmentally conscious customers but also build trust in the brand by showcasing customer testimonials and behind the scenes glimpses of the production process.Through these supportive services, Rajiv has been able to grow Comfort Creations into a successful business that stands out in the competitive furniture market.

Quoting lines from the above paragraph, identify and explain any three auxiliaries to trade used by Rajiv to support his business operations.

Ans. Following are the three auxiliaries to trade used by Rajiv

(i) **Transport and Communication**

"Rajiv partnered with a reputable logistics company, 'Swift Movers', that specialises in ………………… limitations and reach customers in distant markets.'

This line indicates the auxiliary of transport, which removes the hindrance of place by moving goods from the production site to various markets. Transport refers to the movement of raw material, semi-finished and finished goods and passengers from one place to another. Transport removes the hindrance of place by moving good from the place of production to the markets for sale, through road, rail or coastal shipping. Communication facilities such as postal services, telephone, etc. are also necessary so that producers, traders and consumers may exchange information with one another.

(ii) **Banking and Finance**

"Rajiv also relies heavily on banking and finance services. He established a relationship …………..cash flow throughout the production process."

This line highlights the auxiliary of banking and finance, which removes the hindrance of finance by providing loans and credit facilities to support business operations. Banks and financial institutions provide credit facility, loan, etc. to provide finance for smooth flow of business activities. Banks help businessmen to overcome the problem of funds and eliminate the hindrance of finance.

In foreign trade, commercial banks help exporters in collecting money from importers. Commercial banks also help promoters of companies to raise capital from the public.

(iii) **Advertising**

"He runs targeted social media campaigns that highlight the eco-friendly aspects …………………..their features, prices and sustainable origins."

This line demonstrates the auxiliary of advertising, which removes the hindrance of information by promoting products and providing customers with relevant details about the offerings. It makes possible for producers and traders to promote the goods and services available in the market. Thus, it removes the hindrance of information. Advertising helps in providing information about the goods available, its features, price, etc. and inducing customers to buy particular items.

Case Study 14

Katherine, a young entrepreneur with a keen eye for fashion, has long dreamed of opening her own retail store, focusing on trendy and stylish items that appeal to the latest youth fashion trends. She knows that the demand for such items is highly influenced by the ever-changing tastes and preferences of customers. This could lead to situations where her stock might go unsold or require heavy discounts to clear, causing potential losses.

Despite her enthusiasm, Katherine is nervous about the possibility of financial loss. She understands that risks are unavoidable in any business and she worries about whether she is prepared to handle these uncertainties. Wanting reassurance, she turns to her friend Kristina, who successfully runs her own retail business and has experienced the ups and downs of the industry.

Kristina encourages Katherine to pursue her business idea, explaining that, in return for taking risks, business owners have the opportunity to earn profits. She tells Katherine that, while risks are inherent, they also open doors to rewards. Additionally, she advises Katherine to consider business insurance, as it can protect against some of the common risks, such as damage to stock due to fire or theft. Kristina assures her that some risks, like shifts in consumer preferences, will always be there but can be managed through awareness and adaptation.

With newfound confidence, Katherine starts considering the steps she could take to minimise risks and stay resilient in the competitive world of retail.

(i) What is business risk?

(ii) Identify the main features of business risk discussed in the above case. Also, quote the lines for the identified features.

(iii) Is change in taste and preferences of customers a pure risk or a speculative risk? Explain why?

Ans.

(i) Business risk refers to the possibility of inadequate profits or even losses due to uncertainties or unexpected events. Business risk may be defined as the danger of loss due to some unforeseeable, unpredictable and unfavourable event in future.

(ii) Following are the main features of business risk discussed in the above case

- **Uncertainty**

  Business risk arises from uncertainties that cannot be predicted.

  Quoted Line "Change in taste and preferences of customers may result in loss in such type of business."

- **Profit as a Reward for Risk**

  Businesses undertake risks to earn profits, which act as a reward for handling these uncertainties.

  Quoted Line "Kristina advises her to go ahead with her idea as she will get profit as return for undertaking risk."

- **Insurable and Non-insurable Risks**

  Some risks can be covered by insurance, while others, like market risks, cannot.

  Quoted Line "She also told her that some risks in business can be insured by taking insurance policy."

(iii) Change in customer taste and preferences is an example of speculative risk. This is because speculative risks involve the possibility of either a gain or a loss. In this case, shifts in customer preferences could lead to increased demand (if Katherine stocks popular items), resulting in profit or decreased demand (if tastes shift away from her products), leading to a potential loss. Unlike pure risks, which involve only the possibility of loss, speculative risks involve the potential for both outcomes.

Case Study 15

Ankita Mittal is the owner of 'Green Harvest Farms,' an organic farming business that supplies fresh produce to urban markets.

Recently, the farm experienced an unexpected heavy hailstorm that damaged most of the crop, resulting in a significant loss.

While the team was working on recovery, a sudden fluctuation in the market reduced the demand for organic produce, as consumers began preferring budget-friendly options due to an economic downturn. To add to the challenges, a group of employees decided to go on strike, demanding higher wages, which further delayed the restoration process.

On top of these issues, political tensions in the region led to new regulations on farm exports, affecting Green Harvest Farms' distribution channels.

Quoting lines from the above paragraph, identify and explain the different causes of business risk faced by 'Green Harvest Farms.'

Ans. Following are the different causes of business risk faced by the company

(i) **Natural Causes**

"An unexpected heavy hailstorm that damaged most of the crop, resulting in a significant loss."

This line indicates a natural cause of business risk, as natural calamities like hailstorms can lead to damage in production and financial losses. Natural calamities such as flood, drought, famine, hailstorm, etc. result in heavy loss of life, property and income.

(ii) **Economic Causes**

"A sudden fluctuation in the market reduced the demand for organic produce, as consumers began preferring budget-friendly options due to an economic downturn."

This line highlights an economic cause, as changes in consumer preferences and market conditions can impact demand and affect revenue. These are related to a chance of loss due to changes in the market conditions. There can be fluctuations in the market, change in taste, preferences, method of production, competition, etc.

(iii) **Human Causes**

"A group of employees decided to go on strike, demanding higher wages, which further delayed the restoration process."

This is an example of a human cause of business risk, where actions like strikes or negligence from employees can disrupt operations. The human factor is the most common cause of loss in business.

Negligence, carelessness, dishonesty, strikes, riots, etc. on the part of employees are the most important factors of this cause.

SELF ASSESSMENT TEST

Objective Type Questions

1. One single transaction does not constitute business. Business deals in manufacturing or trading goods and provision of services on
   (a) occasional basis (b) regular basis
   (c) periodical basis (d) None of these

2. What is the primary reason why profit is an essential objective for a business?
   (a) It helps the business to expand only in local markets
   (b) It acts as a source of income for the businessman
   (c) It ensures that the business pays taxes on time
   (d) It enables the business to improve its public relations

3. 'No risk no gain' is an important principle which applies to all types of business. Which characteristic of business risk is highlighted in this statement?
   (a) Profit is the reward for risk taking
   (b) No loss is the reward for risk taking
   (c) No profit is the reward for risk taking
   (d) Loss is the reward for risk taking

4. Which of the following is not a major objective of business?
   (a) Innovation (b) Earning profit
   (c) Reducing competition (d) Market standing

5. Business activities are broadly classified into which two categories?
   (a) Production and marketing
   (b) Industry and commerce
   (c) Capital and labour
   (d) Goods and services

6. "Basic raw materials are analysed and separated into different finished products." Identify the type of manufacturing industry in the given statement.
   (a) Analytical industry (b) Synthetical industry
   (c) Primary industry (d) Construction industry

7. Diamond Jewels, an Indian company sells diamond chains to UK. Identify the type of trade.
   (a) Import (b) Export
   (c) Entreport (d) Retail

8. Due to lower wages, workers stop the production work and go on a strike. Identify the cause of risk being portrayed in the case.
   (a) Natural cause (b) Human cause
   (c) Other cause (d) Economic cause

Answers 1. (b) 2. (b) 3. (a) 4. (c) 5. (b) 6. (a) 7. (b) 8. (b)

Short Answer Type Questions

9. "Indigenous bankers constitute the ancient banking system of India. An indigenous banker or bank is an individual or a private firm which receives deposits, deals in hundies or engage itself in lending money." In the light of above statement, explain the important functions of indigenous bankers.

10. "Intermediaries help in facilitating the promotion of trade." Comment.

11. Discuss in brief the position of Indian sub-continent in the world.

12. Explain the three types of economic activities with examples.

13. State any three differences between business and employment.

14. What makes risk an essential element of business? Discuss.

15. Mahesh is running a petrol pump in his town. What possible political causes he can face which may lead to risk in his business?

Long Answer Type Questions

16. "Setting clear objectives is crucial for the success of a business. Without well-defined goals, the organisation may lack direction and focus." In light of the above statement, explain any five objectives of business.

17. Rajneesh wants to start a business and takes help of a consultant as he is confused between industry, trade and commerce. As a consultant, explain him the differences between the three terms.

18. "Commerce can be divided into trade and auxiliaries to trade." Elaborate.

02

CHAPTER

> The form of business organisation should be so strong, that it can continue for a long time and small obstructions should not extinguish it i.e. it may remain static. — *L.H. Haney*

Forms of Business Organisation

▼ YOUR STUDY GOALS

2.1 Sole Proprietorship
2.2 Partnership
2.3 Hindu Undivided Family Business
2.4 Cooperative Society
2.5 Joint Stock Company
2.6 Formation of a Company
2.7 Choice of Form of Business Organisation

▼ YOUR PRACTICE GOAL

- Objective Type Questions (73 Qs ; MCQs, A-R, Statements, Matching)
- Subjective Questions (22 SAs, 10 LAs)
- Case Study Based Questions (Short Case Studies-13, Long Case Studies-5)
- Self Assessment Test (8 MCQs, 7 SAs, 3 LAs)

The form of business organisation that a businessman should choose, is the most important decision that he has to take while starting a new venture. The merits and demerits of each type of organisation should be carefully analysed for choosing the most appropriate form of business.

Various forms of business organisations are

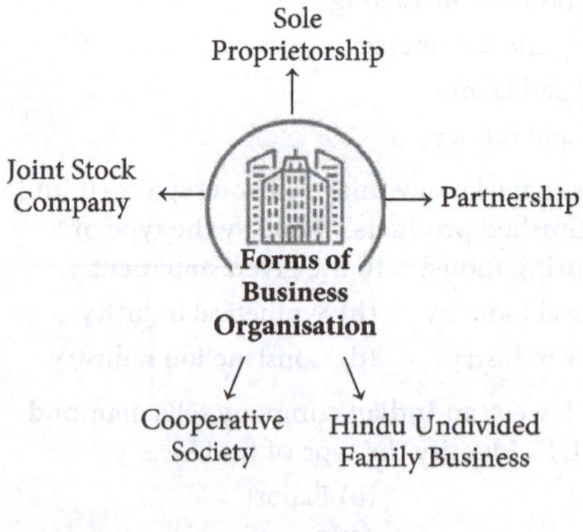

2.1 Sole Proprietorship

Sole proprietorship refers to a form of business organisation which is owned, managed and controlled by an individual, who is the recipient of all profits and bearer of all risks.

Features of Sole Proprietorship

1. **Formation and Closure** There is no legal formality to start this business. Closure can be also done easily.
2. **Liability** Owner's liability is unlimited. In case of losses and repayment of debt, personal property of owner can also be used if the assets of firm are insufficient to meet all the debts.
3. **Sole Risk Bearer and Profit Recipient** In sole proprietorship firm, whole risk is borne by a single individual. Due to this, he is personally liable for all losses and the sole receiver of profits.
4. **Control** This firm is owned, managed and controlled by a single individual.
5. **No Separate Entity** This firm has no legal identity apart from that of its owner. As a result, the owner is held responsible for all the activities of business.
6. **Lack of Business Continuity** As the owner and the business are same in sole proprietorship, death, insanity, imprisonment, physical ailment or bankruptcy of sole trader will directly affect the business and may lead to its closure.

Merits and Limitations of Sole Proprietorship

Merits	Limitations
• **Quick Decision-making** A sole proprietor enjoys freedom in making business decisions. Thus, he can take advantages of market opportunities by taking quick decisions. • **Confidentiality of Information** Sole trader is not expected to share his business decisions and secrets with anybody. He is also not bound by law to publish firm's accounts. • **Direct Incentive** Direct relationship between efforts and reward provide maximum incentive to the sole trader and encourages him to work hard. • **Sense of Accomplishment** If a business is successful, it contributes to the satisfaction of sole proprietor and creates a sense of accomplishment and confidence. • **Ease of Formation and Closure** An important merit of sole proprietorship is the possibility of entering and exiting business with minimal legal formalities.	• **Limited Resources** In sole proprietorship, funds are limited to the owner's personal savings and his borrowing capacity. This limits the scope for expansion of business. • **Limited Life of a Business** Illness, death or insolvency of proprietor affects the business and can lead to its closure. • **Unlimited Liability** Sole trader is personally liable for all the business debts. In case of heavy loss, he may be liable to sell his personal property also, to pay back his debts. • **Limited Managerial Ability** Sole trader's managerial ability is limited. He cannot be an expert in all the aspects of a business, therefore certain tasks could not be performed by him in an optimum manner.

2.2 Partnership

A partnership is a form of organisation in which two or more persons agree to pursue a lawful business.

According to the **Indian Partnership Act, 1932** (Section 4), "Partnership is the relation between persons who have agreed to share the profits of a business carried on by all or any of them acting for all."

Partnership

Features of Partnership

1. **Formation** A partnership firm can be formed through an agreement between the partners. The registration of partnership firm, is not compulsory. The business activity of partnership firm must be lawful, with the motive of earning profit.
2. **Liability** The liability of all the members of this firm is unlimited, i.e. personal assets of partners may also be used to pay the debts in case the business assets are insufficient. The partners are individually and jointly liable to pay back the debts of the firm.

3. **Risk Bearing** The partners bear the risk involved in the business jointly. If a business sustains loss, then partners share the loss in the same ratio in which they share profits.
4. **Decision-making and Control** Each partner has a right to participate in management and decision-making of the organisation. The activities of the firm are managed through joint efforts of all the partners and decisions are taken by mutual consent.
5. **Continuity** The existence of partnership firm is affected by death, retirement, insanity and insolvency (bankruptcy) of any of its partner. It suffers from lack of continuity.
6. **Number of Partners** There must be at least two persons to form a partnership. According to **Section 464** of the Companies Act, 2013, maximum number of partners in a partnership firm can be 100. According to **Rule 10** of the Companies (miscellaneous) Rules 2014, the maximum number of members can be 50.
7. **Mutual Agency** There must be existence of mutual agency relationship among the partners. It means that each partner is both an agent and principal.

Merits and Limitations of Partnership

Merits	Limitations
• **Ease of Formation and Closure** It is very easy to form a partnership firm. Only an agreement among the partners is required to form it and there is no compulsion of registration of the firm. Similarly, it is very easy to close such a firm.	• **Unlimited Liability** The liability of partners is unlimited and they are liable individually as well as jointly.
• **Balanced Decision-making** In partnership, work can be divided among partners according to their skill and knowledge or areas of their expertise. This reduces the burden of work and leads to more balanced decisions.	• **Limited Resources** There is a limit to number of partners in a partnership firm. Therefore, capital investment is also limited and partnership firms face problems in expanding business beyond a certain size.
• **More Funds** It is possible to raise larger amount of funds through partnership as compared to sole proprietorship, as each member contributes to the capital of the firm.	• **Possibility of Conflicts** In this firm, all partners have the power of decision-making. There may be different options on some issues, resulting in dispute. If a partner leaves the firm, it can result in termination of partnership.
• **Sharing of Risks** In partnership, risk gets distributed among partners, which reduces anxiety, burden and stress on individual partners.	• **Lack of Continuity** Partnership comes to an end with the death, retirement, insolvency or lunacy of any of its partners. Thus, it lacks continuity.
• **Secrecy** This firm is not required to publish its accounts and submit its reports. Therefore, the firm is able to maintain confidentiality of information.	• **Lack of Public Confidence** Partnership firms are not required to publish their financial reports and accounts. The true financial status of the partnership firm can not be known. Thus, the confidence of public on partnership firm is low.

Types of Partnership

Partnership can be classified on following two basis

I. Classification on the Basis of Duration

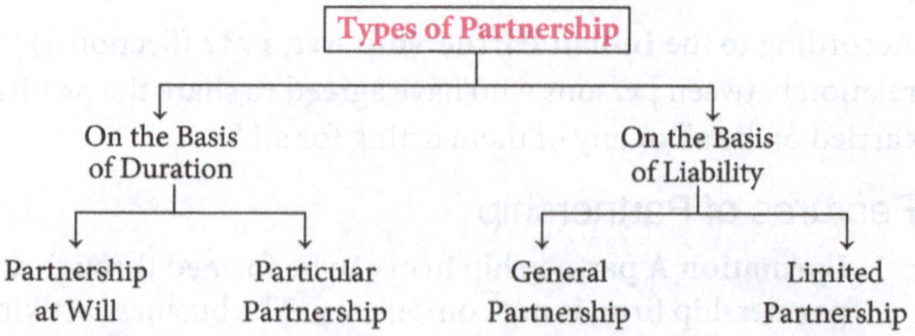

1. **Partnership at Will** This type of partnership can continue for any length of time, depending upon the will of the partners. It can be terminated at the desire of any partner by giving a notice.
2. **Particular Partnership** It is a partnership formed for a specific time period or to achieve a specified objective. It gets automatically dissolved on the expiry of the specified period or on the completion of the specific purpose.

II. Classification on the Basis of Liability

1. **General Partnership** In this form of partnership, the liability of all the partners is unlimited and joint. Each partner can participate in the management of the firm and their acts are binding on each other as well as on the firm. Registration for such partnership is optional.
2. **Limited Partnership** In limited partnership, the liability of at least one partner is unlimited, while other partners enjoy limited liability. The partners with limited liability cannot participate in the management and their acts do not bind the firm or other partner. Registration for such partnership is compulsory.

Partnership Deed

The written agreement containing the terms and conditions of the partnership is known as partnership deed.
The partnership deed contains provisions relating to various matters such as

- Name of the firm
- Nature and location of business
- Duration of business
- Investment made by each partner
- Distribution of profits and losses
- Duties and obligations of the partners
- Salaries and withdrawals of the partners
- Terms governing admission, retirement and expulsion of a partner
- Interest on capital and interest on drawings
- Procedure for dissolution of the firm
- Preparation of accounts and their auditing
- Method of solving disputes

The agreement of partnership deed can be oral or written. However, it is advisable to have a written agreement as it can be used as an evidence of the conditions agreed upon.

Registration of Partnership Firm

Registration means getting the name of partnership firm registered with the Registrar of firms of the area in which the place of business of the firm is situated or proposed to be situated.

It is optional for a partnership firm to get registered. However, non-registration of firm have the following consequences

- A partner of an unregistered firm cannot file a suit against the firm or other partners.
- The firm cannot file a suit against third parties.
- The firm cannot file a case against the partners.

Procedure for Registration of Partnership Firm

The procedure for getting a firm registered is

***Step* 1** Submission of application (signed by all partners) in the prescribed form to the Registrar of firms. The application should contain the following particulars

- Name of the firm
- Location of the firm
- Name of other places where the firm carries on business
- The date when each partner joined the firm
- Names and addresses of the partners
- Duration of partnership

***Step* 2** Deposit the required fee to the Registrar of firms.

***Step* 3** Registrar will verify the information and if satisfied with the authenticity of information, he will issue a certificate of registration.

Types of Partners

Partner	Explanation
Active or Working Partner	An active partner takes active part in management of the firm. He contributes capital, share profit and losses, and has an unlimited liability for the debts or the firm.
Sleeping or Dormant Partner	A sleeping partner contributes capital but does not take active part in the management of the firm. Such type of partner also share profits and losses and bears unlimited liability like other partners.
Secret Partner	A secret partner is one whose association with the firm is hidden from the general public. Such partner also contributes capital, takes active part in business, share profits and losses and bears unlimited liability.
Nominal Partner	A nominal partner is one who allows the use of his name and goodwill for the benefit of the firm, but does not contribute capital and does not take active part in the management or the firm. However, he bears unlimited liability for the debts like other partners.
Partner by Estoppel	A partner by estoppel is one who gives an impression to others by his words or conduct, that he is a partner of the firm. Such partners are also liable for the debts of the firm, even though they does not contribute capital or take part in the management of the firm.
Partner by Holding Out	A partner by holding out is one who is actually not a partner, but allows himself to be represented as a partner by the other partners. Such a person becomes liable to outside creditors, for repayment of any debts which have been extended to the firm on the basis of such representation.

Minor as a Partner

Partnership is based on legal contract between two persons who agree to share the profits or losses of a business carried on by them. Since a minor is incompetent to enter a valid contract with others, he cannot become a partner in any firm. However, a minor can be admitted to the benefits of a partnership firm with the mutual consent of all other partners. In such cases, his liability will be limited to the extent of the capital contributed by him in the firm. A minor can share only the profits and cannot be asked to bear the losses.

2.3 Hindu Undivided Family Business

Hindu Undivided Family (HUF) business or Joint Hindu Family business is that form of business organisation which is owned and managed by the members of HUF.

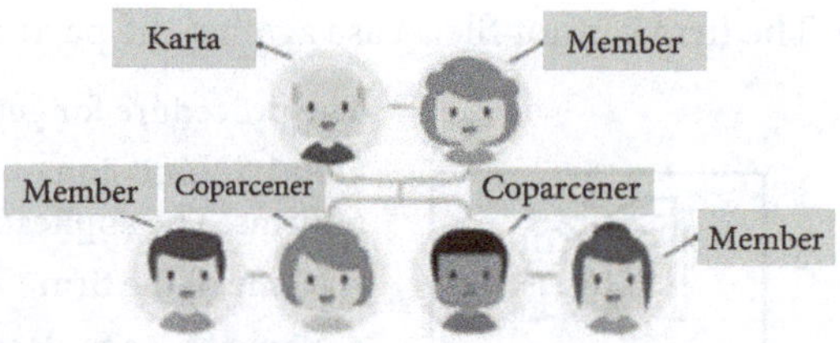

This type of business is governed by Hindu Law, i.e. Hindu Succession Act, 1956. The business is controlled by the head of the family, who is the eldest member of the family and is called *karta*. All members have equal ownership right over the property and they are known as **coparceners**.

Features of Hindu Undivided Family Business

1. **Formation** At least two members and an ancestral property are the basic requirements for the formation of joint hindu family business. The business does not require any agreement as membership is by birth.
2. **Liability** The liability of *karta* is unlimited, but the liability of other members is limited to the extent of their share in the coparcenery property of the business.
3. **Control** The business is managed and controlled by *karta*. He takes all the decisions and these decisions are legally binding on the other members.
4. **Continuity** After the death of *karta*, the next eldest member takes his position and thus, the business continues.
5. **Minor Members** Under HUF business, an individual becomes member by taking birth in the family. Hence, a minor can also be a member of HUF business.

Gender Equality in the Joint Hindu Family

According to the **Hindu Succession (Amendment) Act, 2005**, the daughter of a coparcener of a joint hindu family shall by birth, become a coparcener. At the time of partition of such a joint hindu family, the coparcenary property shall be equally divided to all the coparceners irrespective of their gender (male or female). The eldest member (either male or female of joint hindu family shall become *karta*. Married daughter has equal rights in property of a joint hindu family.

Merits and Limitations of Hindu Undivided Family Business

Merits	Limitations
• **Effective Control** In a HUF business, the *karta* has absolute decision-making power. This facilitates quick and flexible decision-making. • **Continued Business Existence** A HUF business has continued existence. Its existence is not affected by the death of *karta*, as the next eldest member takes up his position. • **Limited Liability of Members** The liability of the coparceners is limited to the extent of their share in the family business. • **Increased Loyalty and Cooperation** The members of a HUF business are loyal to each other. They are willing to cooperate and work towards a common goal, as all of them belong to the same family.	• **Limited Resources** The HUF business depends mainly on the ancestral property. This creates the problem of limited capital. • **Unlimited Liability of *Karta*** In HUF, the liability of the *karta* is unlimited. His personal assets can also be used to discharge the debts of the business. • **Dominance of *Karta*** In HUF, the entire control and management of the business lies with the *karta*. Sometimes, the members may not agree with the decisions taken by the *karta*. This may create conflict among them and consequently operations of the business may break down. • **Limited Managerial Skills** A *karta* has absolute decision-making power related to all aspects of the business. However, he cannot be an expert in all the areas of management.

2.4 Cooperative Society

A cooperative society is a voluntary association of persons, who join together with the motive of welfare of members. To form a cooperative society, consent of 10 adult persons is required and the capital of a society is raised from its members through issue of shares.

Features of Cooperative Society

1. **Voluntary Membership** This society is essentially a voluntary association ofpersons. Any person of 18 years and above is free to join and exit the society any time after serving a notice. Membership is open to all, irrespective of their caste, religion and gender.
2. **Legal Status** The registration of a cooperative society is compulsory. After registration, this society becomes a distinct entity independent of its members. It can enter into contracts and hold property in its name.
3. **Limited Liability** The liability of members is limited to the extent of the amount contributed by them as capital.
4. **Control** In this society, an elected managing committee has the power to take decisions. Members have voting rights to choose the managing committee.
5. **Service Motive** The primary aim of this society is to provide service to its members and not to earn profit. If any surplus is generated as a result of its operations, it is distributed amongst the members as dividend.

Merits and Limitations of Cooperative Society

Merits	Limitations
• **Equality in Voting Status** Cooperative society is governed by the principle of 'one-man-one-vote'. Each member is entitled to equal voting rights, irrespective of capital contribution by them. • **Limited Liability** The liability of every member is limited to the extent of his share in the society's capital. • **Stable Existence** As cooperative society is a separate legal entity, it is not affected by death, lunacy or bankruptcy of the members. • **Economy in Operations** In this society, the members generally offer honorary services to the society. As the society aims to eliminate middleman, it helps in reducing costs. The customers or producers themselves are members of society which also reduces the risk of bad debts. • **Support from Government** The cooperative society gets support from the government in the form of low taxes, subsidies and low interest rates on loans. • **Ease of Formation** It is quite easy to form a cooperative society with any ten adult members. Only few legal formalities are involved in the registration.	• **Limited Resources** A cooperative society is formed by people with limited means. The low rate of dividend discourages members to invest large amount in the society. Therefore, a cooperative society has limited resources. • **Inefficiency in Management** This society is managed by its members who are generally not professional. A cooperative society cannot afford to employ expert managers at high salaries due to limited funds. • **Lack of Secrecy** It is difficult to maintain secrecy about the operations of a cooperative society due to open discussion in the meetings and disclosure obligation according to the Section 7 of Societies Act. • **Government Control** The day-to-day working of a cooperative society is bound by rigid rules and regulations of the government. Keeping accounts, regular audits and inspections is essential. • **Differences of Opinion** The differences arising due to contrary viewpoints may lead to difficulties in decision-making. Personal interests may start to dominate the welfare motive and benefit of other members.

Types of Cooperative Society

1. **Consumer's Cooperative Societies**
   These are established to protect the interest of consumers. These are formed by consumers for obtaining good quality products at reasonable prices. They purchase goods directly from manufacturers or wholesalers in bulk and sells them to the members. Profits (if any) are distributed among the members on the basis of their capital contribution or purchases.
2. **Producer's Cooperative Societies**
   These are formed by producers. The main aim of these societies is to help small producers who cannot easily collect various inputs of production and face problems in marketing. These societies supply raw materials, tools, equipments and other items to their members at reasonable price and also buy their output for sale. Profits are distributed among the members on the basis of the contributions to the total number of goods produced and sold.
3. **Marketing Cooperative Societies**
   These are formed by producers who wish to obtain reasonable prices for their output. They perform various marketing functions like packing, grading, marketing research, etc. for the benefit of its members. These societies eliminate middlemen and improves the competitive position of its members. The profits are distributed among the members according to each member's contribution to the pool of output.
4. **Farmer's Cooperative Societies**
   In these societies, small farmers join together and accumulate their resources for cultivating their land collectively. These societies provides better quality seeds, fertilisers, machineries and other modem techniques for cultivation of crops.
5. **Credit Cooperative Societies**
   These societies comprise of persons who seek financial help in the form of loans. These societies provide loans to their members on easy terms and reasonably low rate of interest. They provide loans out of the amount collected as capital and deposits made by the members.
6. **Cooperative Housing Society**
   The main aim of these societies is to provide houses to people with limited means/income at reasonable price. They also give them the option of paying in installments. These societies construct flats or provide plots to members on which the members themselves can construct the houses as per their choice.

2.5 Joint Stock Company

A joint stock company is an association of persons formed for carrying out business activities and has a legal status independent of its members.

Features of Joint Stock Company

1. **Artificial Person** A joint stock company is an artificial person created by law which do not have any physical body. But, it acts like a natural person who can buy or sell properties, enter into contracts, can lend and borrow money, sue and can be sued in its own name.
2. **Separate Legal Entity** A joint stock company acquires a separate legal entity, from the day of its incorporation, which is distinct from its members. Its assets and liabilities are separate from those of its members.
3. **Formation** The formation of a company is time consuming, expensive and complex process, as it involves preparation of several documents and compliance to several legal requirements. Registration of a company is compulsory under the Companies Act, 2013.
4. **Perpetual Succession** The existence of a company is not affected by death, insolvency, entry or exit of the members. It is created by law and the law can only bring it to an end, by completing a legal procedure called winding up.
5. **Control** The management and control of the affairs of the company is undertaken by the Board of Directors who are appointed by voting. The shareholders do not have the right to be involved in the day-to-day running of the business.
6. **Liability** The liability of the members is limited to the extent of capital contributed by them.
7. **Common Seal** A company is an artifical entity that is created under the law. Unlike human beings, it can not sign official documents. Thus, it signs using common seal of a company.
8. **Risk Bearing** Risk of losses is borne by all the shareholders. In the condition of financial difficulties, all share-holders have to contribute to the extent of their unpaid share in company's capital. Thus, risk is spread over a large number of shareholders.

Merits and Limitations of Joint Stock Company

Merits	Limitations
• **Limited Liability** The shareholders are liable only to the extent of the amount unpaid on the shares held by them. • **Transfer of Interest** The shareholders of a company can easily and freely transfer their shares. They can sell their shares at any time when the share price is high or they are in need of money. • **Perpetual Existence** The existence of a company is not affected by death, insanity, retirement, resignation and insolvency of its members. It can be liquidated only as per the provisions of the Companies Act, 2013. • **Scope for Expansion** A company has large financial resources. Capital can be raised from public through investors, banks or financial institutions.	• **Complexity in Formation** The procedure of formation of a company is complex which requires much time and effort. It is expensive and requires lot of legal formalities to be fulfilled. • **Lack of Secrecy** According to the Companies Act, a public company is required to provide a lot of information to the office of the Registrar of Companies. Such information is available to general public also. • **Impersonal Work Environment** Due to separation between ownership and control, there is no direct link between efforts and reward which leads to a lack of personal interest and incentive. • **Numerous Regulations** A number of regulations are imposed on company such as audit, voting, etc. by different agencies like Registrar of Companies, SEBI, etc. This reduces freedom of operations of a company. • **Delay in Decision-making** All important decisions are taken either by the board of directors or are referred to general meeting which makes decision-making process time consuming. • **Oligarchic Management** A company appears to be democratic as the Board of Directors are the elected representatives of the shareholders.

Merits	Limitations
• **Professional Management** A company can afford to pay high salaries to specialists and professionals. Therefore, as each department is headed by an expert, greater efficiency is observed in company's operations and decision-making.	• **Conflict in Interest** There are much chances of conflict of interests among the stakeholders of a company. e.g. Consumers want better products at lower prices and the shareholders want higher returns. Thus, it becomes very difficult to satisfy such diverse interests.

Liability in Joint Stock Company

Rohan is a shareholder in a company holding 500 shares of ₹ 10 each, on which he has already paid ₹ 7 per share. In the event of losses or company's failure to pay debts, Rohan is liable to pay only ₹ 1,500 (i.e the unpaid amount of ₹ 3 on 500 shares).

Types of Joint Stock Company

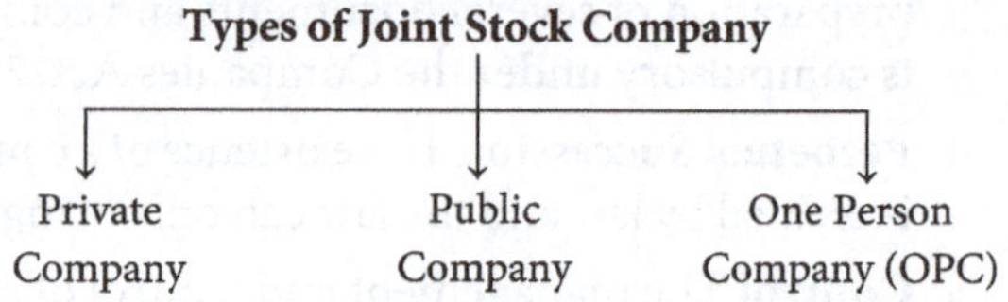

Joint stock company can be classified as

1. Private Company

According to the Companies Act, 2013, a private company means a company that

- restricts the right to transfer its shares.
- has minimum 2 members and maximum 200 members, excluding present and past employees.
- does not invite public to subscribe to its share capital.

It is necessary for a private company to use the word ***private limited*** after its name.

2. Public Company

A public company means a company which is not a private company. According to the Companies Act, 2013, a public company means one that

- has a minimum of 7 members and there is no limit on the maximum number of members.
- has no restriction on transfer of securities.
- is not prohibited from inviting the general public to subscribe its securities.

A private company which is a subsidiary of a public company is also treated as a public company.

Privileges Enjoyed by Private Company Over Public Company

- Only 2 members are required to form a private company as against the minimum requirement of 7 members for a public company.
- Only 2 directors are needed in a private company, as against 3 directors in a public company.
- Private companies are not required to issue a prospectus or the Statement in Lieu of Prospectus.
- Maintaining an index of members is not required by a private company while the same is necessary in the case of a public company.
- Shares of a private company can be allotted, even if minimum subscription is not received.

3. One Person Company (OPC)

This type of company is incorporated by a single person. Before the enforcement of the Companies Act, 2013, a single person was not able to establish a company. An OPC has features of a company and the benefits of the sole proprietorship.

According to Section 2 (62) of the Company's Act, 2013, a company can be formed with just one director and one member. The director and member can also be the same person. An individual who may be a resident or non-resident Indian can register an OPC in India.

Comparative Evaluation of Forms of Organisation

Basis of Comparison	Sole Proprietorship	Partnership	Joint Hindu Family Business	Cooperative Society	Company
Formation	Easiest formation due to minimal legal formalities	Easy formation as registration is optional	Less legal formalities, exemption from registration, easy formation	Registration is compulsory and greater legal formalities	Registration is compulsory and formation process is lengthy and expensive
Members	Only owner	Minimum-2 Maximum-50	Minimum 2 persons for division of family property and no maximum limit	Minimum 10 adults and no maximum limit	**Minimum** Private-2; Public -7 **Maximum** Private-200; Public-Unlimited
Capital Contribution	Limited finance	Limited but more than sole proprietorship	Limited to ancestral property	Limited resources	Large financial resources
Liability	Unlimited	Unlimited and joint	Unlimited for *karta* and limited for other members	Limited	Limited
Control and Management	Owner takes all decisions, quick decision-making	Partners take decisions, consent of all partners is needed	*Karta* takes all business decisions	Elected representative, i.e. managing committee takes all business decisions	Decisions are taken by Board of Directors due to separation between ownership and management
Continuity	Unstable as affected by status of owner	More stable but affected by status of partners	Stable business. It continues event if *karta* dies	Stable because of separate legal status	Stable because of separate legal status

2.6 Formation of a Company

It is a complex process, involving several legal formalities and procedural decisions. It involves following stages

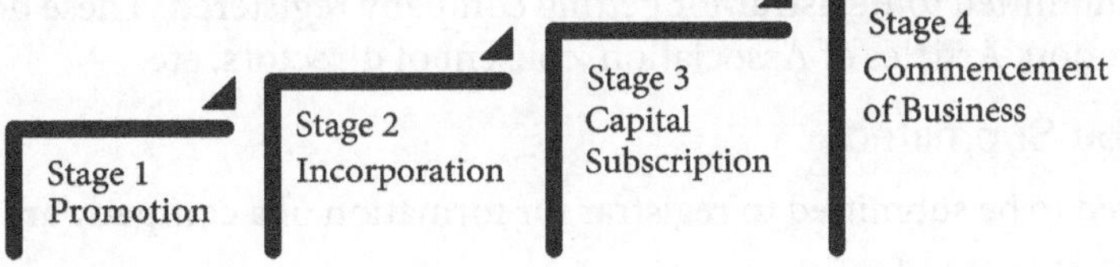

I. Promotion

It includes the steps like identification of business idea, its investigation and arrangement of necessary resources for the formation of a company. The person who performs all the work at promotion stage is known as **promoter**. According to **Section 2(69)** of the Companies Act, 2013, the 'promoter' is defined as the following

- A person who has been named as such in a prospectus or is identified by the company in the annual return referred to in Section 92.
- A person who has control over the affairs of the company, directly or indirectly.

- A person according to whose advice, directions or instructions, the board of directors of the company usually act.

Legal Position of Promoters

- They are neither the agents nor the trustees of the company.
- They are personally liable for preliminary contracts.
- They enjoy a fiduciary position (i.e. depending upon good faith) with the company. This position does not allow a promoter to earn secret profits from the company. If the promoters earn secret profits, the company can cancel the contract, recover the purchase price paid to the promoters and can claim the damages for the loss suffered.

Functions of a Promoter

1. **Identification of Business Opportunity** The primary function of a promoter is to identify a business idea or opportunity which may be related to setting up a new business or to expand the existing business. Promoter also analyse the profitability of an idea, risk involved, resources required, etc.
2. **Feasibility Studies** After identification, the promoters undertake detailed investigation of all aspects of business . The feasibility study includes
   - **Technical Feasibility** To determine whether it is technically possible to produce the product or not.
   - **Financial Feasibility** To determine whether the required finance to float the venture will be arranged or not.
   - **Economic Feasibility** To determine whether the business idea would be profitable or not.
3. **Name Approval** Three names are given in the application to the Registrar of Companies in order of their priority. Resigtrar approves any one name after being satisfied that the name is not identical to name of other companies and also not misleading. However, the proposed name will not be accepted by the Registrar, if
   - it resembles the name of an existing company and it is misleading.
   - it contains the word 'cooperative' and violates the provisions of The Emblem and Names (Prevention of Improper Use) Act, 1950.
   - the name does not end with the word 'Limited' in case of a public company and with the words 'Private Limited' in case of a private company.
4. **Fixing up Signatories to the Memorandum of Association** Promoters make decision regarding the signing of the Memorandum of Association. The written consent of the persons signing the memorandum is taken to act as directors and to take up the qualification shares in the company. The memorandum must be signed by at least 7 persons in case of a public company and 2 persons in case of a private company.
5. **Appointment of Professionals** Promoters appoint merchant bankers, auditors, etc. to assist them in the preparation of necessary documents, which are required to be submitted with the Registrar of Companies.
6. **Preparation of Necessary Documents** Promoter takes up the steps to prepare various legal documents of a company that are to be submitted to Registrar for getting company registered. These documents include Memorandum of Association, Articles of Association, consent of directors, etc.

Documents Required to be Submitted

Important documents required to be submitted to registrar for formation of a company are

1. **Memorandum of Association** (MoA)

   It is the principal document of the company and is also known as charter of the company as it includes the powers and objectives of the company. It defines the scope of its activities and its relations with the investors and outsiders. It contains different clauses which are

Clause	Explanation
Name Clause	Legal and recognised name of the company which has been approved by the Registrar of Companies.
Registered Office Clause	Shows name of the State in which the registered office of the company will be located.

Clause	Explanation
Objects Clause	Main clause of MoA which summarises the purpose for establishing the company. The objects of the company are classified into the following sub-clauses – **Main Objects** Contains the main objects or the basic purpose for which a company is formed. – **Other Objects** Objects not stated in the main object clause can be stated in this sub-clause.
Liability Clause	States the liability of members is limited to the amount unpaid on the shares owned by them.
Capital Clause	States the maximum capital which the company will be authorised to raise through the issue of shares. A company cannot issue share capital in excess of the amount specified in this clause.
Association Clause	The signatories to the MoA state their intention to be associated with the company and also give their consent to purchase qualification shares. The MoA must be signed by atleast 7 persons in case of public company and by 2 persons in case of private company.

2. **Articles of Association** (AoA)

It is a document containing the rules and regulations for the internal management of the company. These are the by laws of a company that define the mode and manner in which the company's business is to be carried on.

Main Contents of Articles of Association

- The amount of share capital of the company.
- The different classes of shares.
- Rights of each type of shareholders.
- Procedure of allotment of shares.
- Procedure for issuing share capital.
- Seal of the company
- Duties, powers and remuneration of directors.
- Procedure regarding winding up of the company.
- Procedure regarding keeping of books of accounts and their audit.
- Procedure for transfer of shares, forfeiture of shares, reissue of forfeited shares.
- Procedure for conducting meetings, appointment and removal of directors, declaration and payment of dividend.

3. **Other Documents to be Submitted**

- **Consent of Proposed Directors** A written consent of each person named as a director, is required for confirming that they agree to buy and pay for qualification shares.
- **Agreement** It is submitted if any company proposes to enter into an agreement with any individual for his appointment as the managing director or a whole time director or manager.
- **Statutory Declaration** It is a declaration stating that all the legal requirements for registration have been complied. It is to be submitted to the Registrar with the above mentioned documents for getting the company registered under the law. This statement can be signed by the following
  - An advocate or a chartered accountant or a cost accountant.
  - Company secretary in practice who is engaged in the formation of a company.
  - A person named in the articles as a director or manager.
  - Secretary of the company.
- **Receipt of Payment of Fee** Along with the above-mentioned documents, necessary fees has to be paid for the registration of the company.

II. Incorporation

It means the registration of a company under the Companies Act, 2013. The following steps are taken by the promoters to get the company incorporated

***Step* 1** **Filing of Necessary Documents** Once the Registrar approves the name, promoter files the following documents

- Memorandum of Association
- Articles of Association
- Statement of authorised capital
- Consent of proposed directors

- Agreement with proposed managing director
- Statutory declaration stating that all formalities are duly completed
- Notice of the exact address of the registered office
- Copy of the Registrar's letter approving the company's name

***Step* 2 Payment of Fee** Alongwith filing of above documents, registration fees has to be deposited.

***Step* 3 Registration** The Registrar verifies all the documents submitted. If he is satisfied with the authenticity of documents, he enters the name of the company in his register.

***Step* 4 Certificate of Incorporation** After entering the name in his register, the Registrar issues a certificate of incorporation. From the date of issue of this certificate, company comes into existence and is considered as separate legal entity.

Effect of Certificate of Incorporation

- A company is legally born on the date printed on the certificate of incorporation. It becomes a legal entity with perpetual succession on the date printed on the certificate of incorporation.
- The company becomes entitled to enter into valid contracts.
- The company becomes a legal business entity irrespective of any deficiency in its registration.
- A private company can immediately commence its business.

III. Capital Subscription

After incorporation, a public company can raise the required funds from the public by means of issue of shares and debentures. For doing the same, it has to issue a prospectus which is an invitation to the public to subscribe to the capital of the company.

Steps for Raising Funds from Public

***Step* 1 SEBI Approval** SEBI regulates the capital market of India to protect the interest of investors. A public company is required to take the approval from SEBI to issue securities.

***Step* 2 Filing of Prospectus or Statement in Lieu of Prospectus** It is a document which invites offers from the public to purchase shares, debentures or make deposits in the company. If a public company having share capital raises funds privately (like through friends, relatives or some private arrangements), then it files a 'Statement in Lieu of Prospectus', with the Registrar of Companies.

***Step* 3 Appointment of Bankers, Brokers and Underwriters** In order to raise funds from the public, experts are appointed. These experts do the following tasks to raise funds from public

- The bankers of the company receive the application money. Brokers encourage the public to apply for the shares.
- If the company is not reasonably assured of receiving good response from public to the issue, it may appoint underwriters. Underwriters undertake to buy the shares if these are not subscribed by public. They receive a commission for underwriting the issue.

***Step* 4 Minimum Subscription** It refers to minimum numbers of shares that must be subscribed by the public before a company proceed further with the allotment of shares.

According to the SEBI guidelines, minimum subscription is 90 per cent of the issue amount. If minimum subscription is not received, the allotment cannot be made and the application money must be returned to the applicants within 30 days.

***Step* 5 Application to Stock Exchange** It is necessary for a public company to list their shares in the stock exchange. If a company fails to get permission from SEBI within 10 weeks from the date of closure of subscription list, the allotment will become void and the money received from applicants will have to be returned.

***Step* 6** **Allotment of Shares** It involves issuance of allotment letters to the shareholders. A return of allotment containing the name, address and number of shares allotted to each shareholder is to be submitted to the Registrar within 30 days of allotment.

IV. Commencement of Business

To commence business, a public company has to obtain a Certificate of Commencement of business. For this, the following documents have to be filed with the Registrar of Companies

- A declaration that minimum subscription of 90 per cent of the issued shares has been received.
- A declaration that all directors have paid in cash in respect of allotment of shares made to them.
- A declaration that no money is pending to pay back to the applicants.
- A statutory declaration that the above requirements have been completed and must be signed by the director or secretary of the company.

The registrar verifies all the documents and declarations submitted by the company. If he finds them satisfactory, then he issues a certificate for commencement of business and the company can start its business from and the issue of the certificate.

2.7 Choice of Form of Business Organisation

Factor	Explanation
Cost and Ease in Setting up the Organisation	Sole proprietorship and partnership are inexpensive and simple to establish, while cooperative societies and companies require registration, making their formation lengthy and costly. Thus, sole proprietorship is ideal for low cost setups.
Liability	Sole proprietors and partners have unlimited liability, as does the *karta* in HUF. In contrast, members of companies and cooperative societies have limited liability, making companies preferable for risk averse individuals.
Continuity	Sole proprietorships and partnerships lack continuity due to owner related disruptions, unlike HUF, cooperative societies and companies. Companies are ideal for permanent ventures, while sole proprietorships and partnerships suit short-term needs.
Management Ability	Sole proprietors may lack managerial expertise, whereas partnerships allow shared skills. Companies can hire professionals, making them suitable for businesses requiring professional management.
Capital Considerations	Companies can raise significant capital by issuing shares while partnerships pool partners' resources. Sole proprietorships, with limited funds, suit small-scale operations, whereas companies cater to larger scales.
Degree of Control	Sole proprietorship offers direct control and decision-making while companies separate ownership and management. Sole proprietorship is ideal for those seeking full control, whereas partnerships or companies suit those who are open to shared decision-making.
Nature of Business	Businesses requiring personal customer contact, like grocery stores, favour sole proprietorship. For large-scale manufacturing without direct customer interaction, the company structure is better suited.

Choice of Forms of Business

Ravi wanted full control over his new bakery business, so he chose a sole proprietorship to make all decisions independently. However, his friend Asha preferred starting a tech startup with shared responsibilities and opted for a partnership. On the other hand, Neha planned to expand her clothing brand nationwide and formed a company to bring in professional management.

Mind Map

FORMS OF BUSINESS ORGANISATION

1 Sole Proprietorship

Sole proprietorship refers to a form of business organisation which is owned, managed and controlled by an individual, who is the recipient of all profits and bearer of all risks.

Merits
- Quick decision-making
- Confidentiality of information
- Direct incentive
- Sense of accomplishment
- Ease of formation and closure

Demerits
- Limited resources
- Limited life of a business
- Unlimited liability
- Limited managerial ability

2 Partnership

A partnership is a form of organisation in which two or more persons agree to pursue a lawful business.

Merits
- Ease of formation and closure
- Balanced decision-making
- More funds
- Sharing of risks
- Secrecy

Demerits
- Unlimited liability
- Limited resources
- Possibility of conflicts
- Lack of continuity
- Lack of public confidence

Types of Partnerships
- On the basis of duration
  - Partnership at will
  - Particular partnership
- On the basis of liability
  - General partnership
  - Limited partnership

Types of Partners
- Active or working
- Sleeping or dormant
- Secret
- Nominal
- Partner by estoppel
- Partner by holding out

3 Hindu Undivided Family Business

Hindu Undivided Family (HUF) business or Joint Hindu Family business is owned and managed by the members of HUF. The business is controlled by the head of the family, who is the eldest member of the family and is called *karta*.

Merits
- Effective control
- Continued business existence
- Limited liability of members
- Increased loyalty and cooperation

Demerits
- Limited resources
- Dominance of *karta*
- Unlimited liability of *karta*
- Limited managerial skills

4 Cooperative Society

A cooperative society is a voluntary association of persons, who join together with the motive of welfare of members. To form a cooperative society, consent of 10 adult persons is required and the capital of a society is raised from its members through issue of shares.

Merits
- Equality in voting status
- Limited liability
- Stable existence and easy formation
- Economy in operations
- Support from government

Demerits
- Limited resources
- Lack of secrecy
- Inefficiency in management
- Differences of opinion, government control

Types of Cooperative society
- Consumer's cooperative societies
- Producer's cooperative societies
- Marketing cooperative societies
- Farmer's cooperative societies
- Credit cooperative societies
- Cooperative housing society

5 Joint Stock Company

A joint stock company is an association of persons formed for carrying out business activities and has a legal status independent of its members.

Merits
- Limited liability
- Transfer of interest
- Perpetual existence
- Scope for expansion
- Professional management

Demerits
- Complexity in formation
- Lack of secrecy
- Impersonal work environment
- Numerous regulations
- Delay in decision-making
- Oligarchic management
- Conflict in interest

Types
- **Private Company** Restricts the right to transfer its shares, does not invite public to subscribe to its share capital, Minimum – 2 members, Maximum – 200 members.
- **Public Company** No restriction on transfer of securities, not prohibited from inviting general public to subscribe to its securities, Minimum – 7 members, maximum – No limit.
- **One Person Company** Can be formed with just one director and one member (director and member can be same person).

6 Formation of a Company

I. Promotion
- Identification of business opportunity
- Feasibility studies
- Name approval
- Fixing up signatories to MoA
- Appointment of professionals
- Preparation of necessary documents

II. Incorporation
- Filing of necessary documents
- Payment of fees
- Registration
- Certificate of incorporation

III. Capital Subscription
- SEBI approval
- Filing of prospectus or statement in lieu of prospectus
- Appointment of bankers, brokers and underwriters
- Minimum subscription
- Application to stock exchange
- Allotment of shares

IV. Commencement of Business

7 Choice of Form of Business Organisation

- Cost and ease in setting-up the organisation
- Liability
- Continuity
- Management ability
- Capital considerations
- Degree of control
- Nature of business

EXAM PATTERN QUESTIONS

Objective Type Questions

Multiple Choice Questions (MCQs)

1. Profits are not shared in case of

(a) company (b) cooperative society
(c) sole proprietorship (d) partnership

2. Which form of business is preferred when the initial cost of setting-up the organisation needs to be low and legal requirements minimal?

(a) Company
(b) Cooperative society
(c) Sole proprietorship
(d) Joint hindu family business

3. After completing high studies in hotel management courses from one of the highly reputed hotel Management Institutes of India, Mahesh decided to start his own bakery in his hometown. His father arranged funds and supported him to commence his business.

He recruited some staff and purchased the required equipment and machines. Within a few months, he started manufacturing bakery products in the market and sold them at reasonable prices. His quality products and reasonable prices helped him in making a good profit. Identify the form of business organisation highlighted in the above case. **Competency Based Que**

(a) Company
(b) Joint hindu family business
(c) Sole trading concern (d) Partnership

4. Identify the form of business organisation in the below picture.

(a) Sole proprietorship
(b) Hindu undivided family
(c) Partnership
(d) Company

5. Which of the following statements is incorrect about a minor partner?

(a) He has to bear losses also
(b) He can inspect books of accounts
(c) He has an option to continue with a firm after attaining majority
(d) He shares only profits

6. Rakesh and Rajesh are two close friends who decided to take the franchise of Tata Sky. Both of them invested equally to get the franchise for their home district. It was agreed mutually between Rakesh and Rajesh to share the profits or losses of the firm on an equal basis. Name the form of business organisations run by the friends referred to in the above case.

Competency Based Que

(a) Partnership (b) One person company
(c) Joint venture (d) Sole trading concern

7. How is the continuity of a partnership firm affected?

(a) It remains unaffected by the death or retirement of a partner
(b) It continues automatically without any legal formalities
(c) It is affected by the death, retirement or insolvency of a partner
(d) It is dissolved upon any disagreement among the partners

8. Sudhanshu is an active partner in a partnership firm, where, the liability of partners is unlimited. Partners are allowed to participate in the management of the firm business.

All the partners are abiding by the rules framed in the partnership. Registration of a partnership firm is optional and the firm business may come to an end in the event of death, insolvency and lunatic of any partner. Which type of partnership is referred to in the above case? **Competency Based Que**

(a) General partnership
(b) Partnership at will
(c) Limited liability partnership
(d) Particular partnership

9. **The partnership deed generally includes the following**
(a) Name of firm (b) Nature of business
(c) Location of business (d) All of these

10. **Identify the form of business organisation depicted in the below picture.**

(a) Sole proprietorship (b) Hindu undivided family
(c) Partnership (d) Company

11. **Why is having a written partnership deed advisable?**
(a) It eliminates the need for registration of the partnership
(b) It can be used as evidence of agreed terms and conditions
(c) It ensures unlimited liability for all partners
(d) It is mandatory under the Indian Partnership Act, 1932

12. **Which of the following is not a consequence of non-registration of a partnership firm?**
(a) A partner cannot file a suit against the firm
(b) The firm cannot file a suit against third parties
(c) The firm cannot take loans from banks
(d) The firm cannot file a case against its partners

13. **A, B and C are the partners in a partnership firm. They mutually decide that A's association with the firm will not be revealed to the general public. According to the above statement, A is a** **Competency Based Que**
(a) nominal partner (b) dormant partner
(c) secret partner (d) partner by estoppel

14. **Ramesh is presenting himself as a partner of ABC Associates through his conduct or behaviour. Clients dealing with the firm accept him as a partner due to his self-acclaimed attitude of being a partner of the firm. Which type of partner Mr. Ramesh is referred to in the above case?** **Competency Based Que**
(a) Active partner (b) Sleeping partner
(c) Secret partner (d) Partner by estoppel

15. **"Allows the use of his name and goodwill for the benefit of the firm." Identify the type of partner mentioned in the statement.** **Competency Based Que**
(a) Active partner (b) Sleeping partner
(c) Nominal partner (d) Secret partner

16. **A partnership firm, ABC Enterprises, was formed by three partners under an agreement to start a garment business. The firm decided not to register the partnership since registration is not mandatory under Indian law. Each partner agreed to share profits and losses equally.**

However, after a year of operation, one of the partners, Mr. X, decided to retire due to personal reasons. The remaining partners discussed continuing the business but faced legal challenges related to the firm's liabilities.

What is the nature of liability for the partners in a partnership firm? **Competency Based Que**
(a) Limited to their investment in the firm
(b) Unlimited, including personal assets
(c) Limited to their share of profits
(d) Limited to the firm's assets

17. **Two friends, Ankit and Raj, started a partnership firm named AR Traders to sell handcrafted products. They decided to form a partnership for a period of five years.**

To ensure clarity, they created a written agreement outlining the profit sharing ratio, duties of each partner and provisions for dispute resolution.

After two years, Ankit decided to withdraw some money as his share of profit, but Raj objected, stating the partnership deed did not mention such provisions. Which type of partnership does AR Traders represent? **Competency Based Que**
(a) Partnership at will
(b) Particular partnership
(c) Limited partnership
(d) General partnership

18. **Rahul, a well-known businessperson, agreed to let a startup firm, TechSpark Solutions, use his name to attract investors and customers.**

He neither contributed any capital nor participated in the firm's management. Meanwhile, another partner, Priya, actively managed the operations and contributed capital.

The firm also had a partner, Vishal, who stayed away from day-to-day operations but contributed capital and shared profits. Unexpectedly, the firm incurred heavy losses and creditors sought repayment from all partners, including Rahul and Vishal.

Which type of partner is Rahul in TechSpark Solutions? **Competency Based Que**
(a) Active partner
(b) Nominal partner
(c) Sleeping partner
(d) Secret partner

19. Identify the form of business organisation in the below picture.

(a) Sole proprietorship (b) Hindu undivided family
(c) Partnership (d) Company

20. In hindu undivided family, ... has absolute decision-making power.

(a) karta (b) coparcener
(c) minor (d) All of these

21. Ramesh, the head of his family, manages a business that has been passed down for generations. The business is run jointly by Ramesh, his two brothers and their families. All members share the profits as per their ancestral rights and the management is guided by the traditions of the family. Identify the form of business organisation described in the case. Competency Based Que

(a) Hindu Undivided Family (HUF)
(b) Partnership
(c) Sole proprietorship (d) Cooperative society

22. Male person become member of a hindu undivided family business by ....

(a) birth (b) death
(c) registration (d) participation

23. A joint hindu family business is run by Mr. Sachin Agarwal, in Hyderabad, Telangana. In a centralised management environment, he is operating and manages all business activities as the eldest member of the family. How Mr. Sachin should be designated or recognised in the family business? Competency Based Que

(a) Elder member (b) Karta
(c) Coparcener (d) Partner

24. In a joint hindu family business named Sharma Traders, the business has been running successfully for years under the management of Karan, the eldest member of the family. Karan, as the Karta, makes all decisions regarding the operations of the business. The business is built on ancestral property and his younger brothers, Rajesh and Amit, are part of the business but do not take active part in its management.

Rajesh, although a minor, is a coparcener in the business due to his birth into the family. If Karan passes away, his position as Karta will be taken over by Rajesh once he becomes the next eldest member.

What is the primary reason for Rajesh being member of Sharma Traders even though he is a minor? Competency Based Que

(a) He holds a significant stake in the business
(b) He has been actively managing the business
(c) Membership in an HUF business is by birth
(d) He has a legal agreement with his family members

25. At least 10 adults but no maximum limit is specified in case of ....

(a) joint hindu family (b) cooperative society
(c) company (d) partnership

26. A group of small farmers decides to pool their resources to collectively cultivate their land. The society they form provides high quality seeds, fertilisers, modern machinery and advanced techniques to improve agricultural productivity.

Identify the type of cooperative society described in the statement. Competency Based Que

(a) Consumer's cooperative society
(b) Producer's cooperative society
(c) Farmer's cooperative society
(d) Marketing cooperative society

27. Green Valley Cooperative Society is a newly formed cooperative society aimed at providing affordable housing solutions to its members. The society operates on a 'one member, one vote' basis and its members are free to join or exit by giving proper notice. After registration, the society became a separate legal entity, allowing it to hold property and enter contracts in its name.

The members contribute a small capital towards the society and their liability is limited to the amount they have contributed. Any surplus generated by the society is distributed among its members as a dividend.

What is the key feature of Green Valley Cooperative Society that ensures its liability is limited to the members' contribution? Competency Based Que

(a) The cooperative society's registration is optional
(b) The society's objective is profit maximisation
(c) The liability of members is limited to the amount contributed as capital
(d) The society is managed by a board of directors

28. It is difficult to maintain secrecy in the operations of a cooperative society due to open discussion in the meetings and disclosure obligation as per the

(a) Section 17 of the Societies Act
(b) Section 7 of the Societies Act
(c) Section 50 of the Societies Act
(d) Section 55 of the Societies Act

29. Which of the following statements is not correct?

(a) A company can refer to Table A if it does not prepare its articles of association

(b) A private limited company can have a maximum of 200 members

(c) A minor as a partner can inspect the books of the firm

(d) One person company is a company, which has one person as its member

30. In which form of business is there complete separation of ownership and management?

(a) Sole proprietorship (b) Partnership
(c) Cooperative society (d) Company

31. The maximum amount up to which a company can issue capital is called

(a) authorised capital (b) called-up capital
(c) issued capital (d) subscribed capital

32. A company has a minimum of 7 members with no upper limit on membership. It freely allows the transfer of its securities and invites the general public to subscribe to its shares.

Identify the type of company described in the statement. **Competency Based Que**

(a) Private company (b) Public company
(c) One person company (d) Government company

33. Rohan is involved in identifying a business idea, investigating its feasibility and arranging the necessary resources to form a company. He also enjoys a fiduciary position with the company but is neither its agent nor trustee.

Identify the legal position of Rohan as described in the statement. **Competency Based Que**

(a) Director (b) Shareholder
(c) Promoter (d) Trustee

34. "In this clause, the signatories to the Memorandum of Association state their intention to be associated with the company and also give their consent to purchase qualification shares."

Identify the type of clause mentioned in the given statement. **Competency Based Que**

(a) Liability clause (b) Association clause
(c) Name clause (d) Capital clause

35. "This step includes the steps like identification of business idea, its investigation and arrangement of necessary resources for the formation of a company." Identify the stage mentioned in the given statement. **Competency Based Que**

(a) Incorporation
(b) Promotion
(c) Commencement of business
(d) Capital subscription

36. A clause in the memorandum of association specifies the maximum amount of capital a company is authorised to raise through the issue of shares and ensures that the company cannot exceed this limit. Identify the clause described in the statement. **Competency Based Que**

(a) Main objects clause (b) Capital clause
(c) Liability clause (d) Association clause

37. A statutory declaration stating that all formalities have been completed is submitted by the promoters during the .... stage.

(a) promotion (b) incorporation
(c) commencement (d) registration

38. A public company must obtain approval from .... are before issuing securities to protect the interest of investors.

(a) Registrar of Companies (b) SEBI
(c) RBI
(d) Ministry of Corporate Affairs

39. Document issued by a public company to invite the public to purchase shares or debentures.

(a) Memorandum of Association
(b) Statement of accounts
(c) Prospectus (d) Articles of Association

40. .... are appointed to manage financial transactions and public subscriptions as well as to facilitate the process of raising funds from the public.

(a) Directors
(b) Bankers, brokers and underwriters
(c) Auditors (d) Shareholders

41. Identify the type of document given below.

> No. ....20......
>
> **I hereby certify that ..... (Name of the company) is this day incorporated under the Companies Act, 2013 and that the company is limited.**
>
> **The CIN of the company is ....**
>
> **Given under my hand at .... (Place) this .... day of .... (month) Two thousand ....**
>
> **Fees : Deed Stamp ` ....**
>
> **Stamp duty Capital ` ....**
>
> **SEAL**
>
> **Sd/–**
>
> **Registrar of Companies**
> **........... (State)**

(a) Certificate of incorporation
(b) Certificate of commencement
(c) Certificate of registration
(d) Certificate of termination

42. **Nitesh is a shareholder in a company holding 1,000 shares of ₹ 10 each on which he has already paid ₹ 8 per share. In the event of losses or company's failure to pay debts, Nitesh is liable to pay amount of**

Competency Based Que

(a) ₹ 1,000 (b) ₹ 1,600
(c) ₹ 2,000 (d) ₹ 10,000

43. **Raj holds 100 shares of ₹ 10 each in ABC Ltd and he has paid ₹ 5 per share. He is liable to contribute to the company maximum to the extent of**

Competency Based Que

(a) ₹ 2 per share (b) ₹ 5 per share
(c) ₹ 10 per share (d) ₹ 1 per share

44. **Which of the following statements is/are correct about public limited company?**

(a) It has minimum 7 members and no limit on the maximum number of members
(b) It has no restriction on the transfer of securities
(c) It is not prohibited to invite the general public to subscribe to its securities
(d) All of the above

Direction *Read the case study and answer the questions 45 to 48 on the basis of the same*

GreenField Cooperative Society is a voluntary association of farmers who have come together to form a cooperative society to market their agricultural products. The society aims to provide services to its members, such as selling their produce at better rates and offering low interest loans for farming.

The society has been registered under the Cooperative Societies Act and has become a distinct legal entity. While it operates with the welfare of its members in mind, members have the right to exit the society by giving a notice. The liability of members is limited to the extent of their capital contribution and they all have equal voting rights, irrespective of their capital share.

However, despite the good intentions, the society is facing challenges due to limited resources, inefficient management and lack of professional expertise in management. The members often argue over decisions in meetings, with personal interests affecting the society's goals. Additionally, the society has been burdened with government control, as it has to adhere to various government regulations like audits and inspections.

45. **Identify the kind of liability which is enjoyed by the members of GreenField Cooperative Society.**

(a) Unlimited liability (b) Limited liability
(c) General liability (d) None of these

46. **Which feature of the cooperative society provides its members with equal voting rights?**

(a) Perpetual succession (b) Equality in voting status
(c) Service motive (d) Limited liability

47. **What is the primary aim of GreenField Cooperative Society?**

(a) To earn maximum profit for its members
(b) To provide services to its members
(c) To control the agricultural market
(d) To form a separate legal entity

48. **Which of the following is a disadvantage of a cooperative society, as mentioned in the case?**

(a) Ease of formation (b) Lack of secrecy
(c) Limited resources
(d) Support from the government

Assertion-Reason

Direction (Q.No. 49 to 58) *Read the following Assertion (A) and Reason (R) and choose the correct alternative from the following*

Alternatives

(a) Both Assertion (A) and Reason (R) are true and Reason (R) is the correct explanation of Assertion (A)
(b) Both Assertion (A) and Reason (R) are true, but Reason (R) is not the correct explanation of Assertion (A)
(c) Assertion (A) is true, but Reason (R) is false
(d) Assertion (A) is false, but Reason (R) is true

49. **Assertion** (A) A sole proprietor enjoys quick decision-making as there is no need to consult others.

Reason (R) Since the sole proprietor has full control, he can make decisions without delays from other stakeholders.

50. **Assertion** (A) A sole proprietor has unlimited liability.

Reason (R) In case of losses, the sole proprietor's personal property can be used to pay-off business debts.

51. **Assertion** (A) A partnership firm must have at least two partners to be legally formed.

Reason (R) A partnership is based on an agreement between two or more persons to jointly manage and share the profits or losses of a business.

52. **Assertion** (A) A partnership firm can be formed through an agreement between the partners.

Reason (R) Registration of the partnership firm is compulsory for the formation of a partnership.

53. **Assertion** (A) In partnership firm, the liability of every partner is limited, joint and several.

Reason (R) Partnership agreement may be oral or written.

54. **Assertion** (A) A partner by holding out allows himself to be represented as a partner, even though he is not one.

Reason (R) This representation leads to liability for the firm's debts, even if the individual did not contribute capital or participate in management.

55. **Assertion** (A) In a Joint Hindu Family (HUF) business, the *karta* has unlimited liability for the business debts, but other members have limited liability.

Reason (R) The *karta's* liability is unlimited because he is the main decision-maker in the business, while the other members only share profits and have no direct role in management.

56. **Assertion** (A) The managing committee elected by members of the cooperative society is generally not professionally equipped to handle the management functions effectively.

Reason (R) Cooperative society is unable to employ experts because of their inability to pay them higher salaries.

57. **Assertion** (A) Joint stock company can raise huge amount of capital.

Reason (R) Joint stock companies have the ability to issue shares to the public.

58. **Assertion** (A) Board of directors exercise direct control over the business.

Reason (R) Board of directors are the owners of the company.

Two Statements Based MCQs

Direction (Q.No. 59 to 68) *Read the following statements carefully and choose the correct alternative*

Alternatives
(a) Statement I is correct, but Statement II is incorrect
(b) Statement II is correct, but Statement I is incorrect
(c) Both the statements are correct
(d) Both the statements are incorrect

59. **Statement I** A sole proprietorship has no separate legal entity.

Statement II It is very difficult to start or close down sole proprietorship.

60. **Statement I** The formation of a Joint Hindu Family (HUF) business requires an agreement.

Statement II Membership in a joint hindu family business is by birth and no agreement is required.

61. **Statement I** In a joint hindu family business, the liability of all members is unlimited.

Statement II The liability of the karta is unlimited, but other members' liability is limited to the extent of their share.

62. **Statement I** In a cooperative society, each member has equal voting rights irrespective of their capital contribution.

Statement II In a cooperative society, members with a higher capital contribution get more voting rights.

63. **Statement I** An One Person Company (OPC) can be incorporated by a single individual in India.

Statement II An OPC must have at least two directors and two members for registration.

64. **Statement I** A private company can issue a prospectus to invite the public to subscribe to its shares.

Statement II A public company can issue a prospectus and can invite the public to subscribe to its shares.

65. **Statement I** A private company restricts the right to transfer its shares.

Statement II A private company does not invite public to subscribe to its share capital.

66. **Statement I** A promoter is a person who performs all the work at the promotion stage of a company, including identifying a business idea, investigating it and arranging the necessary resources for its formation.

Statement II Promoters are legally considered agents or trustees of the company.

67. **Statement I** The Memorandum of Association (MoA) is the principal document of a company, containing various clauses such as the name clause, registered office clause and objects clause, among others.

Statement II The MoA must be signed by at least 7 persons in the case of a public company and 2 persons in the case of a private company.

68. **Statement I** After incorporation, a public company can raise funds from the public by issuing shares and debentures. It must issue a prospectus to invite the public to subscribe to the capital.

Statement II The company is required to take approval from SEBI before raising funds from the public and the approval process includes filing a prospectus or a Statement in Lieu of Prospectus, depending on the method of fund raising.

Matching

69. Match the following

Column I	Column II
A. Active or working partner	(i) Allows use of name without contributing capital, bears liability
B. Sleeping or dormant partner	(ii) Participation hidden from the public, bears unlimited liability
C. Secret partner	(iii) Contributes capital but does not manage, bears unlimited liability
D. Nominal partner	(iv) Actively manages the firm and bears unlimited liability

Codes

	A	B	C	D		A	B	C	D
(a)	(ii)	(i)	(iii)	(iv)	(b)	(iii)	(iv)	(i)	(ii)
(c)	(i)	(iii)	(ii)	(iv)	(d)	(iv)	(iii)	(ii)	(i)

70. Match the following limitations of cooperative society with their correct decription

Column I	Column II
A. Limited resources	(i) Lack of professional expertise due to limited funds
B. Inefficiency in Management	(ii) Members with limited means and low dividends
C. Lack of secrecy	(iii) Bound by rigid rules, regular audits and inspections
D. Government control	(iv) Open discussions and disclosure obligations

Codes

	A	B	C	D		A	B	C	D
(a)	(ii)	(i)	(iv)	(iii)	(b)	(iii)	(iv)	(i)	(ii)
(c)	(i)	(iii)	(ii)	(iv)	(d)	(ii)	(i)	(iii)	(iv)

71. Match the following features with their correct description

Column I	Column II
A. Artificial person	(i) Limited to the extent of capital contributed
B. Separate legal entity	(ii) Not affected by entry or exit of members
C. Perpetual succession	(iii) Assets and liabilities are distinct
D. Liability	(iv) Created by law, can sue and be sued

Codes

	A	B	C	D		A	B	C	D
(a)	(ii)	(i)	iii)	(iv)	(b)	(iv)	(iii)	(ii)	(i)
(c)	(i)	(iii)	(ii)	(iv)	(d)	(ii)	(i)	(iii)	(iv)

72. Match the following

Column I	Column II
A. Private company	(i) Maximum 200 members
B. Public company	(ii) Minimum 7 members
C. Sole proprietorship	(iii) Consent of 10 adult persons
D. Cooperative society	(iv) Maximum 1 member

Codes

	A	B	C	D		A	B	C	D
(a)	(ii)	(i)	(iii)	(iv)	(b)	(iii)	(iv)	(i)	(ii)
(c)	(i)	(ii)	(iv)	(iii)	(d)	(ii)	(i)	(iii)	(iv)

73. Match the following

Column I	Column II
A. Memorandum of Association	(i) Performs activities during the promotion stage
B. Articles of Association	(ii) Invitation to the public to subscribe to shares or debentures
C. Prospectus	(iii) Rules for internal management of the company
D. Promoter	(iv) Defines the scope of company's activities

Codes

	A	B	C	D		A	B	C	D
(a)	(ii)	(i)	(iii)	(iv)	(b)	(iv)	(iii)	(ii)	(i)
(c)	(i)	(iii)	(ii)	(iv)	(d)	(ii)	(i)	(iii)	(iv)

Answers

1. (c) Sole proprietorship 2. (c) Sole proprietorship
3. (c) Sole trading concern 4. (a) Sole proprietorship
5. (a) He has to bear losses also
6. (a) Partnership
7. (c) It is affected by the death, retirement or insolvency of a partner
8. (a) General partnership 9. (d) All of these
10. (c) Partnership
11. (b) It can be used as evidence of agreed terms and conditions
12. (c) The firm cannot take loans from banks
13. (c) secret partner
14. (d) Partner by estoppel 15. (c) Nominal partner
16. (b) Unlimited, including personal assets
17. (b) Particular partnership
18. (b) Nominal partner
19. (b) Hindu undivided family
20. (a) karta
21. (a) Hindu Undivided Family (HUF)
22. (a) birth 23. (b) Karta
24. (c) Membership in an HUF business is by birth
25. (b) cooperative society
26. (c) Farmer's Cooperative Society
27. (c) The liability of members is limited to the amount contributed as capital
28. (b) Section 7 of the Societies Act
29. (c) A minor as a partner can inspect the books of the firm
30. (d) Company 31. (a) authorised capital
32. (b) Public company 33. (c) Promoter
34. (b) Association clause 35. (b) Promotion
36. (b) Capital clause 37. (b) incorporation
38. (b) SEBI 39. (c) Prospectus
40. (b) Bankers, brokers and underwriters
41. (a) Certificate of incorporation
42. (c) ₹ 2,000 43. (b) ₹ 5 per share
44. (d) All of the above 45. (b) Limited liability
46. (b) Equality in voting status
47. (b) To provide services to its members
48. (c) Limited resources
49. (a) Both Assertion (A) and Reason (R) are true and Reason (R) is the correct explanation of Assertion (A)
50. (a) Both Assertion (A) and Reason (R) are true and Reason (R) is the correct explanation of Assertion (A)
51. (a) Both Assertion (A) and Reason (R) are true and Reason (R) is the correct explanation of Assertion (A)
52. (c) While it is true that a partnership is formed through an agreement, registration is not compulsory. Registration is optional and not required for forming a partnership, though it can offer certain legal advantages.
53. (d) The liability of partners is unlimited and they are liable individually as well as jointly.
54. (a) Both Assertion (A) and Reason (R) are true and Reason (R) is the correct explanation of Assertion (A)
55. (a) Both Assertion (A) and Reason (R) are true and Reason (R) is the correct explanation of Assertion (A)
56. (a) Both Assertion (A) and Reason (R) are true and Reason (R) is the correct explanation of Assertion (A)
57. (a) Both Assertion (A) and Reason (R) are true and Reason (R) is the correct explanation of Assertion (A)
58. (c) The board of directors does not own the company, they are elected to represent the interests of the shareholders, who are the actual owners of the company. The shareholders appoint the board to manage the business on their behalf.
59. (a) It is not difficult to start or close down sole proprietorship.
60. (b) In a joint hindu family business, membership is acquired by birth and no formal agreement is needed for the formation of the business.
61. (b) In a joint hindu family business, the liability of all members is limited and liability of karta is unlimited.
62. (a) A cooperative society operates on the principle of 'one man, one vote', meaning each member, regardless of their capital contribution, has equal voting rights.
63. (a) An OPC requires only one director and one member, not two of each. The director and member can be the same person.
64. (b) A private company cannot issue a prospectus to invite the public to subscribe to its shares.
65. (c) Both the statements are correct
66. (a) Promoters are not agents or trustees of the company. They are personally liable for preliminary contracts and enjoy a fiduciary position, but this does not make them agents or trustees of the company.
67. (c) Both the statements are correct
68. (c) Both the statements are correct
69. (d) (iv) (iii) (ii) (i) 70. (a) (ii) (i) (iv) (iii)
71. (b) (iv) (iii) (ii) (i) 72. (c) (i) (ii) (iv) (iii)
73. (b) (iv) (iii) (ii) (i)

Subjective Questions

Short Answer Type Questions

1. William R Bassett has rightfully observed, "The one man control is the best in the world if that man is big enough to manage everything." Do you agree with him? Give reasons for your answer. Competency Based Que

Ans. Yes, I agree with William R Bassett. His assertion that one-man control is the best in the world is based on the merits of sole proprietorship form of organisation.

Following are the merits of sole proprietorship

(i) **Quick Decision-making**

A sole proprietor enjoys freedom in making business decisions. Thus, he can take advantages of market opportunities by taking quick decisions, as there is no need to consult others.

(ii) **Confidentiality of Information**

Sole trader is not expected to share his business decisions and secrets with anybody. He is also not bound by law to publish firm's accounts.

(iii) **Direct Incentive**

Direct relationship between efforts and reward provide maximum incentive to the sole trader and encourages him to work hard.

(iv) **Ease of Formation and Closure**

An important merit of sole proprietorship is the possibility of entering and exiting business with minimal legal formalities.

However, Bassett further observes that a sole trader will be able to capitalise on the above merits only if he is able to manage each and every aspect of business effectively and efficiently. A sole trader should have expert knowledge related to administration, marketing, finance, etc. to make his control best.

2. Mention the businesses for which sole proprietorship is suitable form of organisation.

Ans. Sole proprietorship is suitable for the following business

(i) It is the most suitable form for small businesses such as local grocery shop and small-scale retailers selling clothes, shoes, etc.

(ii) This form is suitable for business which are required to give personal attention to the needs of the customers, such as beauty parlours, boutiques, etc.

(iii) This form is suitable for business in which quick decision-making is required, as in the case of stock broking business.

(iv) It is suitable for professionals such as doctors, lawyers, etc.

3. "Partnership form of business is particularly suitable for certain specific businesses." Enumerate these businesses. Competency Based Que

Ans. Partnership form of business is suitable for the following businesses

(i) Where the size of the business is relatively small.

(ii) Where the capital requirement is limited.

(iii) Where the partners do not trade but use their professional skills, such as Chartered Accountants (CA), lawyers, etc.

4. "The partners of a partnership firm are jointly and individually liable for the debts of the firm." Discuss. Competency Based Que

Ans. The liability of all the members of a partnership firm is unlimited. The partners are individually and jointly liable to pay back the debts of the firm.

Joint and individual liability of partners is explained below

(i) **Jointly**

All partners are responsible for the debts according to the proportion of their share in the business.

(ii) **Individually**

Each partner can be individually held responsible for repaying the debts of business. Such a partner can later recover from other partners an equivalent amount of money to their share in liability (as per partnership agreement).

5. Partnership can be classified into various types. Discuss the types of partnership on the basis of liability.

Ans. On the basis of liability, partnership can be classified as

(i) **General Partnership**

In this form of partnership, the liability of all the partners is unlimited and joint. Each partner can participate in the management of the firm and their acts are binding on each other as well as on the firm. Registration for such partnership is optional.

(ii) **Limited Partnership**

In limited partnership, the liability of at least one partner is unlimited, while other partners enjoy limited liability. The partners with limited liability cannot participate in the management and their acts do not bind the firm or other partner. Registration for such partnership is compulsory.

6. Give the features of partnership at will and particular partnership.

Ans. The features of partnership at will are

(i) This type of partnership exists at the will of the partners.
(ii) It can be dissolved by giving a notice.

The features of particular partnership are

(i) It is formed for a specified time or for a particular project.
(ii) It dissolves automatically at the expiry of time period or completion of project.

7. "Following a systematic procedure for registering a partnership firm ensures legal recognition, minimises disputes and establishes the firm's credibility in business dealings."

In light of the above statement, explain the procedure for registration of a partnership firm. Competency Based Que

Ans. Following is the procedure for registration of a partnership firm

The procedure for getting a firm registered is

***Step* 1** Submission of application in the prescribed form to the Registrar of firms. The application should be signed by all the partners. The application should contain the following particulars

- Name of the firm
- Location of the firm
- Name of other places where the firm carries on business
- The date when each partner joined the firm
- Names and addresses of the partners
- Duration of partnership

***Step* 2** Deposit the required fee to the Registrar of firms.

***Step* 3** Registrar will verify the information and if satisfied with the authenticity of information, he will issue a certificate of registration.

8. If registration is optional, why do partnership firms willingly go through this legal formality and get themselves registered? Explain. NCERT

Ans. Registration is optional, but partnership firms willingly go through this legal formality and get themselves registered because it has some merits

(i) **Settlement of Claims**
Registered firms can file suit against the third parties, so the rights of registered firms are safeguarded by law. But an unregistered firm or its partner cannot enforce its claim against the third parties or its copartner.

(ii) **Protection of Rights**
The rights and privileges of new partner are also protected in registered firm. But if incoming partner fails to register himself, he will incur great risk, because he will not be in a position to file suit for his dues against his firm or his copartners.

(iii) **Protection to Creditors**
Registered firm has to maintain correct, complete and up-to-date record of its partners who will be liable for the obligations of the firm. The statement recorded in the register regarding constitution of firm would afford a strong safeguard against untrue refusal of partnership and the evasion of liability to persons who want to deal with the firm.

9. Discuss the following types of partners
(i) Partner by holding out
(ii) Secret partner

Ans. Following are the types of partners

(i) **Partner by Holding Out**
A partner by holding out is one who is actually not a partner, but allows himself to be represented as a partner by the other partners. Such a person becomes liable to outside creditors, for repayment of any debts which have been extended to the firm on the basis of such representation.

(ii) **Secret Partner**
A secret partner is one whose association with the firm is hidden from the general public. Such partner also contributes capital, takes active part in business, share profits and losses and bears unlimited liability.

10. Differentiate between sole proprietorship and partnership on the basis of any four factors.

Ans. Following are the differences between sole proprietorship and partnership

Basis	Sole Proprietorship	Partnership
Number of Members	In a sole proprietorship, there is only one member/owner.	In a partnership, there can be minimum two members and maximum fifty members.
Agreement	In a sole proprietorship, there is no agreement as there is only one member.	A partnership is based on agreement between/among members.
Sharing of Profits	A sole proprietor is the recipient of all the profits.	Partners have to share profit amongst them in an agreed ratio.
Decision-making	In sole proprietorship, the decision-making power rests with the sole proprietor.	In partnership, all the partners can participate in decision-making.

11. "The Hindu Undivided Family (HUF) business is governed by Hindu law and has unique characteristics, such as the karta managing the business on behalf of all members. While it ensures continuity of the business, it may also lead to conflicts among family members."
In light of the above statement, explain any two merits and two demerits of the hindu undivided family form of business organisation. Competency Based Que

Ans. Following are the merits of hindu undivided family form of business organisation

(i) **Limited Liability of Members**
The liability of the coparceners is limited to the extent of their share in the family business.

(ii) **Increased Loyalty and Cooperation**
The members of a HUF business are loyal to each other. They are willing to cooperate and work towards a common goal, as all of them belong to the same family.

Following are the demerits of hindu undivided family form of business organisation

(i) **Limited Resources**
The HUF business depends mainly on the ancestral property. This creates the problem of limited capital.

(ii) **Unlimited Liability of Karta**
In HUF, the liability of the karta is unlimited. His personal assets can also be used to discharge the debts of the business.

12. Compare the status of a minor in a joint hindu family business with that in a partnership firm. NCERT

Ans. A person becomes a member in the joint hindu family business when he takes birth in such families. Even minors in the family are coparceners in the family business.
On the other hand, partnership is based on legal contract between two persons who agree to share the profits or losses of a business carried on by them and a minor is incompetent to enter into a valid contract with others. Hence, a minor cannot become a partner in any firm. However, a minor can be admitted to the benefits of a partnership firm with the mutual consent of all the other partners.

13. "Cooperative societies are suitable for certain specific business." Enumerate them. Competency Based Que

Ans. Cooperative societies are suitable for certain businesses specified below

(i) Building housing societies for low and middle income groups.
(ii) To provide credit facilities to the rural poor.
(iii) For marketing of agricultural and industrial output of small-scale units.
(iv) For promoting handicraft industry.
(v) For opening retail shops to provide quality products to consumers at fair price.

14. How does a cooperative society exemplify democracy and secularism? Explain. NCERT

Ans. The word cooperative means working together with others for a common purpose. The decision-making power in a cooperative society lies in the hands of an elected managing committee.
Every member has one vote and this right to vote gives the members an equal chance to elect the members of the managing committee. This feature lends the cooperative society a democratic character.
Further, the membership of a cooperative society is open to all, irrespective of their religion, caste and gender. This feature proves the secular nature of cooperative societies.

15. Discuss any three advantages of a joint stock company.

Ans. Following are the advantages of a joint stock company

(i) **Limited Liability**
The shareholders are liable only to the extent of the amount unpaid on the shares held by them.

(ii) **Transfer of Interest**
The shareholders of a company can easily and freely transfer their shares. They can sell their shares at any time when the share price is high or they are in need of money.

(iii) **Perpetual Existence**
The existence of a company is not affected by death, insanity, retirement, resignation and insolvency of its members. It can be liquidated only as per the provisions of the Companies Act, 2013.

16. Explain with the help of an example, how the liability of members in a joint stock company is limited.

Ans. The shareholders are liable only to the extent of the amount unpaid on the shares held by them. It attracts many investors as the personal assets of the members cannot be claimed by creditors in case of losses. In a joint stock company, members are only liable to the extent of the unpaid amount on shares held by them. e.g. If a member holds 20 shares of ₹ 100 each, on which he has paid ₹ 60 per share, then his maximum liability will be limited to only ₹ 800 (20×40), i.e. ₹ 40 per share on 20 shares held by him.

17. "A joint stock company provides the benefit of limited liability to its members, but it also suffers from certain drawbacks that can impact its operations and decision-making process."
In light of the above statement, discuss three limitations of a joint stock company. Competency Based Que

Ans. Following are the limitations of a joint stock company

(i) **Complexity in Formation**

The procedure of formation of a company is more complex and requires much time and effort. It is expensive and also requires lot of legal formalities to be fulfilled.

(ii) **Lack of Secrecy**

According to the Companies Act, a public company is required to provide a lot of information to the office of the registrar of companies. Such information is available to general public also.

(iii) **Impersonal Work Environment**

Due to separation between ownership and control, there is no direct link between efforts and reward which leads to a lack of personal interest and incentive.

18. What is one person company? Explain.

Ans. One person company is a new concept in India that has been introduced with the Company's Act, 2013. One person company in India is incorporated by a single person. Before the enforcement of the Companies Act, 2013, a single person was not able to establish a company. An OPC has features of a company and the benefits of the sole proprietorship.

According to Section 2 (62) of the Company's Act, 2013, a company can be formed with just one director and one member. The director and member can also be the same person. An individual who is an Indian resident, can register an OPC in India.

19. State the important privileges available to a private company. NCERT

Or **Private company enjoys certain privileges that make it attractive. In the light of the given statement, state the privileges.** Competency Based Que

Ans. The important privileges available to a private limited company are

(i) The minimum number of members required to form a private company is only 2, while at least 7 members are needed to form public company.

(ii) A private company does not need to issue a prospectus.

(iii) Allotment of shares can be done without receiving the minimum subscription.

(iv) A private company needs to have only 2 directors as against a minimum of 3 directors in the case of a public company.

(v) A private company is not required to keep an index of members unlike a public company.

(vi) There is no restriction on the amount of loans to directors in a private company while in case of a public company, permission from the government is required.

20. Discuss the legal position of promoters.

Ans. Following points describe the legal position of promoters

(i) They are neither the agents nor the trustees of the company.

(ii) They are personally liable for preliminary contracts.

(iii) They enjoy a fiduciary position (ie., depending upon good faith) with the company. This position does not allow a promoter to earn secret profits from the company. If the promoters earn secret profits, the company can cancel the contract, recover the purchase price paid to the promoters and can claim the damages for the loss suffered.

21. "SEBI plays a crucial role in regulating the formation of a company." In light of the given statement, discuss the stage of formation of company at which a company interacts with SEBI. Competency Based Que

Ans A company interacts with SEBI (Securities and Exchange Board of India) in the third stage of formation that is, in the stage of capital subscription. SEBI is the regulatory authority of capital markets in our country which has issued guidelines for the disclosure of information and investor protection. A company inviting funds from the general public must make adequate disclosure of all relevant information and must not conceal any material information from the potential investors as per SEBI guidelines. Prior approval from SEBI is, therefore, required before going ahead with raising funds from public. SEBI ensures that the proposed issue of securities follows all the guidelines laid down by it.

22. List the documents required for the incorporation of a company.

Ans. The documents required for the incorporation of a company are

(i) The Memorandum of Association duly stamped, signed and witnessed.

(ii) The Articles of Association duly stamped and witnessed as in case of the Memorandum. If company adopts Table A, statement in lieu of the prospectus is submitted, instead of Articles of Association.

(iii) Written consent of the proposed directors to act as directors and an undertaking to purchase qualification shares.

(iv) The agreement, if any, with the proposed managing director, manager or whole-time director.

(v) A copy of the Registrar's letter approving the name of the company.

(vi) A statutory declaration affirming that all legal requirements for registration have been complied with.

(vii) A notice about the exact address of the registered office (can be submitted within 30 days of incorporation).

(viii) Documentary evidence of payment of registration fees.

Long Answer Type Questions

23. Why is partnership considered by some to be a relatively unpopular form of business ownership? Explain the merits and limitations of partnership. NCERT

Or **"Partnership as a form of business ownership often faces criticism for being relatively unpopular."**

In the light of this statement, discuss the merits and limitations of partnership as a business ownership model. Competency Based Que

Ans. Some people consider partnership to be relatively unpopular because of the inherent features of partnership such as joint risk bearing and profit sharing, collective decision-making, unlimited liability of partners, etc. These factors lead to conflicts among partners and undue burden on some of the partners. Besides, public confidence in partnership firm is low due to lack of transparency.

Partnership firm enjoys the following merits

(i) A partnership firm can be formed with minimal legal formalities by an agreement between the prospective partners, whereby they agree to carryout the business of the firm and share risks. Registration of the firm is also not compulsory and closure of the firm can also be done easily.

(ii) The partners can look after different functions according to their areas of expertise. This reduces the burden of work on individual partners and leads to more effective decisions.

(iii) All the partners share the risks involved in running a partnership firm. This reduces the anxiety, burden and stress on individual partners.

(iv) A partnership firm is not legally required to publish its accounts and submit reports. Hence, it can maintain confidentiality of information relating to its operations.

A partnership firm suffers from the following limitations

(i) All partners of a firm have unlimited liability. Personal assets of the partners may be used for repaying debts, if the business assets are insufficient.

(ii) Partnership firms usually do not operate on a large-scale as there is a restriction on the number of partners and hence, contribution in terms of capital investment remains insufficient for business expansion beyond a point.

(iii) Decision-making authority in a partnership is shared by all the partners. Difference in opinion may lead to conflicts between partners.

(iv) Partnership comes to an end with the death, retirement, insolvency or lunacy of any partner. It may result in lack of continuity if the remaining partners do not enter into a fresh agreement to continue the business.

24. Distinguish between a joint hindu family business and partnership. NCERT

Ans. Following are the differences between a joint hindu family business and partnership

Basis	Partnership	Joint Hindu Family Business
Formation	It is formed with an agreement between partners.	It is formed with less legal formalities than partnership.
Registration Requirement	Registration is optional in partnership.	Joint hindu family business exempted from registration.
Members	Minimum members should be 2 and maximum can be 50 in partnership.	There should be at least two persons for division of family property with no maximum limit of members.
Capital Contribution	Limited but more than the capital that can be raised in case of sole proprietorship.	The capital contribution comes from ancestral property.
Liability	Liability of members is unlimited and joint.	Liability is unlimited only for Karta while it is limited for other members.
Control and Management	Partners take decisions jointly and consent of all partners is needed.	Karta takes decisions which are binding on all the other members.
Continuity	Stable but affected by status of partners.	Stable business, continues even if Karta dies, through succession in family.

25. What are the advantages that make cooperative societies stand out compared to other forms of business?

Ans. Following are the advantages of cooperative societies that make them stand out compared to other forms of business

(i) **Equality in Voting Status**
Cooperative society is governed by the principle of 'one man one vote'. Each member is entitled to equal voting rights, irrespective of capital contribution by them.

(ii) **Limited Liability**
The liability of every member is limited to the extent of his share in the society's capital.

(iii) **Stable Existence**
As cooperative society is a separate legal entity, it is not affected by death, lunacy or bankruptcy of the members. Thus, it operates for a long period of time.

(iv) **Economy in Operations**

In cooperative society, the members generally offer honorary services to the society. As the society aims to eliminate middleman, it helps in reducing costs. The customers or producers themselves are members of society which also reduces the risk of bad debts.

(v) **Support from Government**

The cooperative society gets support from the government in the form of low taxes, subsidies and low interest rates on loans.

(vi) **Ease of Formation**

It is quite easy to form a cooperative society. Personal interests may start to dominate the welfare motive and benefit of other members.

26. "Cooperative societies play an important role in the welfare of its members." In the light of given statement, discuss the various types of cooperative societies that function for the welfare of the members. **Competency Based Que**

Ans. Various types of cooperative societies are

(i) Consumer's cooperative societies
(ii) Producer's cooperative societies
(iii) Marketing cooperative societies
(iv) Farmer's cooperative societies
(v) Credit cooperative societies
(vi) Cooperative housing society

For explanation, refer to topic 'Types of Cooperative Society' on page 40.

27. "The distinction between public and private companies plays a crucial role in shaping the ownership, governance and operational flexibility of businesses." In light of the above statement, explain the key differences between public and private companies **Competency Based Que**

Ans. Following are the key differences between public and private companies

Basis	Public Company	Private Company
Minimum number of Members	7	2
Maximum Number of Members	No limit	Two Hundred (excluding past and present employees)
Minimum Number of Directors	3	2
Invitation to Public to Subscribe to Shares	It is free to invite the public to buy its shares and debentures.	It cannot invite the public to buy its shares and debentures.
Commencement of Business	It cannot commence business after incorporation unless certificate of commencement of business is obtained.	It can commence business immediately after incorporation.
Transfer of Shares	It has no restriction on transfer of shares.	It has restriction on transfer of shares.
Index of Members	It is mandatory to maintain the index of members.	There is no compulsion to maintain the index of members.

28. Explain the steps taken by promoters in the promotion of a company. **NCERT**

Ans. The important functions of promoters/steps involved in promotion stage are

(i) **Identification of Business Opportunity**

The first and foremost function of a promoter is to identify a business idea or opportunity. This opportunity may be related to setting-up a new business or to expand the existing business.

Promoter also analyse the profitability of an idea, risk involved, resources required, etc.

(ii) **Feasibility Studies**

After identifying a business opportunity, the promoters undertake detailed investigation of all aspects of business like cost, profitability, production process, demand of the product, etc. While doing so, promoter seek help of specialists like CA, CS, engineers, etc. The feasibility study includes

- **Technical Feasibility**
  This feasibility study is undertaken to determine whether it is technically possible to produce the product or not, i.e. whether required raw material, input, technology, etc. available or not.
- **Financial Feasibility**
  This feasibility study is undertaken to determine whether the promoters would be able to arrange the necessary finance needed to float the venture or not.
- **Economic Feasibility**
  This feasibility study is undertaken to determine whether the business idea would be profitable or not.

(iii) **Name Approval**

After selecting the name of the company, the promoters submit an application to the Registrar of Companies for its approval.

Three names are given in the application to the Registrar of Companies in order of their priority. resigtrar approves any one name after being satisfied that the name is not identical to name of other companies and also not misleading.

However, the proposed name will not be accepted by the registrar, if

- it resembles the name of an existing company.
- it is misleading.
- it contains the word 'cooperative'.
- it violates the provisions of The Emblem and Names (Prevention of Improper Use) Act, 1950.
- the name does not end with the word 'Limited' in case of a public company and with the words 'Private Limited' in case of a private company.

(iv) **Fixing up Signatories to the Memorandum of Association**
Promoters have to decide about the directors who will be signing the Memorandum of Association. Usually the signatories of the memorandum are the first directors of the company. The written consent of the persons signing the memorandum is taken to act as directors and to take up the qualification shares in the company. The memorandum must be signed by at least 7 persons in case of a public company and 2 persons in case of a private company.

(v) **Appointment of Professionals**
Promoters appoint merchant bankers, auditors, etc. to assist them in the preparation of necessary documents, which are required to be submitted with the Registrar of Companies.

(vi) **Preparation of Necessary Documents**
Promoter takes up the steps to prepare various legal documents of a company that are to be submitted to Registrar for getting company registered. These documents include Memorandum of Association, Articles of Association, Consent of Directors, etc.

29. Discuss the stages of formation of a company.

Ans. Formation of a company is a complex activity, involving the following stages

(i) **Promotion**
Promotion is the first stage in the formation of a company. It includes the steps like identification of business idea, its investigation and arrangement of necessary resources for the formation of a company. The person who performs all the work at promotion stage is known as promoter.

(ii) **Incorporation**
It means the registration of a company under the Companies Act, 2013. The following steps are taken by the promoters to get the company incorporated.

(iii) **Capital Subscription**
After incorporation, a public company can raise the required funds from the public by means of issue of shares and debentures. For doing the same, it has to issue a prospectus which is an invitation to the public to subscribe to the capital of the company.

(iv) **Commencement of Business**
To commence business, a public company has to obtain a certificate of commencement of business. For this, the following documents have to be filed with the Registrar of Companies

- A declaration that minimum subscription of 90 per cent of the issued shares has been received.
- A declaration that all directors have paid in cash in respect of allotment of shares made to them.
- A declaration that no money is pending to pay back to the applicants.
- A statutory declaration that the above requirements have been completed and must be signed by the director or secretary of the company.

30. What is a 'Memorandum of Association'? Briefly explain its clauses. NCERT

Or **"Memorandum of Association is an important document." Discuss its meaning and clauses.**

Ans. Memorandum of Association defines the objectives of the company and determines the boundary line, with in which the company has to perform tasks. No company can legally undertake activities that are not contained in its Memorandum of Association.

The Memorandum of Association contains different clauses, which are

(i) **The Name Clause**
This clause contains the name of the company with which the company will be known, which has already been approved by the Registrar of Companies.
According to name clause the name of a company should not be identical or resembling the name of an existing company and should not violate the provisions of The Emblem and Names (Prevention of Improper Use) Act, 1950.

(ii) **Registered Office Clause**
This clause contains the name of the state, in which the registered office of the company is proposed to be situated.
The exact address of the registered office is not required at this stage but the same must be notified to the Registrar within thirty days of the incorporation of the company.

(iii) **Objects Clause**
This clause is the most important one as it defines the purpose for which the company is formed. A company is not legally entitled to undertake an activity, which is beyond the objects stated in this clause. The object clause is divided into two objects

- **Main Objects** The main objects for which the company is formed are listed in this sub-clause.

- **Other Objects** Objects not included in the main objects could be stated in this sub-clause. A company can undertake a business included in this sub-clause, either by passing a special resolution or passing an ordinary resolution and get central government's approval for the same.

(iv) **Liability Clause**

This clause limits the liability of the members to the amount unpaid on the shares owned by them.

(v) **Capital Clause**

This clause specifies the maximum capital which the company will be authorised to raise through the issue of shares. The authorised share capital of the proposed company along with its division into the number of shares having a fixed face value is specified in this clause.

(vi) **Association Clause**

In this clause, the signatories to the Memorandum of Association state their intention to be associated with the company and also give their consent to purchase qualification shares.

The Memorandum of Association must be signed by at least seven persons in case of a public company and by two persons in case of a private company.

31. Distinguish between 'Memorandum of Association' and 'Articles of Association'.

Ans. Following are the differences between Memorandum of Association and Articles of Association

Basis	Memorandum of Association	Articles of Association
Objectives	Memorandum of Association defines the objects for which the company is formed.	Articles of Association are rules of internal management of the company. They indicate how the objectives of the company are to be achieved.
Position	This is the main document of the company and is subordinate to the Companies Act.	This is a subsidiary document and is subordinate to both the Memorandum of Association and the Companies Act.
Relationship	Memorandum of Association defines the relationship of the company with outsiders.	Articles define the relationship of the members and the company.
Validity	Acts beyond the Memorandum of Association are invalid and cannot be ratified even by a unanimous vote of the members.	Acts which are beyond articles can be ratified by the members, provided they do not violate the memorandum.
Necessity	Every company has to file a memorandum of association.	It is not compulsory for a public limited company to file Articles of Association. It may adopt table A of the Companies Act.
Alteration	Alteration of Memorandum of Association is quite difficult and in many cases, approval of certain statutory authority is required.	Articles can be altered by passing a special resolution by the members.

32. "Choosing the right form of organisation is crucial for business success." In the light of the given statement, discuss the various factors that should be kept in mind while choosing an appropriate form of organisation.

Competency Based Que

Ans. Factors to be kept in mind while choosing form of organisations are

(i) Cost and ease in setting up the organisation

(ii) Liability

(iii) Continuity

(iv) Management ability

(v) Capital considerations

(vi) Degree of control

(vii) Nature of business

For explanation, refer to topic 'Choice of form of business organisation' on page 47.

Case Study Based Questions

Short Case Studies

Case Study 1

A Refreshing Start: Coca Cola Owes its Origin to a Sole Proprietor! The product that has given the world its best-known taste was born in Atlanta, Georgia, on 8th May, 1886. Dr. John Stith Pemberton, a local pharmacist, produced the syrup for Coca-Cola and carried a jug of the new product down the street to Jacobs' Pharmacy, where it was sampled, pronounced 'excellent' and placed on sale for five cents a glass as a soda fountain drink. Dr. Pemberton never realised the potential of the beverage he created. He gradually sold portions of his business to various partners and, just prior to his death in 1888, sold his remaining interest in Coca-Cola to Asa G Candler.

An Atlantan with great business acumen, Mr. Candler proceeded to buy additional business rights and acquire complete control.

On 1st May, 1889, Asa Candler published a full-page advertisement in the Atlanta Journal, proclaiming his wholesale and retail drug business as "sole proprietors of Coca-Cola ... Delicious. Refreshing. Exhilarating. Invigorating." Sole ownership, which Mr. Candler did not actually achieve until 1891, needed an investment of $ 2,300. It was only in 1892 that Mr. Candler formed a company called the Coca-Cola Corporation. NCERT

Source *Website of Coca Cola Company*

On the basis of above case, answer the following questions

(i) "Mr. Candler proceeded to buy additional business rights and acquire complete control." Which feature of sole proprietorship is highlighted in the given statement?

(ii) "Dr. Pemberton, as a sole proprietor, decided to sell portions of his business to other partners, while Candler, as a sole proprietor, decided to convert his sole proprietary business into a company form of organisation." Which merit of sole proprietorship is brought forward by the above instances?

(iii) Why do you think Mr. Candler formed a company called 'the Coca-Cola Corporation'?

Ans.

(i) The feature of sole proprietorship which is highlighted in the given statement is 'control.' In sole proprietorship, the right to run the business and make all decisions lies absolutely with the sole proprietor. He can carry out his plans without any interference from another.

(ii) The merit of sole proprietorship brought forward by the above instances is 'quick decision-making'. A sole proprietor enjoys considerable freedom in making business decisions. Further, decision-making is prompt because there is no need to consult others.

(iii) I think Mr. Candler formed a company because of the many limitations faced by sole proprietorship. These are limited resources, limited life of a business concern, unlimited liability and limited managerial ability.

Case Study 2

The business assets of an organisation amount to ₹ 50,000 but the debts that remain unpaid are ₹ 80,000. What course of action can the creditors take, if NCERT

(i) the organisation is a sole proprietorship firm.

(ii) the organisation is a partnership firm with Anthony and Akbar as partners. Which of the two partners can the creditors approach for repayment of debt? Explain giving reasons.

Ans.

(i) Sole proprietors have unlimited liability. This implies that the owner is personally responsible for payment of debts in case the assets of the business are not sufficient to meet all the debts. In the given case, the total debts that remain unpaid are ₹ 80,000 but the organisational assets amount to ₹ 50,000 only.

In such a situation, the creditors can demand from the proprietor to pay ₹ 30,000 from his/her personal sources even if he/she has to sell his/her personal property to repay the firm's debts.

(ii) The partners of a firm have unlimited liability. Personal assets may be used for repaying debts in case the business assets are insufficient. As the total debts that remain unpaid are ₹ 80,000 but the organisational assets amount to ₹ 50,000 only, the creditors can demand ₹ 30,000 from both the partners.

Anthony and Akbar will be required to pay ₹ 30,000 from their personal assets in an agreed ratio. However, if one of them is not available or is unable to pay, the other partner will have to pay the creditors as each partner can be held responsible for repaying the debts of the business.

Such a partner can later recover from the other partner an amount of money equivalent to the share in liability defined in the partnership agreement.

Case Study 3

Amit, Sumit and Priya decided to start a delivery service together. They entered into a written agreement outlining the terms including profit sharing and responsibilities. They agreed to contribute capital and share profits equally. While registration was not mandatory for their business, they ensured that their operations complied with legal requirements.

If the business incurs losses or debts, all three partners are jointly responsible, with their personal assets being used if necessary to clear the liabilities. They also make decisions collaboratively and share the risks and rewards of the business equally.

(i) Identify the form of business ownership discussed in the case.

(ii) State any three features of this form of business ownership.

Ans.

(i) The form of business ownership discussed in the case is partnership. A partnership is a form of organisation in which two or more persons agree to pursue a lawful business. According to the Indian Partnership Act, 1932 (Section 4), Partnership is the relation between persons who have agreed to share the profits of a business carried on by all or any of them acting for all.

(ii) Following are the features of partnership

- **Formation**
  According to Indian Partnership Act, 1932, a partnership firm can be formed on the basis of an agreement between the partners. The registration of partnership firm, for its formation, is not compulsory. The business activity of partnership firm must be lawful, with the motive of earning profit.
- **Liability**
  The liability of all the members of a partnership firm is unlimited, i.e. personal assets of partners may also be used to pay the debts in case the business assets are insufficient. The partners are individually and collectively liable to pay back the debts of the firm.
- **Risk Bearing**
  The partners bear the risk involved in the business jointly. If a business sustains loss, then partners share the loss in the same ratio in which they share profits.

Case Study 4

Price Waterhouse Coopers was a Partnership Firm Earlier

Price Waterhouse Coopers, one of the world's top accountancy firms has been created in 1998 by the merger of two companies, Price Waterhouse and Coopers and Lybrand, each with historical roots going back some 150 years to the 19th century Great Britain.

In 1850, Samuel Lowell Price setup his accounting business in London. In 1865, he was joined in partnership by William H Holyland and Edwin Waterhouse. As the firm grew, qualified members of its professional staff were admitted into the partnership. By the late 1800s, Price Waterhouse had gained significant recognition as an accounting firm. **NCERT**

On the basis of above case, answer the following questions

(i) "Price Waterhouse Coopers was a partnership firm earlier." As per this sentence, what can be interpreted regarding the suitability of partnership business?

(ii) Give any two limitations of partnership, which would have compelled Price Waterhouse Coopers to change into company form of organisation.

Ans.

(i) Price Waterhouse Coopers is one of the world's top accountancy firm. It was created by partnership of two companies, Price Waterhouse and Coopers and Lybrand. This statement conveys that partnership is the best form of organisation for delivering professional services. Doctors, lawyers, chartered accountants, etc. enter into partnership to gain from the expert knowledge of one another.

(ii) Two limitations of partnership, which would have compelled Price Waterhouse Coopers to change into company form of organisation are

- **Unlimited Liability**
  The liability of partners is unlimited and they are liable individually as well as jointly.
- **Limited Resources**
  There is a limit to number of partners in a partnership firm. Therefore, capital investment is also limited and partnership firms face problems in expanding business beyond a certain size.

Case Study 5

Identify and state the type of partner highlighted in the following statements

(i) Ram is a partner but does not take part in the day-to-day activities of the business.

(ii) Mohan gives an impression of his being partner to others by his words or conduct.

(iii) Raj allows the use of his goodwill to benefit the firm and can be represented as a partner.

Ans.

(i) Ram is a sleeping partner. A sleeping partner contributes capital but does not take active part in the management of the firm. Such type of partner also share profits and losses and bears unlimited liability like other partners.

(ii) Mohan is a partner by estoppel. A partner by estoppel is one who gives an impression to others by his words or conduct, that he is a partner of the firm. Such partners are also liable for the debts of the firm, even though they does not contribute capital or take part in the management of the firm.

(iii) Raj is a nominal partner. A nominal partner is one who allows the use of his name and goodwill for the benefit of the firm, but does not contribute capital and does not take active part in the management or the firm. However, he bears unlimited liability for the debts like other partners.

Case Study 6

Rajesh runs a successful retail business in his ancestral property. He is the head of his family and takes all major decisions for the business, which are followed by all other family members. His younger brothers, Ramesh and Suresh, along with their sons, are also part of the business but do not actively participate in decision-making. The business has been passed down through generations and operates without any formal agreement. The profits are shared among all family members, but Rajesh bears unlimited liability while the others have limited liability based on their share in the property.

(i) Identify the type of business ownership discussed in the case.

(ii) State any three features of this form of business ownership.

Ans.

(i) The type of business ownership discussed in the case is hindu undivided family. Hindu Undivided Family (HUF) business or joint hindu family business is that form of business organisation which is owned and managed by the members of HUF. This type of business is governed by Hindu Law. The business is controlled by the head of the family, who is the eldest member of the family and is called karta. All members have equal ownership right over the property and they are known as coparceners.

(ii) Following are the three features of hindu undivided family

- **Formation**
  At least two members and an ancestral property are the basic requirements for the formation of joint hindu family business. The business does not require any agreement as membership is by birth. It is governed by the Hindu Succession Act, 1956.
- **Liability**
  The liability of karta is unlimited, but the liability of other members is limited to the extent of their share in the coparcenery property of the business.
- **Control**
  The business is managed and controlled by karta. He takes all the decisions and these decisions are legally binding on the other members.

Case Study 7

Amit and his brothers started a family business in 2000. As the eldest brother, Amit managed the entire business and was responsible for all decision-making. Over the years, the business saw mixed results, but Amit never allowed his brothers to check the financial records. Recently, due to losses, Amit had to sell a property to repay the business debts. However, his brothers were not held accountable for any debt settlement.

(i) What form of business is being followed?

(ii) Highlighting the lines from the paragraph, give two characteristics of a joint hindu family business.

Ans.

(i) Joint hindu family business is being followed in the case.

(ii) Two characteristics of a joint hindu family business are

- **Right to Accounts**
  The line "Amit never allowed his brothers to check the financial records" shows that only the Karta has the right to inspect the books of accounts.
- **Management and Decision-making**
  The line "Amit managed the entire business and was responsible for all decision-making" reflects that the eldest male member (Karta) manages the business affairs. The business is managed and controlled by karta.

Case Study 8

A group of 15 farmers in a rural village came together to address the challenges they faced in selling their produce at fair prices. They decided to form an organisation where each member would contribute capital by purchasing shares.

The organisation's primary objective was to work collectively for the welfare of its members. With a democratic structure, every member, irrespective of their contribution, had one vote in decision-making. The group also ensured that surplus earnings were distributed among members in proportion to their contributions.

(i) Identify the form of business organisation described in the case.

(ii) State any three features of the form identified in (i).

Ans.

(i) The form of business organisation described in the case is cooperative society.

(ii) Following are the features of cooperative society

- **Voluntary Membership**
  A cooperative society is essentially a voluntary association of persons. Any person is free to join and exit the society any time after serving a notice. Membership is open to all, irrespective of their caste, religion and gender.
- **Legal Status**
  The registration of a cooperative society is compulsory. After registration, a cooperative society becomes a distinct entity independent of its members. It can enter into contracts and hold property in its name.
- **Limited Liability**
  The liability of members is limited to the extent of the amount contributed by them as capital.

Case Study 9

Amul's Amazing Cooperative Ventures!

Everyday Amul collects 4,47,000 litres of milk from 2.12 million farmers (many illiterate), converts the milk into branded, packaged products, and delivers goods worth ₹ 6 crore (60 million) to over 5,00,000 retail outlets across the country. It all started in December, 1946 with a group of farmers keen to free themselves from intermediaries, gain access to markets and thereby ensure maximum returns for their efforts.

Based in the village of Anand, the Khera District Milk Cooperative Union (better known as Amul) expanded exponentially. It joined hands with other milk cooperatives, and the Gujarat network now covers 2.12 million farmers, 10,411 village level milk collection centres and 14 district level plants (unions). Amul is the common brand for most product categories produced by various unions: liquid milk, milk powder, butter, ghee, cheese, coco products, sweets, ice-cream and condensed milk. Amul's sub-brands include variants such as Amulspray, Amulspree, Amulya and Nutramul. **NCERT**

Source *Adapted from Pankaj Chandra. "Rediff.com", Business Special, September, 2005.*

On the basis of above case, answer the following questions

(i) As per your interpretation, which type of cooperative is Amul.

(ii) "Cooperatives are a boon for the underprivileged." In the light of the above statement, give any two merits of a cooperative society.

Ans.

(i) Amul is a producer's cooperative. These are formed by produces. The main aim of these societies is to help small producers who cannot easily collect various inputs of production and face problems in marketing.
These societies supply raw materials, tools, equipments and other items to their members at reasonable price and also buy their output for sale.

(ii) Merits of a cooperative society are as follows

- **Support from Government**
  The cooperative society gets support from the government in the form of low taxes, subsidies and low interest rates on loans.
- **Ease of Formation**
  It is quite easy to form a cooperative society. Personal interests may start to dominate the welfare motive and benefit of other members.

Case Study 10

XYZ Ltd. was established by a group of individuals to manufacture eco-friendly packaging materials. The business is registered under the Companies Act, giving it a distinct legal identity separate from its members.

The shareholders of XYZ Ltd. enjoy limited liability, ensuring that their personal assets are not at risk beyond their investment.

The management of the company is vested in a board of directors elected by the shareholders.

The company can raise large amounts of capital by issuing shares to the public and its operations are governed by strict legal regulations.

(i) Identify the form of business organisation described in the case.

(ii) State any three drawbacks of the form identified in (i).

Ans.

(i) The form of business organisation described in the case is joint stock company.

(ii) Following are the drawbacks of joint stock company

- **Complexity in Formation**
  The procedure of formation of a company is more complex and requires much time and effort. It is expensive and also requires lot of legal formalities to be fulfilled.
- **Lack of Secrecy**
  According to the Companies Act, a public company is required to provide a lot of information to the office of the registrar of companies. Such information is available to general public also.
- **Impersonal Work Environment**
  Due to separation between ownership and control, there is no direct link between efforts and reward which leads to a lack of personal interest and incentive.

Case Study 11

Laksha Limited issued prospectus, inviting people to subscribe for its shares. It came up with public issue of 30 crores of 30 lakhs shares worth ₹ 100 each. It received applications for 15 lakhs shares. Should the company proceed with allotment of shares?

Ans. According to the Companies Act, minimum subscription has been fixed at 90 per cent of the issued amount. If the company did not get minimum subscription within 30 days from the date of the issue of the prospectus, the allotment cannot be made and the application money received must be returned to the applicants.

In this case, the company has received applications for only 15 lakhs shares. This would mean that the amount of minimum subscription (90 per cent of total issue) has not been received by the company. In this case, allotment cannot be made and application money received must be returned to applicants.

Case Study 12

Pen is Mightier than the Sword

The Case of Luxor Writing Instruments Pvt. Ltd. In the year 1963, a young gentleman armed with the power of hardwork and ambition, started a new era in the field of writing instruments. At a tender age of 19, he started a small manual assembly shop in Sadar Bazaar area in Delhi where he manufactured fountain pens under the name Luxor Writing Instruments Pvt. Ltd. (LWIPL). Being awarded the coveted 'Number one writing instruments exporter' award consecutively for three years, LWIPL has been given the exclusive rights of manufacturing and distributing four international brands in India. *viz.*, pilot, papermate, parker and waterman. Luxor Writing Instruments Pvt. Ltd. has the largest share of this market of over 20 per cent, with a turnover pushing way beyond the ₹ 150 crore mark.

As of today, Luxor is a leading manufacturer and exporter of writing instruments from India. It is currently exporting over 15 per cent of the output and has four manufacturing facilities in New Delhi and three at Mumbai. It employs over 600 people. It is the leader in most segments of the market, manufacturing and distributing a wide variety of pens for various applications and needs.

Source *http://www.luxorparker.com.*

On the basis of above case, answer the following questions

(i) Which form of business organisation is Luxor Writing Instruments Pvt. Ltd.?

(ii) Many entrepreneurs prefer to form a private company. Why?

Ans.

(i) Luxor Writing Instruments Pvt. Ltd. is a private company.

(ii) Entrepreneurs prefer to form a private company because of the following privileges enjoyed by this company over a public company.

Refer to Q.No. 19 of short answer type questions.

Case Study 13

Reliance Industries Limited was founded by Dhirubhai Ambani in 1960. Even after his demise, the company continues to flourish under the leadership of his sons, Mukesh and Anil Ambani. The company is involved in several industries, including telecommunications, petrochemicals and retail. It operates across various countries and has become a global leader in several business sectors.

(i) Which form of business organisation does Reliance Industries represent?

(ii) The company continues to operate successfully even after the demise of its founder. Which characteristic of a company is highlighted in this case?

Ans.

(i) Reliance Industries represent public company.

(ii) Perpetual succession is highlighted in the case. The existence of a company is not affected by death, insanity, retirement, resignation and insolvency of its members. It can be liquidated only as per the provisions of the Companies Act, 2013.

Long Case Studies

Case Study 14

Rahul, an ambitious entrepreneur, has been running a small grocery store in his locality for the past five years. Over time, he has built a loyal customer base, and his store has become a reliable source for everyday needs in the community. Recently, Rahul heard about the construction of a new residential complex just a few kilometers from his store. With hundreds of families expected to move in soon, he sees this as a golden opportunity to expand his business into a larger supermarket that can cater to a wider audience.

However, the decision to expand is not as straightforward as it seems. Rahul knows that scaling up his business will require a significant investment in inventory, space, staff and marketing. The primary concern is arranging additional funds to support this growth. Initially, he considers taking a loan from the bank. While this option seems practical, Rahul is apprehensive about the risk of debt and the pressure of repaying it in case the business doesn't perform as expected.

After much thought, Rahul starts contemplating another option—partnering with someone who can bring in financial resources and share the workload.

However, the idea of sharing control and profits doesn't sit well with him. Rahul values the independence and flexibility he currently enjoys in running his business. He takes pride in making decisions without interference and being solely responsible for his store's success.

After weighing all the pros and cons, Rahul finally decides to stick to the form of business he knows best: managing the supermarket on his own as a sole proprietor. Despite the challenges, he is confident that his hardwork and dedication will help him make the most of the upcoming opportunity.

(i) Which form of organisation has Rahul decided to adopt?

(ii) State three merits of the form of organisation identified in (i) that Rahul would enjoy.

(iii) What are the two drawbacks of adopting the form of organisation identified in (i)?

Ans.

(i) Rahul has decided to adopt sole proprietorship. Sole proprietorship refers to a form of business organisation which is owned, managed and controlled by an individual who is the recipient of all profits and bearer of all risks.

(ii) Following are the merits of sole proprietorship

- **Sense of Accomplishment**
  If a business is successful, it contributes to the satisfaction of the sole proprietor and creates a sense of accomplishment and confidence, which motivates the sole trader to work harder.
- **Ease of Formation and Closure**
  An important merit of sole proprietorship is the possibility of entering and exiting business with minimal legal formalities.
- **Direct Incentive**
  Direct relationship between efforts and reward provide maximum incentive to the sole trader and encourages him to work hard.

(ii) Following are the drawbacks of adopting sole proprietorship

- **Unlimited Liability**
  Sole trader is personally liable for all the business debts. In case of heavy loss, he may be liable to sell his personal property also, to pay back his debts.
- **Limited Managerial Ability**
  Sole trader's managerial ability is limited and due to limited resources, he cannot afford to employ experts. He cannot be an expert in all the aspects of a business, therefore certain tasks could not be performed by him in an optimum manner.

Case Study 15

Neha, Raj and Aryan formed a partnership firm called EcoLiving Creations. The firm specialised in crafting eco-friendly home décor products. The firm was started with a simple agreement between the three partners and they decided not to register the firm to save time and effort. Each partner contributed equally to the initial capital. Neha, being an expert in marketing, focused on promoting their products, while Raj managed production and Aryan handled finances.

The division of responsibilities helped the partners make well-informed decisions and effectively manage the workload. As a result, the firm initially grew rapidly and gained recognition in the market. However, during an expansion project, they faced financial strain due to the limited capital, as the number of partners restricted the firm's ability to raise large funds. Additionally, disagreements began to arise when Aryan suggested investing in a new product line, but Neha and Raj disagreed.

Further, when a customer filed a legal complaint regarding one of their products, the partners had to bear the compensation from their personal savings due to the unlimited liability clause. This situation created additional stress among the partners, highlighting the challenges of their business model.

Quoting lines from the above paragraph, identify and explain two advantages and two disadvantages of the partnership form of business.

Ans. Following are the advantages and disadvantages of partnership

Advantages

(i) **Ease of Formation and Closure**

Quoted Line "The firm was started with a simple agreement between the three partners, and they decided not to register the firm to save time and effort."

It is very easy to form a partnership firm. Only an agreement among the partners is required to form it and there is no compulsion of registration of the firm. Similarly, it is very easy to close such a firm.

(ii) **More Funds**

Quoted Line "Each partner contributed equally to the initial capital."

It is possible to raise larger amount of funds through partnership as compared to sole proprietorship, as each member contributes to the capital of the firm.

Disadvantages

(i) **Unlimited Liability**

Quoted Line "The partners had to bear the compensation from their personal savings due to the unlimited liability clause."

The liability of partners is unlimited and they are liable individually as well as jointly.

(ii) **Limited Resources**

Quoted Line "They faced financial strain due to the limited capital, as the number of partners restricted the firm's ability to raise large funds."

There is a limit to number of partners in a partnership firm. Therefore, capital investment is also limited and partnership firms face problems in expanding business beyond a certain size.

Case Study 16

Rural Fresh is a cooperative society formed by a group of farmers to promote organic produce and ensure fair pricing for its members. Each member has an equal say in the decision-making process, irrespective of their financial contribution. This principle of 'one man one vote' fosters equality and collective decision-making. The cooperative society operates independently as a separate legal entity, ensuring stability even when individual members leave or face personal challenges like bankruptcy.

Over the years, the society faced several challenges. Due to limited capital contributions from its members, Rural Fresh struggled to expand its operations and invest in better infrastructure. Furthermore, as most members lacked professional expertise, decision-making often resulted in inefficiencies.

Lastly, open discussions during meetings and mandatory disclosure requirements under the Societies Act made it difficult for Rural Fresh to maintain operational secrecy, which occasionally gave competitors an advantage.

Quoting lines from the above paragraph, identify and explain two advantages and two disadvantages of the cooperative society form of business.

Ans. Following are the advantages and disadvantages of the cooperative society form of business

Advantages

(i) **Equality in Voting Status**

Quoted Line "Each member has an equal say in the decision-making process, irrespective of their financial contribution."

Cooperative society is governed by the principle of 'one man one vote'. Each member is entitled to equal voting rights, irrespective of capital contribution by them.

(ii) **Limited Liability**

Quoted Line "The cooperative society operates independently as a separate legal entity."

The liability of every member is limited to the extent of his share in the society's capital.

Disadvantages

(i) **Limited Resources**

Quoted Line "Due to limited capital contributions from its members, Rural Fresh struggled to expand its operations and invest in better infrastructure."

A cooperative society is formed by people with limited means. The low rate of dividend discourages members to invest large amount in the society. Therefore, a cooperative society has limited resources.

(ii) **Inefficiency in Management**

Quoted Line "As most members lacked professional expertise, decision-making often resulted in inefficiencies."

Cooperative society is managed by its members who are generally not professional.

A cooperative society cannot afford to employ expert managers at high salaries due to limited funds.

Case Study 17

Kiran is a sole proprietor. Over the past decade, her business has grown from operating a neighbourhood corner shop selling accessories such as artificial jewellery, bags, hair clips and nail art to a retail chain with three branches in the city. Although, she looks after the varied functions in all the branches, she is wondering whether she should form a company to better manage the business. She also has plans to open branches countrywide. **NCERT**

(i) Explain two benefits of remaining a sole proprietor.

(ii) Explain two benefits of converting to a joint stock company.

(iii) What role will her decision to go nationwide play in her choice of form of the organisation?

(iv) What legal formalities will she have to undergo to operate business as a company?

Ans.

(i) Kiran may have the following two benefits of remaining a sole proprietor

- Being the sole proprietor, Kiran can enjoy all the profit earned from the business without having the need to share it with anyone.
- She does not have to publish accounts or be regulated under any law which maintains secrecy of the business activities.

(ii) Kiran may have the following two benefits of converting to a joint stock company

- She will be able to acquire more funds required for expansion of her retail chain branches countrywide through share capital in a joint stock company.
- Public has more faith in a joint stock company than in a sole proprietorship firm which will help in increasing the customer base for Kiran's business.

(iii) Her decision to go nationwide involves an increase in her scale of operation, requirement of capital and management abilities. As a sole proprietor, she may face limitations of resources and her limited managerial ability. She may not be good in all managerial tasks such as purchasing, selling, financing, etc. Thus, her decision-making may not be effective in all the situations especially when there are complexities of large-scale operation. Besides, she will have to bear more risk individually if she remains a sole proprietor and her liability will increase to a large extent. All these factors will definitely play a role in her choice of form of organisation and she will have much stronger reasons to form a joint stock company in this case.

(iv) The formation of a company requires greater time, effort and extensive knowledge of legal requirements and the procedures involved. To operate her business as a company,

- Kiran will have to prepare several documents and will have to ensure compliance with several legal requirements before it can start functioning.
- Kiran will have to register her company, as registration of the company is compulsory under the Indian Companies Act, 2013.
- The Companies Act requires each public company to provide a lot of information to the office of the Registrar of Companies from time-to-time which Kiran will have to provide. The functioning of a company is subject to many legal provisions and compulsions.

A company has to comply with various restrictions including audit, voting, filing of reports and preparation of documents, and is required to obtain various certificates from different agencies such as registrar, SEBI, etc.

Case Study 18

Neha, a bright final year student was waiting for her results to be declared. While at home she decided to put her free time to use. Having an aptitude for painting, she tried her hand at decorating clay pots and bowls with designs. She was excited at the praise showered by her friends and acquaintances on her work. She even managed to sell a few pieces of unique hand pottery from her home to people living in and around her colony.

Operating from home, she was able to save on rental payments. She gained a lot of popularity by word of mouth as a sole proprietor. She further perfected her skills of painting pottery and created new motifs and designs. All this generated great interest among her customers and provided a boost to the demand for her products.

By the end of summer, she found that she was able to make a profit oft 2,500 from her paltry investment in colours, pottery and drawing sheets. She felt motivated to take up this work as a career. She therefore, decided to set-up her own artwork business. She can continue running the business on her own as a sole proprietor, but she needs more money for doing business on a larger-scale.

Her father has suggested that she should form a partnership with her cousin to meet the need for additional funds and for sharing the responsibilities and risks. Side by side, he is of the opinion that it is possible that the business might grow further and may require the formation of a company. She is in a fix as to what form of business organisation she should go in for? **NCERT**

On the basis of above case, answer the following questions

(i) Advise Neha regarding the different factors to be considered before choosing a suitable form of organisation.

(ii) Neha's father has suggested that she should consider forming a partnership with her cousin. What benefits will Neha enjoy, as a result of this partnership?

Ans.

(i) Following factors should be considered by Neha before choosing a suitable form of organisation

- Cost and Ease in Setting-up the organisation
- Liability
- Continuity
- Management ability
- Capital considerations
- Degree of control
- Nature of business

For explanation, refer to topic 'Choice form of business organisation' on page 47.

(ii) The benefits that Neha will be able to enjoy by forming a partnership are

- **Balanced Decision-making**
  In partnership, work can be divided among partners according to their skill and knowledge or areas of their expertise. This reduced the burden of work and leads to more balanced decisions.
- **More Funds**
  It is possible to raise larger amount of funds through partnership as compared to sole proprietorship, as each member contributes to the capital of the firm.
- **Sharing of Risks**
  In partnership, risk gets distributed among partners, which reduces anxiety, burden and stress on individual partners.
- **Secrecy**
  The partnership firm is not required to publish its accounts and submit its reports. Therefore, the firm is able to maintain confidentiality of information.

SELF ASSESSMENT TEST

Objective Type Questions

1. Which of the following is an advantage of sole proprietorship?
   (a) Quick decision-making (b) Direct incentive
   (c) Ease of formation and closure
   (d) All of these
2. Every partner acts in the capacity of
   (a) an agent as well as a principal
   (b) only agent of the firm
   (c) only principal of the firm (d) None of the above
3. A minor can be admitted to the benefits of an already existing partnership firm
   (a) with the consent of the managing partner
   (b) with the consent of all existing partner
   (c) with the consent of the court
   (d) None of the above
4. A society operates on the principle of 'one man one vote,' ensuring equal voting rights to all members, regardless of their capital contribution.
   Which feature of a cooperative society is highlighted in the case above?
   (a) Limited liability (b) Equality in voting status
   (c) Stable existence (d) Economy in operations
5. Small farmers joined hands to cultivate their land collectively using modern techniques, better seeds and shared resources for improved efficiency.
   Which type of cooperative society focuses on collective farming and resource sharing among farmers?
   (a) Credit cooperative society
   (b) Marketing cooperative society
   (c) Farmer's cooperative society
   (d) Producer cooperative society
6. What does 'limited liability' mean in the context of a joint stock company?
   (a) Shareholders are personally liable for all debts of the company
   (b) Shareholders are liable only to the extent of the amount unpaid on their shares
   (c) Shareholders cannot transfer their shares
   (d) Shareholders are responsible for the company's day-to-day management
7. .... document is described as the Charter of the Company.
   (a) Prospectus (b) Articles of Association
   (c) Memorandum of Association
   (d) None of the above
8. Which of the following is the most important factor in the choice of form of business organisation?
   (a) Capital/Finance
   (b) Liability
   (c) Education
   (d) Degree of control

Answers 1. (d) 2. (a) 3. (b) 4. (b) 5. (c) 6. (b) 7. (c) 8. (a)

Short Answer Type Questions

9. Briefly outline the main differences between sole proprietorship and partnership.
10. "A limited partnership allows partners to pool their resources while limiting the liability of some partners. This enables businesses to attract investment while safeguarding the interests of certain individuals."
    In light of the above statement, explain the features of a limited partnership.
11. "The process of registration of a partnership firm ensures that the firm gains legal recognition and can avail itself of various rights under the law."
    In light of the above statement, outline the procedure for the registration of a partnership firm.
12. Discuss any four types of partners in a partnership firm.
13. State any three differences between public company and private company.
14. Rajneesh has to give a speech on the drawbacks of cooperative societies. In context to it, state some of the drawbacks that Rajneesh may elaborate.
15. If a company suffers heavy losses and its assets are not enough to pay-off its liabilities, the balance can be recovered from private assets of its members. Do you agree? Give reasons.

Long Answer Type Questions

16. What is meant by joint hindu family business? Discuss its main features.
17. What is Memorandum of Association? State its main clauses.
18. Ravi wants to start a business of apparels. He wants to evaluate the various forms of business organisation. Explain the factors that should be considered for choosing a suitable form of business organisation.

03

CHAPTER

Private, Public and Global Enterprises

After gaining independence, the establishment of public sector enterprises became essential for the country's comprehensive development. Additionally, India was dedicated to a socialistic pattern of economy leading to the adoption of mixed economy model.

▼ YOUR STUDY GOALS

3.1 Introduction
3.2 Forms of Public Sector Enterprises
3.3 Global Enterprises or Multinational Companies (MNCs)
3.4 Joint Ventures
3.5 Public Private Partnership (PPP)

▼ YOUR PRACTICE GOAL

- Objective Type Questions (63 Qs ; MCQs, A-R, Statements, Matching)
- Subjective Questions (12 SAs, 7 LAs)
- Case Study Based Questions (Short Case Studies-11, Long Case Studies-4)
- Self Assessment Test (8 MCQs, 7 SAs, 3 LAs)

3.1 Introduction

India adopted the concept of mixed economy after independence, where different types of business organisations exist. These can be grouped as privately owned organisations and government owned (public) organisations.

Indian Economy

- **Private Sector**
  - Sole Proprietorship
  - Partnership
  - Joint Hindu Family Business
  - Cooperative Societies
  - Multinational Corporation
  - Joint Stock Company
- **Public Sector**
  - Departmental Undertaking
  - Statutory Corporation
  - Government Company

1. Private Sector Enterprises

It refers to all those enterprises which are managed and owned by individuals or group of individuals. It aims at maximising the wealth of the owners.

2. Public Sector Enterprises

It refers to all those enterprises which are managed and owned partly or wholly by the Central or State Government or by both governments. These may be part of a ministry or created by a Special Act of the Parliament. The public welfare or service is the main objective of these enterprises.

3.2 Forms of Public Sector Enterprises

Public enterprises were formed by the government to participate in the economic activities of the country. They are accountable to public through Parliament and public funds are used by them for their activities.

Public sector enterprises can be organised in any of the following forms

- Departmental undertakings
- Statutory corporation/Public corporation
- Government company

I. Departmental Undertakings

They are the oldest and most traditional form of organising public sector enterprises. These undertakings are considered as a department of ministers and have no spearate legal existence e.g. Railways, post and telegraph department, etc.

These undertakings may be run either by Central or by State Government and the rules of Central/State Government are applicable.

Features of Departmental Undertakings

- They are financed from the government treasury and an annual appropriation for it is made in the budget of the government.
- The revenue earned by these undertakings is also deposited into the treasury.
- They are subject to accounting and audit controls, as applicable to other government activities.
- The staff of departmental undertakings include government servants which are headed by civil servants and Indian Administrative Service (IAS) officers. They are transferable from one ministry to another.
- They are managed and controlled by the government and are accountable to concerned ministry.

Merits and Limitations of Departmental Undertakings

Merits	Limitations
• They facilitate the Parliament to exercise **effective control** over their operations. • They are subject to accounting and audit controls. Thus, they have high degree of public accountability. • The revenue of these undertakings is deposited in the treasury of the government, thus, providing **source** of income for the government. • They are most suitable for operations where **national security** is concerned, because of direct control and supervision of the concerned ministry.	• These undertakings work under strict parliamentary control. This **reduces the flexibility and efficiency** of the undertakings. • Decisions can only be taken after approval from concerned ministry. This leads to **delay in decision-making**. • These undertakings are unable to take advantage of business opportunities as they are not allowed to take risky ventures due to the **bureaucrat's over-cautious and conservative** approach. • These undertakings have a number of rules and regulations and lengthy channels of day-to-day operations, which leads to **red tapism** and bureaucracy. • Constant **interference** from the concerned ministry unduly affects the working of these undertakings. • These undertakings are **insensitive to consumers'** needs and do not provide adequate services to them.

II. Statutory or Public Corporation

These are corporate bodies created by the state legislature or by a Special Act of the Parliament. e.g. State Bank of India, Life Insurance Corporation of India, etc. These are financially independent with a control over a specified area or particular type of commercial acitvity. These have power of government and considerable amount of operational flexibility of private enterprises.

Features of Statutory or Public Corporation

- These are wholly owned by the State Government which has the ultimate financial responsibility and power to appropriate their profits or bear the losses.
- These corporations can sue and be sued, enter into contracts and purchase or sell property in its own name.
- These are managed and controlled by board of directors appointed by the government.
- These are independently financed. i.e. obtain funds by borrowings from the government or public and through the revenue.
- They are free from government accounting and audit control procedures applicable to government departments.
- The employees of these corporations are not government or civil servants. They are not governed by government rules and regulations. However at times, some officers are taken from government departments on deputation, to head these organisations.

Merits and Limitations of Statutory or Public Corporation

Merits	Limitations
• They enjoy independence in their functioning and have operational **flexibility**.	• These corporations **do not enjoy much autonomy and operation flexibility** in reality. All their operations and actions are subject to many rules and regulations.
• As they are not financed from central budget, the government **do not interfere** in their financial matters, including their income and receipts.	• There is **government and political interference** in major decisions of the corporations, especially where huge funds are involved.
• Due to **autonomous set-up**, they frame their own rules and regulations, policies and procedures within the powers assigned to them by the Act. But, the act may provide few matters and issues which require prior approval of a particular ministry.	• Government often appoints advisors to the Corporation Board. This **affects freedom in decision-making** and leads to disagreements.
• They are **helpful** in **economic development** as they have a combination of initiative of private enterprises and power of government.	• Corruption is strongly prevalent in these corporations, as the officials may misuse their autonomy and indulge in **unfair practices** while dealing with public.

III. Government Company

According to Section 2(45) of the Companies Act, 2013, a government company means any company in which not less than 51 percent of the paid-up capital is held by either of the following

- The Central Government
- Any State Government
- Partly by Central Government and partly by one or more State Governments and includes a company which is a subsidiary of a government company.

It can be formed as a private limited company or a public limited company. The shares of the company are purchased in the name of President of India. The government being major shareholders, exercises full control over the management of these companies. e.g. Steel Authority of India Litd. (SAIL), etc.

Features of Government Company

- It has a separate legal existence. Thus, it can buy and sell property, and enter into contract in its own name.
- The management of the company is regulated according to the provisions of Indian Companies Act, like any other public limited company.
- It is exempted from the accounting/audit rules and procedures. However, an auditor is appointed by Central Government and an annual report is to be presented in Parliament/State Legislature.
- It obtains funds from government shareholding and other private shareholders. It can also raise the funds from the capital market.

- It can file a suit in court of law against any third party and can be sued.
- The employees of this company are appointed according to the rules and regulations provided under the Memorandum and Articles of Association of the company.

Merits and Limitations of Government Company

Merits	Limitations
• A government company can be **established easily** by fulfilling the requirements of the Indian Companies Act. • It **enjoys autonomy** in all management decisions and takes actions according to business economy. • It has a **separate legal entity**, apart from the government. • This company provides goods and services to consumers at a reasonable price. Thus, it helps to control market and **curb unhealthy business practices.**	• As the government is the only shareholder in some of the companies, it controls affairs of the company and **provisions** of the Companies Act **do not have much relevance.** • This company **evades constitutional responsibility** as it is not answerable directly to the Parliament. • The **government controls the whole management and administration** of the company. It is not needed to be registered, like other companies under the Companies Act.

3.3 Global Enterprises or Multinational Companies (MNCs)

A global enterprise or multinational company is one which operates in two or more than two countries. These enterprises have their head office in their home country and have branches, factories, offices, etc. in different countries. The branches are known as Majority Owned Foreign Affiliates (MOFA).

Global Enterprises

Pepsi and Coca Cola companies are registered in USA, whereas, they operate across the world. They extend their industrial and marketing operations through a network of branches (Majority Owned Foreign Affiliates in several countries.

Features of Global Enterprises

1. **Huge Capital Resources** These enterprises operate on large-scale and have the ability to raise funds from many sources like issue of equity shares, debentures or bonds to the public. They can also avail loans from financial institutions and international banks. Because of their financial strength, they are able to survive under all circumstances.
2. **Foreign Collaboration** MNCs usually collaborate with Indian companies in the public and private sector. They are required to comply with restrictive clauses related to technology, pricing, dividends, payment, tight control by foreign technicians, etc.
3. **Advanced Technology** In production methods, these enterprises have technological superiorities. They are able to conform to international standards and quality specifications. This leads to industrial progress of the home country of such corporations.
4. **Product Innovation** Due to a huge capital base, these enterprises are able to have highly advanced Research and Development Departments. They are continuously engaged in developing new products of better quality and superior design of existing products.
5. **Marketing Strategies** They use aggressive marketing strategies in order to increase the sales in short period. They have effective advertising and sales promotion techniques. They are able to promote sales easily due to their reliability, up-to-date market information system and a well established brand.

6. **Expansion of Market Territory** The operations and activities of these enterprises extend beyond the physical boundaries of their own countries. They operate through a network of subsidiaries, branches and affiliates in host countries. This expands their market territory and enable them to become international brand.
7. **Centralised Control** These enterprises operate through network of branches and subsidiaries in host countries and controls the operations with a centralised system in home country. However, this control is limited to the board policy framework of the parent company. The head office does not interfere in their day-to-day operations.

3.4 Joint Ventures

When two or more firms join together for a common purpose and mutual benefit, it is known as a joint venture. In broader sense, a joint venture is the accumulation of resources and expertise by two or more businesses, to achieve a particular goal.

Joint Venture

The Company, formerly known as Maruti Udyog Limited, was incorporated as a joint venture between the Government of India and Suzuki Motor Corporation, Japan in February, 1981.

MARUTI SUZUKI

Features of Joint Ventures

- In joint ventures, the two organisations that join may be private, government owned or a foreign company.
- Joint ventures share technology, capital, human resources, risks, rewards, etc.
- Joint venture may also arise on the basis of an agreement between businesses of different countries. In such case, businesses will have to comply with the provisions provided by the governments of the two countries.
- Joint venture is the best way of doing business in India. There is no separate law which governs these joint ventures. They are treated as domestic companies in India.
- They are useful to strengthen long-term relationships or collaborating on short-term projects.
- In joint ventures, profits and losses are shared in agreed proportion. If there is no agreement, profits and losses are shared equally.
- Joint ventures should be based on a Memorandum of Understanding (MoU) and signed by both the parties involved, highlighting the basis of an agreement.

Types of Joint Ventures

Joint ventures may be classified into two types which are as follows

Contractual Joint Venture (CJV)	**Equity-based Joint Venture** (EJV)
In this form of joint venture, a new jointly-owned entity is not created. There is only an agreement to work together. The parties only exercise some elements of control and do not share ownership of the business. A franchisee relationship is a typical example of contractual joint venture. In such a relationship, the key elements are • Two or more parties have a common intention of running a business venture. • Each party brings some inputs. • Both parties exercise some control on the business venture. • It is not a transaction-to-transaction relationship, but has a character of relatively longer duration.	In this form of joint venture, a new separate jointly owned business entity is formed by two or more than two parties, according to the agreement of the parties. The form of business entity may be company, partnership, trusts, limited liability partnership firms, venture capital funds, etc. The key elements of such a joint venture are • There is an agreement to either create a new entity or to join into ownership of an existing entity. • In EJV, ownership by the parties is shared. • Management is shared by the jointly-owned parties. • Responsibilities regarding capital investment and other financing arrangements are shared. • Profits and losses are shared according to the agreement.

Benefits of Joint Ventures

- **Increased Resources and Capacity** Joint ventures helps in tapping up more resources. This enhances the capacity to grow and expand more quickly, and take advantage of new opportunities.
- **Access to New Markets and Distribution Networks** When two enterprises join together, they are free to enhance or expand their market. e.g. Indian company and Chinese company form a joint venture. This will help Indian company to sell its products in China also and the same advantage can also be derived by the Chinese company.
- **Access to Technology** Companies who do not have the capacity to develop their own technology, can join with other companies to access advanced technologies. This helps in improving the quality of products, thereby saving time, energy investment, etc.
- **Innovation** Joint ventures allow business to come up with new and innovative products. This helps in raising the new and creative products in the market. The foreign partners who have new ideas and technology, come up with innovative products.
- **Low Cost of Production** Joint ventures take advantage of lower cost of production to obtain quality products for their global market at a low price. Most of the international companies invest in India because of low cost of raw materials, labour, technical workforce, management, etc.
- **Established Brand Name** When two business firms enter a joint venture, one of the involved parties can derive the benefits from the other's goodwill, which has been established in the market since long.

3.5 Public Private Partnership (PPP)

Public Private Partnership means relationship between public sector and private sector entities in the context of financing, designing and developing infrastructural facilities. In such projects, the private sector contributes technical knowhow and managerial expertise.

The **public partners** in PPP are government entities, i.e. ministries, government departments, municipalities or state-owned enterprises while **private partners** include local or international business with technical or financial expertise, NGOs, community based organisations, etc.

PPP Projects

Kundli Manesar Expressway Ltd. PPP model assigns tasks, obligations and risks among the public and private partners in an optimal manner. Nivedita Setu (Kolkata) is one of the first Public Private Partnerships projects in India.

Features of PPP

- PPP is an arrangement between public sector and a private party, in which private sector provides services and/or assets to the public at large.
- PPP arrangement is for a specific period and at the expiry of such period, such partnership comes to an end.
- PPP is suitable for big projects where gestation period is long and also for high priority projects that aimed at creating public goods, like in infrastructure sector.
- The government may provide subsidy, support a project by providing tax breaks and guarantee annual revenues for a fixed period to the PPP.
- Revenue is shared between the government and private enterprise in an agreed ratio.

Mind Map

PRIVATE, PUBLIC AND GLOBAL ENTERPRISES

1 Introduction

- **Private Sector Enterprises** Refers to all those enterprises which are managed and owned by individuals or group of individuals. Includes sole proprietorship, partnership, Hindu Undivided Family, cooperative societies, etc.
- **Public Sector Enterprises** Refers to all those enterprises which are managed and owned by the Central or State Government or by both Governments.

2 Forms of Public Sector Enterprises

Public enterprises were formed by the government to participate in the economic activities of the country. These include departmental undertakings, statutory corporation and government company.

3 Departmental Undertakings

Oldest and most traditional form of organising public sector enterprises.

Features

- Financed from the government treasury
- Revenue earned is deposited into treasuries
- Subject to accounting and auditing controls
- Managed and controlled by the government
- Staff includes government servants which are headed by civil servants and IAS officers

Merits

- Facilitate the Parliament to exercise effective control
- Have high degree of public accountability
- Provide source of income for the government
- Most suitable where national security is concerned

Demerits

- There is lack of flexibility and efficiency
- There is delay in decision-making
- Bureaucracy and conservative approach exists
- Rules and regulations with political intervention
- Insensitive to consumer needs

4 Statutory or Public Corporation

Corporate bodies created by the state legislature or by a Special Act of the Parliament.

Features

- Wholly owned by the State Government
- Can sue, be sued, enter into contracts, purchase or sell property
- Managed and controlled by board of directors
- Independently financed
- Free from government accounting and audit control procedures
- Employees are not government or civil servants

Merits

- Free from interference of government regulation
- Free from interference in financial matters
- There is autonomous set-up
- They are helpful in economic development

Demerits

- There is lack of operational flexibility
- Government and political interference in major decisions
- There is delay in decision-making
- Corruption is strongly prevalent

5 Government Company

Established under the Companies Act, 2013 and is registered and governed by the provisions of the Indian Companies Act.

Features

- Separate legal existence
- Exempted from accounting/auditing rules
- Obtains funds from government shareholding
- Employees appointed according to rules and regulations of MoA
- Can file suit in court of law against any third party
- Management of the company is regulated according to provisions of Indian Companies Act

Merits

- Easy incorporation
- Existence of separate legal entity
- Prevents unhealthy business practices
- There is no government interference

Demerits

- There is lack of accountability
- There is theoretical freedom
- It defeats the main purpose

6 Global Enterprises or Multinational Companies (MNCs)

A global enterprise or multinational company is one which operates in two or more than two countries. These enterprises have their head office in their home country and have branches, factories, offices, etc. in different countries.

Features

- Huge capital resources
- Advanced technology
- Marketing strategies
- Expansion of market territory
- Foreign collaboration
- Product innovation
- Centralised control

7 Joint Ventures

When two or more firms join together for a common purpose and mutual benefit, it is known as joint venture.

Features

- Organisations may be private, government owned or foreign company
- No separate law
- Profits and losses are shared in agreed proportion
- Useful to strengthen long-term relationships
- Share technology, capital, human resources, risks, rewards, etc
- Should be based on Memorandum of Understanding (MoU)

Types

- **Contractual** A new jointly-owned entity is not created. There is only an agreement to work together.
- **Equity-based** A new separate jointly owned business entity is formed by two or more than two parties according to the agreement of the parties.

Benefits

- Increased resources and capacity
- Low cost of production
- Innovation
- Access to technology
- New markets and distribution networks

8 Public Private Partnership (PPP)

Public Private Partnership (PPP) is the relationship between public sector and private sector entities in the context of financing, designing and developing infrastructural facilities.

Features

- It facilitates partnership between public sector and private sector
- There is provision for subsidy
- Revenue is shared between government and private enterprise
- Suitable for big and high priority projects
- Operations or management is for a specified time period

EXAM PATTERN QUESTIONS

Objective Type Questions

Multiple Choice Questions (MCQs)

1. **Indian economy is a .... kind of economy.**

(a) global (b) mixed
(c) capitalist (d) socialist

2. **An enterprise that comes into existence after an Act is passed in Parliament is known as**

(a) government company (b) parliament company
(c) public corporation (d) government corporation

3. **"These enterprises are owned and managed by Central and State Government and are sometimes a part of ministry." Identify the type of enterprise highlighted in the statement.** **Competency Based Que**

(a) Private sector enterprises
(b) Public sector enterprises
(c) Sole proprietorship (d) Public private partnership

4. **Public sector enterprises come into existence by .... of the Parliament.**

(a) union list (b) special act
(c) government provision (d) government order

5. **The main motive of the private sector is**

(a) social service (b) earning profit
(c) Both (a) and (b) (d) None of these

6. **Which of the following is the oldest and most traditional form of public sector enterprises?**

(a) Statutory corporation (b) Public company
(c) Government company (d) Departmental undertaking

7. **An organisation is working for the purpose of public welfare as a ministry of government. It is financed by government and all its income is deposited in government treasury. Identify which kind of public sector enterprise is it?** **Competency Based Que**

(a) Partnership (b) Departmental undertaking
(c) Sole proprietorship (d) Company

8. **The Central Transport Department, a departmental undertaking of the government, is responsible for managing public transportation across the country. It operates under the direct control of the Ministry of Transport, with all revenue deposited into the government treasury. The department is managed by civil servants and follows strict parliamentary procedures for decision-making.**

While this ensures high accountability and effective control, frequent delays are observed in implementing new transportation policies due to extensive bureaucratic processes. Moreover, complaints from consumers regarding inadequate services often go unaddressed, reflecting insensitivity to consumer needs.

Despite this, the department continues to be a significant source of income for the government and is critical for maintaining national security during emergencies.
Which of the following is not a limitation of departmental undertakings? **Competency Based Que**

(a) Red tapism
(b) Insensitivity to consumer needs
(c) Lack of public accountability
(d) Delay in decision-making

9. **A government run organisation is directly controlled by a ministry and subject to the accounting and audit rules applicable to other government activities. It provides a source of income to the government, ensuring public accountability. Identify the type of organisation described in the statement.**
Competency Based Que

(a) Government company
(b) Public corporation
(c) Departmental undertaking
(d) Joint venture

10. **Identify the form of public sector enterprise illustrated in the below picture which is suitable for public utility services and strategic industries.**

(a) Departmental undertaking
(b) Government company
(c) Statutory corporations
(d) None of the above

11. **The State Agricultural Corporation, a public enterprise, operates as a body corporate with the authority to enter into contracts and manage its assets independently. Governed by a Board of Directors appointed by the State Government, it secures funds through government borrowings and revenue from its agricultural products.**

Unlike departmental undertakings, it is not subject to government accounting and audit controls, allowing it greater operational flexibility. However, in case of financial losses, the State Government assumes ultimate responsibility. Its employees are hired directly by the corporation, with only a few officers occasionally deputed from government departments.

Which of the following is a characteristic of the State Agricultural Corporation? **Competency Based Que**

(a) Employees are government civil servants
(b) The corporation is subject to government accounting controls
(c) It operates as a body corporate and can sue or be sued in its own name
(d) The profits and losses are borne solely by the board of directors

12. **Identify the form of public sector enterprise illustrated in the below picture that has the power of government and considerable amount of operating flexibility of private enterprises.**

(a) Departmental undertaking
(b) Government company
(c) Statutory corporations
(d) None of the above

13. **LIC is an example of**

(a) statutory corporation (b) public company
(c) government company (d) departmental undertaking

14. **Navratan Ltd. is a company engaged in the production and distribution of heavy electrical goods. Pattern of shareholding in the company is as follows**

(i) **Government of India –15%**
(ii) **Government of Bihar – 26 %**
(iii) **Government of Assam – 10%**
(iv) **General Public – 49%**

Navratan Ltd. can be classified as which of the following? **Competency Based Que**

(a) Small company
(b) Government company
(c) Private company
(d) None of the above

15. **Maximum degree of autonomy is enjoyed by ....**

(a) government company
(b) statutory corporation
(c) departmental undertaking
(d) None of the above

16. **A government company is a company in which the paid-up capital held by the government is not less than ....**

(a) 49% (b) 51%
(c) 50% (d) 25%

17. **Identify the form of public sector enterprise illustrated in the below picture which is registered and governed by the provisions of the Companies Act.**

(a) Departmental undertaking
(b) Government company
(c) Statutory corporations
(d) None of the above

18. **"A government company enjoys autonomy in management decisions and provides goods and services at reasonable prices to prevent unhealthy business practices."**

Which merit of government companies is highlighted in this statement? **Competency Based Que**

(a) Easy incorporation
(b) No government interference
(c) Prevents unhealthy business practices
(d) Separate legal entity

19. **An enterprise is having huge capital, huge turnover and its branches are spread all over the country. What do we call such kinds of enterprises?**

(a) Joint venture
(b) Global enterprise
(c) Large corporation
(d) Huge company

20. Identify the form of enterprise highlighted in the given picture.

(a) Public sector enterprise
(b) Private sector enterprise
(c) Global enterprise
(d) Government enterprise

21. StarCom Ltd. is a multinational company with operations in over 10 countries. Its branches, known as Majority Owned Foreign Affiliates (MOFA), handle production and distribution across various global markets. The company leverages its international presence to access diverse resources and cater to a broader customer base.

What is the term used for the branches of multinational companies like StarCom Ltd.? Competency Based Que

(a) Subsidiaries
(b) Majority Owned Foreign Affiliates
(c) Joint ventures
(d) Franchises

22. The term 'centralised control' in MNCs means that control is exercised by

(a) branches (b) subsidiaries
(c) headquarters (d) parliament

23. MNCs may collaborate with companies in the public and private sector. These foreign collaborations have given rise to the growth of

(a) capital markets
(b) perfect competition
(c) monopolies
(d) oligopolies

24. Which of the following statements is not true?

(a) Multinational corporations have huge capital resources
(b) Multinational corporations use aggressive marketing techniques
(c) Indian companies have failed to become MNCs
(d) PPP model is a huge success in India

25. Which of the following statements is not true about MNCs?

(a) MNCs have the ability to raise capital from multiple sources like equity shares, debentures and loans
(b) MNCs often collaborate with Indian companies in the public and private sector
(c) MNCs are restricted from using advanced technology in production methods
(d) MNCs focus on product innovation and have advanced R&D departments

26. Multinational Companies have sophisticated Research and Development Departments engaged in the task of developing new products and superior designs of existing products.

Qualitative research requires huge investment which only multinational companies can afford. Identify the feature of MNC's is being discussed in the above statement. Competency Based Que

(a) Marketing strategies
(b) Product innovation
(c) Advanced technology
(d) Centralised control

27. Which of the following multinational corporation is not Indian?

(a) Hindustan Unilever (b) Asian Paints
(c) Piramal Healthcare (d) Infosys

28. TechWorld Ltd., a leading software company, partnered with GreenEnergy Inc., a renewable energy firm, to develop AI-based solutions for sustainable energy management. Both firms pooled their resources and expertise to achieve their shared goal of advancing clean energy technologies. This collaboration is expected to benefit both companies mutually.

Identify the type of collaboration described in the case. Competency Based Que

(a) Merger
(b) Joint venture
(c) Franchise
(d) Strategic alliance

29. Which of the following is not a feature of joint ventures?

(a) Joint ventures share technology, capital, risks and rewards
(b) They are governed by a separate law in India specifically for joint ventures
(c) Profits and losses are shared in agreed proportion or equally if no agreement exists
(d) They may arise from agreements between businesses of different countries

30. Alpha Builders and Omega Developers partnered to construct a high-tech residential complex. Instead of forming a new entity, both companies agreed to share resources and control for the project under a long-term agreement.

Their collaboration is based on mutual inputs without shared ownership of a separate entity. Identify the type of joint venture described in the case. Competency Based Que

(a) Equity-based Joint Venture (EJV)
(b) Contractual Joint Venture (CJV)
(c) Strategic Alliance
(d) Franchise

31. **A company from India forms a joint venture with a company from Germany. This allows the Indian company to leverage advanced German technology while the German company benefits from access to Indian markets and low-cost production. Which benefit of joint ventures does this scenario primarily highlight?** Competency Based Que

(a) Complete managerial control
(b) Access to technology and markets
(c) Higher operational independence
(d) Limited resource utilisation

32. **"Two companies from different countries collaborate, allowing one to utilise the other's advanced technology to improve product quality and efficiency." Identify the benefit of the joint venture described in the statement.** Competency Based Que

(a) Increased resources and capacity
(b) Innovation
(c) Established brand name
(d) Access to technology

33. **Which of the following statements is not true about the forms of joint ventures?**

(a) In a Contractual Joint Venture (CJV), a new jointly-owned entity is not created and parties only exercise some elements of control
(b) In a Contractual Joint Venture (CJV), profits and losses are shared according to the agreement
(c) In an Equity-based Joint Venture (EJV), a new separate jointly-owned business entity is formed
(d) In an Equity-based Joint Venture (EJV), management, capital investment and profits are shared among the parties as per the agreement

34. **A contract has been entered into between government and Techno Pvt Ltd. (a private business firm) for provision of public assets and public services for the benefit of public. Identify the type of association between Techno Pvt Ltd. and government.** Competency Based Que

(a) Public-private partnership
(b) Supernatural companies
(c) General partnership (d) None of these

Direction *Read the case study and answer the questions 35 to 38 on the basis of the same*

India Post is a government-operated postal system in India, under the Ministry of Communications. It provides a wide range of services including mail delivery, financial services, and retail services. India Post is fully owned by the government of India and functions under its control and supervision.

The funding for India Post comes directly from the government treasury, and the revenue generated through its services is deposited into the government treasury. The recruitment of employees and the conditions of their service are similar to those of other government employees.

35. **Identify the type of public sector enterprise, India Post is considered as**

(a) departmental undertaking
(b) statutory corporation
(c) government company
(d) None of the above

36. **How does India Post get its revenue?**

(a) From sale of goods and services
(b) From government shareholding
(c) From government treasury
(d) From private shareholders

37. **What does India Post do with its revenue?**

(a) Spends it on social welfare
(b) Deposits it in the government treasury
(c) Spends it on various government projects
(d) Deposits it in World Bank

38. **It is fully owned by the government and operates under the Ministry of Communications. Identify the status of employees working in India Post on the basis of the above statement.**

(a) Government employees (b) Private sector employees
(c) Dissatisfied employees (d) Global employees

Assertion-Reason

Direction (Q.No. 39 to 48) *Read the following Assertion (A) and Reason (R) and choose the correct alternative from the following*

Alternatives

(a) Both Assertion (A) and Reason (R) are true and Reason (R) is the correct explanation of Assertion (A)
(b) Both Assertion (A) and Reason (R) are true, but Reason (R) is not the correct explanation of Assertion (A)
(c) Assertion (A) is true, but Reason (R) is false
(d) Assertion (A) is false, but Reason (R) is true

39. **Assertion** (A) Public sector enterprises are organisations owned by government.

Reason (R) Public sector enterprises cannot be managed by government properly.

40. **Assertion** (A) Departmental undertakings are controlled directly by the government ministry to ensure accountability.

Reason (R) Since the government directly controls the operations of these undertakings, they are subjected to strict parliamentary oversight, leading to effective control.

41. **Assertion** (A) The revenue earned by departmental undertakings is deposited into the government's treasury.

Reason (R) This helps the government to maintain financial control over the operations of these undertakings.

42. **Assertion** (A) Departmental undertakings are able to take benefits of business opportunities.

Reason (R) Departmental undertakings do not undertake risky ventures due to bureaucrat's over-cautious and conservative approach.

43. **Assertion** (A) Statutory corporations operate with complete independence from government regulations.

Reason (R) Although statutory corporations are government-owned, they are free from interference in their financial matters and operations.

44. **Assertion** (A) Statutory corporations face less interference from the government.

Reason (R) Statutory corporations have greater autonomy in their operations and financial matters.

45. **Assertion** (A) Political interference can affect the working of statutory corporations.

Reason (R) The influence of government and politicians on decision-making within statutory corporations can cause delays and inefficiencies.

46. **Assertion** (A) Statutory corporation is financed by the government through allocation of funds in the annual general budget of the parliament.

Reason (R) Statutory corporations are managed and controlled by board of directors appointed by the government.

47. **Assertion** (A) The Central Government of India has established a department that is considered as an extension of the ministry itself.

Reason (R) LIC is an example of such a department.

48. **Assertion** (A) Political interference is a disadvantage of a government company.

Reason (R) The operational policies of the government companies are formed according to the whims and fancies of the ministers.

Two Statements Based MCQs

Direction (Q.No. 49 to 58) *Read the following statements carefully and choose the correct alternative*

Alternatives

(a) Statement I is correct and Statement II is incorrect
(b) Statement II is correct and Statement I is incorrect
(c) Both the statements are correct
(d) Both the statements are incorrect

49. **Statement I** Departmental undertakings are headed by IAS officers and civil servants who are transferable from one ministry to another.

Statement II Departmental undertakings have separate legal entity.

50. **Statement I** Employees of departmental undertakings are accountable to the concerned minister, who is ultimately responsible to the Parliament.

Statement II There is a lot of political interference through the ministry in case of departmental undertakings.

51. **Statement I** A statutory corporation may be formed either as a private limited company or a public limited company.

Statement II Reserve Bank of India and Food Corporation of India are examples of statutory corporations.

52. **Statement I** Statutory corporations enjoy a high level of operational flexibility and autonomy in their decision-making processes.

Statement II Government interference, delayed decisions and the prevalence of unfair practices are some common drawbacks associated with statutory corporations.

53. **Statement I** MNCs usually collaborate with Indian companies in the public and private sector.

Statement II Due to a huge capital base, these enterprises are able to have highly advanced research and development departments.

54. **Statement I** Multinational Companies (MNCs) typically have advanced technology and use aggressive marketing strategies.

Statement II MNCs operate in only one country and do not have subsidiaries in other countries.

55. **Statement I** A joint venture is a partnership where two or more businesses collaborate for a common purpose.

Statement II A joint venture typically involves creating a new, separately owned business entity.

56. **Statement I** Contractual Joint Ventures (CJVs) involve the creation of a new business entity.

Statement II In a Contractual Joint Venture (CJV), the partners only sign an agreement to work together but do not share ownership.

57. **Statement I** Equity-based joint ventures involve the creation of a new entity where ownership, management and financial responsibilities are shared.

Statement II Contractual joint ventures require the creation of a new business entity, but profits and losses are not shared between the partners.

58. Statement I One of the benefits of a joint venture is that it allows companies to share resources, risks and rewards.
Statement II Joint ventures are regulated by specific laws in India and are not treated as domestic companies.

Matching

59. Match the following

Column I	Column II
A. Departmental undertaking	(i) These are independently financed
B. Statutory corporation	(ii) Obtains funds from government shareholding and other private shareholders
C. Government company	(iii) Financed from the government treasury

Codes

	A	B	C
(a)	(ii)	(i)	(iii)
(b)	(iii)	(ii)	(i)
(c)	(i)	(iii)	(ii)
(d)	(iii)	(i)	(ii)

60. Match the following

Column I	Column II
A. Public sector enterprise	(i) Post and Telegraph
B. Private sector enterprise	(ii) Steel Authority of India
C. Government company	(iii) Reliance Industrial Ltd.
D. Departmental undertaking	(iv) Indian Railways

Codes

	A	B	C	D
(a)	(ii)	(i)	(iii)	(iv)
(b)	(iv)	(iii)	(ii)	(i)
(c)	(i)	(iii)	(ii)	(iv)
(d)	(iii)	(i)	(ii)	(iv)

61. Match the following

Column I	Column II
A. Life Insurance Corporation	(i) Statutory corporation
B. Public Sector Enterprise	(ii) Operates globally
C. Multinational Corporation	(iii) Owned by government

Codes

	A	B	C
(a)	(ii)	(i)	(iii)
(b)	(iii)	(ii)	(i)
(c)	(i)	(iii)	(ii)
(d)	(i)	(ii)	(iii)

62. Match the following

Column I	Column II
A. Increased resources and capacity	(i) Provides companies with advanced technologies they may not have the capacity to develop on their own.
B. Access to new markets and distribution networks	(ii) Facilitates the development of new and creative products.
C. Access to technology	(iii) Companies can leverage combined resources to grow and expand more quickly.
D. Innovation	(iv) Helps in expanding the reach to new geographical areas and markets.

Codes

	A	B	C	D
(a)	(ii)	(i)	(iii)	(iv)
(b)	(iv)	(iii)	(ii)	(i)
(c)	(i)	(iii)	(ii)	(iv)
(d)	(iii)	(iv)	(i)	(ii)

63. Match the following

Column I	Column II
A. Global Enterprise	(i) Relationship between public sector and private sector entities
B. Contractual Joint Venture	(ii) A new separate jointly owned business entity is formed
C. Equity-based Joint Venture	(iii) A new jointly-owned entity is not created
D. Public-Private Partnership	(iv) Operates in two or more than two countries

Codes

	A	B	C	D
(a)	(ii)	(i)	(iii)	(iv)
(b)	(iv)	(iii)	(ii)	(i)
(c)	(i)	(iii)	(ii)	(iv)
(d)	(iii)	(i)	(ii)	(iv)

Answers

1. (b) mixed
2. (c) public corporation
3. (b) Public sector enterprises
4. (b) special act
5. (b) earning profit
6. (d) Departmental undertaking
7. (b) Departmental undertaking
8. (c) Lack of public accountability
9. (c) Departmental undertaking
10. (a) Departmental undertaking
11. (c) It operates as a body corporate and can sue or be sued in its own name
12. (c) Statutory corporations
13. (a) statutory corporation
14. (b) Total shareholding of Central and State Government is 51% (15 + 26 + 10).
15. (a) government company
16. (b) 51%
17. (b) Government company
18. (c) Prevents unhealthy business practices
19. (b) Global enterprise
20. (c) Global enterprise
21. (b) Majority Owned Foreign Affiliates
22. (c) headquarters
23. (c) monopolies
24. (c) Indian companies have successfully expanded globally and many have become Multinational Corporations (MNCs).
25. (c) MNCs are restricted from using advanced technology in production methods
26. (b) Product innovation
27. (a) Hindustan Unilever
28. (b) Joint venture
29. (b) They are governed by a separate law in India specifically for joint ventures
30. (b) Contractual Joint Venture (CJV)
31. (b) Access to technology and markets
32. (d) Access to technology
33. (b) In a Contractual Joint Venture (CJV), profits and losses are shared according to the agreement
34. (a) Public-private partnership
35. (a) departmental undertaking
36. (a) From sale of goods and services
37. (b) Deposits it in the government treasury
38. (a) Government employees
39. (c) Public sector enterprises can be managed properly by the government if there is effective governance, accountability and efficiency in operations.
40. (a) Both Assertion (A) and Reason (R) are true and Reason (R) is the correct explanation of Assertion (A)
41. (a) Both Assertion (A) and Reason (R) are true and Reason (R) is the correct explanation of Assertion (A)
42. (d) Departmental undertakings are typically government-owned entities that are part of a government department and have more rigid structures. They are not as flexible as other types of organisations (like public sector undertakings or private enterprises) in seizing business opportunities because they are tied to government policies and regulations.
43. (b) Government companies are not entirely exempt from government rules, however, they are free from many controls that apply to government departments.
44. (a) Both Assertion (A) and Reason (R) are true and Reason (R) is the correct explanation of Assertion (A)
45. (a) Both Assertion (A) and Reason (R) are true and Reason (R) is the correct explanation of Assertion (A)
46. (d) Statutory corporations are independently financed. They obtain funds by borrowings from the government or public and through revenue generated by sale of goods and services.
47. (c) LIC is an example of statutory corporation and not departmental undertaking.
48. (a) Both Assertion (A) and Reason (R) are true and Reason (R) is the correct explanation of Assertion (A)
49. (a) Departmental undertakings do not have a separate legal entity. They are considered part of the government and do not have independent legal status like a corporation.
50. (c) Both the statements are correct
51. (b) A statutory corporation is a government-owned corporation established by a Special Act of Parliament or state legislature. It is not formed as a private or public limited company.
52. (b) Statutory corporations generally lack operational flexibility. They are subject to various rules, regulations and government oversight, which limits their autonomy in day-to-day operations.
53. (c) Both the statements are correct
54. (a) Multinational companies operate in multiple countries and often have subsidiaries in those countries.
55. (c) Both the statements are correct

56. (b) In a Contractual Joint Venture (CJV), there is no creation of a new business entity.

57. (a) Contractual Joint Ventures (CJVs) do not involve creating a new entity and the profits and losses are still shared between the partners, but through an agreement, not ownership of a new entity.

58. (a) Joint ventures in India are treated as domestic companies, not governed by any specific laws for joint ventures. They are subject to general company laws in India.

59. (d) (iii) (i) (ii)
60. (b) (iv) (iii) (ii) (i)
61. (c) (i) (iii) (ii)
62. (d) (iii) (iv) (i) (ii)
63. (b) (iv) (iii) (ii) (i)

Subjective Questions

Short Answer Type Questions

1. List the names of some enterprises under the public sector and classify them. NCERT

Ans. Some enterprises under the public sector are

(i) Indian Railways – Departmental Undertaking
(ii) Indian Post and Telegraph – Departmental Undertaking
(iii) Life Insurance Corporation (LIC) of India – Statutory Corporation
(iv) State Trading Corporation – Statutory Corporation
(v) Steel Authority of India Limited (SAIL) – Government Company
(vi) Bharat Heavy Electricals Limited (BHEL) – Government Company

2. State the various features of departmental undertakings.

Ans. Following are the features of departmental undertakings

(i) They are financed from the government treasury and an annual appropriation for it is made in the budget of the government. The revenue earned by these undertakings is also deposited into the treasury.
(ii) They are subject to accounting and audit controls, as applicable to other government activities.
(iii) The staff of departmental undertakings include government servants which are headed by civil servants and Indian Administrative Service (IAS) officers. They are recruited and compensated as per the rules of civil services and they are transferable from one ministry to another.
(iv) They are managed and controlled by the government and are subject to direct control of the ministry. As they are under the direct control of concerned ministry, thus, they are accountable to it.

3. Departmental undertakings have several merits as compared to other public sector enterprises. Discuss any four such merits.

Ans. Following are the merits of departmental undertakings

(i) **Effective Control**
They facilitate the Parliament to exercise effective control over their operations.

(ii) **Accountability**
They are subject to accounting and audit controls. Thus, they have high degree of public accountability.

(iii) **Source of Income**
The revenue of departmental undertakings is deposited in the treasury of the government. Thus, these undertakings provide source of income for the government.

(iv) **National Security**
They are most suitable for operations where national security is concerned, because of direct control and supervision of the concerned ministry.

4. "Departmental undertakings, though an essential form of public enterprise, often face challenges such as limited operational flexibility, bureaucratic delays and lack of professional management."
In light of the above statement, list the drawbacks of a departmental undertakings. Competency Based Que

Ans. Following are the drawbacks of a departmental undertakings

(i) **Lack of Flexibility and Efficiency**
The departmental undertakings work under strict parliamentary control. This reduces the flexibility and efficiency of the undertakings.

(ii) **Delay in Decision-making**
Decisions can only be taken after approval from concerned ministry. This leads to delay in decision-making.

(iii) **Bureaucracy and Conservative Approach**
These undertakings are unable to take advantage of business opportunities as they are not allowed to take risky ventures due to the bureaucrat's over-cautious and conservative approach.

(iv) **Red Tapism**
These undertakings have a number of rules and regulations and lengthy channels of day-to-day operations. This causes delay in decision-making and consequently, affects the urgent matters. This leads to red tapism and bureaucracy.

5. "Departmental undertakings are suitable for operations where maintaining strict government control and ensuring public welfare are of utmost importance." In light of the above statement, list the cases where departmental undertakings are suitable. Competency Based Que

Ans. Departmental undertakings are suitable in the following cases

(i) Undertakings which require utmost secrecy. e.g. In case of strategic industries like defence and atomic power.

(ii) Undertakings which require absolute government control. e.g. In case of broadcasting (Ministry of Communication such as India Post, All India Radio and Doordarshan).

(iii) Undertakings in which private sector is unable to enter due to huge capital investment.

(iv) Undertakings in which undertaking is to be used as a source of revenue, like in case of Indian Railways.

6. Give some relative advantages of statutory corporations over departmental undertakings.

Ans. Some relative advantages of statutory corporations over departmental undertakings are

(i) **Funds**
The funds of statutory corporations do not come from the central budget. Thus, the government generally does not interfere in their financial matters, including their income and receipts.
On the other hand, in departmental undertakings, the revenue earned by the enterprise goes directly to the government treasury and government has full control over the financial matters of the enterprise.

(ii) **Operations**
Statutory corporations enjoy independence in their functioning and a high degree of operational flexibility. On the other hand, in departmental undertakings, Parliament exercises full control on operations.

(iii) **Control**
A statutory corporation is an autonomous body, which enjoys flexibility. On the other hand, in departmental undertakings, there is excessive centralisation of control.

7. State two features of a government company that will help in knowing that a particular company is a government company.

Ans. The two features of a government company which help in knowing that it is a government company are

(i) It is any company established under Indian Companies Act, where not less than 51% of paid-up capital is held by Central Government or by any State Government or partly by Central Government and partly by one or more State Governments and includes a company which is a subsidiary of a government company.

(ii) In a government company, an auditor is appointed by the Central Government and the annual report is to be presented in the Parliament or State Legislature.

8. Why is the government company form of organisation preferred to other types in the public sector? NCERT

Ans. The government company form of organisation is preferred to other types in the public sector because of the following advantages

(i) **Simple Procedure of Establishment**
A government company can be easily formed as compared to other public enterprises. There is no need to get a bill passed by the Parliament or State Legislature. It can be formed simply by following the procedure laid down by the Companies Act.

(ii) **Working on Business Principles**
The government company works on business principles. It is independent in financial and administrative matters. Its board of directors usually consists of professionals and persons of repute.

(iii) **Efficient Management**
The management of a government company ensures efficiency in managing the business as it is more accountable than other forms of public enterprises, as the annual report of the government company is placed before both the Houses of Parliament.

(iv) **Competition**
These companies pose a healthy competition to the private sector and ensures availability of good quality products at reasonable prices to the public.

9. "A government company operates with the autonomy of a private entity while enjoying the support of government funding. However, its functioning is often criticised for inefficiencies due to government interference."
In light of the above statement, discuss the limitations of a government company. Competency Based Que

Ans. Following are the limitations of a government company

(i) **Theoretical Freedom**
As the government is the only shareholder in some of the companies, it controls affairs of the company and provisions of the Companies Act do not have much relevance.

(ii) **Lack of Accountability**
A government company evades constitutional responsibi- lity as it is not answerable directly to the Parliament.

(iii) **Defeats Main Purpose**
Being the only shareholder, the government controls the whole management and administration of the company. It is not needed to be registered, like other companies under the Companies Act.

10. **"Joint ventures are strategic alliances formed by two or more entities to achieve a common business objective. They enable partners to pool resources and expertise, while also sharing risks and rewards."**
In light of the above statement, state any four features of joint ventures. Competency Based Que

Ans. Following are the four features of joint ventures

(i) In joint ventures, the two organisations that join may be private, government owned or a foreign company.

(ii) Joint ventures share technology, capital, human resources, risks, rewards, etc.

(iii) A joint venture may also arise on the basis of an agreement between businesses of different countries. In such case, businesses will have to comply with the provisions provided by the governments of the two countries.

(iv) Joint venture is the best way of doing business in India. There is no separate law which governs these joint ventures. They are treated as domestic companies in India.

11. **"Global enterprises, also known as Multinational Corporations (MNCs), operate in multiple countries, leveraging economies of scale and diverse markets. These businesses often play a significant role in shaping global trade and technological advancements."**
In light of the above statement, state any four features of global enterprises. Competency Based Que

Ans. Following are the four features of global enterprises

(i) **Huge Capital Resources**
The assets and sales of these enterprises are quite huge. They operate on large-scale and have the ability to raise funds from many sources like issue of equity shares, debentures or bonds to the public. They can also avail loans from financial institutions and international banks.

(ii) **Foreign Collaboration**
MNCs usually collaborate with Indian companies in the public and private sector. They are required to comply with restrictive clauses related to technology, pricing, dividends, payment, tight control by foreign technicians, etc.

(iii) **Advanced Technology**
In production methods, these enterprises have technological superiorities. They are able to conform to international standards and quality specifications. This leads to industrial progress of the home country of such corporations.

(iv) **Product Innovation**
Due to a huge capital base, these enterprises are able to have highly advanced Research and Development Departments. They are continuously engaged in developing new products of better quality and superior design of existing products.

12. **Discuss the types of joint ventures.**

Ans. Following are the types of joint ventures

(i) **Contractual Joint Venture** (CJV)
In this form of joint venture, a new jointly-owned entity is not created. There is only an agreement to work together. The parties only exercise some elements of control and do not share ownership of the business. A franchisee relationship is a typical example of contractual joint venture. Two or more parties have a common intention of running a business venture.

(ii) **Equity-based Joint Venture** (EJV)
In this form of joint venture, a new separate jointly owned business entity is formed by two or more than two parties, according to the agreement of the parties. Joint ownership by two or more parties is the key operative factor in such case. The form of business entity may be company, partnership, trusts, limited liability partnership firms, venture capital funds, etc.

Long Answer Type Questions

13. **Can the public sector companies compete with the private sector in terms of profit and efficiency? Give reasons for your answer.** NCERT

Ans. It is difficult for the public sector companies to compete with the private sector in terms of profit and efficiency due to the following reasons

(i) **Difference in Objective**
Private sector firms operate with the objective of profit maximisation, while public sector companies have social welfare as the prime objective. Hence, they cannot be completely profit oriented.

(ii) **Difference in Ownership**
The government is the sole or major shareholder in public sector companies. The management and administration of these companies, therefore, are controlled government which may not make economically sound policies due to political considerations interference.

(iii) **Difference in Management**
Public sector companies are managed by government officials who may not be professionally trained, while private sector companies are run and managed by professional managers. This leads to higher efficiency in the private sector.

(iv) **Difference in Area of Operation**
Private sector operates in all areas with adequate return on investment while public sector operates mainly in basic and public utility sectors where returns are not very high.

(v) **Difference in Job Security**
Workers of public sector enjoy job security. It reduces their performance as they know that in spite of bad performance, there is no fear of losing job, while in private sector their is no job security. It leads to efficiency in private sector.

14. "Private sector enterprises play a critical role in driving economic growth by fostering innovation and competition. On the other hand, public sector enterprises focus on providing essential services and promoting social welfare."

In light of the above statement, distinguish between private sector enterprises and public sector enterprises. Competency Based Que

Ans. Following are the differences between private sector and public sector

Basis	Private Sector Enterprise	Public Sector Enterprise
Ownership	It is owned by private individuals.	It is owned by the Central or State Government.
Purpose	It is motivated by the desire to earn profits.	Its main purpose is to promote public welfare.
Social Objectives	Social objectives are not very important.	It is guided by social objectives like development of backward regions, creation of employment, equitable distribution of wealth, etc.
Efficiency	It is likely to be more efficient because of quick decision-making.	Decision-making is not fast. There is red tapism and bureaucratic control, which reduces its efficiency.
Government Control	It is not subject to strict financial control by the government.	It is subject to strict financial control by the government.

15. "Statutory corporations, being created by a special Act of Parliament or state legislature, enjoy operational autonomy and are subject to minimal interference by the government."

In light of the above statement, discuss the features of statutory corporations. Competency Based Que

Ans. Following are the features of statutory corporations

(i) These are wholly owned by the State Government which has the ultimate financial responsibility and power to appropriate their profits. In case of losses, the state also has to bear the same.

(ii) These corporations can sue and be sued, enter into contracts and purchase or sell property in its own name, as they have the status of body corporate .

(iii) These are managed and controlled by board of directors appointed by the government.

(iv) These are independently financed. They obtain funds by borrowings from the government or public and through revenue generated by sale of goods and services.

(v) They are free from government accounting and audit control procedures applicable to government departments.

(vi) The employees of these corporations are not government or civil servants. They are not governed by government rules and regulations.
However at times, some officers are taken from government departments on deputation, to head these organisations.

16. Highlight the key differences between departmental undertaking, statutory corporation and government company.

Ans. Following are the key differences between departmental undertaking, statutory corporation and government company

Basis	Departmental Undertaking	Statutory Corporation	Government Company
Mode of Formation	It is formed as a separate department or ministry of the State or Central Government.	It is formed by passing an Act by the Parliament or the State Legislature.	It is incorporated as per of the provisions of the Companies Act, 2013 or any other act applicable before this Act.
Raising of Finance	It is financed by allocating funds to it in the annual budget of the government. It has no borrowing rights.	It is financed by the government. It can also finance its needs with the help of revenue earned by sale of goods/services. It can also borrow.	It raises finance through issue of shares. At least 51% of the shares are taken up by the government.
Legal Status	It has no separate legal entity.	It enjoys a separate legal status.	It also enjoys a separate legal status.
Ownership	Government is the sole owner.	Government is the sole owner.	Government owns at least 51% of the ownership rights.
Autonomy	It does not enjoy any autonomy.	It enjoys autonomy to a large extent in its day-to-day working.	It enjoys autonomy but in papers only. Politicians, ministers, government officials interfere in its working.

Basis	Departmental Undertaking	Statutory Corporation	Government Company
Flexibility in Operations	It does not enjoy flexibility in operations.	It enjoys a certain amount of flexibility in operations.	Maximum flexibility is enjoyed in operations.
Employees	The employees are government servants recruited through Indian Administrative Services. Civil Service code is the contract of service.	Employees are appointed on the basis of independent contract of service.	Employees are appointed on the basis of independent contract of service.
Public Accountability	It is accountable to the public, through the concerned ministry or department.	It is accountable to Parliament and also to the concerned ministry.	It is accountable to the concerned ministry.
Management	It is managed by the government officers of the ministry.	It is managed by Board of Directors, which are nominated by the government.	It is managed by Board of Directors, which are elected by the shareholders of the company.
Suitability	Suitable for projects of national importance, public utility or which require huge investment.	Suitable for commercial projects, which are of national importance.	Suitable for projects which need government support and flexibility in operations.
Example	Indian Railways, Post and Telegraphs, etc.	Air India, State Bank of India, etc.	Steel Authority of India, Bharat Heavy Electrical Ltd., etc.

17. Explain the benefits that can be enjoyed by entering into joint ventures.

Ans. Following are the benefits that can be enjoyed by entering into joint ventures

(i) **Increased Resources and Capacity**
Joint ventures helps in tapping up more resources. This enhances the capacity to grow and expand more quickly, and take advantage of new opportunities.

(ii) **Access to New Markets and Distribution Networks**
When two enterprises joined together, they are free to enhance or expand their market. e.g. Indian company and Chinese company form a joint venture. This will help Indian company to sell its products in China also and the same advantage can also be derived by the Chinese company.

(iii) **Access to Technology**
Companies who do not have the capacity to develop their own technology, joined with other companies to access advanced technologies. This helps in improving the quality of products, thereby saving time, energy investment, etc.

(iv) **Innovation**
Joint ventures allow business to come up with new and innovative products. This helps in raising the new and creative products in the market. The foreign partners who have new ideas and technology, come up with innovative products.

(v) **Low Cost of Production**
Joint ventures take advantage of lower cost of production to obtain quality products for their global market at a low price.
Most of the international companies invest in India because of low cost of raw materials, labour, technical workforce, management, etc.

(vi) **Established Brand Name**
When two business firms enter a joint venture, one of the involved parties can derive the benefits from the other's goodwill, which has been established in the market since long.

18. "Public-Private Partnership (PPP) facilitates the effective utilisation of resources by combining the expertise of the private sector with the public sector's access to resources and regulatory authority."

In light of the above statement, explain how Public-Private Partnerships help in achieving the goals of economic development and infrastructure growth.
Competency Based Que

Or

State the meaning of public-private partnership. NCERT

Ans. Public-private partnership means relationship between public sector and private sector entities in the context of financing, designing and developing infrastructural facilities.
In such projects, the private sector contributes technical knowhow and managerial expertise.
Public partners in PPP are government entities i.e. ministries, government departments, municipalities or state-owned enterprises.
Private partners include local or international business with technical or financial expertise, NGOs, community based organisations.

Public-private partnerships help in achieving the goals of economic development and infrastructure growth in the following ways

(i) **Facilitate Partnership between Public Sector and Private Sector**
PPP is an arrangement between public sector and a private party, in which private sector provides services and/or assets to the public at large.

(ii) **Operations or Management for a Specified Time Period**
PPP arrangement is for a specific period and at the expiry of such period, such partnership comes to an end.

(iii) **Suitable for Big and High Priority Projects**
PPP is suitable for big projects where gestation period is long and also for high priority projects that aimed at creating public goods, like in infrastructure sector.

(iv) **Provision for Subsidy**
The government may provide subsidy, support a project by providing tax breaks and guarantee annual revenues for a fixed period to the PPP.

(v) **Sharing of Revenues**
Revenue is shared between the government and private enterprise in an agreed ratio.

19. What are the benefits of entering into joint ventures and public-private partnership? **NCERT**

Ans. The major benefits of entering into joint ventures are

(i) **Increased Resources and Capacity**
When two firms come together, it enables the joint venture company to grow and expand more quickly and efficiently as the new business pools in financial and human resources.

(ii) **Access to New Markets and Distribution Networks**
When foreign companies form joint venture with companies in a host country, they gain access to the market of host country.
They can also take advantage of the established distribution channels, i.e. wholesale and retail outlets in different local markets which may be very expensive for them otherwise.

(iii) **Access to Technology**
Most businesses enter into joint ventures to get access to an advanced technology which is not possible or economically feasible to be developed on their own. Technology adds to efficiency and effectiveness, thus, leading to reduction in costs and superior quality products.

(iv) **Low Cost of Production**
When international corporations invest in developing countries through joint ventures, they are able to benefit from low cost of raw materials and labour. The international partner is thus able to produce the product of required quality and specifications at much lower cost than what is prevailing in the home country.

The major benefits of entering into public private partnership are

(i) **Accelerating Project**
The public-private partnership ensure that the project work is accelerated by sharing the tasks and responsibilities with the aim of completing the project on time.

(ii) **Inflow of Private Investment**
Private participation in investment reduces the use of public money, which can be used in other priority areas and projects.

(iii) **Increased Efficiency**
Private parties provide a public service or project and assume substantial financial, technical and commercial responsibilities. Their expertise in their field brings efficiency to the project.

(iv) **Public Welfare**
PPP is used in the government projects targeted at public welfare, e.g. Delhi Metro Railway Corporation (DMRC).

Case Study Based Questions

Short Case Studies

Case Study 1

Airway provides telecom services to millions of people in India. Similarly, Cellia also provides telecom services to many people. Government of India is holding 100% of the share capital of Cellia, whereas airway is not under the direct control of government. Identify the sectors in which these two enterprises are working.

Ans. Airway is working in the private sector. It refers to all those enterprises which are managed and owned by individuals or group of individuals. It aims at maximising the wealth of the owners.

Cellia is working in the public sector. It refers to all those enterprises which are managed and owned by the Central or State Government or by both governments. These may be part of a ministry or created by a special act of the Parliament. The public welfare or service is the main objective of public sector enterprises.

Case Study 2

The government of Country X has established a specialised entity to manage its railway network. This entity operates directly under the Ministry of Transport and all its major decisions are overseen by the minister of the department. The revenue earned by the railway network is deposited into the government treasury and the expenses are funded from the annual budget allocations. The employees of this entity are considered government employees.

(i) Identify the form of public sector enterprise described in the case.

(ii) State any three drawbacks of this form of public sector enterprise.

Ans.

(i) The form of public sector enterprise described in the case is departmental undertaking. They are the oldest and most traditional form of organising public sector enterprises. These undertakings function under the overall control of one ministry or department of government and is managed by the concerned minister.

(ii) Following are the drawbacks of departmental undertakings

- **Bureaucracy and Conservative Approach**
  These undertakings are unable to take advantage of business opportunities as they are not allowed to take risky ventures due to the bureaucrat's over-cautious and conservative approach.
- **Political Interference**
  Constant interference from the concerned ministry and the politicians unduly affects the working of these undertakings.
- **Insensitive to Consumer Needs**
  These undertakings are insensitive to consumers' needs and do not provide adequate services to them.

Case Study 3

The Indian government has set-up various organisations to serve public interests and provide services to the citizens while ensuring flexibility in operations. These organisations are created either by an Act of Parliament or by state legislatures.

They possess the authority of the government but also enjoy the autonomy to operate like private enterprises.

For instance, the State Bank of India (SBI) and Life Insurance Corporation of India (LIC) were established to provide essential banking and insurance services across the country, ensuring wide reach and efficient operations.

(i) Identify the form of public enterprise mentioned in the case.

(ii) State any two benefits of the form identified in (i).

Ans.

(i) The form of public enterprise mentioned in the case is statutory corporation. These are corporate bodies created by the state legislature or by a Special Act of the Parliament.

They have power of government and considerable amount of flexibility of private enterprises. e.g. State Bank of India, Life Insurance Corporation of India.

(ii) Following are benefits of statutory corporation (any two)

- **Flexibility**
  They are free from interference of governments regulation and control. Thus, they enjoy independence in their functioning and have operational flexibility.
- **Free from Interference**
  As they are not financed from central budget, the government do not interfere in their financial matters, including their income and receipts.
- **Autonomous Set-up**
  Due to autonomous set-up, they frame their own rules and regulations, policies and procedures within the powers assigned to them by the act.
  But, the act may provide few matters and issues which require prior approval of a particular ministry.

Case Study 4

The Government of India has set-up an enterprise to manage and operate the country's civil aviation services. The enterprise is established by a Special Act of Parliament, giving it autonomy in operations and ensuring it is free from excessive government interference. It has its own rules and regulations, separate from the government departments and its revenue and expenses are managed independently.

(i) Identify the form of public sector enterprise indicated in the case.

(ii) State the cases in which the form of public sector enterprise identified in (i) would be suitable.

Ans.

(i) The form of public sector enterprise indicated in the case is statutory corporation.

(ii) Statutory corporations are suitable in the following cases

- Undertakings which require special powers defined by an Act or a statute.
- Undertakings which require huge amount of capital.
- Undertakings which require regular grants from the government.
- Undertakings which require proper balance between public accountability and operational autonomy.

Case Study 5

The Central Government and several State Governments have jointly established a company to promote renewable energy projects across the country.

The company, which is owned 60% by the Central Government and 40% by State Governments, aims to reduce the nation's carbon footprint by developing solar and wind power plants.

This partnership ensures that the energy produced is aligned with national goals for sustainable growth, similar to the structure of the National Thermal Power Corporation (NTPC).

(i) Identify the form of the organisation described in the case study.

(ii) State any three merits of the form identified in (i).

Ans.

(i) It is a form of government company.

(ii) Following are the merits of a government company

- **Easy Incorporation**
  A government company can be established easily by fulfilling the requirements of the Indian Companies Act. No separate act in Parliament is required.
- **No Government Interference**
  It enjoys autonomy in all management decisions and takes actions according to business economy.
- **Prevents Unhealthy Business Practices**
  A government company provides goods and services to consumers at a reasonable price. Thus, it helps to control market and curb unhealthy business practices.

Case Study 6

SteelGrid Corporation was established by the Government of India under the Companies Act. The government holds 75% of its equity shares and the remaining shares are publicly traded. The company operates independently with a separate legal identity, managing its operations efficiently to compete with private firms in the market.

(i) Identify the form of public sector enterprise indicated in the case.

(ii) State the cases in which the form of public sector enterprise identified in (i) would be suitable.

Ans.

(i) The form of public sector enterprise indicated in the case is government company.

(ii) Government company is suitable in the following cases

- Where the government wants to control a company in the private sector, without its nationalisation.
- Where the government wants to launch an enterprise in collaboration with certain private enterprise.
- Where a big project requires government planning and funding.

Case Study 7

The government of a country has established various public sector enterprises to ensure the fulfillment of its socio-economic goals. These enterprises are structured differently based on their management and control mechanisms.

(i) One such enterprise operates directly under the control of the concerned minister of the department. This ensures strict government oversight and accountability.

(ii) Another enterprise enjoys significant autonomy in its management activities, allowing it to function like a private enterprise while still being owned by the government.

(iii) Examples of another type of enterprise include organisations such as LIC and Air India, which have been instrumental in serving public interests while generating revenue for the government.

Identify the forms of public sector enterprises mentioned in the case.

Ans.

(i) It is the form of departmental undertaking. They are the oldest and most traditional form of organising public sector enterprises. These undertakings function under the overall control of one ministry or department of government and is managed by the concerned minister. e.g. Railways, post and telegraph department.

(ii) It is the form of government company. A government company means any company in which not less than 51% of the paid-up capital is held by either of the following
- The Central Government
- Any State Government
- Partly by Central Government and partly by one or more State Governments

(iii) It is the form of statutory corporation. These are corporate bodies created by the state legislature or by a Special Act of the Parliament. They have power of government and considerable amount of flexibility of private enterprises. e.g. State Bank of India, Life Insurance Corporation of India.

Case Study 8

ABC Corporation is a company based in America. It is planning to apply for a permission to start a factory in India. The factory will make the product as per the high standards of the corporation and such a product will be highly superior to those similar products produced in India.

Also, the factory will create two thousand new jobs for assembly-line work. Some of the raw material needed by the company will be sourced from India.

On the basis of above case, answer the following questions

(i) Identify which form of business enterprise is ABC Corporation.

(ii) Do you think that the government should grant permission to ABC Corporation for setting-up the factory in India? Your view should be based on the following facts
- Rate of unemployment is high in our country.
- The government cannot afford to establish new factories to generate employment.
- Land for the project will be allotted in the backward rural areas.
- There are domestic producers producing the same product.

Ans.

(i) ABC Corporation is a Multinational Company (MNC). Multinational companies are huge industrial organisations which extend their industrial and marketing operations through a network of branches in several countries.

(ii) Yes, I think that the government should grant permission to ABC Corporation to set-up a factory in India.

My view is based on the following benefits that will accrue to India if such a decision is taken
- As the rate of unemployment in our country is high and the government does not have funds to invest in establishing new factories, then permitting ABC Corporation to establish its business in India, will help in generating employment opportunities in the country.
- As the land for the project will be allotted in rural areas, therefore it will ensure balanced regional development in the country. However, the corporation should be forced to adhere to environment conservation measures.
- ABC Corporation will produce better quality product. This will force the domestic producers to upgrade their technology and produce similar quality products.

Case Study 9

Two companies, Zenith Tech (a software firm) and Bright Solutions (a hardware provider), signed an agreement to collaborate on creating a smart home system. Zenith Tech develops the software, while Bright Solutions handles hardware production.

Both companies retain their individual ownership and only control their respective contributions to the project. The agreement is valid for five years, with both parties sharing control over the project's direction.

(i) Identify the type of joint venture described in the case.

(ii) State the key elements of the type identified in (i).

Ans.

(i) The type of joint venture described in the case is Contractual Joint Venture (CJV). In this form of joint venture, a new jointly-owned entity is not created.

There is only an agreement to work together. The parties only exercise some elements of control and do not share ownership of the business. A franchisee relationship is a typical example of contractual joint venture.

(ii) Following are the key elements of contractual joint venture
- Two or more parties have a common intention of running a business venture.
- Each party brings some inputs.
- Both parties exercise some control on the business venture.
- It is not a transaction-to-transaction relationship, but has a character of relatively longer duration.

Case Study 10

TechNova Pvt. Ltd., a software development firm, collaborates with GreenEnergy Ltd., a renewable energy company, to establish a new entity, EcoTech Solutions LLP. Both companies agree to share ownership, management and responsibilities, including capital investments.

The profits and losses from EcoTech Solutions LLP will be divided as per the agreement between the two parties.

The new entity aims to integrate technology with renewable energy solutions.

(i) Identify the type of joint venture described in the above case.

(ii) State the key elements of the form identified in (i).

Ans.

(i) The type of joint venture described in the above case is equity-based joint venture. In this form of joint venture, a new separate jointly owned business entity is formed by two or more than two parties, according to the agreement of the parties.

(ii) Following are the key elements of equity-based joint venture

- There is an agreement to either create a new entity or to join into ownership of an existing entity.
- In this joint venture, ownership by the parties is shared.
- In this joint venture, management is shared by the jointly-owned parties.
- In this joint venture, responsibilities regarding capital investment and other financing arrangements are shared.
- In this joint venture, profits and losses are shared according to the agreement.

Case Study 11

Government is planning to construct an expressway. For this, government needs management and technical expertise and financial help to complete it. The government makes a contract with a private company to construct the expressway.

(i) Identify the form of enterprise highlighted above.

(ii) State any three features of the form identified in (i).

Ans.

(i) It is a form of public-private partnership. Public-private partnership means relationship between public sector and private sector entities in the context of financing, designing and developing infrastructural facilities. In such projects, the private sector contributes technical knowhow and managerial expertise.

(ii) Features of public-private partnership are

- **Suitable for Big and High Priority Projects**
  PPP is suitable for big projects where gestation period is long and also for high priority projects that aimed at creating public goods, like in infrastructure sector.
- **Provision for Subsidy**
  The government may provide subsidy, support a project by providing tax breaks and guarantee annual revenues for a fixed period to the PPP.
- **Sharing of Revenues**
  Revenue is shared between the government and private enterprise in an agreed ratio.

Long Case Studies

Case Study 12

Which bank has the most number of ATMs across India? Which bank has the largest coverage network across India? State Bank of India is one such bank.

It was formed by the passing of the SBI Act, 1950. Its penetration, particularly in the rural sectors and its sheer tonnage of customers has been well documented in the past.

SBI undertook an enormous image overhauling effort in 2005. SBI, has revamped its operations to make itself more contemporary, tech-savy and customer friendly, shedding the slipshod style of working that has been the bane of PSU banks growing at an annual rate of 16% indicating that all is well for the time being.

If SBI is able to sustain this rate of growth, modernise its operations and increase its visibility among the urban populace, the image of public sector banks will definitely improve.

On the basis of above case, answer the following questions

(i) Which form of public enterprise is SBI?

(ii) What steps have been taken by SBI to project a new image for itself?

(iii) Give the limitations for SBI as a statutory corporation.

Ans.

(i) SBI is a statutory company, which was formed by the passing of the SBI Act, 1950.

(ii) The following steps have been taken by SBI
Modus operandi of banking operations has been made contemporary and technologically efficient. The style of functioning is customer friendly.

(iii) Following are the limitations for SBI as a statutory corporation

- **Lacks Operational Flexibility**
  These corporations do not enjoy much autonomy and operation flexibility in reality. All their operations and actions are subject to many rules and regulations.
- **Government Interference**
  There is government and political interference in major decisions of the corporations, especially where huge funds are involved.
- **Delay in Decisions**
  Government often appoints advisors to the Corporation Board. This affects the freedom in decision-making and leads to disagreements.
  As a result, the matter is referred to the government for final decisions. This further delays the action.

Case Study 13

GlobalReach Inc., a renowned multinational company, operates in over 20 countries, with its branches known as Majority Owned Foreign Affiliates (MOFA). The company boasts an enormous capital base, leveraging various financial instruments like equity shares, bonds and international loans. Known for its foreign collaborations, GlobalReach often partners with local companies, ensuring compliance with technology and financial regulations. With advanced production technology, GlobalReach adheres to international quality standards, driving industrial progress in host countries. Its Research and Development Department constantly innovates, delivering superior products. Aggressive marketing strategies and effective advertising have helped the company establish itself as a trusted brand globally. The company's expensive network of subsidiaries and affiliates has significantly increased its market reach, making it a leading player in the international arena.

(i) Identify and explain three features of multinational companies illustrated by GlobalReach Inc. in the case.

(ii) How do multinational companies like GlobalReach contribute to the industrial progress of host countries?

Ans.

(i) Following are the features of multinational companies illustrated by GlobalReach Inc in the case

- **Huge Capital Resources**
  The assets and sales of these enterprises are quite huge. They operate on large scale and have the ability to raise funds from many sources like issue of equity shares, debentures or bonds to the public. They can also avail loans from financial institutions and international banks.
- **Advanced Technology**
  In production methods, these enterprises have technological superiorities. They are able to conform to international standards and quality specifications. This leads to industrial progress of the home country of such corporations.
- **Expansion of Market Territory**
  The operations and activities of these enterprises extend beyond the physical boundaries of their own countries. They operate through a network of subsidiaries, branches and affiliates in host countries. This expands their market territory and enable them to become international brand.

(ii) Multinational companies like GlobalReach Inc. contribute to industrial progress in host countries through

- **Employment Opportunities**
  Their operations create jobs, both directly and indirectly, benefitting the host country's workforce.
- **Improved Standards**
  By adhering to international quality norms, they encourage local businesses to adopt better practices and improve their standards.
- **Research and Development**
  Their focus on innovation and product improvement fosters a culture of continuous learning and industrial development in the host country.

Case Study 14

Apple Inc. is one of the most iconic companies in the world, particularly known for revolutionising the smartphone industry. With its innovative products like the iPhone, iPod and iMac, Apple has become a leader in the tech space.

- **Revenue** The total revenue generated by Apple is around $156 billion and continues to grow year after year.
- **Country** The company is headquartered in California, USA, with operations in over 50 countries worldwide.
- **Founders** Apple was founded by Steve Jobs in 1977.
- **Core Business** The core business of Apple is in computer hardware and software, with flagship products such as the iPhone, iPod, iMac and more.
- **Number of Employees** Apple employs around 80,000 people across various countries.

(i) Total number of employees that are working for the company in various countries is around 80,000. What does this statement reflect about the nature of this company?

(ii) Quoting lines from the passage given above, identify any two features of MNCs.

Ans.

(i) The above statement clearly reflects that Apple Inc. is a MNC, as it is operating in various countries across the world.

(ii) Following are the features of MNCs

- **Huge Capital Resources**
  Lines from the passage which are indicative of this characteristic are, "The total revenue ...... year after year." The assets and sales of these enterprises are quite huge. They operate on large-scale and have the ability to raise funds from many sources like issue of equity shares, debentures or bonds to the public. They can also avail loans from financial institutions and international banks.

- **Expansion of Market Territory**
  Lines from the passage are "The company is headquartered in .... 50 countries worldwide." The operations and activities of these enterprises extend beyond the physical boundaries of their own countries. They operate through a network of subsidiaries, branches and affiliates in host countries. This expands their market territory and enable them to become international brand.

Case Study 15

TechGlobal Solutions, a software company based in India, decided to enter into a joint venture with a leading Chinese technology firm, TechPro. Both companies agreed to collaborate on developing innovative software products and expanding their market reach.

TechGlobal Solutions saw this as an opportunity to tap into the Chinese market and access advanced technologies that TechPro had developed. The partnership allowed TechGlobal Solutions to quickly enhance its capacity and resources to meet the growing demand for technology solutions.

As a result, TechGlobal Solutions not only gained access to a wider market but also had the opportunity to leverage TechPro's cutting-edge software development techniques. With this new partnership, both companies were able to introduce high quality products in a shorter time frame, increasing their competitiveness in the global market.

However, the partnership also presented challenges. The companies had to align their objectives and manage cultural differences to ensure smooth operations. Despite these challenges, the joint venture proved to be a beneficial move for both parties, allowing them to share resources and expand their reach.

Quoting lines from the above case, identify and explain the three benefits of joint ventures discussed in the case.

Ans. Following are the three benefits of joint venture discussed in the case

(i) **Increased Resources and Capacity**
"The partnership allowed TechGlobal Solutions to quickly enhance its capacity and resources to meet the growing demand for technology solutions." This line highlights how the joint venture helped TechGlobal Solutions tap into more resources, enabling the company to expand its capacity and grow faster. Joint ventures helps in tapping up more resources. This enhances the capacity to grow and expand more quickly, and take advantage of new opportunities.

(ii) **Access to New Markets and Distribution Networks**
"TechGlobal Solutions saw this as an opportunity to tap into the Chinese market..."
This illustrates how the joint venture allowed TechGlobal Solutions to access the Chinese market, broadening its market reach and distribution network.
When two enterprises joined together, they are free to enhance or expand their market. e.g. Indian company and Chinese company form a joint venture. This will help Indian company to sell its products in China also and the same advantage can also be derived by the Chinese company.

(iii) **Access to Technology**
"The partnership allowed them to leverage TechPro's cutting-edge software development techniques."
This line explains how TechGlobal Solutions benefitted from the advanced technology of TechPro, which helped improve the quality of their products and save time in development.
Companies who do not have the capacity to develop their own technology, joined with other companies to access advanced technologies. This helps in improving the quality of products, thereby saving time, energy investment, etc.

SELF ASSESSMENT TEST

Objective Type Questions

1. A private individual can also become a shareholder in ………… form of public sector undertaking.
   (a) statutory corporation
   (b) government company
   (c) departmental undertaking
   (d) None of the above

2. The government recently announced that 60% of the paid-up capital of a company involved in infrastructure development is held jointly by the Central Government and multiple State Governments. This company plays a pivotal role in national development projects. Which type of company is described in the above case?
   (a) Private company (b) Public company
   (c) Government company (d) Multinational company

3. Shares of a government company are held by government in the name of
   (a) ministry concerned (b) minister concerned
   (c) Prime Minister of India
   (d) President of India

4. Which of the following was a major reason for the public sector's involvement in infrastructure development after independence?
   (a) Availability of abundant foreign investment
   (b) High profitability in these sectors
   (c) Lack of private sector interest due to high capital requirements and long gestation periods
   (d) Preference for privatisation

5. How did the public sector helps address the issue of regional imbalance in India?
   (a) By promoting monopolies in industrial areas
   (b) By setting up industries in backward regions to spur development
   (c) By reducing investments in backward areas
   (d) By focusing only on urban industrial zones

6. MNCs typically collaborate with Indian companies in which sectors?
   (a) Public and private sectors
   (b) Only the public sector
   (c) Only the private sector (d) Informal sectors

7. Which financial institution do MNCs typically avail loans from?
   (a) Local rural banks (b) Cooperative societies
   (c) Financial institution and international banks
   (d) Non-Banking Financial Companies (NBFCs)

8. A global automobile company collaborates with an Indian firm to develop electric vehicles, sharing technology, expertise and resources to achieve this goal. What is this collaboration an example of?
   (a) Multinational corporation
   (b) Joint venture
   (c) Sole proprietorship (d) Partnership

Answers 1. (b) 2. (c) 3. (d) 4. (c) 5. (b) 6. (a) 7. (c) 8. (b)

Short Answer Type Questions

9. "Indian economy can be classified into two sector." In the light of the given statement, briefly discuss the two sectors.

10. Rajesh, a business consultant is confused about the rigidity of departmental undertakings. How would you explain Rajesh about the prevalence of rigidity in departmental undertakings?

11. State any four features of statutory corporations.

12. Name a few enterprises operating in the public sector and classify them.

13. Discuss the circumstances in which government company is a suitable form of public enterprise.

14. Discuss how the MNCs are in a position to exercise massive control on the world economy?

15. A government-owned enterprise in India partners with a foreign company to establish a new manufacturing unit. They agree to share technology, capital, risks and profits in an equal ratio, as outlined in a Memorandum of Understanding (MoU). Identify the form of business described in the case and state any three features of this form.

Long Answer Type Questions

16. An electricity board operates under government departments, while a public transport service is set-up as a statutory corporation and a steel manufacturing company functions as a government company with 55% ownership by the Central Government. Explain how the three forms are different by outlining the key differences between them?

17. Define global enterprises. Briefly discuss its various features.

18. Discuss the concept of public-private partnership.

04

CHAPTER

Business Services

Service sector includes various economic activities that are important for uninterrupted production and exchange of goods. Trade and commerce is not possible without the various service sectors like banking, insurance, communication, etc.

YOUR STUDY GOALS

4.1 Meaning of Business Services
4.2 Banking
4.3 Banking Services
4.4 Insurance
4.5 Postal Services
4.6 Telecom Services

YOUR PRACTICE GOAL

- Objective Type Questions (63 Qs ; MCQs, A-R, Statements, Matching)
- Subjective Questions (14 SAs, 6 LAs)
- Case Study Based Questions (Short Case Studies-11, Long Case Studies-4)
- Self Assessment Test (8 MCQs, 5 SAs, 3 LAs)

4.1 Meaning of Business Services

Business services can be defined as various tasks and activities that help to maintain a business, despite not delivering any tangible product. e.g. Information technology assists numerous other business services like procurement, finance and shipping.

Types of Business Services

The types of business services include the following

Types of Business Services

- **Banking** Handles cash, credit and other financial transactions.
- **Insurance** Contract in which an insurer indemnifies another against losses from specific incidents.
- **Communication** Responsible for the transmission of required information to the concerned parties.
- **Transportation** Concerned with the transport of goods and raw materials.
- **Warehousing** Store goods from the time of their production or purchase until they are sold or consumed.

4.2 Banking

Banking is an industry that handles cash, credit and other financial transactions. Banks provide a safe place to store extra cash and credit. They offer savings accounts, certificates of deposit and checking accounts.

Types of Banks

Type	Explanation
Commercial Banks	A commercial bank is that financial institution which accepts deposits from the public and offers loans for the purpose of consumption or investment. There are two types of commercial banks, *viz*, public sector banks and private sector banks.
Cooperative Banks	These banks have a common ownership and generally provide short-term loans to the agricultural sector. They are formed by a group of individuals to extend credit to their members.
Specialised Banks	These banks are established to provide certain specific needs of the target groups. Foreign exchange banks, industrial banks, etc. are examples of specialised banks.
Central Bank	This bank is the apex bank of the country. It supervises and controls the functioning of other banks. Reserve Bank of India is the central bank of our country.

Types of Bank Accounts

A bank account is a record of the financial transactions that take place between banks and their customers. Banks provide various types of accounts to fulfil the needs of their customers, which include the following

Type and Meaning	Characteristics
Savings Account It is meant for individuals who want to save some amount of money out of their incomes.	• In this account, customers can deposit money as per their ease. They can also withdraw money as and when they need it. • The amount deposited is referred to as the demand liability of bank. Depositor is issued a cheque book and passbook. All the transactions are recorded in passbook. • This account enables the depositor to earn income by way of interest. Though, rate of interest is generally lower as compared to that of fixed deposit account. • There are certain restrictions on the number of withdrawals, in this account.
Current Account Such accounts are opened by businessmen. Current account is also known as *demand deposit.*	• In this account, there are no restrictions on the number and amount of deposits and withdrawals. Therefore, it is also referred to as a *running and active account.* • In this account, overdraft and credit limit facility is available for the account holder. • Banks do not pay any interest on these accounts rather bank imposes some service charge for rendering services.
Recurring Deposit Account This account is opened by those individuals who want to save a part of their income regularly and earn a higher interest rate.	• In such accounts, the account holder is required to deposit a specified sum of money every month. They are also termed as *cumulative time deposits.* The amount together with interest is repaid on maturity. • A high rate of interest is paid on these deposits. The interest rate varies as per period and amount of monthly deposits. • The account holder can get a loan facility against the amount deposited. • The period of account may range from 6 months to 10 years.
Fixed Deposit Account In this type of account, the amount is deposited with the bank for a fixed period of time.	• A lumpsum amount is deposited in this account for a specified time period. This deposit is repayable after the expiry of fixed period. • Fixed deposits are also called *time deposits* or *long-term deposits.* • The rate of interest on fixed deposits is higher than on savings account. • A premature withdrawal is allowed in these accounts but a percentage of interest is forfeited.

Type and Meaning	Characteristics
Multiple Option Deposit Account It is a combination of savings account and fixed deposit account.	• In this account, the depositor can enjoy the liquidity of savings account and rate of interest of fixed deposit account. • In this account, the depositor sets a pre-determined limit of deposits in the savings account. • If the deposits cross this limit, then the bank convert the amount above the limit into a fixed deposit. This facility is known as *auto-sweep facility*. It enables the account holder to earn better interest on the money. • The fixed deposit is broken immediately when the account holder wants to withdraw money more than the amount lying as cash in the account. This facility is known as *sweep-out* or *reverse sweep facility*.

4.3 Banking Services

Banks offer a wide range of services to their customers. These services are referred to as banking services. Following are the description of such services

1. **Bank Draft**
   It is an order issued by a bank on any branch of the same bank to pay the specified amount to the person named in it. It is also known as **demand draft**.

2. **Pay Order or Banker's Cheque**
   It means the bank draft which is payable within the city or town. It may be called as a **local bank draft**. Banks issue pay orders for local use while bank drafts are issued for outstations. The commission charged for a pay order is lesser as compared to a bank draft.

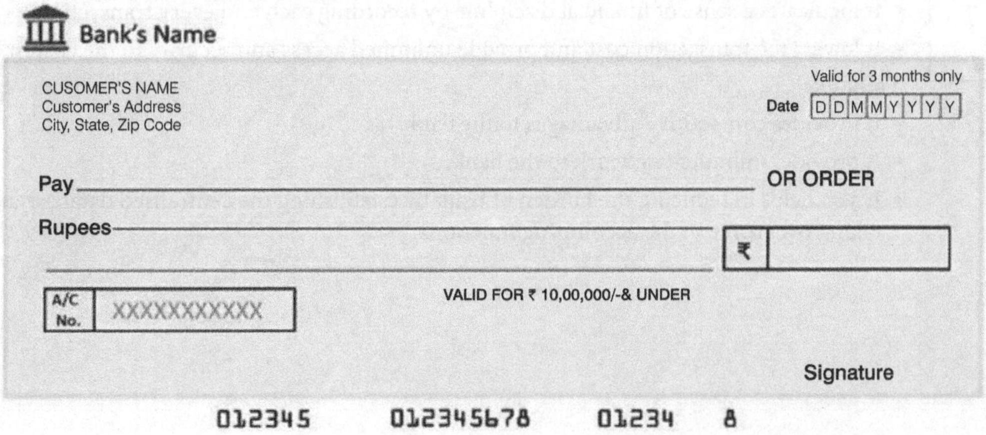

3. **Bank Overdraft**
   It is a facility under which a depositor is allowed to withdraw more amount from his current account upto a specified limit. Overdraft is granted when the borrower has a current account with the bank. This facility is provided against the security of some assets or on the personal guarantee of the borrower. Interest is charged on the exact amount overdrawn by the current account holder.
4. **Cash Credit**
   It is a credit arrangement wherein the bank allows the borrower to borrow money upto a specified limit against some security. Interest is charged only on the amount actually withdrawn or borrowed by the borrower. Cash credit limit is decided by the bank on the basis of the borrower's assets and personal reputation.
5. **Real Time Gross Settlement** (RTGS)
   It is a fund transfer system under which transfer of funds takes place from one bank to another on a real time and gross basis. Settlement on 'real time' means that there is no waiting period and 'gross' settlement means that the transaction is made on one to one basis. The minimum amount to be remitted through RTGS is ₹ 2 lakh. There is no maximum limit for RTGS transactions.
6. **National Electronic Funds Transfer** (NEFT)
   It is a countrywide system by which an individual, firm or company can electronically transfer funds to another individual, firm or company. The funds transfer normally takes place on the same day or the next working day. NEFT functions on net settlement basis. There is no minimum or maximum value limit for NEFT transactions.

e-Banking

e-Banking or electronic banking is a service provided by banks that enables a customer to conduct banking transactions over the internet by using a personal computer, mobile telephone or handheld computer (personal digital assistant). e-Banking includes a range of services like, Automated Teller Machine (ATM), Electronic Data Interchange (EDI), Credit Cards, Electronic or Digital Cash and Electronic Fund Transfer (EFT). The two ways in which EFT can be done arc NEFT (National Electronic Funds Transfer) and RTGS (Real Time Gross Settlement).

Benefits of e-Banking

To Customers

- It facilitates digital payments and promotes transparency in financial statements.
- It provides 24 hours, 365 days a year service to the customers.
- Customers can make the transactions from office, home or while travelling *via* telephone.
- It inculcates a sense of financial discipline by recording each and every transaction.
- It lowers the transaction cost and provide unlimited access and security to the customers.

To Bank

- It provides competitive advantages to the bank.
- It provides unlimited network to the bank.
- It also helps in reducing the burden of bank by establishing the centralised database and by taking over some of the accounting functions.

Types of Digital Payments

Digital payment can be defined as a way of paying for services or goods *via* an electronic medium without the use of cash or cheque. It is also known as **electronic payment system** or **e-payment system.**

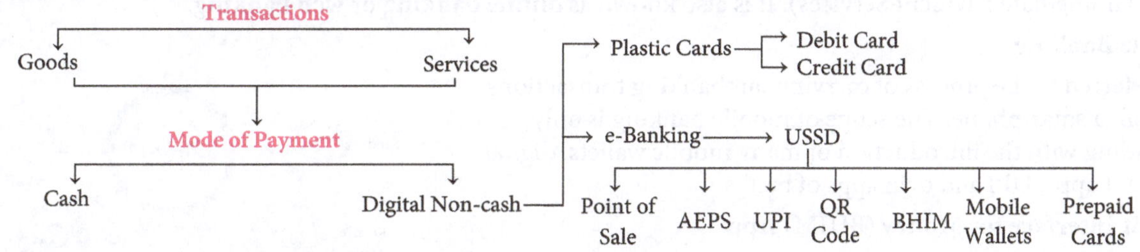

Following are the emerging types/methods of digital payments transactions

1. **Banking Cards**

   These cards have been the most widely used mode of digital payment. Credit cards, debit cards and prepaid cards are the main types of cards with authentication of PIN and OTP for secure payments.

   RuPay, Visa and Master Cards are some of the examples of card payment systems. These cards can be used for online purchases, in digital payment apps, point of sale machines, online transactions, etc. These types of cards are discussed below

Card	Explanation
Debit Card	It refers to the card issued by a bank which can be used to withdraw cash upto the limit present in customer's bank account. It is used to withdraw cash, purchase of goods and services at Point of Sale (PoS)/e-commerce (online purchase), etc.
Credit Card	It is an electronic card issued by a financial institution that authorises the holder to buy goods or services on credit. There is a maximum amount or credit limit, which the user can borrow during a given period.
Prepaid Card	It refers to the card in which money is loaded in advance to make purchases of goods and services at Point of Sale (PoS) and online purchases. Prepaid cards are issued by both banks and non-bank entities.

2. **Unstructured Supplementary Service Data** (USSD)

   This method can be used to carry out mobile banking transactions by dialing USSD code '*99#'. This service can be used without mobile internet data. This service can be used to initiate fund transfer and to make balance queries.

3. **Aadhaar Enabled Payment System** (AEPS)

   It is method to make financial transactions from the bank account with the help of biometric authentication. AEPS can be used for all banking transactions. This service can be availed only when the aadhaar number is registered with bank account.

4. **Unified Payment Interface** (UPI)

   This system enables all bank account holders to send and receive money through UPI based apps in their smartphones without entering bank account information.

5. **Mobile Wallet**

   It is a virtual wallet that stores payment card information on a mobile device. Mobile wallets are convenient for a user to make in-store payments and can be used at merchants listed with mobile wallet service provider.

6. **Point of Sale** (PoS) **Terminals**

   It refers to those machines that are installed at stores where purchases are made by customers using debit/credit cards. It is usually a handheld device that reads banking cards. Some examples are legacy software, cloud computing terminals, mobile terminals and self-service terminals.

7. **Internet Banking**

   It refers to the process of carrying out banking transactions online. Internet banking is usually used to make online fund transfers *via* NEFT (National Electronic Fund Transfer), RTGS (Real Time Gross Settlement) or IMPS (Immediate Payment Services). It is also known as **online banking** or **web banking**.

8. **Mobile Banking**

   It is referred to the process of carrying out banking transactions through a smartphone. The scope of mobile banking is only expanding with the introduction of many mobile wallets, digital payment apps, UPI and own apps of banks.

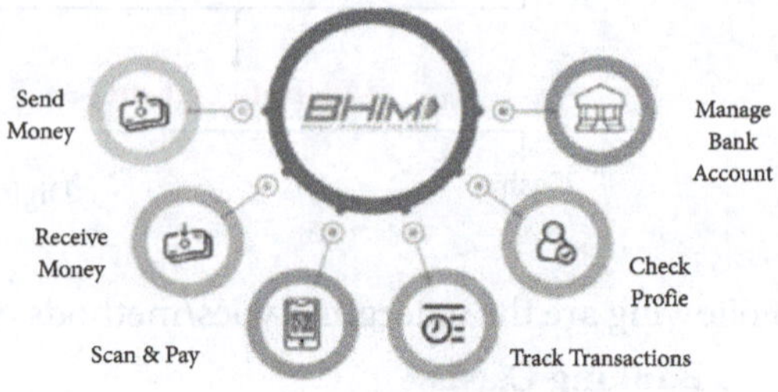

BHIM App

9. **Bharat Interface for Money** (BHIM) **App**

   It is a mobile app developed by National Payments Corporation of India (NPCI), based on Unified Payment Interface (UPI). The app supports all Indian banks through immediate payment service infrastructure and allows the user to instantly transfer money from one bank account to another.

10. **Quick Response Code** (QR Code)

    It is a two-dimensional code and has a pattern of black squares arranged on a square grid with a white background. The user can transfer the desired amount into the receivers bank account by scanning the pattern of QR code.

SAMPLE

4.4 Insurance

Insurance is a contract in which an insurer indemnifies another against losses from specific incidents.In other words, insurance is a contract between two parties, under which one party agrees to pay an agreed amount to another party for the loss suffered by it in return for a consideration of some money, known as premium.

Functions of Insurance

Function	Explanation
Providing Certainty	Insurance cannot remove the uncertainties of the business but it gives certainty of payment of loss. To provide the certainty, the insurer charges premium.
Protection	Insurance cannot stop the happening of a risk or event but can compensate for losses arising out of it. Thus, it provides protection to the insured.
Risk Sharing	On the happening of a risk event, the loss is shared by all the persons exposed to it. The share is obtained from every insured member in form of premiums. In this way, it facilitates risk sharing.
Assist in Capital Formation	The accumulated funds received by way of premium are invested in various income generating schemes. In this way, it assists in capital formation.

Principles of Insurance

Certain principles that are important for a valid insurance contract are

1. Utmost Good Faith

It states that the insurer and insured, both must be transparent and disclose all the essential information required before signing up for an insurance policy. This principle is also known as ***ubberimae fidei*** in Latin. The essential information that needs to be disclosed include

- Insurer and insured should display good faith towards each other in regard to the contract.
- All material facts about the subject to be insured

- Contract of insurance is voidable at the option of the insurer in case of failure to disclose any material fact.
- The insurer must also clear all the terms and conditions in the insurance contract.

e.g. Harshad is a heart patient. But he hides this fact to the LIC while taking a life insurance policy. On his death due to a heart attack, LIC can refuse to pay compensation to his legal representative, as a material fact was not disclosed by Harshad.

Principles of Insurance

- → Utmost Good Faith
- → Insurable Interest
- → Indemnity
- → Proximate Cause
- → Subrogation
- → Contribution
- → Mitigation

2. Insurable Interest

It is defined as the concern of an individual towards obtaining an insurance policy for an item or an individual, against any type of unforeseen events such as losses or death. Insurable interest in any item or an individual is said to arise when the loss of an item or the individual would affect the person to go through financial hardships or any other kind of loss. Insurable interest occurs due to the ownership, possession or through direct relationship with the object/individual.

3. Indemnity

It refers to security against loss. All insurance contracts of fire or marine insurance are contracts of indemnity. According to it, the insurer undertakes to compensate the insured for the loss caused to him/her due to damage or destruction of property insured. The compensation payable and the loss suffered are to be measured in terms of money.

Indemnity

Kamal's shop caught fire and as a result, a part of goods that were stored inside was destroyed. The shop was insured for its full value of ₹ 5 lakh. The insurance company's surveyor examined the damage and estimated that the loss was only ₹ 64,000. The insurance company will pay ₹ 64,000 as compensation. Since, only part of goods were destroyed, only a part of sum insured is paid as compensation under the policy.

This insurance fixes the property issues

Note The principle of indemnity is not applicable to life insurance because loss of life cannot be measured in terms of money.

4. Proximate Cause

According to this principle, the cause or reason for the loss must be related to the subject matter of the insurance policy. When the loss is the result of two or more causes, the proximate cause means the direct, the most dominant and the most effective cause. The insurer is liable to compensate for the loss, only if the proximate cause is covered under the policy.

e.g. Vipin takes a marine insurance policy to protect the rice bags that he is sending through the ship. On the way if a rat spoils the rice, then no compensation will be given to Vipin as loss caused due to rat is a remote cause and not the proximate cause. On the other hand if rat makes a hole in the ship and water enters from the hole and spoils the rice bags, then Vipin is entitled to the compensation as the loss of rice due to sea water is a proximate cause.

5. Subrogation

According to this principle, when the insured is compensated for the loss or damage to the property insured by him/her, the right of ownership of such property passes on to the insurer. This is because the insured should not be allowed to make any profit, by selling the damaged property or from the recovery of the lost property.

Note Principle of subrogation applies to all insurance contracts, which are contracts of indemnity.

Subrogation

Ram took a insurance policy for his car. In an accident, his car totally damaged. Insurer paid the full policy value to the insured. Now, Ram can't sell the scrap remained. After indemnity, the insurer will have all the rights on that scrap of car. This is because Ram should not be allowed to make any profit, by selling the scrap remained.

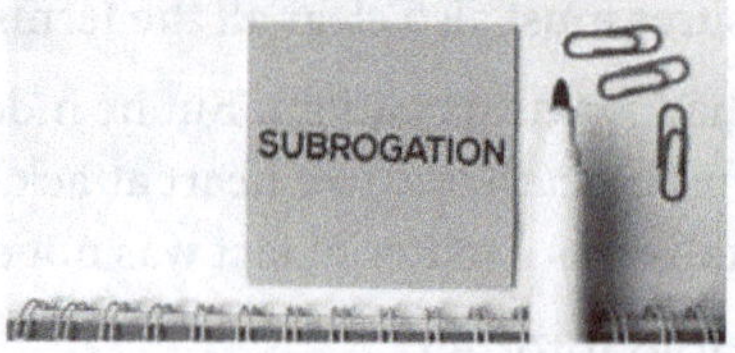

6. Contribution

According to this principle, it is the right of an insurer who has paid claim under an insurance, to call upon other liable insurers to contribute for the loss of payment. It implies that in case of double insurance, the insurers have to share the losses in proportion to the amount assured by each of them.

If there is a loss and there is more than one policy on the same property insured, then the insured will have no right to recover more than full amount of his actual loss.

If the full amount of actual loss is recovered from one insurer only, then the insured have no right to obtain the further payment from other insurer.

7. Mitigation

According to this principle, it is the duty of the insured to take reasonable steps to minimise the loss or damage to the insured property. The insured must behave with great prudence and not be careless just because there is an insurance cover. e.g. If goods kept in a storehouse catch fire, then the owner of the goods should try to recover the goods and save them from fire to minimise the loss or damage.

Types of Insurance

Different types of insurance are discussed below

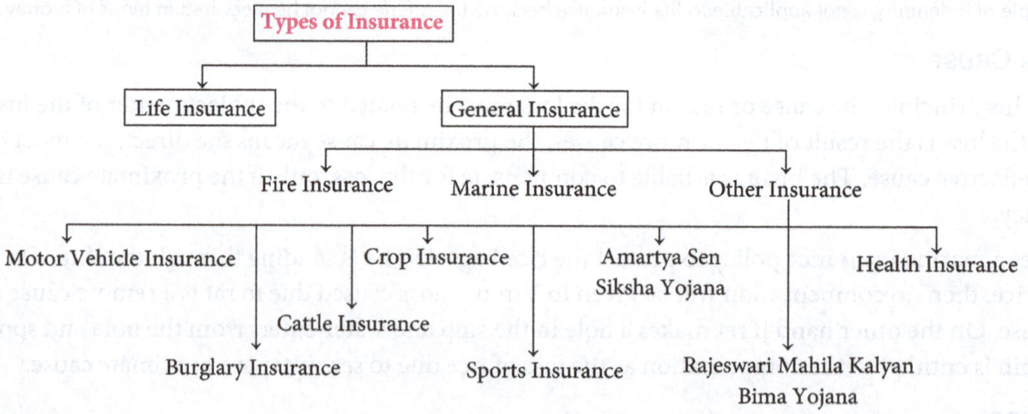

Life Insurance

It is a contract by which the insurer agreed to pay the insured, a certain sum of money on his death or at the expiry of certain period.

The premium of life insurance policy can be paid in one lumpsum or periodically, i.e. monthly, quarterly, half yearly, yearly. The general principles of insurance are also applied to life insurance with a few exceptions like principle of indemnity, principle of contribution and principle of subrogation.

The benefits of life insurance are

- It provides protection to family at the premature death or gives adequate amount at old age when earning capacities are reduced.
- It encourages savings as the amount of premium has to be paid regularly. It thus, provides a sense of security to the insured and his dependents.

Elements of Life Insurance

- The life insurance contract must have all the essentials of a valid contract i.e. proper offer and acceptance, free consent, capacity to enter into a contract, lawful consideration and lawful object.
- The contract of life insurance is a contract of utmost good faith. The insured should be honest and truthful in giving information to the insurance company. He must disclose all material facts about his health to the insurer.
- Without insurable interest, the contract of life insurance is void. In case of life insurance, insurable interest must be present at the time when the insurance is affected.
- Life insurance contract is not a contract of indemnity. The life of a human being cannot be compensated. That is why the amount payable in life insurance on the happening of the event is fixed in advance.

Types of Life Insurance Policies

There are various types of life insurance policies available to suit the requirements of an individual. Some of them are explained below

Policy	Explanation
Whole Life Policy	In this kind of policy, the whole life of the insured is secured and one cannot get the amount before the death of the insured. The premium is payable for fixed period (20 or 30 years) or throughout the life of the insured. In such policies, the rate of premium is very low.
Endowment Life Assurance Policy	In such policies, the insurer undertakes to pay a specified amount when the insured attains a particular age or on his death, whichever is earlier. The sum is payable to the insured if he survives the stipulated period, or to his legal heir/s or nominee if he dies. Thus, the endowment policy matures after a limited number of years.
Joint Life Policy	This policy is taken up by two or more persons. The premium is paid jointly or by either of them in instalments or lumpsum. The assured sum or policy money is payable upon the death of any one person to the other survivor or survivors. Usually, this policy is taken up by husband and wife jointly or by two partners in a partnership firm.
Annuity Policy	Under this policy, the assured sum or policy money is payable in monthly, quarterly, half yearly or annual instalments, after the insured attains a certain age. The premium is paid in instalments over a certain period or single premium may be paid by the assured.
Children's Endowment Policy	This policy is taken by a person for his/her children to meet the expenses of their education or marriage. According to the agreement, when the children attain a particular age, a certain sum is paid by the insurer. The premium is paid by the person entering into the contract but if he dies before maturity, no premium will be paid.

Health Insurance

It is a contract between an insurer and an individual or group, in which the insurer agrees to pay the insured, the expenses related to treatment and hospitalisation of specified diseases.

The premium of health insurance may be payable either in a lumpsum or in instalments. It is a safeguard against rising medical costs.

Types of Health Insurance

- **Individual Mediclaim Policy** This health insurance policy covers the hospitalisation expenses of an individual upto a specified limit.
- **Family Floater Policy** This health insurance policy covers the hospitalisation expenses of an entire family upto a specified limit.
- **Unit Linked Health Plans** This health insurance policy combines health insurance with investment. The insurer pays back a specified amount at the end of the period.

Settlement of Claims

1. **Cashless Settlement** In this form of settlement, the insured gets the amount approved by a third party administrator, who then deposits the amount in the concerned hospital.
2. **Reimbursement** In this form of settlement, the insured settles his bill with the hospital and then asks for reimbursement or compensation from the insurer, by submitting the bills and documents with the third party administrator.

Fire Insurance

It is a contract in which the insurer undertakes to pay the insured for any loss or damage caused by fire, during a specified period of time upto the amount specified in the policy.

Normally, the fire insurance policy is for a period of one year after which it is to be renewed from time to time. The premium may be paid either in lumpsum or instalments.

A claim for loss by fire must satisfy the following two conditions

- There must be actual loss.
- Fire must be accidental and non-intentional.

The risk covered by a fire insurance contract is the loss resulting from fire. If overheating without ignition causes damage, it will not be regarded as a fire loss and the loss will not be recoverable from the insurer.

Elements of Fire Insurance

- The insured must have insurable interest in the subject matter of the insurance. The insurable interest must be present at the time of insurance as well as at the time of loss.
- The contract is based on utmost good faith. The insured should be truthful and honest in giving information to the insurance company. The insurance company should also disclose the facts of the policy to the proposer.
- The contract of fire insurance is a contract of strict indemnity. The insured can recover the actual amount of loss from the insurer in the event of loss. This is subject to the maximum amount for which the subject matter is insured.
- The insurer is liable to compensate only when fire is the proximate cause of damage or loss.

Fire Insurance

Rahul has insured his house for ₹ 5,00,000. The insurer is not necessarily liable to pay that amount, although the house may have been totally destroyed by fire. He will pay the actual loss after deducting depreciation within the maximum limit of ₹ 5,00,000. The purpose is that a person should not be allowed to make profit by insurance.

Marine Insurance

It is a contract whereby the insurer undertakes to compensate the insured for the marine losses. It provides protection against the following

- loss caused by perils of the sea, such as collision of ship with the rock or ship attacked by the enemies or captured by pirates.
- loss due to the actions of the captain and crew of the ship.

The insurer guarantees to compensate for the losses due to damage to the ship or cargo for complete or partial loss at sea. The insurer in this case is known as the **underwriter** and a certain amount of money is paid by the insured in consideration for the guarantee/protection he gets.

Types of Marine Insurance

Insurance	Explanation
Ship or Hull Insurance	This insurance policy provides protection from the losses caused by damage to the ship.
Cargo Insurance	This insurance policy provides protection to the cargo from the risks during its transportation by ship. These risks may be at port, i.e. risk of theft, lost goods or on voyage.
Freight Insurance	If the cargo does not reach the destination due to damage or loss in transit, the shipping company is not paid freight charges. Freight insurance is meant for compensating the loss of freight to the shipping company.

Elements of Marine Insurance

- It is a contract of strict indemnity. But cargo policies provide commercial indemnity rather than strict indemnity. In case of 'Hull Policy', the amount insured is fixed at a level above the current market value.
- It is a contract of utmost good faith. The insured should disclose all facts which include the nature of shipment and the risk of damage exposed to it. Similarly, the insurance company should also disclose the facts of the insurance contract.
- Insurable interest must exist at the time of loss but not necessary at the time when the policy was taken.
- The insurer is liable to compensate only when the particular or nearest cause of damage or loss is covered by the policy. Thus, the principle of causa proximate or proximate cause will apply to it.

Other Insurances

- **Motor Vehicle Insurance** It covers the vehicle for damages against accidents, fire, natural disasters, theft among others and also covers for any injury to the owner. The owner of a motor car may take a comprehensive policy which will cover all these risks.
- **Burglary Insurance** In this policy, the loss of damages of household goods and properties and personal effects due to theft, burglary, house-breaking, etc. are covered. Insurable interest must exist at the time of loss, but not necessary at the time when policy is taken. Also, the principle of proximate cause will apply to it.
- **Cattle Insurance** It is a contract, whereby a sum of money is secured to the insured in the event of death of animals like bulls, buffaloes, cows, etc.
- **Crop Insurance** It is a contract to provide financial support to farmers in the event of a crop failure due to drought or flood.
- **Sports Insurance** This policy assures a comprehensive cover to amateur sportsmen, covering their sporting equipment, personal effects, legal liabilities and personal accident risks. This cover is not available to professional sportsmen.
- **Amartya Sen Siksha Yojana** This policy, offered by the General Insurance Company, secures the education of dependent children, if the insured parent/legal guardian sustains any bodily injury due to an accident leading to his/her death or permanent total disablement.
- **Rajeswari Mahila Kalyan Bima Yojana** This policy has been designed to provide relief to the family members of insured women in case of their death or disablement, which arise due to accidents or problems incidental to women only.

4.5 Postal Services

The Postage and Telegraph Department provides various postal services throughout the country. The Government of India has divided the whole country into 22 postal circles. These circles manage the day-to-day working and perform various services through post offices, sub-post offices and branch post offices. Postal department provides various facilities which are explained below

I. Financial Facilities

These facilities were initiated in the post offices due to lack of banking facilities in the country. These facilities include savings schemes like Public Provident Fund (PPF), Kisan Vihar Patra (KVP) and National Saving Certificates (NSC) in addition to normal retail banking functions of monthly income schemes, recurring deposits, savings account, time deposits and money order facility.

II. Mail Facilities

These facilities includes the following

- Parcel facilities, i.e. transmission of articles from one place to another.
- Registration facility to provide security of articles.
- Insurance facility to provide insurance cover for all risks in the course of transmission by post.

Various types of mail facilities are described below

1. **Registered Post** It is a postal facility under which it is ensured that the mail is either delivered to the address or it comes back to the sender by paying registration charges. The registered mail is marked 'registered post' on its face, to differentiate it from the ordinary mail. In case of loss or damage to the article in the mail, the sender is eligible for compensation.
2. **Parcel** Under this service, parcels of specified size and weight can be sent to domestic and international locations. Postal charges for parcels depend on the weight of the parcel and are reasonably low. Charges for foreign parcel post are higher than that for inland parcel post.
3. **Speed Post** This service is designed for very fast delivery of mail. If the mail is not delivered within the published delivery norms, the fee charged for speed post will be refunded. It has over 1,000 destinations in India and links with 97 major countries across the globe.
4. **Courier** It is a small service provided by private operators in which they collect letters and parcels from the doorstep of senders and delivers them at the place of the addressee. It provides a quick means of communication. No postage is required to be affixed on letters and parcels sent through couriers.

III. Other Facilities

Facility	Explanation
Greeting Post	Through this facility of post offices, greeting cards can be send to friends and relatives on different occasions.
Media Post	Through this facility, business units can send post cards envelopes, etc. to their present and prospective customers to build up their brand.
Direct Post	Through this facility, business units can send addressed or unaddressed direct post to advertise their business.
International Money Transfer	Under this facility, International Money Transfer and Western Union Financial Services, USA have collaborated for remittance of money from 185 countries to India.
Passport Facilities	Under this facility, a partnership between the postal department and Ministry of External Affairs enables applicants to apply for passport through post offices.
e-Bill	Post Under this facility, the post office collect bill payments, like for BSNL and Bharti Airtel.

4.6 Telecom Services

These services refers to the exchange of information through the use of electronic devices. Telecom service is the backbone of every business activity.

The various types of telecom services offered by telecom service providers are

1. **Cellular Mobile Services**
   They include mobile telecom services like voice and non-voice messages, data services and PCO services, utilising any type of network equipment within their service area. They can provide direct interconnectivity with any other type of telecom services.
2. **Fixed Line Services**
   They include voice and non-voice messages and data services to establish linkages for long distance traffic. They utilise any type of network equipment primarily connected through fiber optic cables. They also provide interconnectivity with other types of telecom services.
3. **Cable Services**
   They are one-way entertainment related services provided to subscribers within a licensed area of operation. In future, cable network services are expected to become two way including data, voice and information services.
4. **VSAT** (Very Small Aperture Terminal) **Services**
   They are satellite-based communication services which offer highly flexible and reliable communication solution in both urban and rural areas. VSAT offers the assurance of reliable and uninterrupted service. This service can also be used to provide innovative applications such as tele-medicine, online newspapers, tele-education, etc. even in the most remote areas of our country.
5. **DTH** (Direct to Home) **Services**
   They are satellite-based media services provided by cellular companies. One can receive media services directly through a satellite with the help of a small dish antenna and a set top box. The service provider of DTH services provides a bouquet of multiple channels. It decreases the dependency of the subscriber on services provided by the cable network service providers.

Mind Map

BUSINESS SERVICES

1 Meaning of Business Services

Business services can be defined as various tasks and activities that help to maintain a business, despite not delivering any tangible product.

2 Banking

Banking is an industry that handles cash, credit and other financial transactions.

Types of Bank Accounts

- **Saving** It is meant for individuals who want to save some amount of money out of their incomes.
- **Current** Such accounts are opened by businessmen. Current account is also known as demand deposit.
- **Recurring Deposit** This account is opened by those individuals who want to save a part of their income regularly and earn a higher interest rate.
- **Fixed Deposit** In this type of account, the amount is deposited with the bank for a fixed period of time.
- **Multiple Option Deposit** It is a combination of savings account and fixed deposit account.

3 Banking Services

- **Bank Draft** It is an order issued by a bank on any branch of the same bank to pay the specified amount to the person named in it.
- **Pay Order or Banker's Cheque** It means the bank draft which is payable within the city or town. It may be called as a local bank draft.
- **Bank Overdraft** It is a facility under which a depositor is allowed to withdraw more amount from his current account upto a specified limit.
- **Cash Credit** It is a credit arrangement wherein the bank allows the borrower to borrow money upto a specified limit against some security.
- **Real Time Gross Settlement** (RTGS) It is a fund transfer system under which transfer of funds takes place from one bank to another on a real time and gross basis.
- **National Electronic Funds Transfer** (NEFT) It is a fund transfer system under which transfer of funds takes place on the same day or the next working day.

4 e-Banking

e-Banking or electronic banking is a service provided by banks that enables a customer to conduct banking transactions over the internet by using a personal computer, mobile telephone or handheld computer (personal digital assistant).

Types of Digital Payments

- Banking cards
- Unstructured Supplementary Service Data (USSD)
- Aadhaar Enabled Payment System (AEPS)
- Unified Payment Interface (UPI)
- Mobile wallet
- Point of Sale (PoS) terminals
- Internet banking
- Mobile banking
- Bharat Interface for Money (BHIM) App

5 Insurance

Insurance is a contract in which an insurer indemnifies another against losses from specific incidents.

Types of Insurance

- **Life Insurance** It is a contract by which the insurer agreed to pay the insured, a certain sum of money on his death or at the expiry of certain period.
- **Health Insurance** It is a contract between an insurer and an individual or group, in which the insurer agrees to pay the insured, the expenses related to treatment and hospitalisation of specified diseases.
- **Fire Insurance** It is a contract in which the insurer undertakes to pay the insured for any loss or damage caused by fire.
- **Marine Insurance** It is a contract whereby the insurer undertakes to compensate the insured for the marine losses.

Principles of Insurance

- **Utmost Good Faith** It states that the insurer and insured, both must be transparent and disclose all the essential information.
- **Insurable Interest** It is defined as the concern of an individual towards obtaining an insurance policy for an item or an individual, against any type of unforeseen events such as losses or death.
- **Indemnity** It refers to security against loss.
- **Proximate** The cause or reason for the loss must be related to the subject matter of the insurance policy.
- **Subrogation** When the insured is compensated for the loss or damage to the property insured by him/her, the right of ownership of such property passes on to the insurer.
- **Contribution** It is the right of an insurer who has paid claim under an insurance, to call upon other liable insurers to contribute for the loss of payment.
- **Mitigation** It is the duty of the insured to take reasonable steps to minimise the loss or damage to the insured property.

6 Postal Services

Postal department provides various facilities such as

1. **Financial Facilities** These facilities include savings schemes like Public Provident Fund (PPF), Kisan Vihar Patra (KVP) and National Saving Certificates (NSC) in addition to normal retail banking functions of monthly income.
2. **Mail Facilities** Various types of mail facilities include
   - Registered post
   - Parcel
   - Speed post
   - Courier
3. **Other Facilities** These include greeting post, media post, direct post, international money transfer, passport facilities and e-bill.

7 Telecom Services

Telecom services refers to the exchange of information through the use of electronic devices. It includes the following

- **Cellular Mobile Services** They include mobile telecom services like voice and non-voice messages, data services and PCO services, utilising any type of network equipment within their service area.
- **Fixed Line Services** They include voice and non-voice messages and data services to establish linkages for long distance traffic.
- **Cable Services** They are one-way entertainment related services provided to subscribers within a licensed area of operation.
- **VSAT** (Very Small Aperture Terminal) **Services** They are satellite-based communication services which offer highly flexible and reliable communication solution in both urban and rural areas.
- **DTH** (Direct to Home) **Services** They are satellite-based media services provided by cellular companies.

EXAM PATTERN QUESTIONS

Objective Type Questions

Multiple Choice Questions (MCQs)

1. What is the primary role of the central bank in a country?
(a) To offer loans to businesses
(b) To accept deposits from customers
(c) To regulate and supervise other banks in the country
(d) To provide short-term loans to the agricultural sector

2. "This bank is the apex bank of the country. RBI is the Apex Bank of India." Which type of bank is described in the statement? Competency Based Que
(a) Cooperative bank (b) Specialised bank
(c) Central bank (d) Commercial bank

3. ABC Enterprises maintains a current account with a leading commercial bank. The business often transfers funds to its suppliers in other cities using bank drafts. Additionally, ABC Enterprises utilises locker services for storing important documents. Recently, the company availed a loan to expand its operations and continues to earn interest on its deposits. Which of the following services is not mentioned in the case? Competency Based Que
(a) Locker facilities (b) Bill payments
(c) Transfer of funds (d) Availing loans

4. Which type of bank account offers multiple options to the account holder?
(a) Saving account
(b) Multipurpose account
(c) Fixed deposit account
(d) Current account

5. .... interlinks the savings bank account with a fixed deposit account.
(a) Recurring deposit account
(b) Current account
(c) Multiple option deposit account
(d) None of the above

6. Ankur saves ₹ 3,000 every month. Which type of bank account he should open with the bank? Competency Based Que
(a) Current account
(b) PPF account
(c) Recurring deposit account
(d) Saving account

7. Online-banking provides service to the customers
(a) 24 hours in a day (b) 8 hours in a day
(c) 10 hours in a day (d) None of these

8. "A facility where a depositor is allowed to withdraw more than the available balance in their current account up to a specified limit, with interest charged only on the amount overdrawn." Which banking service is described in this statement? Competency Based Que
(a) Bank draft (b) Pay order
(c) Bank overdraft (d) Cash credit

9. Mr. David, a businessman is involved in daily dealings of cash through the account of his business in Axis Bank. Due to the unavailability of funds and the urgent need to pay his creditors, he approaches the bank to withdraw more than the balance available in his account using the facility provided to him by the bank.

His wife also held an account in the same bank and wanted to transfer ₹ 5,00,000 to her parents but she did not have an e-banking facility in her saving account. But bank helped her to transfer the money.

Name the facility provided by the bank to David when there were no funds in his account to pay his creditors. Competency Based Que
(a) Overdraft facility (b) Transfer facility
(c) Fixed deposits facility (d) All of these

10. Rajesh owns a small business in Mumbai and frequently needs to transfer funds to suppliers in different cities. He uses bank drafts for outstation payments and pay orders for local transactions within the city.

When facing short-term financial needs, Rajesh avails a bank overdraft facility to withdraw more than his account balance, ensuring smooth business operations. For quick fund transfers to other banks, he uses the Real Time Gross Settlement (RTGS) system, especially for large payments exceeding ₹ 2 lakh.

Which of the following is true about RTGS? Competency Based Que
(a) It has a minimum transfer limit of ₹ 1 lakh
(b) It is used only for local transactions
(c) It is the fastest method of transferring funds
(d) It operates on a net settlement basis

11. Meera runs a boutique and uses her bank's services for various needs. For transferring funds to her fabric supplier in another city, she opts for NEFT, which ensures the payment is completed within a day. She occasionally uses the bank overdraft facility to manage cash flow issues, withdrawing more than her account balance against her fixed deposit as security.

Recently, Meera issued a pay order to pay her local carpenter for designing her boutique's interiors, as it was a more cost-effective option compared to a bank draft.

Which of the following statements is incorrect about the services mentioned in the case? **Competency Based Que**

(a) NEFT allows electronic fund transfer within the country
(b) Pay orders are used for outstation payments
(c) Overdraft is granted against a security or personal guarantee
(d) NEFT operates on a net settlement basis

12. Anuj uses two types of payment cards for his transactions. For larger expenses, he uses a card that allows him to spend beyond his account balance, which he repays later within the given limit. For smaller, controlled expenses, he prefers a card where he preloads a fixed amount, ensuring he doesn't overspend.

Which two cards is Anuj using? **Competency Based Que**

(a) Debit card and prepaid card
(b) Credit card and prepaid card
(c) Prepaid card and debit card
(d) Credit card and debit card

13. "A card issued by a bank that allows the holder to withdraw cash up to the limit available in their bank account and make purchases both domestically and internationally." Which type of digital payment method is described in this statement?

Competency Based Que

(a) Credit card (b) Prepaid card
(c) Debit card (d) Banking card

14. There is full guarantee by the issuing bank branch about its payment to the payee. So, there is no risk of .... getting dishonoured.

(a) bank draft (b) cheque
(c) Both (a) and (b) (d) None of these

15. In the new digital market place banks and financial institutions have started providing services over the internet. This type of service is provided by the banks on the internet, lowers the transaction cost, adds value to the banking relationship and empowers customers. Name the service provided by the banks.

Competency Based Que

(a) Electronic fund transfer
(b) Automatic teller machine
(c) Credit card (d) All of the above

16. Which digital payment method allows mobile banking transactions without requiring an internet connection?

Competency Based Que

(a) Aadhaar Enabled Payment System (AEPS)
(b) Unstructured Supplementary Service Data (USSD)
(c) Mobile wallet
(d) Bharat Interface for Money (BHIM) App

17. Identify the method of digital payment in the given picture.

(a) Mobile banking
(b) Bharat Interface for Money App
(c) Point of sale (d) Quick response code

18. Identify the method of digital payment given in the picture

(a) Point of sale (b) Mobile banking
(c) Internet banking (d) Debit card

19. What is the primary feature of the Aadhaar Enabled Payment System (AEPS)?

(a) Virtual storage of payment card information on mobile devices
(b) Banking transactions using biometric authentication
(c) Online fund transfer via NEFT and RTGS
(d) Payments at merchants using debit/credit cards

20. A person gets his stock of ₹ 25,000 insured for ₹ 35,000. A fire occurs and the whole stock gets damaged. The insurance company will pay him only ₹ 25,000, the actual value of his stock and not ₹ 35,000. Which principle of insurance is applied in this case?

Competency Based Que

(a) Principle of contribution (b) Principle of subrogation
(c) Principle of indemnity
(d) Principle of insurable interest

21. A plant manager gets his stock of goods insured but he hides the fact that the electricity board has issued him a statutory warning letter to get his factory wiring changed. Later on, the factory catches fire due to a short circuit. Which principle is violated in the case? Competency Based Que

(a) Principle of subrogation
(b) Principle of utmost good faith
(c) Principle of indemnity
(d) Principle of insurable interest

22. Without disclosing that he is suffering from TB, Mr. A gets himself insured against death for ₹ 10 lakhs. He lives for another three-four years and dies due to TB. The insurance company comes to know about Mr. A's illness only after his death. Now, under these circumstances, the insurance company is not liable to pay anything to the dependents of Mr. A as the contract between the insurance company and Mr. A is void. Identify the principle of insurance to which the above example is related. Competency Based Que

(a) Utmost good faith (b) Insurable interest
(c) Indemnity (d) Subrogation

23. Maximum period limit of general insurance is

(a) 1 year (b) 2 years (c) 3 years (d) No limit

24. A company insures its stock against fire for ₹ 10 lakh. A fire broke down and the total stock was lost. At the time of fire there was stock worth ₹ 15 lakh. What is the value of compensation that company would be entitled to? Competency Based Que

(a) ₹ 5 lakh (b) ₹ 10 lakh
(c) ₹ 15 lakh (d) ₹ 20 lakh

25. A shop owner gets his shop insured against fire for ₹ 10 lakh with insurer A and for ₹ 5 lakh with insurer B. The shop gets fire and he losses ₹ 7.5 lakh. In case under what principle of insurance, he will get ₹ 5 lakh from insurer A and ₹ 2.5 lakh from insurer B? Competency Based Que

(a) Principle of contribution
(b) Principle of insurable interest
(c) Principle of proximate cause
(d) Principle of mitigation

26. Which of the following statements is incorrect regarding types of life insurance policies?

(a) In a whole life policy, the premium is paid throughout the life of the insured and the sum is payable only upon their death
(b) In an endowment life assurance policy, the sum assured is payable at the end of 1 year
(c) In a joint life policy, the policy money is payable upon the death of anyone insured person to the survivor(s)
(d) Endowment life assurance policy ensures payment to the legal heir(s) or nominee in case of the insured's death before the stipulated period

27. Which of the following statements is incorrect regarding elements of fire insurance?

(a) The insured must have an insurable interest in the subject matter both at the time of taking the policy and at the time of loss
(b) Fire insurance is a contract of utmost good faith, requiring the insured and insurer to be honest in disclosing relevant information
(c) Fire insurance provides compensation even if the proximate cause of the loss is not fire
(d) Fire insurance is a contract of indemnity, allowing recovery of the actual loss subject to the maximum insured amount

28. Which of the following statements is incorrect regarding types of health insurance?

(a) An individual mediclaim policy covers hospitalisation expenses of a single person up to a specified limit
(b) A family floater policy provides coverage for hospitalisation expenses of an entire family up to a specified limit
(c) A unit-linked health plan does not include any investment component and only provides health coverage
(d) Unit-linked health plans combine health insurance with investment, offering a specified amount at the end of the period

29. Which of the following is also known as contract of assurance?

(a) Marine insurance (b) Life insurance
(c) Health insurance (d) Fire insurance

30. "Insurance cannot prevent the occurrence of risks, but it compensates for the losses arising from them, providing protection to the insured." Which function of insurance is highlighted in this statement? Competency Based Que

(a) Providing certainty
(b) Risk sharing
(c) Protection
(d) Assist in capital formation

31. Vikas recently purchased an insurance policy to secure the future of his son. The policy ensures that a lumpsum amount will be provided by the insurer once his son turns 18, which Vikas plans to use for his son's higher education. He pays the premium regularly, but if something were to happen to him before the policy matures, the premium payments will stop and the policy benefits will remain intact.
Identify the type of policy Vikas has taken. Competency Based Que

(a) Joint life policy
(b) Endowment life assurance policy
(c) Children's endowment policy
(d) Annuity policy

32. Which type of postal facility ensures that a mail is either delivered to the addressee or returned to the sender, with compensation in case of loss or damage?

(a) Parcel post (b) Speed post
(c) Registered post (d) Media post

33. What is the primary purpose of the media post facility provided by post offices?

(a) Sending greeting cards
(b) Delivering parcels to international locations
(c) Advertising business through postcards and envelopes
(d) Collecting bill payments for utility services

34. The below image shows DTH services. These services are provided by ....

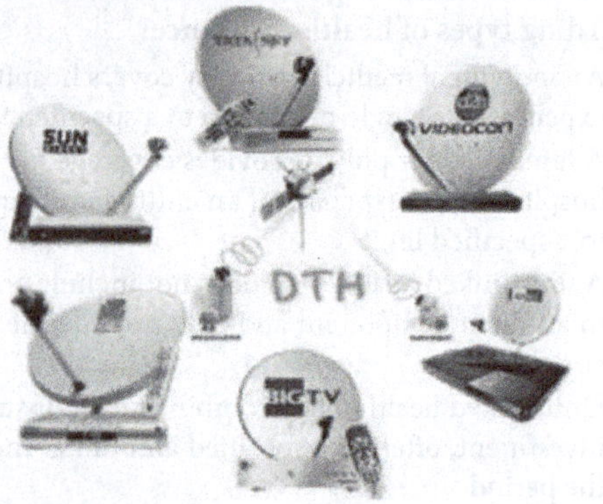

(a) transport companies (b) banks
(c) cellular companies (d) None of these

Direction *Read the case study and answer the questions 35 to 38 on the basis of the same*

Ravi owns a car and gets an insurance policy for ₹ 5 lakh from X Insurance and ₹ 3 lakh from Y Insurance. Unfortunately, the car meets with an accident and the damage amounts to ₹ 4 lakh. Ravi cannot claim ₹ 4 lakh from both X Insurance and Y Insurance because he cannot profit from making full claims from both companies. He can only claim the total loss amount of ₹ 4 lakh from either or both insurance companies in proportion to their coverage. If Ravi claims the entire ₹ 4 lakh from X Insurance, then Y Insurance will pay its proportionate share to X Insurance.

35. Which principle of insurance is highlighted in the above case?

(a) Principle of subrogation
(b) Principle of mitigation
(c) Principle of indemnity
(d) Principle of contribution

36. How much total compensation will Ravi receive?

(a) ₹ 5 lakh (b) ₹ 3 lakh
(c) ₹ 4 lakh (d) ₹ 6 lakh

37. What will be the contribution of X Insurance in the total claim amount?

(a) ₹ 2 lakh (b) ₹ 3 lakh
(c) ₹ 3.2 lakh (d) ₹ 2.5 lakh

38. What will be the contribution of Y Insurance in the total claim amount?

(a) ₹ 1 lakh (b) ₹ 1.5 lakh
(c) ₹ 2 lakh (d) ₹ 2.5 lakh

Assertion-Reason

Direction (Q.No. 39 to 48) *Read the following Assertion (A) and Reason (R) and choose the correct alternative from the following*

Alternatives

(a) Both Assertion (A) and Reason (R) are true and Reason (R) is the correct explanation of Assertion (A)
(b) Both Assertion (A) and Reason (R) are true, but Reason (R) is not the correct explanation of Assertion (A)
(c) Assertion (A) is true, but Reason (R) is false
(d) Assertion (A) is false, but Reason (R) is true

39. Assertion (A) The rate of interest payable is very nominal on current account.

Reason (R) Investment in saving account is risk free.

40. Assertion (A) Banks do not pay any interest on current account. Rather, it imposes service charges for running these accounts.

Reason (R) There is no restriction on number and amount of deposits and withdrawals in case of current account.

41. Assertion (A) AEPS (Aadhaar Enabled Payment System) allows financial transactions through biometric authentication.

Reason (R) AEPS can be used for a wide range of transactions, including balance enquiry, cash withdrawal and payment transactions, but requires aadhaar registration with the bank.

42. Assertion (A) Credit cards allow users to withdraw money even if they don't have sufficient funds in their account.

Reason (R) Credit cards operate on the principle of spending up to a set limit and the withdrawn amount must be repaid within a specified time frame.

43. Assertion (a) Life insurance is a contract of indemnity.

Reason (R) According to principle of indemnity, the insured is entitled to recover the extent of the loss suffered by him, up to the limit of the amount covered by the policy.

44. **Assertion** (A) Insurance helps in risk sharing by pooling premiums from all insured members.

Reason (R) Insurance allows the risk to be shared by all members, thus reducing the financial burden on any one individual.

45. **Assertion** (A) The principle of utmost good faith requires both the insurer and the insured to disclose all material facts related to the insurance policy.

Reason (R) Non-disclosure of material facts by either party can render the insurance contract void.

46. **Assertion** (A) Insurable interest is not required for life insurance policies.

Reason (R) Insurable interest refers to the financial loss that may be suffered due to the loss or damage of an asset, which is not applicable to life insurance.

47. **Assertion** (A) The principle of indemnity applies to life insurance policies.

Reason (R) The principle of indemnity ensures that the insurance payout does not exceed the actual loss suffered.

48. **Assertion** (A) The principle of proximate cause ensures that only the most direct cause of loss is compensated under the insurance policy.

Reason (R) If a loss is caused by multiple factors, the insurer is liable only if the proximate cause is covered by the insurance policy.

Two Statements Based MCQs

Direction (Q.No. 49 to 58) *Read the following statements carefully and choose the correct alternative*

Alternatives

(a) Statement I is correct and Statement II is incorrect
(b) Statement II is correct and Statement I is incorrect
(c) Both the statements are correct
(d) Both the statements are incorrect

49. **Statement I** Business services include intangible services such as information technology, finance and procurement, which help in maintaining a business.

Statement II Business services deliver tangible products directly to consumers for immediate use.

50. **Statement I** Commercial banks help in promoting social welfare by providing loans to industries and businesses.

Statement II Private sector banks primarily focus on social welfare and provide loans at low interest rates to underprivileged sectors.

51. **Statement I** A savings account is used by businesses and allows unlimited withdrawals.

Statement II A current account is typically used by businesses and offers no limit on the number or amount of deposits and withdrawals.

52. **Statement I** Fixed deposit accounts offer a higher rate of interest than savings accounts.

Statement II Fixed deposit accounts are considered a demand liability for the bank.

53. **Statement I** A bank draft is used to transfer funds from one bank to another and it is payable to the receiver on demand.

Statement II A pay order is essentially a bank draft used for out-of-town transactions.

54. **Statement I** AEPS (Aadhaar Enabled Payment System) allows financial transactions using biometric authentication.

Statement II AEPS can be used for transactions only if the aadhaar number is linked with a bank account.

55. **Statement I** Mobile banking enables users to perform banking transactions through their smartphones.

Statement II Mobile banking services are limited to the use of only the bank's official mobile app.

56. **Statement I** Real Time Gross Settlement (RTGS) allows funds to be transferred from one bank to another in real time on a gross basis.

Statement II The minimum transfer amount for RTGS is ₹ 5 lakh.

57. **Statement I** In a life insurance policy, the element of risk is uncertain.

Statement II Marine insurance policy is a contract of indemnity.

58. **Statement I** Fire and marine insurance are contracts of indemnity.

Statement II Principle of subrogation applies to all insurance contracts, which are contracts of indemnity.

Matching

59. Match the following

Column I	Column II
A. Current account	(i) The rate of interest payable is very nominal
B. Savings account	(ii) It is also known as term deposit account
C. Fixed deposit account	(iii) Banks do not pay interest on these accounts

Codes

	A	B	C		A	B	C
(a)	(ii)	(i)	(iii)	(b)	(iii)	(ii)	(i)
(c)	(i)	(iii)	(ii)	(d)	(iii)	(i)	(ii)

60. Match the following

Column I	Column II
A. Endowment Life Assurance Policy	(i) Policy taken by two or more persons, paying the sum on the death of any one person to the other survivors.
B. Children's Endowment Policy	(ii) Policy where the assured sum or policy money is payable after the assured attains a certain age in monthly, quarterly, half yearly or annual instalments.
C. Joint Life Policy	(iii) Policy that pays a sum to the insured at a specified age or to the nominee on the death of the insured.
D. Annuity Policy	(iv) Policy taken by a person for his/her children, paying a sum when the children attain a particular age.

Codes

	A	B	C	D		A	B	C	D
(a)	(iii)	(iv)	(i)	(ii)	(b)	(iv)	(iii)	(ii)	(i)
(c)	(i)	(iii)	(ii)	(iv)	(d)	(ii)	(i)	(iii)	(iv)

61. Match the following

Column I	Column II
A. Ship or hull insurance	(i) A general term used to describe various types of insurance policies protecting goods, ships or freight in marine transport.
B. Cargo insurance	(ii) Protects the ship from damage or losses, ensuring the shipping company's assets are covered against such risks.
C. Freight insurance	(iii) Compensates for the loss of freight charges if the cargo does not reach its destination due to damage or loss in transit.
D. Marine insurance	(iv) Provides protection to the cargo from risks during transportation, such as theft or loss at the port or on voyage.

Codes

	A	B	C	D		A	B	C	D
(a)	(ii)	(i)	(iii)	(iv)	(b)	(iv)	(iii)	(ii)	(i)
(c)	(i)	(iii)	(ii)	(iv)	(d)	(iii)	(i)	(ii)	(iv)

62. Match the following

Column I	Column II
A. Subrogation	(i) It is the duty of the insured to take reasonable steps to the loss to the insured property.
B. Contribution	(ii) Insurer gets all the rights against the third party with respect to subject matter insured after compensating the loss.
C. Mitigation	(iii) This principle ensures equitable distribution of losses between insurers

Codes

	A	B	C
(a)	(ii)	(iii)	(i)
(b)	(iii)	(ii)	(i)
(c)	(i)	(iii)	(ii)
(d)	(ii)	(i)	(iii)

63. Match the following

Column I	Column II
A. Greeting post	(i) Post offices collect bill payments for services like BSNL and Bharti Airtel.
B. International money transfer	(ii) Customers can send greeting cards to friends and relatives on various occasions through this service.
C. Direct post	(iii) A collaboration with Western Union to transfer money from 185 countries to India.
D. e-Bill post	(iv) Business units send addressed or unaddressed direct post for advertising and promotional purposes.

Codes

	A	B	C	D
(a)	(ii)	(i)	(iii)	(iv)
(b)	(ii)	(iii)	(iv)	(i)
(c)	(i)	(iii)	(ii)	(iv)
(d)	(iii)	(i)	(ii)	(iv)

Answers

1. (c) To regulate and supervise other banks in the country
2. (c) Central bank
3. (b) Bill payments
4. (b) Multipurpose account
5. (c) Multiple option deposit account
6. (c) Recurring deposit account
7. (a) 24 hours in a day
8. (c) Bank overdraft
9. (a) Overdraft facility
10. (c) It is the fastest method of transferring funds
11. (b) Pay orders are used for outstation payments
12. (b) Credit card and prepaid card
13. (c) Debit card
14. (a) bank draft
15. (a) Electronic fund transfer
16. (b) Unstructured Supplementary Service Data (USSD)
17. (b) Bharat Interface for Money App
18. (a) Point of sale
19. (b) Banking transactions using biometric authentication
20. (c) Principle of indemnity
21. (b) Principle of utmost good faith
22. (a) Utmost good faith
23. (a) 1 year
24. (b) ₹ 10 lakh
25. (a) Principle of contribution
26. (b) The sum is payable to the insured if he survives the stipulated period or to his legal heir/s or nominee if he dies.
27. (c) Fire insurance only compensates for losses caused by fire or events where fire is the proximate cause.
28. (c) A Unit-Linked Health Plan (ULHP) combines health insurance with an investment component. While it offers health coverage, it also allows the policyholder to invest in various funds, providing returns at the end of the policy term.
29. (b) Life insurance
30. (c) Protection
31. (c) Children's endowment policy
32. (c) Registered post
33. (c) Advertising business through postcards and envelopes
34. (c) cellular companies
35. (d) Principle of contribution
36. (c) The damage amounts to ₹ 4 lakh, so that is the total amount Ravi will receive, irrespective of the total coverage of ₹ 8 lakh (₹ 5 lakh from X Insurance and ₹ 3 lakh from Y Insurance).
37. (d) Contribution of X Insurance = (Coverage by X Insurance/Total Coverage) × Total Claim Amount

    = (5/8) × 4 = ₹ 2.5 lakh
38. (b) Contribution of Y Insurance = (Coverage by Y Insurance/Total Coverage) × Total Claim Amount

    = (3/8) × 4 = ₹ 1.5 lakh
39. (b) Both Assertion (A) and Reason (R) are true, but Reason (R) is not the correct explanation of Assertion (A)
40. (a) Both Assertion (A) and Reason (R) are true and Reason (R) is the correct explanation of Assertion (A)
41. (a) Both Assertion (A) and Reason (R) are true and Reason (R) is the correct explanation of Assertion (A)
42. (a) Both Assertion (A) and Reason (R) are true and Reason (R) is the correct explanation of Assertion (A)
43. (d) Life insurance is not a contract of indemnity because it does not involve compensating for the actual loss suffered. Instead, life insurance provides a pre-determined sum of money in the event of death or specified events.
44. (a) Both Assertion (A) and Reason (R) are true and Reason (R) is the correct explanation of Assertion (A)
45. (a) Both Assertion (A) and Reason (R) are true and Reason (R) is the correct explanation of Assertion (A)
46. (b) Both Assertion (A) and Reason (R) are true, but Reason (R) is not the correct explanation of Assertion (A)
47. (d) Indemnity does not apply to life insurance.
48. (a) Both Assertion (A) and Reason (R) are true and Reason (R) is the correct explanation of Assertion (A)
49. (a) Business services are intangible and assist various tasks like procurement and finance, but they do not involve delivering tangible products.
50. (a) Private sector banks focus on profit making rather than social welfare.
51. (b) A savings account is primarily meant for individuals and has restrictions on the number of withdrawals.
52. (a) Fixed deposit accounts are not considered demand liabilities, unlike savings accounts.
53. (a) Pay order is used for local transactions, while a bank draft is used for out-of-town transactions.
54. (c) Both the statements are correct
55. (a) Mobile banking allows transactions through smartphones, but it is not limited to only the bank's official app; third-party apps like UPI apps can also be used.
56. (a) The minimum amount for RTGS is ₹ 2 lakh, not ₹ 5 lakh.
57. (b) Life insurance policies are based on the likelihood of certain events (like death) happening, which can be estimated statistically, though still uncertain.
58. (a) Principle of subrogation applies only to contracts of indemnity like fire and marine insurance, but not to life insurance in most cases.
59. (d) (iii) (i) (ii)
60. (a) (iii) (iv) (i) (ii)
61. (b) (iv) (iii) (ii) (i)
62. (a) (ii) (iii) (i)
63. (b) (ii) (iii) (iv) (i)

Subjective Questions

Short Answer Type Questions

1. What do you understand by savings account? Discuss its characteristics.

Ans. **Savings Account**

It is meant for individuals who want to save some amount of money out of their incomes.

Following are the characteristics of savings account

(i) In savings account, customers can deposit money as per their ease. They can withdraw money by means of a cheque or a withdrawal slip or ATM as and when they need it.

(ii) The amount deposited in a savings account is referred to as the demand liability of bank. Depositor is issued a cheque book and passbook. All the transactions are recorded in passbook.

(iii) Savings account enables the depositor to earn income by way of interest. Rate of interest of savings account is generally lower as compared to fixed deposit account.

(iv) In these accounts, there are certain restrictions on the number of withdrawals.

2. State the characteristics of recurring deposit account.

Ans. Following are the characteristics of recurring deposit account

(i) In such accounts, the account holder is required to deposit a specified sum of money every month. They are also termed as cumulative time deposits. The amount together with interest is repaid on maturity.

(ii) A high rate of interest is paid on the deposits in these accounts. The interest rate varies as per period and amount of monthly deposits.

(iii) The account holder can get a loan facility against the amount deposited in these accounts.

(iv) The period of account may range from 6 months to 10 years.

3. "Aadhaar Enabled Payment System (AEPS) and Unified Payment Interface (UPI) plays an important role in facilitating digital transactions in India." In the light of the given statement, state the functioning of these services. Competency Based Que

Ans. **Aadhaar Enabled Payment System** (AEPS)

It is method to make financial transactions from the bank account with the help of biometric authentication. AEPS can be used for all banking transactions such as balance enquiry, cash withdrawal, cash deposit, payment transactions, etc. This service can be availed only when the Aadhaar number is registered with bank account.

Unified Payment Interface (UPI)

This system enable all bank account holders to send and receive money through UPI based apps in their smartphones without entering bank account information.

4. State any four functions of insurance.

Ans. Following are the functions of insurance

(i) **Providing Certainty**

Insurance cannot remove the uncertainties of the business but it gives certainty of payment of loss. To provide the certainty, the insurer charges premium.

(ii) **Protection**

Insurance cannot stop the happening of a risk or event but can compensate for losses arising out of it. Thus, it provides protection to the insured.

(iii) **Risk Sharing**

On the happening of a risk event, the loss is shared by all the persons exposed to it. The share is obtained from every insured member in form of premiums. In this way, it facilitates risk sharing.

(iv) **Assist in Capital Formation**

The accumulated funds received by way of premium are invested in various income generating schemes. In this way, it assists in capital formation.

5. What advantages does a life insurance policy give to the holder?

Ans. Following are the advantages of life insurance policy

(i) It provides protection to the dependents of the assured in case of untimely death.

(ii) Through a life insurance, a person can make provision for his old age.

(iii) It encourages people to save money compulsorily.

(iv) These policies can be used as a collateral security to raise loans.

6. "Life insurance policies are comprehensive financial tools designed to provide security, but understanding their key components is crucial for making informed decisions."

In context to the statement, discuss any three main elements of a life insurance policy. Competency Based Que

Ans. Following are the main elements of a life insurance policy

(i) The life insurance contract must have all the essentials of a valid contract i.e. proper offer and acceptance, free consent, capacity to enter into a contract, lawful consideration and lawful object.

(ii) The contract of life insurance is a contract of utmost good faith. The insured should be honest and truthful in giving information to the insurance company. He must disclose all material facts about his health to the insurer.

(iii) Without insurable interest, the contract of life insurance is void. In case of life insurance, insurable interest must be present at the time when the insurance is affected.

7. Name and define the type of insurance wherein insurable interest need not exist when the policy is taken. Competency Based Que

Ans. Marine insurance is the type of insurance wherein insurable interest need not exist when the policy is taken. Under a contract of marine insurance, the insurer undertakes to compensate the insured for marine losses. It is an arrangement by which the insurer undertakes to compensate the owner of a ship or cargo for complete or partial loss at sea. In case of marine insurance, insurable interest is the subject matter which must exist at the time of loss but it need not exist when the policy is taken.

8. Insurable interest is a fundamental principle of insurance. When should it be present in case of
(i) Life insurance policy
(ii) Fire insurance policy
(iii) Marine insurance policy

Ans.

(i) **Life Insurance Policy**
Insurable interest must be present at the time of effecting the policy but need not be necessary at the time when the claim falls due.

(ii) **Fire Insurance Policy**
Insurable interest on the subject matter must be present both at the time of effecting policy as well as when the claim falls due.

(iii) **Marine Insurance Policy**
Insurable interest must be present at the time when claim falls due or at the time of loss only.

9. Give certain examples of facts that should be disclosed before taking the following insurance
(i) Fire (ii) Life
(iii) Motor
(iv) Personal accident insurance

Ans.

(i) **Fire Insurance**
In this insurance, construction of building, fire detection and fire fighting equipment and nature of its use, are to be disclosed.

(ii) **Life Insurance**
In this insurance, age, previous medical history and smoking/drinking habits are to be disclosed.

(iii) **Motor Insurance**
In this insurance, type of vehicle and driver details are to be disclosed.

(iv) **Personal Accident Insurance**
In this insurance, age, height, weight, occupation and previous medical history are to be disclosed.

10. Why is the principle of indemnity not applicable to life insurance?

Ans. The principle of indemnity is not applicable in case of life insurance because in life insurance, the insurer is required to pay the fixed amount agreed upon, in advance, in the event of death or on the expiry of the period of the policy.

The reason is that the life of a person cannot be valued in terms of money and therefore the question of compensation of actual loss does not arise. Thus, a contract of life insurance is a contingent contract or a contract of guarantee. It is not a contract of indemnity.

11. Write short notes on
(i) Burglary insurance (ii) Sports insurance

Ans.

(i) **Burglary Insurance**
In burglary insurance policy, the loss of damages of household goods and properties and personal effects due to theft, burglary, house-breaking, etc. are covered. The actual loss is compensated. The main elements of burglary insurance contract are

- In burglary insurance, insurable interest must exist at the time of loss, but not necessary at the time when policy is taken.
- The insurer is liable to pay only when the particular or nearest cause of damage or loss is covered by the policy. Thus, the principle of proximate cause will apply to it.

(ii) **Sports Insurance**
This policy assures a comprehensive cover to amateur sportsmen, covering their sporting equipment, personal effects, legal liabilities and personal accident risks. This cover is not available to professional sportsmen. The cover is available in respect to the sports like angling, badminton, cricket, golf, lawn tennis, squash, use of sporting guns, etc.

12. "Post office not only transfers our document from one place to other but also provides certain financial facilities." Do you agree? If yes, discuss your answer with proper explanation? Competency Based Que

Ans. Yes, the statement is true as the postal department also provides financial facilities. It operates a network of more than 1.5 lakh postal offices through which they provide postal banking facilities to the general public and mobilise their savings by various schemes such as National Saving Certificate (NSC), Kisan Vikas Patra (KVP), Monthly Income Scheme (MIS), Public Provident Fund (PPF), etc.

13. What are courier services? Give the name of any two courier companies and discuss their functioning.

Ans. Courier service is essentially a postal service offered by private sector enterprises. Couriers carry letters, parcels, etc. and deliver them more quickly and safely than the post office.

First Flight Couriers Limited and Blue Dart are the two examples of courier companies.

Their functions are

(i) These companies perform a very important function of delivering documents, gifts, etc from one place to other.

(ii) These companies facilitate mail services with hundred percent of efficiency.

(iii) These companies allow speedy transmission of articles, documents, gifts, goods, etc. to people in specified cities.

14. Discuss VSAT and DTH as types of telecom services.

Ans.

(i) **VSAT** (Very Small Aperture Terminal) **Services**
They are satellite-based communication services. They offer highly flexible and reliable communication solution in both urban and rural areas. VSAT offers the assurance of reliable and uninterrupted service.
This service can also be used to provide innovative applications such as tele-medicine, online newspapers, tele-education, etc. even in the most remote areas of our country.

(ii) **DTH** (Direct to Home) **Services**
They are satellite-based media services provided by cellular companies. One can receive media services directly through a satellite with the help of a small dish antenna and a set top box.
The service provider of DTH services provides a bouquet of multiple channels. It decreases the dependency of the subscriber on services provided by the cable network service providers.

Long Answer Type Questions

15. "Banks are providing a wide range of services now-a-days." Do you agree? If yes, give the description of such services which are offered by banks? Competency Based Que

Ans. Yes, banks offer a wide range of services to their customers. These services are referred to as banking services. Following is the description of such services

(i) **Bank Draft**
It is an order issued by a bank to a branch of the same bank or another bank, to pay the specified amount to the person in which it is named. It is drawn by a bank either on its own branch or on another bank. It is also known as demand draft.

(ii) **Pay Order or Banker's Cheque**
It means the bank draft which is payable within the city or town. It may be called as a Local Bank Draft. Banks issue pay orders for local use while bank drafts are issued for outstations. The commission charged for a pay order is lesser as compared to a bank draft.

(iii) **Bank Overdraft**
It is a facility under which a depositor is allowed to withdraw more amount from his current account upto a specified limit. Overdraft is granted when the borrower has a current account with the bank. This facility is provided against the security of some assets or on the personal guarantee of the borrower. Interest is charged on the exact amount overdrawn by the current account holder.

(iv) **Cash Credit**
It is a credit arrangement wherein the bank allows the borrower to borrow money upto a specified limit against some security. Interest is charged only on the amount actually withdrawn or borrowed by the borrower. Cash credit limit is decided by the bank on the basis of the borrower's assets and personal reputation.

(v) **Real Time Gross Settlement** (RTGS)
It is a fund transfer system under which transfer of funds takes place from one bank to another on a real time and gross basis. Settlement on 'real time' means that there is no waiting period and 'gross' settlement means that the transaction is made on one to one basis. It is the fastest possible system for transfer of money. The minimum amount to be remitted through RTGS is ₹ 2 lakh. There is no maximum limit for RTGS transactions. RTGS system is maintained and operated by RBI.

(vi) **National Electronic Funds Transfer** (NEFT)
It is a countrywide system by which an individual, firm or company can electronically transfer funds to another individual, firm or company. The funds can be transferred from any branch of the bank. For such transfers, complete details has to be furnished to the bank like the receiver's name, bank account number, account type, etc. The funds transfer normally takes place on the same day or the next working day. NEFT functions on net settlement basis. There is no minimum or maximum value limit for NEFT transactions.

16. Explain briefly the principles of insurance with suitable examples. NCERT

Ans. The specific principles of a valid insurance contract consist of the following

(i) **Principle of Utmost Good Faith**
A contract of insurance is a contract of ubenintae futei i.e. a contract based on utmost good faith.

It is the duty of the insured to voluntarily make full, accurate disclosure of all facts, material to the risk being proposed and the insurer to make clear all the terms and conditions in the insurance contract. e.g. Rakesh is a heart patient.

But he hides this fact while taking a life insurance policy. On his death due to a heart attack, insurer can refuse to pay compensation because a material fact was not disclosed by the insured.

(ii) **Principle of Insurable Interest**

The insured must have an insurable interest in the subject matter of insurance. Insurable interest means some pecuniary interest in the subject matter of the insurance contract.

The insured must have an interest in the preservation of the thing or life insured. e.g. A trustee holding property on behalf of others has an insurable interest in the property.

(iii) **Principle of Indemnity**

According to it, the insurer undertakes to put the insured in the same position that he occupied immediately before the loss due to happening of the event insured against.

The principle of indemnity is not applicable to life insurance. e.g. If an individual suffers a loss of ₹ 50,000 in a fire accident, the insurance company will accept a claim upto ₹ 50,000 and not move.

(iv) **Principle of Proximate Cause**

This principle states that the reason for a loss or damage to the insured object should be the proximate cause, covered under the policy. e.g. If an individual suffers a loss in fire accident due to short circuit, this should be a part of the contract in order to claim the insurance amount.

(v) **Principle of Subrogation**

According to this principle, once the compensation is paid, the right of ownership of the damaged property passes on to the insures, so that the insured cannot sell it to make profits out of loss. e.g. If a person receives ₹ 40,000 for his damaged stock, the ownership of stock will be transferred to the insurer and the insured will hold no control over the damaged stock.

(vi) **Principle of Contribution**

Under this principle, an insurer who has paid a claim under insurance has the right to call upon other liable insurers to contribute for the loss of payment. e.g. If Ram insures his house for ₹ 10 lakh with insurer A and for ₹ 5 lakh with another insurer B, then in case of a loss off ₹ 3 lakh, both the insurers will together pay ₹ 3 lakh and not more.

(vii) **Principle of Mitigation**

This principle states that it is the duty of the insured to take reasonable steps to minimise the loss or damage to the insured property. e.g. If goods kept in a storeroom catch fire, then owner of the goods should try to recover the goods and save them from fire to minimise the loss or damage.

17. Describe various types of insurance and examine the nature of risks protected by each type of insurance. NCERT

Ans. Insurance may be classified as follows

(i) **Life Insurance**

Life insurance provides protection to the family at the premature death or gives adequate amount at old age when earning capacities are reduced. A life insurance policy protects against the uncertainty of life, though its scope has now widened to suit the various insurance needs of an individual. There are various types of life insurance policies as follows

- Whole Life Policy
- Endowment Life Assurance Policy
- Joint Life Policy
- Annuity Policy
- Children's Endowment Policy

(ii) **Fire Insurance**

It is a contract whereby the insurer, in consideration of the premium paid, undertakes to compensate loss or damage caused by fire, during a specified period upto the amount specified in the policy. The fire insurance policy is generally taken for a period of one year, after which it is to be renewed from time to time.

A claim for loss by fire is considered valid only if it satisfies the following two conditions

- There must be actual loss.
- Fire must be accidental and non-intentional.

The risk covered by a fire insurance contract is the loss resulting from fire, which should be the proximate cause of the loss.

(iii) **Marine Insurance**

It is a contract whereby the insurer undertakes to compensate the insured for marine losses. Marine insurance provides protection against loss by marine perils or perils of the sea. There are three risks covered in marine insurance

- **Risk to Ship or Hull** This insurance policy is for indemnifying the insured for losses caused by damage to the ship.
- **Risk to Cargo** This insurance policy provides protection to the cargo from the risks during its transportation by ship.

- **Risk to Freight** Freight insurance is meant for compensating the loss of freight to the shipping company.

(iv) **Health Insurance**

It is a contract between an insurer and an individual or group, in which the insurer agrees to provide the insured, expenses related to treatment and hospitalisation of specified diseases at an agreed-upon price (the premium). Depending upon the policy, premium may be payable either in a lumpsum or in instalments. Health insurance covers the risks of ill-health of an individual or his dependent family members.

18. Discuss the various types of life insurance policies.

Ans. Following are the types of life insurance policies

(i) **Whole Life Policy**

In this kind of policy the whole life of the insured is secured and one cannot get the amount before the death of the insured. The premium is payable for fixed period (20 or 30 years) or throughout the life of the insured. In such policies, the rate of premium is very low.

(ii) **Endowment Life Assurance Policy**

In such policies, the insurer undertakes to pay a specified amount when the insured attains a particular age or on his death, whichever is earlier. The sum is payable to the insured if he survives the stipulated period, or to his legal heir/s or nominee if he dies. Thus, the endowment policy matures after a limited number of years.

(iii) **Joint Life Policy**

This policy is taken up by two or more persons. The premium is paid jointly or by either of them in instalments or lumpsum.

The assured sum or policy money is payable upon the death of any one person to the other survivor or survivors.

Usually, this policy is taken up by husband and wife jointly or by two partners in a partnership firm.

(iv) **Annuity Policy**

Under this policy, the assured sum or policy money is payable in monthly, quarterly, half yearly or annual instalments, after the insured attains a certain age.

The premium is paid in instalments over a certain period or single premium may be paid by the assured. Such policies are useful to those who prefer a regular income after a certain age.

(v) **Children's Endowment Policy**

This policy is taken by a person for his/her children to meet the expenses of their education or marriage. According to the agreement, when the children attain a particular age, a certain sum is paid by the insurer.

The premium is paid by the person entering into the contract but if he dies before maturity, no premium will be paid.

19. Outline the differences between life insurance, fire insurance, marine insurance and health insurance.

Ans. Following are the differences between life insurance, fire insurance, marine insurance and health insurance

Basis	Life Insurance	Fire Insurance	Marine Insurance	Health Insurance
Subject Matter	The subject matter of this insurance is human life.	The subject matter of this insurance is any physical property or assets.	The subject matter of this insurance is a ship, cargo or freight.	The subject matter of this insurance is risk of incurring medical expenses among individuals.
Element	It has the elements of protection and investment.	It has the element of protection only and not the element of investment.	It has the element of protection only.	It has the elements of protection and investment.
Insurable Interest	Insurable interest must be present at the time of effecting the policy but need not be necessary at the time when the claim falls due.	Insurable interest in the subject matter must be present both at the time of effecting policy as well as when the claim falls due.	Insurable interest must be present at the time when claim falls due or at the time of loss only.	Insurable interest must be present at time of effecting the policy or at the time of illness/injury of insured.
Duration	Its policy usually exceeds a year and is taken for longer periods ranging from 5 to 30 years or whole life.	Its policy usually does not exceed a year.	Its policy is for one year or period of voyage or mixed.	Its policy usually does not exceed 1 or 2 years.

Basis	Life Insurance	Fire Insurance	Marine Insurance	Health Insurance
Indemnity	It is not based on the principle of indemnity. The sum assured is paid either on the happening of certain event or on maturity of the policy.	It is a contract of indemnity. The insured can claim only the actual amount of loss from the insurer. The loss due to the fire is indemnified subject to the maximum limit of the policy amount.	It is a contract of indemnity. The insured can claim the market value of the ship and cost of goods destroyed at sea and the loss will be indemnified.	It is a contract of indemnity. The insured can claim on the basis of medical expenses.
Loss Measurement	In this insurance, loss is not measurable.	In this insurance, loss is measurable.	In this insurance, loss is measurable.	In this insurance, loss is measurable.
Surrender Value or Paid-up Value	It has a surrender value or paid-up value.	It does not have any surrender value or paid-up value.	It does not have any surrender value or paid-up value.	It does not have any surrender value or paid-up value.
Policy Amount	In this insurance, one can be insured for any amount.	In this insurance, the amount of the policy can not be more than the value of subject matter.	In this insurance, the amount of the policy can be the market value of the ship or cargo.	In this insurance, the amount of policy depends on the insured i.e., how much amount he wishes to invest.
Contingency of Risk	In this insurance, the event i.e. death or maturity of policy is bound to happen. Thus, claim will be present and there is an element of certainty.	In this insurance, the event i.e. destruction by fire may not happen. Thus, there may be no claim and there is an element of uncertainty.	In this insurance, the event i.e. loss at sea may not happen. Thus, there may be no claim and there is an element of uncertainty.	In this insurance, the event i.e. illness/injury may not happen. Thus, there may be no claim and there is an element of uncertainty.

20. Write a detailed note on various facilities offered by Indian postal department. **NCERT**

Ans. The various facilities provided by Indian postal department are broadly categorised into

(i) **Financial Facilities**

These facilities were initiated in the post offices due to lack of banking facilities in the country. The details of such facilities are

- **Public Provident Fund** (PPF) Any adult residing in India can open a Public Provident Fund account in a post office and in specified banks.
- **Kisan Vikas Patra** (KVP) It is a saving scheme in which invested money is doubled in eight years and seven months.
- **National Savings Certificate** (NSC) One can buy NSC from the post offices. The term of NSC is five years. A new NSC with a maturity of ten years has been introduced. The principal amount alongwith accumulated interest is paid on maturity.

(ii) **Mail Facilities**

These facilities includes parcel facilities that is transmission of articles from one place to another; registration facility to provide security of articles and insurance facility to provide insurance cover for all risks in the course of transmission by post.

(iii) **Other Facilities**

Some other facilities include

- **Greeting Post** Through post offices, greeting cards can be send to friends and relatives on different occasions.
- **Media Post** Business units can send post cards envelopes, etc. to their present and prospective customers to build up their brand.
- **Direct Post** Business units can send addressed or unaddressed direct post to advertise their business.
- **International Money Transfer** Under this facility, Department and Western Union Financial Services, USA have collaborated for 185 countries to India.
- **Passport Facilities**

  A partnership between the postal department and Ministry of External Affairs enables applicants to apply for passport through post offices.
- **e-Bill Post** Under this facility, the post office collect bill payments for BSNL and Bharti Airtel.

Case Study Based Questions

Short Case Studies

Case Study 1

Identify the type of bank account in each of the following cases

(i) It is an account in which Ram deposits his amount with the bank for a fixed period of time.

(ii) The main objective of this account is to enable the business men like Mohan to conduct their business transactions smoothly. Mohan finds this account very useful.

Ans.

(i) It is a type of fixed deposit account. In such accounts, a lumpsum amount is deposited for a specified time period which can range from 15 days to 5 years. This deposit is repayable after the expiry of fixed period.

(ii) It is a type of current account. Such accounts are opened by businessmen. Current account is also known as demand deposit. In this account, there are no restrictions on the number and amount of deposits and withdrawals. Therefore, it is also referred to as a running and active account.

Case Study 2

Rajat recently opened an account in which he is required to deposit a fixed sum of money every month. He chose this account as it offers a higher rate of interest compared to savings accounts, with the rate depending on the amount and duration of deposits. The account has a flexible period ranging from 6 months to 10 years and the accumulated amount, along with interest, is paid on maturity. Rajat is also eligible to take a loan against the amount deposited in this account. This account type is often referred to as a cumulative time deposit account.

(i) Identify the type of bank account.

(ii) State any three characteristics of the type of account identified in (i).

Ans.

(i) The type of bank account mentioned in the case is recurring deposit account. In such accounts, the account holder is required to deposit a specified sum of money every month.

(ii) Following are the characteristics of recurring deposit account

- A high rate of interest is paid on the deposits in these accounts. The interest rate varies as per period and amount of monthly deposits.
- The account holder can get a loan facility against the amount deposited in these accounts.
- The period of account may range from 6 months to 10 years.

Case Study 3

Mr. Rajesh opened an account with ABC Bank to manage his savings and investments more effectively. He wanted an account that would offer him the liquidity of a savings account and the better interest rates of a fixed deposit.

After discussing the options with the bank, Mr. Rajesh opted for a special account type that allowed him to set a pre- determined limit for deposits in his savings account. Any amount exceeding this limit would automatically be converted into a fixed deposit, which the bank referred to as the 'Auto-Sweep Facility.'

Mr. Rajesh appreciated this feature as it helped him earn a higher interest rate on the extra amount. However, whenever he needed more money than was available as cash in the account, the bank immediately broke his fixed deposit to provide him with the additional funds.

(i) Identify the type of account opened by Mr Rajesh.

(ii) State the characteristics of account identified in (i).

Ans.

(i) The type of account opened by Mr. Rajesh is multiple option deposit account. It is a combination of savings account and fired deposit account.

(ii) Following are the characteristics of multiple option deposit account

- In this account, the depositor can enjoy the liquidity of savings account and rate of interest of fixed deposit account.
- In this account, the depositor sets a pre-determined limit of deposits in the savings account.
- If the deposits cross this limit, then the bank convert the amount above the limit into a fixed deposit. This facility is known as auto-sweep facility. It enables the account holder to earn better interest on the money.
- In these accounts, the fixed deposit is broken immediately when the account holder wants to withdraw money more than the amount lying as cash in the account. This facility is known as sweep-out or reverse sweep facility.

Case Study 4

Mr. Sharma, a businessman, needs to pay ₹ 50,000 to a supplier located in another city. He visits his local branch and fills out the necessary form for the draft, paying the amount along with the prescribed commission.

The draft is issued by his bank and sent to the supplier by post. Upon receiving the draft, the supplier deposits it into their own bank account.

The supplier's bank then collects the payment from Mr. Sharma's bank and credits the amount to the supplier's account.

(i) Identify the banking service used by Mr. Sharma for the payment and explain its purpose.

(ii) Explain the procedure involved to withdraw money using banking service identified in (i)

Ans.

(i) The banking service used by Mr. Sharma for the payment is bank draft. It is an order issued by a bank to a branch of the same bank or another bank, to pay the specified amount to the person in which it is named. It is drawn by a bank either on its own branch or on another bank. It is also known as demand draft.

(ii) Following procedure is followed to withdraw money using bank draft

- A person first obtains the bank draft from his bank, fills in a form and pays the amount of the draft alongwith the prescribed commission.
- The person, then sends the bank draft to the receiver by post.
- The receiver then deposit it in his bank.
- The bank collects the payment from the concerned bank and credits it to the customer's account.

Case Study 5

In a modern retail store, customers can choose from various payment methods for their purchases. A young shopper named Ramesh uses his debit card to buy clothes, withdrawing cash from an ATM earlier in the day.

His friend, Priya, prefers using her credit card to make the purchase, which allows her to buy more than her current balance by using the credit limit offered by her card. Meanwhile, an international tourist visiting the store opts for a prepaid card, which had a specific amount pre-loaded for her trip. These cards, including Visa and MasterCard, ensure secure transactions through authentication via PIN or OTP, making the shopping experience convenient for all.

(i) Differentiate between a debit card and a credit card in terms of usage and payment limits.

(ii) How do prepaid cards provide convenience for international travellers?

Ans.

(i) Following are the differences between debit card and credit card.

Basis	Debit Card	Credit Card
Usage	Debit cards are used for withdrawing cash from ATMs, making purchases at PoS (Point of Sale) and transferring funds domestically.	Credit cards are used for purchasing goods and services, both online and at PoS.
Payment/ Withdrawal limit	It allows the user to withdraw or spend money only up to the balance available in their bank account. If the balance is insufficient, the transaction will be declined.	It allows the user to borrow money from the bank or credit institution up to a pre-defined limit, even if there is no balance in the user's account. The borrowed amount must be repaid within a certain time frame, typically with interest if not repaid on time.

(ii) **Prepaid Card**

It refers to the card in which money is loaded in advance to make purchases of goods and services at Point of Sale (PoS) and online purchases. Prepaid cards are issued by both banks and non-bank entities. Prepaid cards are a convenient payment method for international travelers because they are pre-loaded with a specific amount of money, which helps travelers manage their expenses without the need to carry cash.

Case Study 6

Mr. Arvind, a business owner, needs to transfer funds for his various transactions. For his larger payments, he chooses a method where the funds are transferred immediately and settled individually, without any waiting period. This method is ideal for high-value transactions, especially when the amount exceeds ₹ 2 lakh. On the other hand, for smaller payments, Mr. Arvind uses another method that allows him to transfer funds to any bank across the country.

The funds may take a little longer to settle, typically a day or two, but there is no restriction on the minimum or maximum transfer amount.

Identify and explain the two money transfer systems, Mr. Arvind uses for his transactions.

Ans. The two money transfer systems, used by Mr. Arvind for his transactions are

(i) Real Time Gross Settlement (RTGS)

(ii) National Electronic Funds Transfer (NEFT)

For explanation, refer to Q.No. 15 of long answer type questions.

Case Study 7

Mahesh took a marine insurance policy from XYZ insurance company. Under the policy, goods have been insured against damage likely to be caused by sea water. During the voyage, a hole was caused at the bottom of the ship and through the hole, sea water entered into the ship. As a result, the goods insured were damaged and Mahesh suffered loss.

On the basis of above case, answer the following questions

(i) Can Mahesh claim compensation for the damage from the insurance company?

(ii) If Mahesh can claim for compensation, which principle of insurance is applicable?

Ans.

(i) Yes, Mahesh can claim compensation for the damage caused to goods as a result of hole in the ship.

(ii) In this case, the principle of proximate cause would be applicable. Though the sea water entered into the ship due to a hole in the bottom of the ship, but the damage caused to the goods is due to sea page of sea water. Thus, the proximate cause of damage is sea water.

Case Study 8

Rajesh took a marine policy worth ₹ 2,00,000 to protect his goods from the perils of sea. On the way, the goods were spoiled by mice. He suffered a loss of ₹ 1,25,000. He filed a claim for the loss against the insurance company.

(i) Can Rajesh recover ₹ 1,25,000 from the insurance company.

(ii) Which principle of insurance is highlighted in the given case?

Ans.

(i) No, Rajesh cannot recover ₹ 1,25,000 from the insurance company.

(ii) Principle of insurance highlighted in the case is proximate cause. According to this principle, the cause or reason for the loss must be related to the subject matter of the insurance policy.

When the loss is the result of two or more causes, the proximate cause means the direct, the most dominant and the most effective cause. The insurer is liable to compensate for the loss, only if the proximate cause is covered under the policy.

Case Study 9

Sailing Global Inc. operates a fleet of cargo ships that transport goods worldwide. Recently, one of their ships, the 'Ocean Voyager,' encountered a severe storm while crossing the Atlantic. The storm caused significant damage to the ship's hull, resulting in costly repairs.

To mitigate the financial risk of such incidents, Sailing Global Inc. has a comprehensive marine insurance policy that includes coverage for damage to the ship.

As part of their risk management strategy, the company ensures that its vessels are protected and covers any physical damage to the ships. This coverage ensures that Sailing Global Inc. does not have to bear the full financial burden of repairing or replacing damaged vessels after accidents.

(i) Identify the type of marine insurance.

(ii) Discuss the elements of marine insurance.

Ans.

(i) The type of marine insurance is ship or hull insurance This insurance policy provides protection from the losses caused by damage to the ship.

(ii) The elements of marine insurance are as follows

- The contract of marine insurance is a contract of strict indemnity. But cargo policies provide commercial indemnity rather than strict indemnity. In case of 'hull policy', the amount insured is fixed at a level above the current market value.
- The contract of marine insurance is a contract of utmost good faith. The insured should disclose all facts which include the nature of shipment and the risk of damage exposed to it. Similarly, the insurance company should also disclose the facts of the insurance contract.
- In marine insurance, insurable interest must exist at the time of loss but not necessary at the time when the policy was taken.
- The insurer is liable to compensate only when the particular or nearest cause of damage or loss is covered by the policy. Thus, the principle of causa proximate or proximate cause will apply to it.

Case Study 10

Mr. Ramesh, a 45 years old professional, decided to secure his family's health with an insurance plan after hearing about the increasing medical expenses. His doctor had recently informed him that routine check-ups and treatments had become quite expensive. He realised the importance of health insurance to cover unforeseen medical costs, especially considering his family's medical history. He approached a leading insurance company that offers health insurance policies. After evaluating the available options, he decided to go for a Family Floater Policy, which covered his wife, two children and himself. The insurer also mentioned other types of health insurance policies like Individual Mediclaim and Unit Linked Health Plans, which might suit individual needs.

(i) With reference to the case, explain health insurance.

(ii) Discuss the types of health insurance.

Ans.

(i) Health insurance is a contract between an insurer and an individual or group, in which the insurer agrees to pay the insured, the expenses related to treatment and hospitalisation of specified diseases. The premium of health insurance may be payable either in a lumpsum or in instalments. It is a safeguard against rising medical costs. In India, presently the health insurance exists primarily in the form of mediclaim policy, offered to an individual or to any group, association or corporate bodies.

(ii) Generally, there are three types of health insurance. These are

- **Individual Mediclaim Policy**
  This health insurance policy covers the hospitalisation expenses of an individual upto a specified limit.
- **Family Floater Policy**
  This health insurance policy covers the hospitalisation expenses of an entire family upto a specified limit.
- **Unit Linked Health Plans**
  This health insurance policy combines health insurance with investment. The insurer pays back a specified amount at the end of the period.

Case Study 11

Ramesh wanted to send an important legal document to his business associate. He opted for a service that guaranteed delivery to the recipient or a return to the sender, ensuring compensation in case of loss or damage. Meanwhile, his colleague, Neha, needed to send a gift to her cousin abroad. She chose a service where charges were based on the weight of the package, though the international rates were higher than domestic ones. Both were satisfied with the reliability and affordability of their chosen services. Identify and state the two types of mail facilities indicated in the case.

Ans. Following are the two types of mail facilities indicated in the case

(i) **Registered Post**
It is a postal facility under which it is ensured that the mail is either delivered to the address or it comes back to the sender by paying registration charges. The registered mail is marked 'registered post' on its face, to differentiate it from the ordinary mail. In case of loss or damage to the article in the mail, the sender is eligible for compensation.

(ii) **Parcel Post**
Under this service, parcels of specified size and weight can be sent to domestic and international locations. Postal charges for parcels depend on the weight of the parcel and are reasonably low. Charges for foreign parcel post are higher than that for inland parcel post.

Long Case Studies

Case Study 12

Rohit Verma was the operations head of a retail chain, 'QuickMart'. The company aimed to provide a seamless shopping experience to its customers by adopting the latest digital payment technologies. QuickMart installed devices at its outlets that allowed customers to make payments quickly and securely using their banking cards. These devices ensured safe and convenient transactions at the time of purchase.

For online shopping, QuickMart provided a system where customers could transfer funds directly from their bank accounts to the company's account. This system supported various secure and reliable methods for transferring money electronically, eliminating the need to visit the store physically.

Additionally, QuickMart launched a mobile app that allowed customers to pay using features available on their smartphones.

This app supported payments through digital platforms, enabling users to complete transactions from anywhere conveniently.These advanced payment systems helped QuickMart improve its efficiency and cater to its tech-savvy customers effectively.

Quoting lines from the above case, identify and explain the three types of digital payment services used by QuickMart.

Ans. Following are the types of digital payment services used by QuickMart

(i) **PoS Terminals**
Quoted Line "QuickMart installed devices at its outlets that allowed customers to make payments quickly and securely using their banking cards."
It refers to those machines that are installed at all stores where purchases are made by customers using debit/ credit cards. It is usually a handheld device that reads banking cards. Some examples are legacy software, cloud computing terminals, mobile terminals and self-service terminals.

(ii) **Internet Banking**
Quoted Line "QuickMart provided a system where customers could transfer funds directly from their bank accounts to the company's account."
It refers to the process of carrying out banking transactions online.
Internet banking is usually used to make online fund transfers via NEFT (National Electronic Fund Transfer), RTGS (Real Time Gross Settlement) or IMPS (Immediate Payment Services). It is also known as online banking or web banking.

(iii) **Mobile Banking**

Quoted Line "QuickMart launched a mobile app that allowed customers to pay using features available on their smartphones."

Mobile banking is referred to the process of carrying out banking transactions through a smartphone. The scope of mobile banking is only expanding with the introduction of many mobile wallets, digital payment apps, UPI and own apps of banks.

Case Study 13

Anuj took a fire insurance policy for his property worth ₹ 5,00,000 with two insurers: ICICI Lombard General Insurance Co. Ltd for ₹ 4,00,000 and Bajaj Allianz General Insurance Co. Ltd for ₹ 2,00,000. An electric short circuit in his property caused fire and it resulted in a loss of ₹ 1,50,000. He filed a claim for ₹ 1,50,000 against each of the two insurance companies.

(i) Can Anuj recover ₹ 1,50,000 each from the two insurers.
(ii) Which principle of insurance has been highlighted in the given case?
(iii) Determine the liability of each of the two insurers.

Ans.

(i) No, Anuj cannot recover ₹ 1,50,000 each from the two insurers as he has no right to recover more than the full amount of his actual loss. If he recovers ₹ 1,50,000 from one insurer, then he will cease to have any right to obtain further payment from the other insurer.

(ii) Principle of contribution has been highlighted in the above case. According to this principle, it is the right of an insurer who has paid claim under an insurance, to call upon other liable insurers to contribute for the loss of payment. It implies that in case of double insurance, the insurers have to share the losses in proportion to the amount assured by each of them.

If there is a loss and there is more than one policy on the same property insured, then the insured will have no right to recover more than full amount of his actual loss. If the full amount of actual loss is recovered from one insurer only, then the insured have no right to obtain the further payment from other insurer.

(iii) Liability of ICICI Lombard = (Sum Insured with ICICI Lombard/Total Sum Insured) × Actual Loss

= (4,00,000/6,00,000) × 50,000 = ₹ 1,00,000

Liability of Bajaj Allianz = (2,00,000/6,00,000) × 1,50,000 = ₹ 50,000

Case Study 14

A growing business in a small town recently expanded its operations to various parts of India and several international markets.

The company needed a reliable and efficient system to handle its mail and parcel deliveries.

To meet these demands, they decided to leverage the various postal services available in their region, which provided a range of options tailored to different needs. The business had specific requirements for sending marketing materials to both existing and potential customers, so they turned to services that allowed direct mail campaigns, such as sending postcards, greeting cards and other promotional materials.

The company also faced the challenge of managing communication with clients in international markets, so fast and secure mail services were essential. Additionally, to facilitate payments for goods and services, the business explored international money transfer services to manage the financial transactions from customers located abroad.

For domestic operations, the company started using registered post services to ensure secure deliveries of important documents. They also utilised parcel post for sending products to customers within India, taking advantage of reasonably low charges for both domestic and international parcels. As the business grew, they increasingly relied on speed post to meet tight delivery deadlines.

On top of this, the business also wanted to ensure customers received their bills on time and decided to use the e-bill post service to collect payments for utility services like telephone and internet bills.

In addition to these functional needs, the company saw an opportunity to increase its customer engagement through greeting cards sent *via* the postal service during major festivals and holidays.

This personal touch helped strengthen their relationship with clients and contributed to the overall brand-building strategy.

(i) Identify and explain any two types of mail services that the business could have used to enhance its communication with customers.
(ii) Discuss how the use of multiple postal facilities can help a growing business like this one in terms of improving efficiency, customer engagement and financial transactions. Provide at least two examples.

Ans.

(i) Two types of mail services the business could use are

- **Registered Post**

  This service ensures that important documents and parcels are either delivered to the recipient or returned to the sender if delivery fails.

  The business could use registered post to send critical legal or financial documents, ensuring that the materials are secure and that there is a record of delivery or non-delivery.

- **Speed Post**
  This service provides fast delivery of mail, often with a money-back guarantee if the delivery is delayed beyond the stated time. The business could use speed post to deliver time-sensitive items such as promotional materials or customer orders, ensuring quick and reliable delivery within the specified timeline.

(ii) Multiple postal facilities help a growing business in following ways

- **Improving Efficiency**
  The business can use parcel post to send products both domestically and internationally at affordable rates, making it cost-effective for shipping a variety of goods. The service is available for parcels of different sizes and weights, helping the company streamline its logistics and reduce delivery costs.
- **Customer Engagement**
  By using the greeting post service, the business can send personalised greeting cards to clients on festivals and holidays, enhancing customer relationships and fostering brand loyalty. This personal touch makes customers feel valued, which can lead to stronger brand recognition and customer retention.
- **Financial Transactions**
  Through the international money transfer service, the business can receive payments from global customers in a secure and timely manner, supporting international expansion. Additionally, e-bill post allows the business to collect utility bill payments, ensuring timely cash flow for operations and improving overall financial management.

Case Study 15

Ravi Kumar is the Managing Director of 'ConnectPlus Solutions,' a fast-growing telecom company. The company is renowned for providing seamless communication services to its customers across the country. To cater to the diverse needs of customers, ConnectPlus Solutions ensures robust infrastructure and advanced technology.

In urban areas, the company provides mobile-based services that allow customers to make calls, send messages and use data for various purposes.

These services are designed for mobility and ease of use, enabling interconnectivity across networks. For businesses and homes, ConnectPlus offers services that establish long-distance linkages, primarily through high-speed connections utilising fiber optic technology. This ensures uninterrupted communication for large-scale operations. Additionally, ConnectPlus has launched a specialised service for entertainment and information dissemination in specific regions.

These services provide users with access to a variety of media content and are primarily one-directional. However, the company plans to upgrade these services in the near future to include interactive features like voice and data connectivity.

Quoting lines from the above paragraph, identify and explain the three types of telecom services provided by ConnectPlus Solutions.

Ans. Following are the three types of telecom services provided by ConnectPlus Solutions

(i) **Cellular Mobile Services**

"In urban areas, the company provides mobile-based services that allow customers to make calls, send messages and use data for various purposes."

They include mobile telecom services like voice and non-voice messages, data services and PCO services, utilising any type of network equipment within their service area. They can provide direct interconnectivity with any other type of telecom services.

(ii) **Fixed Line Services**

"For businesses and homes, ConnectPlus offers services that establish long-distance linkages, primarily through high-speed connections utilising fiber optic technology."

They include voice and non-voice messages and data services to establish linkages for long distance traffic. They utilise any type of network equipment primarily connected through fiber optic cables, laid across the length and breadth of the country. They also provide interconnectivity with other types of telecom services.

(iii) **Cable Services**

"These services provide users with access to a variety of media content and are primarily one-directional. However, the company plans to upgrade these services in the near future to include interactive features like voice and data connectivity."

They are linkages and switched services within a licensed area of operation to operate media services.

They are essentially one-way entertainment related services. In future, cable network services are expected to become two way including data, voice and information services.

Offering services through the cable network would be similar to providing fixed services.

SELF ASSESSMENT TEST

Objective Type Questions

1. "This service allows the depositor to deposit a specified sum of money every month in his account, which is also known as cumulative time deposit account." Identify the account highlighted in the statement.
   (a) Savings account (b) Current account
   (c) Recurring deposit account
   (d) Joint account
2. Which of the following is not a function of insurance?
   (a) Risk sharing (b) Assist in capital formation
   (c) Handing of funds (d) None of these
3. Which of the following is not applicable in life insurance contract?
   (a) Conditional contract (b) Unilateral contract
   (c) Indemnity contract (d) None of these
4. Sakshi purchased a life insurance policy for her husband but failed to disclose his pre-existing health conditions. Later, the insurer refused to honor the claim.
   Which of the following is an essential element of a valid life insurance contract?
   (a) Insurable interest must be present at the time of claim
   (b) Insurable interest must be present at the time of policy inception
   (c) Disclosure of material facts is optional
   (d) A valid contract requires no lawful consideration
5. Meera and her husband took a life insurance policy that ensures a payout to the survivor in case either of them passes away during the policy term.
   Which type of life insurance policy did Meera and her husband most likely choose?
   (a) Whole Life Policy
   (b) Endowment Life Assurance Policy
   (c) Joint Life Policy
   (d) Term Insurance Policy
6. Satellite based entertainment media services provided by cellular companies over large areas, with the help of a set top box and a small dish antenna are known as
   (a) cable services (b) direct to home
   (c) FM radio (d) None of these
7. A saving scheme run by post offices in India in which the invested money is doubled in eight years and seven months is
   (a) Kisan Vikas Patra
   (b) National Savings Scheme
   (c) National Savings Certificate
   (d) Fixed Maturity Investment Scheme
8. Indian postal department's international money transfer service which enables customers to remit money to countries through a post office is in collaboration with
   (a) COX and kings financial services
   (b) State Bank of India
   (c) Western union financial services
   (d) American express financial services

Answers 1. (c) 2. (c) 3. (c) 4. (b) 5. (c) 6. (b) 7. (a) 8. (c)

Short Answer Type Questions

9. Mention any three advantages which e-banking offers to customers.
10. "With advancements in technology, e-banking has transformed the way banking services are delivered to customers. In the context of this statement, state and explain the various services offered by e-banking."
11. What are the essential elements of life insurance?
12. Discuss marine insurance and fire insurance in brief.
13. Rahul applied for a health insurance policy but did not disclose his history of smoking and diabetes. Later, when he filed a claim for a related illness, the insurer denied the compensation. Explain the principle of utmost good faith in insurance and analyse how it applies to Rahul's situation.

Long Answer Type Questions

14. "The relationship between a bank and a customer begins when the customer opens account with the bank." In context to the statement, discuss some of the accounts that can be opened by a customer in banks.
15. Discuss in brief the various types of digital payments.
16. Mohan is interested in investing the amount in post offices.
    However, he is confused about the available schemes. In context to it, briefly explain any three schemes that Mohan can choose.

05

CHAPTER

Emerging modes of business have evolved with advancements in technology and changing consumer preferences. The rise of the internet in the 1990s paved the way for e-business, while mobile technology further enabled e-commerce, bringing convenience to users.

Emerging Modes of Business

▼ **YOUR STUDY GOALS**

5.1 Concept of e-Business
5.2 Scope of e-Business
5.3 Benefits of e-Business
5.4 Limitations of e-Business

▼ **YOUR PRACTICE GOAL**

- Objective Type Questions (54 Qs ; MCQs, A-R, Statements, Matching)
- Subjective Questions (7 SAs, 4 LAs)
- Case Study Based Questions (Short Case Studies-8, Long Case Studies-4)
- Self Assessment Test (8 MCQs, 5 SAs, 3 LAs)

5.1 Concept of e-Business

e-Business or electronic business refers to the conduct of industry, trade and commerce using a computer network such as the internet.

e-Business *versus* e-Commerce

e-Business is wider term than e-commerce. e-Business includes e-commerce as well as other electronically conducted business functions such as production, inventory management, product development, accounting and finance and human resource management.

On the other hand, e-commerce includes a firm's interaction with its customers and suppliers over the internet.

Thus, e-business is much more than buying or selling over the internet, i.e. e-commerce.

5.2 Scope of e-Business

e-Business includes all the activities of business such as production, finance, marketing personnel administration, planning, organising and controlling, etc. carried out over computer networks.

On the basis of the parties involved in firm's electronic transactions, the scope of e-business extends to the following

- Transactions between two business firms.
- Transactions between a firm and its customers.
- Transactions carried on within a firm itself.

Various constituents of e-business and inter and intra-transactions among them are

Steps of e-Business

- B2B (A firm's interactions with other businesses)
- B2C (A firm's interactions with its customers)
- Intra-B (Firm's internal processes)
- C2C (Customer's interaction with customers)

B2B Commerce

The transactions taking place between two business firms are known as B2B (Business-to-Business) transactions. A business interacts with a number of other business firms which may be suppliers or vendors of diverse inputs. They may also be a part of the channel through which a firm distributes its products to the customers.

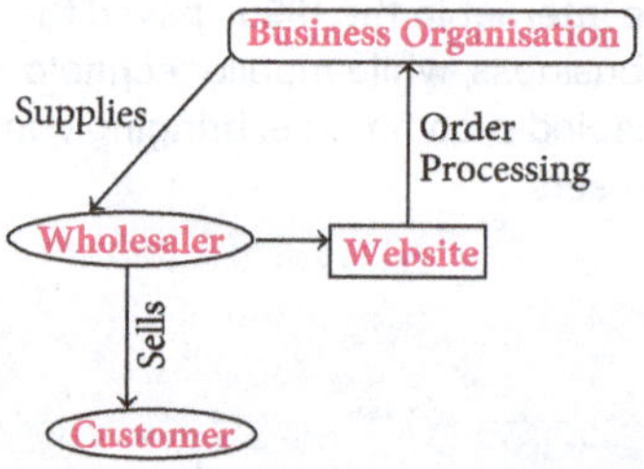

Business-to-Business e-Commerce

B2B transactions may include

- Sharing of information
- Collaborations
- Distribution of goods
- Creation of utilities
- Commercial negotiations

B2B Commerce

An automobile manufacturer makes several B2B transactions. Manufacturing of a car requires large number of components which are manufactured by some other vendors. A network of computers are used to place orders, monitor production, delivery of component and make payments.

B2C Commerce

The transactions taking place between business firms and customers are known as B2C (Business-to-Customers) transactions. This category is related to electronic retailing. This variant of e-business enables a business to be in contact with its customers on round-the-clock basis.

B2C Commerce

The most common and visible B2C transaction is the use of ATM machines for withdrawing cash. Here, the bank is the business firm and the person withdrawing cash is the customer.

B2C transactions may include

- Selling and distribution of goods
- After sales services
- Delivery of products
- Conducting customer surveys
- Promotional activities

B2C transactions also give Customer-to-Business (C2B) transactions.

C2B Commerce

The transactions that provides customers with the freedom of shopping at will are known as C2B transactions. In this commerce, customers can make toll free calls to the call centres set-up by the companies, to make queries and lodge complaints. These transactions are generally outsourced.

Intra-B Commerce

The electronic transactions taking place within a given business firm only, are known as intra-B transactions. It enables the smooth flow of transactions within the different departments of a specific firm. In intra-B commerce, the use of computer-based interaction among the different departments makes it possible for the firm to get the following advantages

- Efficient inventory and cash management
- Effective handling of customers' orders
- Greater utilisation of plant and machinery
- Effective human resource management, etc.

Intra-B commerce transactions may include

- Inventory and cash management.
- Recruitment, selection and training of employees.
- Human resource management, etc.
- Interaction among the different departments.
- Handling of customers' orders.

Intra-B Commerce

A firm's marketing department may interact constantly with production department through intra-B transactions and get the customised products made, as per the requirements of the individual customer.

Intra-B transactions also include firm's interaction with employees, which is referred to as B2E commerce.

e.g. Firms are resorting to personnel recruitment, interviewing and selection, training, development and education through e-commerce. Employees can also use electronic catalogues and ordering forms, and access inventory information for better interaction with the customers.

Use of **Virtual Private Network** (VPN) makes it possible that employees do not have to come to office. They can work from wherever they are and meetings can be held online *via* tele/video conferencing.

C2C Commerce

The transactions taking place between customers are known as C2C (Customer-to-Customer) transactions. These transactions originate from the customer and they end on the customer.

This type of commerce is best suited for dealing in goods for which there is no established market mechanism such as selling used books, clothes, electronics on cash or barter basis.

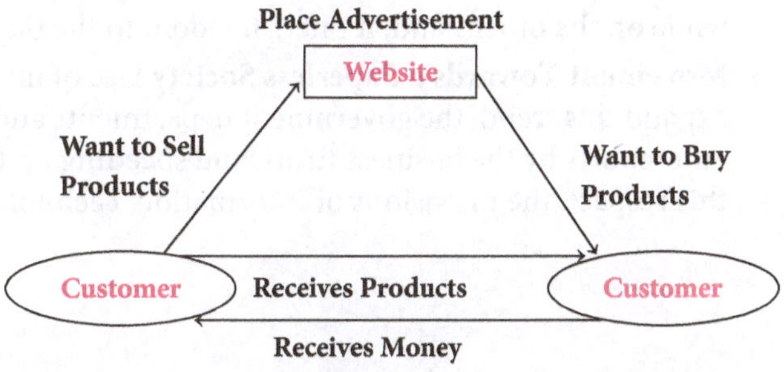

C2C Commerce

Quikr and OLX are examples of this commerce where customers can sell their goods to other customers. Payment intermediary is the technology that supports C2C activities. In this method, instead of purchasing goods directly from seller, the buyer send the money to the intermediary which holds that money until the goods are delivered and accepted by the buyer. PayPal is an example of payment intermediary.

Benefits of e-Commerce

Benefits to Business Organisation

- It expands the marketplace to national and international markets.
- It led to gradual decline in the cost of operations.
- It facilitates 'pull' supply chain management (just-in-time inventory management).
- It gives competitive advantage over competitors.
- It gives proper time management and support business processes.
- It led to small firms co-existing with big firms.

Benefits to Customers and Society

- It provides flexibility.
- It provides competitive price/discounts.
- It provides more options, choices and customised products.
- It provides quick and timely delivery.
- It increases employment potential.
- It facilitate e-auctions and e-tenders.
- It provides opportunity to interact with customers.
- It has a wider outreach.

5.3 Benefits of e-Business

The benefits of e-business are as follows

1. **Ease of Formation and Lower Investment Requirements** e-Business is easy to start and involves less investment. Similar benefits of internet technology are received by big or small business. If a person do not have much of the investment (net worth) but have contacts (network), he can do fabulous business through internet. e.g. To sell electronic products through e-business, a person just need to set-up website, display various pictures of washing machines, TV, etc. and the customer visit the website and place order according to their choice and budget.
2. **Convenience** Internet offers the convenience of doing business 24 hours × 7 days a week. In all 365 days, one can go for shopping or for business at anytime. Such flexibility is available even to the organisational personnel. Thus, e-business offers the advantage of accessing anything, anywhere, anytime.
3. **Speed** Internet is one of the most speedy modes of doing business. One can avail anything, anytime, anywhere at the click of a mouse. Information-intensive products such as softwares, movies, music, e-books and e-journals that can also be delivered online, make it more attractive.
4. **Global Reach/Access** Internet has a wide reach. On one hand, it allows the seller an access to the global market while on the other hand, it offers freedom to the buyer to choose products from almost any part of the world.
5. **Movement Towards a Paperless Society** Use of internet has reduced the dependence on paperwork. In order to expand this trend, the government departments and regulatory authorities are allowing electronic filing of returns and reports by the business firms, and speeding up the process of granting permissions, approvals and licences. In this respect, the provisions of Information Technology Act, 2000 are significant.

Applications of e-Business

- **e-Procurement** It involves internet-based sales transactions between business firms. It includes the following
  - Reverse auctions' that facilitate online trade between a single business purchaser and many sellers.
  - Digital marketplaces that facilitate online trading between multiple buyers and sellers.
- **e-Bidding/e-Auction** Most shopping sites have 'quote your price' option whereby a person can bid for the goods and services (such as airline tickets). It also includes e-tendering whereby a person may submit tender quotations online.
- **e-Communication/e-Promotion** It includes email, publication of online catalogues displaying images of goods, advertisement through banners, pop-ups, opinion poles and customer surveys, etc. It also includes organising meetings and conferences *via* video conferencing.
- **e-Delivery** It includes the following
  - Electronic delivery of computer software, photographs, videos, books (e-books) and journals (e-journals) and other multimedia content to the user's computer.
  - Rendering of legal, accounting, medical and other consulting services electronically.
- **e-Trading** It involves securities trading, i.e. online buying and selling of shares and other financial instruments. e.g. sharekhan.com is the largest online trading firm of India.

5.4 Limitations of e-Business

e-Business suffers from certain limitations, which are listed below

1. **Low Personal Touch** e-Business lacks in personal touch or interactions. Thus, it is less suitable mode of business with respect to certain products such as clothes, food items, toiletries, etc.
2. **Incongruence between Order Taking/Giving and Order Fulfillment Speed** Information can be exchanged quickly in e-business but the physical delivery of the product takes time. This incompatibility may negatively effect the patience of the customers. Sometimes, due to technical reasons, websites take unusually long time to open. This may further frustrate the user.
3. **Need for Technology Capability and Competence of Parties to e-Business** Apart from the traditional 3R's (Reading, WRiting and ARithmetic), both the parties in e-business requires to be familiar with computer or have computer knowledge. This requirement is responsible for digital divide, i.e. the division of society on the basis of familiarity and non-familiarity with digital technology.
4. **Increased Risk due to Anonymity and Non-traceability of Parties** Internet transactions are risky because they occur between cyber personalities. So, it becomes difficult to establish the identity of the two involved parties. Moreover, one does not know even the location from where the parties may be operating. e-Business can also results in hazards of impersonation and leakage of confidential information and other problems such as hacking, virus, etc.
5. **People Resistance** People have a tendency to resist change, as adjustment to new technology and new environment cause a sense of insecurity. Thus, people may resist an organisation's plans of entering into e-business.
6. **Ethical Fallouts** Many companies keep a view on their employees and track their e-mail accounts, files and websites used by them. It is not ethical on the part of the firms.

Despite Limitations, e-Commerce is the Way

Inspite of the above limitations, e-commerce is significant. Most of the limitations of e-business are in the process of being overcomed. This is explained below

- Websites are becoming more and more interactive to overcome the problem of low personal touch.
- Communication technology is continually developing to increase the speed and quality of communication through internet.
- Community telecentres are being established in rural areas with the involvement of government agencies, NGOs and international institutions to overcome the problem of digital divide.

Difference between e-Business and Traditional Business

Basis	e-Business	Traditional Business
Formation	Its formation process is simple.	Its formation process is difficult.
Physical Presence	It does not require physical appearance.	It requires physical appearance.
Locational Requirements	It does not require locational requirements.	It requires location near the sources of raw materials or the market for the products.
Cost of Setting-up	The cost of setting-up e-business is low, as there is no requirement of physical facilities.	The cost of setting-up traditional business is high.
Operating Cost	Its operating cost is low, because of reliance on network of relationships rather than ownership of resources.	Its operating cost is high, because of fixed charges associated with investment in procurement and storage, production, marketing and distribution facilities.
Nature of Contact with Suppliers and Customers	It has direct contact with the suppliers and customers.	It has indirect contact with the suppliers and customers through intermediaries.
Nature of Internal Commmunication	The nature of internal communication is non-hierarchical. It allows direct vertical, horizontal and diagonal communication.	The nature of internal communication is hierarchical i.e. from top level management to middle level management to lower level management to operatives.
Response time for Meeting Customers/Internal Requirements	It gives response to customers/internal requirements instantly.	It take longer time to response to customers/ internal requirements.
Shape of the Organisational Structure	It is horizontal/flat in structure due to directness of command and communication.	It is vertical/tall in structure due to hierarchy or chain of command.
Business Processes and Length of the Cycle	It has simultaneously different processes, therefore business process cycle is shorter.	It has number of sequential processes, i.e. purchase-production/operation-marketing-sales, therefore, business process cycle is longer.
Opportunity for Inter-personal Touch	It has less opportunity for inter-personal touch.	It has much more opportunity for inter-personal touch.
Opportunity for Physical Pre-sampling of the Products	It has less opportunity for physical pre-sampling of the products. However, digitable products have such opportunity as one can pre-sample music, books, journals, software, videos, etc.	It has much more opportunity for physical pre-sampling of the products.
Ease of Going Global	It has more chances of going global, as cyber space has no geographical boundaries.	It has less chances of going global, as various legal formalities are to be completed.
Government Patronage	Its support from government is increasing, as IT sector is among the topmost priorities of the government.	Its support from government is declining.
Nature of Human Capital	It requires technically and professionally qualified personnel.	It requires semi-skilled and even unskilled manpower.
Transaction Risk	It has high risk due to the distance and anonymity of the parties.	It has low risk due to arm's length transactions and face-to-face contact.

Mind Map

EMERGING MODES OF BUSINESS

1 Concept of e-Business

e-Business or electronic business refers to the conduct of industry, trade and commerce using a computer network such as the internet. e-Business is much more than buying or selling over the internet, i.e. e-commerce. e-Commerce includes a firm's interaction with its customers and suppliers over the internet.

2 Scope of e-Business

- **B2B Commerce** The transactions taking place between two business firms are known as B2B (Business-to-Business) transactions. B2B transactions may include sharing of information, creation of utilities, collaborations, etc.
- **B2C Commerce** The transactions taking place between business firms and customers are known as B2C (Business-to-Customers) transactions. B2C transactions may include selling and distribution of goods, after-sales services, delivery of products, etc.
- **Intra-B Commerce** The electronic transactions taking place within a given business firm only, are known as intra-B transactions. It enables the smooth flow of transactions within the different departments of a specific firm.
- **C2C Commerce** The transactions taking place between customers are known as C2C (Customer-to-Customer) transactions. These transactions originate from the customer and they end on the customer.

3 Benefits of e-Commerce

Benefits to Business Organisations

- It expands the marketplace to national and international markets
- It led to gradual decline in the cost of operations
- It facilitates 'pull' supply chain management (just-in-time inventory management)
- It gives competitive advantage over competitors
- It gives proper time management and support business processes
- It led to small firms co-existing with big firms

Benefits to Customers and Society

- It provides flexibility
- It provides competitive price/discounts
- It provides more options, choices and customised products
- It provides quick and timely delivery
- It increases employment potential
- It facilitiate e-auctions and e-tenders
- It provides opportunity to interact with customers
- It has a wider outreach

4 Benefits of e-Business

- **Ease of Formation and Lower Investment Requirements** e-Business is easy to start and involves less investment.
- **Convenience** Internet offers the convenience of doing business 24 hours × 7 days a week. In all 365 days, one can go for shopping or for business at anytime.
- **Speed** One can avail anything, anytime, anywhere at the click of a mouse. Information-intensive products such as softwares, movies, music, e-books and e-journals that can also be delivered online, make it more attractive.
- **Global Reach/Access** Internet has a wide reach. On one hand, it allows the seller an access to the global market while on the other hand, it offers freedom to the buyer to choose products from almost any part of the world.
- **Movement Towards a Paperless Society** Use of internet has reduced the dependence on paper work.

5 Limitations of e-Business

- **Low Personal Touch** e-Business lacks in personal touch or interactions.
- **Incongruence between Order Taking/Giving and Order Fulfillment Speed** Information can be exchanged quickly in e-business but the physical delivery of the product takes time. This incompatibility may negatively effect the patience of the customers.
- **Need for Technology Capability and Competence of Parties to e-Business** Both the parties in e-business requires to be familiar with computer or have computer knowledge. This requirement is responsible for digital divide, i.e. the division of society on the basis of familiarity and non-familiarity with digital technology.
- **Increased Risk due to Anonymity and Non-traceability of Parties** Internet transactions are risky because they occur between cyber personalities. So, it becomes difficult to establish the identity of the two involved parties.
- **People Resistance** People have a tendency to resist change, as adjustment to new technology and new environment cause a sense of insecurity.
- **Ethical Fallouts** Many companies keep a view on their employees and track their e-mail accounts, files and websites used by them. It is not ethical on the part of the firms.

6 Difference between e-Business and Traditional Business

- The formation process of e-business is simple while the formation process of traditional business is difficult
- e-Business does not require physical presence while traditional business requires physical presence
- e-Business does not require locational requirements while traditional business requires location near the sources of raw materials or the market for the products
- The cost of setting up e-business is low while cost of setting traditional business is high
- e-Business has high transaction risk due to the distance and anonymity of the parties while traditional business has low risk due to arm's length transactions and face-to-face contact
- e-Business has more chances of going global, as cyber space has no geographical boundaries while traditional business has less chances of going global, as various legal formalities are to be completed
- e-Business has less opportunity for inter-personal touch while traditional business has much more opportunity for inter-personal touch

EXAM PATTERN QUESTIONS

Objective Type Questions

Multiple Choice Questions (MCQs)

1. Cost of setting a business is .... in e-business.

(a) low (b) high
(c) medium (d) very high

2. Which payment mechanism is typical to e-business?

(a) Cash on Delivery (CoD) (b) Cheques
(c) Credit and debit cards (d) e-Cash

3. "This form of business is wider than e-commerce, encompassing activities like production, inventory management and human resource management, conducted electronically."
Identify the type of business described.

Competency Based Que

(a) e-Commerce (b) e-Business
(c) B2B commerce (d) digital trade

4. Length of the business cycle is generally .... in the case of e-business.

(a) longer (b) shorter (c) narrower (d) wider

5. Interaction between any two departments of one firm is a common feature of .... commerce.

(a) B2B (b) B2C
(c) C2C (d) intra-B

6. Mail sent by the marketing department to the purchase department is an example of Competency Based Que

(a) B2B (b) B2C (c) C2C (d) Intra-B

7. Which of the following is an example of a B2B transaction?

(a) Selling products to customers through an online store
(b) Conducting customer surveys to understand preferences
(c) Collaborating with suppliers for raw materials
(d) Delivering products directly to customers

8. What is the primary benefit of intra-B commerce for a business?

(a) Efficient handling of customer surveys
(b) Round-the-clock interaction with customers
(c) Smooth flow of transactions between departments
(d) Conducting commercial negotiations with vendors

9. Which type of commerce allows customers to make toll-free calls to lodge complaints?

(a) B2B (b) B2C (c) C2B (d) Intra-B

10. "These transactions occur between two business firms and involve interactions such as suppliers or distributors, forming a critical part of a company's operations."
Identify the type of e-commerce transaction.

Competency Based Que

(a) C2B commerce (b) B2B commerce
(c) Intra-B commerce (d) C2C commerce

11. Mr. A wanted to sell his old smartphone to upgrade to a newer model. He used an online platform, OLX, to post an advertisement for his phone. Within a day, he received several responses and finally sold his phone to someone who offered him the highest price.
Identify the branch of e-business being described above. Competency Based Que

(a) C2C commerce (b) B2C commerce
(c) B2B commerce (d) C2B commerce

12. Ritu's Boutique, an online clothing retailer, uses Amazon Marketplace to sell its products directly to customers across the country. Customers can browse, select and purchase the items online and the boutique ensures quick delivery.
Identify the component of e-business being described above. Competency Based Que

(a) C2C commerce (b) B2C commerce
(c) B2B commerce (d) None of these

13. Identify the type of transaction illustrated in the below picture

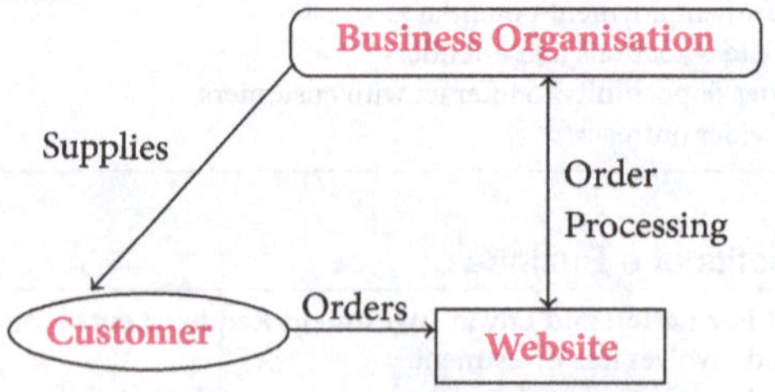

(a) B2B commerce (b) B2C commerce
(c) C2B commerce (d) C2C commerce

14. Amrita is the owner of a popular online clothing store, 'Trendy Styles'. Through her e-commerce platform, she is able to sell clothes and accessories to customers across the country, with 24×7 customer support and easy return policies.

She also conducts periodic customer surveys to improve her services and engages in promotional activities like discount offers and flash sales.

Amrita ensures that products are delivered to customers within 3-5 business days. Recently, she introduced a feature allowing customers to suggest designs, which the store may feature for sale based on customer feedback.

What type of transaction does 'Trendy Styles' primarily engage in? **Competency Based Que**

(a) B2B (Business-to-Business)
(b) B2C (Business-to-Customer)
(c) C2B (Customer-to-Business)
(d) B2G (Business-to-Government)

15. Which of the following statements is incorrect regarding C2B and intra-B commerce?

(a) C2B commerce allows customers to freely shop and make toll-free calls to company call centers for queries and complaints
(b) Intra-B commerce involves electronic transactions between departments within a single firm, helping in inventory and cash management
(c) C2B commerce transactions are generally performed within the company's internal departments, such as inventory management and order fulfillment
(d) Intra-B commerce facilitates efficient human resource management and greater utilisation of plant and machinery within a firm

16. Hero Automobiles Ltd. is a well-known manufacturer in the field of cars. The company makes online transactions for purchase of tyres, battery, etc. from different business units. Use of internet has given them much wider choice of suppliers and company finds this online buying very convenient and time saving. Identify the component of e-business being described above. **Competency Based Que**

(a) B2B commerce (b) B2C commerce
(c) C2B commerce (d) None of these

17. Identify the type of transaction illustrated in the below picture.

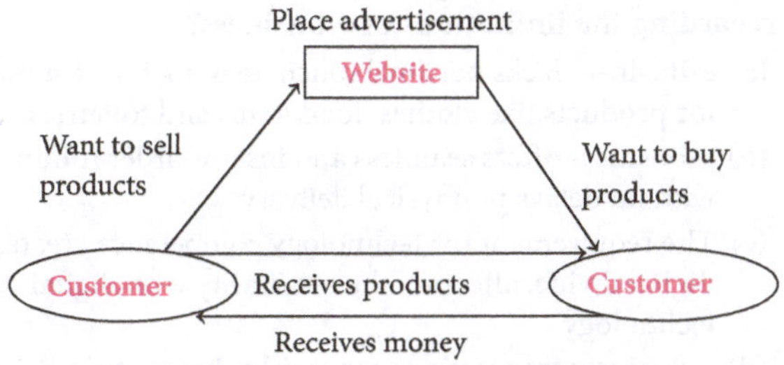

(a) B2B commerce (b) B2C commerce
(c) C2B commerce (d) C2C commerce

18. In recent years, a popular online platform has allowed individuals to directly sell products to each other. This platform enables users to list items they no longer need, ranging from used electronics to handmade goods and other users can browse, purchase, and sometimes negotiate prices.

The entire transaction process, including payment and shipping, is managed through the platform, ensuring security and convenience for both buyers and sellers. This type of business model has gained significant attention due to its ease of use and growing consumer base.

Which component of e-business is being discussed in the case above? **Competency Based Que**

(a) B2B commerce (b) B2C commerce
(c) C2C commerce (d) C2B commerce

19. TechCorp Pvt. Ltd., a leading IT firm, buys software licenses and computer peripherals directly from other companies *via* an online marketplace. This platform allows TechCorp to compare prices and features before making purchases.

Identify the component of e-business being described above. **Competency Based Que**

(a) B2C commerce (b) C2B commerce
(c) B2B commerce (d) C2C commerce

20. Identify the type of transaction illustrated in the below picture

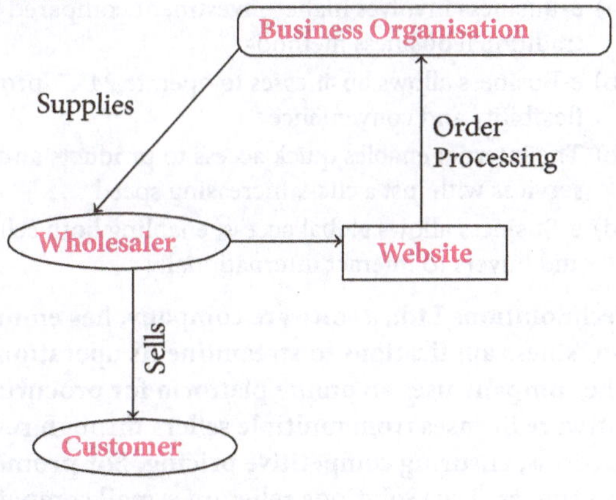

(a) B2B commerce
(b) B2C commerce
(c) C2B commerce (d) C2C commerce

21. "This mode of business allows transactions to happen 24×7 and enables buyers to access products from any part of the world, ensuring flexibility and global reach." Identify the benefit of e-business described in the statement. **Competency Based Que**

(a) Ease of formation (b) Convenience
(c) Speed (d) Global reach

22. Which one of the following is a factor which gives advantage to e-business over traditional business?
(a) Transaction risks (b) Investment requirement
(c) Ethical fallouts
(d) Personal touch with customers

23. Amit is an entrepreneur who recently started his e-business venture. He set-up a simple website showcasing electronic gadgets like smartphones, laptops and accessories. Customers can browse, compare products and place orders anytime, ensuring convenience for both buyers and Amit's team. The speed of online transactions has significantly reduced delivery times for digital products like e-books and software.

With his website accessible globally, Amit receives orders from various countries, enhancing his business reach. Furthermore, he has minimised paperwork by electronically filing returns and reports with regulatory authorities, leveraging the provisions of the Information Technology Act, 2000.
Which of the following benefits of e-business is not mentioned in the case above? **Competency Based Que**
(a) Global access and better business reach
(b) Movement towards a paperless society
(c) Flexibility and convenience
(d) Enhanced customer interaction through surveys

24. Which of the following statements is incorrect regarding the benefits of e-business?
(a) e-Business involves higher investment compared to traditional business methods
(b) e-Business allows businesses to operate 24×7, providing flexibility and convenience
(c) The internet enables quick access to products and services with just a click, increasing speed
(d) e-Business allows global access, enabling both sellers and buyers to interact internationally

25. TechSolutions Ltd., a software company, has embraced e-business applications to streamline its operations. The company uses an online platform for procuring software licenses from multiple sellers through reverse auctions, ensuring competitive pricing. For promoting its services, TechSolutions relies on e-mail campaigns, online catalogs showcasing their products and video conferencing for client meetings.

Additionally, the company provides its clients with e-books and multimedia guides electronically. Recently, it has also started offering clients access to an online trading platform for buying and selling financial instruments.
Which of the following e-business applications is not explicitly mentioned in the case above?
Competency Based Que
(a) e-Procurement (b) e-Delivery
(c) e-Bidding/e-Auction (d) e-Trading

26. Mr. Ramesh buys and sells shares and securities of various companies online, through a platform provided by the Bombay Stock Exchange. Mr. Ramesh is engaged in which of the following applications of e-business?
Competency Based Que
(a) e-Procurement (b) e-Trading
(c) e-Bidding (d) None of these

27. Which of the following is a limitation of e-business?
(a) Global reach
(b) Movement towards a paperless society
(c) Incongruence between order taking and order fulfillment
(d) Convenience of 24×7 operations

28. An emerging fashion brand, StyleTrendz, launched its e-commerce platform to sell trendy clothing online. While the website gained significant traffic, many customers expressed dissatisfaction due to delays in the delivery of their orders, even after making payments instantly. Moreover, some users found it challenging to navigate the website due to a lack of familiarity with digital platforms.
Which of the following limitations of e-Business is highlighted in the case above? **Competency Based Que**
(a) People resistance
(b) Need for technology capability and competence
(c) Increased risk due to anonymity and non-traceability
(d) Incongruence between order taking/giving and order fulfillment

29. "Online transactions face risks such as impersonation, hacking and the anonymity of parties, making it difficult to trace identities or locations."
Identify the limitation of e-business described in the statement. **Competency Based Que**
(a) Low personal touch
(b) Increased risk due to anonymity
(c) Incongruence between order taking and fulfillment speed
(d) People resistance

30. Which of the following statements is incorrect regarding the limitations of e-business?
(a) e-Business lacks personal touch, making it less suitable for products like clothes, food items and toiletries
(b) e-Business offers seamless and instant order fulfilment with no delays in physical delivery
(c) The requirement for technology competence creates a digital divide, affecting the familiarity with digital technology
(d) e-Business transactions carry risks due to the anonymity and non-traceability of parties involved

Direction *Read the following case study and answer the questions 31 to 34 on the basis of the same*

"Let's explore something new," said Aryan to his cousin Priya, who had come to Mumbai for her holidays. Priya curiously asked, "What do you have in mind?" Aryan replied, "Have you tried ordering fresh fruits and vegetables online? It saves a lot of time and energy." Priya looked surprised and said, "I have never done that! Are you sure the quality will be good?" Aryan smiled and explained, "Most platforms provide quality checks and even have a return policy if you're dissatisfied with the products. Let's give it a try and I'll show you how convenient it is."

31. Out of the following items, which item(s) can be ordered online?

(i) Fruits **(ii) Vegetables**
(iii) Meat **(iv) Bakery products**

Codes

(a) Only (i) (b) (i) and (ii)
(c) (i), (ii) and (iii) (d) (i), (ii), (iii) and (iv)

32. How can you ensure the quality of the products ordered online?

(a) By visiting the warehouse before placing an order
(b) By relying on quality checks and return policies provided by the platform
(c) By checking the reviews and ratings of the seller
(d) Both (b) and (c)

33. Identify the advantage(s) of ordering groceries online.

(a) Saves time (b) Home delivery
(c) Wide range of options (d) All of these

34. Identify the limitation(s) of ordering groceries online.

(a) No opportunity to personally inspect the products
(b) Delivery delays (c) Additional delivery charges
(d) All of the above

Assertion-Reason

Direction (Q. No. 35 to 42) *Read the following Assertion (A) and Reason (R) and choose the correct alternative from the following*

Alternatives

(a) Both Assertion (A) and Reason (R) are true and Reason (R) is the correct explanation of Assertion (A)
(b) Both Assertion (A) and Reason (R) are true, but Reason (R) is not the correct explanation of Assertion (A)
(c) Assertion (A) is true, but Reason (R) is false
(d) Assertion (A) is false, but Reason (R) is true

35. Assertion (A) e-Business is referred to as the emerging mode of business.

Reason (R) It is a way of conducting the business according to the recent trends taking place.

36. Assertion (A) C2B commerce allows customers to shop at will and provides them the convenience of toll-free calls to call centers for queries and complaints.

Reason (R) C2B transactions are often outsourced to improve customer service and streamline business operations.

37. Assertion (A) The volume of B2B transactions is much higher than the volume of B2C transactions.

Reason (R) To facilitate a single B2C transaction, there are number of B2B transactions.

38. Assertion (A) There are more chances of going global in case of e-Business.

Reason (R) e-Business has considerably reduced dependence on paperwork.

39. Assertion (A) e-Business provides global reach and allows customers to access products from anywhere at any time.

Reason (R) e-Business is limited by geographical boundaries and only supports local transactions.

40. Assertion (A) One of the major limitations of e-business is the lack of personal interaction, which affects certain types of products like clothes or food.

Reason (R) The absence of face-to-face interaction in e-business reduces the customer's confidence in purchasing goods that they typically prefer to inspect in person.

41. Assertion (A) e-Procurement enables online sales transactions between business firms, facilitating efficient procurement processes through reverse auctions and digital marketplaces.

Reason (R) e-Procurement is primarily used for Consumer-to-Business (C2B) transactions, where individual consumers sell goods to businesses.

42. Assertion (A) e-Business is easier to form and involves lower investment compared to traditional business.

Reason (R) In traditional business, there is a need for substantial physical infrastructure, which increases investment and makes formation more complex.

Two Statements Based MCQs

Direction (Q. No. 43 to 50) *Read the following statements carefully and choose the correct alternative*

Alternatives

(a) Statement I is correct and Statement II is incorrect
(b) Statement II is correct and Statement I is incorrect
(c) Both the statements are correct
(d) Both the statements are incorrect

43. **Statement I** The payment mechanism typical to e-Business is cash on delivery.

Statement II One of the methods of payment in e-Business can be cash on delivery.

44. **Statement I** e-Commerce is a wider term as compared to e-Business.

Statement II B2C process enables the business to remain in touch with its customers on round-the-clock basis.

45. **Statement I** B2C transactions can include promotional activities.

Statement II B2C transactions involve the exchange of goods and services.

46. **Statement I** Intra-B commerce allows transactions between customers and businesses.

Statement II Intra-B commerce is limited to internal transactions within a single business firm.

47. **Statement I** C2B transactions allow customers to initiate the shopping process.

Statement II C2B transactions involve customers making toll free calls to companies for inquiries.

48. **Statement I** One of the benefits of e-business is global reach, which allows access to international markets.

Statement II e-Business provides a limitation of having slow physical delivery of products despite fast information exchange.

49. **Statement I** There are more chances of going global in case of e-business.

Statement II There is greater opportunity for inter personal touch in case of e-business.

50. **Statement I** Low personal touch in e-business makes it unsuitable for the sale of certain products.

Statement II e-Business eliminates the need for technology competency from both parties involved.

Matching

51. Match the following

Column I	Column II
A. B2B commerce	(i) Interactions and dealings among various departments and persons within firms.
B. C2C commerce	(ii) Transactions taking place between business and customers.
C. B2C commerce	(iii) Transactions taking place between two or more customers.
D. Intra-B commerce	(iv) Transactions taking place between business firms.

Codes

	A	B	C	D
(a)	(ii)	(i)	(iv)	(iii)
(b)	(iii)	(iv)	(i)	(ii)
(c)	(i)	(iii)	(ii)	(iv)
(d)	(iv)	(iii)	(ii)	(i)

52. Match the following

Column I	Column II
A. B2B, B2C, C2C, intra-B	(i) e-Payment methods
B. UPI, plastic money, net-banking	(ii) Traditional business
C. Personal inspection, facial interaction	(iii) Scope of e-business

Codes

	A	B	C		A	B	C
(a)	(ii)	(i)	(iii)	(b)	(iii)	(i)	(ii)
(c)	(i)	(iii)	(ii)	(d)	(ii)	(iii)	(i)

53. Match the following

Column I	Column II
A. e-Cash	(i) Service providers of e-banners and pop-ups
B. e-Promotion	(ii) Payment mechanism of e-business
C. Job works	(iii) Advantage of e-business over traditional business
D. Investment required	(iv) Contract manufacturing

Codes

	A	B	C	D		A	B	C	D
(a)	(ii)	(i)	(iv)	(iii)	(b)	(iii)	(iv)	(i)	(ii)
(c)	(i)	(iii)	(ii)	(iv)	(d)	(iv)	(iii)	(ii)	(i)

54. Match the following

Column I	Column II
A. e-Business	(i) Personal contact between buyer and seller
B. Traditional business	(ii) Firm's interaction with its customers and suppliers over the internet
C. e-Commerce	(iii) Possibility of higher transaction risk

Codes

	A	B	C		A	B	C
(a)	(iii)	(i)	(ii)	(b)	(i)	(ii)	(iii)
(c)	(ii)	(iii)	(i)	(d)	(i)	(iii)	(ii)

Answers

1. (a) low
2. (d) e-Cash
3. (b) e-Business
4. (b) shorter
5. (d) intra-B
6. (d) intra-B
7. (c) Collaborating with suppliers for raw materials
8. (c) Smooth flow of transactions between departments
9. (c) C2B
10. (b) B2B commerce
11. (a) C2C commerce
12. (b) B2C commerce
13. (b) B2C commerce
14. (b) B2C (Business-to-Customer)
15. (c) C2B commerce involves transactions where customers interact with businesses, often for services or complaints. Intra-B commerce, on the other hand, refers to internal transactions within a business firm.
16. (a) B2B commerce
17. (d) C2C commerce
18. (c) C2C commerce
19. (c) B2B commerce
20. (a) B2B commerce
21. (d) Global reach
22. (b) Investment requirement
23. (d) Enhanced customer interaction through surveys
24. (a) e-Business is generally easy to start and involves lower investment requirements, unlike traditional business methods
25. (c) e-Bidding/e-Auction
26. (b) e-Trading
27. (c) Incongruence between order taking and order fulfilment
28. (d) Incongruence between order taking/giving and order fulfillment
29. (b) Increased risk due to anonymity
30. (b) Although information can be exchanged quickly in e-business, physical delivery often takes time, which can create issues with order fulfilment speed.
31. (d) (i), (ii), (iii) and (iv)
32. (d) Both (b) and (c)
33. (d) All of these
34. (d) All of the above
35. (a) Both Assertion (A) and Reason (R) are true and Reason (R) is the correct explanation of Assertion (A)
36. (b) Both Assertion (A) and Reason (R) are true, but Reason (R) is not the correct explanation of Assertion (A)
37. (a) Both Assertion (A) and Reason (R) are true and Reason (R) is the correct explanation of Assertion (A)
38. (a) Both Assertion (A) and Reason (R) are true and Reason (R) is the correct explanation of Assertion (A)
39. (c) e-Business breaks geographical limitations, not limited by them.
40. (a) Both Assertion (A) and Reason (R) are true and Reason (R) is the correct explanation of Assertion (A)
41. (c) e-Procurement does not focus on C2B transactions but rather on B2B (Business-to-Business) transactions.
42. (a) Both Assertion (A) and Reason (R) are true and Reason (R) is the correct explanation of Assertion (A)
43. (b) Cash on Delivery (CoD) is just one of several possible payment mechanisms in e-business, not the typical or exclusive one. e-Business platforms usually offer multiple payment options such as credit/debit cards, online wallets and bank transfers.
44. (b) e-Business is wider than e-commerce. e-Business includes e-commerce as well as other electronically conducted business functions such as production, inventory management, product development, accounting and finance and human resource management.
45. (c) Both the statements are correct
46. (b) Intra-B commerce (intra-business commerce) refers to electronic transactions that occur within the same business, such as communication between different departments of a company. It doesn't involve customers or businesses outside the company.
47. (c) Both the statements are correct
48. (c) Both the statements are correct
49. (a) e-Business typically operates through digital platforms, reducing the need for interpersonal interactions, which are more common in traditional face-to-face business models.
50. (a) e-Business requires both the business and the customer to have some level of technological competency. Customers need to know how to navigate websites and businesses need to know how to manage online platforms.
51. (d) (iv) (iii) (ii) (i)
52. (b) (iii) (i) (ii)
53. (a) (ii) (i) (iv) (iii)
54. (a) (iii) (i) (ii)

Subjective Questions

Short Answer Type Questions

1. "e-Business is the new way of doing a business." Do you agree? Justify your answer. **Competency Based Que**

Ans. Yes, I agree with the given statement. e-Business is not new business but is merely new way of doing business. In e-business, a firm uses a computer and internet to access its customers.

This way of doing business have been evolved by entrepreneurs to successfully meet competitive pressures and customer demands.

2. What is meant by the term 'e-business'? How it is different from e-commerce?

Ans. Electronic business refers to conducting business activities over internet or any other computer network.

e-Business is wider than e-commerce. Following are the differences between e-business and e-commerce

Basis	e-Business	e-Commerce
Meaning	e-Business is a more elaborate term and comprises various business transactions and functions conducted electronically, including e-commerce, i.e. buying and selling over a computer network.	e-Commerce means buying and selling products and services over a computer network.
Coverage	e-Business includes not only e-commerce but also other electronically conducted business transactions like production, inventory management, product development, finance, marketing and human resource development.	e-Commerce is concerned with buying and selling, therefore it covers firm's interaction with its customers and suppliers over a computer network.

3. Describe any three applications of e-business.

Or **Describe briefly any two applications of e-business.** **NCERT**

Ans. Following are the applications of e-business

(i) **e-Procurement**

It involves internet-based sales transactions between business firms. It includes the following

- 'Reverse auctions' that facilitate online trade between a single business purchaser and many sellers.
- Digital marketplaces that facilitate online trading between multiple buyers and sellers.

(ii) **e-Bidding/e-Auction**

Most shopping sites have 'quote your price' option whereby a person can bid for the goods and services (such as airline tickets). It also includes e-Tendering whereby a person may submit tender quotations online.

(iii) **e-Communication/e-Promotion**

It includes e-mail, publication of online catalogues displaying images of goods, advertisement through banners, pop-ups, opinion polls and customer surveys, etc. It also includes organising meetings and conferences *via* video conferencing.

4. "B2B commerce involves transactions between businesses, such as manufacturers and wholesalers or wholesalers and retailers, often conducted through electronic platforms."

In the context of the statement, explain the concept of B2B commerce and illustrate it with an example. **Competency Based Que**

Ans. The transactions taking place between two business firms are known as B2B (Business-to-Business) transactions. A business interacts with a number of other business firms which may be suppliers or vendors of diverse inputs. They may also be a part of the channel through which a firm distributes its products to the customers.

e.g. An automobile manufacturer makes several B2B transactions. Manufacturing of a car requires large number of components which are manufactured by some other vendors. A network of computers are used to place orders, monitoring production, delivery of component and making payments.

B2B transactions may include sharing of information, creation of utilities, collaborations, commercial negotiations and distribution of goods.

5. Discuss the concept of intra-B commerce. How it is useful for the firm?

Ans. The electronic transactions taking place within a given business firm only are known as intra-B transactions. It enables the smooth flow of transactions within the different departments of a specific firm.

Intra-B commerce transactions may include

(i) Inventory and cash management.
(ii) Interaction among the different departments.
(iii) Recruitment, selection and training of employees.
(iv) Handling of customers' orders.
(v) Human resource management, etc.

In intra-B commerce, the use of computer-based interaction among the different departments makes it possible for the firm to get the following advantages
(i) Efficient inventory and cash management.
(ii) Greater utilisation of plant and machinery.
(iii) Effective handling of customers' orders.
(iv) Effective human resource management, etc.

6. "e-Commerce has revolutionised the way business organisations operate, enabling them to reach customers globally and streamline operations through digital platforms."

In the context of the statement, discuss the benefits of e-commerce to business organisations. Competency Based Que

Ans. Following are the benefits of e-commerce to business organisations
(i) It expands the marketplace to national and international markets.
(ii) It led to gradual decline in the cost of operations.
(iii) It facilitates 'pull' supply chain management (just-in-time inventory management).
(iv) It gives competitive advantage over competitors.
(v) It gives proper time management and support business processes.

7. State the benefits of e-commerce to customers and society.

Ans. Following are the benefits of e-commerce to customers and society
(i) It provides flexibility.
(ii) It provides competitive price/discounts.
(iii) It provides more options, choices and customised products.
(iv) It provides quick and timely delivery.
(v) It increases employment potential.
(vi) It facilitiate e-auctions and e-tenders.
(vii) It provides opportunity to interact with customers.

Long Answer Type Questions

8. Discuss the salient aspects of B2C commerce. NCERT

Ans. The salient aspects of B2C commerce are as follows

(i) **Online Selling**
B2C commerce involves selling the products online to customers who register for online shopping.

(ii) **Online Marketing**
B2C commerce includes a wide range of marketing activities such as promotion and sometimes even delivery of products (e.g. Music or e-books) that are carried out online at a much lower cost and high speed.

(iii) **Adaptation to Customer Requirements**
B2C commerce has made it possible for firms to manufacture the product with customised features to suit the requirements of the customers and also to provide the convenience of home delivery and cash on delivery to the customers.

(iv) **Customer Feedback**
B2C enables a business to be in continuous touch with its customers through online surveys about demand, fashion trends and customer satisfaction.

(v) **C2B Interactions**
C2B interactions provide the customers with the freedom of shopping-at-will. Customers can also make use of call centres set up by companies to make toll-free calls to make queries and lodge complaints round-the-clock at no extra cost.

(vi) **Outsourcing**
The call centres or helplines for B2C commerce interactions may be outsourced and are not necessary to be set-up by the business itself.

9. "e-Business has revolutionised traditional business practices by facilitating transactions and interactions through electronic platforms." In the context of the statement, discuss the benefits of e-business. Competency Based Que

Ans. Following are the benefits of e-business

(i) **Ease of Formation and Lower Investment Requirements**
e-Business is easy to start and involves less investment. Similar benefits of internet technology are received by big or small business. If a person do not have much of the investment (networth) but have contacts (network), he can do fabulous business through interne.
e.g. To sell electronic products through e-business, a person just need to set-up website, display various pictures of washing machines, refrigerators, TV, etc. and the customer visit the website and place order according to their choice and budget.

(ii) **Convenience**
Internet offers the convenience of doing business 24 hours × 7 days a week. In all 365 days, one can go for shopping or for business at anytime. Such flexibility is available even to the organisational personnel. Thus, e-business offers the advantage of accessing anything, anywhere, anytime.

(iii) **Speed**
Internet is one of the most speedy modes of doing business. One can avail anything, anytime, anywhere at the click of a mouse. Information-intensive products such as softwares, movies, music, e-books and e-journals that can also be delivered online, make it more attractive.

(iv) **Global Reach/Access**
Internet has a wide reach. On one hand, it allows the seller an access to the global market while on the other hand, it offers freedom to the buyer to choose products from almost any part of the world.

(v) **Movement Towards a Paperless Society**
Use of internet has reduced the dependence on paperwork. In order to expand this trend, the government departments and regulatory authorities are allowing electronic filing of returns and reports by the business firms and speeding up the process of granting permissions, approvals and licences. In this respect, the provisions of Information Technology Act, 2000 are significant.

10. Discuss the limitations of electronic mode of doing business. Are these limitations severe enough to restrict its scope? Give reasons for your answer. NCERT

Ans. e-Business has its own limitations as discussed below

(i) **Low Personal Touch**
e-Business lacks the warmth of interpersonal interactions and personal touch for satisfaction of customer. Thus, it is relatively less suitable mode of business for product categories such as garments, toiletries, food items, etc.

(ii) **Incongruence between Order Taking/ Giving and Order Fulfillment Speed**
In e-business, orders can be placed at the click of a mouse, but the physical delivery of the product takes time. Customers are sometimes not patient enough to bear with this delay. At times, the users even get frustrated due to technical reasons when websites take unusually long time to respond.

(iii) **Need for Technology Capability and Competence of Parties to e-Business**
The parties need to be fairly familiar with computers and interne. The digital divide has thus limited the scope of e-business.

(iv) **Increased Risk due to Anonymity and Non-traceability of Parties**
Internet transactions occur between cyber personalities and it is difficult to establish the identity of the parties or know the location from where the parties may be operating. e-Business is also risky due to additional hazards of impersonation and leakage of confidential information such as credit card details. Problems of 'virus' attacks and 'hacking' also pose security concerns in e-business.

(v) **People Resistance**
The process of adjustment to new technology and new way of doing things causes stress and a sense of insecurity among people in business firms.

As a result, people may resist a change from traditional business to e-business.

(vi) **Ethical Fallout**
Companies use to keep a view and track of the computer files, e-mail account and the websites visited by their employees or others, who use their network systems, which is not considered right on ethical grounds.

These limitations are not that severe which restricts the scope of e-business as most of the limitations discussed above are in the process of being overcome in the following ways

(i) Websites are becoming more and more interactive to overcome the problem of 'personal touch.'

(ii) Speed and quality of communication through internet is being improved through communication technology innovations.

(iii) Efforts are on to overcome the digital divide through setting-up of community tele-centres in villages and rural areas with the involvement of government agencies, NGOs and international institutions.

(iv) The transaction risks and data transmission risks can be minimised with the use of secure payment sites, use of anti-virus programs and encrypting of data to safeguard the customers.

Thus, we can say that despite limitations, e-business is here to stay and bring a positive change in the business, governance and the economies.

11. Outline any six points of difference between e-business and traditional business.

Or

State any three differences between e-business and traditional business. NCERT

Ans. Following are the differences between e-business and traditional business

Basis	e-Business	Traditional Business
Formation	Its formation process is simple.	Its formation process is difficult.
Physical Presence	It does not require physical appearance.	It requires physical appearance.
Locational Requirements	It does not require locational requirements.	It requires location near the sources of raw materials or the market for the products.
Cost of Setting-up	The cost of setting-up e-business is low, as there is no requirement of physical facilities.	The cost of setting-up traditional business is high.
Operating Cost	It operating cost is low, because of reliance on network of relationships rather than ownership of resources.	Its operating cost is high, because of fixed charges associated with investment in procurement and storage, production, marketing and distribution facilities.
Nature of Contact with the Suppliers and the Customers	It has direct contact with the suppliers and customers.	It has indirect contact with the suppliers and customers through intermediaries.

Case Study Based Questions

Short Case Studies

Case Study 1

'Let us do some shopping,' Rita woke up Rekha, her friend from the home-village who had come to Delhi during the vacations. 'At this hour well past midnight' said Rekha rubbing her eyes. 'Who would be sitting with his shop open for you?' 'Oh! Perhaps I could not convey it properly. We are not going anywhere. I am talking about online shopping over the internet' told Rita. 'Oh yes I have heard of online shopping, but have never done any.' Imagining yourself as Rita, answer the following questions of Rekha.

(i) What can we buy online?

(ii) How does the e-vendor deliver the goods ordered?

(iii) Why is internet not yet popular in villages?

Ans.

(i) We can buy a number of things ranging from clothes, accessories, footwear, jewellery and even groceries and vegetables online.

(ii) The e-vendor delivers the goods ordered through courier service.

(iii) It may be due to the fact that infrastructure is not much developed in the villages and there is, in general, a lack of communication and transport facilities. Also, power supply continues to be a major issue in rural India.

Case Study 2

Rahul wanted to sell his old laptop but didn't know how to find a buyer. After a quick online search, he found a platform where individuals could list their used products and directly connect with interested buyers. Rahul created a listing, and within a week, he successfully sold his laptop to someone in his city. This platform facilitated transactions between individuals without involving any intermediaries.

(i) State the type of e-business discussed in the case.

(ii) Give a suitable example in support of the type of e-business identified in (i).

Ans.

(i) The type of e-business discussed in the case is C2C commerce. The transactions taking place between customers are known as C2C (Customer-to-Customer) transactions. These transactions originate from the customer and they end on the customer. This type of commerce is best suited for dealing in goods for which there is no established market mechanism such as selling used books, clothes, electronics on cash or barter basis.

(ii) Etsy and Ebay are examples of C2C commerce where customers can sell their goods to other customers. Payment intermedia is the technology that supports C2C activities. In this method, instead of purchasing goods directly from seller, the buyer sends the money to the intermediary which holds that money until the goods are delivered and accepted by the buyer. PayPal is an example of payment intermediary.

Case Study 3

Raj operates an online electronics store called TechMart, where he sells gadgets like smartphones, laptops and accessories directly to customers. Customers can browse products, compare specifications, read user reviews and place orders online. The platform offers multiple payment options, including cash on delivery and UPI. Additionally, TechMart provides doorstep delivery and post-purchase support through a dedicated customer service team.

(i) State the type of e-business discussed in the case.

(ii) List some of the transactions conducted in the type of e-business identified in (i).

Ans.

(i) The transactions taking place between business firms and customers are known as B2C (Business-to-Customers) transactions. This category is related to electronic retailing. This variant of e-business enables a business to be in contact with its customers on round-the-clock basis. The most common and visible B2C transaction is the use of ATM machines for withdrawing cash. Here, the bank is the business firm and the person withdrawing cash is the customer.

(ii) B2C transactions may include

- Selling and distribution of goods
- Conducting customer surveys
- After sales services
- Promotional activities
- Delivery of products

Case Study 4

Identify and state the type of e-business transaction highlighted in the following cases

(i) Rajesh is a customer and lodges a complaint at the company's call centre as his mixer grinder is not working properly.

(ii) Mohan and Ram work in Technesia Ltd. and send their daily report through e-mail.

Ans.

(i) The type of e-business transaction highlighted in the case is C2B Commerce. The transactions that provides customers with the freedom of shopping at will are known as C2B transactions. In this commerce, customers can make toll free calls to the call centres set up by the companies to make queries and lodge complaints. These transactions are generally outsourced.

(ii) The type of e-business transaction highlighted in the case is intra-B commerce. The electronic transactions taking place within a given business firm only are known as intra-B transactions. It enables the smooth flow of transactions within the different departments of a specific firm. Intra-B commerce transactions may include inventory and cash management, interaction among the different departments, etc.

Case Study 5

Technart Enterprises is dealing in electronic accessories. With the continuous increase in the demand, their business is expanding. However, the Managing Director (MD) observed that the decision-making process in the enterprise is very slow and level of coordination is decreasing between the various departments. Ramesh, an IT professional suggested that the company should have its own internet to interact and deal between various departments and persons within the firm.

(i) Identify the branch of e-business suggested by Ramesh.

(ii) Mention some areas in which this branch of e-business can be conducted.

Ans.

(i) The branch of e-business suggested by Ramesh is intra-B commerce. The electronic transactions taking place within a given business firm only are known as intra-B transactions. It enables the smooth flow of transactions within the different departments of a specific firm.

(ii) Areas in which intra-B commerce can be conducted are

- Inventory and cash management.
- Interaction among the different departments.
- Recruitment, selection and training of employees.
- Handling of customers' orders.
- Human resource management, etc.

Case Study 6

Ram is a manufacturer of readymade kids garments. He sells his products through various dealers across the country. However, his sales are decreasing over the years. Recently, his wife gifted him a jacket, which she had ordered through Jabong (an online shopping site for fashion).

This gave Ram an idea to start selling his products online. State any three benefits that Ram can get through e-business.

Ans. Following are the benefits that Ram can get through e-business

(i) **Ease of Formation and Lower Investment Requirements**

e-Business is easy to start and involves less investment. Similar benefits of internet technology are received by big or small business. If a person do not have much of the investment (net worth) but have contacts (network), he can do fabulous business through interne. e.g. To sell electronic products through e-business, a person just need to set-up website, display various pictures of washing machines, refrigerators, TV, etc. and the customer visit the website and place order according to their choice and budget.

(ii) **Convenience**

Internet offers the convenience of doing business 24 hours × 7 days a week. In all 365 days, one can go for shopping or for business at anytime. Such flexibility is available even to the organisational personnel. Thus, e-business offers the advantage of accessing anything, anywhere, anytime.

(iii) **Speed**

Internet is one of the most speedy modes of doing business. One can avail anything, anytime, anywhere at the click of a mouse.

Information-intensive products such as softwares, movies, music, e-Books and e-Journals that can also be delivered online, make it more attractive.

Case Study 7

An IT company has launched a new platform where users can access a wide range of services from the comfort of their homes. The platform provides access to e-books, e-journals, videos and software that users can download directly onto their devices.

It also offers multimedia content such as educational videos and photography collections. Additionally, the platform facilitates professional services like legal advice, accounting and medical consultations through virtual sessions, making it highly convenient for users.

(i) Identify the type of e-business application described in the case.

(ii) State any two components of the e-business application mentioned in the case.

Ans.

(i) The type of e-business application described in the case is e-delivery.

(ii) e-Delivery includes the following

- Electronic delivery of computer software, photographs, videos, books (e-books) and journals (e-journals) and other multimedia content to the user's computer. Rendering of legal, accounting, medical and other consulting services electronically.
- e-Trading It involves securities trading, that is online buying and selling of shares and other financial instruments. e.g. sharekhan.com is the largest online trading firm of India.

Case Study 8

'TechSpark Innovations' is a start-up that designs customised mobile accessories such as phone cases, screen protectors and chargers. The company operates entirely online, using e-commerce platforms to sell its products. By eliminating the need for physical stores and maintaining a just-in-time inventory model, TechSpark has reduced its costs significantly.

Customers can customise their products on the company's website, selecting designs, colours and materials tailored to their preferences. The founder of TechSpark highlights that their e-commerce platform has not only widened their market but also reduced administrative and operational costs.

However, some customers express concerns regarding e-business operations. They find it challenging to assess the product's quality without a physical store. Additionally, some customers worry about the security of their personal information while making online transactions.

(i) How has e-commerce helped TechSpark produce customised products and services at a lower cost?

(ii) Mention any two limitations of e-business.

Ans.

(i) e-Commerce has helped in the production of customised products and services at lower costs because of the reasons enumerated below

- e-Commerce widens the market at no extra cost. Also, the transaction costs are reasonably reduced.
- e-Commerce saves on various administrative costs, so a customer pays only for the customised product.
- There is no need to maintain inventory. This also plays an important factor responsible for cost reduction.

(ii) Following are the limitations of e-business

- **Increased Risk due to Anonymity and Non-traceability of Parties**
  Internet transactions are risky because they occur between cyber personalities. So, it becomes difficult to establish the identity of the two involved parties. Moreover, one does not know even the location from where the parties may be operating.
  e-Business can also results in hazards of impersonation and leakage of confidential information and other problems such as hacking, virus, etc.
- **People Resistance**
  People have a tendency to resist change, as adjustment to new technology and new environment cause a sense of insecurity. Thus, people may resist an organisation's plans of entering into e-Business.

Long Case Studies

Case Study 9

TechHub is a dynamic online platform designed to bridge the gap between manufacturers, wholesalers, retailers and consumers. Established as a leading e-business model, it offers both two types of e-business services. The platform connects manufacturers and wholesalers with retailers, facilitating bulk ordering, streamlining the supply chain and ensuring cost-effective transactions. Retailers can easily place large orders and negotiate deals directly with manufacturers, reducing intermediary costs and ensuring timely deliveries.

TechHub also runs a e-commerce store, where individual consumers can purchase a wide range of products such as electronics, home appliances, clothing and accessories. The site is designed for a seamless shopping experience, offering product customisation options, exclusive promotions and discounts. TechHub also values customer feedback, allowing users to review products and share their shopping experiences, which in turn helps improve product offerings and customer service.

The platform integrates secure payment gateways and offers a hassle-free return policy, which has contributed to its growing popularity. Over time, TechHub has expanded its operations and now collaborates with a diverse array of local and international vendors. The business has also taken steps to improve its technological infrastructure, allowing faster transactions and better inventory management. In line with market trends, TechHub has adopted innovative tools like artificial intelligence for personalised product recommendations, making the platform more attractive to both businesses and consumers.

TechHub's success is driven by its ability to cater to the needs of both businesses and individual customers while maintaining an efficient and user-friendly digital environment.

It has positioned itself as a powerful e-Business entity, poised for future growth.

(i) Identify and state the type of e-business mentioned in the case.

(ii) Explain any two other types of e-business not mentioned in the case.

Ans.

(i) The two types of e-business mentioned in the case are B2B and B2C commerce.

- **B2B Commerce**
  The transactions taking place between two business firms are known as B2B (Business-to-Business) transactions. A business interacts with a number of other business firms which may be suppliers or vendors of diverse inputs. They may also be a part of the channel through which a firm distributes its products to the customers. B2B transactions may include
  - Sharing of information
  - Creation of utilities
  - Collaborations
  - Commercial negotiations
  - Distribution of goods
- **B2C Commerce**
  The transactions taking place between business firms and customers are known as B2C (Business-to-Customers) transactions. This category is related to electronic retailing. This variant of e-business enables a business to be in contact with its customers on round-the-clock basis. B2C transactions may include
  - Selling and distribution of goods
  - Conducting customer surveys
  - After sales services
  - Promotional activities
  - Delivery of products

(ii) The two other types of e-business not mentioned in the case are as follows

- **Intra-B Commerce**
  The electronic transactions taking place within a given business firm only are known as intra-B transactions. It enables the smooth flow of transactions within the different departments of a specific firm. In intra-B commerce, the use of computer-based interaction among the different departments makes it possible for the firm to get the following advantages
  - Efficient inventory and cash management
  - Greater utilisation of plant and machinery
  - Effective handling of customers' orders
  - Effective human resource management, etc.
- **C2C Commerce**
  The transactions taking place between customers are known as C2C (Customer-to-Customer) transactions. These transactions originate from the customer and they end on the customer.
  This type of commerce is best suited for dealing in goods for which there is no established market mechanism such as selling used books, clothes, electronics on cash or barter basis.

Case Study 10

ABC Enterprises, a retail company, recently launched an online platform to complement its brick-and-mortar stores. Through their e-commerce website, customers can browse, compare and purchase products from the comfort of their homes. The company offers a wide range of products, including electronics, clothing, and home essentials. They also provide secure payment options, doorstep delivery, and a flexible return policy.

The new platform has significantly increased their sales and customer base, particularly in remote areas where physical stores are unavailable. Customers appreciate the convenience of 24×7 shopping and the ability to compare prices. Society has also benefitted, as the platform supports small sellers to reach wider markets.

(i) Define the term e-commerce.

(ii) State any four advantages of e-commerce to businesses organisations.

(iii) Mention any five advantages of e-commerce to society and customers.

Ans.

(i) e-Commerce refers to the buying and selling of goods and services over the internet, including activities such as online shopping, payment processing and digital delivery.

(ii) Following are the advantages of e-commerce to business oragnisations

- It expands the marketplace to national and international markets.
- It led to gradual decline in the cost of operations.
- It facilitates 'pull' supply chain management (just-in-time inventory management).
- It gives competitive advantage over competitors.

(iii) Following are the advantages of e-commerce to society and customers

- It provides flexibility.
- It provides competitive price/discounts.
- It provides more options, choices and customised products.
- It provides quick and timely delivery.
- It increases employment potential.

Case Study 11

Rajesh Kumar is the Managing Director of 'TechLink Solutions', a start-up specialising in online education platforms. The company offers a wide range of courses, including programming, design and management, catering to learners from different age groups. Rajesh was quick to recognise the potential of digital business and ensured that TechLink Solutions operated entirely online, eliminating the need for physical premises or extensive paperwork.

With the company's efficient e-business model, learners could instantly access course materials and resources from anywhere in the world at the click of a button. This speedy delivery made TechLink Solutions a preferred choice for students who valued convenience.

Additionally, the company allowed learners to enroll in courses offered by renowned international instructors, expanding its global reach.

TechLink Solutions also took significant steps toward a paperless society by encouraging students to submit assignments and receive certifications electronically. The regulatory authorities supported this move by enabling online filing of documents and approvals, ensuring seamless operations.

Quoting lines from the above paragraph, identify and explain three benefits of e-business discussed in the case.

Ans. Following are the benefits of e-business discussed in the case

(i) **Speed**

"Learners could instantly access course materials and resources from anywhere in the world at the click of a button."

Internet is one of the most speedy modes of doing business. One can avail anything, anytime, anywhere at the click of a mouse. Information-intensive products such as softwares, movies, music, e-books and e-journals that can also be delivered online, make it more attractive.

(ii) **Global Reach**

"The company allowed learners to enroll in courses offered by renowned international instructors, expanding its global reach."

Internet has a wide reach. On one hand, it allows the seller an access to the global market while on the other hand, it offers freedom to the buyer to choose products from almost any part of the world.

(iii) **Movement Toward a Paperless Society**

"TechLink Solutions encouraged students to submit assignments and receive certifications electronically."

Use of internet has reduced the dependence on paper-work. In order to expand this trend, the government departments and regulatory authorities are allowing electronic filing of returns and reports by the business firms and speeding up the process of granting permissions, approvals and licences. In this respect, the provisions of Information Technology Act, 2000 are significant.

Case Study 12

Sneha Verma was the founder of GreenBuy, an online store specialising in sustainable and eco-friendly products. The store gained popularity for its unique range and convenient shopping experience. However, Sneha faced several challenges in managing the operations of GreenBuy effectively. While the website allowed instant order placements, many customers complained that the delivery of their orders was delayed compared to expectations. Some buyers expressed frustration over this delay as they had anticipated faster delivery based on the platform's promises.

Additionally, Sneha realised that some customers were unable to navigate the website properly or complete their purchases because they lacked the technical knowledge required for online shopping. GreenBuy received several e-mails and calls from users who found the process of ordering online overwhelming.

Moreover, despite taking precautions, GreenBuy experienced incidents of online fraud and hacking. One customer reported that their personal details were misused after shopping on the website. These issues not only affected GreenBuy's reputation but also made Sneha reconsider the risks associated with operating an e-Business platform.

Quoting lines from the above paragraph, identify and explain three limitations of e-business.

Ans. Following are the limitations of e-business

(i) **Incongruence between Order Taking and Fulfillment Speed**

"While the website allowed instant order placements, many customers complained that the delivery of their orders was delayed compared to expectations."

Information can be exchanged quickly in e-business but the physical delivery of the product takes time. This incompatibility may negatively effect the patience of the customers. Sometimes, due to technical reasons, websites take unusually long time to open. This may further frustrate the user.

(ii) **Need for Technology Capability and Competence**

"Some customers were unable to navigate the website properly or complete their purchases because they lacked the technical knowledge required for online shopping."

Apart from the traditional 3R's (Reading, Writing and Arithmetic), both the parties in e-business requires to be familiar with computer or have computer knowledge. This requirement is responsible for digital divide, i.e. the division of society on the basis of familiarity and non-familiarity with digital technology.

(iii) **Increased Risk Due to Anonymity and Non-traceability**

"Despite taking precautions, GreenBuy experienced incidents of online fraud and hacking."

Internet transactions are risky because they occur between cyber personalities. So, it becomes difficult to establish the identity of the two involved parties. Moreover, one does not know even the location from where the parties may be operating. e-Business can also results in hazards of impersonation and leakage of confidential information and other problems such as hacking, virus, etc.

SELF ASSESSMENT TEST

Objective Type Questions

1. e-Business is defined as the conduct of industry, trade and commerce using the
   (a) internet (b) social network
   (c) society (d) All of these
2. Physical presence is required in .... business.
   (a) e-business (b) traditional business
   (c) Both (a) and (b) (d) None of these
3. .... is a pre-requisite for implementation of e-business.
   (a) Website (b) Virtual private network
   (c) Antivirus (d) Payment mechanism
4. The withdrawal of money from ATM is an example of
   (a) C2C commerce (b) B2B commerce
   (c) Intra-B commerce (d) B2C commerce
5. Rajeshwari found that there are some books which are of no use for her. She tries to sell them on one of the website. It is an example of
   (a) B2C commerce
   (b) C2C commerce
   (c) Intra-B commerce
   (d) B2B commerce
6. Which of the following is a key advantage of e-business?
   (a) High investment and complex formation
   (b) Ease of formation and lower investment requirements
   (c) Limited market reach
   (d) Requires a large physical storefront
7. M/S Sharma is engaged in the preparation and publications of online advertisements through banners and pop-ups, etc. These services are an example of
   (a) e-delivery (b) e-bidding
   (c) e-promotion
   (d) e-procurement
8. Which one of the following is a factor which gives advantage to e-business over traditional business?
   (a) Transaction risks
   (b) Investment requirement
   (c) Ethical fallouts
   (d) Personal touch with customers

Answers 1. (a) 2. (b) 3. (a) 4. (d) 5. (b) 6. (b) 7. (c) 8. (b)

Short Answer Type Questions

9. Are e-business and e-commerce identical concepts? Discuss their differences with examples.
10. An online retailer allows customers to purchase products directly from their website, offering convenient payment options and home delivery services. This B2C business model enables seamless transactions between the company and individual customers. Discuss the salient aspects of B2C commerce.
11. TechKart implemented e-Business strategies to expand its customer base, streamline operations and improve sales. State any three benefits of e-business that can be enjoyed by TechKart.
12. "With the rise of online platforms, businesses are increasingly relying on digital methods to conduct transactions, interact with customers and manage operations. This trend has led to various innovative applications that cater to different aspects of business functioning." In the light of the given statement, describe any three applications of e-business.
13. "The growing digital landscape has transformed the way businesses operate, allowing them to reach global markets, enhance customer interactions and streamline operations."

    In the context of the statement, state any four differences between e-business and traditional business.

Long Answer Type Questions

14. "e-Business has a wider scope." In the light of the given statement, elaborate the scope of e-business with the help of examples.
15. Explain the benefits of e-commerce to business organisation and consumers.
16. "While e-business offers flexibility and a wide reach, it also presents challenges such as data security concerns, technological issues and the lack of personal interaction. These factors may impact the overall customer experience and operational efficiency." Explain the drawbacks of e-business.

06

CHAPTER

> Social responsibility refers to the businessman's decisions and actions taken for reasons at least partially beyond the firm's direct economic or technical interest.
>
> — *Keith Davis*

▼ YOUR STUDY GOALS

- 6.1 Concept of Social Responsibility
- 6.2 Social Responsibility towards Different Interest Groups
- 6.3 Business and Environmental Protection
- 6.4 Business Ethics

▼ YOUR PRACTICE GOAL

- Objective Type Questions (62 Qs ; MCQs, A-R, Statements, Matching)
- Subjective Questions (12 SAs, 6 LAs)
- Case Study Based Questions (Short Case Studies-8, Long Case Studies-4)
- Self Assessment Test (8 MCQs, 7 SAs, 3 LAs)

Social Responsibility of Business and Business Ethics

A business has some obligations towards society and has to respect its norms and values while fulfilling the profit earning motive.

Socially desirable practices include supply of goods and services, providing goods and services at fair price, creating healthy and better working conditions, installing devices to control pollution, etc.

Socially undesirable practices that should be avoided include production and sale of bad quality products and services, polluting the environment, unfair trade practices, fraudulent practices, etc.

Thus, the success of business depend upon its socially responsible and ethically upright behaviour.

6.1 Concept of Social Responsibility

Social responsibility refers to the obligation of business to take those decisions which are desirable for the various groups in the society.

Social responsibility is a much wider concept than legal responsibility. Legal responsibility can be fulfilled by a mere compliance with law whereas social responsibility is an obligation (covered or not covered by law) on business enterprises to work for the welfare of society.

In other words, social responsibility involves element of voluntary action on the part of business for the benefit of society.

***Corporate Social Responsibility** (CSR)*

CSR refers to the responsibilities and duties of the corporates towards the society. It includes contribution towards economic, social and environmental development that creates positive impact on society at large.

The CSR, in India, is governed by Clause 135 of the Companies Act, 2013. It applies to the companies which have either of the following

- annual turnover of ₹ 1,000 crore and more
- a net worth of ₹ 500 crore and more
- a net profit of ₹ 5 crore and more

Need for Social Responsibility

- It is required to serve the interest of certain sections of society such as customers, employees, suppliers, community, etc.
- It gives the moral understanding to an entrepreneur, as to what is right and what is wrong.
- It also helps in addressing legal, ethical and commercial issues.

Case of Social Responsibility

People have different views about whether a business should care only for its owners or also take responsibility for the society it impacts. Thus, there are arguments both in favour of and against the social responsibility.

Arguments for Social Responsibility

Favourable Point	Explanation
Justification for Existence and Growth	Business exists to provide goods and services to satisfy human needs. Profit making is an important objective of business activity but it should be considered as an outcome of the service to the people.
Long-term Interest of the Firm	A business will be able to survive in the long-run only if the members of society including workers, consumers, shareholders, government officials, etc. feel that business enterprise is serving for their best interest.
Avoidance of Government Regulation	Government regulations are undesirable from the business point of view because they limit their freedom. By assuming social responsibility voluntarily, government regulations can be avoided.
Maintenance of Society	It is desirable that business enterprises should assume social responsibilities, otherwise people who are not getting their due from the business may resort to anti-social activities.
Availability of Resources with Business	Business institutions have valuable financial and human resources. e.g. Managerial talent and capital resources. The business should use these resources for producing socially desirable and good quality products.
Converting Problems into Opportunities	Business can convert problems into profitable deals by being socially responsible. e.g. Problem of electricity supply led to invention of generators and inverters.
Better Environment for Doing Business	A society with fewer problems provides better environment for a firm to conduct its business. So, in order to ensure proper environment for growth and sustenance, a business should be responsible towards the society.
Holding Business Responsible for Social Problems	Environmental pollution, unsafe workplaces, corruption in public institutions and discriminatory practices in employment are some of the problems which are created by business enterprises. Social responsibility helps a business in recognising these problems and get involved in solving these problems.

Arguments against Social Responsibility

Unfavourable Point	Explanation
Violation of Profit Maximisation Objective	Business exists only for profit maximisation. Involvement of business in social activities may shift its focus from economic productivity and reduce the profits of the organisation. It can fulfill its social responsibility by maximising its profits through increased efficiency and reduced costs.
Burden on Consumers	Businessmen are likely to simply shift their burden of social responsibilities like pollution control and environmental protection, by charging higher prices from the consumers instead of bearing it themselves. It is unfair to shift the burden to the consumers in the name of social responsibility.
Lack of Social Skills	A businessman does not have the necessary understanding and training to solve certain social problems. Therefore, social problems should be solved by other specialised agencies.
Lack of Broad Public Support	Generally, the public does not like business involvement or interference in social programmes. Therefore, business cannot participate successfully in solving social problems due to lack of public confidence and cooperation.

Kinds of Social Responsibility

- **Economic Responsibility** Basically, a business enterprise is an economic entity. Its primary social responsibility is economic, i.e. to produce goods and services that society wants and sell them at a profit.
- **Legal Responsibility** A law abiding enterprise is a socially responsible enterprise. Therefore, every business has a responsibility to operate within the laws of the society.
- **Ethical Responsibility** This includes the behaviour of the firm that is expected by society. It is not included in law so it is not compulsory for business to assume this responsibility.
- **Discretionary Responsibility** It signifies a voluntary obligation that an enterprise assumes. e.g. Providing charitable contribution to educational institutions.

6.2 Social Responsibility towards Different Interest Groups

A business is socially responsible towards a diverse group of people. Some of the specific responsibilities of enterprises towards specific groups are as follows

Responsibility towards the Shareholders (Investors) or Owners

- To provide a fair return to the shareholders or owners on their capital investment.
- To ensure the safety of their investment.
- To provide accurate updates and information about its working and schemes of future growth.

Shareholders

Responsibility towards the Workers

- To provide opportunities to the workers for meaningful work.
- Try to give right kind of working conditions.
- To respect the democratic rights of the workers to form unions.
- To ensure the worker a fair wage and a fair deal.

Responsibility towards the Consumers

- To supply the right quality and quantity of goods and services to consumers at reasonable prices.
- To take proper precaution against unfair trade practices like adulteration, poor quality, misleading and dishonest advertisement, etc.
- To provide information about the product, the company and other matters related to the consumer.

Responsibility towards the Government and Community

- To ensure timely and honest payment of taxes.
- To work according to various rules and regulations laid down by the government.
- To ensure that environment is not polluted.
- To act according to the well-accepted values of the society.
- To develop a proper image in society through continuous interaction with various groups of people.

6.3 Business and Environmental Protection

The environment is defined as the entire surroundings of men, both natural and man-made. The environment quality is deteriorating rapidly particularly due to industrial activities. Thus, it is reasonable to link environment protection with business.

The protection of the environment is directly related to the control of pollution.

Causes of Pollution

The introduction of harmful substances into environment is referred to as pollution. Business activities such as production, distribution, storage and consumption of goods and services are most critical source of environmental pollution.

Business enterprises are responsible for causing four types of pollution, which are as follows

Type	Explanation
Air Pollution	It is caused by the usage of chemicals in industries, factories and plants or by the emission of carbon monoxide by vehicles. These emissions degrade the quality of air and create a hole in the ozone layer which results in global warming. It led to warming of the Earth and is dangerous for all living beings.
Water Pollution	It is mostly caused by the dumping of chemical wastes into big rivers, streams, lakes, etc. by business enterprises. It has led to the death of several aquatic animals and posed a threat to human life.
Land Pollution	It is caused by dumping of toxic wastes on land. This damages the quality of land and makes it unfit for agriculture or plantation.
Noise Pollution	It is caused by the noise produced during running of factories and vehicles. Continuous exposure to noise is not only annoying, but also causes serious health problems such as loss of hearing, mental disorder, etc.

Environmental Problems

The United Nations has identified eight problems that cause damage to the natural environment. These are

- Ozone depletion
- Global warming
- Solid and hazardous wastes
- Water pollution
- Fresh water quality and quantity
- Deforestation
- Land degradation
- Danger to biological diversity

Need for Pollution Control

Pollution control means the control of emissions and effluents into air, water or soil.

Following are the specific reasons which make pollution control necessary

Need for Pollution Control

- Reduction of Health Hazards
- Reduced Risk of Liability
- Cost Savings
- Improved Public Image
- Other Social Benefits

Reason	Explanation
Reduction of Health Hazards	Diseases such as cancer, heart attacks and lung complications are caused by pollutants in the environment. In respect to this, pollution control measures should be adopted to check the spread of such diseases.
Reduced Risk of Liability	Factories emit toxic gases, liquid and solid wastes into the environment. This poses a risk of penalties and fines on enterprises. Therefore, every business enterprise should install pollution control devices in its premises to reduce pollution and avoid penalties.
Cost Savings	Improper production technology results in greater wastes. It leads to higher cost of waste disposal and cleaning the plants. An effective pollution control programme helps in reducing the costs of operating business.
Improved Public Image	Society has become conscious of environmental quality. In this respect, a firm should try to control the pollution to improve its public image.
Other Social Benefits	If the pollution is controlled, this will help in gaining other benefits like clean rivers, better quality of life, smoke free air, clearer visibility, cleaner buildings and availability of natural products in much purer form.

Role of Business in Environmental Protection

It is the social responsibility of every business to take steps to check pollution and to protect environmental resources. Business enterprises have all the resources and knowledge to solve environmental problems at the source.

Business should take the following steps to protect the environment

- Top management of the enterprise should be committed to create, maintain and develop work culture for environmental protection and pollution prevention. This commitment should be shared throughout the enterprise by all divisions and employees.
- The management of the enterprise should develop policies to purchase good quality raw materials, employing superior technology, using scientific techniques of disposal and treatment of wastes, developing employee skills, etc. to control pollution.
- It should respect the laws and regulations that are enacted by the government for prevention of pollution.
- It should participate in government programmes that are related to management of hazardous substances, cleaning of rivers, plantation of trees and checking deforestation.
- It should conduct periodical assessment of pollution control programmes in terms of costs and benefits, in order to increase the progress with respect to environmental protection.
- It should arrange for educational workshops and training materials to share technical information and experience with suppliers, dealers and customers, to get them actively involved in pollution control programmes.

6.4 Business Ethics

Ethics is concerned with what is right and what is wrong. It establishes linkage between individual good and social good. It is a set of principles that may be written or unwritten, governing a professional or human activity.

Business ethics refer to the socially determined moral principles which should govern business activities. It gives the standard which managerial executives follow for practices and give equal and fair treatment to the employees, stakeholders, agents, customers, etc.

Some examples of business ethics are

- Charging fair prices from customers.
- Using fair weights for measurement of commodities.
- Giving fair treatment to workers.
- Earning reasonable profits.

Ethics vs Law

Ethical standards are frequently incorporated into laws, yet ethical behaviour surpasses the requirements of legal compliance. Unlike laws, ethics are not mandatory but serve as general principles outlining actions to avoid and practices to refrain from. Since adhering to ethics is voluntary, they are not punishable under law (except some unethical aspects like black marketing, adulteration, etc).

Elements of Business Ethics

Some of the basic elements of business ethics while running a business are

Element	Explanation
Top Management Commitment	Business ethics can be followed by a business only if its top level management is openly and strongly committed towards the ethical conduct. It must give continuous leadership for developing and upholding the values of the organisation.
Publication of a Code	Enterprises with effective ethics programmes define the 'principles of conduct' or the 'code of conduct' for the whole organisation in the form of a written document, which is known as **code**. The code may cover subjects like fundamental honesty and adherence to laws, product safety and quality, health and safety in the workplace, conflicts of interests, employment practices, fair dealing in selling/marketing practices and financial reporting.
Establishment of Compliance Mechanisms	Suitable mechanisms should be established by the business enterprise to ensure that the actual decisions and actions comply with the firm's ethical standards. e.g. – Paying attention to values and ethics in recruiting and hiring. – Emphasising corporate ethics in training. – Auditing performance regularly to analyse the degree of compliance. – Instituting communication systems to help employees report incidents of unethical behaviour, etc.
Involving Employees at all Levels	The involvement of employees in ethical programmes is necessary as they are responsible at different levels to implement ethical policies, to make a business ethical. e.g. Small groups of employees can be formed to discuss the vital ethical policies of firms and examine attitude of employees towards these policies.
Measuring Results	It is difficult to accurately measure the end results of ethics programmes, but the firms can do this by auditing or monitoring the compliance with ethical standards.

Mind Map

SOCIAL RESPONSIBILITY OF BUSINESS AND BUSINESS ETHICS

1 Concept of Social Responsibility

Social responsibility refers to the obligation of business to take those decisions which are desirable for the various groups in the society. It involves element of voluntary action on the part of business for the benefit of society.

Arguments for Social Responsibility
- Justification for existence and growth
- Long-term interest of the firm
- Avoidance of government regulation
- Maintenance of society
- Availability of resources with business
- Converting problems into opportunities
- Better environment for doing business
- Holding business responsible for social problems

2 Case of Social Responsibility

There are arguments both in favour of and against the social responsibility.

Arguments against Social Responsibility
- Violation of profit maximisation objective
- Burden on consumers
- Lack of social skills
- Lack of broad public support

3 Social Responsibility towards Different Interest Groups

Responsibility towards the Shareholders or Owners
- To provide a fair return to the shareholders or owners on their capital investment
- To ensure the safety of their investment
- To provide accurate updates and information about its working and schemes of future growth

Responsibility towards the Workers
- To provide opportunities to the workers for meaningful work
- Try to give right kind of working conditions
- To respect the democratic rights of the workers to form unions
- To ensure the worker a fair wage and a fair deal

Responsibility towards the Consumers
- To supply the right quality and quantity of goods and services to consumers at reasonable prices
- To take proper precaution against unfair trade practices
- To provide information about the product, the company and other matters related to the consumer

Responsibility towards the Government and Community
- To ensure timely and honest payment of taxes
- To work according to various rules and regulations laid down by the government
- To ensure that environment is not polluted
- To act according to the well-accepted values of the society
- To develop a proper image in society through continuous interaction with various groups of people

5 Business Ethics

Business ethics refer to the socially determined moral principles which should govern business activities. It gives the standard which managerial executives follow for practices and give equal and fair treatment to the employees, stakeholders, agents, customers, etc.

Elements of Business Ethics
- **Top Management Commitment** Business ethics can be followed by a business only if its top level management is openly and strongly committed towards the ethical conduct.
- **Publication of a Code** Enterprises with effective ethics programmes define the 'principles of conduct' or the 'code of conduct' for the whole organisation in the form of a written document known as code.
- **Establishment of Compliance Mechanisms** Suitable mechanisms should be established by the business enterprise to ensure that the actual decisions and actions comply with the firm's ethical standards.
- **Involving Employees at all Levels** The involvement of employees in ethical programmes is necessary as they are responsible at different levels to implement ethical policies, to make a business ethical.
- **Measuring Results** The firms can measure results by auditing or monitoring the compliance with ethical standards.

4 Business and Environmental Protection

The environment is defined as the entire surroundings of men, both natural and man-made. The protection of the environment is directly related to the control of pollution.

Need for Pollution Control
- It helps in reduction of health hazards
- It helps in reducing the risk of liability
- It helps in saving costs
- It helps in improving the public image and gaining other social benefits

Causes of Pollution
- **Air Pollution** It is caused by the usage of chemicals in industries, factories and plants or by the emission of carbon monoxide by vehicles.
- **Water Pollution** It is mostly caused by the dumping of chemical wastes into big rivers, streams, lakes, etc. by business enterprises.
- **Land Pollution** It is caused by dumping of toxic wastes on land.
- **Noise Pollution** It is caused by the noise produced during running of factories and vehicles.

Role of Business in Environmental Protection
- Top management of the enterprise should be committed to create, maintain and develop work culture for environmental protection and pollution prevention
- The management of the enterprise should develop policies to purchase good quality raw materials, employing-superior technology, etc
- It should respect the laws and regulations that are enacted by the government for prevention of pollution
- It should participate in government programmes that are related to management of hazardous substances
- It should conduct periodical assessment of pollution control programmes in terms of costs and benefits
- It should arrange for educational workshops and training materials to share technical information and experience with suppliers, dealers and customers

EXAM PATTERN QUESTIONS

Objective Type Questions

Multiple Choice Questions (MCQs)

1. To develop faith and trust in business by assuming various social responsibilities creates .... for the business.

(a) problems
(b) chaos
(c) cost (d) goodwill

2. A socially undesirable practice for a business enterprise is

(a) fair pricing of goods
(b) abiding by government regulations
(c) production and sale of substandard products
(d) developing a better environment for business growth

3. "Some businesses oppose CSR, arguing that involvement in social activities may reduce profits and shift the burden to consumers."

Which of the following is being described in this statement? Competency Based Que

(a) Arguments for social responsibility
(b) Reality of social responsibility
(c) Arguments against social responsibility
(d) Legal requirements of CSR

4. Laws cannot be passed for all possible circumstances. People who feel that they are not getting their due from the business may resort to anti-social activities, not necessarily governed by law. This may harm the interest of business itself. Therefore, business enterprises should assume social responsibilities.

Identify the argument in favour of social responsibility being discussed in the above statement. Competency Based Que

(a) Maintenance of society
(b) Better environment for doing business
(c) Avoidance of government regulation
(d) Availability of resources with business

5. "The primary objective of businesses should be to maximise profits and any involvement in social causes can distract from this goal."

Which argument against social responsibility is reflected in the statement? Competency Based Que

(a) Violation of profit maximisation objective
(b) Burden on consumers
(c) Lack of social skills
(d) Lack of broad public support

6. Identify the business concept illustrated in the below picture.

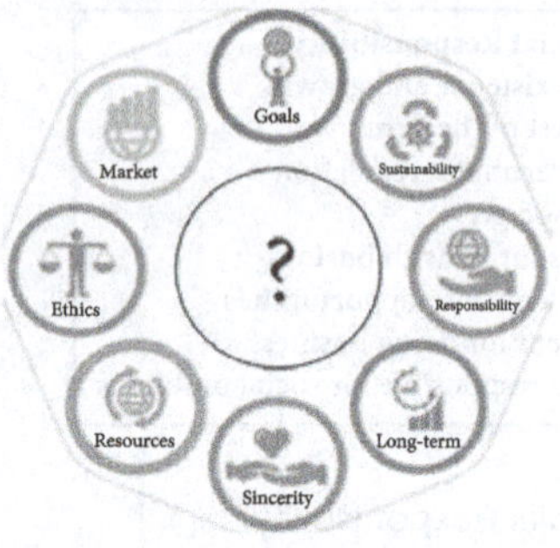

(a) Corporate social responsibility
(b) Corporate social ethics
(c) Corporate social values
(d) None of the above

7. This refers to purely voluntary obligation that an enterprise assumes, for instance, providing charitable contributions to educational institutions or helping the affected people during floods or earthquakes. Identify the kind of responsibility being discussed in the above statement. Competency Based Que

(a) Economic responsibility (b) Legal responsibility
(c) Discretionary responsibility (d) Ethnical responsibility

8. "This category of responsibility involves actions that are not required by law but are expected by society, such as respecting religious sentiments in advertisements."

Which type of responsibility is being referred to? Competency Based Que

(a) Legal responsibility
(b) Discretionary responsibility
(c) Ethical responsibility
(d) Economic responsibility

9. Greenline Industries, a leading manufacturing company, has been recognised for its efforts to reduce its carbon footprint by adopting eco-friendly practices such as recycling waste, using renewable energy and planting trees around its facilities. Although there are no legal obligations requiring the company to undertake these initiatives, it believes in contributing to environmental sustainability and societal welfare. The company also runs a scholarship programme for underprivileged students and provides financial support to local health clinics.

Which of the following concepts is being demonstrated by Greenline Industries in the given case? Competency Based Que

(a) Legal responsibility (b) Social responsibility
(c) Economic responsibility (d) Ethical responsibility

10. Which of the following statements is incorrect regarding the responsibilities of a business enterprise towards its shareholders or owners?

(a) To provide a fair return on their capital investment
(b) To ensure the safety of their investment
(c) To prioritise the interests of customers over shareholders
(d) To provide accurate updates and information about its working and future growth schemes

11. The given picture depicts the responsibility towards one of the groups. Identify the group

(a) Responsibility towards government
(b) Responsibility towards workers
(c) Responsibility towards customers
(d) Responsibility towards shareholders

12. A renowned manufacturing company, XYZ Ltd., ensures that its employees are provided with meaningful work opportunities and fair wages. The company actively creates a safe and conducive working environment, prioritising the well-being of its workers.
In addition, XYZ Ltd. respects the democratic rights of employees by allowing them to form unions and express their concerns freely. These practices have earned the company a reputation for being employee-friendly and socially responsible. Identify the interest group being prioritised by XYZ Ltd. in the given case. Competency Based Que

(a) Shareholders (b) Workers
(c) Consumers (d) Government

13. When business firms use eco-friendly methods of production, then they are performing social responsibilities towards which group?

(a) Customer (b) Employees
(c) Community (d) Shareholders

14. To protect and assist small-scale suppliers by placing orders with them is the responsibility of the business towards ....

(a) community (b) government
(c) employees (d) suppliers

15. Providing fair compensation and safe working conditions, is related to social responsibilities towards

(a) customer (b) employees
(c) community (d) shareholders

16. The given picture depicts the responsibility towards one of the groups. Identify the group.

(a) Responsibility towards government
(b) Responsibility towards workers
(c) Responsibility towards customers
(d) Responsibility towards shareholders

17. e-Choupal is an initiative on Indian Tobacco Corporation (ITC) Limited to link directly with rural farmers to procurement of agriculture produce. e-Choupal was conceived to tackle the challenge posed by the unique features on Indian agriculture characteristics by fragmented farms, weak infrastructures and the involvement of numerous intermediaries. Through e-Choupal, IKTC aims to change the quality of life and the entire outlook of Indian farmers. Towards which interest group, is ITC discharging its social responsibility? Competency Based Que

(a) Social responsibility towards customers
(b) Social responsibility towards community
(c) Social responsibility towards society
(d) Both (a) and (b)

18. XYZ Pvt. Ltd., a well-known manufacturer of household appliances, recently launched a new mixer grinder. The company ensured that the product met high quality standards and was available in different models at reasonable prices. It also provided detailed information about the product's features, warranty and usage instructions through brochures and advertisements. Additionally, the company promised to avoid any misleading advertisements and maintain transparency with consumers.
Which responsibility towards consumers is not being highlighted in the case? Competency Based Que

(a) Supplying the right quality and quantity at reasonable prices
(b) Avoiding unfair trade practices
(c) Providing information about the product
(d) Precautions against adulteration

19. **Manana Ltd. decided to donate 3% of its sales to 'Child Rights and You (CRY)' for improving the condition of children in India. This initiative by the company was highly appreciated by the public and their sales increased by 10%. Identify the interest group towards which Manana Ltd. is discharging its social responsibility?** **Competency Based Que**

(a) Shareholders (b) Customers
(c) Employees (d) Community and society

20. **Identify the type of pollution illustrated in the below picture.**

(a) Air pollution (b) Noise pollution
(c) Water pollution (d) Land pollution

21. **Identify the type of pollution illustrated in the below picture.**

(a) Water pollution (b) Land pollution
(c) Noise pollution (d) Air pollution

22. **Greenfield City has witnessed a significant rise in respiratory problems among its residents. The Air Quality Index (AQI) often shows alarming levels due to the increased usage of chemicals in factories and plants. Additionally, heavy vehicular traffic contributes to the emission of carbon monoxide, further worsening the situation.**

Scientists have observed that these emissions not only degrade air quality but also damage the ozone layer, leading to global warming. Rising temperatures have adversely affected the local ecosystem, causing harm to plants, animals and humans. Environmentalists are urging the government to take strict measures to combat this issue. The situation has raised concerns among citizens about their health and the planet's future. Identify the type of pollution discussed in the above case. **Competency Based Que**

(a) Water pollution (b) Air pollution
(c) Soil pollution (d) Noise pollution

23. **Automobiles emit carbon monoxide. This directly contributes to**

(a) water pollution (b) noise pollution
(c) land pollution (d) air pollution

24. **What is the primary purpose of installing pollution control devices in factories?**

(a) To increase production efficiency
(b) To reduce penalties and fines
(c) To increase profit margins
(d) To improve employee relations

25. **Which of the following is not a benefit of pollution control?**

(a) Improved public image
(b) Reduced health hazards
(c) Increased legal complications
(d) Cost savings

26. **Senith Enterprises operates in a heavily industrialised zone and emits toxic gases into the air. Recently, the company installed modern pollution control equipment and adopted superior waste disposal methods. These steps not only reduced emissions but also enhanced its reputation in the market.**

What specific benefit of pollution control is highlighted in the case? **Competency Based Que**

(a) Reduction of health hazards
(b) Improved public image
(c) Reduced risk of liability
(d) Cost savings

27. **Bhsuan Pvt. Ltd. faced penalties from regulatory authorities for not adhering to environmental laws. To address this, the company implemented an environment action plan, conducted training for employees and partnered with a government tree plantation initiative.**

Which step towards environmental protection is reflected in XYZ Pvt. Ltd.'s actions? **Competency Based Que**

(a) Developing employee skills
(b) Respecting laws and regulations
(c) Conducting periodic assessments
(d) Participating in government programmes

28. **DEF Corporation noticed high costs due to waste disposal issues caused by outdated production techniques. By switching to scientific waste treatment methods and superior technology, the company managed to cut costs and streamline its operations.**

Which reason for pollution control is primarily addressed by DEF Corporation's actions? **Competency Based Que**

(a) Reduced health hazards (b) Cost savings
(c) Improved public image (d) Reduced risk of liability

29. Which of the following statement(s) is/are not true?
(a) Pollution causes danger to biological diversity
(b) Controlling pollution can result in reduction of health hazards
(c) Dumping of toxic waste on land leads to air pollution
(d) None of the above

30. Use of synthetic fertilisers and pesticides in agriculture leads to
(a) water pollution (b) noise pollution
(c) land pollution (d) air pollution

31. .... has resulted in ozone depletion, which is leading to climate change and dangerous warming of the earth.
(a) Noise pollution (b) Land pollution
(c) Water pollution (d) Air pollution

32. GreenWay Ltd., a company producing eco-friendly products, aims to ensure its business activities are ethically sound. The CEO of the company, Mr. Arun, emphasises ethical conduct in all operations, from product safety to marketing practices. The company has published a detailed code of conduct that outlines principles such as fair dealing, employee health and adherence to laws.

To ensure compliance, the HR department integrates ethical considerations into recruitment and provides ethics training for employees. Additionally, regular audits are conducted to monitor adherence to ethical standards and employees are encouraged to report any unethical behaviour through a dedicated communication system. Small teams are formed at different levels to review policies and foster a culture of ethics across the organisation.
Which element of business ethics is GreenWay Ltd. focusing on by publishing a detailed code of conduct?
Competency Based Que
(a) Top management commitment
(b) Publication of a code
(c) Involvement of employees at all levels
(d) Measuring results

33. Which of the following statements is incorrect regarding the elements of business ethics?
(a) Top management commitment is crucial for upholding the ethical conduct in a business
(b) A code of conduct is essential for defining the principles of ethical behaviour in the organisation
(c) Employees are not involved in the process of ethical decision-making in the organisation
(d) Compliance mechanisms should be established to ensure that business decisions align with ethical standards

Direction *Read the case study and answer the questions 34 to 37 on the basis of the same*

EcoTech Industries, a leading manufacturing company in India, had been facing increasing pressure from environmental organisations and consumers due to the high level of pollution caused by its production processes. The company was producing electronic components and generating large amounts of toxic waste, contributing to air and water pollution in nearby areas. This situation started affecting the public perception of EcoTech and its market share began to decrease.

In response, the management decided to implement a comprehensive pollution control programme. They installed modern pollution control devices, improved waste management processes and adopted cleaner production technologies. The company also initiated a community outreach programme, engaging with local residents and environmental groups to promote awareness about its efforts.

Over time, EcoTech's public image improved and it was able to mitigate the risk of penalties, all while reducing operational costs and ensuring a cleaner environment.

34. What was the main reason, EcoTech Industries faced increased pressure from the public?
(a) Poor product quality
(b) High pollution levels
(c) Low production capacity
(d) Employee disputes

35. What action did EcoTech take to address the pollution issue?
(a) Ignored the problem
(b) Implemented a pollution control programme
(c) Reduced production
(d) Outsourced production to another country

36. What is one of the benefits EcoTech experienced after implementing pollution control measures?
(a) Increased fines and penalties
(b) Improved public image
(c) Higher production costs
(d) Lower product demand

37. How did EcoTech engage with the community to improve its public image?
(a) By providing financial donations to environmental organisations
(b) By initiating a community outreach programme
(c) By reducing its product prices
(d) By increasing its advertising budget

Assertion-Reason

Direction (Q. No. 38 to 47) *Read the following Assertion (A) and Reason (R) and choose the correct alternative from the following*

Alternatives

(a) Both Assertion (A) and Reason (R) are true and Reason (R) is the correct explanation of Assertion (A)
(b) Both Assertion (A) and Reason (R) are true, but Reason (R) is not the correct explanation of Assertion (A)
(c) Assertion (A) is true, but Reason (R) is false
(d) Assertion (A) is false, but Reason (R) is true

38. **Assertion** (A) A business exists primarily to make a profit, but it should consider social responsibility as part of its operations.

Reason (R) A business will only survive in the long-run if it serves the best interests of society, including workers, consumers and the government.

39. **Assertion** (A) Socially desirable practices include providing goods and services at fair prices, ensuring healthy working conditions and installing devices to control pollution.

Reason (R) Socially desirable practices enable businesses to align their operations with societal expectations, contributing to both social welfare and environmental sustainability.

40. **Assertion** (A) The development of professional managerial education has enhanced businesses' focus on social responsibility.

Reason (R) Professional managers are more likely to prioritise profit maximisation over social goals.

41. **Assertion** (A) Businesses must respect ethical responsibilities, such as the dignity of people in advertisements, to meet societal expectations.

Reason (R) Ethical responsibilities are legally binding and must be followed by businesses.

42. **Assertion** (A) Employee involvement in developing ethical programmes helps create a strong ethical culture.

Reason (R) When employees are part of the decision-making process, they are more likely to adhere to ethical standards.

43. **Assertion** (A) Business enterprises have tremendous social power because of huge resources in hand.

Reason (R) Business enterprises should supply right quality and quantity of goods and services at reasonable prices.

44. **Assertion** (A) Legal responsibility has a broader scope than social responsibility.

Reason (R) Legal responsibility may be fulfilled by mere compliance with law, while social responsibility involves voluntary efforts of business for the benefit of society.

45. **Assertion** (A) Pollution control measures are crucial for the survival of a business in the long-run.

Reason (R) Businesses that ignore environmental protection may face health hazards, penalties and loss of public trust.

46. **Assertion** (A) Businesses should install pollution control devices to comply with regulations.

Reason (R) The emission of toxic gases and wastes without control leads to penalties and fines.

47. **Assertion** (A) Ethics is not synonymous with religious morality or moral theology.

Reason (R) Ethics is the principle that guides the human behaviour.

Two Statements Based MCQs

Direction (Q. No. 48 to 57) *Read the following statements carefully and choose the correct alternative*

Alternatives

(a) Statement I is correct and Statement II is incorrect
(b) Statement II is correct and Statement I is incorrect
(c) Both the statements are correct
(d) Both the statements are incorrect

48. **Statement I** Corporate Social Responsibility (CSR) refers to a business's duty towards society, covering economic, social and environmental aspects.

Statement II According to Clause 135 of the Companies Act, 2013, CSR applies only to businesses with an annual turnover of ₹ 500 crore or more.

49. **Statement I** Social responsibility is only about complying with laws and regulations in society.

Statement II Social responsibility includes ethical behaviour, such as respecting the religious sentiments of people, even if not mandated by law.

50. **Statement I** Violation of the profit maximisation objective is a valid argument against social responsibility.

Statement II Social responsibility helps in converting problems into opportunities and creating a better environment for business growth.

51. **Statement I** A business that focuses only on maximising profits will be able to survive and grow in the long-run.

Statement II Businesses must consider the interests of society to ensure long-term survival and success.

52. **Statement I** Social responsibility of businesses should be limited to economic and legal aspects only.

Statement II Ethical responsibility includes behaving in a way that is expected by society, even if it is not legally required.

53. **Statement I** A business enterprise has the responsibility to provide a fair return on the capital investment of its shareholders or owners.

Statement II A business enterprise must ensure the safety of the investment made by its shareholders or owners.

54. **Statement I** Pollution control measures are necessary to improve public health by reducing diseases caused by environmental pollutants.

Statement II Pollution control only helps businesses to avoid penalties and fines and does not provide any other long-term benefits.

55. **Statement I** A business enterprise has a responsibility to ensure environmental protection, including adopting pollution control measures.

Statement II Government regulations and laws regarding pollution control are unnecessary since businesses voluntarily address environmental issues.

56. **Statement I** Top management should be committed to creating and maintaining a work culture focused on environmental protection and pollution prevention, which should be shared throughout the enterprise.

Statement II The management should develop policies for purchasing good quality raw materials, employing superior technology, and using scientific techniques for waste disposal and treatment to control pollution.

57. **Statement I** Business should adopt eco-friendly production and marketing processes to ensure environmental protection.

Statement II Expenditure on social cause is a drain on business resources.

Matching

58. Match the following

Column I	Column II
A. Business existence and growth	(i) Business survives in the long-run when it serves the best interests of society members.
B. Long-term interest of the firm	(ii) Business should assume social responsibility to avoid restrictions imposed by government regulations.
C. Avoidance of government regulation	(iii) Business can turn challenges like electricity shortages into profitable solutions, like generating electricity through inverters.
D. Converting problems into opportunities	(iv) Business exists to meet human needs and makes profits as a result of serving society.

Codes

	A	B	C	D		A	B	C	D
(a)	(ii)	(i)	(iv)	(iii)	(b)	(iii)	(iv)	(i)	(ii)
(c)	(i)	(iii)	(ii)	(iv)	(d)	(iv)	(i)	(ii)	(iii)

59. Match the following

Column I	Column II
A. Violation of profit maximisation objective	(i) Business may lose focus on profitability, as social activities can reduce efficiency and profits.
B. Burden on consumers	(ii) Business may pass on the cost of social responsibilities, such as pollution control, to consumers through higher prices.
C. Lack of social skills	(iii) Businessmen may not have the required expertise to solve complex social problems, which should be handled by specialised agencies.
D. Lack of broad public support	(iv) Public skepticism and lack of trust in businesses' involvement in social issues can prevent successful participation in social programmes.

Codes

	A	B	C	D		A	B	C	D
(a)	(ii)	(i)	(iv)	(iii)	(b)	(iii)	(iv)	(i)	(ii)
(c)	(i)	(ii)	(iii)	(iv)	(d)	(iv)	(iii)	(ii)	(i)

60. Match the following

Column I	Column II
A. Payment of taxes on time	(i) Responsibility towards shareholders
B. Provide the right quality and quantity of goods	(ii) Responsibility towards workers
C. Provide right kind of working conditions	(iii) Responsibility towards customers
D. Provide fair return to the shareholders	(iv) Responsibility towards government

Codes

	A	B	C	D
(a)	(ii)	(i)	(iv)	(iii)
(b)	(iii)	(iv)	(i)	(ii)
(c)	(i)	(iii)	(ii)	(iv)
(d)	(iv)	(iii)	(ii)	(i)

61. Match the following

Column I	Column II
A. Release of carbon monoxide	(i) Land pollution
B. Sewage disposal in rivers	(ii) Noise pollution
C. Use of loud machines	(iii) Water pollution
D. Dumping of toxic waste	(iv) Air pollution

Codes

	A	B	C	D
(a)	(ii)	(i)	(iv)	(iii)
(b)	(iii)	(iv)	(i)	(ii)
(c)	(i)	(iii)	(ii)	(iv)
(d)	(iv)	(iii)	(ii)	(i)

62. Match the following

Column I	Column II
A. Social responsibility	(i) What is right what is wrong, is judged on basis of socially determined standards of human behaviour.
B. Environment	(ii) Business enterprises should take some steps like top management commitment, periodical assessment of pollution control programmes, etc.
C. Business ethics	(iii) It is the obligation to take decisions and perform actions which are desirable in terms of objective and value of our society.

Codes

	A	B	C
(a)	(ii)	(i)	(iii)
(b)	(iii)	(i)	(ii)
(c)	(i)	(iii)	(ii)
(d)	(iii)	(ii)	(i)

Answers

1. (d) goodwill
2. (c) production and sale of substandard products
3. (c) Arguments against social responsibility
4. (a) Maintenance of society
5. (a) Violation of profit maximisation objective
6. (a) Corporate social responsibility
7. (c) Discretionary responsibility
8. (c) Ethical responsibility
9. (b) Social responsibility
10. (c) The primary responsibility towards shareholders is to ensure fair returns, safety of investment and transparency, while customer interests are handled as a separate responsibility.
11. (c) Responsibility towards customers
12. (b) Workers **13.** (c) Community
14. (d) suppliers **15.** (b) employees
16. (b) Responsibility towards workers
17. (b) Social responsibility towards community
18. (d) Precautions against adulteration
19. (d) Community and society
20. (b) Noise pollution **21.** (a) Water pollution
22. (b) Air pollution **23.** (d) Air pollution
24. (b) To reduce penalties and fines
25. (c) Increased legal complications
26. (b) Improved public image
27. (d) Participating in government programmes
28. (b) Cost savings
29. (c) Dumping of toxic waste on land leads to land pollution.
30. (c) land pollution **31.** (d) Air pollution
32. (b) Publication of a code
33. (c) Employees at all levels should be involved in ethical programmes to ensure the effective implementation of ethical policies and standards.
34. (b) High pollution levels
35. (b) Implemented a pollution control programme
36. (b) Improved public image
37. (b) By initiating a community outreach programme
38. (a) Both Assertion (A) and Reason (R) are true and Reason (R) is the correct explanation of Assertion (A)
39. (a) Both Assertion (A) and Reason (R) are true and Reason (R) is the correct explanation of Assertion (A)
40. (c) Professional managers are now more likely to address both social and profit related goals due to modern management education.
41. (c) Ethical responsibilities are expected by society but not enforceable by law.
42. (a) Both Assertion (A) and Reason (R) are true and Reason (R) is the correct explanation of Assertion (A)

43. (b) Both Assertion (A) and Reason (R) are true, but Reason (R) is not the correct explanation of Assertion (A)
44. (d) Legal responsibility is more limited in scope than social responsibility. Legal responsibilities are obligations that businesses must follow according to laws and regulations, whereas social responsibility goes beyond legal obligations and includes voluntary efforts for the welfare of society, like environmental sustainability, philanthropy and ethical practices.
45. (a) Both Assertion (A) and Reason (R) are true and Reason (R) is the correct explanation of Assertion (A)
46. (a) Both Assertion (A) and Reason (R) are true and Reason (R) is the correct explanation of Assertion (A)
47. (b) Both Assertion (A) and Reason (R) are true, but Reason (R) is not the correct explanation of Assertion (A)
48. (a) CSR applies to companies with an annual turnover of ₹ 1,000 crore or more a net worth of ₹ 500 crore or more, or a net profit of ₹ 5 crore or more.
49. (b) Social responsibility also includes ethical responsibility, which goes beyond legal compliance.
50. (b) While profit maximisation is important, social responsibility can also create opportunities and improve the business environment.
51. (b) A business must serve societal interests to ensure long-term growth and survival.
52. (b) Social responsibility includes ethical and discretionary responsibilities, not just economic and legal.
53. (c) Both the statements are correct
54. (a) Pollution control offers other benefits, such as cost savings and improved public image.
55. (a) Government regulations and laws exist to enforce pollution control if businesses fail to take action voluntarily.
56. (c) Both the statements are correct
57. (a) Expenditures can lead to long-term benefits like enhanced brand image, customer loyalty and a stronger market position. Many businesses find that contributing to social causes improves their overall profitability and sustainability.
58. (d) (iv) (i) (ii) (iii)
59. (c) (i) (ii) (iii) (iv)
60. (d) (iv) (iii) (ii) (i)
61. (d) (iv) (iii) (ii) (i)
62. (d) (iii) (ii) (i)

Subjective Questions

Short Answer Type Questions

1. State the need for social responsibility.

Ans. Social responsibility is needed because of the following reasons

(i) It is required to serve the interest of certain sections of society such as customers, employees, suppliers, community, etc.

(ii) It gives the moral understanding to an entrepreneur, as to what is right and what is wrong.

(iii) It also helps in addressing legal, ethical and commercial issues.

2. What do you understand by social responsibility of business? How is it different from legal responsibility? NCERT

Ans. Social responsibility refers to the obligation of business to take those decisions which are desirable for the various groups in the society. As per this concept, a businessman should not only consider his own interests, but he should keep in mind the interests of the society as a whole. Social responsibility of business implies that a business should respect the aspiration of society alongwith its profit interest.

Social responsibility is a much wider concept than legal responsibility. Legal responsibility can be fulfilled by a mere compliance with law whereas social responsibility is an obligation (covered or not covered by law) on business enterprises to work for the welfare of society. In other words, social responsibility involves element of voluntary action on the part of business for the benefit of society.

3. "Social responsibility in business is often seen as a means to contribute to societal well-being, but it also raises concerns about the allocation of resources and its potential distraction from business goals." In the context of the statement, present arguments against social responsibility of business. Competency Based Que

Ans. Following are the arguments against social responsibility

(i) **Violation of Profit Maximisation Objective**
Business exists only for profit maximisation. Involvement of business in social activities may shift its focus from economic productivity and reduce the profits of the organisation. It can fulfil its social responsibility by maximising its profits through increased efficiency and reduced costs.

(ii) **Burden on Consumers**
Businessmen are likely to simply shift their burden of social responsibilities like pollution control and environmental protection, by charging higher prices from the consumers instead of bearing it themselves. It is unfair to shift the burden to the consumers in the name of social responsibility.

(iii) **Lack of Social Skills**
A businessman does not have the necessary understanding and training to solve certain social problems. Therefore, social problems should be solved by other specialised agencies.

(iv) **Lack of Broad Public Support**
Generally, the public does not like business involvement or interference in social programmes. Therefore, business cannot participate successfully in solving social problems due to lack of public confidence and cooperation.

4. "Businesses today are expected to contribute positively to society, not just through profits but by addressing the needs of various stakeholders." In light of this statement, discuss the social responsibility of business towards the government and the community.
Competency Based Que

Ans. A business enterprise has the following responsibilities towards the government and community

(i) To ensure timely and honest payment of taxes.
(ii) To work according to various rules and regulations laid down by the government.
(iii) To ensure that environment is not polluted.
(iv) To act according to the well-accepted values of the society.
(v) To develop a proper image in society through continuous interaction with various groups of people.

5. "Businesses today have a significant impact on societal welfare, extending their focus beyond financial gains to address the needs and expectations of different stakeholders." In the context of this statement, discuss the social responsibility of businesses towards investors. **Competency Based Que**

Ans. Following are the social responsibilities of business towards investors

(i) To ensure reasonable dividends and capital appreciation.
(ii) To prevent insider trading and financial manipulation.
(iii) To facilitate investor involvement in key decisions.
(iv) To provide truthful and timely financial updates.
(v) To adopt measures for long-term stability and growth.

6. What is environment? What is environmental pollution? **NCERT**

Ans. The environment is defined as the totality of man's surroundings including both natural resources like land, water, air, fauna and flora, minerals, etc. and man-made resources such as cultural heritage, socio-economic institutions, etc.

Environmental pollution refers to the introduction of harmful substances into the environment which cause change in the physical, chemical and biological characteristics of air, land and water, that further harm the life of humans and other species.

7. Write short notes on
(i) Air pollution
(ii) Water pollution

Ans.
(i) **Air Pollution**
It is caused by the usage of chemicals in industries, factories and plants or by the emission of carbon monoxide by vehicles. These emissions degrade the quality of air and create a hole in the ozone layer which results in global warming. It led to warming of the earth and is dangerous for all living beings.

(ii) **Water Pollution**
It is mostly caused by the dumping of chemical wastes into big rivers, streams, lakes, etc. by business enterprises. It has led to the death of several aquatic animals and posed a threat to human life. It degrades the quality of water.

8. "Pollution control is necessary to save the environment." In the light of the given statement, give any four reasons why pollution control is necessary?
Competency Based Que

Or **Why do the enterprises need to adopt pollution control measures?** **NCERT**

Ans. Pollution control is necessary because of the following reasons

(i) **Reduction of Health Hazards**
Diseases such as cancer, heart attacks and lung complications are caused by pollutants in the environment. In respect to this, pollution control measures should be adopted to check the spread of such diseases.

(ii) **Reduced Risk of Liability**
Factories emit toxic gases, liquid and solid wastes into the environment. This poses a risk of penalties and fines on enterprises. Therefore, every business enterprise should install pollution control devices in its premises to reduce pollution and avoid penalties.

(iii) **Cost Savings**
Improper production technology results in greater wastes. It leads to higher cost of waste disposal and cleaning the plants. An effective pollution control programme helps in reducing the costs of operating business.

(iv) **Improved Public Image**
Society has become conscious of environmental quality. In this respect, a firm should try to control the pollution to improve its public image.

9. State any four steps that a business should take to protect the environment.

Or **What steps can an enterprise take to protect the environment from the dangers of pollution?** NCERT

Ans. Following are the steps that a business should take to protect the environment

(i) Top management of the enterprise should be committed to create, maintain and develop work culture for environmental protection and pollution prevention. This commitment should be shared throughout the enterprise by all divisions and employees.

(ii) The management of the enterprise should develop policies to purchase good quality raw materials, employing superior technology, using scientific techniques of disposal and treatment of wastes, developing employee skills, etc. to control pollution.

(iii) It should respect the laws and regulations that are enacted by the government for prevention of pollution.

(iv) It should participate in government programmes that are related to management of hazardous substances, cleaning of rivers, plantation of trees and checking deforestation.

10. What do you understand by business ethics? Give examples.

Ans. Business ethics refer to the socially determined moral principles which should govern business activities. It is concerned with what is right and what is wrong. Ethics establishes linkage between individual good and social good. Ethics are a set of principles that may be written or unwritten, governing a professional or human activity.

Some examples of business ethics are

(i) Charging fair prices from customers.
(ii) Using fair weights for measurement of commodities.
(iii) Giving fair treatment to workers.
(iv) Earning reasonable profits.

11. State the features of business ethics.

Ans. Business ethics exhibits certain features which are enumerated below

(i) Business ethics is applicable to those individuals and organisations which are engaged in business.

(ii) Business ethics promotes honesty and transparency in business dealings.

(iii) Business ethics are often guided by law to provide a basic framework that business may choose to follow in order to gain public acceptance.

12. What are the various factors influencing business ethics?

Ans. The factors that influence business ethics are

(i) The individual's personal code of behaviour is the result of the complex environment that influences one's life.

(ii) The ethical standards imposed on a manager by his superiors also influence him in his decisions as to the morality of behaviour. If the superior condones unethical activities such as padding expenses accounts, the subordinate is encouraged to look upon this activity as an acceptable practice.

(iii) The policies of the company also influence the determination of ethical conduct. Standards of behaviour in an industry are often greatly influenced by the dominant firms in that industry. The authors of the company policy obviously have an effect that is decisive.

Long Answer Type Questions

13. "Business is essentially a social institution and not merely a profit-making activity." Explain.

NCERT; Competency Based Que

Ans. Business is essentially a social institution and not merely a profit-making activity. Like every individual living in society, business also has certain obligations towards society in terms of respect for social values and norms of behaviour. It is obligatory for the business concern to focus on social benefits for the society.

A business need to focus on following points

(i) **Justification for Existence and Growth**
Though profit motive is an important justification for undertaking business activity, it should be looked upon as an outcome of the social objectives fulfilled by the business firm. The prosperity and growth of business are possible only through continuous service to society.

(ii) **Long-term Interest of the Firm**
The public image of any firm would be improved if the increasing number of members of society like workers, consumers, shareholders, government officials. Feel that business enterprise is serving its best interest. Therefore, it is in own interest of a firm fulfils its social responsibility.

(iii) **Avoidance of Government Regulation**
It is believed that a business organisation can avoid the problem of undesired government regulations and actions by voluntarily assuming the social responsibility which helps to reduce the need for new laws, which restricts their freedom.

(iv) **Maintenance of Society**
When the stakeholders of the business fell that they are cheated, exploited and not getting their dues from the business, may resort to anti-social activities, for which there is no protection by law. They may harm the business itself, therefore, it is desirable that a business enterprise should assume social responsibility.

So, with the help of above mentioned points, we can conclude that "Business is essentially a social institution and not merely a profit-making activity."

14. "Social responsibility in business is often seen as a means to build goodwill and trust, but it also raises questions about its impact on profitability and focus on core objectives." In the context of the statement, present arguments for social responsibility of business. Competency Based Que

Ans. Following are the arguments for social responsibility

(i) **Justification for Existence and Growth**
Business exists to provide goods and services to satisfy human needs. Profit-making is an important objective of business activity but it should be considered as an outcome of the service to the people.

(ii) **Long-term Interest of the Firm**
A business will be able to survive in the long-run only if the members of society including workers, consumers, shareholders, government officials, etc. feel that business enterprise is serving for their best interest.

(iii) **Avoidance of Government Regulation**
Government regulations are undesirable from the business point of view because they limit their freedom. By assuming social responsibility voluntarily, government regulations can be avoided.

(iv) **Maintenance of Society**
It is desirable that business enterprises should assume social responsibilities, otherwise people who are not getting their due from the business may resort to anti-social activities.

(v) **Availability of Resources with Business**
Business institutions have valuable financial and human resources e.g. Managerial talent and capital resources. The business should use these resources for producing socially desirable and good quality products.

(vi) **Converting Problems into Opportunities**
Business can convert problems into profitable deals by being socially responsible. e.g. Problem of electricity supply led to invention of generators and inverters.

(vii) **Better Environment for Doing Business**
A society with fewer problems provides better environment for a firm to conduct its business. So, in order to ensure proper environment for growth and sustenance, a business should be responsible towards the society.

15. "Businesses today play a pivotal role in shaping societal outcomes, going beyond profit-making to meet the expectations of various stakeholders." In the context of the statement, discuss the social responsibility of business towards shareholders, workers and consumers. Competency Based Que

Ans. The social responsibility of business towards different interest groups is as follows

Responsibility towards the Shareholders or Owners

A business enterprise has the following responsibilities towards the shareholders or owners

(i) To provide a fair return to the shareholders or owners on their capital investment.

(ii) To ensure the safety of their investment.

(iii) To provide accurate updates and information about its working and schemes of future growth.

Responsibility towards the Workers

A business enterprise has the following responsibilities towards the workers

(i) To provide opportunities to the workers for meaningful work.

(ii) Try to give right kind of working conditions.

(iii) To respect the democratic rights of the workers to form unions.

(iv) To ensure the worker a fair wage and a fair deal.

Responsibility towards the Consumers

A business enterprise has the following responsibilities towards the consumers

(i) To supply the right quality and quantity of goods and services to consumers at reasonable prices.

(ii) To take proper precaution against unfair trade practices like adulteration, poor quality, misleading and dishonest advertisement, etc.

(iii) To provide information about the product, the company and other matters related to the consumer.

16. Discuss the guidelines enumerated by the Companies Act, 2013 for corporate social responsibility. NCERT

Ans. The corporate social responsibility in India as governed by the Companies Act, 2013 (under Clause 135) applies to those companies which have annual turnover of ₹ 1,000 crore and more or those having as net worth of ₹ 500 crore and more or a net profit of ₹ 5 crore and more.

CSR as per Companies Act, 2013 can be understood with the help of the following guidelines

(i) As per the new rules applicable from fiscal year 2014-15 onwards, the companies are required to set-up a committee for CSR consisting of their board members, including at least one independent director.

(ii) The companies should spend at least 2% of their average net profits earned during previous three years on CSR activities.

(iii) The indicative activities, which can be undertaken by a company under CSR, have been specified under Schedule VII of the Act.

(iv) Only CSR activities undertaken in India will be taken into consideration.

(v) The activities which are exclusively meant for employees of the organisation or their family members will not be considered as a part of CSR.

17. Write detailed note on role of business in environment protection.

Ans. Environment is very essential for the survival of humans or any species. We humans depend so much on the environment in our day-to-day life. Trees provide us with fresh oxygen for breathing and fruits, pulses and cereals for sustaining life. The rivers provide us with water which is an essential part of our existence.

The role of the environment is crucial in the survival of society and the businesses. Therefore, it is extremely necessary on the part of businesses to conserve and protect the environment to prevent global emergencies.

A business organisation or the businesses around the globe can take the following steps in order to reduce environmental pollution and thereby protect the environment

(i) Companies involved in the production of various utilities or products can go for eco-friendly, low waste and clean technology for equipment used in such industries.

(ii) Industrial wastes should be recycled every time so that it minimises the chances of pollution.

(iii) The machinery should be upgraded so that it complies with the pollution norms, which will be beneficial in reducing the levels of pollution.

(iv) Conduct quarterly/yearly audits for checking the effectiveness of the pollution control programmes and making changes so as to bring about more success in pollution control programmes.

(v) The companies and industries should comply with the rules laid down by the government with respect to prevention of environmental pollution.

(vi) The businesses should take steps to save the environment by setting up campaigns of planting trees, cleaning of rivers.

18. "Business ethics serve as the guiding principles that shape the moral foundation of an organisation, ensuring responsible decision-making and conduct in its operations." In the context of the statement, discuss the elements of business ethics. **Competency Based Que**

Or

Explain the various elements of business ethics. **NCERT**

Ans. Following are the elements of business ethics

(i) **Top Management Commitment**

Business ethics can be followed by a business only if its top level management (chief executive officer and other high level managers) is openly and strongly committed towards the ethical conduct. It must give continuous leadership for developing and upholding the values of the organisation.

(ii) **Publication of a Code**

Enterprises with effective ethics programmes define the 'principles of conduct' or the 'code of conduct' for the whole organisation in the form of a written document, which is known as code.

The code may cover subjects like fundamental honesty and adherence to laws, product safety and quality, health and safety in the workplace, conflicts of interests, employment practices, fair dealing in selling/marketing practices and financial reporting.

(iii) **Establishment of Compliance Mechanisms**

Suitable mechanisms should be established by the business enterprise to ensure that the actual decisions and actions complied with the firm's ethical standards. e.g.

- Paying attention to values and ethics in recruiting and hiring.
- Emphasising corporate ethics in training
- Auditing performance regularly to analyse the degree of compliance.
- Instituting communication systems to help employees report incidents of unethical behaviour, etc.

(iv) **Involving Employees at all Levels**

Involvement of employees at all levels in ethics programmes is essential as it is the employees who implement ethics policies to make ethical business a reality.

e.g. Small groups of employees can be formed to discuss the important ethics policies of firms and examine attitudes of employees towards these policies.

(v) **Measuring Results**

The firms must audit to monitor compliance with ethical standards to measure the end results of ethics programmes as far as possible and further course of action should then be decided by the top management team in discussion with other employees.

Case Study Based Questions

Short Case Studies

Case Study 1

Dinesh is the CEO of a pharmaceutical company 'Alpha-Beta' with an annual turnover of ₹ 1,000 crore. The company is based in Jabalpur which is famous for its soft marble. Many craftsmen make beautiful statues from the marble. However, they made barely enough to fulfil their basic needs.

On researching about the probable reasons for their plight, Dinesh found that they were unorganised and lacked the financial strength to market their produce. Dinesh created a fund and advanced them a certain sum which enabled them to stock over their inventory.

He also opened a school and a health centre for these craftsmen.

(i) Is Dinesh fulfilling his social responsibility?

(ii) Why there is a need for social responsibility?

(iii) State some socially desirable practices.

Ans.

(i) Yes, Dinesh is fulfilling his social responsibility.

(ii) Social responsibility is required because of the following reasons

- It is required to serve the interest of certain sections of society such as customers, employees, suppliers, community, etc.
- It gives the moral understanding to an entrepreneur, as to what is right and what is wrong.
- It also helps in addressing legal, ethical and commercial issues.

(iii) Socially desirable practices include supply of goods and services, providing goods and services at fair price, creating healthy and better working conditions, installing devices to control pollution, etc.

Case Study 2

A leading apparel brand launched a new advertising campaign featuring a vibrant and bold theme. However, the advertisement unintentionally used symbols and phrases that were deemed offensive to the cultural and religious sentiments of a particular community.

Recognising the backlash, the company immediately withdrew the advertisement, issued a public apology and re-released the campaign with appropriate changes. This act of self-regulation, even in the absence of any legal obligation, was appreciated by society and highlighted the brand's commitment to respecting societal values.

(i) Identify and state the type of social responsibility exhibited by the company in the above case.

(ii) A businessman has to fulfil certain social obligations. List them.

Ans.

(i) The type of social responsibility exhibited by the company in the case is ethical responsibility. This includes the behaviour of the firm that is expected by society.

It is not included in law so it is not compulsory for business to assume this responsibility. e.g. Respecting the religious sentiments of people and dignity of people while advertising its product.

(ii) Social responsibilities of a businessman include

- He should ensure that the investors get a satisfactory rate of return to them.
- He must provide a good salary, security and suitable working conditions for his employees.
- He should offer them quality products at reasonable rates.
- He should see to it that the business does not cause harm to the environment in any way.

Case Study 3

Zenith Enterprises pays wages to its employees at a rate which is much lower than the minimum wages prescribed by the government.

The working conditions in the factory are inappropriate as there is lack of proper ventilation and there is a strict rule against formation of trade union. Against which 'group', Zenith Enterprises has ignored the social responsibility.

Mention any four responsibilities which the firm should have towards this 'group'.

Ans. Zenith Enterprises has ignored the social responsibility towards 'workers'.

Following are the four responsibilities, which Zenith Enterprises should have towards workers

(i) To create and provide proper and safe working conditions.

(ii) To ensure fair wages and a fair deal from the management.

(iii) To provide opportunities for personal growth and development.

(iv) To provide opportunities to the workers for meaningful work.

Case Study 4

Business has various social responsibilities towards several interest groups. Identify and state the relevant interest group and any one responsibility in the following cases

(i) Reeyan Enterprises has a chain of apparel business and is expected to supply good quality products at reasonable prices.

(ii) Mahesh Textiles is required to pay taxes regularly and honestly.

Ans.

(i) The relevant interest group is customers.
Responsibility To take proper precaution against unfair trade practices like adulteration, poor quality, misleading and dishonest advertisement, etc.

(ii) The relevant interest group is government.
Responsibility To develop a proper image in society through continuous interaction with various groups of people.

Case Study 5

XYZ Electronics launched a new model of their air purifiers, advertising it as '100% effective against pollutants.' However, the product was found to be of poor quality, with many customers complaining about its inefficiency and durability issues. Despite repeated complaints, XYZ Electronics ignored the grievances and continued to make misleading claims in their advertisements.

(i) Identify the group whose interest is being ignored by XYZ Electronics.

(ii) State three responsibilities that XYZ Electronics should follow towards this group.

Ans.

(i) The group whose interest is being ignored by XYZ Electronics is consumers.

(ii) XYZ Electronics should fulfill the following responsibilities towards consumers

- To supply the right quality and quantity of goods and services to consumers at reasonable prices.
- To take proper precaution against unfair trade practices like adulteration, poor quality, misleading and dishonest advertisement, etc.
- To provide information about the product, the company and other matters related to the consumer.

Case Study 6

Paras Enterprises, a leading manufacturing company, recently announced its decision to reinvest all its profits into expanding its production facilities. Despite achieving record profits this year, the company chose not to declare dividends for shareholders. Additionally, shareholders have been raising concerns about the lack of transparency in financial reports and the management's future growth plans.

(i) Identify the group whose interest is being ignored by the company.

(ii) State three responsibilities the company should follow towards this group.

Ans.

(i) The group whose interest is being ignored by the company is 'shareholders'.

(ii) The company should fulfil the following responsibilities towards the shareholders

- To provide a fair return to the shareholders or owners on their capital investment.
- To ensure the safety of their investment.
- To provide accurate updates and information about its working and schemes of future growth.

Case Study 7

A manufacturing company, Zephyr Industries, has been releasing harmful gases into the atmosphere due to outdated machinery and lack of filtration systems in its factories. Residents of nearby areas have reported respiratory problems, thick smog covering the skies and an unpleasant odor around the factory premises. This has raised concerns about environmental safety and the health of the local community.

(i) Identify and state the type of pollution discussed in the above case.

(ii) State any three reasons why pollution control is necessary.

Ans.

(i) The type of pollution discussed in the case is air pollution. It is caused by the usage of chemicals in industries, factories and plants or by the emission of carbon monoxide by vehicles.
These emissions degrade the quality of air and create a hole in the ozone layer which results in global warming. It led to warming of the earth and is dangerous for all living beings.

(ii) Pollution control is necessary because of the following reasons

- **Cost Savings**
  Improper production technology results in greater wastes. It leads to higher cost of waste disposal and cleaning the plants. An effective pollution control programme helps in reducing the costs of operating business.
- **Improved Public Image**
  Society has become conscious of environmental quality. In this respect, a firm should try to control the pollution to improve its public image.

- **Other Social Benefits**
  If the pollution is controlled, this will help in gaining other benefits like clean rivers, better quality of life, smoke free air, clearer visibility, cleaner buildings and availability of natural products in much purer form.

Case Study 8

Varun is working as a manager and his work is to formulate ethical practices, which will be followed by the organisation.

(i) Enumerate certain ethical practices that can be formulated by Varun.

(ii) How would one ensure that one has made a right ethical decision? Elaborate with suitable example.

Ans.

(i) Ethical practices that can be formulated by Varun are
- Providing good quality products to the customers.
- Making goods available in the market at reasonable prices.
- Providing employment to the weaker sections of the society.
- Abide by the rules and regulations laid down by the government and paying the taxes on time.
- Paying the minimum and fair wages to workers.
- Not to use child labour in production process.
- Judicious use of natural resources, etc.

(ii) One can ensure that one has made a right ethical decision by asking oneself the following questions
- Will his decision harm anyone?
- Is his decision in compliance with the legal laws of the country?
- Will his decision promote social welfare?

If the answer to the first question is a 'No' and to the other two questions is a 'Yes', then one can be sure that one has made an ethical decision. e.g. The top management takes a decision to retrench 50 labourers. Now, this decision is not ethical because, it harms the interest of the retrenched labourers and does not promote social welfare.

Long Case Studies

Case Study 9

XYZ Ltd., a well-established manufacturing company in the consumer goods sector, has been in operation for more than 20 years. While its primary focus has always been on producing high quality goods to meet the demands of society and generate profits, the company has also begun incorporating Corporate Social Responsibility (CSR) into its business model.

Recently, the company introduced environmentally friendly production processes, reduced its carbon footprint and began supporting local communities by providing educational scholarships to underprivileged students.

However, despite these efforts, a group of investors has raised concerns, arguing that the company's emphasis on CSR activities could be a distraction from its main objective maximising profits. On the other hand, the management believes that balancing economic and social responsibilities is crucial for sustainable business growth.

They are committed to producing goods that meet market needs while also contributing positively to society and the environment.

(i) State the meaning of social responsibility.

(ii) Give any three arguments in favour of social responsibility.

(iii) Give any two arguments against social responsibility.

Ans.

(i) Social responsibility refers to the obligation of business to take those decisions which are desirable for the various groups in the society. Social responsibility is a much wider concept than legal responsibility.

(ii) Arguments in favour of social responsibility are as follows
- **Justification for Existence and Growth**
  Business exists to provide goods and services to satisfy human needs. Profit-making is an important objective of business activity but it should be considered as an outcome of the service to the people.
- **Long-term Interest of the Firm**
  A business will be able to survive in the long-run only if the members of society including workers, consumers, shareholders, government officials, etc. feel that business enterprise is serving for their best interest.
- **Avoidance of Government Regulation**
  Government regulations are undesirable from the business point of view because they limit their freedom. By assuming social responsibility voluntarily, government regulations can be avoided.

(iii) Arguments against social responsibility are as follows
- **Violation of Profit Maximisation Objective**
  Business exists only for profit maximisation. Involvement of business in social activities may shift its focus from economic productivity and reduce the profits of the organisation. It can fulfill its social responsibility by maximising its profits through increased efficiency and reduced costs.

- **Burden on Consumers**
  Businessmen are likely to simply shift their burden of social responsibilities like pollution control and environmental protection, by charging higher prices from the consumers instead of bearing it themselves. It is unfair to shift the burden to the consumers in the name of social responsibility.

Case Study 10

Rajiv Textiles is a clothing manufacturing company known for its wide range of affordable garments. The company was recognised for its quality standards and was often praised for introducing stylish and durable clothing at competitive prices. Rajiv Textiles had built a strong customer base and employed a large workforce, many of whom had been with the company for years.

However, in its pursuit of cost cutting, the company started using low quality raw materials that caused skin irritation for some customers. This led to a decline in customer satisfaction. Additionally, the company delayed wage payments to its workers and failed to provide safe working conditions in its factories, resulting in widespread dissatisfaction among employees.

To complicate matters, the company diverted funds allocated for product development to other ventures without informing its shareholders. This reduced the profitability of the company and caused its share value to drop significantly.

As a result, the reputation of Rajiv Textiles was severely damaged and it faced backlash from multiple stakeholders.

(i) Quoting lines from the above paragraph, identify three interest groups towards which the business failed to fulfill its social responsibility.

(ii) Also, state two responsibilities towards each interest group.

Ans.

(i) Following are the interest groups towards whom the business failed to fulfil the social responsibility

- **Customers**
  Quoting line "The company started using low quality raw materials that caused skin irritation for some customers."
- **Workers**
  Quoting line "The company delayed wage payments to its workers and failed to provide safe working conditions in its factories."
- **Shareholders**
  Quoting line "The company diverted funds allocated for product development to other ventures without informing its shareholders."

(ii) Following are the responsibilities towards various interest groups

Responsibility towards the Consumers
A business enterprise has the following responsibilities towards the consumers

- To supply the right quality and quantity of goods and services to consumers at reasonable prices.
- To take proper precaution against unfair trade practices like adulteration, poor quality, misleading and dishonest advertisement, etc.

Responsibility towards the Workers
A business enterprise has the following responsibilities towards the workers

- To provide opportunities to the workers for meaningful work.
- Try to give right kind of working conditions.

Responsibility towards the Shareholders or Owners
A business enterprise has the following responsibilities towards the shareholders or owners

- To provide a fair return to the shareholders or owners on their capital investment.
- To ensure the safety of their investment.

Case Study 11

Eclipse Automobiles, a renowned car manufacturing company, has always been proactive in its production planning. Each year, the company conducts an in-depth analysis of market trends, consumer preferences and emerging technologies to guide its manufacturing process.

Last year, the company launched an electric car, which gained significant attention due to the increasing demand for environment friendly alternatives.

This planning helped Eclipse Automobiles maintain a competitive edge and position itself as a leader in the electric vehicle market. However, this year, a sudden shift in government regulations focused on reducing vehicle emissions and promoting sustainable energy.

Eclipse Automobiles, having already finalised their production schedules, found it difficult to quickly adjust to these changes. While Eclipse struggled to modify their plans, another company, EcoDrive, quickly adapted and launched new models that complied with the latest environmental standards, helping it capture a larger share of the market.

(i) Quoting lines from the above paragraph, identify and state the type of pollution discussed in the case.

(ii) Discuss the steps that should be taken by business in the protection of the environment.

Ans.

(i) **Air Pollution**

"... a sudden shift in government regulations focused on reducing vehicle emissions and promoting sustainable energy." It is caused by the usage of chemicals in industries, factories and plants or by the emission of carbon monoxide by vehicles. These emissions degrade the quality of air and create a hole in the ozone layer which results in global warming. It led to warming of the earth and is dangerous for all living beings.

(ii) Business should adopt the following steps in the protection of the environment

- Top management of the enterprise should be committed to create, maintain and develop work culture for environmental protection and pollution prevention. This commitment should be shared throughout the enterprise by all divisions and employees.
- The management of the enterprise should develop policies to purchase good quality raw materials, employing superior technology, using scientific techniques of disposal and treatment of wastes, developing employee skills, etc. to control pollution.
- It should respect the laws and regulations that are enacted by the government for prevention of pollution.
- It should participate in government programmes that are related to management of hazardous substances, cleaning of rivers, plantation of trees and checking deforestation.
- It should conduct periodical assessment of pollution control programmes in terms of costs and benefits, in order to increase the progress with respect to environmental protection.

Case Study 12

ABC Ltd., a well-known manufacturing company, had always prided itself on its high quality products and customer satisfaction. However, recently, the company faced a major ethical issue when it was discovered that a few of its suppliers were using child labour in their factories. The company's leadership, after discovering this, was divided on how to respond.

Some executives believed that continuing business with these suppliers was necessary for maintaining low production costs, while others argued that it would tarnish the company's reputation. After much deliberation, the management decided to sever ties with the unethical suppliers and adopt more stringent measures to ensure ethical sourcing of materials.

This decision was not easy, as it meant a short-term increase in production costs, but the leadership was committed to aligning with its core values of fairness and social responsibility.

(i) Discuss the concept of business ethics as discussed in the case.

(ii) State any four elements of business ethics.

Ans.

(i) Business ethics refer to the socially determined moral principles which should govern business activities. In the case, business ethics refers to the moral principles and standards that guide the company's decisions and actions. ABC Ltd. faced a dilemma when it discovered that its suppliers were engaging in unethical practices, such as child labour.

The company had to choose between maintaining lower production costs by continuing to do business with these suppliers or acting in accordance with ethical values like fairness, social responsibility and respect for human rights.

The decision to sever ties with unethical suppliers and adopt ethical sourcing practices highlights the importance of business ethics in maintaining the company's integrity, reputation and commitment to socially responsible practices.

(ii) Following are the elements of business ethics

- **Top Management Commitment**

  Business ethics can be followed by a business only if its top level management (chief executive officer and other high level managers) is openly and strongly committed towards the ethical conduct. It must give continuous leadership for developing and upholding the values of the organisation.
- **Publication of a Code**

  Enterprises with effective ethics programmes define the 'principles of conduct' or the 'code of conduct' for the whole organisation in the form of a written document, which is known as code.

  The code may cover subjects like fundamental honesty and adherence to laws, product safety and quality, health and safety in the workplace, conflicts of interests, employment practices, fair dealing in selling/marketing practices and financial reporting.
- **Involving Employees at all Levels**

  The involvement of employees in ethical programmes is necessary as they are responsible at different levels to implement ethical policies, to make a business ethical. e.g. Small groups of employees can be formed to discuss the vital ethical policies of firms and examine attitude of employees towards these policies.
- **Measuring Results**

  It is difficult to accurately measure the end results of ethics programmes, but the firms can do this by auditing or monitoring the compliance with ethical standards.

SELF ASSESSMENT TEST

Objective Type Questions

1. Which of the following is a responsibility of a business enterprise towards its workers?
   (a) To provide workers with opportunities for meaningless work
   (b) To ignore workers' right to form unions
   (c) To ensure fair wages and a fair deal for workers
   (d) To create unhealthy working conditions

2. Social responsibility of a business refers to ... efforts on the part of a business to contribute to the welfare of society.
   (a) compulsory (b) voluntary
   (c) legal (d) ethical

3. Which of the following amount to unethical business practices towards customers?
   (a) Dishonest advertising
   (b) Unfair pricing
   (c) Improper after-sales servicing
   (d) All of the above

4. "To supply the right quantity of goods." It is an example of responsibility of business towards ....
   (a) owners (b) workers
   (c) government (d) consumers

5. Pollution control is necessary due to which of the following reasons?
   (a) It increases the cost of production
   (b) It reduces the risk of diseases like cancer and heart attacks
   (c) It decreases the quality of life
   (d) It harms the public image of the business

6. Which of the following is capable of doing maximum good to the society?
   (a) Business success (b) Laws and regulations
   (c) Ethics (d) Professional management

7. United Nations has identified ozone depletion as one of the major problems that causes damage to natural environment. It is caused by
   (a) emission of carbon monoxide by industries and vehicles
   (b) increase of O_2 in environment
   (c) dumping of chemical wastes into water bodies
   (d) dumping of toxic wastes on land

8. Shalu Apparels is selling its products at higher prices and is not providing proper working conditions to the workers. The activities of the company are also causing pollution. Which concept is lacking?
   (a) Concept of social responsibility
   (b) Concept of business ethics
   (c) Both (a) and (b)
   (d) None of the above

Answers 1. (c) 2. (b) 3. (d) 4. (d) 5. (b) 6. (c) 7. (a) 8. (c)

Short Answer Type Questions

9. Give any three arguments against social responsibility.

10. "Shareholders are crucial to the success and growth of a company, with their interests often aligning with the company's performance." In the context of the statement, state the responsibilities of business towards shareholders.

11. Mohan is a consumer. List certain responsibilities that he will expect from a businessman.

12. "Pollution can significantly impact the environment, posing serious threats to public health and biodiversity." In the context of the statement, state any three types of pollution.

13. Satakshi is an environment protection professional. Suggest any three points that could have been enumerated by her to show the need of pollution control.

14. State any three features of business ethics.

15. Give any four examples of business ethics.

Long Answer Type Questions

16. "Corporate social responsibility extends beyond financial gains, focusing on creating value for society as a whole, including ethical and environmental considerations." In the context of the statement, discuss the arguments in favour of social responsibility.

17. Rajesh wants to understand that why it is the moral duty of business to take positive steps for controlling the problem of pollution. As a consultant, explain him the role of business in the protection of environment.

18. "Business ethics are essential in fostering trust and fairness in corporate environments, guiding companies to act responsibly beyond legal requirements." In the context of the statement, explain the various elements of business ethics.

07

CHAPTER

Sources of Business Finance

The activity concerned with planning, developing, managing, administering and increasing of the capital used for business purposes is known as finance.

▼ **YOUR STUDY GOALS**

7.1 Meaning of Business Finance
7.2 Sources of Finance
7.3 Owner's Funds
7.4 Borrowed Funds

▼ **YOUR PRACTICE GOAL**

- Objective Type Questions (57 Qs ; MCQs, A-R, Statements, Matching)
- Subjective Questions (14 SAs, 6 LAs)
- Case Study Based Questions (Short Case Studies-8, Long Case Studies-4)
- Self Assessment Test (8 MCQs, 7 SAs, 3 LAs)

7.1 Meaning of Business Finance

The requirement of funds by business to carry out its various activities is called business finance.

It is that activity which is concerned with the acquisition and conservation of capital funds in meeting the financial need and overall objectives of business enterprise.

Nature of Business Finance

- The concept of business finance is very wide and is used in every type of business house whether it is small or large.
- It includes all types of funds and capital that are needed to start, run, expand and diversify the business.
- The primary goal of business finance is to increase the corporate value.

Importance of Business Finance

1. **Necessary to Start Business** Every new venture needs money to buy plant and machinery, land and building, raw material, etc. So, finance is significant to start a business.
2. **Necessary to Face Economic Cycle** During recession and depression, the sales of the business go down and the profitability is adversely affected. To overcome problems during such times, finance is significant.

3. **Necessary for Growth** Sometimes, in order to attain more or to achieve greater success, a company needs significant financial investment to acquire new capital, staff or inventory.
4. **Necessary for the Payments of Debts** It is necessary that a business firm meets its liabilities in time. Prompt payment of debts can be possible only because of adequate arrangement of finance.
5. **Necessary for Availing the Opportunities** Business can take the advantage of upcoming opportunities and can earn more, only if it has adequate finance at its disposal.

Importance of Business Finance
- → Necessary to Start Business
- → Necessary to Face Economic Cycle
- → Necessary for Growth
- → Necessary for the Payments of Debts
- → Necessary for Availing the Opportunities

Financial Needs of Business

The financial needs of the business can be categorised into the following

Fixed Capital Requirements	Working Capital Requirements
Fixed assets such as land, plant, machinery, etc. are required to start a business. The amount which is required to purchase these assets is known as fixed capital requirements of the enterprise. This amount remains invested in the business for a long period of time. The following points should be kept in mind regarding fixed capital requirements • A manufacturing firm require more fixed capital as compared to a trading firm. • A business operating on a large-scale requires more fixed capital than a small enterprise. • Fixed capital requirements should be financed through long-term sources of finance.	A business also needs finance to carry out the day-to-day operations or activities. The amount required to meet these activities is known as the working capital requirements of the business. Following points should be kept in mind regarding the working capital requirements • If operating cycle of a business is shorter, then amount required will be lesser and *vice-versa*. • These requirements are generally met through short-term sources of finance. • A business selling goods on credit or having slow sales turnover require more working capital. • Working capital requirement increases during festive season, expansion of business, shifting to a new location and payments of current debts.

7.2 Sources of Finance

A business can raise funds or finance from a number of sources. Sources of finance can be classified on the basis of period, source of generation and ownership.

Classification of Sources of Finance

On the basis of period

Long-term
- Equity shares
- Retained earnings
- Preference shares
- Debentures
- Loan from financial institutions
- Loan from banks

Short-term
- Trade credit
- Factoring
- Banks
- Commercial paper

Medium-term
- Loan from banks
- Public deposits
- Loan from financial institution
- Lease financing

On the basis of source of generation

Internal Sources
- Equity share capital
- Retained earnings

External Sources
- Financial institutions
- Loan from banks
- Preference shares
- Public deposits
- Debenture
- Lease financing
- Commercial papers
- Trade credit
- Factoring

On the basis of ownership

Owner s Funds
- Equity shares
- Retained earnings
- Preference shares
- Global depository receipts
- American depository receipts
- Indian depository receipts

Borrowed Funds
- Debentures
- Loans from banks
- Loans from financial institutions
- Public deposits
- Lease financing
- Commercial papers

I. Classification on the Basis of Period

Period	Explanation
Long-term Sources	• These sources provide finance to business firms for a period exceeding five years. Such capital is invested in fixed or permanent assets of a business. • These sources include issue of shares, debentures, long-term borrowings, loans from financial institutions, etc.
Medium-term Sources	• These sources provide finance to business firms for a period exceeding one year but less than five years. Such capital is used for modernisation of plant and machinery or introduction of a new product or an advertisement campaign. • These sources include finance from financial institutions, public deposits, commercial banks, lease financing, etc.
Short-term Sources	• These sources provide finance to business firms for less than one year. Such capital is required to meet day-to-day requirements and for holding stock of raw material, spare parts, etc. It is often called **working capital.** • These sources indude trade credit, loans from commercial banks, commercial papers, etc.

II. Classification on the Basis of Source of Generation

Source	Explanation
Internal Sources	These include all those funds which are generated from within the business, i.e. funds from collection of receivables, disposing-off surplus inventories and ploughing back of profit. These sources can fulfil only limited needs of the business.
External Sources	These include all those funds which are generated from outside the business, i.e. include issue of debentures, borrowing from commercial banks and financial institutions and accepting public deposits. These sources are costly but large amounts can be raised through these sources. In some cases, business is required to mortgage its assets for raising finance from these sources.

III. Classification on the Basis of Ownership

On the basis of ownership, sources of finance can be classified as

- Owner's funds
- Borrowed funds

7.3 Owner's Funds

Funds or finance provided by the owners (a sole trader or partners or shareholders) of the business is referred to as owner's funds. Besides capital, it also include profits reinvested in the business. The funds provided by the owners are not required to be paid back during the life of the business, therefore they are a permanent source of finance. These sources include the following

1. Retained Earnings

A business does not distribute all its trading profits as dividends among the shareholders. It retain a part of these profits for future expansion of the company. This part is known as retained earning. This is also referred to as **ploughing back of profits.**

Merits and Demerits of Retained Earnings

Merits	Demerits
• It is a permanent source of funds for an organisation. • It does not involve any explicit cost in the form of interest, dividend or floatation cost. • It offers a greater degree of operational freedom and flexibility. • It enhances the capacity of business to absorb unexpected losses. • It may lead to an increase in market price of equity shares issued.	• Excessive ploughing back may cause dissatisfaction amongst the shareholders, as they would get lower dividends. • As the profits of business are fluctuating, it is an uncertain source of fund. • Firms do not recognise the opportunity cost associated with this source, which lead to insignificant use of funds.

2. Equity Shares

A business can raise necessary finance by issue of shares. The capital obtained by issue of shares is known as **share capital** and person holding the shares is referred to as **shareholders**. Shares are classified as equity shares and preference shares.

The money raised by issue of equity shares is known as **equity share capital**. The holders of equity shares are called **equity shareholders**. The **features** of equity shares are

- Equity shares represent the ownership of a company.
- Equity shareholders do not get a fixed dividend but are paid on the basis of earnings of the company. They are referred to as residual owners as they receive what is left after all other claims on the company's income and assets have been settled.
- Equity shareholders enjoy the reward as well as bear the risk of ownership. Their liability is limited to the extent of capital contributed by them in the company.
- Through their right to vote, equity shareholders have a right to participate in the management of the company.

Merits and Demerits of Equity Shares

Merits	Demerits
• Equity shares are suitable for those investors who are willing to assume risk for higher returns. • Payment of dividend to shareholders is not compulsory. Therefore, there is no burden on the company. • It is a permanent source of capital as it is repaid only at the time of dissolution of company. • Equity capital provides creditworthiness to the company and confidence to prospective loan providers. • Funds can be raised through equity shares without creating any charge on the assets of the company.	• Investors who want steady income may not prefer equity shares due to fluctuating returns. • The cost of equity shares is more as compared to other sources of funds. • Every successive issue of equity shares reduces the voting power and earnings of existing equity shareholders. • Many formalities and procedural delays are involved while raising funds through equity.

3. Preference Shares

The capital raised by issue of preference shares is called **preference share capital**. The **features** of preference shares are

- Preference shares confer following two preferential rights to its holders
  - Right to receive dividend at a fixed rate, before dividend is paid to equity shareholders.
  - Right to receive repayment of capital at the time of dissolution of the company. This right authorises them to receive payment against capital before any amount is paid to equity shareholders.
- Preference shares resemble debentures as they bear a fixed rate of return.
- Preference shares also resemble equity shares as the dividend is payable only at the discretion of the directors and only out of profit after tax.
- Preference shareholders are like creditors of the company. They do not enjoy voting rights. They cannot take part in management of the company.

Merits and Demerits of Preference Shares

Merits	Demerits
• The dividends to be paid to shareholders are fixed. • These shares are suitable for those investors who want fixed income with comparatively low risk. • It does not affect the control of equity shareholders as these shares do not carry voting rights.	• These shares are not suitable for those investors who are willing to take risk and are interested in higher returns. • These shares reduce the claim of equity shareholders over the assets of the company. • Company has to pay higher rates of dividends to the preference shareholders as compared to interest on debentures.

Merits	Demerits
• Payment of fixed dividends to preference shareholders enable a company to declare higher dividends for equity shareholders. • Assets are not required to be mortgaged for raising preference share capital.	• Dividend on these shares is to be paid only when company earns profit. Thus, returns are not assured. • The dividend paid on preference shares is not deductible from profits as expense. Thus, there is no tax savings.

Types of Preference Shares

- **Cumulative Preference Shares** These shares give shareholders the right to receive accumulate dividend from the company even if they are not profitable. These dividends will be counted as arrears in years when the company is not profitable. These will be paid in full from the year when the business is profitable.
- **Non-cumulative Preference Share** These shares provide the shareholder a fixed dividend amount each year. If the company fails to pay the dividend on such preference shares in any year, then such dividend cannot be claimed by the shareholder in the future.
- **Participating Preference Shares** These shares provide shareholders the right to share (participate) in the surplus of company's profit after paying dividend on preference and equity shares.
- **Non-participating Preference Shares** These shares do not provide shareholder the right to share (participate) in the surplus profits of the company.
- **Convertible Preference Shares** These shares can be converted into equity shares after a specified time period.
- **Non-convertible Preference Shares** These shares cannot be converted into equity shares.

7.4 Borrowed Funds

The funds that are raised by way of loans and credit from the public, banks and financial institutions are termed as borrowed funds. These funds are raised from external source and are required to be paid back after a fixed period. These sources include the following

1. Debentures/Bonds

Debenture issued by a company is basically a written acknowledgement that the company has borrowed a certain amount of money and promises to repay it at a future date.

The **features** of debentures are

- Debentures are basically borrowed funds due to which, the debenture holders are deemed to be the creditors of the company.
- Debenture holders receive a fixed rate of interest at a specified interval of six months or one year.
- Public issue of debentures requires that the issue be rated by a credit rating agency like CRISIL (Credit Rating and Information Services of India Ltd.) on the basis like track record of company, its profitability, debt servicing capacity, credit worthiness and the perceived risk of lending.

Merits and Demerits of Debentures

Merits	Demerits
• It is preferred by those investors who want fixed income at lesser risk. • Debentures are fixed charge funds and do not participate in the profits of the company. • The issue of debentures is suitable in the situation when the sales and earnings are relatively stable. • Debentures do not carry voting rights. So, financing through debentures does not reduce control of equity shareholders on management. • Financing through debentures is less costly as compare to cost of share capital, as the interest payment on debentures is deductible.	• Debentures put a permanent burden on the earnings of a company. There is a greater risk when earnings of the company fluctuate. • In case of redeemable debentures, the company has to make provisions for repayment on the specified date, even during periods of financial difficulty. • Each company has certain borrowing capacity. With the issue of debentures, the capacity of a company reduces to further borrow funds.

Types of Debentures

- **Secured Debentures** These create charge on the assets of the company by mortgaging the assets of the company.
- **Unsecured Debentures** These do not create any charge or security on the assets of the company.
- **Registered Debentures** These debentures are recorded in the register of debentureholders maintained by the company. They can be transferred through a regular instrument of transfer.
- **Bearer Debentures** These are not recorded and are transferred by delivery only.
- **Convertible Debentures** These debentures are convertible into equity shares after a specific period.
- **Non-convertible Debentures** These are not convertible into equity shares after a specific period.
- **First Debentures** These debentures are repaid before the repayment of any other debentures.
- **Second Debentures** These are paid after the first debentures have been paid back.
- **Zero Interest Debentures** These debentures do not carry any explicit rate of interest. The difference between the face value of the debenture and its purchase price is the return that investor receives.

2. Loans from Commercial Banks

Commercial banks extend loans to the business firms for different purposes and different time periods. The conditions of loans from commercial banks are

- Banks extend credit in many ways, like, cash credits, overdrafts, discounting of bills of exchange and issue of letter of credit.
- The repayment of loan or credit is made by the borrower in lumpsum or in instalments as per the agreement between the bank and the borrower.
- Interest charged by banks depends upon a number of factors, such as nature of advance, period for which the loan is taken, etc.
- Loan is generally offered by banks on security of assets.

Merits and Demerits of Loan from Commercial Banks

Merits	Demerits
• Banks provide timely assistance to business by providing funds as and when needed. • Secrecy of business can be maintained as the information supplied to the bank by the borrowers is kept confidential. • Formalities such as issue of prospectus and underwriting are not required for raising loans from a bank. • It is a flexible source of finance as the loan amount can be increased according to business needs and can be repaid in advance when funds are not needed.	• Funds are generally available for short periods and its extension or renewal is uncertain and difficult. • Banks make detailed investigation of the company's affairs, financial structure, etc. This makes the procedure slightly difficult. • In some cases, difficult terms and conditions are imposed by banks for the grant of loan.

3. Loans from Financial Institutions

The government has established a number of financial institutions all over the country. The **features** of financial institutions are

- These institutions are established by the Central as well as State Governments.
- These institutions provide loan for medium and long-term needs of a business.
- These institutions provide for specialised finance, keeping in view, the diverse requirements of business units.
- These institutions are also called **development banks** as they facilitate industrial development in the country.

Merits and Demerits of Loans from Financial Institutions

Merits	Demerits
• They provide long-term finance, that are not provided by commercial banks. • These institutes also extend technical and managerial support to business firms. • Getting a loan from these institutes, raises the goodwill of the borrowing company in the capital market. • Repayment can be made in easy instalments, therefore, it does not prove to be a burden on the business. • As these institutions are owned by State, they can provide funds during the period of depression also.	• Many formalities are required by these institutes to grant a loan. • Restrictions are imposed by these institutes on companies such as restrictions on the payment of dividends or restrictions on the autonomy of management. • The financial institutions may interfere in the management of the company by nominating representatives in the board of directors of the borrowing company. This restricts their powers and the borrowing companies feel helpless in certain cases.

Special Financial Institutions

- **Industrial Finance Corporation of India** (IFCI) It was established in July 1948 to assist for balanced regional development and encourage new entrepreneurs to enter into the priority sectors of the economy.
- **State Financial Corporation** (SFC) It was established under the State Financial Corporations Act, 1951. It provides medium and short-term finance to industries, which are outside the scope of the IFCI.
- **Industrial Credit and Investment Corporation of India** (ICICI) It was established in 1955 and assists the creation, expansion and modernisation of industrial enterprises exclusively in the private sector.
- **Industrial Development Bank of India** (IDBI) It was established in 1964 under the Industrial Development Bank of India Act, 1964. Its objective is to coordinate the activities of other financial institutions including commercial banks.
- **State Industrial Development Corporations** (SIDCs) These have been set-up by many State Governments for the purpose of promoting industrial development in their respective States.
- **Unit Trust of India** (UTI) It was established by the Government of India in 1964 under the Unit Trust of India Act, 1963. The basic objective of UTI is to mobilise the community's savings and channelise them into productive ventures.
- **Life Insurance Corporation of India** (LIC) It was set-up in 1956 under the LIC Act, 1956. It mobilises the community's savings in the form of insurance premiums and provide these savings to industrial concerns (both public as well as private) in the form of direct loans.

4. Public Deposits

The deposits that are raised by business organisations directly from the public are known as public deposits. It is a source of both medium and short-term finance. Under it, a company directly raises loans from the public, in the form of deposits for a fixed period of time at a fixed rate of interest. This rate is generally higher than that offered on bank deposits.

Companies generally invite public deposits for a period upto three years. Its acceptance is regulated by the Reserve Bank of India. Any person who is interested in depositing money with a company can do so by filling a prescribed form. The company issues a deposit receipt as acknowledgement of debt.

Merits and Demerits of Public Deposits

Merits	Demerits
• The procedure of obtaining deposits is simple and does not contain restrictive conditions. • Cost of public deposits is generally lower than the cost of borrowings from banks and others institutions. • Public deposits do not usually create any charge on assets of company. • As the depositors do not have voting rights, the control of the company is not reduced.	• New companies generally find it difficult to raise funds through public deposits. • It is an unreliable source of finance as the public may not respond when the company needs money. • Collection of public deposits may prove difficult, when a large size of deposits is required.

5. Trade Credit

The credit extended by one trader to another for the purchase of goods and services is called trade credit. The conditions of trade credit are

- Such credit appears in the accounts of the buyer of goods as sundry creditors or accounts payable.
- It is commonly used by business organisation as a source of short-term financing.
- The terms of trade credit may vary from industry to industry and person to person.
- The amount and period of trade credit depends on the following factors
  - Goodwill or reputation of the purchasing firm.
  - The amount of purchases made.
  - Past record of the buyer and his financial position.

Merits and Demerits of Trade Credit

Merits	Demerits
• Trade credit is a convenient and continuous source of funds. • It is readily available, in case the credit worthiness of the customers is known to the seller. • It helps to promote sales of an organisation by ensuring regular supply of tradeable goods and raw materials. • It can be used to finance the increase in inventory of goods if an organisation expects higher sales in the near future. • It does not create any charge on the assets of the firm.	• Trade credit may motivate a firm to overtrade. Overtrading occurs when a firm purchases more goods than it needs, only because they are being offered on credit. • Only limited amount of funds can be raised through this source. • It is generally a costly source of funds as compared to others. It is because the seller charges a high rate of interest for goods sold on credit.

6. Inter-Corporate Deposits (ICDs)

The unsecured short-term deposits that are made by one company with another company for a period of minimum 7 days which can be extended up to one year are called inter-corporate deposits. ICDs are generally unsecured.

Companies having surplus funds lend it to other companies who are in need of funds. This arrangement is mutually benefitting. The lending company earns interest on its idle funds and the borrowing company is able to fulfill its short-term financial needs.

Following are the **types** of inter-corporate deposits

- **Call Deposits** Such deposits can be withdrawn by the lending company by giving a one day notice. The interest on call deposits is around 10 per cent per annum.
- **Three Months Deposits** These deposits are made for a period of three months. The rate of interest on three months deposits is around 12 per cent per annum.
- **Six Months Deposits** These are made for a period of six months, only with the companies which enjoy a high credit rating. The rate of interest on six months deposits is around 15 per cent per annum.

Merits and Demerits of Inter-Corporate Deposits

Merits	Demerits
• There are not much legal formalities involved in it. • They are generally facilitated through brokers, who maintain absolute secrecy about the lending and borrowing companies. • They are a good source of working capital. It can be availed quickly, when the need for funds arise.	• They are short-term and unsecured deposits. Thus, they are not suitable for the long-term financial needs of the business. • The rate of interests on these deposits is higher than that of banks. • They are risky deposits from the point of view of lenders. • They have no organised market, where they can be bought and sold.

Owner's Fund *Vs* Borrowed Fund

Basis	Owner's Fund	Borrowed Fund
Meaning	It refers to the funds provided by the owner of the business enterprise.	It refers to the funds raised through loans and borrowings.
Period of Investment	It is a permanent source of capital for business.	It is for a specified period, depending upon the nature of need.
Requirement of Security	It does not require any security.	It is provided on the security of some fixed assets.
Control	The providers of owners' funds have a control over the management of business.	The providers of borrowed funds do not get the right to control.
Risk of Refund	There is a risk involved in the refund of owners' funds as they are the primary risk bearer.	There is negligible risk involved in the refund of borrowed funds.
Return	Return is known as dividend, which varies with earnings of the company.	The providers of borrowed funds get interest at a fixed rate at regular intervals.
Sources	Equity shares, preference shares, retained earnings, etc.	Debentures and bonds, loans, inter-corporate deposits, trade credit, public deposits, etc.

Mind Map

1 Business Finance

The requirement of funds by business to carry out its various activities is called business finance.

Nature

- The concept of business finance is very wide and is used in every type of business house whether it is small or large
- It includes all types of funds and capital that are needed to start, run, expand and diversify the business
- The primary goal of business finance is to increase the corporate value

2 Sources of Finance

1. **Classification on the Basis of Period**
   - Long-term sources (for exceeding five years)
   - Medium-term sources (for exceeding one year but less than five years)
   - Short-term sources (for less than one year)
2. **Classification on the Basis of Source of Generation**
   - **Internal Sources** These include all those funds which are generated from within the business.
   - **External Sources** These include all those funds which are generated from outside the business.
3. **Classification on the Basis of Ownership**
   On the basis of ownership, sources of finance can be classified as owner's funds and borrowed funds.

SOURCES OF BUSINESS FINANCE

3 Owner's Funds

Funds or finance provided by the owners of the business is referred to as owner's funds. These sources include retained earnings and shares.

Retained Earnings

Business retain a part of profits for future expansion of the company. This part is known as retained earnings. This is also referred to as ploughing back of profits.

Merits

- Permanent source of funds
- Does not involve explicit cost
- Operational freedom and flexibility
- Enhances capacity of business
- Increase in the market price of equity shares

Demerits

- Excessive ploughing back may cause dissatisfaction amongst the shareholders
- Uncertain source of fund
- Lack of recognition of opportunity cost leads to insignificant use of funds

Equity Shares

The money raised by issue of equity shares is known as equity share capital. The holders of equity shares are called equity shareholders. Equity shares represent the ownership of a company. Payment of dividend to equity shareholders is not compulsory. Therefore, there is no burden on the company. Every successive issue of equity shares reduces the voting power and earnings of equity shareholders.

Preference Shares

The capital raised by issue of preference shares is called preference share capital. They have right to receive dividend at a fixed rate, before dividend is paid to equity shareholders and right to receive repayment of capital at the time of dissolution of the company. This right authorises them to receive payment against capital before any amount is paid to equity shareholders.

4 Borrowed Funds

The funds that are raised by way of loans and credit from the public, banks and financial institutions are termed as borrowed funds.

Loans from Financial Institutions

The government has established a number of financial institutions all over the country. These institutions are established by the Central as well as State Governments. These institutions provide loan for medium and long-term needs of a business. They provide long-term finance, that are not provided by commercial banks. These institutions also extend technical and managerial support to business firms.

Loans from Commercial Banks

Commercial banks extend loans to the business firms for different purposes and different time periods. Banks provide timely assistance to business by providing funds as and when needed. Secrecy of business can be maintained as the information supplied to the bank by the borrowers is kept confidential. However, funds are generally available for short periods and its extension or renewal is uncertain and difficult.

Debentures/Bonds

Debenture issued by a company is basically a written acknowledgement that the company has borrowed a certain amount of money and promises to repay it at a future date.

Debentures are basically borrowed funds due to which, the debenture holders are deemed to be the creditors of the company. Debenture holders receive a fixed rate of interest at a specified interval of six months or one year.

Public Deposits

The deposits that are raised by business organisations directly from the public are known as public deposits. Cost of public deposits is generally lower than the cost of borrowings from banks and others institutions. Public deposits do not usually create any charge on the assets of the company. As the depositors do not have voting rights, the control of the company is not reduced.

Trade Credit

The credit extended by one trader to another for the purchase of goods and services is called trade credit. Trade credit is a convenient and continuous source of funds. It is readily available, in case the credit worthiness of the customers is known to the seller. However, trade credit may motivate a firm to overtrade. Overtrading occurs when a firm purchases more goods than it needs, only because they are being offered on credit. Only limited amount of funds can be raised through this source.

Inter-Corporate Deposits (ICDs)

The unsecured short-term deposits that are made by one company with another company for a period of minimum 7 days which can be extended up to one year are called inter-corporate deposits. ICDs are generally unsecured. There are not much legal formalities involved in it. They are generally facilitated through brokers, who maintain absolute secrecy about the lending and borrowing companies.

EXAM PATTERN QUESTIONS

Objective Type Questions

Multiple Choice Questions (MCQs)

1. The amount required for purchasing building, plant and machinery is known as ....

(a) working capital (b) authorised capital
(c) fixed capital (d) permanent capital

2. Every business requires funds to face the economic cycle. Economic cycle refers to the time period between ....

(a) buying raw material and making sales
(b) growth and recession
(c) borrowing money and repaying it
(d) commencement and winding up of business

3. TechnoCraft Pvt. Ltd. is a manufacturing company that specialises in producing heavy machinery. The company recently decided to expand its operations by setting-up a new plant. For this, it required significant investment in purchasing land, machinery and other equipment. TechnoCraft's management financed these needs through long-term loans and equity.

Additionally, the company needs funds for day-to-day operations, such as buying raw materials, paying electricity bills and employee salaries. The management observed that during the festive season, demand for their machinery surges, which requires them to maintain higher inventories and extend credit to customers. To manage this, they utilise short-term sources of finance.

What type of financial need is required to purchase land and machinery? Competency Based Que

(a) Fixed capital requirements
(b) Working capital requirements
(c) Short-term loans
(d) Contingency funds

4. The given image illustrates the payment of electricity bill. Identify the type of financial need indicated.

(a) Fixed capital requirements
(b) Working capital requirements
(c) Short-term loans
(d) Contingency funds

5. Identify the type of financial need illustrated in the below picture where plant and machinery are used to carry out the operations of the business.

(a) Fixed capital requirements
(b) Working capital requirements
(c) Short-term loans
(d) Contingency funds

6. When comparing sources of finance, owner's funds do not require repayment and provide the owner with control over the business. On the other hand, borrowed funds come with a fixed repayment period. Identify the characteristic of owner's funds mentioned in the statement. Competency Based Que

(a) Owner's funds do not require security
(b) Borrowed funds do not require repayment
(c) Borrowed funds offer control to the owner
(d) Owner's funds are temporary

7. "Retained earnings offer a permanent source of capital without involving explicit costs. However, excessive ploughing back of profits may cause dissatisfaction among shareholders."
Identify the disadvantage of retained earnings discussed in the above statement. Competency Based Que

(a) They may lead to dissatisfaction among shareholders due to lower dividends
(b) They are not suitable for long-term financial needs
(c) They are uncertain and fluctuate with profits
(d) They require the payment of interest

8. Elite Ltd. has been operating successfully in the textile industry for over a decade. Instead of distributing all its profits as dividends, the company retains a significant portion of its earnings every year to fund future expansion plans.

This approach has helped the company maintain operational flexibility and absorb unexpected market fluctuations. However, some shareholders have expressed dissatisfaction due to reduced dividend payouts. Despite this, Elite Ltd. believes this strategy will enhance its long-term growth and increase the market value of its shares. Which characteristic of owner's funds is highlighted by Elite Ltd.'s strategy of retaining earnings? Competency Based Que

(a) Permanent source of funds
(b) Dependence on external funding
(c) Regular dividend distribution
(d) Short-term operational freedom

9. Bright Future Ltd. is a manufacturing company planning to expand its operations by setting-up a new production unit. The company requires funds for the project and is exploring various sources of finance. For purchasing land and building, it is looking for a reliable source that can provide finance for more than five years. For the advertisement of its new product, it needs a source of finance for about three years.

Additionally, the company requires funds to maintain sufficient working capital to meet its daily operational needs. The management is also considering reinvesting a portion of the company's retained earnings to minimise external borrowing. Which source of finance is most suitable for purchasing land and building? Competency Based Que

(a) Trade credit (b) Issue of shares
(c) Commercial paper (d) Public deposits

10. Which of the following preferential rights is/are enjoyed by preference shareholders over equity shareholders?

(a) Right to receive repayment of capital before that of equity
(b) Right to receive fixed rate of dividend
(c) Both (a) and (b)
(d) Voting rights

11. Rohit, an investor, is analysing various options for long-term investment. He is interested in investing in a company where he can participate in its management and take advantage of higher returns, even if it involves some risk.

While reviewing the company's proposal, he learns that the company plans to raise funds without creating any charge on its assets.

Which source of finance is the company planning to use? Competency Based Que

(a) Debentures (b) Equity shares
(c) Preference shares (d) Public deposits

12. Meera is a cautious investor who prioritises a stable income with minimal risk. She is considering investing in a company's financial instrument that offers fixed dividends but does not provide voting rights or a share in management decisions.

The company assures her that its assets will not be mortgaged to raise these funds.

Which financial instrument is the company offering to Meera? Competency Based Que

(a) Equity shares
(b) Debentures
(c) Preference shares
(d) Public deposits

13. A company is planning to issue shares that ensure fixed annual dividends but do not allow shareholders to claim any unpaid dividends in future years. The company clarifies that these shares will not grant holders the right to share in surplus profits or convert them into equity shares.

What type of preference shares is the company offering? Competency Based Que

(a) Cumulative convertible preference shares
(b) Non-cumulative non-participating preference shares
(c) Participating convertible preference shares
(d) Non-cumulative participating preference shares

14. Debentures are a preferred investment option for those who seek fixed income with lesser risk. This makes them suitable for investors who want predictable returns. Identify the merit of debentures discussed in the statement. Competency Based Que

(a) They provide variable returns based on company profits
(b) They are suited for investors seeking fixed income at lesser risk
(c) They offer high returns with high risk
(d) They carry voting rights for investors

15. XYZ Pvt. Ltd. required additional capital to expand its operations. The company approached a bank and secured a loan of ₹ 50 lakh. It also issued debentures worth ₹ 30 lakh to raise funds from the public. These sources of finance will be repaid over time with interest. The management believes this approach will help achieve the expansion objectives while keeping ownership unaffected.

Which of the following is the key characteristic of borrowed funds as used by XYZ Pvt. Ltd.? Competency Based Que

(a) No repayment obligation
(b) Ownership remains unaffected
(c) They represent the capital of shareholders
(d) They do not involve any interest payment

16. **ABC Ltd. planned to raise funds by issuing various types of debentures. It issued secured debentures by mortgaging its property and convertible debentures, which could be converted into equity shares after five years.**

Additionally, the company also issued registered debentures to a select group of investors, ensuring they were recorded in the company's register. To attract investors seeking no interest payments, it issued zero-interest debentures at a discounted price, redeemable at par after maturity.

Which type of debenture issued by ABC Ltd. ensures the holder's name is recorded in the company's register? Competency Based Que

(a) Bearer debentures
(b) Registered debentures
(c) Convertible debentures
(d) Secured debentures

17. **"Commercial banks offer loans to business firms for various purposes and periods, including options like cash credits and overdrafts. The repayment terms can vary depending on the agreement."**

Identify the characteristic of loans from commercial banks mentioned in the above statement.

Competency Based Que

(a) They are provided without any security
(b) They have fixed repayment terms that cannot be altered
(c) Repayment is flexible and based on mutual agreement
(d) Interest rates are fixed and unchangeable

18. **Sharma Enterprises required additional funds to expand its production capacity. The company approached a commercial bank and secured a loan. The funds were disbursed promptly and the enterprise appreciated the confidentiality maintained by the bank. The loan process was straightforward, without the need for issuing a prospectus. However, the bank imposed stringent terms and conditions and the company was concerned about the loan's short repayment period, which might hinder its financial planning.**

What is one key disadvantage of taking loans from commercial banks as faced by Sharma Enterprises? Competency Based Que

(a) Secrecy of business is compromised
(b) Funds are usually available only for short periods
(c) Formalities for raising funds are complex
(d) Loan amounts cannot be adjusted to business needs

19. **ABC Pvt. Ltd., a medium-scale enterprise, sought financial assistance to expand its manufacturing unit. The company approached the Industrial Finance Corporation of India (IFCI) for long-term funding, as it focuses on regional development and supports new entrepreneurs.**

However, the firm also explored other options like the State Financial Corporation (SFC) in their region for medium-term finance and ICICI, which specialises in providing assistance to private sector enterprises for modernisation.

ABC Pvt. Ltd. found that these institutions had varying objectives but shared a common goal of industrial development. Which financial institution is primarily focused on providing medium-term and short-term finance to industries within a specific State?

Competency Based Que

(a) Industrial Development Bank of India (IDBI)
(b) State Financial Corporation (SFC)
(c) Industrial Credit and Investment Corporation of India (ICICI)
(d) Unit Trust of India (UTI)

20. **Which of the following statements is incorrect regarding public deposits?**

(a) The procedure of obtaining deposits is simple and does not contain restrictive conditions
(b) Public deposits generally create a charge on the assets of the company
(c) The cost of public deposits is generally lower than the cost of borrowings from banks and other institutions
(d) New companies generally find it difficult to raise funds through public deposits

21. **XYZ Ltd. is a company that raises funds directly from the public in the form of public deposits. It offers a fixed rate of interest, which is generally higher than the interest offered on bank deposits. The company invites deposits for a period of 2 years and the acceptance of these deposits is regulated by the Reserve Bank of India. A person wishing to deposit money with XYZ Ltd. must fill out a prescribed form, and the company provides a deposit receipt as an acknowledgment of the debt.**

Which of the following statements is true regarding public deposits? Competency Based Que

(a) Public deposits are a source of long-term finance for companies
(b) Public deposits can be raised without the regulation of the Reserve Bank of India
(c) Companies generally raise public deposits for a period of upto three years
(d) The interest rate on public deposits is generally lower than that on bank deposits

22. **Jupiter Ltd. is well-known manufacturer of sanitary fittings. Recently, company was short of funds for meeting its day-to-day expenses. So, the company approached one of its suppliers to grant 60 days credit on purchase of raw material. On the basis of credit worthiness of Jupiter Ltd. the supplier granted the credit.**

Identify the source of finance highlighted in the given case. Competency Based Que

(a) Commercial papers
(b) Trade credit
(c) Bills of exchange
(d) Cash credit

23. Which of the following statements is incorrect regarding trade credit?

(a) Trade credit is a convenient and continuous source of funds
(b) Trade credit can be used to finance the increase in inventory of goods if an organisation expects higher sales in the near future
(c) Trade credit is generally a less costly source of funds compared to other sources
(d) Trade credit may motivate a firm to overtrade, resulting in purchasing more goods than necessary

24. If the credit is extended by one trader to another for the purchase of goods and services it is called

(a) trade credit (b) loan
(c) debt (d) asset

25. Identify the type of source of finance illustrated in the below picture.

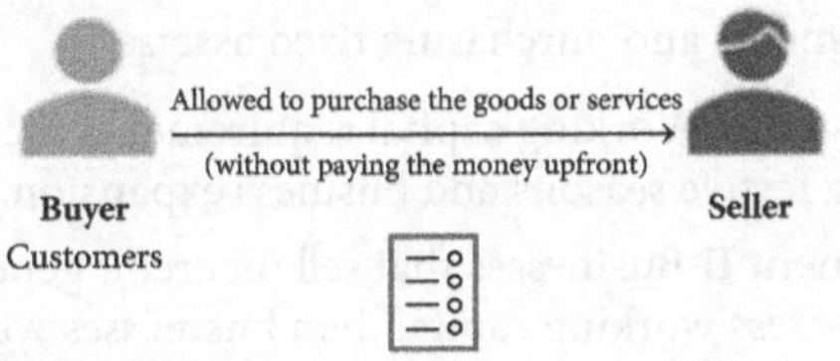

(a) Trade credit (b) Public deposit
(c) Equity shares (d) Debentures

26. To meet the problem of short-term capital inadequacy, Harman Ltd. borrowed ₹ 4 crore from Rana Ltd. which had surplus funds. Although Rana Ltd. charged higher interest rates as compared to bank borrowings, still Harman Ltd. preferred this source as no security had to be given to raise funds. Identify the source of finance being discussed in the given case. Competency Based Que

(a) Equity shares (b) Preference shares
(c) Public deposits (d) Inter-corporate deposits

27. Which of the following statements is incorrect regarding Inter-Corporate Deposits (ICDs)?

(a) ICDs are generally unsecured and can be made for a minimum of 7 days
(b) The interest rate on three month deposits is typically around 15 per cent per annum
(c) Call deposits can be withdrawn by the lending company with a one day notice
(d) Six months deposits are made only with companies that have a high credit rating

28. "Laws cannot cover every circumstance and businesses must deal with urgent capital needs. Inter-Corporate Deposits (ICDs) offer a quick solution to such needs." Identify the merit of ICDs discussed in the above statement. Competency Based Que

(a) They are short-term and unsecured deposits
(b) They are a good source of working capital
(c) They require a lengthy approval process
(d) They are generally low-risk deposits

Direction *Read the case study and answer the questions 29 to 32 on the basis of the same*

PQR Ltd., a company engaged in the production of electronic gadgets, is looking to expand its operations. The management is considering two options: either to diversify into manufacturing smartwatches or to venture into the production of electric vehicles.

The company plans to invest in setting-up a new manufacturing facility in the outskirts of Bengaluru. To finance the investment, the finance manager is tasked with identifying suitable sources of long-term funds for capital expenditures and short-term sources for working capital needs.

29. Identify which of the following is not the long-term source of finance?

(a) Equity shares (b) Retained earnings
(c) ADR (d) Public deposits

30. Which of the following sources of finance would involve the least financial risk for PQR Ltd. in financing its expansion?

(a) Equity shares
(b) Retained earnings
(c) Debentures
(d) Public deposits

31. "It facilitates the purchase of materials for manufacturing without immediate payment." Which source of finance is being described for working capital needs?

(a) Commercial paper
(b) Retained earnings
(c) Subsidy
(d) Trade credit

32. Which of the following long-term sources of finance would PQR Ltd. use if it wanted to reinvest its profits for further expansion without involving external investors?

(a) Preference shares
(b) Lease financing
(c) Retained earnings
(d) Bank loans

Assertion-Reason

Direction (Q. No. 33 to 42) *Read the following Assertion (A) and Reason (R) and choose the correct alternative from the following*

Alternatives

(a) Both Assertion (A) and Reason (R) are true and Reason (R) is the correct explanation of Assertion (A)
(b) Both Assertion (A) and Reason (R) are true, but Reason (R) is not the correct explanation of Assertion (A)
(c) Assertion (A) is true, but Reason (R) is false
(d) Assertion (A) is false, but Reason (R) is true

33. **Assertion** (A) Retained earnings can only be used by an established firm and not by a new firm.

Reason (R) A newly established firm has not yet earned any profits to be used as reserves.

34. **Assertion** (A) Equity share capital acts as a temporary source of capital for the business.

Reason (R) Equity capital is to be repaid at the time of liquidation of a company.

35. **Assertion** (A) Equity shares create an additional source of capital in a business.

Reason (R) Equity share capital is the best source of long-term capital.

36. **Assertion** (A) Debentures are preferred by investors who seek fixed income with lower risk.

Reason (R) Debentures offer a fixed charge on funds and do not participate in the company's profits.

37. **Assertion** (A) Secured debentures create a charge on the company's assets.

Reason (R) Debenture holders have a claim over the assets in case of default by the company.

38. **Assertion** (A) Debentures put a permanent burden on a company's earnings.

Reason (R) The risk increases if a company's earnings fluctuate.

39. **Assertion** (A) Loans from commercial banks are flexible as they can be repaid in advance when funds are not needed.

Reason (R) Loans from commercial banks require formalities like issuing a prospectus and underwriting.

40. **Assertion** (A) Loans from financial institutions are a better option for long-term finance.

Reason (R) Financial institutions provide technical and managerial support along with financial assistance.

41. **Assertion** (A) Loans from financial institutions can be repaid in easy instalments.

Reason (R) The repayment process may be burdensome if strict terms are imposed.

42. **Assertion** (A) Financial institutions may interfere in the management of a company by nominating representatives to the Board of Directors.

Reason (R) This interference can restrict the powers of the management of the borrowing company.

Two Statements Based MCQs

Direction (Q. No. 43 to 52) *Read the following statements carefully and choose the correct alternative*

Alternatives

(a) Statement I is correct and Statement II is incorrect
(b) Statement II is correct and Statement I is incorrect
(c) Both the statements are correct
(d) Both the statements are incorrect

43. **Statement I** Fixed capital is required for purchasing assets like land and machinery and is needed for long-term investments.

Statement II Working capital is used for long-term investments and purchasing fixed assets.

44. **Statement I** Working capital requirements increase during festive seasons and business expansion.

Statement II Businesses that sell on credit generally require less working capital than businesses with cash sales.

45. **Statement I** Owners' funds does not require any security.

Statement II The providers of borrowed funds do not get the right to control.

46. **Statement I** Owner's funds are a permanent source of capital for a business while borrowed funds are for a fixed period of time.

Statement II Borrowed funds do not require any security while owner's funds are secured by the assets of the company.

47. **Statement I** Preference shareholders enjoy the right to receive fixed rate of dividend before any dividend is paid to equity shareholder.

Statement II The issue of preference shares reduces the capacity of the company to further borrow funds.

48. **Statement I** The providers of borrowed funds have control over the business management.

Statement II The providers of owner's funds are entitled to interest payments at a fixed rate.

49. **Statement I** Public deposits are a source of both medium and short-term finance for businesses.

Statement II The interest rate on public deposits is usually lower than that offered by banks.

50. **Statement I** Trade credit is an unsecured form of credit extended by one trader to another for the purchase of goods.

Statement II The conditions for trade credit are fixed and remain the same across all industries.

51. **Statement I** Interest is not payable on trade credit.

Statement II The control of the company is not diluted in case of public deposits.

52. **Statement I** Call deposits under ICDs can be withdrawn by the lending company with a one day notice.

Statement II The rate of interest for call deposits is lower than that of six months deposits.

Matching

53. Match the following

Column I	Column II
A. Shares	(i) The capital which is required for long period
B. Working capital	(ii) The capital which is required for day-to-day operations
C. Fixed capital	(iii) External source of funds

Codes

	A	B	C		A	B	C
(a)	(ii)	(iii)	(i)	(b)	(i)	(iii)	(ii)
(c)	(iii)	(ii)	(i)	(d)	(ii)	(i)	(iii)

54. Match the following

Column I	Column II
A. Retained earnings	(i) Have voting rights in proportion to the shares held by shareholders.
B. Equity shares	(ii) Right to receive repayment of capital at the time of dissolution.
C. Preference shares	(iii) Part of profits which is kept as reserve for use in the future.

Codes

	A	B	C		A	B	C
(a)	(iii)	(i)	(ii)	(b)	(iii)	(ii)	(i)
(c)	(i)	(iii)	(ii)	(d)	(ii)	(i)	(iii)

55. Match the following

Column I	Column II
A. Secured debentures	(i) Not recorded and transferred by delivery only
B. Unsecured debentures	(ii) Recorded in the register of debentureholders
C. Registered debentures	(iii) Do not create any charge on the assets
D. Bearer debentures	(iv) Create charge on the assets

Codes

	A	B	C	D		A	B	C	D
(a)	(ii)	(i)	(iii)	(iv)	(b)	(iv)	(iii)	(ii)	(i)
(c)	(i)	(iii)	(ii)	(iv)	(d)	(ii)	(iii)	(i)	(iv)

56. Match the following

Column I	Column II
A. Debentures	(i) They do not create charge on assets
B. Trade credit	(ii) They create charge on assets
C. Public deposits	(iii) These include call deposits.
D. Inter-corporate deposits	(iv) These are not issued in a foreign currency

Codes

	A	B	C	D		A	B	C	D
(a)	(ii)	(i)	(iv)	(iii)	(b)	(iii)	(ii)	(i)	(iv)
(c)	(i)	(iii)	(ii)	(iv)	(d)	(iv)	(ii)	(iii)	(i)

57. Match the following

Column I	Column II
A. Trade credit	(i) Commercial banks such as State Bank of India, Canara Bank, etc. extend loans to the business firms.
B. Inter-corporate deposits	(ii) The deposits that are raised by business organisations directly from the public.
C. Public deposits	(iii) Unsecured short-term deposits that are made by one company with another company for a period of minimum 7 days.
D. Loans from commercial banks	(iv) Credit extended by one trader to another for the purchase of goods and services.

Codes

	A	B	C	D		A	B	C	D
(a)	(ii)	(i)	(iii)	(iv)	(b)	(iv)	(iii)	(ii)	(i)
(c)	(i)	(iii)	(ii)	(iv)	(d)	(ii)	(i)	(iv)	(iii)

Answers

1. (c) fixed capital
2. (b) growth and recession
3. (a) Fixed capital requirements
4. (b) Working capital requirements
5. (a) Fixed capital requirements
6. (a) Owner's funds do not require security
7. (a) They may lead to dissatisfaction among shareholders due to lower dividends
8. (a) Permanent source of funds
9. (b) Issue of shares
10. (c) Both (a) and (b)
11. (b) Equity shares
12. (c) Preference shares
13. (b) Non-cumulative non-participating preference shares
14. (b) They are suited for investors seeking fixed income at lesser risk
15. (b) Ownership remains unaffected
16. (b) Registered debentures
17. (c) Repayment is flexible and based on mutual agreement
18. (b) Funds are usually available only for short periods
19. (b) State Financial Corporation (SFC)
20. (b) Public deposits typically do not create a charge on the assets of the company. This is one of the advantages of public deposits, as they do not require collateral or security, unlike borrowings from banks or financial institutions.
21. (c) Companies generally raise public deposits for a period of upto three years
22. (b) Trade credit
23. (c) Trade credit is often considered a costly source of finance compared to other sources like bank loans or public deposits.
24. (a) trade credit
25. (a) Trade credit
26. (d) Inter-corporate deposits
27. (b) The correct interest rate for three month deposits is around 12 per cent per annum, not 15 per cent.
28. (b) They are a good source of working capital
29. (d) Public deposits
30. (a) Equity shares
31. (d) Trade credit
32. (c) Retained earnings
33. (a) Both Assertion (A) and Reason (R) are true and Reason (R) is the correct explanation of Assertion (A)
34. (d) Equity share capital is a permanent source of capital for a business, not a temporary one. It represents ownership in the company.
35. (b) Both Assertion (A) and Reason (R) are true, but Reason (R) is not the correct explanation of Assertion (A)
36. (a) Both Assertion (A) and Reason (R) are true and Reason (R) is the correct explanation of Assertion (A)
37. (a) Both Assertion (A) and Reason (R) are true and Reason (R) is the correct explanation of Assertion (A)
38. (b) Both Assertion (A) and Reason (R) are true, but Reason (R) is not the correct explanation of Assertion (A)
39. (c) Loans from commercial banks do not require the formalities of issuing a prospectus and underwriting, which are usually needed for equity financing.
40. (a) Both Assertion (A) and Reason (R) are true and Reason (R) is the correct explanation of Assertion (A)
41. (b) Both Assertion (A) and Reason (R) are true, but Reason (R) is not the correct explanation of Assertion (A)
42. (b) Both Assertion (A) and Reason (R) are true, but Reason (R) is not the correct explanation of Assertion (A)
43. (a) Working capital is for day-to-day operations, while fixed capital is for long-term investments.
44. (a) Credit sales typically require more working capital than cash sales.
45. (c) Both the statements are correct
46. (a) Owner's funds are permanent, and borrowed funds are typically secured by assets.
47. (a) The issue of preference shares may have an impact on the company's capital structure and the perception of lenders, but it doesn't reduce borrowing capacity in a straightforward manner.
48. (d) Borrowed funds do not give control over management and owner's funds are not paid a fixed interest.
49. (a) Public deposits typically offer higher interest rates than bank deposits to attract investors.
50. (a) Trade credit varies from industry to industry and person to person.
51. (c) Both the statements are correct
52. (c) Both the statements are correct
53. (c) (iii) (ii) (i)
54. (a) (iii) (i) (ii)
55. (b) (iv) (iii) (ii) (i)
56. (a) (ii) (i) (iv) (iii)
57. (b) (iv) (iii) (ii) (i)

Subjective Questions

Short Answer Type Questions

1. What is business finance? Why does business need funds? Explain. NCERT

Ans. Requirements of funds by business to carry out its various activities is called business finance. Funds are required to commence and carry on business.

All business activities such as planning, organising, managing, controlling, purchasing, selling, directing, marketing, etc. cannot take place without finance.

Businesses need funds due to the following reasons

(i) An organisation needs machinery, buildings, furniture, etc. to set-up operations and to purchase all these items, funds are needed. This is called fixed capital requirement. The amount varies with the type of business.

(ii) To run day-to-day operations like purchasing raw materials requires regular funds, also called working capital requirement.

2. Discuss the significance of business finance.

Ans. Business significance is important because of the following reasons

(i) **Necessary to Start Business**
Every new venture needs money to buy plant and machinery, land and building, raw material, etc. So, finance is significant to start a business.

(ii) **Necessary to Face Economic Cycle**
During recession and depression, the sales of the business go down and the profitability is adversely affected. To overcome problems during such times, finance is significant.

(iii) **Necessary for Growth**
Sometimes, in order to attain more or to achieve greater success, a company needs significant financial investment to acquire new capital, staff or inventory.

(iv) **Necessary for the Payments of Debts**
It is necessary that a business firm meets its liabilities in time. Prompt payment of debts can be possible only because of adequate arrangement of finance.

(v) **Necessary for Availing the Opportunities**
Business can take the advantage of upcoming opportunities and can earn more, only if it has adequate finance at its disposal.

3. Write a short note on 'working capital requirements'.

Ans. A business also needs finance to carry out the day-to-day operations such as purchase of raw material, payment of electricity bill, rent, salaries, wages, taxes, etc. The amount required to meet these needs is known as the working capital requirements of the business.

The following points should be kept in mind regarding the working capital requirements

(i) If the operating cycle of a business, is shorter, then the amount of working capital required will be lesser and *vice-versa.*

(ii) Working capital requirements are generally met through short-term sources of finance.

(iii) A business selling goods on credit or having slow sales turnover require more working capital than other concern selling on cash basis or having a faster sales turnover.

(iv) Working capital requirement increases during festive season, expansion of business, shifting to a new location and payments of current debts.

4. What is the difference between internal and external sources of raising funds? Explain. NCERT

Ans. Following are the differences between internal and external sources of funds (any four)

Basis	Internal Sources	External Sources
Meaning	Internal sources of funds are those that are generated within the business.	External sources of funds include those sources that lie outside an organisation, such as suppliers, lenders and investors.
Examples	The examples of these sources are accelerating collection of receivables, disposing-off surplus inventories and ploughing back of profit.	The examples of these sources are issue of debentures, borrowing from commercial banks and financial institutions and accepting public deposits.
Purpose	The internal sources of funds can fulfill only limited needs of the business.	Large amount of money can be raised through external sources.
Cost	Cost of internal funds is low.	External funds are more costly.
Security Required	Business is not required to provide security while obtaining funds from internal sources.	Business is required to mortgage its assets as security while obtaining funds from external sources.

5. What do you understand by share, share capital and shareholders? Explain with the help of an example.

Ans. Shares

The capital of a company is divided into small units and each such unit is referred to as a 'share'.

Each share forms a unit of ownership and is offered for sale to raise the capital of the company. Shares are classified as equity shares and preference shares.

Share Capital
Total amount raised by issue of shares constitute the share capital of the company.

Shareholders
The persons who buy shares are referred to as 'shareholders'. e.g. Sun Rise company issues 10,000 shares of ₹ 10 each for a total value of ₹ 1,00,000.
In the above example, number of shares issued are 10,000, share capital is of ₹ 1,00,000 and the persons who purchase these shares are shareholders.

6. "Equity shares provide companies with a permanent source of capital without any obligation to repay the funds. However, they dilute the control of existing shareholders and involve higher costs due to dividend expectations and regulatory compliance."
In light of the above statement, explain the drawbacks of equity shares. **Competency Based Que**

Ans. Following are the drawbacks of equity shares
(i) Investors who want steady income may not prefer equity shares due to fluctuating returns.
(ii) The cost of equity shares is more as compared to other sources of funds.
(iii) Every successive issue of equity shares reduces the voting power and earnings of existing equity shareholders.
(iv) Many formalities and procedural delays are involved while raising funds through equity.

7. "Preference shareholders often hold a unique position in a company, benefitting from rights such as priority in dividend distribution and repayment of capital in liquidation. However, these rights also limit their influence on company management."
In light of the above statement, list the two preferential rights enjoyed by preference shareholders compared to equity shareholders. **Competency Based Que**

Or **What preferential rights are engaged by preference shareholders? Explain.** **NCERT**

Ans. Preference shares confer following two preferential rights to its holders
(i) Right to receive dividend at a fixed rate, before dividend is paid to equity shareholders.
(ii) Right to receive repayment of capital at the time of dissolution of the company. This right authorises them to receive payment against capital before any amount is paid to equity shareholders.

8. "Debentures are a popular means of raising long-term funds, characterised by fixed interest rates, transferability and legal obligations to repay. Despite their advantages, they pose repayment risks to companies during financial crises."
Based on the above statement, discuss the various characteristics of debentures. **Competency Based Que**

Ans. The characteristics of debentures are
(i) Debentures are basically borrowed funds due to which, the debentureholders are deemed to be the creditors of the company.
(ii) Debentureholders receive a fixed rate of interest at a specified interval of six months or one year.
(iii) Public issue of debentures requires that the issue be rated by a credit rating agency like CRISIL (Credit Rating and Information Services of India Ltd.) on the basis like track record of company, its profitability, debt servicing capacity, credit worthiness and the perceived risk of lending.

9. What advantages does issue of debentures provide over the issue of equity shares? **NCERT**

Ans. Debentures provide the following advantages over equity shares
(i) Issuing equity shares makes the shareholders own the company and they become entitled to voting rights, while debentureholders do not have any rights in the organisation. They get a fixed amount in the form of payment. Debentures thus, do not contribute towards the dilution of ownership of the company and can be issued without any risk.
(ii) For issuing shares, the company has to bear huge costs; also, dividends payment is not tax deductible. For interest paid to debentures, the company receives tax deductions, so issuing debentures is beneficial.
(iii) Debentures have a fixed rate of return. So, if no profit is also earned, then also the company needs to pay the dividend, which is at a fixed rate. On the other hand, a company issuing equity shares and making profit needs to share more with the shareholders, which varies with the profit earned. Thus, it is better to issue debentures.

10. "Loans from commercial banks offer companies an accessible source of finance with structured repayment options, yet they often come with stringent documentation requirements and collateral demands."
In light of the above statement, state the conditions of loans from commercial banks. **Competency Based Que**

Ans. The conditions of loans from commercial banks are

(i) Banks extend credit in many ways, like, cash credits, overdrafts, discounting of bills of exchange and issue of letter of credit.

(ii) The repayment of loan or credit is made by the borrower in lumpsum or in instalments as per the agreement between the bank and the borrower.

(iii) Interest charged by banks depends upon a number of factors, such as nature of advance, period for which the loan is taken, etc.

(iv) Loan is generally offered by banks on security of assets.

11. State any three demerits of 'loans from commercial banks' as a source of finance.

Ans. Following are the demerits of 'loans from commercial banks' as a source of finance

(i) Funds are generally available for short periods and its extension or renewal is uncertain and difficult.

(ii) Banks make detailed investigation of the company's affairs, financial structure, etc. This makes the procedure of obtaining funds slightly difficult.

(iii) In some cases, difficult terms and conditions are imposed by banks for the grant of loan.

12. State any four types of special finance institutions that aid in providing finance.

Ans. Following are the types of special finance institutions that aid in providing finance

(i) **Industrial Finance Corporation of India** (IFCI)

It was established in July 1948, as a statutory corporation under the Industrial Finance Corporation Act, 1948. Its objectives include assistance towards balanced regional development and encouraging new entrepreneurs to enter into the priority sectors of the economy.

(ii) **State Financial Corporations** (SFCs)

It was established under the State Financial Corporations Act, 1951. This act empowered the State Governments to establish State Financial Corporations in their respective regions. These provide medium and short-term finance to industries, which are outside the scope of the IFCI.

(iii) **Industrial Credit and Investment Corporation of India** (ICICI)

It was established in 1955 as a public limited company under the Companies Act. It assists the creation, expansion and modernisation of industrial enterprises exclusively in the private sector.

(iv) **Industrial Development Bank of India** (IDBI)

It was established in 1964 under the Industrial Development Bank of India Act, 1964. Its objective is to coordinate the activities of other financial institutions including commercial banks.

13. Discuss in brief the types of Inter-Corporate Deposits (ICDs).

Ans. Three types of Inter-Corporate Deposits (ICDs) are

(i) **Call Deposits**

It is a deposit which can be withdrawn by the lender by giving a one day notice. The annual interest rate is around 10 per cent.

(ii) **Three Months Deposit**

It is a deposit made for a period of three months. It is used to finance short-term needs of funds such as payment of tax, payment of dividend, etc. The annual interest rate is around 12 per cent.

(iii) **Six Months Deposit**

It is a deposit made for a period of six-months. It is usually made with first class borrowers. The annual interest rate is around 15 per cent.

14. "Owners' funds represent the shareholders' commitment to the business and remain a permanent source of capital, whereas borrowed funds provide short-term liquidity but add financial leverage to the company."

In the context of the above statement, distinguish between owners' funds and borrowed funds.

Competency Based Que

Ans. Following are the differences between owners' fund and borrowed fund (any four)

Basis	Owner's Fund	Borrowed Fund
Meaning	It refers to the funds provided by the owner of the business enterprise.	It refers to the funds raised through loans and borrowings.
Requirement of Security	It does not require any security.	Borrowed funds are generally provided on the security of some fixed assets.
Control	The providers of owners' funds have a control over the management of business.	The providers of borrowed funds do not get the right to control.
Risk of Refund	There is a risk involved in the refund of owners' funds as they are the primary risk bearer.	There is negligible risk involved in the refund of borrowed funds.
Return	Return is known as dividend, which varies with earnings of the company.	The providers of borrowed funds get interest at a fixed rate at regular intervals.
Sources	Equity shares, preference shares, retained earnings, etc.	Debentures and bonds, loans, inter-corporate deposits, trade credit, public deposits, etc.

Long Answer Type Questions

15. Discuss the sources from which a large industrial enterprise can raise capital for financing, modernisation and expansion. NCERT

Ans. The following sources of capital are suitable for raising capital for expansion

(i) **Equity Shares**

These are the shares that are part of the owner's capital. The persons holding such shares are known as equity shareholders and they enjoy decision-making capacity in management, they also get high returns when the profits of the business get higher.

(ii) **Preference Shares**

This is a type of share that gives shareholders a preferential right with regard to the repayment of capital and earning payments after a period of time. The payment to preference shareholders is done as per Section 80 of the Companies Act, 1956.

(iii) **Loans**

A business can borrow funds from banks and similar financial institutions for a fixed time at a fixed rate/variable rate, and they have to pay interest.

(iv) **Retained Earnings**

These are parts of profit that are kept for use in the future.

(v) **Debentures**

These are instruments that are helpful in raising long-term capital. Debentures are like loans having a fixed rate of return.

16. "Ploughing back of profits, also known as retained earnings, is a key method of internal financing where profits earned by the business are reinvested rather than distributed as dividends. While it provides a cost-effective and readily available source of funds, this approach can sometimes lead to shareholder dissatisfaction and limit diversification opportunities." In light of the above statement, write a short note on ploughing back of profits and state its merits and demerits. Competency Based Que

Ans. A business does not distribute all its trading profits as dividends among the shareholders. It retain a part of these profits for future expansion of the company. This part is known as retained earning. This is also referred to as ploughing back of profits.

Following are the merits of retained earnings

(i) Retained earnings is a permanent source of funds for an organisation.

(ii) It do not involve any explicit cost in the form of interest, dividend or floatation cost.

(iii) It offers a greater degree of operational freedom and flexibility.

(iv) It enhances the capacity of business to absorb unexpected losses.

(v) It may lead to an increase in the market price of equity shares issued by the company.

Following are the demerits of retained earnings

(i) Excessive ploughing back may cause dissatisfaction amongst the shareholders, as they would get lower dividends.

(ii) As the profits of business are fluctuating, it is an uncertain source of fund.

(iii) Firms do not recognise the opportunity cost associated with this source, which lead to insignificant use of funds.

17. Distinguish between equity shares and preference shares.

Ans. Following are the differences between equity shares and preference shares

Basis	Equity Shares	Preference Shares
Participation in Management	They have full right to participate.	They did not have right to participate.
Sequence of Dividend	In these shares, dividend is paid last of all.	In these shares, preference is given in payment of dividend.
Sequence of Refund of Capital	On winding up of the company, capital is refunded after preference shares.	In these shares, preference is given in refunding the capital.
Refund of Capital During Lifetime	In these shares, capital cannot be refunded at all.	In these shares, capital can be refunded in case of redeemable preference shares.
Permanency of Dividend	In these shares, dividend is uncertain as it fluctuates with the amount of divisible profits decision of board of directors.	In these shares, dividend is certain and fixed.

18. Explain the various types of debentures.

Ans. Following are the various types of debentures

(i) **Secured Debentures**

These create charge on the assets of the company by mortgaging the assets of the company.

(ii) **Unsecured Debentures**

These do not create any charge or security on the assets of the company.

(iii) **Registered Debentures**

These debentures are recorded in the register of debentureholders maintained by the company. They can be transferred through a regular instrument of transfer.

(iv) **Bearer Debentures**
These are not recorded and are transferred by delivery only.

(v) **Convertible Debentures**
These debentures are convertible into equity shares after a specific period.

(vi) **Non-convertible Debentures**
These are not convertible into equity shares after a specific period.

(vii) **First Debentures**
These debentures are repaid before the repayment of any other debentures.

(viii) **Second Debentures**
These are paid after the first debentures have been paid back.

(ix) **Zero Interest Debentures**
No interest is paid on these debentures. These debentures are issued at discount and are redeemed at par. The difference between the issue price. The redemption value is deemed to be the interest.

19. "Public deposits, as a source of business finance, are simple to raise and do not dilute ownership. However, they are often criticised for their limited duration and dependency on the trust of depositors."
In light of the above statement, list the merits and demerits of public deposits. **Competency Based Que**

Ans. Following are the merits of public deposits

(i) The procedure of obtaining deposits is simple and does not contain restrictive conditions.
(ii) Cost of public deposits is generally lower than the cost of borrowings from banks and others institutions.
(iii) Public deposits do not usually create any charge on the assets of the company.
(iv) As the depositors do not have voting rights, the control of the company is not reduced.

Following are the demerits of public deposits

(i) New companies generally find it difficult to raise funds through public deposits.
(ii) It is an unreliable source of finance as the public may not respond when the company needs money.
(iii) Collection of public deposits may prove difficult, when a large size of deposits is required.

20. Explain trade credit and inter-corporate deposits as sources of finance for business enterprises.

Ans. **Trade credit** is the credit extended by one trader to another for the purchase of goods and services. It facilitates the purchase of supplies without immediate payment and is commonly used by business organisations as a source of short-term financing.

Trade credit appears in the records of the buyer as 'sundry creditors' or 'accounts payable'. It is granted prudently to those customers who have reasonable amount of financial standing and goodwill.

The volume and period of credit extended depends on factors such as reputation of the purchasing firm, financial position of the seller, volume of purchases, past record of payment and degree of competition in the market.

Terms of trade credit may vary from industry to industry and from person to person. As we know, trade is the purchase and sale of goods for profit motive. So, trade credit strictly refers to the routine business activity.

Benefits of trade credit are

(i) It helps a company accumulate inventories for increasing sales in future.
(ii) Trade creditors do not have any rights over company assets. Therefore, assets can be mortgaged to raise money from other sources.

Inter-corporate deposits are unsecured short-term deposits that are made by one company with another company for a period of minimum 7 days which can be extended up to one year. ICDs are generally unsecured. Companies having surplus funds lend it to other companies who are in need of funds.

This arrangement is mutually benefitting. The lending company earns interest on its idle funds and the borrowing company is able to fulfill its short-term financial needs.

Benefits of inter-corporate deposits are

(i) There are not much legal formalities involved in it.
(ii) They are generally facilitated through brokers, who maintain absolute secrecy about the lending and borrowing companies.
(iii) They are a good source of working capital.
It can be availed quickly, when the need for funds arise.

Case Study Based Questions

Case Study 1

ABC Co. Ltd. has decided to expand its scale of operation for which it needs funds. A major portion of funds is required for purchasing plant and machinery, while the requirement of funds for its day-to-day operations will also increase due to such decisions. The sources of funds are generally classified into owners fund and borrowed funds. ABC Co. Ltd. can raise required funds by employing both the above mentioned sources to fulfill its needs.

(i) Which two types of capital requirements of ABC Co. Ltd. are discussed above? Give examples of each.

(ii) Name and explain two sources of owner's fund which ABC Co. Ltd. use to raise finance.

Ans.

(i) The two types of capital requirements are as follows

- **Fixed Capital**
  Fixed assets such as land, plant, machinery, etc. are required to start a business. The amount which is required to purchase these assets is known as fixed capital requirements of the enterprise
- **Working Capital**
  A business also needs finance to carry out the day-to-day operations such as purchase of raw material, payment of electricity bill, rent, salaries, wages, taxes, etc. The amount required to meet these needs is known as the working capital requirements of the business.

(ii) Two sources of owner's funds which ABC Co. Ltd use to raise finance are as follows

- **Equity Share Capital**
  Capital is raised by issue of equity shares. These are the most important source of raising long-term finance.
- **Retained Earnings**
  It is that part of profits which is not distributed as dividend and is retained for use in future. A business does not distribute all its trading profits as dividends among the shareholders.

Case Study 2

Amar owns a small farm in which he grows flowers. He is able to earn a small amount of profit, but being of an ambitious nature, he wants to take over a neighbouring farm and increase the range of flowers he is selling.

He is of the view that he will need long-term finance for this purpose and plans to take a bank loan to pay for the take over. He has already borrowed money to buy a new tractor. On the basis of above case, answer the following questions

(i) What is meant by long-term source of finance?

(ii) Identify and explain a form of internal finance Amar could have used to buy the tractor.

(iii) What factors would the bank consider before granting loan to Amar?

Ans.

(i) Long-term sources of finance means those sources which provide finance to business firms for a period exceeding five years.

(ii) A form of internal finance which Amar could have used to buy the tractor is 'retained earnings'. These earnings are a part of trading profits which are not withdrawn by the proprietor, but are reinvested by them in the business.

(iii) The bank would consider the following factors before granting loan to Amar

- Amount of loan required.
- Period for which the loan is required.
- Security offered.
- Profit earning capacity of the business.
- Repayment schedule of any previous loan taken.

Case Study 3

Meenakari Ltd. has good prospects. So it is planning to expand their business. For this the company needs additional funds. The finance manager reports that the company is not in a position to bear extra burden of paying any fixed financial charges like interest or dividend.

They do not want to bear any floatation cost even. Also, the equity shareholders insist not to issue further shares as there is risk of dilution of control.

(i) Identify the source of finance most suitable for Meenakari Ltd.

(ii) State any three benefits of the source of finance identified in (i).

Ans.

(i) The source of finance most suitable for Meenakari Ltd is retained earnings. A business does not distribute all its trading profits as dividends among the shareholders. It retain a part of these profits for future expansion of the company. This part is known as retained earning.

(ii) The benefits of retained earnings are as follows

- It offers a greater degree of operational freedom and flexibility.
- It enhances the capacity of business to absorb unexpected losses.
- It may lead to an increase in the market price of equity shares issued by the company.

Case Study 4

XYZ Ltd., a growing enterprise in the manufacturing sector, plans to expand its operations by raising additional funds. After deliberating on various options, the company decides to choose a source of finance that aligns with its vision. This source does not burden the company with compulsory payouts and offers long-term financial stability.

Moreover, it boosts the company's creditworthiness and ensures that the company's assets remain unencumbered, allowing flexibility for future borrowing. This option is also suitable for investors willing to take risks in exchange for potentially higher returns.

(i) Identify the source of finance used by XYZ Ltd.

(ii) State three merits of this source of finance.

Ans.

(i) The source of finance used by XYZ Ltd. is equity shares. These are the most important source of raising long-term finance. The money raised by issue of equity shares is known as equity share capital. The holders of equity shares are called equity shareholders.

(ii) Following are the merits of equity shares

- Equity shares are suitable for those investors who are willing to assume risk for higher returns.
- Payment of dividend to the equity shareholders is not compulsory. Therefore, there is no burden on the company.
- It is a permanent source of capital. A company is not required to pay back the equity capital during its lifetime. It is repaid only at the time of dissolution of company.

Case Study 5

Sumanti Enterprises. is looking to raise funds for its expansion project. The company decides to issue a new class of shares that will offer a fixed dividend to investors but will not carry voting rights. This option is being chosen as the company wants to raise funds without diluting control over its operations.

The shares will be issued to institutional investors who are seeking a stable income with relatively lower risk compared to equity shares. The decision is based on the company's need for additional capital without increasing its debt burden.

(i) Identify the source of finance.

(ii) State the various types of the source identified in (i).

Ans.

(i) The source of finance used in the case is preference shares. The capital raised by issue of preference shares is called preference share capital.

(ii) Following are the various types of preference shares

- **Cumulative Preference Shares**
  These shares give shareholders the right to receive accumulate dividend from the company even if they are not profitable. These dividends will be counted as arrears in years when the company is not profitable. These will be paid in full from the year when the business is profitable.
- **Non-cumulative Preference Share**
  These shares are provide the shareholder a fixed dividend amounts each year from the company's net profit. If the company fails to pay the dividend on such preference shares to the shareholder in any year, then such dividend cannot be claimed by the shareholder in the future.
- **Participating Preference Shares**
  These shares provide share holders the right to share (participate) in the surplus of company's, after paying dividend on preference and equity shares.
- **Non-participating Preference Shares**
  These shares do not provide shareholder the right to share (participate) in the surplus profits of the company.
- **Convertible Preference Shares**
  These shares can be converted into equity shares after a specified time period.
- **Non-convertible Preference Shares**
  These shares cannot be converted into equity shares.

Case Study 6

Companies issuing different debentures Mahindra and Mahindra was the first company in India to issue convertible zero interest debentures in January, 1990. Recently, the board of Titan Industries has approved the issue of partly convertible debentures on a right's basis to raise around ₹ 126.83 crore. The issue will comprise 21 lakh partly convertible debentures of ₹ 600 each in the ratio of one partly convertible debenture for every 20 equity shares held in the company to the shareholders.

(i) Explain the meaning of convertible zero interest debentures issued by Mahindra and Mahindra.

(ii) Explain the meaning of partly convertible debentures on right's basis.

(iii) State one merit of debentures.

Ans.

(i) Convertible zero interest debentures are debentures which carry no interest and are convertible into equity shares at the end of a specified period.

(ii) Partly convertible debentures on right's basis means that a part of these debentures will be converted into equity shares at the end of the stipulated period and that these debentures can be subscribed by only existing equity shareholders of the company.

(iii) Financing through debentures is less costly as compared to the cost of preference or equity capital, as the interest payment on debentures is deductible.

Case Study 7

Reena Ltd. is a well-known manufacturer of sanitary fittings. Recently, company was short of funds for meeting its day-to-day expenses. So, the company approached one of its suppliers to grant 60 days credit on purchase of raw material. On the basis of creditworthiness of Reena Ltd. the supplier granted the credit. **Competency Based Que**

(i) Identify the source of finance highlighted in the given case.

(ii) State any four merits of the source identified in (i).

Ans.

(i) The source of finance highlighted in the given case is trade credit.

(ii) Following are the merits of trade credit

- Trade credit is a convenient and continuous source of funds.
- It is readily available, in case the credit worthiness of the customers is known to the seller.
- It helps to promote sales of an organisation by ensuring regular supply of tradeable goods and raw materials.
- It can be used to finance the increase in inventory of goods if an organisation expects higher sales in the near future.

Case Study 8

Classic Furnishings, a leading manufacturing company, recently found itself with surplus funds after a profitable quarter. To utilise these idle funds effectively, the management decided to lend them to another company, ABC Pvt. Ltd., which was facing a temporary liquidity crunch.

This arrangement, structured for a period of three months, allowed ABC Pvt. Ltd. to meet its short-term financial obligations while Classic Furnishings earned interest on its excess funds. However, the management of Classic Furnishings was aware that the arrangement was unsecured and depended heavily on the financial stability of ABC Pvt. Ltd.

(i) Identify the source of finance described in the case.

(ii) What are the drawbacks of using the source of finance identified in (i)?

Ans.

(i) The source of finance described in the case is inter-corporate deposits.

(ii) The drawbacks of using inter-corporate deposits is as follows

- They are short-term and unsecured deposits. Thus, they are not suitable for the long-term financial needs of the business.
- The rate of interests on these deposits is higher than that of banks.
- They are risky deposits from the point of view of lenders.
- They have no organised market, where they can be bought and sold.

Long Case Studies

Case Study 9

Ritu Verma was the Chief Financial Officer of Prime Textiles Ltd., a company specialising in high quality fabrics. The company had recently decided to raise additional funds for its upcoming expansion plans. Ritu suggested issuing preference shares as the mode of financing. She emphasised that these shares would ensure fixed dividends to the investors, providing them with secure and stable returns. This decision attracted a group of risk averse investors who preferred assured income over high returns.

However, as the company's profits increased significantly due to the success of its expansion, many investors started showing interest in higher returns through equity shares. Some stakeholders criticised the decision, highlighting that preference shares reduced the equity shareholders' claim on the company's growing assets. Meanwhile, competitors like Elite Fabrics Ltd., who focused more on equity financing, attracted investors willing to take risks for potentially higher returns.

Quoting lines from the above paragraph, identify and explain two merits and two demerits of preference shares as discussed in the case.

Ans. Following are the merits of preference shares as discussed in the case

(i) **Fixed Returns to Investors**

"She emphasised that these shares would ensure fixed dividends to the investors, providing them with secure and stable returns." The dividends to be paid to the preference shareholders are fixed. This ensures the security of fixed returns to the investors.

(ii) **Attracts Risk-averse Investors**

"This decision attracted a group of risk-averse investors who preferred assured income over high returns." These shares are suitable for those investors who want fixed income with comparatively low risk.

Following are the demerits of preference shares as discussed in the case

(i) **Unsuitable for High Risk Investors**

"Many investors started showing interest in higher returns through equity shares." Preference shares are not suitable for those investors who are willing to take risk and are interested in higher returns.

(ii) **Reduces Equity Shareholders' Claims**

"Some stakeholders criticised the decision, highlighting that preference shares reduced the equity shareholders' claim on the company's growing assets." These shares reduce the claim of equity shareholders over the assets of the company.

Case Study 10

Ravi Mehta is the Chief Financial Officer (CFO) of 'Ecostar Industries,' a company known for its eco-friendly consumer appliances. To fund a major expansion project, the company decided to issue debentures worth ₹ 50 crore. Ravi ensured the debenture issuance was structured carefully, offering a competitive interest rate to attract investors.

However, after the issuance, the company faced fluctuating earnings due to market volatility and rising input costs. Despite reduced profits, Ecostar Industries had to meet its fixed interest obligations, which created financial strain.

Additionally, the debentures were redeemable within seven years, requiring the company to make provisions for repayment even during challenging financial periods. This significantly affected the company's ability to allocate funds for other business needs.

Furthermore, with the issue of these debentures, Ecostar Industries reached its borrowing capacity. This restricted the company's ability to secure additional loans when an unexpected opportunity arose to acquire a smaller competitor in the market.

(i) Quoting lines from the above case, identify and explain three demerits of issuing debentures faced by 'Ecostar Industries.'

(ii) State any two features of debentures.

Ans.

(i) Following are the demerits of issuing debentures faced by 'Ecostar Industries'.

- **Fixed Financial Burden**

  "Despite reduced profits, Ecostar Industries had to meet its fixed interest obligations, which created financial strain."

  Debentures put a permanent burden on the earnings of a company. There is a greater risk when earnings of the company fluctuate.

- **Mandatory Repayment Obligation**

  "The debentures were redeemable within seven years, requiring the company to make provisions for repayment even during challenging financial periods." In case of redeemable debentures, the company has to make provisions for repayment on the specified date, even during periods of financial difficulty.

- **Limitation on Borrowing Capacity**

  "With the issue of these debentures, Ecostar Industries reached its borrowing capacity." Each company has certain borrowing capacity. With the issue of debentures, the capacity of a company reduces to further borrow funds.

(ii) Following are the features of debentures

- Debentures are basically borrowed funds due to which, the debentureholders are deemed to be the creditors of the company.
- Debentureholders receive a fixed rate of interest at a specified interval of six months or one year.

Case Study 11

Sunrise Textiles Pvt. Ltd., a leading player in the textile industry, has been experiencing significant growth in demand for its high quality products. To capitalise on this opportunity, the company decided to expand its manufacturing capacity and establish new distribution networks. However, this ambitious expansion required a substantial amount of funding. After evaluating various options, the company approached a well-known financial institution, State Bank of India, for assistance.

The bank presented Sunrise Textiles with several financing options, including cash credit, overdrafts, discounting of bills of exchange and the issuance of letters of credit for trade transactions. These options provided the company with the flexibility to choose the one that best suited its needs. According to the agreement between the bank and the company, the repayment of the loan could be made either in lumpsum or through regular instalments over a specified period, ensuring convenience for the borrower.

The interest rate charged by the bank was influenced by factors such as market conditions, the company's creditworthiness and the duration of the loan. The management of Sunrise Textiles appreciated the convenience and accessibility of this financing option but was aware of the need to adhere strictly to the repayment terms to maintain a good credit history and financial stability.

This move was seen as a strategic step to support the company's growth and strengthen its market position.

(i) Identify the source of finance and list the conditions to raise finance.

(ii) State any three merits of this source of finance.

Ans.

(i) The source of finance used in the case is loan from commercial banks.
Following are the conditions

- Banks extend credit in many ways, like, cash credits, overdrafts, discounting of bills of exchange and issue of letter of credit.
- The repayment of loan or credit is made by the borrower in lumpsum or in instalments as per the agreement between the bank and the borrower.
- Interest charged by banks depends upon a number of factors, such as nature of advance, period for which the loan is taken, etc.
- Loan is generally offered by banks on security of assets.

(ii) Following are the merits of loans from commercial banks

- Banks provide timely assistance to business by providing funds as and when needed.
- Secrecy of business can be maintained as the information supplied to the bank by the borrowers is kept confidential.
- Formalities such as issue of prospectus and underwriting are not required for raising loans from a bank. Therefore, this is an easier source of funds.

Case Study 12

ABC Industries is a small-scale enterprise located in Maharashtra, India. Recently, the company decided to expand its operations by setting-up a new production unit in a neighbouring state.

For this purpose, the management approached Maharashtra State Financial Corporation to secure funding. This financial institution, established by the state government, specialises in providing medium and long-term loans to businesses for expansion and modernisation.

The financial institution evaluated the company's proposal and approved a loan of ₹ 5 crore for a tenure of 8 years.

The management of ABC Industries was pleased with the terms, as the loan came with specialised financial assistance, including expert advice on project implementation.

They also appreciated how such institutions play a crucial role in industrial development by offering favourable loan conditions and expert guidance.

Based on this case, answer the following questions

(i) Identify the source of funds being used by ABC Industries.

(ii) State any two features of financial institutions as mentioned in the case.

(iii) State any four merits of loans from financial institutions.

Ans.

(i) The source of fund that is being used by ABC Industries is loan from financial institutions. The government has established a number of financial institutions all over the country.

(ii) Following are the features of loans from financial institutions

- These institutions provide for specialised finance, keeping in view, the diverse requirements of business units.
- These institutions are also called development banks as they facilitate industrial development in the country.

(iii) Following are the merits of loans from financial institutions

- Financial institutions provide long-term finance, that are not provided by the commercial banks.
- These institutes not only provide funds but also extend technical and managerial support to business firms.
- If a firm gets a loan from these institutes, then it will also help in raising the goodwill of the borrowing company in the capital market.
- Repayment can be made in easy instalments, therefore, it does not prove to be a burden on the business.

SELF ASSESSMENT TEST

Objective Type Questions

1. Retained earnings does not involve any cost in the form of
   (a) dividend (b) interest
   (c) floatation cost (d) All of these
2. XYZ Ltd. has been retaining a portion of its annual profits for future expansion, instead of distributing all profits as dividends to its shareholders. This practice is known as ploughing back of profits, helping the company grow without incurring additional financing costs. What is the major disadvantage of retaining earnings as a source of funds?
   (a) It offers operational freedom and flexibility
   (b) Excessive retention may lead to shareholder dissatisfaction due to lower dividends
   (c) It increases the market price of equity shares
   (d) It ensures a fixed return to the company
3. ABC Corporation is raising funds through the issue of equity shares. Equity shareholders of the company have voting rights and are entitled to a share of the company's profits, but their dividends are not fixed. Which of the following is a disadvantage of raising funds through equity shares?
   (a) Investors do not have voting rights
   (b) It provides a permanent source of capital
   (c) Successive issues of equity shares dilute the voting power of existing shareholders
   (d) Equity shares ensure fixed dividends to shareholders
4. Which of the following is not a feature of borrowed funds?
   (a) No control over management of the business
   (b) Periodic interest payment
   (c) Permanent capital
   (d) All of the above
5. Payment of interest is a legal compulsion on the company when funds are raised through issue of
   (a) equity shares (b) debentures
   (c) Both (a) and (b) (d) None of these
6. The acceptance of public deposits is regulated by the …………… in India.
   (a) RBI (b) SEBI
   (c) commercial banks (d) All of these
7. What is a source of internal financing or self-financing?
   (a) Trade credit (b) Factoring
   (c) Retained earnings (d) Lease financing
8. Trade credit is the example of
   (a) long-term finance (b) medium-term finance
   (c) short-term finance (d) All of these

Answers 1. (d) 2. (b) 3. (c) 4. (c) 5. (b) 6. (a) 7. (c) 8. (c)

Short Answer Type Questions

9. Discuss in brief the significance of business finance.
10. State the sources of finance on the basis of ownership.
11. State any four features of equity shares.
12. "Preference shares provide a fixed return to investors and have priority over equity shareholders in the event of liquidation. However, they do not offer voting rights and are less flexible compared to equity shares."
    In light of the above statement, state two preferential rights which preference shareholders enjoy over equity shareholders.
13. Distinguish between equity shares and preference shares on the following basis
    (i) Participation in management
    (ii) Sequence of refund capital
    (iii) Sequence of dividend
14. Premlata Ltd. seeks financial support for its new project and considers various financial institutions. These institutions provide funding to businesses for expansion, research and infrastructure development while supporting economic growth. Name any three financial institutions and discuss their objectives.
15. Discuss 'trade credit' as a source of finance.

Long Answer Type Questions

16. Differentiate between shares and debentures.
17. Debentures provide companies with a fixed source of capital and typically offer lower interest rates compared to loans. However, they come with a legal obligation to repay the principal amount and pay interest regularly, which can impact the company's cash flow. Additionally, issuing debentures increases the company's debt burden and can affect its creditworthiness. In light of the above statement, discuss the features and advantages of debentures.
18. Discuss the various features, merits and demerits of 'loans from financial institutions'.

08 CHAPTER

Small Business and Enterprises

Small-scale industries in India are a part of modern industries which come under village and small industries sector. Village and small industries together provide the largest employment opportunities in India.

▼ YOUR STUDY GOALS

▼ YOUR PRACTICE GOAL

- Objective Type Questions (62 Qs ; MCQs, A-R, Statements, Matching)
- Subjective Questions (12 SAs, 6 LAs)
- Case Study Based Questions (Short Case Studies-9, Long Case Studies-4)
- Self Assessment Test (8 MCQs, 7 SAs, 3 LAs)

8.1 Concept of Entrepreneurship Development

Entrepreneurship development is the process by which the skills and knowledge of entrepreneurs can be improved through training and programmes.

Entrepreneur refers to those persons who set-up their business. The business unit i.e. the output of the process of entrepreneurship is called an **enterprise**. The main objective of entrepreneurship development is to increase the number of entrepreneurs.

Characteristics of Entrepreneurship Development

1. **Systematic Activity** Entrepreneurship is a systematic and step-by-step activity. It has certain competency requirements, temperamental, skill and other knowledge which can be acquired, learnt and developed by both formal educational and vocational training as well as by observation and work experience.

2. **Lawful and Purposeful Activity** Lawful business is the objective of entrepreneurship. Its purpose is to create value for personal profit and social gain.
3. **Innovation** Entrepreneurship involves continuous search for new ideas. An entrepreneur recognises the need for change and he always initiates new and better ways to do the work.
4. **Organisation of Production** Entrepreneur mobilises the resources required for production into a productive enterprise or firm. These resources or factors of production include land, labour, capital and technology.
5. **Risk Taking** Risk is an inherent element of entrepreneurship. An entrepreneur runs an enterprise for profit motive but there is also the risk of loss. If an entrepreneur does not have willingness to assume risk, then entrepreneurship will never succeed.

Need of Entrepreneurship Development

Reason	Explanation
Employment Opportunities	Entrepreneurship enables entrepreneurs to create more/additional employment opportunities for youth.
Economic Independence	Entrepreneurs develop and produce substituted products of imported goods and prevent the over-dependence on the other countries.
Capital Formation	Entrepreneurship encourages the establishment of new industries in economy which increase the capital formation rate in country.
Development of Backward and Tribal Areas	Entrepreneurship leads to scattering of economic activities in all areas of the country.
More Utilisation of Natural Resources	Entrepreneurship enables the economy to utilise and explore the abundant of natural resources.
Economic Growth and Development	Entrepreneurship provides the base of industrialisation in economy which is the main cause of economic growth and economic development.

Entrepreneurship Development Process (EDP)

The various steps involved in the process of entrepreneurship development are

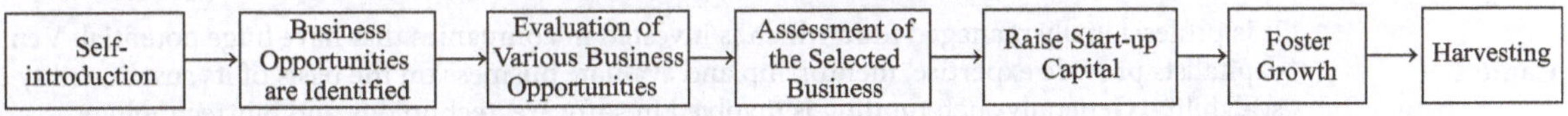

1. **Self-introduction** The person concerned in the process does an self-introspection to determine his relative strengths and weaknesses.
2. **Business Opportunities are Identified** The various forth coming business opportunities are identified in terms of unsatisfied needs and wants of people.
3. **Evaluation of Various Business Opportunities** The evaluation of various business opportunities is done and the selection is narrowed down to one best business idea.
4. **Assessment of the Selected Business Idea** The assessment of selected business idea is done in terms of its feasibility to become a viable business venture, by conducting varied types of researches.
5. **Raise Start-up Capital** By using business plan, entrepreneur tries to attract venture capitalist and partners.
6. **Foster Growth** To foster growth of business, new ideas are developed and implemented through effective environmental scanning.
7. **Harvesting** The final stage relates to harvesting where in the entrepreneurs may sell their business and gain reward of their endeavours.

8.2 Start-up India Scheme

Start-up means when a business is being started. Start-up India is an initiative launched on 16th January, 2016 with an objective to carve a strong ecosystem for innovation and start-ups in the country.

According to the Ministry of Commerce and Industry, a start-ups means

- An entity incorporated or registered in India.
- A private limited company or partnership firm or a limited liability partnership which is not older than 5 years.
- A company with an annual turnover not exceeding ₹ 25 crore for any of the financial years since incorporation.
- A company working towards innovation, development or improvement of products or processes.

Objectives of Start-up India Scheme

- To generate an entrepreneurial culture and promote entrepreneurial values in the society at large and influence the mindset of people towards entrepreneurship.
- To create awareness about the benefits of being an entrepreneur and the process of entrepreneurship.
- To encourage more dynamic start-ups by motivating educated youth, scientists and technologists to consider entrepreneurship as a profitable, preferred and viable career.
- Expanding the base of entrepreneurial supply by meeting specific needs of under represented target groups, like women, socially and economically backward communities, under represented regions to achieve inclusiveness and sustainable development to address the needs of the population at the bottom of the pyramid.

Ways to Fund Start-up

Way	Explanation
Bootstrapping	It means starting a business without external capital. Entrepreneur can invest from his/her past saving or can get from family or friends. It is suitable only if the initial requirement is small.
Crowd Funding	Crowd sourced funding is a means of raising money for a creative project (i.e. music, film, book). It is a collection of funds from multiple investors through social networking sites for a specific project.
Angel Funding	Angel investors are individuals with surplus cash who are interested to invest in upcoming start-ups. Many household names, like Google, Facebook were financed in their earliest stages by angel investors.
Venture Capital	It is professionally managed fund which is invested in companies that have huge potential. Venture capitalists provide expertise, mentorship and evaluate business on the basis of its sustainability and scalability. Generally such funding is involved in software, technology and bio-technology.
Business Incubators	Incubators provide professional services that facilitates the development of new business by providing resources, support and advice.
Business Accelerators	Accelerators offer a range of support service and funding opportunities for start-ups. They provide capital and investment in return for start-up equity.
Microfinance and NFBCs	Microfinance means access to financial services to those who do not have access to conventional banking services or have not qualified for a bank loan. NBFCs (Non-Banking Financial Corporation) provides banking services without meeting legal requirement of a bank.

Bootstrapping

Suraj wanted to start a homemade candle business but lacked external funding. He used his personal savings and a small loan from his brother to buy materials and set-up his workshop. With this bootstrap funding, he managed to launch his business on a small-scale.

8.3 Intellectual Property Rights (IPRs)

Intellectual Property (IP) is defined as the creation of the mind, inventions, literary, artistic works, symbols names, images and designs used in business. It is intangible as it cannot be identified or defined by its own physical parameters.

Intellectual property is divided into two broad categories

1. **Industrial Property** It includes inventions (patents), trademarks, industrial designs and geographical indications.
2. **Copyright** It includes literary works such as novels, poems, plays, films, musical works and artistic works such as drawings, paintings, photographs, sculptures and architectural designs.

With the establishment of WTO and India being a signatory to the agreement of Trade Related Intellectual Property System (TRIPS), several legislations were passed for the protection of intellectual property rights to meet the international obligations. These included

- Trademark Act, 1999
- The Geographical Indications of Goods (Registration and Protection) Act, 1999
- Design Act, 2000
- Protection of Plant Varieties and Farmers Rights Act, 2001
- The Patents Act, 2005
- The Copyright (Amendment) Act, 2012

Features of IPRs

1. **Legal Rights** Intellectual property rights are legal rights of the creator/IP owner, to prevent others from using the protected subject matter.
2. **Technology** It is essential for IPR that the creation has to be original. The creator has to bring something creative into existence. IPR covers various aspects of information technology, automobiles, pharmaceuticals, biotechnology, etc.
3. **Business and Economics** The basics of IPRS help in the development of the industry and in the success of businesses. IPRS provide rights to the proprietors of the businesses.

Importance of IPRs for Entrepreneurs

- It encourages creation of new, path breaking inventions, such as cancer cure medicines.
- It encourages creators, authors, creators, etc. for their work by providing incentives.
- It allows creators and inventors to have control over their creations and inventions, so that work created by a person can be distributed and communicated to the public only with his/her permission. This helps in the prevention of loss of income.
- It helps authors, creators, developers and owners to get recognition for their works.

Types of IPRs

The following types of IPR are recognised in India

Type	Explanation
Copyright	It is the right to 'not copy'. It is offered when an original idea is expressed by the creator or author. The copyright is an exclusive right of the creator to prevent the unauthorised use of the content, which includes reproducing and distributing copies of the subject matter.
Trademark	A trademark is any word, name or symbol (or their combination) that helps to identify the goods made by an individual, company, organisation, etc. It helps in distinguishing similar products in the market from its competitors.

Type	Explanation
	Trademark may be categorised into the following • **Conventional Trademark** This category includes works, colour combination, label, logo, packaging, shape of goods, etc. • **Non-conventional Trademark** This category includes those marks which were not considered distinctive previously, but started getting recognition with the passage of time, i.e. sound mark, dynamic mark, etc.
Geographical Indication (GI)	It is primarily an indication which identifies agricultural, natural or manufactured products (handicrafts, industrial goods and food stuffs) that possesses the qualities of the geographical location in which they originate. Goods protected and registered as GI are categorised into agricultural products, natural, handicrafts, manufactured goods and food stuffs. Darjeeling Tea, Kangra Painting, Kashmir Pashmina, etc. are some of the examples of GI.
Patent	It is a type of IPR which protects the scientific inventions (products and or process). It is an exclusive right granted by the government which prevent any body from making, using, offering for sale, selling or importing the invention. Following conditions are required for an invention to be patentable • It must be new, i.e. it should not already exist in the current knowledge anywhere in the world. • It must be non-obvious to any person who is skilled in the relevant field of technology. • It must be capable of industrial application, i.e. capable of being used or manufactured in the industry.
Design	It includes shape, pattern and arrangement of lines or colour combination that is applied to any article. It is a protection given to aesthetic appearance or eye catching features. The period of protection of a design is 10 years, which can be renewed for further 5 years after expiration. During this period, a registered design can only be used after getting a license from its owner.
Plant Variety	It refers to grouping of plants into categories on the basis of their botanical characteristics. It is a type of variety which is produced and developed by farmers. This helps in conserving, improving and making available plant genetic resources, e.g. Hybrid versions of potatoes.
Semiconductor Integrated Circuits Layout Design	Semiconductor integrate circuit is any product that contains transistors and other circuitry elements which are formed on a semiconductor material or an insulating material or inside the semiconductor material. It is designed to perform an electronic circuitry function.

IP and Business

It is important for a business enterprise to protect and manage the intellectual property. The IP of other businesses should be respected both on ethical and legal grounds. Intellectual Property Rights (IPRs) are important in supporting new ventures for monetisation of ideas and establishment of competitiveness in the market.

8.4 Meaning of Small-scale Enterprises

Small-scale enterprise is defined on the basis of investment made in the plant and machinery equipment. The Micro, Small and Medium Enterprises Development (MSMED) Act, 2006 was launched in India to develop micro, small and medium enterprises.

The **features** of small scale industries are as follows

1. **Personal Character** Small-scale industries enjoy the personal character. It is generally owned by a single entrepreneur or partnership.
2. **Simple Managerial Structure** They are managed by owners only. Thus, they can reap the benefits of direct motivation, secrecy, flexibility, etc.
3. **Labour Incentive Techniques** There is a predominance of labour in these industries. They use labour incentive techniques of production instead of mechanised methods of production.

4. **Local Area of Operations** The operations of these industries are localised. They depend mainly on local resources but products are exported all over the world.
5. **Simple Technology** The machinery and equipment used for the production of goods are operated manually and are not very sophisticated.

Micro, Small and Medium Enterprises Development (MSMED) Act, 2006

The MSMED Act came into force in October, 2006. It addresses the issues relating to credit, marketing and technology upgradation of micro, small and medium enterprises. Service related enterprises are also included under this Act.

MSMED Act identifies the following enterprises and specifies the limits for their categorisation

Enterprise	Investment and Turnover
Micro Enterprise	In micro enterprise, the investment in plant and machinery is less than ₹ 1 crore and the turnover does not exceed ₹ 5 crore.
Small Enterprise	In small enterprise, the investment in plant and machinery is less than ₹ 10 crore and the turnover does not exceed ₹ 50 crore.
Medium Enterprise	In medium enterprise, the investment in plant and machinery is less than ₹ 50 crore and the turnover does not exceed ₹ 250 crore.

Village and Cottage Industries

Village Industry It is defined as any industry which is located in a rural area and produces goods or renders services with or without the use of power. In such industries, the fixed capital investment per head or artisan or worker is specified by the Central Government from time to time.

Cottage Industry It is also known as rural industry or traditional industry. It is not defined by capital investment criteria as in the case of other small-scale industries.

Role of Small Business in India

The small business or small-scale industries play the following roles in India

Role	Explanation
Contribution in GDP	Small-scale industries in India account for 95% of the industrial units of the country. They contribute almost 40% of the gross industrial value added and 45% of the total exports (direct and indirect) from India.
Employment Generation	In India, small-scale industries are the second largest employers of human resources, after agriculture. They generate more employment opportunities per unit of capital invested as compared to large industries. Thus, they are considered good for countries like India, that have surplus labour and less capital.
Supply Variety of Products	Small-scale industries in India supply enormous variety of products which include the following • Goods of mass consumption such as readymade garments, hosiery goods, etc. • Sophisticated goods such as electrical goods, engineering goods, drugs, etc. • Handlooms, handicrafts and other products which have high export value.
Balanced Regional Development	Small-scale industries produce products using simple technologies and depend on locally available resources in terms of both material and labour. Thus, they can be opened anywhere in the country, without any locational constraints and the benefits of industrialisation can be received by every region.
Provide Business Opportunities	Small-scale industries provide opportunity for the growth of entrepreneurship. By utilising skills and talent, an individual can become entrepreneur as less capital investment is required for setting-up business in small sector.
Low Cost of Production	Small-scale industries have the advantage of low cost of production as their establishment and running cost are minimum. This provides competitive strength to small-scale industries.
Quick Decisions	As the small-scale industries are small in size, quick and timely decisions can be taken without consulting many people, this helps to save time which enables the business to capture the opportunities at the right time.
Customised Production	Small-scale industries are best suited for customised production, i.e. designing the product as per the tastes/ preferences/needs of an individual customer, with simple and flexible production techniques.

Role of Small-Business in Rural India

- **Non-farm Employment** Small businesses have encouraged rural people to involve in a wide range of agricultural activities, along with the traditional activities of farming and agricultural labour. They provide varied and multiple sources of income to the rural people.
- **Employment for Artisans** Cottage and rural industries play an important role in providing employment opportunities in the rural areas, especially to the traditional artisans and the weaker sections of society.
- **Prevention of Migration** Development of rural and village industries can also prevent migration of rural population to urban areas in search of employment.
- **Socio-economic Aspects** Small businesses contribute towards socio-economic aspects such as reduction in income inequalities, dispersed development of industries and linkage with other sectors of the economy.

8.5 Problems of Small Business

Following are the major problems that are faced by small business

1. **Finance** One of the severe problems faced by small business is the non-availability of adequate finance to carry out its operations. These units lack in credit worthiness and have a small capital base. As a result, they heavily depend on local financial resources and frequently exploited by the moneylenders.
2. **Raw Material** Shortage of raw material is another problem of small business. If the required materials are not available, small businesses have to compromise on the quality or have to pay high price to get good quality materials. Their bargaining power is relatively low due to the small quantity of purchases made by them.
3. **Managerial Skills** Small business is generally promoted and operated by a single person, who may not possess technical and managerial skills to run the business.
4. **Marketing** Small-scale enterprises are unable to meet the expenses of marketing activities. They depend on middlemen who exploit them by paying low prices for their goods and delaying their payments.

Problems of Small Business
- → Finance
- → Raw Material
- → Managerial Skills
- → Marketing
- → Quality
- → Capacity Utilisation
- → Technology
- → Global Competition

5. **Quality** Many small business organisations do not adhere to desired standards of quality. Instead, they concentrate on cutting the cost and keeping the prices low. As they do not maintain quality, they are not able to compete in global markets.
6. **Capacity Utilisation** Due to lack of marketing skills or lack of demand, many small business have to operate below full capacity, due to which their operating costs tend to increase. This leads to sickness and closure of the business.
7. **Technology** Use of outdated technology is another serious problem of small business. This results in low productivity and uneconomical production.
8. **Global Competition** The Liberalisation, Privatisation and Globalisation (LPG) policies being followed by several countries across the world have created following problems for small business
   - They have to compete from medium and large industries as well as multi-national companies.
   - They have difficulty to withstand high quality standards, technological skills, financial credit worthiness, managerial and marketing capabilities of large industries.
   - Due to strict requirements of quality certification like ISO 9000, small industries have limited access to markets of developed countries.

Problems of Small Business

Rahul started a small handicrafts business in his hometown but soon faced multiple challenges. He struggled to secure a loan from banks due to his limited credit history and had to rely on local moneylenders charging high interest rates.

Procuring good quality raw materials at reasonable prices became difficult because suppliers favoured larger buyers. Moreover, he lacked the managerial expertise to expand operations and could not afford to offer competitive salaries, leading to high employee turnover.

8.6 Government Assistance to Small Industries and Small Business Units

Government has been actively participating in promoting, establishing and developing small industries, particularly the rural, cottage and village industries. It also have been promoting self-employment opportunities in rural areas. It has introduced various schemes and has extended institutional support to the small and rural industries.

Forms of support offered to small industries by the government are

- Institutional support in respect of credit facilities.
- Provision of developed sites for construction of sheds.
- Provision of training facilities.
- Supply of machinery on hire export marketing.
- Technical and financial assistance for technological upgradation.
- Special incentives for setting up of enterprises in backward areas.

Institutional Support

The government has extended institutional support to SSIs by opening special institutions which cater to the financial and other needs of the SSIs.

It includes the following

I. National Small Industries Corporation (NSIC)

NSIC was set-up in 1955 to promote, aid and foster the growth of small-scale units in India. It performs the following functions

- It supplies indigenous and imported machines and raw materials to small-scale industries on hire purchase schemes.
- It exports the product of small units and help to establish their creditworthiness.
- It helps in upgradation of technology.
- It provides mentoring and advisory services.
- It develops software technology parks and technology transfer centres.
- It launches various schemes and extends support to help small-scale entrepreneurs.

Various Schemes and Support Programmes launched by NSIC

1. **Performance and Credit Rating Scheme**

   This scheme is implemented by NSIC to achieve the following objectives

   - Sensitising the small industries about the need of credit rating.
   - Encouraging the small business units to maintain good financial track record. This helps to ensure that their credit rating is high, when they approach financial institutions for their working capital and fixed capital requirements.

2. **Marketing Assistance Scheme**

Under this scheme, the Ministry of Micro, Small and Medium Enterprises, through NSIC, has been providing marketing support to micro and small industries.

The objectives of this scheme are

- To enhance marketing capabilities and competitiveness of micro and small enterprises.
- To exhibit the competencies of these enterprises.
- To update these enterprises about the prevalent market scenario and its impact on their activities.
- To facilitate formation of groups of micro and small enterprises, so that they are able to collectively market their products and services.
- To provide a platform for these enterprises to interact with large institutional buyers.
- To provide information regarding various programmes of the government aimed at their development and growth.
- To enrich the marketing skills of micro and small entrepreneurs.

3. **Marketing Support Extended to MSMEs**

NSIC extends marketing support to MSMEs through the following activities

- NSIC organises International Technology Exhibitions in foreign countries where micro, small and medium enterprises can showcase their products.
- NSIC also organises domestic exhibitions where MSMEs can showcase their products.
- NSIC organises buyer-seller meets for MSMEs, where bulk and departmental buyers such as the railways, defence, large companies, etc. are invited.
- NSIC conducts intensive campaigns to spread awareness regarding the various schemes of the government which are for the benefit of micro, small and medium enterprises.
- NSIC also benefit the micro, small and medium enterprises by various other support activities which are
  - Development of display centres, show windows, hoarding, etc. for promoting the products and services of MSMEs.
  - Printing brochures and catalogues and preparing CDs and short films to spread information related to the products offered by MSMEs.
  - Development of websites which help MSMEs to market their products.
  - Development and disbursement of material which spreads awareness related to various programmes/ schemes and events that aim to benefit MSMEs.
  - Preparing a directory which contains updated information related to various MSMEs.
  - Documentation of success stories of MSMEs.
  - Conducting studies to explore and access new markets, businesses and product ranges for both domestic and international markets.
  - Hosting international delegations and networking events.

II. District Industries Centre (DICs)

The District Industries Centre Programme was launched on 1st May, 1978, with a view to provide all the services and support facilities to entrepreneurs, to set-up small and village industries at district level.

Following functions are performed by DICs

- Identification of suitable schemes for the entrepreneurs interested to set-up small industries in rural areas.
- Preparing feasibility reports for proposed projects.
- Helping the entrepreneurs in arranging for credit.
- Helping the entrepreneurs to have access to raw material and machinery.
- Extending various support services to entrepreneurs.

III. Some More Institutions

1. **National Bank for Agriculture and Rural Development** (NABARD)
   The NABARD was set-up on 15th July, 1982 to provide finance to rural areas in order to promote integrated rural development.
   It is an apex institution that provides finance to rural and small industries and organises training and development programmes for rural entrepreneurs.
2. **The Rural Small Business Development Centre** (RSBDC)
   It was set-up by the world association for small and medium enterprises and is sponsored by NABARD.

It aims at providing managerial and technical support to current and prospective micro and small entrepreneurs in rural areas. It has organised various programmes on rural entrepreneurship, skill upgradation workshops, training programmes and counselling camps in various villages, to provide rural employment.

3. **Small Industries Development Bank of India** (SIDBI)
   It was established in April, 1990 as a wholly owned subsidiary of IDBI, under the Small Industries Development Bank of India Act, 1990. Its main objective is to promote, finance and develop the small-scale sector in India. It provides direct and indirect financial assistance to small business organisations under various schemes. It coordinates the functions of other institutions engaged in similar activities.

4. **National Commission for Enterprises in the Unorganised Sector** (NCEUS)
   It was constituted in September, 2004 with the following objectives
   - To suggest measures which help to improve productivity of small-scale enterprises.
   - To generate more employment opportunities in rural areas.
   - To develop linkage between small-scale sector and institutions in the area of credit, raw materials, infrastructure, technology upgradation and marketing.
   - To enhance the competitiveness of small sector in the global market.

5. **Rural and Women Entrepreneurship Development** (RWED) **Programme**
   This programme encourages rural people and women to establish entrepreneurial ventures. It aims at promoting a conducive business environment, and at building institutional and human capacities to support entrepreneurial initiatives.

   It provides the following services
   - Creating a business environment which encourages initiative of rural and women entrepreneurs.
   - To enhance human and institutional capacities.
   - To provide training for women entrepreneurs.
   - To render other advisory services.

6. **World Association for Small and Medium Enterprises** (WASME)
   It is an international non-governmental organisation for micro, small and medium scale enterprises based in India, which set-up an international committee for rural industrialisation. It offers various schemes for promotion of business and sustained growth of such enterprises.

7. **Scheme of Fund for Regeneration of Traditional Industries** (SFURTI)
   A special fund has been created by the government to make the traditional industries more productive and competitive. The government started this fund in 2005 by investing ₹ 100 crore.

   This scheme is implemented by the Ministry of Agro and Rural Industries, in collaboration with State Governments. The main objectives of this scheme are
   - To improve the technology of traditional units to make them competitive, profitable and sustainable.
   - To create sustained employment opportunities.
   - To set-up traditional industries in various parts of the country.

Mind Map

SMALL BUSINESS AND ENTERPRISES

1 Concept of Entrepreneurship Development

Entrepreneurship Development (ED) is the process by which the skills and knowledge of entrepreneurs can be improved through training and programmes. Entrepreneur refers to those persons who set up their business.

2 Characteristics of ED

- Systematic activity
- Lawful and purposeful activity
- Innovation
- Organisation of production
- Risk taking

3 Need of ED

- Employment opportunities
- Economic independence
- Capital formation
- Development of backward and tribal areas
- More utilisation of natural resources
- Economic growth and development

4 Entrepreneurship Development Process (EDP)

- Self introduction
- Business opportunities are identified
- Business opportunities are evaluated
- Assessment is carried out of the selected business idea
- Start-up capital is raised
- New ideas are developed to foster growth
- Entrepreneurs may sell their business, i.e. harvesting

5 Start-Up India Scheme

Start-up means when a business is being started. According to the Ministry of Commerce and Industry, a start-ups means

- An entity incorporated or registered in India
- A private limited company or partnership firm or a limited liability partnership which is not older than 5 years.
- A company with an annual turnover not exceeding ₹ 25 crore for any of the financial years since incorporation
- A company working towards innovation, development or improvement of products or processes

Ways to Fund Start-up

- **Bootstrapping** It means starting a business without external capital.
- **Crowd Funding** Crowd sourced funding is a means of raising money for a creative project (i.e. music, film, book).
- **Angel Funding** Angel investors are individuals with surplus cash who are interested to invest in upcoming start-ups.
- **Venture Capital** It is professionally managed fund which is invested in companies that have huge potential.
- **Business Incubators** Incubators provide professional services that facilitates the development of new business by providing resources, support and advice.
- **Business Accelerators** Accelerators offer a range of support service and funding opportunities for start-ups. They provide capital and investment in return for start-up equity.
- **Microfinance and NFBCs** Microfinance means access to financial services. NBFCs (Non-Banking Financial Corporations) provide banking services without meeting legal requirement of a bank.

8 Institutional Support

1. National Small Industries Corporation (NSIC)
Various schemes and support programmes launched by NSIC include

- **Performance and Credit Rating Scheme** This scheme is implemented by NSIC to sensitise the small industries about the need of credit rating and encouraging the small business units to maintain good financial track record.
- **Marketing Assistance Scheme** Under this scheme, the Ministry of Micro, Small and Medium Enterprises, through NSIC, has been providing marketing support to micro and small industries.
- **Marketing Support Extended to MSMEs** NSIC organises International Technology Exhibitions in foreign countries where micro, small and medium enterprises can showcase their products, etc.

2. District Industries Centre (DICs) It was launched on 1st May, 1978, with a view to provide all the services and support facilities to entrepreneurs, to set-up small and village industries at district level. DICs perform number of functions like identification of suitable schemes, preparing feasibility reports, helping entrepreneurs in arranging for credit, etc.

Role of Small Business in India

- Contribution in GDP
- Employment generation
- Supply variety of products
- Balanced regional development
- Provide business opportunities
- Low cost of production
- Quick decisions
- Customised production

Role of Small Business in Rural India

- Non-farm employment
- Employment for artisans
- Prevention of migration
- Socio-economic aspects

7 Small-Scale Enterprises

Small-scale enterprise is defined on the basis of investment made in the plant and machinery equipment. The Micro, Small and Medium Enterprises Development (MSMED) Act, 2006 was launched in India to develop micro, small and medium enterprises.

- **Micro Enterprise** Investment in plant and machinery is less than ₹ 1 crore and the turnover does not exceed ₹ 5 crore.
- **Small Enterprise** Investment in plant and machinery is less than ₹ 10 crore and the turnover does not exceed ₹ 50 crore.
- **Medium Enterprise** Investment in plant and machinery is less than ₹ 50 crore and the turnover does not exceed ₹ 250 crore.

Problems of Small Business

- Finance
- Managerial skills
- Marketing
- Capacity utilisation
- Raw material
- Global competition
- Quality
- Technology

6 Intellectual Property Rights (IPRs)

Intellectual Property (IP) is defined as the creation of the mind, inventions, literary, artistic works, symbols names, images and designs used in business.

Types of IPRs include

- Copyright
- Geographical indication
- Design
- Semi-conductor integrated circuits layout design
- Trademark
- Patent
- Plant variety

EXAM PATTERN QUESTIONS

Objective Type Questions

Multiple Choice Questions (MCQs)

1. People who own, operate and take risk for a business venture is called

(a) aptitude (b) employee
(c) entrepreneur (d) entrepreneurship

2. Entrepreneurship provides

(a) capital investment (b) self-employment
(c) administration (d) marketing

3. Nidhi noticed the increasing demand for eco-friendly home décor items. She launched a business creating products using recycled materials and traditional artisan techniques. Nidhi secured initial funding through bootstrapping and later received a grant under the start-up India initiative.

Her products gained popularity due to their unique designs and environmental sustainability, attracting customers both domestically and internationally. Which characteristic of entrepreneurship is reflected in Nidhi's business approach? Competency Based Que

(a) Goal-oriented activity
(b) Related to innovation
(c) Economic independence
(d) Risk bearing

4. Rajesh started a small food processing unit in a tribal region, using locally grown produce and hiring local workers. His venture improved the economic condition of the area by providing employment and utilising underused natural resources.

Rajesh obtained a MUDRA Shishu loan to meet his initial funding requirements and plans to expand his business to other backward areas. Which need of entrepreneurship development does Rajesh's business fulfill? Competency Based Que

(a) Development of backward and tribal areas
(b) Fostering growth in urban areas
(c) Raising global investment
(d) Increasing export dependence

5. What is the main purpose of entrepreneurship development?

(a) To increase foreign trade
(b) To increase number of entrepreneurs
(c) To increase GDP
(d) To increase literacy

6. Ravi, an aspiring entrepreneur, identified a business opportunity in developing solar-powered gadgets. He evaluated the feasibility of his idea by conducting thorough research and decided to launch a company. To fund his start-up, he approached an angel investor and also used crowd funding platforms.

His business idea was recognised under the Start-up India initiative as it was innovative and met all the eligibility criteria. Ravi aims to expand his venture by utilising government schemes like MUDRA and promoting environmental sustainability through his products.

Which step of the entrepreneurship development process did Ravi perform when he conducted research on his business idea's feasibility? Competency Based Que

(a) Self-introduction
(b) Assessment of selected business idea
(c) Raising start-up capital (d) Fostering growth

7. Which of the following statements is incorrect?

(a) Entrepreneurship involves lawful activities and aims to create both personal profit and social gain
(b) Entrepreneurship is primarily concerned with static processes and avoids frequent changes in the enterprise
(c) Entrepreneurs mobilise resources like land, labour, capital and technology to establish productive enterprises
(d) Entrepreneurship involves risk bearing as an inherent element, with the possibility of both profit and loss

8. Which of the following statements is incorrect regarding the start-up India scheme?

(a) A start-up under the start-up India initiative must be incorporated or registered in India
(b) A start-up can only be a public limited company to qualify under the scheme
(c) A start-up should have a turnover not exceeding ₹ 25 crore for any of the financial years since incorporation
(d) A start-up must focus on innovation, development or improvement of products or processes

9. As per the notification issued by the Ministry of Commerce and Industry, a start-up means, with reference to the period

(a) not older than 5 years
(b) not older than 10 years
(c) not older than 12 years (d) not older than 13 years

10. An entrepreneur decides to start a business using their past savings and financial support from friends. This funding option is suitable for ventures requiring a small initial investment. Identify the funding method used. **Competency Based Que**

(a) Crowd funding (b) Bootstrapping
(c) Angel funding (d) Business accelerators

11. A start-up receives funding from a professionally managed fund in exchange for mentorship and evaluation based on scalability. This type of funding is commonly used in the software and technology sector. Identify the funding method. **Competency Based Que**

(a) Angel funding (b) Venture capital
(c) Micro-finance (d) Business incubators

12. Which of the following statements is incorrect?

(a) Crowd funding involves raising money from multiple investors through social networking sites for a specific project
(b) Angel investors typically invest in start-ups at their earliest stages and require majority equity ownership
(c) Venture capitalists focus on companies with high scalability and often provide mentorship
(d) Micro-finance provides financial services to individuals who lack access to conventional banking services

13. A small business seeks support services and resources from an organisation that facilitates its growth and development. The organisation also provides advice to help launch the start-up. What is this funding option called? **Competency Based Que**

(a) Business accelerators (b) Business incubators
(c) Angel funding (d) Crowd funding

14. Identify the way of funding the start up illustrated in the given picture in which surplus cash is used to invest in upcoming start-ups. Many household names, like Google, Facebook were financed in their earliest stages by this method.

(a) Venture capital
(b) Angel investors
(c) Government programmes
(d) Bootstrapping

15. .... is the practice of funding a project by raising money from a large number of people for a common goal.

(a) Venture capital (b) Angel investors
(c) Government programmes
(d) Crowd funding

16. Rahul, an entrepreneur, developed a new, energy efficient battery technology that could significantly reduce carbon emissions. To secure his invention, he applied for one of the intellectual property right. He ensured that his invention met all the criteria for patentability. It was new, involved a non-obvious technical advancement and had industrial applications. After receiving the patent, Rahul gained exclusive rights to manufacture and sell the technology, preventing competitors from copying his innovation. What type of intellectual property right did Rahul use to protect his invention? **Competency Based Que**

(a) Copyright (b) Trademark
(c) Patent (d) Geographical indication

17. Sakshi started her line of organic skincare products named 'Nature's Glow.' She created a unique logo and packaging to differentiate her products in the market. To safeguard her brand identity and prevent others from misusing her logo and name, she registered them under the Trademark Act, 1999.

This ensured that her products could stand out in a competitive market. What type of intellectual property right did Sakshi use to protect her brand identity? **Competency Based Que**

(a) Patent (b) Trademark
(c) Copyright (d) Design

18. A group of artisans in Kashmir decided to promote their traditional handwoven Pashmina shawls. These shawls were known for their unique texture and quality, attributed to the region's specific climatic and geographical conditions. To prevent fake products from being sold under the same name, they registered 'Kashmir Pashmina' as a geographical indication under the GI Act, 1999. What does the registration of 'Kashmir Pashmina' as a geographical indication help to protect? **Competency Based Que**

(a) Industrial designs (b) Artistic works
(c) Regional product authenticity
(d) Semi-conductor designs

19. A .... includes shape, pattern and arrangement of lines or colour combination that is applied to any article.

(a) design (b) copyright
(c) patent (d) trademark

20. In the case of service enterprise, where investment in equipment is more than ₹ 10 lakh but does not exceed ₹ 2 crore is

(a) micro enterprise (b) small enterprise
(c) medium enterprise (d) cottage industries

21. **Khadi and village industries are identified as**
(a) large-scale industries
(b) traditional small-scale industries
(c) modern small-scale industry
(d) medium-scale industry

22. **Chandan started a business of offering home Cleaning Services under the name of 'Care Home'. His total investment in the equipment is ₹ 7,50,000. Identify the category in which his business will fall under Micro, Small and Medium Enterprises Development Act, 2006.** **Competency Based Que**
(a) Micro enterprise (b) Small enterprise
(c) Medium enterprise (d) None of these

23. **As per the government of India, size of small-scale industry can be decided on the basis of**
(a) number of employees working
(b) volume of output
(c) power consumed for business
(d) investment in plant and machinery

24. **Which of the following is not a problem for small business?**
(a) Finance (b) Technology
(c) Sickness (d) Regional balance

25. **Vikram runs a small handloom business in a rural area. His products, including handwoven sarees and shawls, are highly appreciated for their unique designs and quality. The business uses locally available raw materials and employs artisans from the nearby villages.**

Despite the popularity of his products, Vikram often faces issues such as difficulty in acquiring adequate finance and raw materials. Additionally, his business struggles with outdated weaving techniques, leading to lower productivity. Which of the following problems is Vikram's business primarily facing? **Competency Based Que**
(a) Capacity utilisation (b) Finance and technology
(c) Labour shortage (d) Marketing

26. **Meera operates a small-scale soap making unit in her hometown. Her products are made using traditional methods and the demand for her soaps has been steadily growing. However, due to limited marketing resources, Meera relies on local middlemen to distribute her products.**

These middlemen often delay payments and offer lower prices, making it difficult for her to scale her business. What is the primary problem faced by Meera's business? **Competency Based Que**
(a) Managerial skills (b) Marketing
(c) Quality (d) Labour

27. **Small businesses often lack creditworthiness and have a small capital base, leading to dependence on local financial resources. Identify the major problem discussed in the statement.** **Competency Based Que**
(a) Shortage of raw material
(b) Inadequate managerial skills
(c) Limited availability of finance
(d) Low productivity of labour

28. **Small-scale enterprises often pay high prices for good quality raw materials due to their low bargaining power.**
This problem arises because they make purchases in smaller quantities. Identify the issue faced by small businesses. **Competency Based Que**
(a) High employee turnover
(b) Marketing limitations
(c) Shortage of raw material
(d) Outdated technology

29. **Pradeep started a manufacturing unit of electrical accessories. He is facing severe shortage of adequate finance to carry out the business activities. His manufacturing unit is also suffering from shortage of required inputs and he is unable to buy inputs in bulk due to lack of shortage facilities.**
Pradeep wants his product to be world class quality, but he is unable to hire professional experts due to shortage of funds. His manufacturing unit is operating below the full capacity level due to shortage of demand.
Identify the problems of small-scale business faced by Pradeep in his business in the given case. **Competency Based Que**
(a) Shortage of finance, raw material, managerial skills and idle capacity
(b) Shortage of fmance, suppliers, managerial skills and idle capacity
(c) Shortage of finance, raw material, technical skills and idle capacity
(d) None of the above

30. **Which of the following points highlight the role of small-scale business in the development of the country?**
(a) Promotes balanced regional development
(b) Employment generation
(c) Low cost of production
(d) All of the above

31. **Jagmohan established a factory to manufacture formal jackets and blazers. Encouraged by the favourable response in the market, Jagmohan now wants to export his products to Europeans. Name the institution, with the help of given picture, which can help Jagmohan in achieving his objective.**

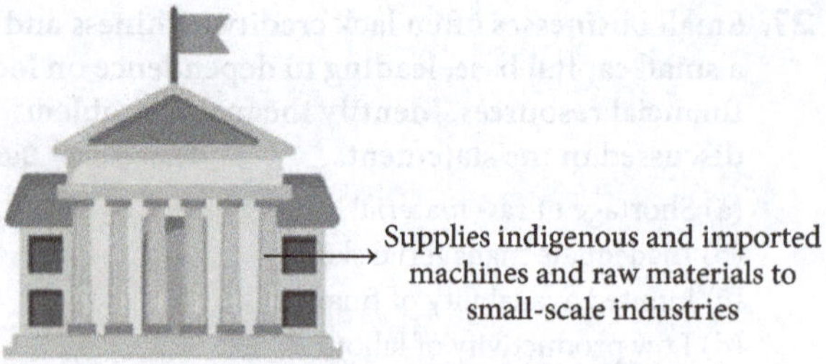

(a) National Small Industries Commission (NSIC)
(b) National Small Industries Council (NSIC)
(c) National Small Industries Corporation (NSIC)
(d) None of the above

32. Rupa is starting a business of cotton saree making at home in her village. She is also investing her savings and also acquire loans from the bank. Now she is facing problem in promotion of her business. Name the institution, with the help of given picture which can help Rupa in achieving his objective.

(a) Khadi and Village Industries Commission (KVIC)
(b) Khadi and Village Industries Council (KVIC)
(c) Khadi and Village Industries Corporation (KVIC)
(d) None of the above

33. Out of the many government agencies and corporations, working for the promotion and welfare of small business, ... is at the bottom of hierarchy and implements government policies at ground level.
(a) Ministry of Agro and Rural Industries
(b) District Directorate of Industries
(c) State Governments (d) District Industries Centres

Direction *Read the case study and answer the questions 34 to 37 on the basis of the same*

After completing their MBA, three friends decided to venture into the textile industry and provide employment opportunities to local artisans. They set-up 'Vibrant Textiles' in their hometown.

After experiencing positive market response, one of the friends, Ramesh, is planning to expand their business by opening a new unit called 'Elegant Fabrics' in a rural area of Rajasthan. The unit will focus on producing eco-friendly garments using sustainable resources. They plan to invest ₹ 1.5 crore for machinery and ₹ 60 lakh for initial operational costs. The new unit will adopt a capital-intensive technique due to the need for advanced machinery and technology.

34. Which category of SSI does 'Elegant Fabrics' belong to?
(a) Micro enterprises (b) Small enterprises
(c) Medium enterprises (d) Cottage industry

35. Which of the following is not a feature of entrepreneurship?
(a) Innovation (b) Risk taking
(c) Ownership of business (d) Dynamic process

36. Post-training stage of the Entrepreneurship Development Programme (EDP) does not include
(a) management skill development
(b) guidance in project implementation
(c) sustaining motivation
(d) providing follow-up

37. The Finance Manager estimates an investment of ₹ 1.5 crore for machinery and ₹ 60 lakh for operating expenses. Identify the type of source required to finance these requirements.
(a) Equity capital
(b) Long-term loans
(c) Preference capital
(d) Loans from commercial banks

Assertion-Reason

Direction (Q.No. 38 to 47) *Read the following Assertion (A) and Reason (R) and choose the correct alternative from the following*

Alternatives
(a) Both Assertion (A) and Reason (R) are true and Reason (R) is the correct explanation of Assertion (A)
(b) Both Assertion (A) and Reason (R) are true, but Reason (R) is not the correct explanation of Assertion (A)
(c) Assertion (A) is true, but Reason (R) is false
(d) Assertion (A) is false, but Reason (R) is true

38. Assertion (A) The start-up India scheme aims to encourage entrepreneurship by promoting an entrepreneurial culture in society.

Reason (R) The scheme creates awareness about the benefits and processes of entrepreneurship, motivating youth to consider it as a career.

39. Assertion (A) Venture capitalists provide financial assistance only to businesses with high growth potential.

Reason (R) Venture capital funding involves professional management, mentorship and an evaluation of the sustainability and scalability of a business.

40. Assertion (A) Crowd funding is a popular method for raising money for creative projects like films and books.

Reason (R) It involves collecting funds from a large number of investors through social networking platforms for specific projects.

41. **Assertion** (A) Business incubators provide only financial support to start-ups.

Reason (R) Incubators offer a range of professional services including advice, resources and support to facilitate business development.

42. **Assertion** (A) Intellectual Property Rights (IPRs) are important for entrepreneurs as they allow control over their inventions.

Reason (R) IPR enables creators to prevent unauthorised use of their creations, which helps in protecting income.

43. **Assertion** (A) The Patents Act protects scientific inventions and gives exclusive rights to the inventor.

Reason (R) A patent prevents others from making, using or selling the patented invention without the permission of the patent holder.

44. **Assertion** (A) Small-Scale Industries (SSIs) contribute significantly to India's GDP.

Reason (R) SSIs account for 95% of the industrial units in India and contribute nearly 40% of the gross industrial value.

45. **Assertion** (A) Micro, Small and Medium Enterprises (MSMEs) are important for regional development.

Reason (R) MSMEs can be set-up anywhere in the country without locational constraints, thus spreading industrialisation benefits to all regions.

46. **Assertion** (A) Small-scale industries often employ labour-intensive production methods.

Reason (R) These industries rely on manual labour and simple technologies for production.

47. **Assertion** (A) Government programmes like MUDRA, offer capital for the growth of start-ups at various stages.

Reason (R) MUDRA provides three products, i.e. 'Shishu', 'Kishore' and 'Tarun' to meet different funding needs based on the stage of growth.

Two Statements Based MCQs

Direction (Q.No. 48 to 57) *Read the following statements carefully and choose the correct alternative*

Alternatives

(a) Statement I is correct and Statement II is incorrect
(b) Statement II is correct and Statement I is incorrect
(c) Both the statements are correct
(d) Both the statements are incorrect

48. **Statement I** Entrepreneurs improve the standard of living of many people, directly and indirectly.

Statement II Entrepreneurship involves bigger risk as compared to career in employment or practice of a profession.

49. **Statement I** The start-up India scheme aims to create an entrepreneurial culture by motivating educated youth and technologists.

Statement II The scheme mainly focuses on expanding large-scale enterprises and supporting established businesses.

50. **Statement I** Bootstrapping refers to the practice of funding a project or venture by raising money from a large number of people for a common goal.

Statement II Bootstrapping is a good option of funding only if the initial requirement is small and handy.

51. **Statement I** Angel investors provide funding for early stage start-ups in exchange for equity.

Statement II Venture capitalists are individuals who fund start-ups through personal savings without requiring equity.

52. **Statement I** Crowd funding is a method of raising funds for creative projects using social media platforms.

Statement II Crowd funding is commonly used to finance large industrial projects rather than small creative initiatives.

53. **Statement I** Intellectual Property Rights (IPRs) encourage the creation of new inventions by providing creators exclusive rights.

Statement II IPR allows others to freely use and reproduce a creator's work to encourage innovation.

54. **Statement I** A patent protects scientific inventions and grants the inventor exclusive rights to their product or process.

Statement II Copyrights protect only physical inventions and exclude artistic or literary works.

55. **Statement I** Small industries are the largest employers of human resources.

Statement II Small industries promote balanced regional development of the country.

56. **Statement I** The MSMED Act, 2006 defines small-scale enterprises based on investment in plant and machinery.

Statement II The MSMED Act only covers large enterprises and does not include small or micro enterprises.

57. **Statement I** Small-scale industries are generally managed by large teams and have a complex managerial structure.

Statement II Small-scale industries benefit from quick decision-making and flexibility due to their simple managerial structure.

Matching

58. Match the following

Column I	Column II
A. Bootstrapping	(i) Investment from individuals with surplus cash, often in the early stages of a start-up like Google or Facebook.
B. Venture capital	(ii) Raising money from multiple investors through social networking for creative projects like music, films, etc.
C. Crowd funding	(iii) Professionally managed fund which is invested in companies that have huge potential.
D. Angel funding	(iv) Starting a business without external capital, using personal savings or funds from family/ friends.

Codes

	A	B	C	D		A	B	C	D
(a)	(ii)	(iii)	(i)	(iv)	(b)	(iv)	(iii)	(ii)	(i)
(c)	(i)	(iii)	(ii)	(iv)	(d)	(ii)	(i)	(iii)	(iv)

59. Match the following

Column I	Column II
A. Patent	(i) Identifies goods whose qualities are tied to the geographical location, such as Darjeeling Tea or Kashmir Pashmina.
B. Copyright	(ii) A mark (word, name, symbol, etc.) that identifies and distinguishes goods, with categories like conventional and non-conventional trademarks.
C. Trademark	(iii) Provides exclusive rights to creators or authors to prevent unauthorised use, reproduction or distribution of content.
D. Geographical Indication (GI)	(iv) Protects scientific inventions (products or processes) that are new, non-obvious and capable of industrial application.

Codes

	A	B	C	D		A	B	C	D
(a)	(ii)	(i)	(iii)	(iv)	(b)	(iv)	(iii)	(ii)	(i)
(c)	(i)	(iii)	(ii)	(iv)	(d)	(ii)	(iii)	(i)	(iv)

60. Match the following

Column I	Column II
A. Entrepreneurship	(i) Scheme for nurturing innovation
B. Start-up	(ii) Investment does not exceed ₹ 1 crore
C. Cottage industries	(iii) Process of setting one's business
D. Micro industries	(iv) Rural industries uses family labour

Codes

	A	B	C	D		A	B	C	D
(a)	(ii)	(i)	(iii)	(iv)	(b)	(iv)	(iii)	(ii)	(i)
(c)	(i)	(iii)	(ii)	(iv)	(d)	(iii)	(i)	(iv)	(ii)

61. Match the following

Column I	Column II
A. Micro enterprise	(i) Investment in plant and machinery is less than ₹ 50 crore
B. Small enterprise	(ii) Investment in plant and machinery is less than ₹ 10 crore
C. Medium enterprise	(iii) Investment in plant and machinery is less than ₹ 1 crore

Codes

	A	B	C
(a)	(iii)	(ii)	(i)
(b)	(i)	(ii)	(iii)
(c)	(i)	(iii)	(ii)
(d)	(ii)	(i)	(iii)

62. Match the following

Column I	Column II
A. SFURTI	(i) 1978
B. NABARD	(ii) 2005
C. NSIC	(iii) 1982
D. DIC	(iv) 1955

Codes

	A	B	C	D		A	B	C	D
(a)	(ii)	(i)	(iii)	(iv)	(b)	(iv)	(iii)	(ii)	(i)
(c)	(i)	(iii)	(ii)	(iv)	(d)	(ii)	(iii)	(iv)	(i)

Answers

1. (c) entrepreneur
2. (b) self-employment
3. (b) Related to innovation
4. (a) Development of backward and tribal areas
5. (b) To increase number of entrepreneurs
6. (b) Assessment of selected business idea
7. (b) Entrepreneurship is a dynamic process that requires regular adaptation and innovation to remain competitive in a changing environment.
8. (b) The start-up India scheme allows private limited companies, partnership firms or limited liability partnerships, not just public limited companies, to qualify as start-ups.
9. (a) not older than 5 years
10. (b) Bootstrapping
11. (b) Venture capital
12. (b) Angel investors do not always require majority equity ownership, they often invest smaller amounts compared to venture capitalists and may take minority stakes.
13. (b) Business incubators
14. (b) Angel investors
15. (d) Crowd funding
16. (c) Patent
17. (b) Trademark
18. (c) Regional product authenticity
19. (a) design
20. (b) small enterprise
21. (b) traditional small-scale industries
22. (a) Micro enterprise
23. (d) investment in plant and machinery
24. (d) Regional balance
25. (b) Finance and technology
26. (b) Marketing
27. (c) Limited availability of finance
28. (c) Shortage of raw material
29. (a) Shortage of finance, raw material, managerial skills and idle capacity
30. (d) All of the above
31. (c) National Small Industries Corporation (NSIC)
32. (a) Khadi and Village Industries Commission (KVIC)
33. (d) District Industries Centres
34. (b) Small enterprises
35. (c) Ownership of business
36. (a) management skill development
37. (b) Long-term loans
38. (a) Both Assertion (A) and Reason (R) are true and Reason (R) is the correct explanation of Assertion (A)
39. (a) Both Assertion (A) and Reason (R) are true and Reason (R) is the correct explanation of Assertion (A)
40. (a) Both Assertion (A) and Reason (R) are true and Reason (R) is the correct explanation of Assertion (A)
41. (d) Incubators offer more than financial support, i.e. they provide a variety of professional services to help new businesses grow.
42. (a) Both Assertion (A) and Reason (R) are true and Reason (R) is the correct explanation of Assertion (A)
43. (a) Both Assertion (A) and Reason (R) are true and Reason (R) is the correct explanation of Assertion (A)
44. (a) Both Assertion (A) and Reason (R) are true and Reason (R) is the correct explanation of Assertion (A)
45. (a) Both Assertion (A) and Reason (R) are true and Reason (R) is the correct explanation of Assertion (A)
46. (a) Both Assertion (A) and Reason (R) are true and Reason (R) is the correct explanation of Assertion (A)
47. (a) Both Assertion (A) and Reason (R) are true and Reason (R) is the correct explanation of Assertion (A)
48. (c) Both the statements are correct
49. (a) The focus of the scheme is on promoting start-ups and new businesses, not large-scale or established businesses.
50. (b) Bootstrapping refers to funding a business or project using personal savings or revenue from the business itself, not by raising money from a large number of people.
51. (a) Venture capitalists are professional investors who provide funding to start-ups, usually in exchange for equity, not just from personal savings.
52. (a) Crowd funding is generally not used for large industrial projects, which require more formal and substantial funding.
53. (a) IPR actually restricts others from using or reproducing a creator's work without permission.
54. (a) Copyrights protect literary, artistic and musical works, not just physical inventions.
55. (b) Small industries are the second largest employer after agriculture.
56. (a) MSMED Act specifically includes micro, small and medium enterprises, not just large enterprises.
57. (b) Small-scale industries typically have a simple managerial structure with fewer individuals managing operations.
58. (b) (iv) (iii) (ii) (i)
59. (b) (iv) (iii) (ii) (i)
60. (d) (iii) (i) (iv) (ii)
61. (a) (iii) (ii) (i)
62. (d) (ii) (iii) (iv) (i)

Subjective Questions

Short Answer Type Questions

1. "Entrepreneurship development plays a vital role in driving economic growth and societal progress." In the light of the given statement, discuss the need of entrepreneurship development for a developing country like India. Competency Based Que

Ans. For a developing economy like India, need of entrepreneurship development arises due to the following reasons (any four)

(i) **Employment Opportunities**
Entrepreneurship enables entrepreneurs to create more/additional employment opportunities for youth.

(ii) **Economic Independence**
Entrepreneurs develop and produce substituted products of imported goods and prevent the over-dependence on the other countries.

(iii) **Capital Formation**
Entrepreneurship encourages the establishment of new industries in economy which increase the capital formation rate in country.

(iv) **Development of Backward and Tribal Areas**
Entrepreneurship leads to scattering of economic activities in all areas of the country.

(v) **More Utilisation of Natural Resources**
Entrepreneurship enables the economy to utilise and explore the abundance of natural resources.

(vi) **Economic Growth and Development**
Entrepreneurship provides the base of industrialisation in economy which is the main cause of economic growth and economic development.

2. State the main objectives of start-up India scheme.

Ans. Following are the objectives of start-up India scheme

(i) To generate an entrepreneurial culture and promote entrepreneurial values in the society at large and influence the mindset of people towards entrepreneurship.

(ii) To create awareness about the benefits of being an entrepreneur and the process of entrepreneurship.

(iii) To encourage more dynamic start-ups by motivating educated youth, scientists and technologists to consider entrepreneurship as a profitable, preferred and viable career.

(iv) Expanding the base of entrepreneurial supply by meeting specific needs of under represented target groups, like women, socially and economically backward communities, under represented regions to achieve inclusiveness and sustainable development to address the needs of the population at the bottom of the pyramid.

3. "Intellectual Property Rights (IPRs) play a crucial role in fostering innovation and protecting the creations of individuals and organisations. These rights provide creators with exclusive control over their inventions, designs or artistic works, encouraging investment in research and development.

However, the proper enforcement of IPR is essential to prevent unauthorised use and ensure fair competition."
In light of the above statement, discuss the importance of intellectual property rights. Competency Based Que

Ans. The importance of IPR for entrepreneurship is

(i) It encourages creation of new, path breaking inventions, such as cancer cure medicines.

(ii) It encourages creators, authors, creators, etc. for their work by providing incentives.

(iii) It allows creators and inventors to have control over their creations and inventions so that the work created by a person can be distributed and communicated to the public only with his/her permission. This helps in the prevention of loss of income.

(iv) It helps authors, creators, developers and owners to get recognition for their works.

4. Discuss the concept of trademark.

Ans. A trademark is any word, name or symbol (or their combination) that helps to identify the goods made by an individual, company, organisation, etc.

A trademark helps in distinguishing similar products in the market from its competitors. A competitor cannot use the same or similar trademark to sell their products in the market.

Trademark may be categorised into the following

(i) **Conventional Trademark**
This category includes works, colour combination, label, logo, packaging, shape of goods, etc.

(ii) **Non-Conventional Trademark**
This category includes those marks which were not considered distinctive previously, but started getting recognition with the passage of time, i.e. sound mark, dynamic mark, etc.

5. "MSME and entrepreneurship are connected." Do you agree? Give two reasons. NCERT; Competency Based Que

Ans. Yes, entrepreneurship and MSMEs are inter-connected, as to start a small business one needs innovation and creativity which is a base for entrepreneurship.

Two reasons to support the answer would be

(i) MSME are the second largest employers of human resources, after agriculture.
They generate a greater number of employment opportunities per unit of capital invested compared to large industries. Therefore, it provides an attractive place to start for most entrepreneurs.

(ii) The skills and talents of people can be channelled into business ideas which can be converted into reality with little capital investment and almost nil formalities to start a small business.
Thus, MSME is often a starting point for most entrepreneurs.

6. What is MSME? NCERT

Ans. The Ministry of Micro, Small and Medium Enterprises is the ministry in the Government of India. It is the apex executive body for the formulation and administration of rules, regulations and laws relating to micro, small and medium enterprises in India.

MSME identifies the following enterprises and specifies the limits for their categorisation

(i) **Micro Enterprise**
In micro enterprise, the investment in plant and machinery is less than ₹ 1 crore and the turnover does not exceed ₹ 5 crore.

(ii) **Small Enterprise**
In small enterprise, the investment in plant and machinery is less than ₹ 10 crore and the turnover does not exceed ₹ 50 crore.

(iii) **Medium Enterprise**
In medium enterprise, the investment in plant and machinery is ₹ 50 crores and the turnover does not exceed ₹ 250 crore.

7. Distinguish between a small-scale business unit and large-scale business unit on the basis of nature, type of labour, scale of operation and capital.

Ans. The differences between a small-scale business unit and large-scale business unit are

Basis	Small-scale Business Unit	Large-scale Business Unit
Nature	It is labour intensive.	It is capital intensive.
Type of Labour	It uses labour of family.	It uses hired labour.
Scale of Operation	It operates on small-scale.	It operates on large-scale.
Capital	In this unit, capital does not exceed ₹ 10 crore.	In this unit, capital can be increased above ₹ 10 crore.

8. State any four features of small-scale industries.

Ans. Following are the features of small-scale industries

(i) **Personal Character**
Small-scale industries enjoy the personal character. It is generally owned by a single entrepreneur or partnership.

(ii) **Simple Managerial Structure**
They are managed by owners only. Thus, they can reap the benefits of direct motivation, secrecy, flexibility, etc.

(iii) **Labour Incentive Techniques**
There is a predominance of labour in these industries. They use labour incentive techniques of production instead of mechanised methods of production.

(iv) **Local Area of Operations**
The operations of these industries are localised. They depend mainly on local resources but products are exported all over the world.

9. Discuss how small-scale industries play an important role in India.

Ans. Following are the ways in which small-scale industries play an important role in India (any four)

(i) **Contribution in GDP**
Small-scale industries in India account for 95% of the industrial units of the country. They contribute almost 40% of the gross industrial value added and 45% of the total exports (direct and indirect) from India.

(ii) **Employment Generation**
In India, small-scale industries are the second largest employers of human resources, after agriculture. They generate more employment opportunities per unit of capital invested as compared to large industries. Thus, they are considered good for countries like India, that have surplus labour and less capital.

(iii) **Supply Variety of Products**
Small-scale industries in India supply enormous variety of products which include the following

- Goods of mass consumption such as readymade garments, hosiery goods, stationery items, soaps and detergents, domestic utensils, etc.
- Sophisticated goods such as electrical goods, engineering goods, drugs, etc.
- Handlooms, handicrafts and other products which have high export value.

(iv) **Balanced Regional Development**
Small-scale industries produce products using simple technologies and depend on locally available resources in terms of both material and labour. Thus, they can be opened anywhere in the country, without any locational constraints and the benefits of industrialisation can be received by every region.

(v) **Provide Business Opportunities**
Small-scale industries provide opportunity for the growth of entrepreneurship. By utilising skills and talent, an individual can become entrepreneur as less capitals investment is required for setting-up business in small sector.

10. What is a cottage industry? NCERT

Ans. Cottage industries are also known as rural industries or traditional industries. They are not defined by capital investment criteria as in the case of other small-scale industries. They perform agricultural activities along with other supplementary activities at home. The following are some important features of cottage industries

(i) They are owned and operated by individuals who invest their private resources in these units.
(ii) They employ family members as labour.
(iii) They require talent and skills that are generally passed on from one generation to the next in the family.
(iv) They are highly labour-intensive and indigenous, with very less amount of capital required.
(v) They sell a small portion of the output in the local market.

11. "Small-scale industries (SSIs) in rural areas have emerged as a significant factor for local economic growth by generating employment, reducing migration to urban centers and utilising local resources effectively.

These industries help in balancing regional development but may face challenges in terms of limited access to technology, finance and skilled labour."

In light of the above statement, write a short note on the role of small-scale industries in rural areas. Competency Based Que

Or **Describe the role of small business in rural India.** NCERT

Ans. To improve the standard of living of these people, small-scale enterprises (commerce and manufacturing) are launched and encouraged in the rural areas. The role of small business in rural India can be explained through the following points

(i) **Non-farm Employment**
Small-scale industries have encouraged rural people to involve in a wide range of agricultural activities, along with the traditional activities of farming and agricultural labour. They provide varied and multiple sources of income to the rural people.

(ii) **Employment for Artisans**
Cottage and rural industries play an important role in providing employment opportunities in the rural areas, especially to the traditional artisans and the weaker sections of society.

(iii) **Prevention of Migration**
Development of rural and village industries can also prevent migration of rural population to urban areas in search of employment.

(iv) **Socio-economic Aspects**
Small-scale industries contribute towards socio-economic aspects such as reduction in income inequalities, dispersed development of industries and linkage with other sectors of the economy.

12. District Industries Centres (DIC) play a crucial role in promoting industrial development at the district level by offering support in various administrative and regulatory aspects. They assist entrepreneurs in setting-up businesses by providing necessary infrastructure, technical guidance and financial support.

In the light of the above statement, discuss the functions of DICs. Competency Based Que

Ans. The main objective of DICs is to make available all necessary services related to opening of micro, small and medium enterprises at one place.

The following are the functions of DICs

(i) It acts as the focal point of industrialistion of the district.
(ii) It identifies projects for setting-up of SSI units.
(iii) It issues permanent registration certificate to SSI units.
(iv) It provides marketing support to SSI units.
(v) It acts as a link between the entrepreneurs and the lead bank of the district.
(vi) It helps businessman in obtaining licence from electricity board, water supply board, etc.

Long Answer Type Questions

13. "Entrepreneurship is marked by innovation, risk taking and the ability to create opportunities. Entrepreneurs are often seen as catalysts for economic growth, fostering competition and employment. However, entrepreneurship also requires a keen understanding of market trends and customer needs, and it involves challenges related to funding, scalability and sustainability."

In light of the above statement, discuss any five features of entrepreneurship development. Competency Based Que

Ans. Following are the features of entrepreneurship development

(i) **Systematic Activity**
Entrepreneurship is a systematic and step-by-step activity. It has certain competency requirements, temperamental, skill and other knowledge which can be acquired, learnt and developed by both formal educational and vocational training as wells as by observation and work experience.

(ii) **Lawful and Purposeful Activity**
Lawful business is the objective of entrepreneurship. Its purpose is to create value for personal profit and social gain.

(iii) **Innovation**
Entrepreneurship involves continuous search for new ideas. An entrepreneur recognises the need for change and he always initiates new and better ways to do the work.

(iv) **Organisation of Production**
Entrepreneur mobilises the resources required for production into a productive enterprise or firm. These resources or factors of production include land, labour, capital and technology.

(v) **Risk Taking**
Risk is an inherent element of entrepreneurship. An entrepreneur runs an enterprise for profit motive but there is also the risk of loss. If an entrepreneur does not have willingness to assume risk, then entrepreneurship will never succeed.

14. "Funding a start-up can be achieved through various sources such as venture capital, crowd funding, bank loans and angel investors. Each of these funding methods has its own set of advantages, such as quicker access to capital or the possibility of mentorship. However, challenges like equity dilution, high interest rates or a lack of investor interest may arise."

In light of the above statement, discuss the various methods to fund a start-up. Competency Based Que

Ans. Following are the different methods to fund a start-up

(i) **Bootstrapping**
It means starting a business without external capital. Entrepreneur can invest from their past saving or can get from family or friends. It is suitable only if the initial requirement is small.

(ii) **Crowd Funding**
Crowd sourced funding is a means of raising money for a creative project (i.e. music, film, book). It is a collection of funds from multiple investors through social networking sites for a specific project.

(iii) **Angel Funding**
Angel investors are individuals with surplus cash who are interested to invest in upcoming start-ups. Many household names, like Google, Facebook were financed in their earliest stages by angel investors.

(iv) **Venture Capital**
It is professionally managed fund which is invested in companies that have huge potential. Venture capitalists provide expertise, mentorship and evaluate business on the basis of its sustainability and scalability. Generally such funding is involved in software, technology and bio-technology.

(v) **Business Incubators**
Incubators provide professional services that facilitates the development of new business by providing resources, support and advice.

(vi) **Business Accelerators**
Accelerators offer a range of support service and funding opportunities for start-ups. They provide capital and investment in return for start-up equity.

(vii) **Micro-finance and NBFCs**
Micro-finance means access to financial services to those who do not have access to conventional banking services or have not qualified for a bank loan.
NBFCs (Non-Banking Financial Corporation) provides banking services without meeting legal requirement of a bank.

15. "Innovation is integral to MSME." Discuss giving reasons to your answer. NCERT; Competency Based Que

Ans. Innovation is integral to MSME due to the following reasons

(i) Innovation is a driving force in any economy. Due to its rapid development and use, technology has become a crucial element affecting almost all industries, including agriculture, manufacturing and services.

(ii) Innovations and technical advancements greatly influence the extent to which businesses and initiatives contribute to the country's economic growth and worldwide expansion.

(iii) The current state of the world requires constant innovation from businesses, including introducing new technology to raise quality standards and creating proper infrastructure support.
There have been attempts to construct appropriate laboratories, technology centres and incubation units to assist all businesses in improving their tools and machines.

(iv) Infrastructure assistance is necessary for companies to develop innovative ideas that benefit MSMEs and the overall industrial sector to modernise technology.

(v) It is also necessary for business incubators to help entrepreneurs with commercialisation to accelerate the process of turning such technologies from basic ideas into successful enterprises that generate jobs.

In conclusion, inventions take place when individuals think outside the box. To be a successful invention, it must be simple, basic and focused on only one task. Any technology or invention must be understandable to the average person for it to be helpful. A brilliant mind is driven to succeed by all these original ideas and the desire to make them happen. These enterprises and innovators are supported by the Ministry of MSME, which encourages them to follow their lofty goals of creating something useful and novel.

16. Small businesses are often considered the backbone of the economy, yet they encounter significant challenges that hinder their growth and sustainability. In the context of the given statement, discuss the various problems faced by small businesses. Competency Based Que

Or **Discuss the problems faced by small-scale industries.** NCERT

Ans. Following are the problems faced by small businesses

(i) **Finance**
One of the severe problems faced by small business is the non-availability of adequate finance to carry out its operations. These units lack in credit worthiness and have a small capital base. As a result, they heavily depend on local financial resources and frequently exploited by the moneylenders.

(ii) **Raw Material**
Shortage of raw material is another problem of small business. If the required materials are not available, small businesses have to compromise on the quality or have to pay high price to get good quality materials. Their bargaining power is relatively low due to the small quantity of purchases made by them.

(iii) **Managerial Skills**
Small business is generally promoted and operated by a single person, who may not possess technical and managerial skills to run the business.

(iv) **Marketing**
Small-scale enterprises are unable to meet the expenses of marketing activities. They depend on middlemen who exploit them by paying low prices for their goods and delaying their payments.

(v) **Quality**
Many small business organisations do not adhere to desired standards of quality. Instead, they concentrate on cutting the cost and keeping the prices low. As they do not maintain quality, they are not able to compete in global markets.

(vi) **Capacity Utilisation**
Due to lack of marketing skills or lack of demand, many small business have to operate below full capacity, due to which their operating costs tend to increase. This leads to sickness and closure of the business.

17. What measures has the government taken to solve the problem of finance and marketing in the small-scale sector? NCERT

Ans. Government has provided the following institutional support to solve the problem of finance and marketing in the small-scale sector

(i) **National Bank for Agriculture and Rural Development** (NABARD) It was set-up in 1982, to promote integrated rural development.
Apart from agriculture, it supports small industries, cottage and village industries and rural artisans.
It provides credit and offers counselling and consultancy services, and organises training and development programmes for rural entrepreneurs.

(ii) **The Rural Small Business Development Centre** (RSBDC)
It was set-up by the world association for small and medium enterprises and is sponsored by NABARD. It works for the benefit of socially and economically disadvantaged individuals and groups. It aims at providing management and technical support to current and prospective micro and small entrepreneurs in rural areas.

(iii) **National Small Industries Corporation** (NSIC)
It was set-up in 1955, with a view to promote, aid and foster the growth of small business units in the country.

(iv) **Small Industries Development Bank of India** (SIDBI)
It was set-up as an apex bank to provide direct/indirect financial assistance under different schemes, to meet credit needs of small business organisations and to coordinate the functions of other institutions in similar activities.

(v) **The National Commission for Enterprises in the Unorganised Sector** (NCEUS)
It was constituted in September, 2004, with the objectives of recommending measures considered necessary for improving the productivity of small enterprises in the informal sector and to enhance the competitiveness of the sector in the emerging global environment by developing linkages of the sector with other institutions in the areas of credit, raw materials, infrastructure, technology upgradation, marketing, etc.

(vi) **Rural and Women Entrepreneurship Development** (RWED)
This programme aims at promoting a conducive business environment and at building institutional and human capacities that will encourage and support the entrepreneurial initiatives of rural people and women by providing training and advisory services.

(vii) **Scheme of Fund for Regeneration of Traditional Industries** (SFURTI)
The Central Government set-up this fund to make the traditional industries more productive and competitive and to facilitate their sustainable development. The main objectives of SFURTI are to develop clusters of traditional industries in various parts of the country; build innovative and traditional skills, improve technologies, encourage public private partnerships, develop market intelligence, etc.

(viii) **The District Industries Centres** (DICs)

District Industries Centre is the institution at the district level which provides all the services and support facilities to the entrepreneurs for setting-up small and village industries including identification of suitable schemes, preparation of feasibility reports, arranging for credit, machinery and equipment, provision of raw materials and other extension services. This was launched on 1st May, 1978.

18. Discuss the various schemes and support programmes launched by National Small Industries Corporation.

Ans. The various schemes and support programmes which are launched by NSIC are

(i) **Performance and Credit Rating Scheme**

This scheme is implemented by NSIC to achieve the following objectives

- Sensitising the small industries about the need of credit rating.
- Encouraging the small business units to maintain good financial track record.

(ii) **Marketing Assistance Scheme**

Under this scheme, the Ministry of Micro, Small and Medium Enterprises, through NSIC, has been providing marketing support to micro and small industries.

The objectives of this scheme are

- To enhance marketing capabilities and competitiveness of micro and small enterprises.
- To exhibit the competencies of these enterprises.
- To update these enterprises about the prevalent market scenario and its impact on their activities.
- To facilitate formation of groups of micro and small enterprises.
- To provide a platform for these enterprises to interact with large institutional buyers.
- To provide information regarding various programmes of the government.
- To enrich the marketing skills of micro and small entrepreneurs.

(iii) **Marketing Support Extended to MSMEs**

NSIC extends marketing support to MSMEs through the following activities

- NSIC organises International Technology Exhibitions in foreign countries where Micro, Small and Medium Enterprises can showcase their products.
- NSIC also organises domestic exhibitions where MSMEs can showcase their products.
- NSIC organises buyer-seller meets for MSMEs.
- NSIC conducts intensive campaigns to spread awareness regarding the various schemes of the government.
- NSIC also benefit the micro, small and medium enterprises by various other support activities such as development of display centres, show windows, hoarding, printing brochures, development of websites, preparing a directoty, etc.

Case Study Based Questions

Short Case Studies

Case Study 1

The government of Country X has launched several initiatives aimed at boosting employment, such as 'Youth Empowerment Programme' and 'Innovation for Growth.' However, these programmes have not yielded the expected results and experts suggest that the root cause lies in the lack of entrepreneurial skills among the youth.

Despite the availability of resources and opportunities, many young individuals are unable to harness their potential in the job market, leading to a rise in unemployment.

(i) Identify the concept which can reduce the unemployment problem in Country X.

(ii) State the need of this concept in India.

Ans.

(i) The concept which can reduce the unemployment problems in Country X is entrepreneurship development.

(ii) For a developing economy like India, need of entrepreneurship development arises due to the following reasons (any three)

- **Employment Opportunities**

  Entrepreneurship enables entrepreneurs to create more/additional employment opportunities for youth.

- **Economic Independence**

  Entrepreneurs develop and produce substituted products of imported goods and prevent the over-dependence on the other countries.

- **Capital Formation**
  Entrepreneurship encourages the establishment of new industries in economy which increase the capital formation rate in country.
- **Development of Backward and Tribal Areas**
  Entrepreneurship leads to scattering of economic activities in all areas of the country.

Case Study 2

Amit, a young scientist, has developed a device that can purify water using a completely new and innovative process. He claims that his invention is unique, has never been developed before and is based on a breakthrough technology in water filtration.

The device is easy to manufacture and can be scaled for industrial production. Amit wants to ensure that no one else can copy, sell or use his invention without his permission. He approaches a legal expert to secure his intellectual property rights for this invention.

(i) Identify the type of intellectual property right. Amit should apply for, to protect his invention.

(ii) State the conditions required for this type of intellectual property right to be granted.

Ans.

(i) The type of intellectual property right Amit should apply for to protect his invention is patent. A patent is a type of IPR which protects the scientific inventions (products and or process). It is an exclusive right granted by the government which prevent any body from making, using, offering for sale, selling or importing the invention.

(ii) Following conditions are required for an invention to be patentable

- It must be new, i.e. it should not already exist in the current knowledge anywhere in the world.
- It must be non-obvious to any person who is skilled in the relevant field of technology.
- It must be capable of industrial application, i.e. capable of being used or manufactured in the industry.

Case Study 3

Ravi and Rohan, two enthusiastic tech-savvy friends, launched their company, 'AgriTech Solutions,' in 2022. The primary aim of their business is to develop a mobile application to help farmers increase productivity by providing real-time data on soil health, weather conditions and crop management techniques.

Their company is registered in India, is a private limited entity and its annual turnover is ₹ 15 crore. Since their focus is on innovative solutions for agriculture, they believe they qualify for benefits under the start-up India initiative.

(i) Would Ravi and Rohan's company be classified as a start-up under the start-up India initiative? Justify your answer.

(ii) State any two objectives of the start-up India scheme.

Ans.

(i) Yes, Ravi and Rohan's company, AgriTech Solutions, would be classified as a start-up under the start-up India initiative. The company meets the criteria for being a start-up

- It is registered in India.
- It is a private limited company.
- It was established in 2022, making it less than 5 years old.
- Its annual turnover is ₹ 15 crore, which is under the ₹ 25 crore limit.
- The company focuses on innovation by developing a farming efficiency app.

(ii) Two objectives of the start-up India scheme

- To generate an entrepreneurial culture and promote entrepreneurial values in the society at large and influence the mindset of people towards entrepreneurship.
- To create awareness about the benefits of being an entrepreneur and the process of entrepreneurship.

Case Study 4

After completing MBA from IIM, Ahemdabad, Arun decided to enter into a start-up business. After analysing the market, he found that there is considerable scope in Food Delivery business. However, Arun is not sure of the ways in which he can finance his start-up.

So, he consulted his friend, Saubhagya, who himself started a start-up one year back. Saubhagya suggested him a number of ways to finance the start-up. State any four ways to finance start-up, which were suggested by Saubhagya.

Ans. Following are the ways to finance start-up

(i) **Crowd Funding**
Crowd sourced funding is a means of raising money for a creative project (i.e. music, film, book). It is a collection of funds from multiple investors through social networking sites for a specific project.

(ii) **Angel Funding**
Angel investors are individuals with surplus cash who are interested to invest in upcoming start-ups. Many household names, like Google, Facebook were financed in their earliest stages by angel investors.

(iii) **Venture Capital**
It is professionally managed fund which is invested in companies that have huge potential. Venture capitalists provide expertise, mentorship and evaluate business on the basis of its sustainability and scalability.

Generally such funding is involved in software, technology and bio-technology.

(iv) **Bootstrapping**

It means starting a business without external capital. Entrepreneur can invest from their past saving or can get from family or friends. It is suitable only if the initial requirement is small.

Case Study 5

After completing the graduation, three close friends (Prakash, Samaksh and Mahesh) decided to start their own business.

(i) Prakash established a factory to produce readymade garments and invested ₹ 9 crore in plant and machinery.

(ii) Samaksh established a factory to produce readymade garments and invested ₹ 35 crore in plant and machinery.

(iii) Mahesh established a factory to produce readymade garments and invested ₹ 80 lakhs in plant and machinery.

Identify the category in which their business will fall under Micro, Small and Medium Enterprises Development Act, 2006.

Ans. All three business will be classified as manufacturing enterprises. As per Micro, Small and Medium Enterprises Development Act, 2006, their business will be categorised as

(i) Prakash, small enterprise

(ii) Samaksh, medium enterprise

(iii) Mahesh, micro enterprise

Case Study 6

Vishal and Priya, two young entrepreneurs, decided to set-up a small-scale enterprise in their hometown to produce eco-friendly jute bags. Their business required a modest investment in machinery, which they funded through a government scheme promoting small enterprises. They employed a team of 15 workers who operated the machinery manually, ensuring high-quality production with minimal environmental impact.

The enterprise was managed by Vishal and Priya themselves, allowing them to maintain direct control, ensure flexibility and keep operational secrets. The raw materials were sourced locally, but their eco-friendly bags quickly gained popularity and were exported to various countries.

The simplicity of their operation and the labour-intensive techniques allowed them to keep costs low while providing employment in their community.

The use of basic technology ensured that their workers could easily learn and operate the equipment.

(i) Identify and explain two features of small-scale enterprises highlighted in the case.

(ii) How does the localised operation of small-scale enterprises benefit the community?

Ans.

(i) Two features of small-scale enterprises highlighted in the case are

- **Simple Managerial Structure**

  They are managed by owners only. Thus, they can reap the benefits of direct motivation, secrecy, flexibility, etc.

- **Labour Incentive Techniques**

  There is a predominance of labour in these industries. They use labour incentive techniques of production instead of mechanised methods of production.

(ii) The localised operation benefits the community by

- Providing employment opportunities for local workers, improving their standard of living.
- Utilising local resources efficiently, supporting local suppliers and businesses.
- Promoting regional development through economic activity and increased income circulation in the area.

Case Study 7

Meena runs a small weaving business in her village, where she makes handwoven mats and baskets using locally sourced bamboo. The entire family, including her children, contributes to the work, which is carried out in a small shed attached to their house.

The tools used are basic and inexpensive and the products are sold in nearby markets. Meena emphasises that their work reflects traditional techniques passed down through generations, helping preserve the cultural heritage of their community.

Identify any three features of the cottage industry as highlighted in Meena's weaving business.

Ans. The three features of the cottage industry highlighted in Meena's weaving business are

(i) **Use of Family Labour**

The entire family, including children, contributes to the production process.

(ii) **Use of Simple Equipment**

The tools used for weaving are basic and inexpensive.

(iii) **Production Using Indigenous Technology**

Traditional techniques passed down through generations are employed in making the products.

Case Study 8

After obtaining M. Tech, degree from a national level technical institute, Raj joined a big enterprise as a mechanical engineer.

He worked there for about 4 years, but felt suffocated as he had no scope for doing something new and taking his own decisions. He has recently decided to leave the job and start his own small industrial unit in a rural backward area notified by the government.

(i) Do you agree with Raj's decision? Give your justification.

(ii) What institution should he contact to get support for his industrial venture?

Ans.

(i) Yes, I agree with Raj's decision to set-up his own small industrial unit. The reasons are

- Self-employment
- Scope for creativity and innovation
- Complete control
- Generation of employment for others.

(ii) Raj can get in touch with the officials of the following institutions to get the needed support to set up his small industrial unit

- National Small Industries Corporation (NSIC)
- District Industries Centre (DIC)
- Rural Small business Development Centre (RSBDC)
- Khadi and Village Industries Commission (KVIC)
- Small Industries Development Bank of India (SIDBI)

Case Study 9

The National Small Industries Corporation Ltd. is a Government of India enterprise under the Ministry of Micro, Small and Medium Enterprises (MSME). It operates through a countrywide network of offices and technical centres in the country. NSIC has a B2B web portal. The portal provides small and medium sized enterprises in India, an access to customers around the globe exclusively, once they get themselves listed with NSIC portal for an annual fee.

The portal facilitates transactions between buyers and sellers without any intervention. It has features which will enable virtual buyer-seller meets and assist in request of quotations for business orders.

It also host a database of small and medium companies' details, products, catalogues and pictures, in addition to providing market intelligence services (services such as product and tender tracking) to registered companies at a little extra cost.

(i) With reference to the case, state the meaning of NSIC.

(ii) The above text tells about the assistance provided by NSIC to the small and medium enterprises for marketing their products. Give any one more mode of marketing assistance provided by NSIC.

Ans.

(i) NSIC was set-up in 1955 to promote, aid and foster the growth of small-scale units in India. It works under the Ministry of Micro, Small and Medium Enterprises (MSME) operates through a countrywide network of offices and technical assistance.

(ii) **'Organising International Technology Exhibitions in Foreign Countries and Participation in International Exhibitions/Trade Fairs**

NSIC organises international technology exhibitions in foreign countries where micro, small and medium enterprises can showcase their products. This helps the enterprises to boost the sales of their products, form joint ventures with foreign collaborators and enter into agreements related to technology transfers and marketing arrangements.

In addition to organising international exhibitions, NSIC also helps these enterprises to participate in international exhibitions and trade fairs hosted by other bodies. Participation in such events helps in image building of MSMEs and exposes them to international practices.

Long Case Studies

Case Study 10

An aspiring entrepreneur named Raj decided to explore the world of business. Raj began his entrepreneurial journey through a process of self-reflection. He spent considerable time assessing his strengths and weaknesses, determining that his strategic thinking and risk taking abilities would be his greatest assets in this journey.

Once confident in his skills, Raj began identifying potential business opportunities. He noticed an increasing demand for sustainable consumer goods in the market, particularly eco-friendly packaging solutions. Raj believed that there was a gap in the market for affordable and practical eco-friendly alternatives. Raj analysed several opportunities, weighing their potential to meet consumer needs and generate profits.

After evaluating various ideas, Raj narrowed down his focus to a sustainable packaging start-up, which he believed could succeed due to growing environmental concerns. He then assessed the feasibility of this business idea by conducting thorough market research, analysing competitors and consulting with industry experts.

His research confirmed that there was a strong demand for eco-friendly packaging and that the concept was viable.

The next step in his entrepreneurial process was raising capital. Raj created a comprehensive business plan outlining his business idea, goals, financial projections and strategies for market penetration.

Armed with this plan, Raj approached venture capitalists and potential business partners. His well-prepared pitch attracted the necessary funding. With the capital in place, Raj worked on fostering growth for his start-up. He focused on developing innovative packaging solutions that could offer more value than existing products in the market. Raj implemented a robust environmental scanning process.

After several successful years, Raj's business grew significantly and became one of the leading players in the sustainable packaging sector. At this point, Raj decided to consider his exit strategy. After a thorough evaluation, he sold the business to a larger corporation that wanted to expand its eco-friendly product line. Raj successfully harvested the rewards of his entrepreneurial efforts.

(i) Identify the concept described in the case study.

(ii) Discuss the process of entrepreneurship development as illustrated in the case study.

Ans.

(i) The concept described in the case study is entrepreneurship development. Entrepreneurship development is the process of enhancing entrepreneurial skills and knowledge through structured training and institution building programmes.

(ii) The process of entrepreneurship development as illustrated in the case study is as follows

- **Self-introduction**
  The person concerned in the process does an self-introspection to determine his relative strengths and weaknesses.
- **Business Opportunities are Identified**
  The various forth coming business opportunities are identified in terms of unsatisfied needs and wants of people.
- **Evaluation of Various Business Opportunities**
  The evaluation of various business opportunities is done and the selection is narrowed down to one best business idea.
- **Assessment of the Selected Business Idea**
  The assessment of selected business idea is done in terms of its feasibility to become a viable business venture, by conducting varied types of researches.
- **Raise Start-up Capital**
  By using business plan, entrepreneur tries to attract venture capitalist and partners.
- **Foster Growth**
  To foster growth of business, new ideas are developed and implemented through effective environmental scanning.
- **Harvesting**
  The final stage relates to harvesting where in the entrepreneurs may sell their business and gain reward of their endeavours.

Case Study 11

Neha Verma, an ambitious young entrepreneur, launched her start-up 'TechSolutions,' aiming to provide innovative software solutions for small businesses. However, Neha quickly realised that one of the most challenging aspects of building her start-up was securing the necessary funds for development and expansion.

To gather initial capital, Neha utilised a popular modern approach where small contributions from a large number of individuals were collected through online platforms, allowing people who supported her vision to invest in her project. This method not only helped raise funds but also created a community of supporters.

Additionally, Neha sought funding from wealthy individuals who had experience in the business world and were looking to support emerging companies. These investors provided her with the initial boost, offering not just money but valuable advice to guide the early phases of her venture.

Lastly, to further expand her company, Neha approached a professional fund management firm. The firm, known for investing in businesses with high growth potential, provided both financial resources and strategic guidance to help 'TechSolutions' scale quickly, especially in technology and software development.

Quoting lines from the above paragraph, identify and explain three methods of funding the start-up discussed in the case.

Ans. Following are the three methods of funding the start-up discussed in the case

- **Crowd Funding**
  "Neha utilised a popular modern approach where small contributions from a large number of individuals were collected through online platforms, allowing people who supported her vision to invest in her project."

  Crowd sourced funding is a means of raising money for a creative project (i.e. music, film, book). It is a collection of funds from multiple investors through social networking sites for a specific project.
- **Angel Funding**
  "Neha sought funding from wealthy individuals who had experience in the business world and were looking to support emerging companies. These investors provided her with the initial boost, offering not just money but valuable advice to guide the early phases of her venture."

Angel investors are individuals with surplus cash who are interested to invest in upcoming start-ups. Many household names, like Google, Facebook were financed in their earliest stages by angel investors.

- **Venture Capital**

  "Neha approached a professional fund management firm. The firm, known for investing in businesses with high growth potential, provided both financial resources and strategic guidance to help 'TechSolutions' scale quickly, especially in technology and software development."

  It is professionally managed fund which is invested in companies that have huge potential.

  Venture capitalists provide expertise, mentorship and evaluate business on the basis of its sustainability and scalability. Generally such funding is involved in software, technology and bio-technology.

Case Study 12

Riya Verma, the Managing Director of InnovateTech Solutions, strongly believed in the importance of protecting intellectual property rights to sustain innovation. The company developed unique designs for consumer electronics and also invested heavily in the development of hybrid plant varieties for agricultural purposes. The designs were meticulously created to ensure the aesthetic appeal of their products. These designs were registered under the Design Act, ensuring their protection for 10 years, with an option for renewal.

Additionally, the company's research division focused on creating high yielding hybrid plant varieties, grouping them based on their unique botanical characteristics. These varieties were crucial for conserving plant genetic resources and enhancing agricultural productivity.

InnovateTech Solutions also created innovative semi-conductor integrated circuits for their electronic products, with the layout designs being protected under the Semiconductor Integrated Circuits Layout Design Act, 2000. This protection ensured that the company retained exclusive rights to their intricate circuit designs, preventing unauthorised replication.

Quoting lines from the above paragraph, identify and explain three types of intellectual property rights discussed in the case.

Ans. Following are the three types of intellectual property rights discussed in the case

(i) **Design**

"The designs were meticulously created to ensure the aesthetic appeal of their products. These designs were registered under the Design Act, ensuring their protection for 10 years, with an option for renewal."

It includes shape, pattern and arrangement of lines or colour combination that is applied to any article. It is a protection given to aesthetic appearance or eye-catching features.

The period of protection of a design is 10 years, which can be renewed for further 5 years after expiration. During this period, a registered design can only be used after getting a license from its owner.

(ii) **Plant Variety**

"The company's research division focused on creating high yielding hybrid plant varieties, grouping them based on their unique botanical characteristics."

It refers to grouping of plants into categories on the basis of their botanical characteristics.

It is a type of variety which is produced and developed by farmers. This helps in conserving, improving and making available plant genetic resources, e.g. Hybrid versions of potatoes.

(iii) **Semiconductor Integrated Circuits Layout Design**

"InnovateTech Solutions also created innovative semiconductor integrated circuits for their electronic products, with the layout designs being protected under the Semiconductor Integrated Circuits Layout Design Act, 2000."

A semiconductor is an integral part of every computer chip. Semiconductor integrate circuit is any product that contains transistors and other circuitry elements which are formed on a semiconductor material or an insulating material, or inside the semiconductor material.

It is designed to perform an electronic circuitry function. Semiconductor Integrated Circuits Layout Design Act, 2000 was enacted to provide protection to semiconductor integrated circuits layout designs.

Case Study 13

In a small town nestled in the hills of West Bengal, tea farmers have been growing a special variety of tea for centuries.

This tea, known for its delicate flavour and aroma, has become a symbol of the region's heritage. Over time, other tea producers across the country started using the same name for their products, which led to confusion among consumers.

To protect the unique characteristics of the tea and the reputation of its origin, the local farmers and government decided to seek legal protection for this tea, ensuring that only the tea grown in that specific region could be sold under its distinctive name.

Similar steps have been taken for other unique regional products, such as handcrafted textiles from Kashmir and intricate paintings from Himachal Pradesh, allowing these products to be recognised for their authenticity and connection to their place of origin.

(i) Identify the type of Intellectual Property Right (IPR).

(ii) State any three features of IPR.

(iii) State why IPR is important.

Ans.

(i) The type of intellectual property right described in the case is Geographical Indication (GI). It is primarily an indication which identifies agricultural, natural or manufactured products (handicrafts, industrial goods and food stuffs) that possesses the qualities of the geographical location in which they originate.

Goods protected and registered as GI are categorised into agricultural products, natural, handicrafts, manufactured goods and food stuffs. Darjeeling Tea, Kangra Painting, Kashmir Pashmina, etc. are some of the examples of GI.

(ii) Following are the features of IPR

- **Legal Rights**
  Intellectual property rights are legal rights of the creator/IP owner, to prevent others from using the protected subject matter.
- **Technology**
  It is essential for IPR that the creation has to be original. The creator has to bring something creative into existence.
  IPR covers various aspects of information technology, automobiles, pharmaceuticals, biotechnology, etc.
- **Business and Economics**
  The basics of IPRS help in the development of the industry and in the success of businesses.
  IPRS provide rights to the proprietors of the businesses.

(iii) The importance of IPR for entrepreneurship is

- It encourages creation of new, path breaking inventions, such as cancer cure medicines.
- It encourages creators, authors, creators, etc. for their work by providing incentives.
- It allows creators and inventors to have control over their creations and inventions.
  So that work created by a person can be distributed and communicated to the public only with his/her permission. This helps in the prevention of loss of income.
- It helps authors, creators, developers and owners to get recognition for their works.

SELF ASSESSMENT TEST

Objective Type Questions

1. Which of the following is a method of raising capital by starting a business with personal savings or funds from family and friends?
(a) Crowd funding
(b) Bootstrapping
(c) Angel funding (d) Venture capital

2. Which of the following is a funding option where multiple investors contribute money through social networking sites for a specific project?
(a) Government programmes
(b) Crowd funding
(c) Angel funding (d) Business incubators

3. ………….. helps in distinguishing similar products in the market from its competitors.
(a) Copyright (b) Patent
(c) Trademark (d) Design

4. A company has created a unique logo and packaging design to distinguish its product from others in the market. This design helps consumers identify the product easily and prevents competitors from using similar packaging. Which category of trademark does the unique logo and packaging design of the product fall under?
(a) Non-conventional trademark
(b) Conventional trademark
(c) Sound mark (d) Dynamic mark

5. Investment limit in plant and machinery for micro-manufacturing enterprises is
(a) must not exceed ₹ 1 crore (b) must not exceed ₹ 5 crore
(c) must not exceed ₹ 10 crore
(d) must exceed ₹ 1 crore

6. Kavita established a manufacturing unit to produce all types of electrical wires. She invested ₹ 3.5 crores in Plant and machinery. Identify the type of manufacturing enterprise as per Micro, Small and Medium Enterprises Development Act, 2006.
(a) Micro enterprise (b) Small enterprise
(c) Medium enterprise (d) None of these

7. Government has various departments and programmes for the welfare of small businesses in organised sector. For the development of unorganised sector, government constituted.
(a) NCEUS (b) WASME
(c) DIC's Programme (d) SFURTI

8. There are many programmes for the welfare of women in India. Which of the following is a programme to encourage women to establish entrepreneurial ventures?
(a) WASME (b) SPURT (c) RWED (d) IRDP

Answers 1. (b) 2. (b) 3. (c) 4. (b) 5. (a) 6. (b) 7. (a) 8. (c)

Short Answer Type Questions

9. State any four characteristics of entrepreneurship development.

10. State any three needs of entrepreneurship development.

11. "The start-up India scheme is a government initiative aimed at promoting and supporting innovation, entrepreneurship and job creation in India. The scheme provides various benefits such as tax exemptions, funding support and easier regulatory procedures to help new businesses thrive. It aims to create an environment where start-ups can grow and scale rapidly, contributing to the overall economic development."
In light of the above statement, state the main objectives of the Start-Up India scheme.

12. Discuss patent as a type of intellectual property right.

13. "Creativity and innovation is the key to MSME." Justify the statement.

14. Discuss the role played by SIDBI in promoting SSIs.

15. "The National Small Industries Corporation (NSIC) plays a pivotal role in the development of small-scale industries by offering financial and technical support. It provides assistance in areas like marketing, technology upgradation, and credit facilitation. The NSIC has contributed significantly to fostering the growth and sustainability of small industries in India."
In light of the above statement, state the main functions of the National Small Industries Corporation.

Long Answer Type Questions

16. Small-scale enterprises exist in every part of India. If you had a work given to identify these industries, what features you may remember of such industries?

17. Discuss the various measures adopted by government to promote SSIs in India.

18. "Small-scale Industries (SSIs) are often vital to the economy, providing employment opportunities and fostering local growth. However, these industries face various challenges that hinder their development and sustainability. These factors contribute to their struggle to scale up and compete with larger firms in the market."
In light of the above statement, discuss the problems faced by small-scale industries.

09

CHAPTER

Internal Trade

The significance of trade has increased considerably in the modern times because of the development of the new products every day. Trade helps in creating a link between producers and consumers.

▼ **YOUR STUDY GOALS**

9.1 Meaning of Internal Trade
9.2 Types of Retail Trade
9.3 Goods and Services Tax (GST)

▼ **YOUR PRACTICE GOAL**

- Objective Type Questions (56 Qs ; MCQs, A-R, Statements, Matching)
- Subjective Questions (10 SAs, 8 LAs)
- Case Study Based Questions (Short Case Studies-9, Long Case Studies-4)
- Self Assessment Test (8 MCQs, 7 SAs, 3 LAs)

The buying and selling of goods and services with the objective of earning profit is known as trade. Trade can be broadly classified into two categories that are

1. **Internal Trade** It is a trade which takes place within the country.
2. **External Trade** It is a trade which takes place between two or more countries.

9.1 Meaning of Internal Trade

Internal trade means buying and selling of goods within the boundaries of the nation or country.

Following are the **features** of internal trade

- Internal trade aims at equitable distribution of goods within a nation fastly and at a reasonable cost.
- Internal trade is also known as home trade or inland trade.
- No custom duty or import duty is levied on such trade as goods are part of domestic production and are meant for domestic consumption.

Types of Internal Trade

Internal trade can be classified into two broad categories as

Types of Internal Trade
- Wholesale Trade
- Retail Trade

I. Wholesale Trade

Wholesale trade refers to buying and selling of goods and services in large quantities for the purpose of resale or intermediate use. In other words, in this trade, good and services are purchased in large quantity from manufacturers and resold to retailers, who then sells them to the ultimate consumers.

Traders dealing in **wholesale** trade are called wholesalers. They are the first middlemen in the chain of distribution.

Following are the **features** of wholesale trade

- This trade provides link between the manufacturers and the retailers but there is usually no direct dealing with the ultimate consumers.
- The wholesalers buy goods in large quantities and sells in smaller quantities.
- Wholesalers maintain large stock of goods and provide credit facilities to the retailers.
- The wholesalers usually specialise in one particular line of goods.
- Wholesalers undertake various activities such as grading of products, packing into smaller lots, storage, transportation, promotion of goods, collection of small and scattered orders of retailer and distribution of supplies to them.

Wholesale Trade

A farmer produces 10,000 kg of wheat and sells it to a wholesaler in bulk. The wholesaler stores the wheat, divides it into smaller packets and sells them to multiple grocery store retailers. These retailers then sell the wheat packets to individual consumers.

Services of Wholesalers to Manufacturers

Service	Explanation
Facilitating Large-scale Production	Wholesalers collect small orders from a number of retailers and make purchases in bulk quantities from the producers. This enables the producers to undertake production on a large-scale.
Bearing Risk	The wholesalers deal in goods in their own name, take delivery of the goods and keep them in large lots in their warehouses. In this process, they bear risks like fall in prices, theft, spoilage, fire, etc. which would have been borne by the manufacturer.
Financial Assistance	The wholesalers provide financial assistance to the manufacturers as they generally make cash payment for the goods purchased by them. Sometimes they also advance money to the producers for bulk orders placed by them.
Expert Advice	The wholesalers are in direct contact with the retailers, therefore they can advice the manufacturers about various aspects related to customer's tastes and preferences, market conditions, etc.
Help in the Marketing Function	The wholesalers distribute goods to a number of retailers, who in turn sell these goods to a large number of customers. Thus, they help in marketing the product.
Facilitate Production Continuity	The wholesalers facilitate continuity of production activity throughout the year by purchasing the goods as and when they are produced and storing them till they are demanded by retailers or consumers in the market.
Storage	The wholesalers take delivery of goods when they are produced and keep them in their godowns/warehouses. Thus, they help the manufacturers in storage of goods.

Services of Wholesalers to Retailers

Service	Explanation
Availability of Goods	The wholesalers make available the products of various manufacturers to the retailers. Thus, the retailers are able to offer a variety of goods to their customers.
Marketing Support	The wholesalers perform various marketing functions to convince customers to purchase the goods. This increases the demand of the products which results in increased profits for the retailer.
Grant of Credit	The wholesalers provide credit facilities to retailers by selling goods on credit to them. This enables them to manage their business with relatively small amount of working capital.
Specialised Knowledge	The wholesalers specialise in one line of products. They inform the retailers about the new products, their uses, quality, prices, etc.
Risk Sharing	The wholesalers purchase in bulk quantities and sell in small quantities to the retailers. It protects the retailers from the risk of storage, reduction in prices, demand fluctuations, etc.

II. Retail Trade

Retail trade refers to sale of goods and services directly to the ultimate consumers in small quantities. Traders dealing in retail trade are called **retailers.**

Following are the **features** of retail trade
- Retailer is the last link in the chain of distribution.
- Retailers sell goods or services to consumers for final consumption.
- They deal in a wide variety of products.
- They are generally located in residential areas.
- They act as a middlemen between the wholesalers and customers.
- They buy and sell small quantity of goods.
- They maintain personal relations with customers.

Retail Trade

A grocery store in a neighbourhood buys various products like rice, flour and snacks in small quantities from wholesalers. The store then sells these items directly to customers for their personal use. Customers often visit the store because it's convenient and located nearby.

Services of Retailers to Manufacturers and Wholesalers

Service	Explanation
Help in Distribution of Goods	Retailers help in the distribution of products by making them available to the final consumers, thus creating place utility.
Personal Selling	The retailers make individual sales to customers in small quantities. Thus, they relieve the producers from personal selling efforts and greatly help them in the process of actualising the sale of the products.
Enabling Large-scale Operations	As retailer services relieved the manufacturers and wholesalers from the botheration of making individual sales to consumers in small quantities, they are enabled to operate at large-scale.
Collecting Market Information	As retailers remain in direct contact with the customers, they provide important market information about the tastes, preferences and attitudes of customers.
Help in Promotion	Manufacturers and distributors carry on various promotional activities, in order to increase the sale of their products. Retailers participate in these activities and help to promote the sale of the products.

Services of Retailers to Consumers

Service	Explanation
Regular Availability of Products	The most important service of a retailer to consumers is to maintain regular availability of various products produced by different manufacturers. It enables the customers to buy product as and when needed.
New Products Information	The retailers provide important information about the arrival, special features, etc. of new products to the customers, by arranging effective display of products.
Convenience in Buying	Retailers generally sell goods in small quantities, according to the requirements of their customers. They are situated very near to residential areas and remain open for long hours. This offers great convenience to the customers.
Wide Selection	Retailers generally keep stock of a variety of products. This enables the consumers to make their choice.
After-sales Services	Retailers provide important after-sales services such as home delivery, supply of spare parts and attending to customers.
Provide Credit Facilities	The retailers sometimes provide credit facilities to their regular customers. This led to increased level of consumption and better standard of living of the customers.

Terms of Trade

- **Cash on Delivery** (COD) It refers to a type of transaction in which payment for goods or services is made at the time of delivery.
- **Free on Board or Free on Rail** (FOB or FOR) It refers to a contract between the seller and the buyer in which all the expenses, from the point of delivery to a carrier, are to be borne by seller.
- **Cost, Insurance and Freight** (CIF) It is the price of goods which includes the cost of goods as well as the insurance and freight charges payable on goods upto destination port.
- **Errors and Omissions Excepted** (E&OE) It refers to that term which is used in trade documents to state that mistakes and things which have been ignored should be taken into account.

9.2 Types of Retail Trade

The different types of retailers are given in the chart below

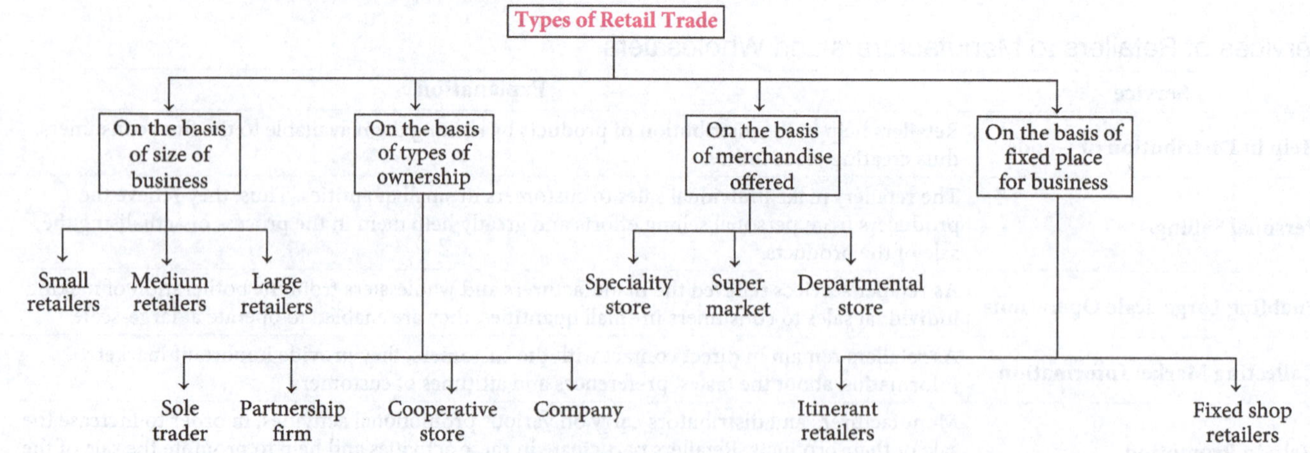

Itinerant Retailers

These are traders that do not have a fixed place of business to operate from. They keep on moving with their wares/ goods from street to street or place to place, in search of customers.

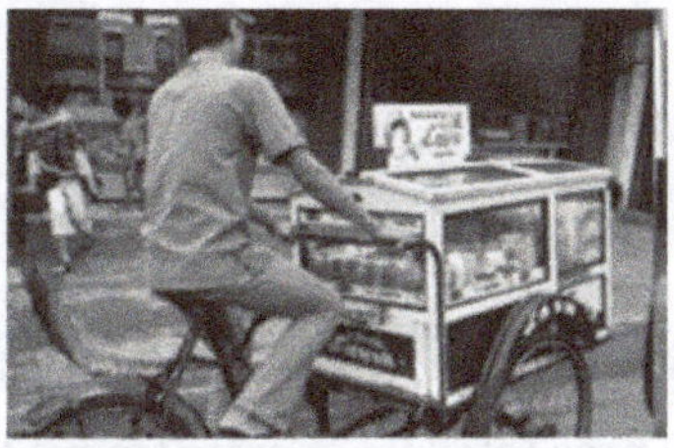

Following are the **characteristics** of itinerant retailers
- They are small traders operating with limited resources.
- They normally deal in products of daily use such as toiletry products, fruits and vegetables, etc.
- The emphasis of such traders is to provide greater customer service by making the products available at the doorstep of the customers.
- They have to keep their limited inventory at their homes or at some other suitable place.

Types of Itinerant Retailers

Types of Itinerant Retailer	Features
Hawkers and Peddlers They are traders who move from place to place selling their goods. They usually carry their goods in a bag, or on a cart, or a cycle or on animals. They can be seen on streets of residential areas, place of exhibition, outside schools and restaurants.	• They sell their merchandise at the doorsteps of customers. • They generally deal in non-standardised and low-value goods such as toys, vegetables, fruits, fabrics, snacks, ice-cream, etc. • They bargain with customers and try to charge maximum possible price for their products. • The products offered by them are generally not reliable in terms of quality and price.
Periodic Market Traders These traders sell their articles on fixed days in different market places. A special feature of these traders is that their weekly market day is fixed. e.g. Saturdays (Shani Bazaar) or Mondays (Som Bazaar), etc.	• These traders can deal in a particular merchandise or they can be general traders. • They deal in low-priced customer goods of daily use, such as readymade garments, fabrics, toys, etc. • They cater to the requirements of lower income customers. • Their shops are temporary structures. • They can also sell their goods in fairs and during festivals.
Street Traders/Pavement Vendors These retailers display their goods at street crossings, or on pavements, or in the corridors of markets. They can also display their goods on railway platforms, bus stands, cinema halls, etc.	• They sell goods of common use such as newspapers and magazines, stationery items, readymade garments, etc. • They deal in low-priced products. • They do not change their place of business frequently.
Cheap Jacks They are petty retailers who have independent shops in residential colonies or business localities but for a temporary period.	• They keep on changing their business from one locality to another, depending upon the potential of the area. However, change is not as frequent as in the case of hawkers or market traders. • They deal in consumer items as well as services such as repair of watches, shoes, etc.

Fixed Shop Retailers

These are retail shops which maintain permanent establishment to sell their merchandise. Therefore, they do not move from place to place to serve their customers.

Following are the **characteristics** of fixed shop retailers
- They have greater resources and operate on a relatively large-scale as compared to itinerant traders.
- They deal in different products, including consumer durables as well as non-durables products.
- They have greater credibility in the minds of customers and they provide greater service to the customers such as home delivery, repairs, credit facilities, etc.

Types of Fixed Shop Retailers

On the basis of size of operation, fixed shop retailers can be classified as

Types of Fixed Shop Retailers
- Fixed Shop-Small Retailers
- Fixed Shop-Large Retailers

I. Fixed Shop-Small Retailers

These retailers operate from a fixed shop, but their area of operation is limited.

Types of Small Retailers

Types	Features
General Stores These stores deal in items of daily use like groceries, confectionery, etc. They generally operate in residential areas and satisfy the day-to-day needs of the consumers.	• These have a large variety in each line of goods. • These stores remain open for long hours at convenient timings. • These stores provide credit to some of their regular customers.
Single Line Stores/Speciality Shops These stores deal in a specific product line. The product line may consist of readymade garments, textiles, medicines, shoes, stationery or books.	• These shops are located in a central place of the market, where a large number of customers can be attracted. • They provide a wide choice to the customers in the selection of a particular line of goods.
Street Stall Holders These small vendors are commonly found at street crossings or other places where flow of traffic is heavy. They deal mainly in goods of cheap variety like hosiery products, toys, soft drinks, etc.	• They attract floating customers and provide convenient service to the customers in buying some of the items of their needs. • They get their supplies from local suppliers, as well as wholesalers. • They operate on a small-scale.
Second-hand Goods Shop These shops sell second-hand goods of different kinds like furniture, books, clothes and other household articles. These shops are suitable for customers with moderate means.	• These shops generally sell goods at low prices, but if it is dealing in rare objects of historical importance or antique goods, then the price charged by them is high. • These shops have no fixed location. They may be located at street crossings or in busy streets. • The shops may operate from a table or a temporary structure, or it may have reasonable good structure. It can also operate through e-commerce (e.g. OLX.com).

II. Fixed Shop-Large Retailers

These retailers operate from a fixed shop on a very large-scale. Their area of operation is wide. They are of the following types

- Departmental store
- Chain stores
- Mail order houses

1. Departmental Store

A departmental store is a large establishment that offers a wide variety of products and aimed at satisfying every customer's need under one roof. These stores have a number of departments, each one confining its activities to a specific kind of product.

Features of Departmental Store

- These stores are centrally located so that they can cater to large number of customers and try to maximise customer satisfaction by providing additional facilities such as restaurants, travel, etc.
- These stores cater to that segment of customers for whom price is secondary.

- The form of organisation for such stores is joint stock companies, managed by board of directors.
- These stores purchase goods directly from the manufacturers and maintain their own warehouses to store goods.
- These stores have a centralised purchasing department, whereas sales are decentralised in different departments.

Advantages of Departmental Store

Advantages	Explanation
Attract Large Number of Customers	These stores are centrally located, thus they attract a large number of customers.
Convenience in Buying	These stores offer a large variety of goods under one roof. Therefore, it is convenient for customers to purchase goods from these stores.
Attractive Services	These stores provide extra services to the customers, such as home delivery of goods, accepting orders through telephone and online, provision of rest rooms, restaurants, etc.
Economy of Large-scale Operations	These stores are organised and managed on a large-scale. Therefore, they are able to enjoy economies of large-scale operations and increase their profits.
Promotion of Sales	These stores spend considerable amount of money on advertising and other promotional activities which help in strengthening the sales.

Disadvantages of Departmental Store

Disadvantage	Explanation
Lack of Personal Attention	These stores are not able to give personal attention to each and every customer because of large-scale operations.
High Operating Costs	These stores provide a number of additional services to their customers, thus their operating costs are also high.
High Possibility of Loss	These stores operate on large-scale and incur high operating costs, thus their exposure to risk is also high.
Inconvenient Location	These stores are generally located in a central location. Customers encounter traffic problems while visiting these stores. It is also not convenient for the purchase of goods that are needed at short notice.

2. Chain Stores or Multiple Shops

Chain stores are networks of retail shops that are owned and operated by manufacturers or intermediaries. Under this type of arrangement, a number of shops with similar appearance are established in localities, spread over different parts of the country.

These shops normally deal in standardised and branded customer products, which have rapid sales turnover. e.g. An outlet of Reebok.

Features of Chain Stores

- These shops are located in populous localities, so that customers can be served at a place near their residence.
- Each retail outlet is under the direct supervision of a Branch Manager, who is responsible for its day-to-day operations.
- All branches are controlled by the head office.
- Purchasing of all goods for all these stores is done by the head office which dispatch goods to these stores according to their requirements.
- In these stores, the price of the goods is fixed and sales are made on cash basis. Daily sales are deposited in a local bank account.
- The head office appoints inspectors, who supervise the day-to-day operations of the store in respect of quality of customer service provided, adherence to rules and regulations, etc.

Advantages of Chain Stores

Advantages	Explanation
Economies of Scale	These stores operate on a large-scale as the goods are purchased in bulk. Therefore, they are able to enjoy economies of scale.
Elimination of Middlemen	Through these stores, the manufacturers sells goods directly to the consumers, thus eliminating unnecessary middlemen in the sale and purchase of goods.
No Bad Debts	All the sales in these stores are made on cash. Therefore, there is no question of bad debts.
Diffusion of Risk	The risk is spread over a number of shops. Loss from one shop can be recovered from the profit of another shop.
Transfer of Goods	In case of lack of demand, goods from one store can be transferred to another store. This reduces the chances of dead stock in these shops.
Low Cost	These stores have low operational costs because of centralised purchasing, elimination of middlemen and centralised promotion of sales.
Flexibility	This system of chain stores offers the advantage of flexible operations. If a shop is incurring loss, then it can be closed down or shifted to some other place, without any significant effect on the organisation.

Disadvantages of Chain Stores

Disadvantages	Explanation
Limited Selection of Goods	Majority of the multiple shops (especially stores owned and operated by manufacturers) deal only in limited range of products. e.g. Reebok deals in sports wear and foot wear. These stores do not sell products of other manufacturers. Therefore, customers visiting these stores have only selected items to choose from.
Lack of Initiative	The employees working in these stores work according to the instructions of the head office. Due to this, they became habitual of getting guidance from the head office on all matters. This also takes away the initiative from them to use their creative skills to satisfy the customers.
Lack of Personal Touch	Due to operating on a large-scale and lack of initiative in the employees, their dealings with customers lack personal touch.
Difficult to Change Demand	If the demand for the merchandise handled by multiple shops change rapidly, the management may have to sustain huge losses because of large stocks lying unsold at the central depot.

3. Mail Order Houses

Mail order houses are the retail outlets that sell their merchandise through mail. There is generally no direct personal contact between the buyers and the sellers in this type of trading.

In the absence of any personal contact, the transaction is settled in the following ways

- The seller prepares a list of potential customers. Telephone directories, list of members of clubs, etc. can be used for preparing the list.
- The potential customers are approached with the help of pamphlets, specific advertisements, offer letter through mail, samples, etc.
- The customers send their orders through mail according to their need.
- On receiving the order, the seller packs the goods of the required specifications and delivers it to the post office, from where it is delivered to the customer.

The payment of the goods can be made in the following ways

- The customer can be asked to make full payment in advance.
- The goods may be sent through VPP (Value Payable Post). Under this arrangement, the goods are sent through post and are delivered to the customers only on making full payment for the same.
- The goods may be sent through bank, which deliver the goods only on receiving the payment.

Suitability of Mail Order Houses

Mail order business is suitable only for the categories of goods that

- are not perishable in nature.
- can be graded and standardised.
- have a ready demand in the market.
- can be described through pictures.
- are not bulky.
- are easily transportable, at low cost.
- are available in large quantities throughout the year.
- involve least possible competition in the market.

Advantages of Mail order Houses

Advantages	Explanation
Limited Capital Requirement	This business needs limited capital because it does not require fixed capital investment for big buildings and other infrastructural facilities.
Elimination of Middlemen	This business eliminates unnecessary middlemen between the buyers and sellers.
Absence of Bad Debts	Mail order houses do not extend credit facilities to their customers. Goods are delivered only when the payment has been received. Therefore, there is no question of bad debts.
Wide Reach	Under this system, goods can be sent to all the places having postal services. This ensures wide reach of the business.
Convenience	This system is convenient for the customers, as goods are delivered at their doorsteps.

Disadvantages of Mail Order Houses

Disadvantages	Explanation
Lack of Personal Contact	This business is characterised by the lack of personal contact between the buyers and sellers. This might create misunderstanding and mistrust among buyers and sellers and create following problems • The buyers cannot examine the goods before purchasing. • The sellers cannot pay personal attention to the likes and dislikes of every individual customer. • The sellers cannot clear all the doubts of the buyers through catalogues and advertisements.
High Promotion Cost	This type of business has a high promotion cost due to heavy expenditure on advertisement and other methods of promotion.
No After Sales Service	In this form of business, there is absence of after sales services which is very important for the satisfaction of customers.
No Credit Facilities	This business does not extend credit facilities to its customers.
Delayed Delivery	In this business, there is no immediate delivery of goods to the customers. There is a considerable time gap between placing of order and receiving goods.
Possibility of Abuse	In this type of business, there is greater possibility of being cheated as dishonest traders can cheat their customers, by making false claims related to the product.
High Dependence on Postal Services	This type of business has limited prospects for a country like India, where many places are still without postal facilities.

9.3 Goods and Services Tax (GST)

GST is an indirect tax levied in India on the sale of goods and services. GST was implemented from 1st July, 2017 in India. It is based on the philosophy of 'One Nation and One Tax'. GST was introduced to replace multiple indirect taxes levied by State and Central Governments, in order to simplify the indirect tax system.

Key Features of GST

- GST is applicable on the 'supply' of goods and services as compared to the earlier concept of tax which was levied on the manufacture or sale of goods or provision of services.
- GST is spread in the whole country.
- CGST, SGST and IGST are levied at rates mutually agreed upon by the Centre and the States, under the assistance of the GST Council.
- Import of goods and services is treated as inter-state supplies and would be subject to IGST, in addition to the applicable customs duties.
- GST is based on the principle of destination-based consumption tax which replaced the principle of origin-based taxation.
- There are four tax slabs namely 5%, 12%, 18% and 28% for all goods or services.
- Exports and supplies to SEZ (Special Economic Zones) are zero-rated.
- There are various modes of payment of tax available to the taxpayer such as internet banking, debit/credit card and National Electronic Funds Transfer (NEFT)/ Real Time Gross Settlement (RTGS).

Benefits of GST

- It has eliminated the need for filing multiple returns and assessments, and rationalising the tax treatment of goods and services along the supply chain from producers to consumers.
- The GST network is a self-regulating mechanism, which checks tax frauds and tax evasion. It also brings more businesses into the formal economy.
- GST has anti-profiteering measure which prevent entities from making excessive profits.
- With the implementation of GST, luxury goods have become costlier, while items of mass consumption have become cheaper.
- It has also led to the following
  - Reduction in overall tax burden.
  - Development of a harmonised national market for goods and services.
  - Higher disposable income in hand, education and essential needs.
  - It enables customers to have wider choice.
  - It increases economic activity.
  - It provide more employment opportunities.

GST Council-Constitution

- **Chairperson** Union Finance Minister
- **Vice-Chairperson** It is chosen amongst the ministers of State Government
- **Members** Minister of State Finance and all ministers of Finance/Taxation of each State
- **Quorum** 50% of total members
- **Weightage** States have 2/3rd and Centre has 1/3rd of total votes
- **Decision** Supported by atleast 75% majority
- **Recommendation** Council shall make recommendations on everything related to GST including, rules and rates, etc.

Mind Map

INTERNAL TRADE

1 Meaning of Internal Trade

Internal trade means buying and selling of goods within the boundaries of the nation or country. Types of internal trade include wholesale and retail trade.

Wholesale Trade

It refers to buying and selling of goods and services in large quantities for the purpose of re-sale or intermediate use.

Services of Wholesalers to Manufacturers
- Facilitating large-scale production
- Bearing risk
- Financial assistance
- Expert advice
- Storage
- Help in the marketing function
- Facilitate production continuity

Services of Wholesalers to Retailers
- Availability of goods
- Marketing support
- Grant of credit
- Specialised knowledge
- Risk sharing

Retail Trade

It refers to sale of goods and services directly to the ultimate consumers in small quantities. Traders dealing in retail trade are called retailers.

Services of Retailers to Manufacturers and Wholesalers
- Help in distribution of goods
- Personal selling
- Enabling large-scale operations
- Collecting market information
- Help in promotion

Services of Retailers to Consumers
- Regular availability of products
- New products information
- Convenience in buying
- Wide selection
- After sales services
- Provide credit facilities

2 Types of Retail Trade

On the basis of fixed place for business, it can be divided into itinerant retailers and fixed shop retailers.

Fixed Shop Retailers

These are retail shops which maintain permanent establishment to sell their merchandise. Therefore, they do not move from place to place to serve their customers. They can be divided into fixed shop-small retailers and fixed shop-large retailers.

Itinerant Retailers

They are traders that do not have a fixed place of business to operate from. They keep on moving in search of customers. Following are the types of itinerant retailers
- **Hawkers and Peddlers** They are traders who move from place to place selling their goods. They usually carry their goods in a bag, or on a cart, or a cycle, or on animals.
- **Periodic Market Traders** These traders sell their articles on fixed days in different market places.
- **Street Traders/Pavement Vendors** These retailers display their goods at street crossings, or on pavements, or in the corridors of markets.
- **Cheap Jacks** They are petty retailers who have independent shops in residential colonies or business localities but for a temporary period.

5 Goods and Services Tax (GST)

GST is an indirect tax levied in India on the sale of goods and services. GST was introduced to replace multiple indirect taxes levied by State and Central Governments, in order to simplify the indirect tax system.

Features
- GST is applicable on the 'supply' of goods and services
- GST is spread in the whole country. The GST levied by the centre is called Central GST (CGST) and the GST levied by the states is called State GST (SGST)
- Import of goods and services is treated as inter-State supplies and would be subject to IGST, in addition to the applicable customs duties
- There are four tax slabs namely 5%, 12%, 18% and 28% for all goods or services

4 Fixed Shop-Large Retailers

These retailers operate from a fixed shop on a very large-scale. Their area of operation is wide.

Types
- **Departmental Stores** It is a large establishment that offers a wide variety of products and aimed at satisfying every customer's need under one roof. These stores cater to that segment of customers for whom price is secondary.
- **Chain Stores or Multiple Shops** Chain stores are networks of retail shops that are owned and operated by manufacturers or intermediaries. Under this type of arrangement, a number of shops with similar appearance are established in localities, spread over different parts of the country. The purchasing of all goods for all these stores are done by the head office which dispatch goods to these stores according to their requirements.
- **Mail Order Houses** These are the retail outlets that sell their merchandise through mail. There is generally no direct personal contact between the buyers and the sellers in this type of trading. It is suitable only for the categories of goods that are not perishable in nature, are not bulky, can be graded and standardised, are easily transportable at low cost, etc.

3 Fixed Shop-Small Retailers

These retailers operate from a fixed shop, but their area of operation is limited.

Types
- **General Stores** These stores deal in items of daily use like groceries, confectionery, etc.
- **Single Line Stores/Speciality Shops** These stores deal in a specific product line. The product line may consist of readymade garments, textiles, medicines, shoes, stationery or books.
- **Street Stall Holders** These small vendors are commonly found at street crossings or other places where flow of traffic is heavy.
- **Second-hand Goods Shop** These shops sell second-hand goods of different kinds like furniture, books, clothes and other household articles.

EXAM PATTERN QUESTIONS

Objective Type Questions

Multiple Choice Questions (MCQs)

1. Wholesaler not just buys goods from manufacturers, but they also help manufacturer in marketing of the product by

(a) storing goods in bulk quantities
(b) making cash payment
(c) transportation facilities
(d) conveying retailers' feedback to manufacturer

2. Which of the following is a service offered by the wholesaler to a retailer?

(a) Facilitate production continuity
(b) Facilitates large-scale production
(c) Risk sharing (d) Storage

3. ABC Pvt. Ltd., a leading toy manufacturer, recently expanded its production capacity. To ensure seamless distribution and efficient marketing, they partnered with several wholesalers. These wholesalers purchased toys in bulk, stored them in their warehouses and distributed them to retailers across the country.

Despite seasonal variations in demand, the wholesalers ensured that ABC Pvt. Ltd.'s production process continued without interruption by consistently placing large orders and storing the surplus stock.

Additionally, they provided the company with valuable insights about consumer preferences, helping the manufacturer align its product designs with market trends. How do wholesalers help manufacturers to ensure continuity in their production process? Competency Based Que

(a) By producing goods on their behalf
(b) By storing goods and purchasing them as they are produced
(c) By directly selling goods to consumers
(d) By reducing manufacturing costs

4. XYZ Wholesalers, specialising in electronic gadgets, has been a reliable partner for numerous retail stores across the region. By offering a wide range of products from different manufacturers, XYZ ensures that retailers can provide variety to their customers.

The company frequently runs promotional campaigns to boost the demand for these gadgets, benefitting the retailers with increased sales. Additionally, XYZ extends credit facilities to small retailers, enabling them to operate smoothly with limited working capital.

They also keep the retailers informed about the latest gadgets, their features and pricing, helping them make informed decisions.

Which service provided by wholesalers helps retailers to manage their business with limited funds? Competency Based Que

(a) Marketing support (b) Risk sharing
(c) Grant of credit (d) Availability of goods

5. Fresh Bakes Pvt. Ltd., a popular bakery products manufacturer, relies on its network of retailers to reach its customers. The retailers ensure that Fresh Bakes' products, including bread, cakes and cookies, are available in every neighbourhood store.

By engaging directly with customers, these retailers collect feedback on new flavours and packaging, which they share with the company. Additionally, the retailers actively participate in promotional campaigns, such as 'Buy One Get One' offers, increasing product visibility and boosting sales.

How do retailers help manufacturers and wholesalers in large-scale operations? Competency Based Que

(a) By purchasing goods in bulk quantities
(b) By making individual sales to final consumers
(c) By conducting promotional activities
(d) By providing credit facilities

6. Green Mart, a neighbourhood grocery store, is known for its wide range of products and excellent customer service. The store always stocks essential items from multiple brands, ensuring regular availability for its customers. Green Mart also keeps customers informed about new arrivals through attractive displays and promotional banners.

Located in a convenient residential area, it operates extended hours, making shopping easier for busy families. Additionally, the store offers home delivery and occasional credit facilities to its loyal customers, enhancing their shopping experience.

Which service provided by retailers enhances customers' convenience in buying? Competency Based Que

(a) Providing after-sales services
(b) Selling goods in small quantities and being located near residential areas
(c) Offering credit facilities
(d) Arranging effective product displays

7. Retailers provide essential services to manufacturers and wholesalers, including distribution of goods, personal selling, enabling large-scale operations, collecting market information and promotion of products.

Identify the key service provided by retailers that directly aids manufacturers in understanding customer preferences. **Competency Based Que**

(a) Distribution of goods
(b) Personal selling
(c) Collecting market information
(d) Enabling large-scale operations

8. Giriraj is a small trader who carry different types of vegetables in a wheeled vehicle and move from one colony to another to sell vegetables at the doorstep of the customers. Giriraj does not have a fixed price policy and price varies depending on the bargaining power of the customers.

Identify the type of retailer under which Giriraj should be placed. **Competency Based Que**

(a) Itinerant retailer (b) Hawker
(c) Both (a) and (b) (d) None of these

9. Which of the following is not a type of itinerant retailers?

(a) Market traders (b) Street stallholders
(c) Cheap jacks (d) Peddlers and hawkers

10. Small retailers who are commonly found in places with huge populations are called ....

(a) market traders (b) second-hand goods shop
(c) peddlers and hawkers (d) street retailers

11. Arjun runs a small shop that operates every Friday in the local Shukravar Bazaar. His temporary stall offers a variety of low-priced readymade garments and toys, attracting many customers from nearby villages. During festival seasons, Arjun also sets-up his stall at fairs, catering to the needs of low income families. His business thrives on weekly market days when customers look for affordable daily-use items.

What type of trader is Arjun? **Competency Based Que**

(a) Hawker (b) Periodic market trader
(c) Fixed shop small retailer (d) Wholesaler

12. They are small retailers who deal in consumer items. They have shops in business localities on a temporary basis. They change their business place from one locality to another on the basis of potentiality of the area.

Identify the type of 'itinerant retailer'.

(a) Hawkers (b) Street traders
(c) Market traders (d) Cheap jacks

13. Identify from the below which of the folllowing is not the characteristic of fixed shop retailers?

(a) Dealing with different products
(b) Have greater resources
(c) Independent shops of temporary nature facilities
(d) Mostly provides credit

14. Neha owns a stationery and gift shop located in the city's main market. Her shop is permanently established and well-known among locals for its wide range of products, including notebooks, pens, gift items consumer durables like lamps.

Customers trust her shop for quality products and reliable services such as home delivery and occasional credit facilities for regular buyers. What type of retailer is Neha? **Competency Based Que**

(a) Street trader/pavement vendor
(b) Hawker
(c) Fixed shop retailer
(d) Periodic market trader

15. 'Fashion Hub,' located in the heart of the city market, specialises in readymade garments. The shop offers a wide variety of clothing options for all age groups, providing customers with an extensive selection within the garment category.

Its central location attracts a large number of shoppers who trust the store for its exclusive focus on quality apparel. What type of retail shop is 'Fashion Hub'? **Competency Based Que**

(a) Departmental store
(b) Periodic market trader
(c) Single line store/Speciality shop
(d) General store

16. Which of the following statements is incorrect about fixed shop-small retailers?

(a) General stores deal in items of daily use such as groceries, confectionery, stationery and soft drinks
(b) Single line stores/speciality shops offer a wide choice to customers in the selection of a particular line of goods.
(c) General stores remain open for long hours at convenient timings
(d) Single line stores provide credit facilities to all customers

17. "They operate on a small-scale, dealing mainly in inexpensive, non-standardised goods and serve a transient customer base."

Identify the retail format being described. **Competency Based Que**

(a) Chain stores (b) Street stallholders
(c) Speciality stores (d) Franchise outlets

18. **"These shops provide a wide choice to the customers in the selection of a particular line of goods." Identify the retail format being described.** **Competency Based Que**

(a) Chain stores (b) Street stallholders
(c) Speciality shops (d) Second hand goods shops

19. **Shops selling second-hand goods cater to a niche market, offering a variety of used items at lower prices. However, when dealing with rare or antique goods of historical importance, the prices are significantly higher.**

These shops often have no fixed location and may be found on street crossings or in busy areas. They may operate from temporary set-ups like tables or simple structures, especially in the case of second-hand books or other items.

What is a common characteristic of shops selling second-hand goods? **Competency Based Que**

(a) Fixed locations
(b) High prices for rare antiques
(c) Permanent structures (d) Limited variety of products

20. **'School uniforms shop' is an example of**

(a) general store (b) street stallholders
(c) speciality shop (d) None of these

21. **Which of the following statements is incorrect about a departmental store?**

(a) They are centrally located to cater to a large number of customers
(b) They provide additional facilities such as restaurants, travel and information bureaus, free wi-fi zones, kids zones and restrooms
(c) They focus primarily on a price sensitive customer segment
(d) They purchase goods directly from manufacturers and maintain their own warehouses

22. **Identify the type of store illustrated in the given picture.**

BIG BAZAAR™
Making India *Beautiful*

(a) Departmental store (b) Chain store
(c) Mail order house (d) Speciality store

23. **"Chain stores operate with a unified brand identity and standardised products across multiple locations." Which of the following best describes chain stores?** **Competency Based Que**

(a) Shops with unique and non-standardised products
(b) Retail outlets with a common brand identity and standardised products
(c) Independent shops operating in a single locality
(d) Shops selling perishable goods

24. **Identify the type of store illustrated in the given picture.**

Café COFFEE Day ®

(a) Departmental store (b) Chain store
(c) Mail order house (d) Speciality store

25. **The orders are received and goods are mailed directly to the buyers in which form.**

(a) Departmental store (b) Chain store
(c) Shopping mall (d) Mail order house

26. **Which of the following statements is not correct about GST?**

(a) GST is like a last point retail tax. GST is going to be collected at point of sale
(b) GST will abolish all the direct tax levied in India
(c) It will be implemented from 1st July, 2017 throughout the country
(d) It will unify the tax structure in India

27. **Chairperson of the GST council is**

(a) President (b) Finance Minister
(c) Prime Minister (d) None of these

Direction *Read the case study and answer the questions 28 to 31 on the basis of the same*

Elegant Kitchens Pvt. Ltd., based in Bengaluru, is a well-known manufacturer of modular kitchen units and accessories. Its products are in high demand across South India due to their premium quality and aesthetic designs. To cater to the festive season rush in October and November, the company's marketing team has introduced a special 'Festive Kitchen Combo,' which includes a set of accessories at a discounted price. These combos are attractively packaged to appeal to customers.

For efficient distribution across South India, Elegant Kitchens has partnered with Supreme Distributors, who buy the combos in bulk and supply them to local retailers in major cities. Additionally, the company has its own showroom in Bengaluru named 'Elegant Spaces,' which has been receiving an excellent response. Inspired by its success, the company is planning to open showrooms in Hyderabad, Chennai and Kochi.

28. **Which of the following is not a service provided by wholesalers to manufacturers?**

(a) Facilitating large-scale production
(b) Providing credit facilities to customers
(c) Reducing storage costs for manufacturers
(d) Assisting in product promotion

29. **Identify the type of fixed retail shop represented by 'Elegant Spaces' in Bengaluru.**

(a) Departmental stores (b) Multiple shops
(c) Super markets (d) General stores

30. **Supreme Distributors, who partner with the company for bulk purchasing and supplying to retailers, are an example of which type of intermediary?**

(a) Retailers (b) Wholesalers
(c) Brokers (d) Commission agents

31. **The company's plan to open showrooms in Hyderabad, Chennai and Kochi showcases which feature of such retail outlets?**

(a) Decentralised operations
(b) Independent management
(c) Centralised control (d) Multiple ownership

Assertion-Reason

Direction (Q. No. 32 to 41) *Read the following Assertion (A) and Reason (R) and choose the correct alternative from the following*

Alternatives

(a) Both Assertion (A) and Reason (R) are true and Reason (R) is the correct explanation of Assertion (A)
(b) Both Assertion (A) and Reason (R) are true, but Reason (R) is not the correct explanation of Assertion (A)
(c) Assertion (A) is true, but Reason (R) is false
(d) Assertion (A) is false, but Reason (R) is true

32. **Assertion** (A) Wholesalers provide financial assistance to manufacturers.

Reason (R) Wholesalers often sell goods on credit to manufacturers to enable large-scale production.

33. **Assertion** (A) Wholesale trade acts as a link between manufacturers and retailers but does not deal directly with ultimate consumers.

Reason (R) Wholesalers buy goods in large quantities from manufacturers and sell them in smaller quantities to retailers.

34. **Assertion** (A) Wholesalers act as a link between manufacturers and retailers by purchasing goods in large quantities and selling them in smaller quantities.

Reason (R) Wholesalers provide services such as storage, grading, transportation and credit facilities to retailers, which enhance the distribution process.

35. **Assertion** (A) The wholesaler performs various marketing functions and provide support to the consumers.

Reason (R) Wholesalers provide after-sale services to the consumers in the form of home delivery of goods.

36. **Assertion** (A) Retailers assist manufacturers in marketing their products to consumers by providing information about customer preferences.

Reason (R) Retailers are directly involved in promotional activities that influence the sale of products.

37. **Assertion** (A) Retailers are the last link in the chain of distribution, directly serving the ultimate consumers.

Reason (R) Retailers deal only in durable goods like furniture and electronics.

38. **Assertion** (A) Fixed shop retailers have greater credibility among customers compared to itinerant traders.

Reason (R) Fixed shop retailers operate from a permanent establishment and provide services like home delivery and credit facilities.

39. **Assertion** (A) GST is based on the principle of destination-based consumption.

Reason (R) GST replaced the earlier principle of origin-based taxation to ensure a fair distribution of revenue to the States where goods and services are consumed.

40. **Assertion** (A) Import of goods and services is treated as inter-state supplies under GST.

Reason (R) Imports are subject to Integrated GST (IGST) in addition to customs duties to maintain uniformity in taxation.

41. **Assertion** (A) The GST council determines the tax rates under CGST, SGST and IGST.

Reason (R) The GST council consists of representatives from the Centre and States, fostering cooperative federalism in tax governance.

Two Statements Based MCQs

Direction (Q. No. 42 to 51) *Read the following statements carefully and choose the correct alternative*

Alternatives

(a) Statement I is correct and Statement II is incorrect
(b) Statement II is correct and Statement I is incorrect
(c) Both the statements are correct
(d) Both the statements are incorrect

42. **Statement I** Internal trade is also known as home trade or inland trade.

Statement II Internal trade involves the import of goods, which are subject to custom duties.

43. **Statement I** General stores deal in a large variety of goods required for daily use.

Statement II General stores are generally located in central market areas to attract more customers.

44. Statement I Specialty shops provide a wide choice of goods within a specific product line.

Statement II Specialty shops generally operate in residential areas to satisfy daily consumer needs.

45. Statement I Street stall holders operate on a large-scale, dealing in premium goods.

Statement II Street stall holders attract floating customers by selling goods of a cheap variety.

46. Statement I Second-hand goods shops often sell goods at low prices, but antique goods may have high prices.

Statement II Second-hand goods shops are always located in a fixed location within residential areas.

47. Statement I Mail order houses involve direct personal contact between buyers and sellers.

Statement II Goods ordered through mail order houses can be sent *via* VPP or bank transfer.

48. Statement I Mail order houses prepare a list of potential customers using telephone directories and other resources.

Statement II Payment for goods in mail order houses can be made in advance or through VPP.

49. Statement I GST is applicable on the supply of goods and services.

Statement II GST applies only to luxury goods and excludes items of mass consumption.

50. Statement I The principle of GST is origin-based taxation.

Statement II GST has replaced multiple indirect taxes and cesses in India.

51. Statement I GST has resulted in the development of a harmonised national market for goods and services.

Statement II GST only benefits businesses and not consumers.

Matching

52. Match the following

Column I	Column II
A. Wholesale trade	(i) Buying of goods in small quantities and selling them to ultimate consumers
B. Retail trade	(ii) Buying and selling of goods within the boundaries of a nation
C. Internal trade	(iii) Buying and selling of goods in large quantities for resale

Codes

	A	B	C		A	B	C
(a)	(ii)	(i)	(iii)	(b)	(iii)	(ii)	(i)
(c)	(iii)	(i)	(ii)	(d)	(ii)	(iii)	(i)

53. Match the following

Column I	Column II
A. Undertake advertising and other sales promotion activities	(i) Availability of goods
B. Helps them to manage their business with small amount	(ii) Grant of credit
C. Maintain adequate stock of commodities to offer variety to customers	(iii) Marketing support

Codes

	A	B	C		A	B	C
(a)	(ii)	(i)	(iii)	(b)	(iii)	(ii)	(i)
(c)	(i)	(iii)	(ii)	(d)	(ii)	(iii)	(i)

54. Match the following

Column I	Column II
A. Hawkers and peddlers	(i) They are petty retailers who have independent shops in residential colonies or business localities but for a temporary period.
B. Periodic market traders	(ii) These retailers display their goods at street crossings or on pavements, or in the corridors of markets.
C. Street traders/ pavement vendors	(iii) A special feature of these traders is that their weekly market day is fixed.
D. Cheap jacks	(iv) They usually carry their goods in a bag or on a cart, or a cycle or on animals.

Codes

	A	B	C	D		A	B	C	D
(a)	(ii)	(i)	(iii)	(iv)	(b)	(iv)	(iii)	(ii)	(i)
(c)	(i)	(iii)	(ii)	(iv)	(d)	(ii)	(iii)	(i)	(iv)

55. Match the following

Column I	Column II
A. General stores	(i) These shops sell second-hand goods of different kinds like furniture, books, clothes and other household articles.
B. Single line stores	(ii) These small vendors are commonly found at street crossings or other places where flow of traffic is heavy.
C. Street stall holders	(iii) These stores deal in a specific product line. The product line may consist of readymade garments, textiles, medicines, shoes, stationery or books.

Column I		Column II
D. Second-hand goods shop	(iv)	These stores deal in items of daily use like groceries, confectionery, stationery, soft drinks, etc.

Codes

	A	B	C	D
(a)	(ii)	(i)	(iii)	(iv)
(b)	(iv)	(iii)	(ii)	(i)
(c)	(i)	(iii)	(ii)	(iv)
(d)	(ii)	(iii)	(i)	(iv)

56. Match the following

Column I		Column II
A. Departmental stores	(i)	Cafe Coffee Day
B. Chain stores	(ii)	Office supplies
C. Main order houses	(iii)	Spencers

Codes

	A	B	C
(a)	(ii)	(i)	(iii)
(b)	(iii)	(i)	(ii)
(c)	(i)	(iii)	(ii)
(d)	(ii)	(iii)	(i)

Answers

1. (d) conveying retailers' feedback to manufacturer
2. (c) Risk sharing
3. (b) By storing goods and purchasing them as they are produced
4. (c) Grant of credit
5. (b) By making individual sales to final consumers
6. (b) Selling goods in small quantities and being located near residential areas
7. (c) Collecting market information
8. (c) Both (a) and (b)
9. (b) Street stallholders
10. (d) street retailers
11. (b) Periodic market trader
12. (d) Cheap jacks
13. (c) Independent shops of temporary nature facilities
14. (c) Fixed shop retailer
15. (c) Single line store/Speciality shop
16. (d) Single line stores provide credit facilities to all customers
17. (b) Street stallholders
18. (c) Speciality shops
19. (b) High prices for rare antiques
20. (c) speciality shop
21. (c) They focus primarily on a price sensitive customer segment
22. (a) Departmental store
23. (b) Retail outlets with a common brand identity and standardised products
24. (b) Chain store
25. (d) Mail order house
26. (b) GST will abolish all the direct tax levied in India
27. (b) Finance Minister
28. (b) Providing credit facilities to customers
29. (b) Multiple shops
30. (b) Wholesalers
31. (c) Centralised control
32. (c) Wholesalers do not sell goods on credit to manufacturers; instead, they buy goods in bulk and pay manufacturers directly.
33. (a) Both Assertion (A) and Reason (R) are true and Reason (R) is the correct explanation of Assertion (A)
34. (a) Both Assertion (A) and Reason (R) are true and Reason (R) is the correct explanation of Assertion (A)
35. (c) Wholesalers generally do not provide after-sale services like home delivery, this function is typically handled by retailers.
36. (a) Both Assertion (A) and Reason (R) are true and Reason (R) is the correct explanation of Assertion (A)
37. (c) Retailers deal in both durable and non-durable goods, not just durable goods.
38. (a) Both Assertion (A) and Reason (R) are true and Reason (R) is the correct explanation of Assertion (A)
39. (a) Both Assertion (A) and Reason (R) are true and Reason (R) is the correct explanation of Assertion (A)
40. (a) Both Assertion (A) and Reason (R) are true and Reason (R) is the correct explanation of Assertion (A)
41. (a) Both Assertion (A) and Reason (R) are true and Reason (R) is the correct explanation of Assertion (A)
42. (a) Internal trade does not involve import duties, as goods are meant for domestic consumption.
43. (a) General stores are located in residential areas, to meet daily needs conveniently.
44. (a) Specialty shops are located in central places of markets, to attract more customers for a specific product line.
45. (b) Street stall holders operate on a small-scale and primarily deal in goods of cheap variety.

46. (a) Second-hand goods shops do not always have a fixed location; they can operate from various places, including temporary set-ups

47. (b) Mail order houses do not involve direct personal contact. The interaction is typically through catalogs, phone calls or online ordering.

48. (c) Both the statements are correct

49. (a) GST is applicable to both luxury goods and items of mass consumption.

50. (b) GST follows the principle of destination-based taxation, not origin-based taxation.

51. (a) GST benefits both businesses and consumers by reducing tax burdens and increasing economic activity.

52. (c) (iii) (i) (ii)

53. (b) (iii) (ii) (i)

54. (b) (iv) (iii) (ii) (i)

55. (b) (iv) (iii) (ii) (i)

56. (b) (iii) (i) (ii)

Subjective Questions

Short Answer Type Questions

1. What do you understand by wholesale trade? State its features.

Ans. Wholesale trade refers to buying and selling of goods and services in large quantities for the purpose of resale or intermediate use.

Following are the features of wholesale trade

(i) This trade provides link between the manufacturers and the retailers but there is usually no direct dealing with the ultimate consumers.

(ii) The wholesalers buy goods in large quantities and sells in smaller quantities.

(iii) Wholesalers maintain large stock of goods and provide credit facilities to the retailers.

(iv) The wholesalers usually specialise in one particular line of goods.

(v) Wholesalers undertake various activities such as grading of products, packing into smaller lots, storage, transportation, promotion of goods, collection of small and seattered orders of retailer and distribution of supplies to them.

2. What purpose is served by wholesalers by providing warehousing facilities? NCERT

Ans. Two-way purpose is served by wholesalers by providing warehousing facilities in the following manner

(i) Wholesalers take delivery of goods when these are produced in factory and keep them in their godowns/warehouses, which reduces the burden on manufacturers for providing storage facilities for the finished products.

(ii) Warehousing by wholesalers relieves the retailers of the work of collecting goods from several producers and keeping huge inventory of the same.

3. Briefly discuss the services that are provided by wholesalers to retailers.

Ans. Following are the services that are provided by wholesalers to retailers (any four)

(i) **Availability of Goods**

The wholesalers make available the products of various manufacturers to the retailers. Thus, the retailers are able to offer a variety of goods to their customers.

(ii) **Marketing Support**

The wholesalers perform various marketing functions such as advertisements and other sales promotional activities to convince customers to purchase the goods. This increases the demand of the products which results in increased profits for the retailer.

(iii) **Grant of Credit**

The wholesalers provide credit facilities to retailers by selling goods on credit to them. This enables them to manage their business with relatively small amount of working capital.

(iv) **Specialised Knowledge**

The wholesalers specialise in one line of products. They inform the retailers about the new products, their uses, quality, prices, etc.

(v) **Risk Sharing**

The wholesalers purchase in bulk quantities and sell in small quantities to the retailers. It protects the retailers from the risk of storage, reduction in prices, demand fluctuations, etc.

4. Define retail trade. State its features.

Ans. Retail trade refers to sale of goods and services directly to the ultimate consumers in small quantities. Traders dealing in retail trade are called retailers.

Following are the features of retail trade

(i) Retailer is the last link in the chain of distribution.
(ii) Retailers sell goods or services to consumers for final consumption.
(iii) They deal in a wide variety of products.
(iv) They buy and sell small quantity of goods.
(v) They are generally located in residential areas.
(vi) They maintain personal relations with customers.
(vii) They act as a middlemen between the wholesalers and customers.

5. "Itinerant retailers form a vital part of the unorganised retail sector, catering to the diverse needs of customers with their mobility and accessibility." Briefly discuss the various types of itinerant retailers. Competency Based Que

Ans. Various types of itinerant retailers are as follows

(i) **Hawkers and Peddlers**
They are traders who move from place to place selling their goods. They usually carry their goods in a bag or on a cart, or a cycle, or on animals. They can be seen on streets of residential areas, place of exhibition, outside schools and restaurants.

(ii) **Periodic Market Traders**
These traders sell their articles on fixed days in different market places.
A special feature of these traders is that their weekly market day is fixed. e.g. Saturdays (Shani Bazaar) or Mondays (Som Bazaar), etc.

(iii) **Street Traders/Pavement Vendors**
These retailers display their goods at street crossings or on pavements, or in the corridors of markets. They can also display their goods on railway platforms, bus stands, cinema halls, etc.

(iv) **Cheap Jacks**
They are petty retailers who have independent shops in residential colonies or business localities but for a temporary period.

6. Distinguish between single line stores and speciality stores. Can you identify such stores in your locality? NCERT

Ans. Following are the differences between single line stores and speciality stores

Basis	Single Line Stores	Speciality Stores
Meaning	These are small shops where one thing works, e.g. Clothing or electrical items.	These stores only work on some kind of product from selected product lines, e.g. Gents' clothes.
Product Variety	These stores used to offer a great variety of products.	These stores are usually selling all products of a particular niche. They are special stores for those products.
Example	If a store is working with clothes, it will have a wide variety of clothes of all sizes of nakedness men, women and children.	If the store is especially for men clothing, then it will be having all kinds of men's clothing.

Based on the above features, we can identify single line stores and speciality stores.

7. "Departmental stores offer a wide variety of goods under one roof, making them a convenient shopping destination for customers." State and explain any four merits of departmental stores that contribute to their popularity. Competency Based Que

Ans. Following are the merits of departmental stores that contribute to their popularity

(i) **Attract Large Number of Customers**
These stores are centrally located, thus they attract a large number of customers.

(ii) **Convenience in Buying**
These stores offer a large variety of goods under one roof. Therefore, it is convenient for customers to purchase goods from these stores.

(iii) **Attractive Services**
These stores provide extra services to the customers, such as home delivery of goods, accepting orders through telephone and online, provision of rest rooms, restaurants, etc.

(iv) **Economy of Large-scale Operations**
These stores are organised and managed on a large-scale. Therefore, they are able to enjoy economies of large-scale operations and increase their profits.

8. "Departmental stores are considered a one-stop solution for diverse customer needs, offering a wide variety of goods under a single roof. However, they face several challenges that limit their effectiveness and efficiency." In the context of the given statement, discuss the drawbacks of departmental stores. Competency Based Que

Ans. Following are the drawbacks of departmental stores

(i) **Lack of Personal Attention**
These stores are not able to give personal attention to each and every customer because of large-scale operations.

(ii) **High Operating Costs**

These stores provide a number of additional services to their customers, thus their operating costs are also high.

(iii) **High Possibility of Loss**

These stores operate on large-scale and incur high operating costs, thus their exposure to risk is also high.

(iv) **Inconvenient Location**

These stores are generally located in a central location. Customers encounter traffic problems while visiting these stores. It is also not convenient for the purchase of goods that are needed at short notice.

9. "Chain stores have revolutionised retail by maintaining consistency in products, pricing and services across locations." What is meant by a chain store? Discuss its concept and state three merits of this retail format. Competency Based Que

Ans. Chain stores are networks of retail shops that are owned and operated by manufacturers or intermediaries. Under this type of arrangement, a number of shops with similar appearance are established in localities, spread over different parts of the country. These shops normally deal in standardised and branded customer products, which have rapid sales turnover.

Following are the merits of chain stores

(i) **Elimination of Middlemen**

Through these stores, the manufacturers sells goods directly to the consumers, thus eliminating unnecessary middlemen in the sale and purchase of goods.

(ii) **No Bad Debts**

All the sales in these stores are made on cash. Therefore, there is no question of bad debts.

(iii) **Transfer of Goods**

In case of lack of demand, goods from one store can be transferred to another store. This reduces the chances of dead stock in these shops.

10. "The Goods and Services Tax (GST) council has been pivotal in ensuring uniformity in taxation across the nation. However, its role extends beyond tax regulation to fostering cooperative federalism."

In the context of the statement, write a short note on the GST Council. Competency Based Que

Ans. GST council is a governing body to regulate and direct each and every step for the implementation of GST in the nation with decisions over tax rates.

Following are the designated personnel included in GST Council

(i) **Chairman**

Union Finance Minister is the Chairman of GST Council.

(ii) **Vice Chairman**

It is chosen amongst the ministers of State Government.

(iii) **Members**

Minister of State Finance and all ministers of Financial/ Taxation of each state are members of GST Council.

The points related to quorum and decision making of GST council are

(i) For a valid meeting of the members of GST council, at least 50% of the total number of members should be present at the meeting.

(ii) Every decision made during the meeting should be supported by at least 75% majority.

(iii) The vote of Central Government shall have the weightage of 1/3rd of the total votes in the meeting.

(iii) The vote of State Government shall have the weightage of 2/3rd of the total votes in the meeting.

(iv) The council shall make recommendations on everything related to GST including rules and rates, etc.

Long Answer Type Questions

11. "Retailers play a crucial role in the distribution chain by acting as a link between wholesalers, manufacturers and the end consumers."

Explain the various services rendered by retailers to customers in ensuring the efficient flow of goods. Competency Based Que

Ans. Retailers provide the following services to the consumers

(i) **Regular Availability of Products**

The most important service of a retailer to consumers is to maintain regular availability of various products produced by different manufacturers. It enables the customers to buy product as and when needed.

(ii) **New Products Information**

The retailers provide important information about the arrival, special features, etc. of new products to the customers, by arranging effective display of products.

(iii) **Convenience in Buying**

Retailers generally sell goods in small quantities, according to the requirements of their customers. They are situated very near to residential areas and remain open for long hours. This offers great convenience to the customers.

(iv) **Wide Selection**

Retailers generally keep stock of a variety of products. This enables the consumers to make their choice.

(v) **After-sales Services**

Retailers provide important after-sales services such as home delivery, supply of spare parts and attending to customers.

(vi) **Provide Credit Facilities**

The retailers sometimes provide credit facilities to their regular customers. This leads to increased level of consumption and better standard of living of the customers.

12. Discuss the various services that are provided by wholesalers to manufacturers

Ans. Following are the services that are provided by wholesalers to manufacturers

(i) **Facilitating Large-scale Production**

Wholesalers collect small orders from a number of retailers and make purchases in bulk quantities from the producers.

This enables the producers to undertake production on a large-scale.

(ii) **Bearing Risk**

The wholesalers deal in goods in their own name, take delivery of the goods and keep them in large lots in their warehouses.

In this process, they bear risks like fall in prices, theft, spoilage, fire, etc. which would have been borne by the manufacturer.

(iii) **Financial Assistance**

The wholesalers provide financial assistance to the manufacturers as they generally make cash payment for the goods purchased by them. Sometimes they also advance money to the producers for bulk orders placed by them.

(iv) **Expert Advice**

The wholesalers are in direct contact with the retailers, therefore they can advice the manufacturers about various aspects related to customer's tastes and preferences, market conditions, etc.

(v) **Help in the Marketing Function**

The wholesalers distribute goods to a number of retailers, who in turn sell these goods to a large number of customers. Thus, they help in marketing the product.

(vi) **Facilitate Production Continuity**

The wholesalers facilitate continuity of production activity throughout the year by purchasing the goods as and when they are produced, and storing them till they are demanded by retailers or consumers in the market.

(vii) **Storage**

The wholesalers take delivery of goods when they are produced and keep them in their godowns/warehouses. Thus, they help the manufacturers in storage of goods.

13. Distinguish between wholesalers and retailers.

Ans. Following are the differences between wholesalers and retailers

Basis	Wholesalers	Retailers
Purchases and Sales	They purchase goods from manufacturers and sell them to retailers.	They purchase goods from wholesalers and sell them to ultimate consumers.
Quantity of Goods	They buy and sell goods in large quantities.	They buy and sell goods in small quantities.
Specialisation	They specialise, generally, in purchase and sale of one commodity only.	They do not specialise in only one good, but provide all types of goods.
Capital	They require a large amount of capital.	They require comparatively less capital.
Price	Wholesale price is less than retail price.	Retail price is more than wholesale price.

14. Imagine life without your local market. What difficulties would a consumer face if there is no retail shop? NCERT; Competency Based Que

Ans. There are many difficulties that people can face if there is no retail store. These serve as a link between manufacturers/ retailers and consumers as they buy goods from supermarkets/retailers and sell them directly to consumers. If there are no retail stores available neighbours at that time life will be difficult.

By buying a simple product or for everyday use we will have to go a long way. We can buy certain things as and when required if other retail stores are within transit not far from our house.

In an emergency, we can easily find medicine and other necessary items if any shops are nearby. Otherwise, life can be very difficult.

Retail shops or retailers play an important role in following things

(i) **Product Availability**

The most important service of a retailer to consumers is to maintain regular availability of various products produced by different manufacturers. It enables the customers to buy product as and when needed.

(ii) **Product Information**

The retailers provide important information about the arrival, special features, etc. of new products to the customers, by arranging effective display of products.

(iii) **Convenience in Purchase**
Retailers generally sell goods in small quantities, according to the requirements of their customers. They are situated very near to residential areas and remain open for long hours. This offers great convenience to the customers.

(iv) **Wide Choice**
Retailers generally keep stock of a variety of products. This enables the consumers to make their choice.

(v) **After-sales Services**
Retailers provide important after sales services such as home delivery, supply of spare parts and attending to customers.

(vi) **Credit Facilities**
The retailers sometimes provide credit facilities to their regular customers. This led to increased level of consumption and better standard of living of the customers.

15. Itinerant traders have been an integral part of internal trade in India. Analyse the reasons for their survival inspite of competition from large-scale retailers. NCERT

Ans. Itinerant retailers are traders who do not have a fixed place of business to operate from. They keep on moving with their wares from street to street or place to place, in search of customers.

Following are the reasons for their survival inspite of competition from large-scale retailers

(i) They are small traders and hence rural customers and consumers from backward areas find themselves more comfortable dealing with them.

(ii) They normally deal in consumer products of daily use such as toiletry products, fruits and vegetables, etc. demand for which does not fall much with time.

(iii) The emphasis of such traders is on providing greater customer service by making the products available at the very doorsteps of the customers. This makes it convenient for the consumers and helps in the survival of itinerant sellers.

(iv) Their cost of operation is very low as compared to large-scale retailers as they do not have to incur expenses of fixed shops and inventory costs. Therefore, they are in a position to offer lower prices to consumers for their products.

16. Explain the usefulness of mail orders houses. What type of products are generally handled by them? Specify. NCERT

Ans. Mail order houses are the retail outlets that sell their merchandise through mail. There is generally no direct personal contact between the buyers and the sellers in this type of trading.

Mail order houses are useful because of the following reasons

(i) **Limited Capital Requirement**
Mail order business can be started with relatively low amount of capital, as it does not require heavy expenditure on building and other infrastructural facilities.

(ii) **Elimination of Middlemen**
The biggest advantage of mail order business for consumers is that unnecessary middlemen between the buyers and sellers are eliminated which results in savings to the buyers as well as to the sellers.

(iii) **Absence of Bad Debt**
Since, the mail order houses do not extend credit facilities to the customers, there are no chances of any bad debt on account of non-payment by the customers.

(iv) **Wide Reach**
This system has a wide reach as a large number of people throughout the country can be served through mail and the goods can be sent to all the places having postal services.

(v) **Convenience**
This system is very convenient for the consumers as the goods are delivered at the doorsteps of the customers.

Mail order houses usually deals only in the goods that can be

(i) graded and standardised
(ii) easily transported at low cost
(iii) have ready demand in the market
(iv) are available in large quantity throughout the year
(v) involve least possible competition in the market
(vi) described through pictures, etc.

17. "Mail order houses have become a unique way of conducting business, offering convenience to customers while also facing certain drawbacks."
In the context of this business model, discuss the concept and limitations of mail order houses.
Competency Based Que

Ans. Mail order houses are the retail outlets that sell their merchandise through mail. There is generally no direct personal contact between the buyers and the sellers in this type of trading.

In the absence of any personal contact, the transaction is settled in the following ways

(i) The seller prepares a list of potential customers. Telephone directories, list of members of clubs, etc. can be used for preparing the list.

(ii) The potential customers are approached with the help of pamphlets, specific advertisements, offer letter through mail, samples, etc.

(iii) The customers send their orders through mail according to their need.

(iv) On receiving the order, the seller packs the goods of the required specifications and delivers it to the post office, from where it is delivered to the customer.

(v) The payment of the goods can be made in the following ways

- The customer can be asked to make full payment in advance.
- The goods may be sent through VPP (Value Payable Post). Under this arrangement, the goods are sent through post and are delivered to the customers only on making full payment for the same.
- The goods may be sent through bank, which deliver the goods only on receiving the payment.

Following are the limitations of mail order houses

(i) **High Promotion Cost**

This type of business has a high promotion cost due to heavy expenditure on advertisement and other methods of promotion.

(ii) **No After-sales Service**

In this form of business, there is absence of after sales services which is very important for the satisfaction of customers.

(iii) **No Credit Facilities**

This business does not extend credit facilities to its customers.

(iv) **Delayed Delivery**

In this business, there is no immediate delivery of goods to the customers. There is a considerable time gap between placing of order and receiving goods.

(v) **Possibility of Abuse**

In this type of business, there is greater possibility of being cheated as dishonest traders can cheat their customers, by making false claims related to the product.

(vi) **High Dependence on Postal Services**

This type of business has limited prospects for a country like India, where many places are still without postal facilities

18. Discuss the various features of GST

Ans. Following are the main features of GST

(i) GST is applicable on the 'supply' of goods and services as compared to the earlier concept of tax which was levied on the manufacture or sale of goods or provision of services.

(ii) GST is spread in the whole country. The GST levied by the centre is called Central GST (CGST) and the GST levied by the states (including Union Territories with own legislature) is called State GST (SGST). Union territories without legislature levy Union Territory GST (UTGST). For inter-state supplies, Integrated GST (IGST) is levied.

(iii) CGST, SGST and IGST are levied at rates mutually agreed upon by the Centre and the States, under the assistance of the GST Council.

(iv) Import of goods and services is treated as inter-State supplies and would be subject to IGST, in addition to the applicable customs duties.

(v) GST is based on the principle of destination-based consumption which replaced the principle of origin-based taxation.

(vi) There are four tax slabs namely 5%, 12%, 18% and 28% for all goods or services.

(vii) Exports and supplies to SEZ (Special Economic Zones) are zero-rated.

(viii) There are various modes of payment of tax that are available to the taxpayer such as Internet banking, debit/credit card and National Electronic Funds Transfer (NEFT)/Real Time Gross Settlement (RTGS).

(ix) The GST has replaced 17 indirect taxes (8 Central + 9 State levels) and 23 cesses of the Centre and the States.

Case Study Based Questions

Short Case Studies

Case Study 1

Pad Chihan Limited is a large-sized company manufacturing durable consumer goods, specifically shoes. The company faces a crucial decision regarding its distribution strategy whether to rely on wholesalers as interme- diaries or set-up its own chain stores for direct retail.
This decision impacts how efficiently and effectively the company can reach its target customers and maintain control over its brand image and customer service. What alternatives would you suggest? Give reasons in support of your answer.

Ans. In the above case, we find there are two alternatives before the company

(i) To have wholesalers as middlemen.
(ii) To have its own multiple shops.

Both the alternatives have their own merits and demerits. I would suggest that multiple shops are the better alternative than the wholesalers due to following reasons

(i) Multiple shops eliminate middlemen. Hence, there is direct contact between the company and consumers. All advantages of elimination of wholesalers can be enjoyed.
(ii) Since the company is large sized, it means company has sufficient financial resources to have its own shops. Thus, the company is in a position to eliminate middlemen.
(iii) Company is manufacturing shoes i.e. durable consumer product, therefore, multiple shops are better alternative.
(iv) Company can approach maximum customers through its own shops. Wholesalers may not find it profitable to deal in shoes of a new company and therefore, wholesalers will not be taking interest.
(v) Multiple shops have a better appeal to consumers. Bata Shoe Company is a good example.

Case Study 2

Giridhar is a small trader who carry different types of vegetables in a wheeled vehicle and move from one colony to another to sell vegetables at the doorstep of the customers. Giridhar does not have a fixed price policy and price varies depending on the bargaining power of the customers.

(i) Identify the type of retailer under which Giridhar should be placed.
(ii) State any three features of the type of retailer identified in (i).

Ans.

(i) Giridhar is an itinerant retailer (Hawker) as he does not have a fixed place of business to operate from.
(ii) Following are the features of hawkers
- They sell their merchandise at the doorsteps of customers.
- They generally deal in non-standardised and low-value goods such as toys, vegetables, fruits, fabrics, snacks, ice-cream, etc.
- They bargain with customers and try to charge maximum possible price for their products.

Case Study 3

Rajneesh is a retailer who is generally seen in areas having high population like bus stands, railway stations, etc. He deals in common use products, like newspapers, magazines, toys, stationery items, etc. He does not change his place of business frequently.

(i) Identify the type of itinerant retailer in the above case.
(ii) State any three features of the type of retailer identified in (i).

Ans.

(i) The type of itinerant retailer in the above case is street trader or pavement vendor. These retailers display their goods at street crossings, or on pavements, or in the corridors of markets. They can also display their goods on railway platforms, bus stands, cinema halls, etc.
(ii) Following are the features of street traders
- They sell goods of common use such as newspapers and magazines, stationery items, readymade garments, etc.
- They deal in low-priced products.
- They do not change their place of business frequently.

Case Study 4

At a bustling street crossing, Ramesh sets-up his small stall everyday, selling affordable items like toys, hosiery products and cold drinks. His location ensures a steady flow of customers due to the heavy traffic in the area. Ramesh keeps his inventory small and focuses on serving immediate needs at a low cost. He doesn't have a permanent shop and operates with minimal infrastructure, relying on the heavy footfall of the area. His quick service and affordable pricing attract daily commuters and passersby.

(i) Identify the type of fixed shop small retailer.
(ii) State any three features of the type of retailer identified in (i).

Ans.

(i) The type of fixed shop small retailer is street stall holder. These small vendors are commonly found at street crossings or other places where flow of traffic is heavy. They deal mainly in goods of cheap variety like hosiery products, toys, soft drinks, etc.

(ii) Following are the features of street stall holder

- They attract floating customers and provide convenient service to the customers in buying some of the items of their needs.
- They get their supplies from local suppliers, as well as wholesalers.
- They operate on a small-scale.

Case Study 5

Deepak is a dealer of used books and runs a shop under the name of 'Ravi Bookshop' in Kamla Nagar, Delhi. As the bookshop is located within the area of college campus, it is very famous among the college students as they can get the used books in good condition and that too at a price much less than the MRP.

(i) Identify the category of the type of retail trade under which Deepak should be placed.

(ii) State any three features of the type of retailer as identified in (i).

Ans.

(i) The category of the type of retail trade under which Deepak should be placed is second-hand goods shop. These shops sell second-hand goods of different kinds like furniture, books, clothes and other household articles. These shops are suitable for customers with moderate means.

(ii) Following are the features of second-hand goods shops

- The shops selling second-hand goods generally sell goods at low prices, but if it is dealing in rare objects of historical importance or antique goods, then the price charged by them is high.
- The shops selling second-hand goods have no fixed location. They may be located at street crossings or in busy streets.
- The shops may operate from a table or a temporary structure (as in case of second-hand books), or it may have reasonable good structure (as in case of shops selling second-hand furniture or vehicles). It can also operate through e-commerce (e.g. OLX.com).

Case Study 6

Akbarally was the first departmental store of India. There were two full line department stores and eight supermarkets called mini-Akbarallys across Mumbai.

This store was generating phenomenal profits upto 1990s, but with the onset of the retail boom in 1990s and the subsequent proliferation of speciality stores, malls and branded stores, the downward slide of Akbarally began. In 2009, not being able to sustain losses, Akbarally closed down.

(i) What are departmental stores?

(ii) State the limitations of departmental stores which could have been the cause of Akbarally's failure

Ans.

(i) Departmental store is a large establishment offering a wide variety of products, classified into well-defined departments. A departmental store aims at satisfying practically all the needs of the consumers under one roof. It has a number of departments, each one confining its activities to a specific kind of product.

(ii) Following are the limitations of departmental stores which could have been the cause of Akbarally's failure

- **Lack of Personal Attention**
  These stores are not able to give personal attention to each and every customer because of large-scale operations.
- **High Operating Costs**
  These stores provide a number of additional services to their customers, thus their operating costs are also high.
- **High Possibility of Loss**
  These stores operate on large-scale and incur high operating costs, thus their exposure to risk is also high.
- **Inconvenient Location**
  These stores are generally located in a central location. Customers encounter traffic problems while visiting these stores. It is also not convenient for the purchase of goods that are needed at short notice.

Case Study 7

A group of retail stores known as 'SuperShop' has been established across various cities in the country. These stores operate under a unified brand and follow a standardised approach in terms of store layout, product display and customer service.

The shops offer a variety of branded products such as clothing, electronics and household goods. SuperShop is managed by a parent company that oversees the operations of each store, ensuring consistent quality and customer experience.

(i) Identify and state the type of fixed shop large retailer described in the case.

(ii) Discuss any three limitations of the type of retailer identified in (i).

Ans.

(i) The type of fixed shop large retailer in the case is chain store. Chain stores or multiple shops are networks of retail shops that are owned and operated by manufacturers or intermediaries. Under this type of arrangement, a number of shops with similar appearance are established in localities, spread over different parts of the country.

These shops normally deal in standardised and branded customer products, which have rapid sales turnover.

(ii) Following are the limitations of chain store

- **Lack of Initiative**
  The employees working in these stores work according to the instructions of the head office. Due to this, they became habitual of getting guidance from the head office on all matters. This also takes away the initiative from them to use their creative skills to satisfy the customers.
- **Lack of Personal Touch**
  Due to operating on a large scale and lack of initiative in the employees, their dealings with customers lack personal touch.
- **Difficult to Change Demand**
  If the demand for the merchandise handled by multiple shops change rapidly, the management may have to sustain huge losses because of large stocks lying unsold at the central depot.

Case Study 8

Seller receives orders from the customers by post and delivers the products by post. It is referred to as 'non-store impersonal retailing'. So, it is a 'retail selling by post' from the seller's end and a 'shopping through post' by a customer. This type of retail institution solicits patronage by means of catalogues sent through post and contain detailed descriptions of merchandise offered for sale.

(i) Identify the type of retail outlet being highlighted in the given case.

(ii) State three limitations of the type of retail outlet as identified in (i).

Ans.

(i) The type of retail outlet highlighted in the case is mail order house. Mail order houses are the retail outlets that sell their merchandise through mail. There is generally no direct personal contact between the buyers and the sellers in this type of trading.

(ii) Following are the limitations of mail order houses

- **Lack of Personal Contact**
  This business is characterised by the lack of personal contact between the buyers and sellers. This might create misunderstanding and mistrust among buyers and sellers.
- **High Promotion Cost**
  This type of business has a high promotion cost due to heavy expenditure on advertisement and other methods of promotion.
- **Delayed Delivery**
  In this business, there is no immediate delivery of goods to the customers. There is a considerable time gap between placing of order and receiving goods.

Case Study 9

The introduction of the Goods and Services Tax (GST) in India has brought a significant change in the taxation system. GST is a single tax that applies to the supply of goods and services across the country, eliminating the need for multiple indirect taxes. It rationalises the tax treatment along the entire supply chain, from producers to consumers, ensuring a seamless flow of goods and services. The GST network is a self-regulating mechanism designed to check tax fraud and evasion, promoting greater transparency and bringing more businesses into the formal economy.

Additionally, GST incorporates an anti- profiteering measure to ensure that businesses pass on the benefits of reduced costs to consumers. As a result, luxury goods have become more expensive, while goods of mass consumption have become relatively cheaper.

(i) Discuss the meaning of GST.

(ii) State any four benefits of GST.

Ans.

(i) GST is an indirect tax levied in India on the sale of goods and services. GST was implemented from 1st July, 2017 in India. It is based on the philosophy of 'One Nation and One Tax'. GST was introduced to replace multiple indirect taxes levied by State and Central Governments, in order to simplify the indirect tax system.

(ii) Following are the benefits of GST

- It has eliminated the need for filing multiple returns and assessments, and rationalising the tax treatment of goods and services along the supply chain from producers to consumers.
- The GST network is a self-regulating mechanism, which checks tax frauds and tax evasion. It also brings more businesses into the formal economy.
- GST has anti-profiteering measure which prevent entities from making excessive profits. National Anti-profiteering Authority (NAA) is to be set-up to ensure that the benefits accrued to entities due to reduction in costs is passed on to the consumers.
- With the implementation of GST, luxury goods have become costlier, while items of mass consumption have become cheaper.

Long Case Studies

Case Study 10

Sana Retailers is a well-established chain of stores that specialises in selling everyday household products. The company has a wide network across urban and rural areas, which enables them to bring goods from manufacturers to the hands of the end consumers. The company's marketing team works closely with manufacturers and wholesalers, offering insights into customer preferences and new market trends.

Sana Retailers also actively participates in promotional campaigns initiated by manufacturers, such as offering discounts and loyalty points to increase product sales. Their stores are known for providing personalised customer service, which has helped foster customer loyalty.

Additionally, Sana Retailers focuses on maintaining small, frequent stock replenishments in their stores, relieving manufacturers from the need to handle individual sales to consumers. This enables manufacturers and wholesalers to focus on large-scale production and operations.

Quoting lines from the above case, identify and explain five services provided by retailers to manufacturers and wholesalers.

Ans. The following are the five services provided by retailers to manufacturers and wholesalers, as highlighted in the case study

(i) **Help in Distribution of Goods**

"Sana Retailers is a well-established chain of stores that specialises in selling everyday household products… bring goods from manufacturers to the hands of the end consumers." Retailers help in the distribution of products by making them available to the final consumers, thus creating place utility.

(ii) **Personal Selling**

"Their stores are known for providing personalised customer service, which has helped foster customer loyalty." The retailers make individual sales to customers in small quantities. Thus, they relieve the producers from personal selling efforts and greatly help them in the process of actualising the sale of the products.

(iii) **Enabling Large-scale Operations**

"Sana Retailers focuses on maintaining small, frequent stock replenishments in their stores, relieving manufacturers from the need to handle individual sales to consumers." As retailers services relieved the manufacturers and wholesalers from the botheration of making individual sales to consumers in small quantities, they are enabled to operate at large-scale.

(iv) **Collecting Market Information**

"The company's marketing team works closely with manufacturers and wholesalers, offering insights into customer preferences and new market trends." As retailers remain in direct contact with the customers, they provide important market information about the tastes, preferences and attitudes of customers.

(v) **Help in Promotion**

"Sana Retailers also actively participates in promotional campaigns initiated by manufacturers, such as offering discounts and loyalty points to increase product sales."

Manufacturers and distributors carry on various promotional activities, in order to increase the sale of their products.

Retailers participate in these activities and help to promote the sale of the products.

Case Study 11

In a quiet residential area, a small shopping district has emerged, providing essential services to the local community. Among the various stores present, two types of retailers stand out.

One offer a wide range of everyday items such as groceries, household goods, soft drinks and stationery. These stores cater to the basic and frequent needs of the residents, ensuring convenience for daily life.

On the other hand, another one focus on specific product lines, such as garments, books or pharmaceuticals.

These stores provide a more in-depth selection and expertise in their particular category, making them ideal for customers looking for specific, quality-focused products. Together, these stores contribute significantly to the smooth functioning of the community's shopping experience.

(i) Identify and state the type of fixed shop small retailers in the case.

(ii) Discuss the various features of the types of retailers identified in (i).

Ans.

(i) Following are the type of fixed shop small retailers in the case

- **General Stores**

  These stores deal in items of daily use like groceries, confectionery, stationery, soft drinks, etc. They generally operate in residential areas and satisfy the day-to-day needs of the consumers.

- **Single Line Stores/Speciality Shops**

  These stores deal in a specific product line. The product line may consist of readymade garments, textiles, medicines, shoes, stationery or books.

(ii) Following are the features of general stores
- These have a large variety in each line of goods.
- These stores remain open for long hours at convenient timings.
- These stores provide credit to some of their regular customers.

Following are the features of single line stores/speciality shops
- These shops are located in a central place of the market, where a large number of customers can be attracted.
- They provide a wide choice to the customers in the selection of a particular line of goods.

Case Study 12

Anita Sinha was the managing director of a large retail chain, 'Prime Emporium', which operated several departmental stores across metropolitan cities in India. These stores were strategically located in bustling city centers, ensuring accessibility to a large customer base.

Anita believed in offering more than just shopping, hence, all Prime Emporium outlets provided additional facilities such as multi-cuisine restaurants, kids' play zones, free Wi-Fi and customer lounges to enhance customer satisfaction.

The stores targetted customers for whom price was not the primary concern but quality and convenience were paramount. Goods were sourced directly from manufacturers, allowing Prime Emporium to maintain their own warehouses and control stock efficiently. Anita ensured that the stores were managed by a board of directors, reflecting the joint stock company form of organisation. This centralised management structure facilitated seamless decision-making and consistent service across all outlets.

However, in recent months, competition from online retail platforms and specialised stores began to challenge Prime Emporium. While the stores maintained their loyal customer base, the inability to compete on price and niche product offerings put them under some pressure.

Quoting lines from the above case, identify and explain four features of departmental stores discussed in the above case.

Ans. Following are the four features of departmental stores discussed in the above case

(i) **Centrally Located to Cater to a Large Number of Customers**

"These stores were strategically located in bustling city centers, ensuring accessibility to a large customer base."

These stores are centrally located so that they can cater to large number of customers.

These stores try to maximise customer satisfaction by providing additional facilities such as restaurants, travel and information bureau, free wi-fi zone, kids zone, rest rooms, etc.

(ii) **Provision of Additional Facilities to Maximise Customer Satisfaction**

"These stores provided additional facilities such as multi-cuisine restaurants, kids' play zones, free wi-fi and customer lounges."

These stores try to maximise customer satisfaction by providing additional facilities such as restaurants, travel and information bureau, free wi-fi zone, kids zone, rest rooms, etc.

(iii) **Target Segment of Customers who Prioritise Quality and Convenience Over Price**

"The stores targeted customers for whom price was not the primary concern but quality and convenience were paramount."

This emphasises that departmental stores cater to a segment that values quality service and convenience over price alone.

(iv) **Combination of Retailing and Warehousing Functions for Efficiency**

"Goods were sourced directly from manufacturers, allowing Prime Emporium to maintain their own warehouses and control stock efficiently."

These stores purchase goods directly from the manufacturers and maintain their own warehouses where goods are stored. Thus, these stores combine the functions of retailing and selling.

Case Study 13

Cafe Coffee Day (CCD), a popular coffee chain, operates a network of cafes across multiple cities in India. Each outlet has a uniform appearance, layout and branding, providing a standardised experience to customers. These cafes are owned and managed by the parent company, ensuring consistent quality and service. CCD specialises in serving branded coffee and snacks, catering to a broad customer base.

With outlets in malls, airports, and prime localities, CCD has a high turnover of its products. The company also maintains a centralised purchasing system, which helps in cost efficiency and quality control. To enhance customer loyalty, CCD offers various promotional schemes and discount cards. Moreover, the company strategically selects locations with high footfall, ensuring better visibility and accessibility.

This arrangement allows CCD to maintain its brand identity while continuously expanding its reach across the country.

(i) Identify the type of retail outlet being described in the given case.

(ii) State any three features of the retail outlet identified in (i).

(iii) State any three advantages of the retail outlet identified in (i).

Ans.

(i) The retail outlet described in the given case is chain store.

(ii) Following are the features of chain stores

- These shops are located in populous localities, so that customers can be served at a place near their residence.
- Each retail outlet is under the direct supervision of a branch manager, who is responsible for its day-to-day operations.
- All branches are controlled by the head office. The head office formulates policies and gets them implemented.
- The purchasing of all the goods for all these stores are done by the head office which dispatched goods to these stores according to their requirements. This results in saving the cost of operation of these stores.
- In these stores, The prices of the goods is fixed and sales are made on cash basis. Daily sales are deposited in a local bank account and details regarding this are sent to the head office.
- The head office appoints inspectors, who supervise the day-to-day operations of the store in respect of quality of customer service provided, adherence to rules and regulations, etc.

(iii) Following are the advantages of chain stores

- **No Bad Debts**

  All the sales in these stores are made on cash. Therefore, there is no question of bad debts.
- **Transfer of Goods**

  In case of lack of demand, goods from one store can be transferred to another store. This reduces the chances of dead stock in these shops.
- **Diffusion of Risk**

  The risk is spread over a number of shops. Loss from one shop can be recovered from the profit of another shop.

SELF ASSESSMENT TEST

Objective Type Questions

1. Retailers who have no fixed place of sale are called
   (a) itinerant retailers
   (b) street traders
   (c) market traders
   (d) hawkers

2. A small trader sells fruits and vegetables door-to-door, moving from one residential area to another in search of customers. Their limited inventory is stored at home for easy accessibility. What is a characteristic of itinerant retailers?
   (a) They operate from a fixed location
   (b) They deal in luxury goods
   (c) They move from place to place to provide products directly to customers
   (d) They manage large warehouses for storage

3. Small retailers who are commonly found at places with huge population are called
   (a) market traders
   (b) second hand goods shop
   (c) peddlers and hawkers
   (d) street retailers

4. Which type of retailers provides door-to-door services to their customers?
   (a) Street traders (b) Peddlers and hawkers
   (c) General stores (d) Street stallholders

5. General stores primarily deal with which of the following types of items?
   (a) Electronics and appliances
   (b) Daily use items such as groceries and confectionery
   (c) Furniture and home décor
   (d) Clothing and accessories

6. ………… is a type of retail trading where business is carried on through post.
   (a) Departmental store (b) Chain store
   (c) Mail order house (d) Automatic vending machine

7. In order to eliminate bad debts in full, under which arrangement, goods may be sent to customers through bank and are delivered only on making full payment?
   (a) Departmental stores (b) Peddlars
   (c) Mail order houses (d) Chain stores

8. A manufacturer based in Delhi supplies goods to customers across India, including states like Maharashtra and Gujarat. Additionally, imported goods are also part of the business operations.
   What type of GST would apply to the supply of goods and services between states like Maharashtra and Gujarat?
   (a) CGST (b) SGST
   (c) IGST (d) UTGST

Answers 1. (a) 2. (c) 3. (d) 4. (b) 5. (b) 6. (c) 7. (c) 8. (c)

Short Answer Type Questions

9. Define internal trade. What are its two types?
10. State any three points of difference between 'wholesaler' and 'retailer'.
11. A manufacturer wants to expand its market reach by collaborating with retailers who can help distribute products efficiently to end consumers. However, the manufacturer faces challenges in ensuring smooth supply chain management and brand representation. Discuss the services of retailers to manufacturers and wholesalers, focusing on how they contribute to marketing, inventory management and customer engagement.
12. ABC Enterprises operates in rural areas where access to retail stores is limited. The company uses itinerant traders like hawkers and street vendors to distribute its products directly to customers, ensuring wider reach and convenience.
    Discuss the four types of itinerant traders.
13. What are general stores? Discuss its key features.
14. State any three features of chain stores.
15. Discuss any four key features of goods and services tax.

Long Answer Type Questions

16. Describe the various services provided by wholesalers to manufacturers and retailers.
17. Different types of fixed shops under retail trade include specialty stores, department stores and convenience stores. Discuss how these shops differ in terms of product variety, customer experience and target audience?
18. Despite their convenience, large departmental stores face challenges such as intense competition from online shopping, high operational costs and changing consumer preferences in India. In the context of the given statement, discuss why are departmental stores not popular in India?

10

CHAPTER

International Business

International business consists of transactions that are devised and carried out across national borders to satisfy the objectives of the individuals, companies and organisations. These transactions take on various forms which are often interrelated. — *Michael R. Czinkota*

YOUR STUDY GOALS

10.1 Meaning of International Business
10.2 Export Trade
10.3 Import Trade
10.4 World Trade Organisation (WTO)

YOUR PRACTICE GOAL

- Objective Type Questions (62 Qs ; MCQs, A-R, Statements, Matching)
- Subjective Questions (10 SAs, 5 LAs)
- Case Study Based Questions (Short Case Studies-6, Long Case Studies-4)
- Self Assessment Test (8 MCQs, 7 SAs, 3 LAs)

10.1 Meaning of International Business

Manufacturing and trading beyond the boundaries of one's own country is known as international or external business. It can be defined as those business activities that take place across the national frontiers.

Advantages of International Business

International business provides benefits to nations as well as business firms.

Advantages to Nations

Advantages	Explanations
Earning of Foreign Exchange	International business helps a country to import those goods and services which it cannot produce efficiently such as petroleum products and fertilisers, etc. Thus, it helps to earn foreign exchange.
More Efficient use of Resources	International business operates on a principle that the countries should tend to produce goods in which they have a comparative advantage or which they can produce efficiently. This results in prevention of wasteful duplication of resources.

Advantages	Explanations
Improving Growth Prospects and Employment Potentials	International business results in increase in employment opportunities directly or indirectly. It results in increase in production and for this demand, requirement of labour also increases.
Increased Standard of Living	In the absence of international business, it would not have been possible for the world community to consume goods and services produced in other countries that the people in these countries are able to consume and enjoy a higher standard of living.

Advantages to Firms

Advantages	Explanations
Prospects for Higher Profits	When prices in the domestic market are low, firms can earn more profits by selling their products in those countries in which prices are high.
Increased Capacity Utilisation	Many business and industrial enterprises have unused capacity, that can be efficiently utilised for further production. Thus, surplus production can be used to generate extra profits from foreign trade.
Prospects for Growth	When the domestic demand for a firm's product or services start getting saturated in the domestic market, then firms can considerably improve prospects of their growth by venturing out in the international market.
Way Out to Intense Competition in Domestic Market	Highly competitive domestic market drives many companies to go international in search of markets for their products.
Improved Business Vision	Most enterprises have an urge to grow, to become more competitive, to diversify and derive the benefits of going global through international business.

Disadvantages of International Business

1. **Distance** Due to long distances between countries, it is difficult to establish personal and quick contacts between traders from different countries. There is a large time gap between the placement of order and receipt of goods from foreign countries.

2. **Different Currency** Each country has its own currency. Payment for imported goods is made in foreign currency and payment for export is also received in foreign currency.
3. **Different Languages** Different languages are spoken and written in different countries. It is therefore, difficult for traders to understand each other. One must know the foreign language or appoint someone to read the price lists of foreign countries.
4. **Legal Formalities** International business is monitored by the government. Prior permission has to be obtained before exporting or importing goods or services. A large number of documents have to be filed and custom duties are paid on imports and exports.
5. **Blocked Capital** Traders have to often depend upon a chain of intermediaries in international business. There is a long time gap between the dispatch of goods by the exporter and their receipt and payment by the importer. Therefore, the capital of the exporter is blocked for a long period.

Reasons for International Business

The countries cannot produce equally and cheaply all the things that they need. This is because of the following reasons

- Unequal distribution of natural resources among them or differences in their productivity levels.
- Availability of various factors of production such as labour, capital and raw materials, differ among nations.
- Labour productivity and production cost differ among nations due to various socio-economic, geographical and political reasons.

Scope of International Business

1. **Merchandise Exports and Imports** It includes trade in goods that are tangible. They can be touched and seen like machinery, garments, etc.
2. **Services Exports and Imports** This involves trade in intangibles and therefore it is also known as invisible trade. It cannot be seen and touched but can only be felt like tourism, travel, insurance, etc. They are the major constituents of world trade.
3. **Licensing** It is permitting another party in a foreign country to produce and sell goods under one's own trademark, patents or copyrights in lieu of some fee.
4. **Franchising** It is similar to licensing but it is used in connection with services only. Pizza Hut, Dominos, etc. operate through this system. They also pay a fee for the use of the name.
5. **Foreign Investments** This is the investment of funds in abroad in exchange of financial return from that country in the form of profit, interest or dividend. It is of two types
   (i) **Foreign Direct Investments** (FDI) It takes place when a company directly invests in properties such as plant and machinery, land and building to undertake production and marketing of goods and services in those countries.
   (ii) **Portfolio Investments** It takes place when a company invests in another company by acquiring shares of that company or giving them loans and earn dividend on shares and interest on loans.

Scope of International Business
- → Merchandise Exports and Imports
- → Services Exports and Imports
- → Licensing
- → Franchising
- → Foreign Investments

10.2 Export Trade

It is a mode of international trade in which goods produced in the domestic country are sold to the residents of another country. Following are the **objectives** of export trade

1. **Sell Surplus Goods** A country may produce a commodity in such quantities that are more than its needs. The country can sell its surplus output to foreign countries. In this way, export trade is undertaken to make productive use of surplus goods.
2. **Better Utilisation of Resources** Export trade widens the market for goods. A country can make better utilisation of its resources by producing goods on a large-scale, both for domestic use and for export.
3. **Earn Foreign Exchange** A country can earn valuable foreign exchange through export.
4. **Increase National Income** Export trade helps a country to increase its national income.
5. **Generate Employment** The growth of export trade also creates employment opportunities.
6. **To Create International Cooperation** Export trade improves mutual understanding and cooperation between nations.

Procedure for Conducting Export Trade

A number of steps are required to be taken to complete an export transaction. These steps are explained below

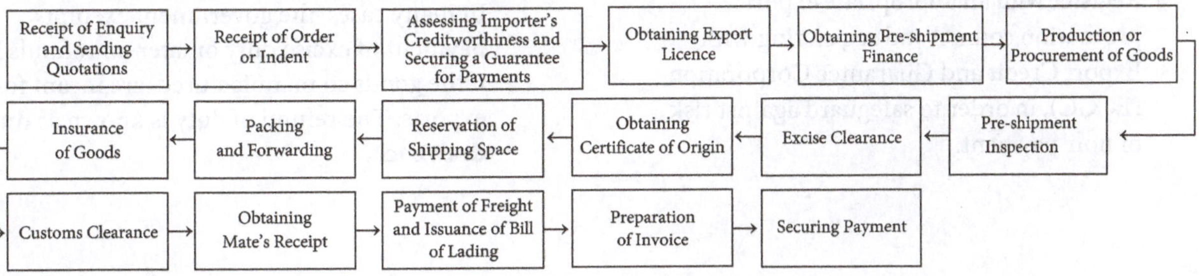

Step 1 **Receipt of Enquiry and Sending Quotations** The prospective buyer of a product sends an enquiry to different exporters, requesting them to send information regarding price, quality and terms and conditions for export of goods. The exporter sends a reply to the enquiry in the form of a quotation, referred to as proforma invoice.

Step 2 **Receipt of Order or Indent** If the prospective buyer finds the export price and other terms and conditions acceptable, he places an order for the goods to be dispatched. This order (also known as indent) contains a description of the goods ordered, prices to be paid, delivery terms, packing and marking details and delivery instructions.

Step 3 **Assessing Importer's Creditworthiness and Securing a Guarantee for Payments** After receipt of the indent, the exporter makes necessary enquiry about the creditworthiness of the importer. The purpose of the enquiry is to assess the risk of non-payment by the importer, once the goods reach the import destination. To minimise such risk, most of the exporters demand a letter of credit from the importer.

Step 4 **Obtaining Export Licence** After becoming assured about payments, the exporting firm initiates the steps relating to compliance of export regulations and take following steps to obtain licence

- Open a bank account in any bank authorised by the Reserve Bank of India (RBI) and get an account number.
- Obtain Import Export Code (IEC) number from the Directorate General Foreign Trade (DGFT) or Regional Import Export Licensing Authority.
- Register with an appropriate export promotion council and registering with Export Credit and Guarantee Corporation (ECGC), in order to safeguard against risk of non-payment.

Step 5 **Obtaining Pre-shipment Finance** Once a confirmed order and a letter of credit have been received, the exporter approaches his banker for obtaining pre-shipment finance to undertake export production.

Step 6 **Production or Procurement of Goods** After obtaining finance, the exporter proceeds to get the goods ready as per the specifications of the importer.

Step 7 **Pre-shipment Inspection** The exporter is required to get the goods inspected before shipment.

The government has passed Export Quality Control and Inspection Act, 1963 for this purpose and has authorised some agencies to act as inspection agencies.

Step 8 **Excise Clearance** According to Central Excise Tariff Act, excise duty is payable on the materials used in manufacturing goods. The exporter, therefore, has to apply to the concerned Excise Commissioner in the region with an invoice. If the Excise Commissioner is satisfied, he may issue the excise clearance.

In many cases, the government exempts payment of excise duty or later on refunds it, if the goods so manufactured are meant for exports. The refund of duty is known as **duty drawback**.

Step 9 **Obtaining Certificate of Origin** Some importing countries provide tariff concessions or other exemptions to the goods coming from a particular country. For availing such benefits, the importer may ask the exporter to send a certificate of origin.

Step 10 **Reservation of Shipping Space** The exporting firm applies to the shipping company for provision of shipping space. It has to specify the type of goods to be exported, probable date of shipment and the port of destination. On acceptance of application, the shipping company issues a shipping order.

Step 11 **Packing and Forwarding** After reservation of shipping space, the goods are properly packed and marked with necessary details such as name and address of the importer, gross and net weight, port of shipment and destination, country of origin, etc.

The exporter then makes necessary arrangement for transportation of goods to the port. On loading goods into the railway wagon, the railway authorities issue a 'railway receipt' which serves as a title to the goods. The exporter endorses the railway receipt in favour of his agent to enable him to take delivery of goods at the port of shipment.

Step 12 **Insurance of Goods** The exporter gets the goods insured with an insurance company to protect against the risks of loss or damage of the goods, due to the perils (hazards) of the sea during the transit.

Step 13 **Customs Clearance** The goods must be cleared from the customs before loading on the ship. For obtaining customs clearance, the exporter starts preparing the shipping bill.

Five copies of the shipping bill, alongwith the following documents are to be submitted before the Customs Appraiser at the Customs House

- Export contract or export order
- Letter of credit
- Commercial invoice
- Certificate of origin
- Certificate of inspection, where necessary
- Marine insurance policy

After submission of these documents, the superintendent of the concerned port trust is approached for obtaining the carting order. It is the instruction to the staff at the gate of the port to permit the entry of the cargo inside the dock.

Step 14 **Obtaining Mate's Receipt** The mate or the captain of the ship issues mate's receipt to the port superintendent for the goods to be loaded on the ship. The port superintendent hands over the mate's receipt to the C&F agent.

Step 15 **Payment of Freight and Issuance of Bill of Lading** The C&F agent surrenders the mate's receipt to the shipping company for computation of freight. After receiving the receipt of the freight, the shipping company issues a bill of lading which serves as an evidence that the shipping company has accepted the goods for carrying them to the designated destination. In case, goods are being sent by air, this document is referred to as airway bill.

Step 16 **Preparation of Invoice** After sending the goods, an invoice of the dispatched goods is prepared. The invoice states the quantity of goods sent and the amount to be paid by the importer. The C&F agent gets it duly attested by the customs.

Step 17 **Securing Payment** After the shipment of goods, the exporter informs the importer about it. The importer needs various documents to claim the title of goods on their arrival in his/her country and getting them customs cleared.

The documents that are needed in this connection include certified copy of invoice, bill of lading, packing list, insurance policy, certificate of origin and letter of credit.

The exporter sends these documents through his/her banker with the instruction that these may be delivered to the importer, after acceptance of the bill of exchange.

Submission of the relevant documents to the bank for the purpose of getting the payment from the bank is called negotiation of the documents. The documents are handed over to the importer only against payment.

Documents used in Export Trade

Documents related to goods exported, shipment of exported goods and payment of exported goods are discussed below

I. Documents Related to Goods Exported

Document	Explanations
Export Invoice	It is a seller bill information about goods like quantity, number of packages, name of ship, terms of delivery, payments, etc.
Packing List	This document provides complete details regarding the goods exported and the form in which they are being sent.
Certificate of Origin	It specifies the country in which the goods are being manufactured. This certificate enables the importer to claim tariff concessions or other exemptions. It is also used in the case when there is a ban on imports of some goods from certain countries.
Certificate of Inspection	It is the certificate that states that the consignment has been inspected as required under the Export (Quality Control and Inspection) Act, 1963. It is issued by some authorised agency Export Inspection Council of India (EICI).

II. Documents Related to Shipment of Exported Goods

Document	Explanations
Mate's Receipt	This receipt is issued by the captain or mate of the ship to the exporter after the goods are loaded on board of the ship. Such receipts contain name of the vessel, description of packages, marks, condition of the cargo, etc.
Shipping Bill	With the help of this document, permission is granted for the export of goods by the customs office. It contains details regarding the goods being exported, name of the vessel, exporters name and address, country of final destination, etc.
Bill of Lading	It acts as an evidence regarding the acceptance of shipping company to carry the goods to the port of destination. It is also referred to as document of title to the goods and is freely transferable by endorsement and delivery.
Shipping Order	It is an instruction to the captain of the ship to receive the specified goods on board after their customs clearance at a designated port.
Airway Bill	It is a document issued by the airline company on receiving the goods on board, its aircraft and at the same time giving its acceptance to carry them to the port of destination.
Marine Insurance Policy	It is a document containing contract between the exporter and the insurance company to indemnify against loss.
Cart Ticket	It is also known as cart chit or gate pass. It is prepared by the exporter and contains details regarding export cargo like number of packages, shipping bill number, port of destination, etc.

III. Documents Related to Payment of Exported Goods

Document	Explanations
Letter of Credit	It is a guarantee letter issued by the importer bank stating that it will honour the export bills to the bank of the exporter, upto a certain amount.
Bill of Exchange	It is a written document in export and import transactions in which, exporter asks the importer to pay a specified amount to a certain person or the bearer of the document. The importer claim the title of exported goods only when he accepts the order in bill of exchange.
Bank Certificate of Payment	It is a certificate specifying that necessary documents relating to the particular export consignment have been negotiated and payment has been received in accordance with the exchange control regulations.

Letter of Credit : Procedure

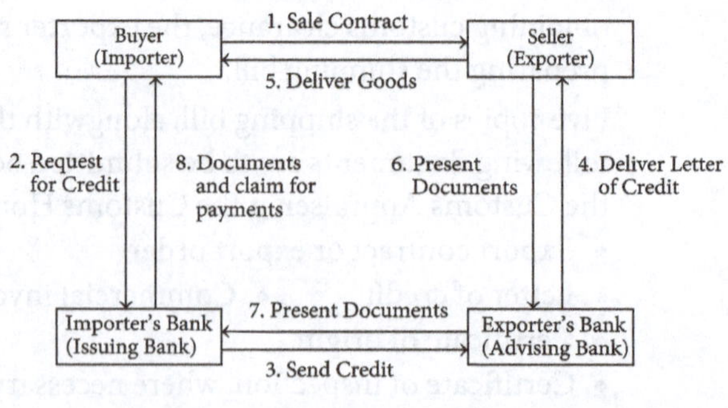

Note Document like letter of credit, bill of lading, airway bill and bill of exchange are also used in import trade.

10.3 Import Trade

It is a mode of international trade in which the residents of a domestic country purchases goods from a foreign country.

Following are the **objectives** of import trade

1. **Speed Up Industrialisation** Developing countries import scarce raw materials and capital goods and advanced technology required for rapid industrial development.
2. **Meet Consumer Demand** The goods which are in demand but are not available in the country are imported to meet consumer demand.
3. **Overcome Famine** During famine, a country can import foodgrains and other essential commodities to prevent starvation.
4. **Ensure National Defense** Countries like India import equipment for its armed forces Army, Air Force and Navy. Such imports enable the country to ensure its sovereignty and territorial integrity.

Procedure for Conducting Import Trade

Following steps are required to be followed to import goods from a foreign country

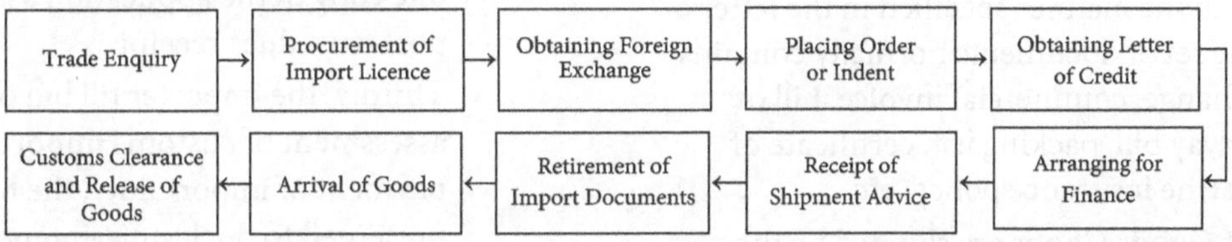

Step 1 **Trade Enquiry** Firstly, the importing firm has to gather information about the countries and firms which export the given product. The importer can gather such information from the trade directories and/or trade associations and organisations.

After identification, the importing firm approaches the export firms for collecting information about their export prices and terms of exports.

After receiving a trade enquiry, the exporter prepares a quotation and sends it to the importer. This quotation is known as **proforma invoice**.

Step 2 **Procurement of Import Licence** There are certain goods that can be imported freely, while others need licensing. The importer needs to consult the Export Import (EXIM) policy in order to know whether the goods that he/she wants to import are subject to import licensing or not.

Step 3 **Obtaining Foreign Exchange** In India, all foreign exchange transactions are regulated by the Exchange Control Department of the Reserve Bank of India (RBI). According to the rules, every importer is required to secure the sanction of foreign exchange.

For obtaining such a sanction, the importer has to make an application to a bank authorised by RBI, to issue foreign exchange. After proper scrutiny of the application, the bank sanctions the necessary foreign exchange for the import transaction.

Step 4 **Placing Order or Indent** After obtaining the import licence, the importer places an import order or indent with the exporter for supply of the specified products.

Step 5 **Obtaining Letter of Credit** If the payment terms between the importer and the overseas supplier is accepted by both parties, then the importer should obtain the letter of credit from its bank and forward it to the overseas supplier.

Step 6 **Arranging for Finance** The importer should make arrangements in advance to pay to the exporter on arrival of goods at the port. Advanced planning for financing imports is necessary, so as to avoid huge penalties to be paid on the imported goods, lying uncleared at the port.

Step 7 **Receipt of Shipment Advice** After loading the goods on the vessel, the overseas supplier dispatches the shipment advice to the importer. A shipment advice contains information about the shipment of goods.

Step 8 **Retirement of Import Documents** After shipping the goods, the overseas supplier prepares a set of necessary documents according to the terms of contract and letter of credit. The supplier hand it over to his/her banker for their onward transmission and negotiation to the importer, in the manner specified in the letter of credit. The set of documents normally contains bill of exchange, commercial invoice, bill of lading/airway bill, packing list, certificate of origin, marine insurance policy, etc.

Step 9 **Arrival of Goods** Goods are shipped by the overseas supplier according to the contract. The person incharge of the carrier (ship or airway) informs the officer incharge at the dock or the airport about the arrival of goods in the importing country. He provides the document called import general manifest.

Step 10 **Customs Clearance and Release of Goods** All the goods imported into India have to pass through customs clearance after they cross the Indian borders.

The clearance involves the following steps

- Firstly, the firm has to obtain a delivery order also known as endorsement for delivery.
  This order entitle as the importer to take delivery of goods after paying freight charges.
- Secondly the importer has to pay dock charges and obtain port trust dues receipt. The importer has to submit two copies of an application known as application to import, to the landing and shipping dues officer.
  This officer collects dock charge and gives back one copy of the application as receipt known as port trust dues receipt.
- Thirdly, the importer fill bill of entry for assessment of customs import duty. After payment of import duty, the bill has to be presented to dock superintendent for examination.
- Fourthly, upon the satisfaction of the dock superintendent, the bill will be presented to the port authority who will issue release order of the goods after receiving necessary charges.

Documents used in Import Trade

Documents used in Import Trade
- Trade Enquiry
- Proforma Invoice
- Import Order or Indent
- Shipment Advice
- Bill of Entry
- Sight Draft
- Usance Draft
- Import General Manifest
- Dock Challan

1. **Trade Enquiry** It is a written request made by an importing firm to the overseas supplier for providing information regarding the price and various terms and conditions for exporting goods.
2. **Proforma Invoice** A proforma invoice is a document that contains details of the quality, grade, design, size, weight and price of the import export product and the terms and conditions on which their import/export will take place.
3. **Import Order or Indent** It is a document in which the importer orders for supply of requisite goods to the supplier. The order contains information such as quantity and quality of goods, price of goods, method of forwarding the goods, nature of packing, mode of payment, etc.
4. **Shipment Advice** The exporter sends shipment advice to the importer for informing him that the shipment of goods has been made. It contains invoice number, bill of lading/airways bill, name of the vessel with date, the port of export, description of goods, quantity and the date of sailing of the vessel.

5. **Bill of Entry** It is a form supplied by the customs office to the importer who filled it at the time of receiving the goods. It has to be submitted to the customs office. It contains information such as name and address of the importer, name of the ship, number of packages, marks on the packages, description of goods, quantity and value of goods, name and address of the exporter, port of destinations and customs duty payable.

Bill of Entry											
Vessel		Master or Agent			Port of Shipment		Port of Destination		Importer's Name and Address		
Packages		Quantity		Description of each Class of Goods	Real Value as per Sea Customs Act		Value on which Duty is Assessed			Duty	
Number	Marks	Unit	Amount		Rate	Amount	Tariff Rate	Add Value	Amount	Rate	Amount
							Total Value ₹ ________				
							Total Duty ₹ ________				

Specimen Bill of Entry

6. **Sight Draft** It is a type of bill of exchange, wherein the drawer instructs the bank to hand over the relevant documents to the importer only against payment.
7. **Usance Draft** It is a type of bill of exchange, wherein the drawer instructs the bank to hand over the relevant documents to the importer only against the acceptance of the bill.
8. **Import General Manifest** It is a document that contains details of the imported goods. It is on the basis of this document only that unloading of cargo takes place.
9. **Dock Challan** Dock charges are to be paid when all formalities of custom are completed. While paying the dock dues, the importer or his clearing agent specifies the amount of dock dues in a form, which is known as dock challan.

10.4 World Trade Organisation (WTO)

It was setup on 1st January, 1995, replacing the General Agreement on Tariffs and Trade (GATT). The headquarters of WTO is at Geneva in Switzerland. WTO has an international status, similar to that of the International Monetary Fund (IMF) and the World Bank.

It was set-up to promote free and fair trade amongst nations. India is a founding member of WTO. All the members of WTO are required to adopt laws and policies framed under WTO rules.

Objectives of WTO

- To ensure reduction of tariffs and other trade barriers imposed by different countries.
- To engage in activities that improve the standards of living, create employment, increase income and effective demand, facilitate production, etc.
- To promote an integrated, viable, durable trading system and ensure international peace.
- To settle disputes among member nations.
- To ensure a smooth process for international trade by framing common rules and regulations.
- To accelerate economic growth of developing countries.

World Trade Organisation

Role or Functions of WTO

- **Supervision and Liberalisation** WTO is an international organisation which supervise international trade. It deals with regulation of trade between countries.
- **Lays Code of Conduct** It lays down a commonly accepted code of conduct which contains rules and regulations, so as to eliminate trade barriers.
- **Dispute Settlement Body** All disputes between member nations are settled by WTO with mutual consultations, in order to promote international peace and good trade relations. It ensures that all the member countries follow the rules and regulations prescribed in the WTO agreement act for the settlement of their disputes.
- **Operation of Revised Agreements** WTO supervises the operations of the revised agreements and ministerial declarations about the goods, services and Trade Related Intellectual Property Rights (TRIPS).

Benefits of WTO

- It helps to promote international peace and facilitates international business.
- Rules by WTO make international trade and relations very smooth and predictable.
- Free trade through WTO improves the living standard of the people by increasing the income level. Free trade also provides ample scope of getting varieties of qualitative products.
- Economic growth has been fastened because of free trade.
- The system encourages good government.
- It helps fostering growth of developing countries by providing them with special and preferential treatment in trade related matters.

Mind Map

1 Meaning of International Business

Manufacturing and trading beyond the boundaries of one's own country is known as international or external business. It can be defined as those business activities that take place across the national frontiers.

2 Advantages of International Business

To Nations
- Earning of foreign exchange
- More efficient use of resources
- Increase in employment
- Increase in standard of living
- Stability in prices

To Firms
- Prospects for higher profits
- Increased capacity utilisation
- Prospects for growth
- Way out to intense competition in domestic market
- Improved business vision

3 Scope of International Business

- **Merchandise Exports and Imports** It includes trade in goods that are tangible.
- **Services Exports and Imports** This involves trade in intangibles and therefore it is also known as invisible trade.
- **Licensing** It is permitting another party in a foreign country to produce and sell goods under one's own trademark, patents or copyrights in lieu of some fee.
- **Franchising** It is similar to licensing but it is used in connection with services only.
- **Foreign Investments** This is the investment of funds in abroad in exchange of financial return from that country in the form of profit, interest or dividend. It is of two types, i.e. Foreign Direct Investment (FDI) and portfolio investments.

4 Export Trade

It is a mode of international trade in which goods produced in the domestic country are sold to the residents of another country.

Following are the **objectives** of export trade
- To sell surplus goods
- To ensure better utilisation of resources
- To earn foreign exchange
- To increase national income
- To generate employment
- To create international cooperation

5 Procedure for Conducting Export Trade

- Receipt of enquiry and sending quotations
- Receipt of order or indent
- Assessing importer's creditworthiness and securing a guarantee for payments
- Obtaining export licence
- Obtaining pre-shipment finance
- Production or procurement of goods
- Pre-shipment inspection
- Excise clearance
- Obtaining certificate of origin
- Reservation of shipping space
- Packing and forwarding
- Insurance of goods
- Customs clearance
- Obtaining mate's receipt
- Payment of freight and issuance of bill of lading
- Preparation of invoice
- Securing payment

Documents related to Goods Exported
- Export invoice
- Packing list
- Certificate of origin
- Certificate of inspection

Documents related to Shipment of Exported Goods
- Mate's receipt
- Shipping bill
- Bill of lading
- Shipping order
- Airway bill
- Marine insurance policy
- Cart ticket

Documents related to Payment of Exported Goods
- Letter of credit
- Bill of exchange
- Bank certificate of payment

6 Import Trade

It is a mode of international trade in which the residents of a domestic country purchases goods from a foreign country.

Following are the **objectives** of import trade
- To speed up industrialisation
- To meet consumer demand
- To overcome famine
- To ensure national defense

7 Procedure for Conducting Import Trade

- Trade enquiry
- Procurement of import licence
- Obtaining foreign exchange
- Placing order or indent
- Obtaining letter of credit
- Arranging for finance
- Receipt of shipment advice
- Retirement of import documents
- Arrival of goods
- Customs clearance and release of goods

Documents used in Import Trade
- Trade enquiry
- Proforma invoice
- Import order or indent
- Shipment advice
- Bill of entry
- Sight draft
- Usance draft
- Import general manifest
- Dock challan

8 World Trade Organisation (WTO)

WTO was set-up to promote free and fair trade amongst nations. India is a founding member of WTO. All the members of WTO are required to adopt laws and policies framed under WTO rules.

Objectives
- To ensure reduction of tariffs and other trade barriers imposed by different countries
- To engage in activities that improve the standards of living, create employment, increase income and effective demand, facilitate production, etc
- To promote an integrated, viable, durable trading system and ensure international peace
- To settle disputes among member nations and ensure a smooth process for international trade by framing common rules and regulations

EXAM PATTERN QUESTIONS

Objective Type Questions

Multiple Choice Questions (MCQs)

1. Intangible aspect of services in international business is known as

(a) home trade (b) foreign trade
(c) invisible trade (d) local trade

2. Which factor of production is not part of the domestic business?

(a) Land
(b) Labour
(c) Customer (d) Capital

3. A country experiencing a surplus in the production of high quality coffee decides to export it to other nations, as domestic consumption is limited. This move not only stabilises coffee prices in the local market but also generates foreign exchange, boosts employment in the coffee industry and allows people in other countries to enjoy premium coffee.

Which of the following is not an advantage of international business? **Competency Based Que**

(a) Earning foreign exchange
(b) Better utilisation of resources
(c) Decline in employment opportunities
(d) Increase in standard of living

4. A smartphone manufacturer in a saturated domestic market decides to expand internationally. By exporting to countries with high demand and less competition, the company effectively utilises its surplus production capacity and earns higher profits. This move also aligns with its vision of becoming a global leader in the technology sector.

Which of the following is not an advantage of international business to firms? **Competency Based Que**

(a) Prospects for higher profits
(b) Intense competition in foreign markets
(c) Increased capacity utilisation
(d) Improved business vision

5. International business involves various complexities, such as managing different currencies, dealing with language barriers and complying with legal formalities. Traders often face challenges due to long distances, making quick communication difficult. Additionally, blocked capital becomes a significant issue as exporters experience delays in receiving payments, tying up their funds for extended periods.

Which of the following is a disadvantage of international business? **Competency Based Que**

(a) Language barriers
(b) Low transportation costs
(c) Standardised products
(d) Easy exchange rates

6. A textile exporter in India faces challenges due to delayed payments from an overseas buyer, leading to blocked capital. Additionally, the company must navigate complex legal formalities and convert payments received in foreign currency to Indian Rupees. Despite these hurdles, the business continues due to India's advantage in low cost labour and high quality raw materials.

Which of the following is a disadvantage of international business? **Comptency Based Que**

(a) Unequal distribution of natural resources
(b) Blocked capital due to delayed payments
(c) Availability of low cost labour
(d) Differences in productivity levels

7. Which of the following statements is incorrect?

(a) Merchandise exports and imports include trade in tangible goods such as machinery and garments
(b) Services exports and imports involve intangible goods like tourism and insurance, known as invisible trade
(c) Licensing allows a party in a foreign country to produce and sell goods under one's own trademark, patents or copyrights in exchange for a fee
(d) Foreign investments include only portfolio investments, where a company acquires shares or gives loans to another company to earn dividends and interest

8. Which of the following is a primary objective of export trade?

(a) Sell surplus goods (b) Reduce national income
(c) Import foreign goods (d) Minimise employment

9. An agricultural country, with surplus wheat production, decides to export to neighbouring nations to avoid wastage and earn foreign exchange. By exporting wheat, the country utilises its resources more effectively and generates employment opportunities in farming and logistics. This move also fosters better cooperation and trade relations with importing nations, contributing to the country's national income growth. Which of the following is not an objective of export trade? **Competency Based Que**

(a) To sell surplus goods
(b) To earn foreign exchange
(c) To reduce imports from other countries
(d) To generate employment

10. **.......... is an important step in export procedure where the prospective buyer sends an enquiry to different exporters to seek information about availability of goods.**

(a) Receipt of enquiry (b) Export license
(c) Indent (d) Production of goods

11. **Pradeep wants to export auto spare parts to Mr. David in Switzerland. Mr. David has asked for an enquiry to seek information about availability of goods, price, quality and terms and conditions for export of goods. In response to the enquiry, Pradeep sends a reply in the form of proforma invoice.**

Mr. David found the price and terms and conditions acceptable. So, he placed the order for goods. After verifying the creditworthiness of Mr. David, Pradeep obtains an export licence and arranges the pre-shipment finance.

On the basis of given case study, state the next step to be followed by Pradeep related to the procedure of export trade. **Competency Based Que**

(a) Procurement of goods (b) Pre-shipment inspection
(c) Excise clearance (d) None of these

12. **Raj Exports received an enquiry from a French buyer requesting details about their textile products, including pricing and delivery terms. After sending a quotation, the French buyer placed an order, agreeing to the stated terms. Before proceeding, Raj exports assessed the buyer's creditworthiness and requested a letter of credit to secure payment.**

Once assured, they initiated steps to obtain an export licence, including registration with the export promotion council and obtaining an import export code.

Which document ensures the exporter minimises the risk of non-payment by the importer?

Competency Based Que

(a) Commercial invoice (b) Certificate of origin
(c) Letter of credit (d) Duty drawback

13. **Which of the following statements is incorrect?**

(a) Mate's receipt is issued by the captain or mate of the ship after loading the goods on board
(b) Certificate of inspection is issued by the Export Inspection Council of India to certify that the consignment has been inspected as required under the Export (Quality Control and Inspection) Act, 1963
(c) Marine insurance policy provides a contract between the exporter and the insurance company to indemnify against loss or damage to goods during transit
(d) Sight draft is a type of bill of exchange where the importer accepts the bill only after receiving the goods

14. **Which of the following statements is incorrect?**

(a) Packing list provides complete details regarding the goods exported and how they are packed
(b) Import order or indent specifies the quantity and quality of goods, price, method of forwarding and mode of payment
(c) Bill of entry contains information such as the importer's name, ship name, description of goods and customs duty payable
(d) Pre-shipment finance is required after production or procurement of goods to facilitate the shipment process

15. **Cart ticket is also known as**

(a) cart chit (b) gate pass
(c) vehicle pass (d) All of these

16. **Certificate of inspection is issued by**

(a) captain of the ship (b) exporter's bank
(c) insurance company
(d) Export Inspection Council of India

17. **The exporter has to open a bank account in any bank authorised by .... to deal in foreign exchange.**

(a) State Bank of India
(b) Reserve Bank of India
(c) Central Government
(d) State Government

18. **With the help of picture given below, identify the document which is issued by commanding officer of the ship to the exporter after the cargo is loaded on the ship.**

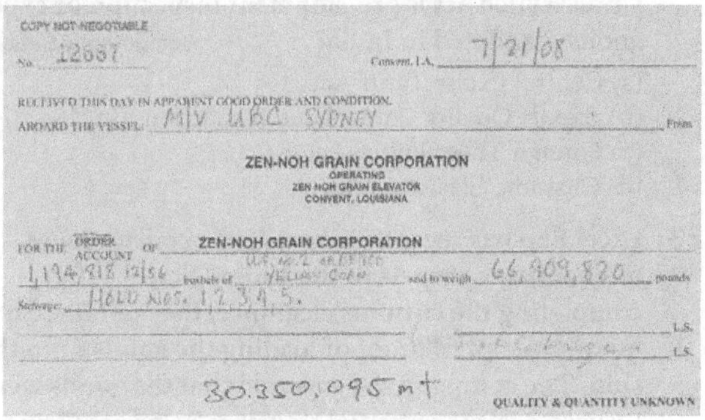
COPY NOT NEGOTIABLE
No. 12687 Convent, LA. 7/21/08
RECEIVED THIS DAY IN APPARENT GOOD ORDER AND CONDITION,
ABOARD THE VESSEL M/V UBC SYDNEY From
ZEN-NOH GRAIN CORPORATION
OPERATING
ZEN NOH GRAIN ELEVATOR
CONVENT, LOUISIANA
FOR THE ORDER ACCOUNT OF ZEN-NOH GRAIN CORPORATION
1,194,918 12/56 bushels of YELLOW CORN said to weigh 66,909,820 pounds
Stowage HOLD NOS. 1,2,3,4,5.
L.S.
L.S.
30.350,095 mt
QUALITY & QUANTITY UNKNOWN

(a) Certificate of origin (b) Mate's receipt
(c) Letter of credit (d) None of these

19. **With the help of picture given below, identify the document which is prepared by the importer and it show the details of goods imported and is used by custom authorities to determine import duty.**

Vessel		Master or Agent			Port of Shipment	Port of Destination			Importer's Name and Address		
Packages		Quantity		Description of each Class of Goods	Real Value as per Sea Customs Act		Value on which Duty is Assessed			Duty	
Number	Marks	Unit	Amount		Rate	Amount	Tariff Rate	Add Value	Amount	Rate	Amount
									Total Value ₹ ________ Total Duty ₹ ________		

(a) Certificate of Origin (b) Mate's Receipt
(c) Bill of Entry (d) None of these

20. **Mohan, an exporter sent complete information about the quality, grade, size, weight and type of packing of the product on his enquiry. Such an above quotation prepared is known as** **Competency Based Que**

(a) performa invoice (b) intent
(c) letter of information (d) enquiry performa

21. **Performa invoice is issued by the**

(a) shipping company of importer
(b) exporter to importer
(c) importer to exporter
(d) exporter to the shipping company

22. **Global Traders, a spice exporter, completed production as per the importer's specifications and obtained pre-shipment finance for packing and transport. Before shipment, the goods underwent mandatory inspection under the Export Quality Control and Inspection Act, 1963.**

The exporter then arranged insurance to safeguard the goods against damage during transit and submitted the required documents, including a shipping bill, to the customs office for clearance.

Under which act is pre-shipment inspection of export goods mandated in India? **Competency Based Que**

(a) Central Excise Tariff Act
(b) Export Quality Control and Inspection Act, 1963
(c) Foreign Trade Policy Act
(d) Customs Clearance Act

23. **Excel Exports recently dispatched a consignment of handmade carpets to the United States. After completing the customs clearance, they obtained a mate's receipt as proof of loading the goods onto the ship. The company also ensured that the goods were insured against potential transit risks by acquiring a marine insurance policy.**

Additionally, a bill of lading was issued by the shipping company, which served as evidence of acceptance to transport the goods and acted as the title to the consignment. The importer required a certificate of origin to avail of tariff concessions for the carpets.

Which document serves as evidence of acceptance by the shipping company to transport goods and acts as the title to the consignment? **Competency Based Que**

(a) Export invoice (b) Bill of lading
(c) Marine insurance policy
(d) Mate's receipt

24. **TechWave Solutions, a domestic company in India, recently imported large quantities of foodgrains from neighbouring countries due to a poor harvest caused by unexpected droughts in the region. The company, alongside government initiatives, aimed to ensure a steady food supply to the public and prevent a potential food crisis.**

By importing these grains, TechWave Solutions helped meet the immediate demand for food and contribute to national food security. This decision was made in light of the country's limited domestic production and the urgent need to address the food shortage. Which of the following is an objective of import trade? **Competency Based Que**

(a) Export surplus goods
(b) Overcome famine
(c) Strengthen international cooperation
(d) Increase national income

25. **An Indian exporter wants to export electronic goods to Japan. He prepares a document and includes the details of the cargo in terms of the shippers name, the name of the vessel, port where goods are to be discharges, etc. What is this document called?** **Competency Based Que**

(a) Shipping bill (b) Shipping order
(c) Airway bill (d) Bill of lading

26. **"The goods were not loaded on the ship as they did not get the customs clearance due to lack of one of the main documents."**

Identify the document which was required among the following. **Competency Based Que**

(a) Bill of clearance (b) Custom bill
(c) Shipping bill (d) Bill of exchange

27. **Which of the following is not the objective of import trade?**

(a) To meet consumer demand
(b) To improve the standard of living
(c) To speed up industrialisation
(d) To earn foreign exchange

28. **Having identified the countries and firms that export the product, the importing firm approaches the export firms with the help of**

(a) trade enquiry
(b) proforma invoice
(c) mate's receipt 186 advertisement
(d) sight draft

29. **Which of the following document is required in connection with an import transaction?**
(a) Certificate of origin (b) Shipping bill
(c) Letter of credit (d) Mate's receipt

30. **The document used in import trade that provides details about the imported goods and is necessary for unloading the cargo. Identify the correct document from the options below.**
(a) Proforma invoice (b) Bill of entry
(c) Shipment advice (d) Import general manifest

31. **World Trade Organisation (WTO) was founded in 1995 to deal with rules and regulations of international trade. Which of the following is not an objective of WTO?**
(a) Raising standards of living
(b) Raising income
(c) Ensuring full employment
(d) Boosting growth of developed countries

32. **The WTO Acts as a dispute settlement body, where disputes between member nations are resolved through mutual consultations to ensure international peace and good trade relations.**

Identify the role of WTO highlighted in the above statement. **Competency Based Que**
(a) Supervision and liberalisation
(b) Lays code of conduct
(c) Dispute settlement body
(d) Operation of revised agreements

33. **WTO aims to reduce tariffs and other trade barriers, promote economic growth and create a smooth process for international trade by establishing common rules and regulations. Identify the primary objectives of WTO mentioned in the above statement.** **Competency Based Que**
(a) To ensure reduction of tariffs and other trade barriers
(b) To engage in export activities
(c) To deal only with trade of goods
(d) All of the above

Direction *Read the case study and answer the questions 34 to 37 on the basis of the same*

Green Earth Handicrafts Ltd. a reputed name in the handicrafts industry, has been producing eco-friendly decorative items for over 15 years.
Known for its intricate designs and sustainable practices, the company has a strong local customer base. However, due to increasing competition in the domestic market and the rise of cheaper alternatives, the company's sales have been declining over the past five years.

To counter this challenge, the marketing team suggested exploring international markets and collaborating with distributors nationwide to enhance their reach. The financial manager highlighted that government policies encourage handicrafts exports by offering incentives and marketing assistance. The company believes this approach could open new avenues for growth while supporting the national economy.

34. **Which of the following is not a benefit of foreign trade to a nation?**
(a) Promotes cultural exchange
(b) Reduces unemployment
(c) Leads to overdependence on foreign markets
(d) None of the above

35. **A distributor helps a manufacturer to enjoy economies of scale by**
(a) providing storage facilities
(b) delivering goods on credit
(c) bearing promotional expenses
(d) placing bulk orders

36. **International trade can help resolve challenges of intense domestic competition by**
(a) exploring new foreign markets
(b) increasing focus on rural domestic markets
(c) reducing production costs
(d) developing a monopoly in the domestic market

37. **International business activities include which of the following?**
(a) Export and import of goods and services
(b) Joint ventures and strategic alliances
(c) Technology transfer and foreign direct investment
(d) All of the above

Assertion-Reason

Direction (Q. No. 38 to 47) *Read the following Assertion (A) and Reason (R) and choose the correct alternative from the following*

Alternatives
(a) Both Assertion (A) and Reason (R) are true and Reason (R) is the correct explanation of Assertion (A)
(b) Both Assertion (A) and Reason (R) are true, but Reason (R) is not the correct explanation of Assertion (A)
(c) Assertion (A) is true, but Reason (R) is false
(d) Assertion (A) is false, but Reason (R) is true

38. **Assertion** (A) International business and international trade are one and the same thing.

Reason (R) International business involves the international movements of goods and services, capital, personnel, technology and intellectual property.

39. **Assertion** (A) Countries exchange their surplus production with goods that they are in short supply with other countries.

Reason (R) All the countries cannot produce equally well due to uneven distribution of natural resources.

40. **Assertion** (A) Obtaining an export licence is a crucial step in completing an export transaction.

Reason (R) An export licence ensures compliance with export regulations and allows goods to be legally exported.

41. **Assertion** (A) Pre-shipment finance is essential for exporting goods.

Reason (R) Pre-shipment finance is required for acquiring raw materials and packaging goods for export.

42. **Assertion** (A) A certificate of origin helps in availing tariff concessions in import trade.

Reason (R) It specifies the country of origin and enables exemptions from certain import restrictions.

43. **Assertion** (A) An exporter must secure payment after the shipment of goods.

Reason (R) Documents like letter of credit and bill of Exchange are used to ensure payment.

44. **Assertion** (A) Excise clearance is necessary for exported goods.

Reason (R) Excise duty can be exempted or refunded for goods meant for exports.

45. **Assertion** (A) Shipping documents such as mate's receipt and bill of lading are used in export trade.

Reason (R) They act as evidence of goods being accepted by the shipping company.

46. **Assertion** (A) Letter of credit is the most appropriate and secure method of payment to settle international transactions.

Reason (R) Letter of credit is a guarantee issued by the exporter's bank.

47. **Assertion** (A) The WTO supervises the liberalisation of international trade.

Reason (R) It establishes rules to eliminate trade barriers between member countries.

Two Statements Based MCQs

Direction (Q. No. 48 to 57) *Read the following statements carefully and choose the correct alternative*

Alternatives

(a) Statement I is correct and Statement II is incorrect
(b) Statement II is correct and Statement I is incorrect
(c) Both the statements are correct
(d) Both the statements are incorrect

48. **Statement I** Customers are more homogeneous in their taste, preferences, consumption patterns and buying behaviour in case of international business.

Statement II Production cost of a particular good differs in different countries due to difference in socio economic, geographical and political conditions.

49. **Statement I** Exporters need to secure a letter of credit to minimise the risk of non-payment by the importer.

Statement II The Bill of Lading Acts as proof of goods ownership and transportation.

50. **Statement I** Pre-shipment inspection is mandatory for all exports as per the Export (Quality Control and Inspection) Act, 1963.

Statement II Excise duty is exempted for goods meant for export.

51. **Statement I** The certificate of origin is required for availing tariff concessions in importing countries.

Statement II A packing list provides details regarding the shipping and delivery instructions.

52. **Statement I** A railway receipt serves as a title document for goods transported via railway to the port of shipment.

Statement II Pre-shipment finance is used for acquiring raw materials and other components needed for export production.

53. **Statement I** The shipping bill contains details regarding the goods being exported and port of destination.

Statement II Mate's receipt is issued after the goods are loaded onto the ship.

54. **Statement I** WTO helps in promoting free trade and economic growth.

Statement II India is not a member of WTO.

55. **Statement I** WTO supervises and liberalises international trade between member countries.

Statement II Disputes between member countries under WTO are settled through bilateral agreements.

56. **Statement I** The World Trade Organisation (WTO) facilitates Trade Related Intellectual Property Rights (TRIPS).

Statement II India obtained its Import Export Code (IEC) from the Directorate General Foreign Trade (DGFT).

57. **Statement I** The WTO was established on 1st January, 1995, to replace GATT.

Statement II WTO headquarters are located in Washington, DC.

Matching

58. Match the following

Column I	Column II
A. Export invoice	(i) Information about goods including quantity, number of packages, ship name, delivery terms and payments.
B. Packing list	(ii) Specifies the country of manufacture, used for tariff concessions or exemptions.
C. Certificate of origin	(iii) Details regarding the goods exported and the form in which they are sent.
D. Certificate of inspection	(iv) Certifies that the consignment has been inspected under the Export (Quality Control and Inspection) Act.

Codes

	A	B	C	D		A	B	C	D
(a)	(ii)	(i)	(iii)	(iv)	(b)	(iv)	(iii)	(ii)	(i)
(c)	(i)	(iii)	(ii)	(iv)	(d)	(ii)	(iii)	(i)	(iv)

59. Match the following

Column I	Column II
A. Mate's receipt	(i) Instruction to the ship's captain to receive goods on board after customs clearance.
B. Shipping bill	(ii) Evidence of goods being accepted by the shipping company.
C. Bill of lading	(iii) Grants permission for export by customs office, includes details such as vessel name and destination country.
D. Shipping order	(iv) Issued by the ship's captain after loading goods on board.

Codes

	A	B	C	D		A	B	C	D
(a)	(ii)	(i)	(iii)	(iv)	(b)	(iv)	(iii)	(ii)	(i)
(c)	(i)	(iii)	(ii)	(iv)	(d)	(ii)	(iii)	(i)	(iv)

60. Match the following

Column I	Column II
A. Proforma invoice	(i) Form filled by the importer at customs, containing details like importer's name, ship name and package descriptions.
B. Import order or indent	(ii) Sent by the exporter to inform the importer about the shipment.
C. Shipment advice	(iii) A document ordering the supply of goods from the supplier, detailing quantity, quality, etc.
D. Bill of entry	(iv) Contains details of quality, grade, design, size, weight, price and terms for import/export.

Codes

	A	B	C	D		A	B	C	D
(a)	(ii)	(i)	(iii)	(iv)	(b)	(iv)	(iii)	(ii)	(i)
(c)	(i)	(iii)	(ii)	(iv)	(d)	(ii)	(iii)	(i)	(iv)

61. Match the following

Column I	Column II
A. Country in which the goods are produced	(i) Shipment advice
B. Quality of goods	(ii) Certificate of origin
C. Description of goods and quantity	(iii) Trade inquiry
D. Written request by the importer	(iv) Certificate of inspection

Codes

	A	B	C	D		A	B	C	D
(a)	(ii)	(iv)	(i)	(iii)	(b)	(iv)	(iii)	(ii)	(i)
(c)	(i)	(iii)	(ii)	(iv)	(d)	(ii)	(iii)	(i)	(iv)

62. Match the following

Column I	Column II
A. Supervision and liberalisation	(i) WTO oversees the implementation of revised agreements and ministerial declarations related to goods, services and TRIPS.
B. Lays code of conduct	(ii) WTO resolves disputes between member nations through mutual consultations and promotes good trade relations.
C. Dispute settlement body	(iii) WTO establishes a code of conduct with rules and regulations to eliminate trade barriers.
D. Operation of revised agreements	(iv) WTO supervises international trade and regulates trade between countries.

Codes

	A	B	C	D		A	B	C	D
(a)	(ii)	(i)	(iii)	(iv)	(b)	(iv)	(iii)	(ii)	(i)
(c)	(i)	(iii)	(ii)	(iv)	(d)	(ii)	(iii)	(i)	(iv)

Answers

1. (c) invisible trade
2. (c) Customer
3. (c) Decline in employment opportunities
4. (b) Intense competition in foreign markets
5. (a) Language barriers
6. (b) Blocked capital due to delayed payments
7. (d) Foreign investments include both Foreign Direct Investments (FDI) and portfolio investments.
8. (a) Sell surplus goods
9. (c) To reduce imports from other countries
10. (a) Receipt of enquiry
11. (a) Procurement of goods
12. (c) Letter of credit
13. (d) Sight draft is a type of bill of exchange, in which the drawer (i.e. exporter) instructs the bank to hand over the relevant documents to the importer only against payment.
14. (d) Pre-shipment finance is actually required before the production or procurement of goods.
15. (d) All of these
16. (d) Export Inspection Council of India
17. (b) Reserve Bank of India
18. (b) Mate's receipt
19. (c) Bill of Entry
20. (a) performa invoice
21. (b) exporter to importer
22. (b) Export Quality Control and Inspection Act, 1963
23. (b) Bill of lading
24. (b) Overcome famine
25. (a) Shipping bill
26. (c) Shipping bill
27. (d) To earn foreign exchange
28. (a) trade enquiry
29. (c) Letter of credit
30. (d) Import general manifest
31. (d) Boosting growth of developed countries
32. (c) Dispute settlement body
33. (a) To ensure reduction of tariffs and other trade barriers
34. (c) Leads to overdependence on foreign markets
35. (d) placing bulk orders
36. (a) exploring new foreign markets
37. (d) All of the above
38. (d) International business including trade, also encompasses other activities such as foreign direct investment, strategic alliances and cross border movement of resources beyond just goods and services.
39. (a) Both Assertion (A) and Reason (R) are true and Reason (R) is the correct explanation of Assertion (A)
40. (a) Both Assertion (A) and Reason (R) are true and Reason (R) is the correct explanation of Assertion (A)
41. (a) Both Assertion (A) and Reason (R) are true and Reason (R) is the correct explanation of Assertion (A)
42. (a) Both Assertion (A) and Reason (R) are true and Reason (R) is the correct explanation of Assertion (A)
43. (a) Both Assertion (A) and Reason (R) are true and Reason (R) is the correct explanation of Assertion (A)
44. (a) Both Assertion (A) and Reason (R) are true and Reason (R) is the correct explanation of Assertion (A)
45. (a) Both Assertion (A) and Reason (R) are true and Reason (R) is the correct explanation of Assertion (A)
46. (c) Letter of credit is issued by a bank, which guarantees payment to the exporter through a third party bank rather than directly issued by the exporter's bank.
47. (a) Both Assertion (A) and Reason (R) are true and Reason (R) is the correct explanation of Assertion (A)
48. (b) Customers are not homogenous as their tastes, preferences, consumption patterns and buying behaviour differ.
49. (c) Both the statements are correct
50. (c) Both the statements are correct
51. (c) Both the statements are correct
52. (c) Both the statements are correct
53. (c) Both the statements are correct
54. (a) India is a founding member of WTO and it plays a significant role in international trade under WTO.
55. (a) WTO settles disputes through a structured Dispute Settlement Body (DSB), not bilateral agreements.
56. (c) Both the statements are correct
57. (a) WTO's headquarters are located in Geneva, Switzerland, not Washington, DC
58. (c) (i) (iii) (ii) (iv)
59. (b) (iv) (iii) (ii) (i)
60. (b) (iv) (iii) (ii) (i)
61. (a) (ii) (iv) (i) (iii)
62. (b) (iv) (iii) (ii) (i)

Subjective Questions

Short Answer Type Questions

1. "International business plays a significant role in expanding market reach and increasing profitability for firms. By engaging in cross border trade, businesses can access new markets and reduce dependence on domestic demand." In the context of the given statement, discuss any four advantages of international business to firms. **Competency Based Que**

Ans. Following are advantages of international business to firms

(i) **Prospects for Higher Profits**
When prices in the domestic market are low, firms can earn more profits by selling their products in those countries in which prices are high.

(ii) **Prospects for Growth**
When the domestic demand for a firm's product or services start getting saturated in the domestic market, then firms can considerably improve prospects of their growth by venturing out in the international market.

(iii) **Way Out to Intense Competition in Domestic Market**
Highly competitive domestic market drives many companies to go international in search of markets for their products.

(iv) **Increased Capacity Utilisation**
Many business and industrial enterprises have unused capacity, that can be efficiently utilised for further production. Thus, surplus production can be used to generate extra profits from foreign trade.

2. "While international business opens up opportunities for firms to grow and thrive globally, it also poses several challenges that can hinder their operations. These challenges may include economic risks, cultural differences and compliance with foreign regulations." In the context of the given statement, discuss any four disadvantages of international business. **Competency Based Que**

Ans. Following are the disadvantages of international business

(i) **Distance**
Due to long distances between countries, it is difficult to establish personal and quick contacts between traders from different countries. There is a large time gap between the placement of order and receipt of goods from foreign countries.

(ii) **Different Currency**
Each country has its own currency. Payment for imported goods is made in foreign currency and payment for export is also received in foreign currency.

(iii) **Different Languages**
Different languages are spoken and written in different countries. It is therefore, difficult for traders to understand each other.

One must know the foreign language or appoint someone to read the price lists of foreign countries.

(iv) **Legal Formalities**
International business is monitored by the government. Prior permission has to be obtained before exporting or importing goods or services. A large number of documents have to be filed and custom duties are paid on imports and exports.

3. Briefly discuss the various reasons which justify the need for international business.

Or **What is the major reason underlying trade between nations?** **NCERT**

Ans. Need for international business exists because of the following reasons

(i) Unequal distribution of natural resources among them or differences in their productivity levels.

(ii) Availability of various factors of production such as labour, capital and raw materials, differ among nations.

(iii) Labour productivity and production cost differ among nations due to various socio-economic, geographical and political reasons.

4. Differentiate between international trade and international business. **NCERT**

Ans. Following are the differences between international trade and international business.

Basis	International Trade	International Business
Meaning	International trade refers to the exchange of goods and services across the international boundaries of countries.	International business not only includes movement of capital, of goods and services, but also of capital personnel, technology and intellectual property like patents, trademark, know how and copyrights.
Movement	International trade means movement of goods only.	A business transaction that takes place between two or more countries is known as international business.
Scope	International trade is a narrow term.	International business is much broader than international trade.

5. Discuss the objectives of import trade.

Ans. Following are the objectives of import trade

(i) **Speed Up Industrialisation**
Developing countries import scarce raw materials and capital goods and advanced technology required for rapid industrial development.

(ii) **Meet Consumer Demand**
The goods which are in demand but are not available in the country are imported to meet consumer demand.

(iii) **Overcome Famine**
During famine, a country can import foodgrains and other essential commodities to prevent starvation.

(iv) **Ensure National Defense**
Countries like India import equipment for its armed forces army, air force and navy. Such imports enable the country to ensure its sovereignty and territorial integrity.

6. "Export trade is an essential component of international business that facilitates economic growth, employment generation and foreign exchange earnings. Countries and firms engage in export trade to achieve specific economic and strategic objectives." In the context of the given statement, discuss the objectives of export trade. Competency Based Que

Ans. Following are the objectives of export trade (any four)

(i) **Sell Surplus Goods**
A country may produce a commodity in such quantities that are more than its needs. The country can sell its surplus output to foreign countries. In this way, export trade is undertaken to make productive use of surplus goods.

(ii) **Better Utilisation of Resources**
Export trade widens the market for goods. A country can make better utilisation of its resources by producing goods on a large-scale, both for domestic use and for export.

(iii) **Earn Foreign Exchange**
A country can earn valuable foreign exchange through export.

(iv) **Increase National Income**
Export trade helps a country to increase its national income.

(v) **Generate Employment**
The growth of export trade also creates employment opportunities.

7. Write a short note
(i) Mate's receipt
(ii) Letter of credit

Ans.

(i) **Mate's Receipt**
A mate receipt is issued by the commanding officer of the ship when the cargo is loaded on board and contains the information about the name of the vessel, berth, date of shipment, description of packages, markings and number, cargo condition when received on board the ship and so on. The port superintendent, on receipt of port dues, hands over the mate's receipt to the C&F agent.

(ii) **Letter of Credit**
A letter of credit is guarantee issued by the importer's bank that it will honour payment, up to a certain amount of export bills, to the bank of the exporter. Most exporters want a letter of credit from the importer to mitigate such risks.

8. What is bill of lading? How does it differ from bill of entry? NCERT

Or **"The bill of lading is a crucial shipping document that serves as evidence of the contract of carriage. On the other hand, the bill of entry is an import document filed for customs clearance."**
In the light of the above statement, highlight the differences between bill of lading and bill of entry. Competency Based Que

Ans. Bill of lading is issued by the shipping company after the receipt of freight. It serves as an evidence that the shipping company has accepted the goods for carrying them to the designated destination. In case the goods are being sent by air, this document is referred to as airway bill.

On the other hand, bill of entry' is filled by the importer for assessment of customs import duty. An appraiser examines the document carefully and gives the examination order.

The importer procures the said document prepared by the appraiser and pays the duty, if any. After payment of the import duty, the bill of entry has to be presented to the dock superintendent. The examiner gives his report on the bill of entry which is then presented to the port authority, which issues the release order after receiving necessary charges.

9. "The World Trade Organisation (WTO) plays a pivotal role in regulating international trade and ensuring a smooth flow of goods and services across countries. By setting trade rules and resolving disputes, the WTO promotes free and fair trade globally." In the context of the given statement, briefly explain the role of the WTO in international business. Competency Based Que

Ans. The role or functions of WTO are

(i) **Supervision and Liberalisation**
WTO is an international organisation which supervise international trade. It deals with regulation of trade between countries.

(ii) **Lays Code of Conduct**
It lays down a commonly accepted code of conduct which contains rules and regulations, so as to eliminate trade barriers.

(iii) **Dispute Settlement Body**
All disputes between member nations are settled by WTO with mutual consultations, in order to promote international peace and good trade relations. It ensures that all the member countries follow the rules and regulations prescribed in the WTO Agreement Act for the settlement of their disputes.

(iv) **Operation of Revised Agreements**
WTO supervises the operations of the revised agreements and ministerial declarations about the goods, services and Trade Related Intellectual Property Rights (TRIPS).

10. Discuss the benefits of WTO.

Ans. Following are the benefits of WTO (any four)

(i) It helps to promote international peace and facilitates international business.

(ii) Rules by WTO make international trade and relations very smooth and predictable.

(iii) Free trade through WTO improves the living standard of the people by increasing the income level. Free trade also provides ample scope of getting varieties of qualitative products.

(iv) Economic growth has been fastened because of free trade.

(v) The system encourages good government.

(vi) It helps fostering growth of developing countries by providing them with special and preferential treatment in trade related matters.

Long Answer Type Questions

11. "International business is more than international trade." Comment. NCERT

Ans. It is right to say that international business is more than international trade as international trade is a part of international business. International business includes the following

(i) **International Trade**
It comprises of buying and selling of goods and services beyond the geographical borders of the country. It is also referred to as 'foreign trade' or 'external trade'. It can also be understood as exchange of goods and services between residents of different countries.It involves the use of foreign exchange to discharge trade obligations.

(ii) **Exporting and Importing**
Exporting refers to selling of goods and services by a firm of home country to a firm of foreign country. Importing refers to buying of goods and services by a firm of home country from a firm of foreign country.

(iii) **Licencing and Franchising**
Licencing is a contractual arrangement in which one firm grants access to its patents, trademarks or technology to another firm in a foreign country. Franchising is a contractual agreement which involves grant of rights by one party to another for use of technology, trademarks and patents in return of the agreed payment for a certain period of time.

(iv) **Foreign Investments**
This is the investment of funds in abroad in exchange of financial return from that country in the form of profit, interest or dividend. It is of two types

- **Foreign Direct Investments** (FDI) It takes place when a company directly invests in properties such as plant and machinery, land and building to undertake production and marketing of goods and services in those countries.
- **Portfolio Investments** It takes place when a company invests in another company by acquiring shares of that company or giving them loans and earn dividend on shares and interest on loans.

12. "Domestic businesses primarily cater to customers within the geographical boundaries of a single country, while international businesses expand beyond these boundaries to serve global markets."
In the context of the given statement, highlight the key differences between domestic business and international business. Competency Based Que

Ans. Following are the differences between domestic business and international business

Basis	Domestic Business	International Business
Nationality of Buyers and Sellers	It involves dealings between people or organisation from the same country.	It involves dealings between people or organisation from the different countries.
Nationality of Other Stakeholders	Other stakeholders such as suppliers, employees, middlemen, shareholders and partners are usually citizens of the same country.	Other stakeholders such as suppliers, employees, middlemen, shareholders and partners are from different countries.

Basis	Domestic Business	International Business
Mobility of Factors of Production	The mobility of factors of production like labour and capital is relatively more within a country.	The mobility of factors of production like labour and capital across nations is relatively less.
Customer Heterogeneity Across Markets	The customers are homogeneous in the domestic market.	The customers are heterogeneous in the international market.
Differences in Business Systems	The business systems are likely to be more similar within a country.	The variation in business system is likely to be more across countries.
Currency Used	Currency of domestic country is used.	It involves use of currencies of more than one country.

13. Rekha Garments has received an order to export 2000 men's trousers to Swift Imports Limited located in Australia.

Discuss the procedure that Rekha Garments would need to go through for executing the export order.

NCERT; Competency Based Que

Ans. Steps involved in executing the export order are

(i) **Assessing Creditworthiness of Swift Imports Limited and Securing a Guarantee for Payments**
After receiving the receipt of indent, Rekha Garments should make necessary enquiry about the creditworthiness of Swift Imports Limited in order to assess the risks of non-payment by the importer.

(ii) **Obtaining Export Licence**
After assuring about payments, the exporting firm Rekha Garments would initiate the steps relating to compliance of export regulations which demand that the export firm must have an export licence before it proceeds with exports.

(iii) **Obtaining Pre-shipment Finance**
Rekha Garments would then approach its banker for obtaining pre-shipment finance to undertake export production, for procuring raw materials and other components, processing and packing of goods and transportation of goods to the port of shipment.

(iv) **Production or Procurement of Goods**
Rekha Garments would proceed to get the goods ready as per the specifications of the importer. Either the firm would itself produce the goods or else buy them from the market.

(v) **Pre-shipment Inspection**
If the product to be exported comes under the category of compulsory inspection, Rekha Garments needs to contact the Export Inspection Agency (EIA) or any other designated agency for obtaining inspection certificate.

(vi) **Excise Clearance**
Rekha Garments would then have to apply to the concerned Excise Commissioner in the region with an invoice. If the Excise Commissioner is satisfied, he would issue the excise clearance. Rekha Garments may get the refund of excise duty known as duty drawback, as it is exporting the goods.

(vii) **Obtaining Certificate of Origin**
Some importing countries provide tariff concessions or other exemptions to the goods coming from a particular country. If such benefits are available, the importer may ask the exporter to send a certificate of origin.

(viii) **Reservation of Shipping Space**
The exporting firm applies to the shipping company for provision of shipping space. It has to specify the types of goods to be exported, probable date of shipment and the port of destination. On acceptance of application for shipping, the shipping company issues a shipping order.

(ix) **Packing and Forwarding**
The goods are then properly packed and marked with necessary details such as name and address of the importer, gross and net weight, port of shipment and destination, country of origin, etc. Rekha Garments would then have to make necessary arrangement for transportation of goods to the port.

(x) **Insurance of Goods**
Rekha Garments would then get the goods insured with an insurance company to protect against the risks of loss or damage of the goods due to the perils of the sea during the transit.

(xi) **Customs Clearance**
The goods must be cleared from the customs before these can be loaded on the ship. For obtaining customs clearance, Rekha Garments would have to prepare the shipping bill. Five copies of the shipping bill alongwith the other required documents would then be submitted to the Customs Appraiser at the customs house.

(xii) **Obtaining Mate's Receipt**
The goods are then loaded on the ship for which the mate or the captain of the ship issues mate's receipt to the port superintendent.

(xiii) **Payment of Freight and Issuance of Bill of Lading**
After the receipt of freight, the shipping company would issue a bill of lading, which serves as an evidence that the shipping company has accepted the goods for carrying them to the designated destination.

(xiv) **Preparation of Invoice**

After sending the goods, an invoice of the dispatched goods would be prepared. The invoice states the quantity of goods sent and the amount to be paid by the importer and would be presented to Swift Imports Limited for payment.

14. Your firm is planning to import textile machinery from Canada. Describe the procedure involved in importing. NCERT

Ans. Following procedure is involved in importing textile machinery from Canada

(i) **Trade Enquiry**

The importing firm will approach the textile machinery export firms in Canada with the help of trade enquiry and collect information about their export prices and terms of exports.

After receiving a trade enquiry, the exporter will prepare a quotation called proforma invoice and send it to our firm.

(ii) **Procurement of Import Licence**

We will consult the Export Import (EXIM) Policy to know whether the textile machinery imports are subject to import licensing.

In case it can be imported only against the license, we will procure an import license.

(iii) **Obtaining Foreign Exchange**

As payment for imports will be made in Canadian dollars, our firm will have to make an application to a bank authorised by RBI to issue foreign exchange.

(iv) **Placing Order or Indent**

After obtaining the import license, our firm will place an import order or indent with the exporter for supply of the specified products containing information about the price, quantity, grade and quality of machinery and the instructions relating to packing, shipping, ports of shipment and destination, delivery schedule, insurance and mode of payment.

(v) **Obtaining Letter of Credit**

If the payment terms are agreed between us and the overseas supplier, then our firm should obtain the letter of credit from its bank and forward it to the overseas supplier.

(vi) **Arranging for Finance**

Our firm would make arrangements in advance to pay to the exporter on arrival of goods at the port.

(vii) **Receipt of Shipment Advice**

After loading the ordered textile machinery on the vessel, the overseas supplier will dispatch the shipment advice to our firm which contains information about the shipment of goods.

(viii) **Retirement of Import Documents**

After shipping the machinery, the overseas supplier will prepare a set of necessary documents including bill of exchange, commercial invoice, bill of lading/airway bill, packing list, certificate of origin, marine insurance policy, etc.

He will hand it over to his or her banker for their onward transmission. The acceptance of bill of exchange for the purpose of getting delivery of the documents is known as retirement of import documents, after which the bank will handover the import documents to the importer.

(ix) **Arrival of Goods**

Goods will be shipped by the overseas supplier as per the contract. The officer incharge at the dock will provide the document called Import General Manifest on the basis of which unloading of cargo will take place.

(x) **Customs Clearance and Release of Goods**

Textile machinery imported into India will have to pass through customs clearance. Firstly, the firm will have to obtain a delivery order, pay dock dues and obtain port trust dues receipt. Then it fill in a form 'bill of entry' for assessment of customs import duty. After payment of the import duty, the bill of entry has to be presented to the dock superintendent.

The examiner will give his report on the bill of entry and we will present the bill of entry to the port authority who will issue the release order after receiving necessary charges.

15. Explain the meaning of the following documents used in connection with import transactions.

(i) Trade enquiry **(ii) Proforma invoice**
(iii) Shipment advice **(iv) Import general manifest**
(v) Bill of entry

Ans.

(i) **Trade Enquiry**

It is a written request by an importing firm to the exporter for supply of information regarding the price and various terms and conditions on which the latter is ready to exports goods.

(ii) **Proforma Invoice**

A proforma invoice is a document that contains details of the quality, grade, design, size, weight and price of the import export product and the terms and conditions on which their import/export will take place.

(iii) **Shipment Advice**

It contains information about the shipment of goods. The information provided in the shipment advice includes details such as invoice number, bill of lading/airways bill number and date, name of the vessel with date, the port of export, description of goods and quantity and the date of sailing of vessel.

The overseas supplier dispatches the shipment advice to the importer after loading the goods on the vessel.

(iv) **Import General**

Manifest It is a document that contains the details of the imported goods.

It is a document on the basis of which unloading of cargo takes place. It is provided by the person incharge of the carrier (ship or airway) to the officer in charge at the dock.

(v) **Bill of Entry**

It is a form supplied by the customs office to the importer who filled it at the time of receiving the goods. It has to be submitted to the customs office. It contains information such as name and address of the importer, name of the ship, number of packages, marks on the packages, description of goods, quantity and value of goods, name and address of the exporter, port of destinations and customs duty payable.

Case Study Based Questions

Short Case Studies

Case Study 1

XYZ Ltd., a leading Indian textile company, recently expanded its operations by exporting its premium quality fabrics to Europe and Asia.

This move not only increased its revenue but also enhanced its global reputation. The government of India supported such initiatives as they contribute to the country's foreign exchange reserves.

The company's management reported that the expansion allowed them to utilise their production capacity efficiently and generate employment opportunities in the domestic market.

The success of XYZ Ltd. highlights the growing significance of international business in today's interconnected world.

(i) Define international business.

(ii) State any one benefit of international business to the nation as well as to firms.

Ans.

(i) Manufacturing and trading beyond the boundaries of one's own country is known as international or external business. International business can be defined as those business activities that take place across the national frontiers.

(ii) **Benefit of International Business to Nation**

Earning of Foreign Exchange International business helps a country to import those goods and services which it cannot produce efficiently such as petroleum products and fertilisers, etc.

Benefit of International Business to Firm

Improved Business Vision Most enterprises have an urge to grow, to become more competitive, to diversify and derive the benefits of going global through international business.

Case Study 2

Global Tech Industries, a software development firm headquartered in Country X, has expanded its operations to Country Y. This move has allowed Global Tech to access a skilled talent pool in Country Y at competitive wages, enabling them to offer high quality software solutions at lower costs.

Additionally, the company has entered new markets, providing a wider customer base and increased revenues. However, local businesses in Country Y have expressed concerns about increased competition, potential job displacement and the dominance of foreign firms in the local economy, leading to economic disparities.

(i) State any two advantages of international business to nations.

(ii) State any two disadvantages of international business.

Ans.

(i) Following are the advantages of international business to nations

- **Increase in Employment**
  International business results in increase in employment opportunities directly or indirectly. It results in increase in production and for this demand, requirement of labour also increases, which creates employment opportunities.
- **Increase in Standard of Living**
  In the absence of international business, it would not have been possible for the world community to consume goods and services produced in other countries that the people in these countries are able to consume and enjoy a higher standard of living.

(ii) Following are the disadvantages of international business

- **Legal Formalities**
  International business is monitored by the government. Prior permission has to be obtained before exporting or importing goods or services. A large number of documents have to be filed and custom duties are paid on imports and exports.

- **Blocked Capital**
  Traders have to often depend upon a chain of intermediaries in international business. There is a long time gap between the dispatch of goods by the exporter and their receipt and payment by the importer. Therefore, the capital of the exporter is blocked for a long period.

Case Study 3

Rajneesh is a successful businessman who is engaged in the manufacturing of high quality auto spare parts. He ensures that his products meet international standards, making them highly competitive in the global market.

His manufacturing unit is located in India, where he sells products domestically through a network of distributors and retailers.

At the same time, Rajneesh has expanded his operations internationally, exporting auto spare parts to countries like Singapore, Switzerland and Belgium, which has helped him earn foreign exchange and build a global reputation.

On the basis of the given case, answer the following questions

(i) Identify the two kinds of business in which Rajneesh is engaged.

(ii) Differentiate between the two types of business as identified in part (i) of the question.

Ans.

(i) The two kinds of business in which Rajneesh is engaged are domestic business and international business.

(ii) Following are the differences between domestic business and international business

Basis	Domestic Business	International Business
Nationality of Buyers and Sellers	It involves dealings between people or organisation from the same country.	It involves dealings between people or organisation from the different countries.
Political System and Risks	Political factors have a profound impact on domestic business. It subject to political system and risks of one single country.	Different countries have different forms of political systems and degrees of risks which often became barrier to international business.
Business Regulations and Policies	Domestic business is subjected to rules, laws and policies, taxation system, of a single country.	International business transactions are subject to rules, laws and policies, tariffs and quotas, etc of multiple countries.

Case Study 4

Mr. X runs a leather factory and produces leather garments for exports to different countries. Mr. X has obtained all environmental clearances for his business after installing the state of the art machinery. He has taken every precaution to ensure that no pollution is caused to the areas surrounding his factory.

Further to contribute to the reputation of brand India, Mr. X goes extra miles to ensure quality of leather garments to be exported. There is zero tolerance level as far as quality of export items is concerned. Because of all this, his profit margin is very low. On the basis of above case, answer the following questions

(i) Comment on the conduct of Mr. X as a manufacturer and an exporter.

(ii) Is it advisable to sacrifice profits to take care of environment surrounding the factory?

(iii) What objectives are being attained by the export efforts of Mr. X?

Ans.

(i) Mr. X is a responsible manufacturer and exporter as he has taken all environmental clearances by installing necessary equipment to check pollution of any kind.

(ii) Yes, it is advisable to invest money on environmental protection even if the profit margin declines. Taking care of environment is an important social responsibility of a businessman.

(iii) The export objectives being achieved are
- Earning of foreign exchange.
- Building up India's image by exporting quality products.

Case Study 5

Identify the document highlighted in the following cases

(i) This document is prepared by the importer and it shows the details of goods imported and is used by custom authorities to determine import duty.

(ii) On the basis of this document, imported goods are unloaded from the carrier.

Ans.

(i) Bill of entry is prepared by the importer and it shows the details of goods imported and is used by custom authorities to determine import duty. It is a form supplied by the customs office to the importer who filled it at the time of receiving the goods. It has to be submitted to the customs office.

It contains information such as name and address of the importer, name of the ship, number of packages, marks on the packages, description of goods, quantity and value of goods, name and address of the exporter, port of destinations and customs duty payable.

(ii) On the basis of import general manifest, imported goods are unloaded from the carrier. It is a document that contains details of the imported goods. It is on the basis of this document only that unloading of cargo takes place.

Case Study 6

Global trade has become increasingly interconnected over the years. A leading international organisation plays a key role in ensuring smooth trade relations between nations by setting rules and resolving disputes. Recently, this organisation mediated a trade conflict between two major economies regarding tariffs on electronic goods, ensuring both countries adhered to fair trade practices.

The organisation also provides a platform for member countries to negotiate agreements aimed at reducing trade barriers and promoting free trade. With over 160 member nations, it works toward fostering economic cooperation globally.

(i) Identify the organisation highlighted in the given case.

(ii) State any three objectives of the organisation identified in (i).

Ans.

(i) The organisation highlighted in the given case is World Trade Organisation (WTO). It was set-up to promote free and fair trade amongst nations. India is a founding member of WTO. All the members of WTO are required to adopt laws and policies framed under WTO rules.

(ii) Following are the objectives of WTO

- To ensure reduction of tariffs and other trade barriers imposed by different countries.
- To engage in activities that improve the standards of living, create employment, increase income and effective demand, facilitate production, etc.
- To promote an integrated, viable, durable trading system and ensure international peace.

Long Case Studies

Case Study 7

Raj Industries, a well-established manufacturing company, decided to expand its operations internationally to enhance its market reach. After thorough market research, they chose to adopt different strategies for entering foreign markets. They explored three methods

(i) Raj Industries permitted a foreign company in Germany to produce and sell their products under the Raj Industries trademark. The foreign company paid a fee in return for the use of the brand, trademarks and patents.

(ii) Raj Industries entered into a franchising agreement with a local partner in Australia for their restaurant chain. The local partner paid a fee for the right to use the Raj Industries brand name and operational procedures.

(iii) Raj Industries invested directly in a plant in China, establishing a production unit to manufacture goods and market them locally in the region.

Quoting lines from the above case, identify and explain three forms of foreign business operations discussed in the case.

Ans. Following are the three forms of foreign business operations discussed in the case

(i) **Licensing**

"Raj Industries permitted a foreign company in Germany to produce and sell their products under the Raj Industries trademark."

Licensing involves allowing another party in a foreign country to produce and sell goods under the company's trademark, patents or copyrights in exchange for a fee. Raj Industries granted a German company the right to use their brand in return for a fee, allowing them to leverage the local market without direct investment.

(ii) **Franchising**

"Raj Industries entered into a franchising agreement with a local partner in Australia for their restaurant chain."

Franchising is similar to licensing, but it focuses on services rather than goods. The local partner pays a fee to operate under the Raj Industries brand name and utilise the company's business model and operational systems. This allows the company to expand without managing operations directly in the foreign market.

(iii) **Foreign Investment**

"Raj Industries invested directly in a plant in China, establishing a production unit to manufacture goods and market them locally in the region."

It involves making investments directly in properties such as land, buildings or machinery in a foreign country to undertake production and marketing. Raj Industries set-up a production facility in China to manufacture and market goods locally, ensuring direct control over operations. Foreign investment is the investment of funds in abroad in exchange of financial return from that country in the form of profit, interest or dividend.

It is of two types

- **Foreign Direct Investments** (FDI) It takes place when a company directly invests in properties such as plant and machinery, land and building to undertake production and marketing of goods and services in those countries.

- **Portfolio Investments** It takes place when a company invests in another company by acquiring shares of that company or giving them loans and earn dividend on shares and interest on loans.

Case Study 8

XYZ Industries, a leading manufacturer of organic food products, recently decided to expand its operations by exploring the export market. With a strong domestic customer base, XYZ Industries aimed to enter the global market, particularly in regions where demand for healthy and sustainable products was growing. The company partnered with distributors in countries like the United States, Canada and Australia to export its range of packaged organic snacks and beverages.

However, this expansion came with its own set of challenges. XYZ Industries had to ensure that its products met stringent international health and safety regulations. They also had to establish efficient supply chain management, secure the necessary export documentation and maintain quality control throughout the process.

Export trade not only helps businesses like XYZ Industries grow by tapping into new markets but also enhances their competitive advantage through product differentiation and specialisation.

Additionally, it contributes to fostering bilateral trade relationships, leading to stronger economic ties between nations.

(i) Define export trade.

(ii) Discuss the objectives of export trade.

(iii) Discuss the documents related to goods exported.

Ans.

(i) Export trade is a mode of international trade in which goods produced in the domestic country are sold to the residents of another country.

(ii) Following are the objectives of export trade

- **Sell Surplus Goods**
  A country may produce a commodity in such quantities that are more than its needs. The country can sell its surplus output to foreign countries. In this way, export trade is undertaken to make productive use of surplus goods.
- **Better Utilisation of Resources**
  Export trade widens the market for goods. A country can make better utilisation of its resources by producing goods on a large-scale, both for domestic use and for export.
- **Earn Foreign Exchange**
  A country can earn valuable foreign exchange through export.
- **Increase National Income**
  Export trade helps a country to increase its national income.
- **Generate Employment**
  The growth of export trade also creates employment opportunities.

(iii) Following are the documents related to goods exported

- **Export Invoice**
  It is a seller bill information about goods like quantity, number of packages, name of ship, terms of delivery, payments, etc.
- **Packing List**
  This document provides complete details regarding the goods exported and the form in which they are being sent.
- **Certificate of Origin**
  It specifies the country in which the goods are being manufactured. This certificate enables the importer to claim tariff concessions or other exemptions. It is also used in the case when there is a ban on imports of some goods from certain countries.
- **Certificate of Inspection**
  It is the certificate that states that the consignment has been inspected as required under the Export (Quality Control and Inspection) Act, 1963. It is issued by some authorised agency Export Inspection Council of India (EICI).

Case Study 9

Ravi Exporters, a company based in India, recently received an export order from a client in Germany for 500 units of handcrafted home decor items.

After accepting the order, the company began the process of fulfilling the shipment. Ravi, the owner, first secured an Importer Exporter Code (IEC) and ensured that the export items were registered under the Export Promotion Council.

He then collaborated with a freight forwarder to arrange transportation and insurance for the goods. Ravi prepared all necessary documents such as packing list, bill of lading and shipping bill. He also filed a Customs Declaration Form with the customs authority for the shipment clearance.

Once the goods were inspected and cleared by customs, they were loaded onto the ship. Ravi sent the commercial invoice and certificate of origin to his German buyer for final payment.

Upon confirmation, the goods were successfully shipped and Ravi tracked the shipment until it reached the buyer's port.

(i) Explain the export procedure in brief.

(ii) Also, explain bill of exchange and shipping bill in context with export procedure.

Ans.

(i) For detailed explanation of export procedure, refer to topic 'Procedure for conducting export trade' on page 273 to 275.

(ii) **Bill of Exchange**

It is a written document in export and import transactions in which, exporter ashs the importer to pay a specified amount to a certain person or the bearer of the document. The importer claim the title of exported goods only when he accepts the order in bill of exchange.

Shipping Bill

With the help of this document, permission is granted for the export of goods by the customs office. It contains details regarding the goods being exported, name of the vessel, exporters name and address, country of final destination, etc.

Case Study 10

Arvind owns a textile company in India and plans to expand his business by importing high quality cotton fabric from Egypt. He is aware that importing goods involves several legal and procedural steps, but he is unsure of the exact process.

To ensure compliance with the regulations, Arvind contacts a trade consultant who advises him to obtain an Importer Exporter Code (IEC) from the directorate general of goreign trade. He also needs to finalise the terms of trade with the supplier, place an order and arrange for foreign exchange payment.

After placing the order, the supplier ships the goods and sends the shipment documents, including the bill of lading, invoice and packing list.

Once the goods arrive at the Indian port, Arvind will need to submit these documents to customs for verification. Customs authorities inspect the goods and calculate the import duty before issuing clearance.

The trade consultant emphasises that understanding each step, from documentation to payment of import duty, is crucial to avoid delays or penalties. **Competency Based Que**

(i) Explain the import procedure in brief.

(ii) Explain 'import order or indent' and 'shipment advice' in context with import procedure.

Ans.

(i) For detailed explanation of import procedure, refer to topic 'Procedure for conducting import trade' on page 277 and 278.

(ii) **Import Order or Indent**

It is a document in which the importer orders for supply of requisite goods to the supplier. The order contains information such as quantity and quality of goods, price of goods, method of forwarding the goods, nature of packing, mode of payment, etc.

Shipment Advice

The exporter sends shipment advice to the importer for informing him that the shipment of goods has been made.

It contains invoice number, bill of lading/airways bill, name of the vessel with date, the port of export, description of goods, quantity and the date of sailing of the vessel.

SELF ASSESSMENT TEST

Objective Type Questions

1. Labour productivity and production cost differ among nations due to
   (a) geographical reasons (b) agricultural reasons
   (c) personal reasons (d) government policies
2. XYZ Ltd., an Indian company, has recently entered the international market by exporting goods to the USA. However, they are facing challenges due to long distances, different currencies and legal formalities. What is one major disadvantage XYZ Ltd. is experiencing in their international business dealings?
   (a) Easy and quick communication
   (b) Fluctuation in exchange rates
   (c) Immediate receipt of payment
   (d) High import duties without delays
3. Which of the following reasons explains why countries engage in international business?
   (a) Unequal distribution of natural resources among nations
   (b) Differences in labour productivity and production costs
   (c) Availability of various factors of production such as labour, capital and raw materials
   (d) All of the above
4. India produces a large quantity of textiles but has a limited domestic market. By exporting these textiles to foreign countries, India can utilise its surplus resources efficiently and earn valuable foreign exchange. This contributes to increasing the overall national income as well. Why does India engage in export trade?
   (a) To hoard resources
   (b) To sell surplus goods and earn foreign exchange
   (c) To reduce domestic production
   (d) To import more goods
5. Which of the following is not an advantage of exporting?
   (a) Easier way to enter into international markets
   (b) Comparatively lower risk
   (c) Limited presence in foreign markets
   (d) Less investment requirements
6. The exporter approaches his bank to obtain………, once he received a confirmed order from the importer for the purpose of export production.
   (a) letter of credit (b) pre-shipment finance
   (c) post-shipment finance (d) bank guarantee
7. Certificate of Inspection is issued by
   (a) captain of the ship (b) exporter's bank
   (c) insurance company
   (d) Export Inspection Council of India
8. Which one of the following is not part of export documents?
   (a) Export invoice
   (b) Certificate of origin
   (c) Bill of entry
   (d) Mate's receipt

Answers 1. (a) 2. (b) 3. (d) 4. (b) 5. (c) 6. (b) 7. (d) 8. (c)

Short Answer Type Questions

9. "International business encompasses more than just international trade." How is international business different from international trade?
10. "International business involves various challenges." State any four disadvantages of international business.
11. What is the major reason underlying trade between nations?
12. State any three differences between domestic business and international business.
13. XYZ Company, a manufacturing firm, imports raw materials from abroad to meet its production needs. This allows them to access high quality materials that are not available domestically. Discuss the objectives of import trade for businesses like XYZ Company.
14. "The World Trade Organisation (WTO) plays a crucial role in regulating global trade." In light of the given statement, discuss the role of WTO.
15. State the benefits of WTO.

Long Answer Type Questions

16. A company in India expands its operations to multiple countries, increasing its market reach and boosting exports. This leads to job creation, economic growth and improved global competitiveness.
    In context of the given case, discuss the benefits of international business to a nation as well as individual firms.
17. Briefly describe the various important documents used in export transactions.
18. The procedure for the import of goods involves several steps. Briefly explain the procedure to be followed for the import of goods.

Project Report

A project report is a written document of what the *analyser* analyses in his/her project work. The project report needs to be prepared with great care and consideration.

A project report should

- be handwritten
- be concise
- be clear
- have diagrammatic presentation
- have a length of 25 to 30 pages
- have topics with suitable headings
- end up with conclusion
- should be presented in a neat folder

Elements

Try to ensure that your report contains the following elements

Title Page

This should include the project title, name of the company/product on which you are conducting your research and name of the student. Your can also list the name of your school, class and subject teacher.

Acknowledgement

It is usual to thank those individuals, who have provided particularly useful assistance, technical or otherwise, during your project through acknowledgement.

Content Page

This should list the main sections and sub-sections of your report. Choose self-explanatory titles with their respective pages and use double spacing for clarity. Content should be impressive and explanatory, so that the reader would clearly understand the purpose of the project.

Try to avoid too many levels of sub-heading.

Project Work

Introduction

This is one of the most important component of the project report. It should begin with a clear statement of what the project is about, so that the nature and scope of the project can be understood by the reader. It should summarise everything which you set out to achieve and provide a clear summary of the project's background, relevance and main contributions. The introduction should set the context for the project and should provide the reader with a summary of the key things to look out for, in the remainder of the report. It is useful in stating the main objectives of the project as part of the introduction.

Background

The background section of the report should set the project into action. It specifies the problem, what remedial actions are taken, what are its effects etc. It proposes the layout of the whole project.

Body of Report

The central part of the report usually consists of three or four sections detailing the technical work undertaken during the project. The structure of these sections is highly project dependent. They can reflect the chronological development of the project. It includes the detailed description regarding the matter of the project.

Evaluation

This might involve quantitative and qualitative evaluation such as expressibility, functionality, ease-of-use, etc of a product. At some point, you should also evaluate the strengths and weaknesses of what you have done. It includes certain questionnaires, sampling test, etc. which help in evaluating the result on the basis of truths and facts.

Conclusion

The conclusion should list the things, which have been learnt as a result of the work you have done. It shows the ultimate response of the project undertaken by a student. It should be expressive and impressive, so that a reader would clearly evaluate the result and rate you on the basis of your presentation.

ASSESSMENT OF THE PROJECT REPORT

The teacher assesses the project report on the following parameters

1.	Initiative, cooperativeness and participation	1 Mark
2.	Creativity in presentation	1 Mark
3.	Content, observation and research work	2 Mark
4.	Analysis of situations	2 Mark
5.	Viva	4 Mark
	Total	10 Marks

Project Work

Title of the Project : Case Study on Orchids from Meghalaya and Sikkim

Objective : The case study will help to understand the reasons for geographical specialisation of the product, demand and supply situation of the product and effect on prices due to absence of effective transport system and suitable warehouse facilities

Name : ....

School : ....

Year : ....

Class : XI A

Submitted To : ....

Orchid Flower

Acknowledgement

I would like to express my special thanks of gratitude to my teacher_________ as well as our Principal _________ who gave me the golden opportunity to do this wonderful project on the topic 'Case Study on Orchids from Meghalaya and Sikkim'.

This project helped me a lot in gaining adequate knowledge about the topic. I have completed this project after proper analysis and research and I came to know about so many new things.

I am really thankful to all of my friends, co-partners and guide, who have devoted their precious time in completing my project. Secondly, I would also like to thank my parents or guardians who helped me a lot in finishing this project within the prescribed time.

I am making this project not only for marks but also to increase my knowledge and intellect development.

Thanks again to all who helped me.

Certificate

This is to Certify that the project work 'Case Study on Orchids from Meghalaya and Sikkim' is the bonafide work of .... (Name of the student) who carried out the work under my supervision ....

(Name and Signature of Teacher/Supervisor)

Contents

Introduction To Orchids

Orchids are considered as the most beautiful flowering plants for the exquisite beauty of the flower, variety of fragrance, brilliance in colour, unusual shapes, variation in form and attractive growth habits. There are about 24,000 species and 32,000 hybrids of orchids.

All orchids are perennial herbs that lack any permanent woody structure. They can grow according to two patterns

- **Monopodial** The stem grows from a single bud, leaves are added from the apex each year and the stem grows longer accordingly. The stem of orchids with a monopodial growth can reach several metres in length, as in *Vanilla.*

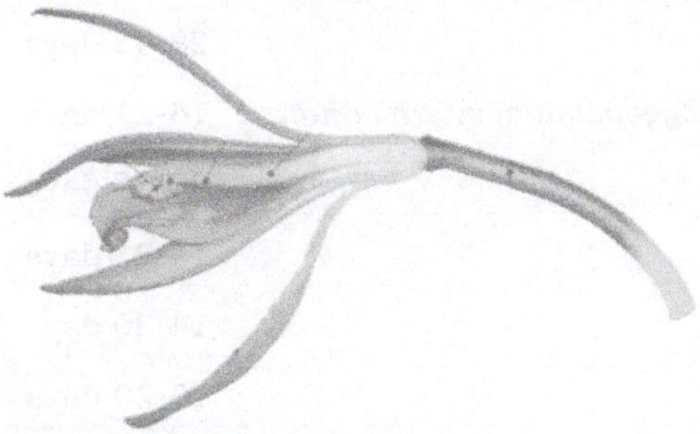

Longitudinal section of a flower of Vanilla planifolia

- **Sympodial** Sympodial orchids have a front (the newest growth) and a back (the oldest growth). The plant produces a series of adjacent shoots which grow to a certain size, bloom and then stop growing and are replaced. *Ophrys* grows according to this pattern.

Ophrys apifera

Unique Characteristic Of Orchids : A High Shelf Life

Orchids are the most pampered of the plants and occupy top position among all the flowering plants, valued for cut flower production and as potted plants, because of their bewitchingly beautiful flowers, which have a long lasting shelf life. The shelf life or vase life of some important orchids is given below

Name of Species/Hybrids	Shelf life/Vase life (days)
Aerides odoratum, Aerides multiflorum, Cymbidium iridioides, Dendrobium nobile, Renant.hera imschootiana	28-56 days
Paphiopdilum hirtussimum, P. wardianum	56 days
Phaius tankervillae	28-42 days
Vanda coerulea, Vanda teres, Zygopetalum intermedium	14-21 days
Cymbidium hybrids	20-55 days
Dendrobium hybrids	14-21 days
Vanda, Mokara hybrids	14-30 days
Cattleya hybrids	10-20 days
Phalaenopsis hybrids	25-30 days
Aranda	18-28 days

This high shelf life of orchids enhances its use as a decorative flower and help it to fetch a very high price in the international market.

Conditions Favourable for the Growth of Orchids

Orchids are delicate flowers which bloom only in ideal climatic conditions, which are explained below

The Ideal Temperature

For growth of orchids, daytime temperature should range between 70 to 80 degrees Fahrenheit (21 to 27 degrees Celsius). Also, the night temperature should be 60 to 62 degrees Fahrenheit (15.5 to 17 degrees Celsius). A day night fluctuation of 10 to 15 degrees Fahrenheit is essential to produce beautiful, long-lasting blooms. This is due to the fact that orchids must produce energy in the form of carbohydrates during the day, when the temperature is high and store that energy at night, when the temperature drops.

The Ideal Light

The orchid plant should have exposure to sunlight. Indirect sunlight is ideal but very poor light tends to produce weak plants and retards flowering. A plant which has been grown in shades should be gradually shifted to sunlight conditions.

Potting and Compost

An ideal compost for orchids should be one which provides high degree of porosity and ensure adequate oxygen for root respiration. Also, water should drain out freely through the compost and the pot, and it should be resistant to rapid decomposition and decay. Also, the pot selected for planting orchids require special consideration. Epiphytic orchids like *Cattleya, Dendrobium* etc are best grown in specially designed orchid pots with holes at the bottom and slits or perforations on the sides. Monopodial epiphytes like *Aerides, Vanda* etc are particularly suited for basked culture, because of large aerial roots produced from these plants. Many orchids are conveniently grown on the branches of the trees, charred wooden slabs or tree term blocks.

Orchid Flower Pot with Perforations

Orchid Flowers on Branches of Trees

Orchid Flowers in Basket

Humidity and Watering

As orchids are grown in a light and porous compost, watering is very important. Newly potted plants should not be watered frequently, but the compost should be kept moist by fine spraying. As new root emerges and growth starts, the plants need more frequent watering and it should be decreased again after flowering. Fine spraying of water is also very beneficial to plants during the period of growth and on warm days. Alkaline water is injurious to orchids and slight acidic water at pH upto 7 should be used.

Also, orchids, in general, prefer high relative humidity. But, it should be kept in mind that in high humid atmosphere, watering should be less frequent. It is also a good idea to have a water tank or pool in the centre of the orchidaria to maintain humidity, which should not be less than 30% at night and 80% during day time.

Nutrients

A balanced mix of nitrogen, phosphate and potash in the ratio of 5 : 6 : 5 and very small amount of magnesium, calcium, manganese, iron, boron and zinc has been found very effective on a large number of species and hybrids of orchids. For best results, two table spoonfuls of the above mixture is mixed in 10 litres of water and is sprayed once a week on the roots and leaves of the orchid plant.

Commercial Cultivation of Orchids

Uses of Orchids

Orchids are commercially used for the following purposes

For Decorations in Weddings and Other Social Events

The first and foremost use of orchids it to decorate the venues of weddings and other social events. For decorations, orchids can be joined together into garlands and hung or draped from ceiling, plants and other centrepieces. The garlands can also be used to decorate the stage and the entrance gate. Bouquets of orchids can be used to decorate cars in which the bride and bridegroom travel.

Entrance area decorated by Orchids

Beautiful Wedding Decoration by Orchids

Car Decoration By Orchids

Other Uses of Orchids

Orchids are used as decorative items in homes, offices and public places. It is most important commercial use.

However, orchids have certain other uses also which are enumerated below

- In Turkey, orchids are used for making a traditional beverage called salep. It is a type of flour that is produced by grinding tubers of *Orchis militaris, Orchis mascula* and other kinds of orchids with ovoid tubers. It is also consumed in Saudi Arabia, Syria and Iran and is said to be effective in curing sore throat, digestive problems and gum disease.
- *Vanilla*, an aromatic oil that exudes from the seed pods of *Vanilla* is the most famous orchid product. It is used to flavour dishes. Its medicinal uses relate to relieving nausesea and improving food intake in patients receiving chemo therapy, It is also used as a diagnostic aroma for Alzheimer's disease. loss of the sense of smell being an early manifestation of this condition.
- An orchid product called 'Shihu' is made from several *dendrobium* species. It is recommended for indigestion, rehydration and as an anti-pyretic, to increase white cells in the blood.
- Moscatilin, derived from *Dendrobium loddigesii*, has anti-cancer activity for stomach and lung cancer cell lines. It is also an anti-platelet agent.
- Shihu 'Eguang wan', which contains *Dendrobium products*, is recommended for eye problems.
- *Gastrodia elata* is grown commercially, and is used to treat allergies and relieve headache and fatigue. Many herbal formulas for treating hypertension, convulsions, migraine and cramps include this preparation.

Gastrodia elata

Dendrobium loddigesii

Dendrobium nagasaki

Project Work

Orchid Growing Areas of The World

Majority of the cultivated orchids are native of tropical countries and occur in their greatest diversity in humid tropical forests of

- Netherlands
- Mexico
- Ceylon
- South China
- Malaysia
- New Guinea
- South and Central America
- India
- Burma
- Thailand
- Phillippines
- Australia

Global Orchid Trade

The orchid has taken a significant position in the cut flower industry due to its attractiveness, long shelf life, high productivity, right season of bloom, ease of packing and transportation. Orchids account for a large share of global floriculture trade, both as cut flowers and as potted plants and are estimated to comprise around 10% of the international fresh cut flower trade.

The average trade value of fresh cut orchids and buds trade during 2007-2012 was US $ 483 million. As of 2016, there are more than 40 exporting countries and more than 60 importing countries of orchids, around the World, and the total size of global trade is more than US $ 700 million.

Value of fresh cut orchids and buds global trade (2007-2012) (Unit : Million US $)

Year	2007	2008	2009	2010	2011	2012
Import	233,734,023	252,647,645	232,568,129	251,445,523	265,702,077	267,196,847
Export	230,470,421	238,702,950	217,781,745	227,389,789	244,996,271	237,543,797
Total	464,204,444	491,350,595	450,349,874	478,835,312	510,698,348	504,740,644

Source : *Department of Foreign Trade, Thailand (2013)*

The Netherlands is the top orchid exporting country in the World (39.67% of world orchid market) followed by Thailand (28.41%), Taiwan (10%), Singapore (10%) and New Zealand (6%). Importing countries are mainly Japan (30%), UK (12%), Italy (10%), France (7%) and the USA (6%).

The total orchid cut flower trade of the world mostly consists of 85% *Dendrobium* species and 15% *Phalaenopsis* and *Cymbidium* species.

Orchid Growing Areas in India

Orchids are an important component of the Indian floriculture industry. It forms around 9% of our flora and are the largest botanical family of higher plants in India. India is endowed with 160 genra and more than 1300 species of orchids, including commercially important species like *Arachnis, Cattleya, Phalaenopsis, Cymbidium, Dendrobium, Paphiopedilum, Vanda* and *Renanthera.*

Important orchid growing areas in India are

- Arunachal Pradesh
- Assam
- Manipur
- Meghalaya
- Mizoram
- Nagaland
- Sikkim
- Tripura
- Kerala
- Karnataka
- Tamil Nadu

North-East India : An Important Orchid Growing Area

The Northeast India, comprising of eight states, viz. Arunachal Pradesh, Assam, Manipur, Meghalaya, Mizoram, Nagaland, Sikkim and Tripura is the most important orchid growing area. It sustains around 856 species of orchids, 34 amongst them are identified as threatened plants of India.

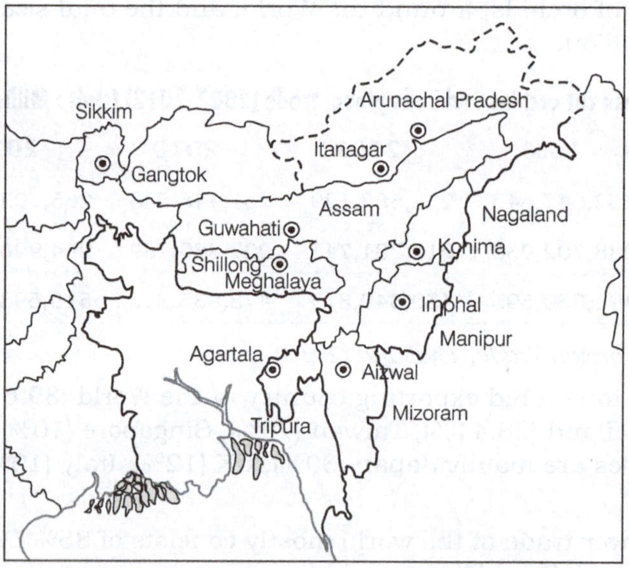

Important Orchid Growing States of India

Orchid Distribution under Forest Cover in North East (Kataki et al. 1984)

State	Area	Dense Forest	% Forest Cover	Orchid	
	000 km^2			Genera	Species
Arunachal Pradesh	83,743	54,542	65.13	130	600
Assam	78,438	15,842	20.19	74	182
Manipur	22,327	5,309	23.77	67	207
Meghalaya	22,429	3,305	14.73	98	352
Mizoram	21,081	4,279	20.29	74	249
Nagaland	16,579	3,531	21.29	64	241
Sikkim	7,096	2,403	38.86	132	540
Tripura	10,488	1,825	17.40	37	66

Production of Orchids in Sikkim and Meghalaya

The tropical, humid climate of Sikkim and Meghalaya is ideal for orchid cultivation. As per the data collected by National Horticulture Board (NHB), in 2014-15, Meghalaya produced 500 tonnes of orchid flowers and Sikkim produced 250 tonnes of orchid flowers. Sikkim and Meghalaya, together are home to 750 species of orchids, 450 species in Sikkim and 300 species in Meghalaya. In the months of April-May and September-October, lovely orchids can be found in bloom, everywhere in these states.

In Sikkim, the Deorali Orchid Sanctuary and National Research Centre for orchids are the places to visit. Sikkim also plays host to the International Flower Festival that showcases rare varieties of orchids. The Noble Orchid is the state's official flower, conveying the importance of orchids for the state.

In Meghalaya, orchids form a very observable element of the vegetation available. The two forests-Mawsmai and Mawmluh inhabits the highest number of orchid species in the whole region. Soharim is another forest in Meghalaya which is a paradise for orchid lovers. Meghalaya government has promoted various tour packages and holiday trips to explore the orchids of this region.

Noble Orchid : State flower of Sikkim

Notable Genera of the Orchid Family Grown in Sikkim and Meghalaya

- Anthogonium Wall. **Ex Lindl.**
- Acrochaene **Lindl.**
- Cremastra **Lindl.**
- Dickasonia **L.O. Williams**
- Eriodes **Rolfe**
- Jejosephia **A.N. Rao and Mani**
- Myrmechis **(Lindl.) Bl.**
- Ornithochilus **(Lindl.) Wall. Ex Benth.**
- Renanthera **Lour.**
- Arundina **Bl.**
- Bulleyia **Schltr.**
- Cleisocentron **Bruhl**
- Diglyphosa **bl.**
- Herpysma **Lindl.**
- Mischobulbum **schltr.**
- Neogyne **reichb.f.**
- Risleya **King and Pantl.**
- Tipularia **Nutt.**

Threatened Orchids of Sikkim and Meghalaya

- Acanthephippium sylhetense
- Cymbidium eburneum
- Cym. tigrinum
- Den. densiflorum
- Eria fragrans
- P. insigne
- Ps. villosum
- Vanda coerulea
- Vanda pumila
- Bulleyia yunnanensis
- Cym. devonianum
- Dendrobium chrysotoxum
- Den. falconeri
- Paphiopedilum fairreanum
- P. venustum
- Renanthera imschootiana
- Vanilla pilfera
- Epigeneium rotundatum

Marketing of Orchids Grown in Sikkim and Meghalaya

Orchids are tender and hence highly perishable. This poses great problems in their marketing, particularly long distance marketing. But with the development of quick transport vehicles and refrigerated and insulated vans, orchids are now transported to distant markets, including foreign markets.

In the marketing of orchids, the following two aspects are important

1. Channels of Marketing

In the marketing of orchids, there are two main agencies, *viz* the local buyer and the distant market florists. Because of this, there are two channels of marketing

Channel I Producer → Local Buyer → Consumer

Channel II Producer → Wholesaler → Retailer → Consumer

2. Cost of Orchid

The cost of an orchid plant can range from ₹ 7 to ₹ 300. It depends upon a number of factors, such as

- **Type of Orchid Plant** For example, a common variety such as *Acampe papillosa* is available for ₹ 20, where as exotic variety such as *Camalex* can fetch ₹ 300.
- **Age of Orchid Plant** The cost of orchid plant also depends upon its age, as is explained below
  - A deflashed seedling without hardening is the cheapest.
  - 3 months to 1 year old hardened seedlings/off shoots/back bulbs are next in line.
  - They are followed by 1 year to 2 year old plants.
  - The most expensive are 2 year old and above, flowering size plants.

Rate List of Orchid Plants

The table given below shows the rate list of some common orchid plants.

Rate of Orchid Seedlings, Off-shoots, Backbulbs and Plants (Without Containers)

Name of Species	Deflasked seedlings without hardening (₹)	3 months-1 year old hardened seedlings/off shoots/backbulbs (₹)	1 year-2 year old (₹)	2 year old and flowering size (₹)
C. fuscescens	7/-	10/-	15/-	20/-
C. occultata	7/-	10/-	15/-	20/-
C. ovalis	7/-	10/-	15/-	20/-
Crytochilus sanguinia	8/-	15/-	20/-	30/-
Cymbidium aloifolium	7/-	10/-	15/-	20/-
C. devonianum	7/-	10/-	15/-	20/-
C. eburnium	9/-	20/-	30/-	60/-
C. elegans	7/-	10/-	15/-	20/-
C. giganteum	9/-	20/-	30/-	60/-
C. grandiflorum	9/-	20/-	30/-	60/-

Rate List of Cut Orchid Flowers

The rate of cut flowers depend on the fact that whether they are single, spike, bouquet or a corsage. It also depends on the fact that they are species or hybrids.

The table given below gives the rate of cut flowers

Rate For Cut Flowers : Single, Spike, Bouquet And Corsage

Grades	Species	Spike (Rupees/spike)			Single flower	Bouquet (Rupees)		Corsage (Rupees)
		<8fls	8-15 fls	> 15 fls		- A	B	
I.	Highly ornamental, longlasting bright colour and large	3/-	5/-	6/-	2/-	15/-	30/-	10/-
II.	Ordinary	2/-	4/-	5/-	1/-	10/-	20/-	5/-

Grades	Hybrids	Spike (Rs./spike)			Single flower Rs./pc.	Bouquet Rs./pc.		Corsage Rs./pc.
		<8fls	8-15 fls	> 15 fls		- A	B	
I.	Highly ornamental longlasting awarded hybrids	12/-	18/-	25/-	3/-	50/-	150/-	18/-
II.	Ornamental hybrids of older generations	10/-	15/-	20/-	2/-	40/-	120/-	15/-
III.	Native F1 hybrids	6/-	8/-	10/-	1.5/-	25/-	75/-	12/-

The above rates are inclusive of the cost of marketing, which is around 30% of the cost stated above. The highest component of the marketing cost in the cost associated to transportation and packing.

MARKETING CHANNEL OF ORCHID

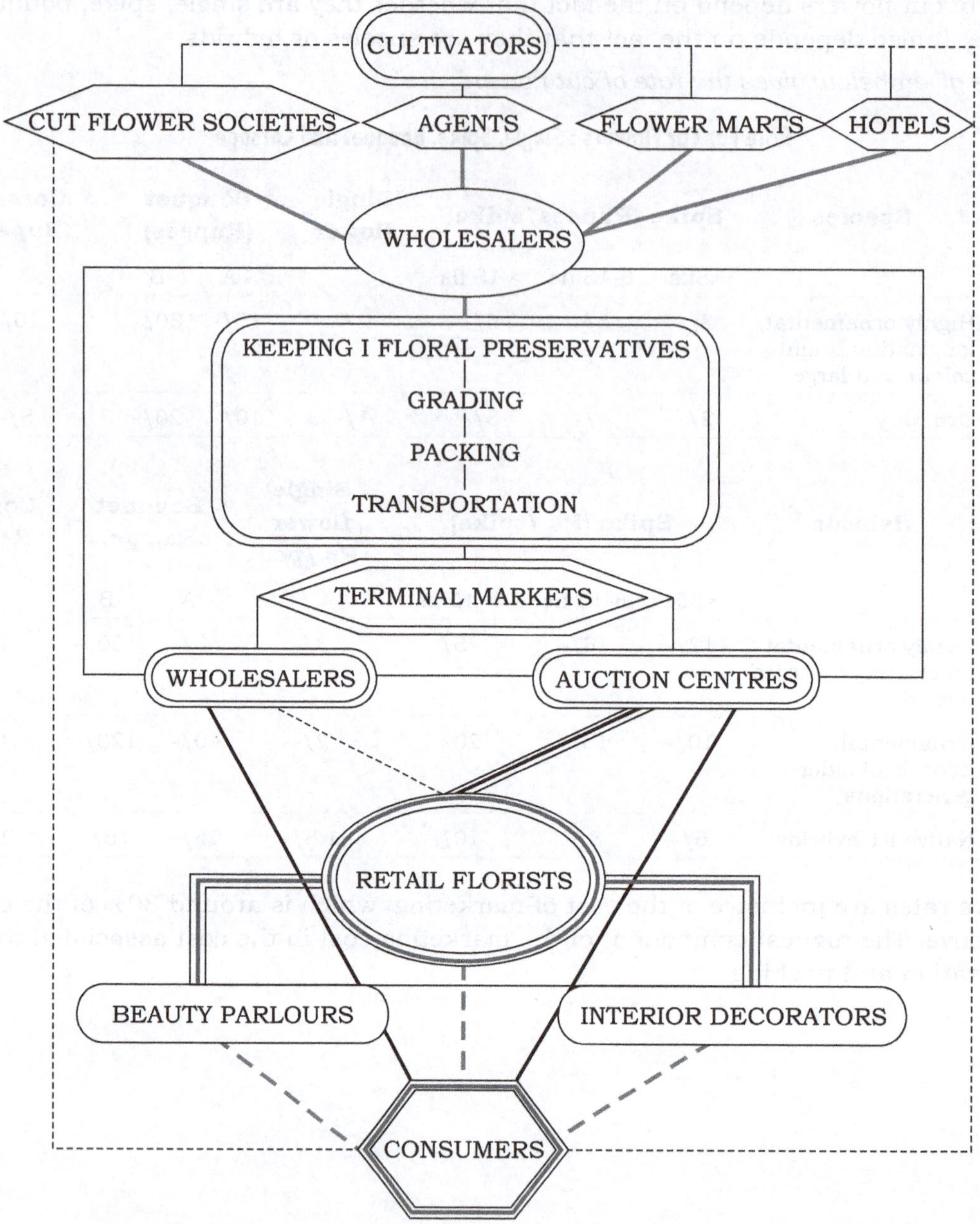

Post Harvest Management of Orchids

Post harvest management of orchids is very important in the marketing process, as it helps to increase the shelf life of the orchids.

The following processes are important as a part of post harvest management

Pre-Cooling

All flowers should be precooled immediately after harvest by placing them in cold storage, without packing or in open boxes, till they reach the desired temperature.

Conditioning

Conditioning or hardening is a simple process, where flowers are kept standing loosely in a big container so that air can circulate around the stems. The purpose of the treatment is to restore the turgidity of cut flowers with water stress during storage and transport. Flowers stems should be placed in warm water or in a preservative solution in plastic jars at a depth of 2-4 cm and held at room temperature or in cold storage for several hours.

Impregnation

Sometimes, the cut ends of the flower stems are impregnated for a short time with chemicals. This treatment protects the blockage of the water vessel in the stem by microbial growth and stem decay. Impregnation of cut bases of flowers with high concentration (1000 ppm-1500 ppm) of silver nitrate, nickel chloride or cobalt chloride for 10-15 minutes improves the longevity of several flowers such as *Aster, Gerbera, Gladiolus, carnation, Chrysanthemum, Cymbidium, Phalaenopsis* and snapdragon.

Bud opening

It is a procedure of harvesting flowers at a stage earlier than normally considered as the cutting stage and then opening the buds off the plant. Such types of post harvest handling may be applied by growers or wholesalers. Bud opening of flowers increases longevity of cut flowers by reducing the sensitivity of flowers to extreme temperatures, low humidity and ethylene, saving space during shipment and extending the useful storage life.

Preservatives

Preservatives are used in the holding solutions in the form of tablets containing a mixture of chemicals such as sugars, germicides, salts, growth regulators etc. Besides, the chemicals are employed during conditioning, pulsing and for making bud opening solutions to improve flower shape, size and opening and colour of the flowers.

Grading

Grading is done based on the basis of parameters like appearance, stage of maturity, blemishes or injuries due to diseases, infestations caused by insets, pests, colour and size of the bud, straightness, strength as well as length of stem.

Grading of Cymbidium Cut Flowers

Cymbidium	Grades	Flower count	Spike length	Other consideration
Cymbidium Standard	AAA	>12	1.25m	Strong straight stems, uniform length, no marks on flowers.
	AA	8	90 cm	
Cymbidium Miniature	XL	>15	65 +	Bent crooked spikes but with perfect flowers
	L	12-14	55-64	
	M	8-11	40-54	
	S	<5	30-39	

Packaging of Orchids

Flowers are generally grouped into bunches of 5, 10, 12 or 20 stems and loosely tied with rubber bands. Before placing them in the package, individual flower bunches are wrapped with suitable packing materials like cellophane paper, kraft paper, newspaper, tissue paper or corrugated cardboard sheet. For local markets, the bunches are held in buckets containing water or preservative solution. It is advisable that for long distance transport and storage, flower bunches are held in dry cardboard boxes. The minimum length of boxes should be about twice the width and its width about twice the height. Use of telescope-style boxes made of CFB is ideal. Ethylene scrubbers with $KMnO_4$ or purafil may also be kept in the box. For export purpose, packing of flowers in two piece box is a better option.

Storage of Cut Flowers

Low temperature treatment during storage or shipment period reduces the entire metabolism in the tissues, slows down the respiration, transpiration and ethylene action and retards the multiplication of bacteria and fungi. In general, temperate orchids are stored at lower temperature even at 5°C in cold chambers, whereas tropical orchids are stored at 7-10°C. A 90-95% relative humidity is necessary during storage to minimize moisture loss and to prevent wilting.

There are two types of cold storage methods, namely 'Wet storage' and 'Dry storage'. In wet storage, flowers are stored with their bases dipped in water or preservative solution for a short time. Dry storage methods are used for long term storage.

In this method, fresh flowers are harvested in the morning, graded and sealed in plastic bags or boxes to prevent the loss of moisture. In Controlled Atmosphere (CA) storage, cut flowers are kept in gas tight cool chambers equipped with cooling systems at a higher level of CO_2 and lower level of O_2 to reduce the respiration rate and production and action of ethylene. Generally, the concentration of CO_2 should be maintained higher than 4% and not below 0.4% in CA storage.

Storage of Orchid Cut Flowers

Name of Orchid	Storage Temperature	Storage Period
Oncidium, Phalaenopsis, Odontoglossum, Cattleya	7-10°C	2 weeks
Dendrobium	5-7°C	10-14 days
Cymbidium	1-4°C	14 days
Paphiopedilum	-0.5-3.0°C	20 days
Arachnis, Aranda, Aranthera, Ascocenda, Epidendrum	8-13°C	10-14 days

Transport

Being short lived and perishable in nature, flowers should be delivered to destination as early as possible immediately after harvest. For long distance markets, cut flowers are transported by cargo planes, merchant ships and trucks. Other modes of transportation are head loads, bicycles, two-three wheelers, cars, vans etc. Hence, for long distance transportation, advanced methods of post-harvest handling like cooling, conditioning, impregnation, pulsing, bud opening and packaging are followed. Orchids are supplied with water for long distance transportation. The base of the flower stem is placed in a vial or rubber balloon filled with water or wrapped in wet tissue.

The best method of transport of most of the cut flowers is under refrigeration from the grower to final consumers.

Conclusion

This case-study introduces is to the beautiful world of orchids. It tells us about its scientific classification, ideal condition for its growth, its uses and important orchid growing areas of the World and India.

The above case-study also helps us to reach to the conclusion that orchid cultivation is of immense importance for the states of Sikkim and Meghalaya. Orchids enhance the tourism industry of the state and help it to earn foreign exchange also. Also, this case-study helps us to become aware of the marketing process of orchids and its channels of distribution.

This case-study also helps us to have an assessment of the price of orchid plant and that of a cut-flower. It also gives us an insight about various marketing costs.

This case study also makes us aware of the post-harvest management of orchid, and various techniques which help to increase the shelf-life of orchids.

Viva Voce Questions

1. *Why have you chosen this project?*

Ans. Orchids have always been my favourite flower. I found this project as an opportunity to find out more about this beautiful and exotic flower.

2. *How many species of orchids are found in the World?*

Ans. There are about 24,000 species of orchids found in the World.

3. *Which feature of the orchid flower makes it suitable for decorations in weddings and social events?*

Ans. Orchid flowers have a longer lasting shelf life, which makes it suitable for decorations in weddings and social events.

4. *If you are baking a cake, then which orchid can you use for flavouring?*

Ans. Vanilla

5. *Name any two orchid growing countries of the World.*

Ans. Netherlands and Mexico.

6. *Why are Sikkim and Meghalaya important orchid growing states in India?*

Ans. Sikkim and Meghalaya are important orchid growing states because of their tropical and humid climate and ideal soil composition.

7. *State any two techniques of post harvest management of orchids.*

Ans. Pre-cooling and conditioning are two techniques related to post harvest management of orchids.

SUGGESTED PROJECTS

As per CBSE guidelines, the students can prepare a project-report on any of the following topics

I. Project One : Field Visit

The objective of introducing this project among the students is to give a first hand experience to them regarding the difference types of business units operating in their surroundings, to observe their features and activities and relate them to the theoretical knowledge given in their text books. The students should select a place of field visit form the following : (Add more as per local area availability.)

1. Visit to a Handicraft unit.
2. Visit to an Industry.
3. Visit to a wholesale market. (vegetables, fruits, flowers, grains, garments, etc.)
4. Visit to a Departmental store.
5. Visit to a Mall.

II. Project Two : Case Study on a Product

Take a product having seasonal growth and regular demand with which students can relate. For example,

1. Apples form Himachal Pradesh, Kashmir.
2. Oranges from Nagpur.
3. Mangoes form Maharashtra/ U.P./Bihar/Andhra Pradesh etc.
4. Strawberries from Panchgani.

III. Project Three : Aids to Trade

The student can prepare a project on various aids to trade which are stated below

1. Transport
2. Communication
3. Advertising
4. Insurance
5. Warehousing

IV. Project Four : Import/Export Procedure

Student can prepare a detailed project report on either import procedure or export procedure.

V. Project Five : A visit to any State Emporium

Student can visit a state emporium and prepare a project report on the visit. It should however, be kept in mind that the state emporium should be other than your school state.

SAMPLE QUESTION PAPER 1

A Highly Simulated Sample Question Paper for CBSE Class XI Examination

BUSINESS STUDIES

Time : 3 Hours **Max. Marks : 80**

General Instructions

1. This question paper contains 34 questions. All questions are compulsory.
2. Marks are indicated against each question.
3. Answer should be brief and to the point.
4. Answer to questions carrying 3 marks may have about 50 to 75 words.
5. Answer to questions carrying 4 marks may have about 150 words.
6. Answer to questions carrying 6 marks may have about 200 words.

1. Submission of tender quotations online is known as ………. . (1)

(a) e-promotion (b) e-delivery
(c) e-trading (d) e-bidding

2. If compared to e-business transaction risks in a traditional business are (1)

(a) higher
(b) lower
(c) transaction risks are same in both
(d) no risk at all

3. "Business 2 Customer (B2C) commerce includes a variety of activities and transactions." Which of the following is not a part of B2C commerce activities? (1)

(a) Online selling
(b) Online advertising
(c) Customer to business interaction
(d) Customer to customer interaction

4. Which of the following statements is incorrect regarding inter-corporate deposits? (1)

(a) Call deposits can be withdrawn by the lending company with a one-day notice and usually carry an interest rate of around 10% per annum.
(b) Three-month deposits are made for a period of three months and the interest rate on these deposits is around 15% per annum.
(c) Six-month deposits are only given to companies with a high credit rating and the interest rate is approximately 15% per annum.
(d) Inter-corporate deposits serve as a short-term financing option between companies.

5. Identify the three stages in the formation of a company as per the correct sequence. (1)

(a) Incorporation, promotion, subscription of a company
(b) Promotion, subscription of a company, incorporation
(c) Subscription of a company, promotion, incorporation
(d) Promotion, incorporation, subscription of a company

6. International trade offers many benefits to the nation, one such benefit is that it provides a way out to intense competition in domestic market, which implies (1)

(a) winding-up internal business
(b) doing international business
(c) doing technological upgradation
(d) promotion of goods and services

7. **Statement I** Small industries are more labour intensive and less capital intensive.

Statement II MSMEs are the second largest employer of human resources after agriculture. (1)

Alternatives

(a) Statement I is correct and Statement II incorrect
(b) Statement II is correct and Statement I is incorrect
(c) Both the statements are correct
(d) Both the statements are incorrect

8. Choose the correct statement from the following (1)

(a) Intellectual Property (IP) includes only industrial property such as patents and trademarks.
(b) Copyright protects inventions, industrial designs and geographical indications.
(c) TRIPS agreement led to the establishment of WTO for intellectual property rights protection.

(d) Intellectual Property Rights (IPR) in India are governed by laws in compliance with international obligations under TRIPS.

9. Nitin a small businessman deals in buying and selling different fast moving consumer goods. The scope of business is limited to his local market. He purchased different types of goods from the wholesaler each weekend located at the State capital.
Identify the type of trade followed by the businessman referred in the above case. (1)

(a) Wholesale trade (b) Retail trade
(c) International trade (d) Entrepot trade

10. "International trade is settled by use of foreign exchange." Who earns foreign exchange during the course of international trade? (1)

(a) Importing countries (b) Exporting country
(c) World trade organisation
(d) All of the above

11. Rohan a grocery shop owner suffered a lot of damages due to cyclonic effect. Government declared a relief package to the affected people of the affected areas.
Identify the type of risk caused to the shopkeepers highlighted in the above case. (1)

(a) Natural cause (b) Human cause
(c) Economic cause (d) None of these

12. **Assertion** (A) Business must procure supplies from large enterprises.

Reason (R) Business is also a part of system. It makes use of resources of society. (1)

Alternatives

(a) Both Assertion (A) and Reason (R) are true and Reason (R) is the correct explanation of Assertion (A)
(b) Both Assertion (A) and Reason (R) are true, but Reason (R) is not the correct explanation of Assertion (A)
(c) Assertion (A) is true, but Reason (R) is false
(d) Assertion (A) is false, but Reason (R) is true

13. Match the following (1)

Column I	Column II
A. Shipping order	(i) Excise commission
B. Inspection certificate	(ii) Captain of the ship
C. Railway receipt	(iii) EIA
D. Excise clearance	(iv) Railway authorities

Codes

	A	B	C	D		A	B	C	D
(a)	(i)	(ii)	(iii)	(iv)	(b)	(iv)	(iii)	(ii)	(i)
(c)	(iii)	(ii)	(i)	(iv)	(d)	(ii)	(i)	(iv)	(iii)

14. "International trade requires movement of goods across the boundaries of a nation." Which of the following is the cheapest mode of transporting goods to longer distances? (1)

(a) Road (b) Rail
(c) Ships (d) Air

15. Aman Woollen Ltd. a leading woollen items manufacturing company established 20 years ago by Aman, is well-known for its quality goods and consumers have high brand loyalty for its products especially shawls.

The company was doing very well but due to riots, terrorism, unrest in the area for past 10 years, their sales are consistently slashing down.

To solve this problem, the marketing manager of the company suggested to explore the possibility of going international and to appoint wholesalers country wide. The financial manager supported his suggestion and informed that government is also providing subsidies and technical and marketing support to such export-oriented industries as international trade offers many benefits to the nation.

Which of the following is not the benefit of foreign trade to a nation? (1)

(a) Economic growth
(b) Earning of forest
(c) Higher profits
(d) Price stability

16. "Every source of finance has some costs associated with them." Which is the costliest source of finance from the company's point of view? (1)

(a) Equity share capital
(b) Preference share capital
(c) Debentures
(d) Inter-corporate deposits

17. **Statement I** A company can commence business after incorporation.
Statement II It is necessary to get every company incorporated, whether private and public. (1)

Alternatives

(a) Statement I is correct and Statement II incorrect
(b) Statement II is correct and Statement I is incorrect
(c) Both the statements are correct
(d) Both the statements are incorrect

18. **Assertion** (A) In partnership firm, the liability of every partner is limited, joint and several.
Reason (R) Partnership agreement may be oral or written. (1)

Alternatives

(a) Both Assertion (A) and Reason (R) are true and Reason (R) is the correct explanation of Assertion (A)

(b) Both Assertion (A) and Reason (R) are true, but Reason (R) is not the correct explanation of Assertion (A)

(c) Assertion (A) is true, but Reason (R) is false

(d) Assertion (A) is false, but Reason (R) is true

19. Poonam and Radha are manufacturing leather belts and wallets. Both of them share profits and losses in the ratio of 3 : 2. Poonam has invested a capital of ₹ 10 lakh, while Radha has invested ₹ 7 lakh in the business.

Identify the form of business organisation in which both of them have promoted their business. (1)

(a) Sole proprietorship

(b) Partnership

(c) Hindu undivided family

(d) None of the above

20. With the help of picture given below, identify the form of public sector enterprises which are set-up under a Special Act of Parliament. (1)

(a) Statutory corporation

(b) Departmental undertaking

(c) Government corporation

(d) None of the above

21. Pinkmate Limited is a company engaged in the production of cosmetics, specially targeting the young girls. The company conducts all its transactions through bank accounts.

Which account is suitable according to you, for Pinkmate Limited? Also give any two features of such an account. (3)

Or Distinguish between public company and private company.

22. Olx.com is an e-commerce website that provides a platform to its users to buy and sell second hand items. Identify and explain the type of e-business transaction facilitated by Olx.com. (3)

23. According to Henry Fayol, "The purpose of business is not only earning profit but also discharging responsibilities towards society." In context to the above statement, explain any two social responsibilities of a business. (3)

Or What do you understand by social responsibility of business? How is it different from legal responsibility?

24. Rohit is a safe investor and for this reason he prefers to invest in debentures issued by companies. Recently, he purchased debentures issued by Safe Locks Limited.

The terms of issue of debentures revealed that they created a charge on the assets of the company. Also, Rohit's name was entered in the register of debenture-holders maintained by the company.

(i) Identify the type of debentures issued by Safe Lock Limited.

(ii) Explain the type of debentures identified in point (i). (3)

25. Explain briefly the concept of mail order business. (4)

26. Describe briefly the history of commerce in India. (4)

27. Explain briefly the nature of small business in India. (4)

28. (i) 'Easy Day', 'Vishal Mega Mart' and 'Big Bazaar' are examples of which type of fixed shops?

(ii) Give any two merits and one demerit of the type identified. (4)

Or

Zumbara is a small African country. Although endowed with a lot of natural resources, there are quite a few industries in the country. Also, the government of the country has a very rigid trade policy due to which the people of Zumbara finds it very difficult to import goods from other countries. Because of this policy of the government, the people of the country face scarcity of many goods in their daily life and this has led to unrest in the country.

As an advisor to the government, how will you convince the Zumbara government to encourage international trade?

29. Ashutosh is working as sales executive in ABC Limited company. His job is to enhance the sale of the company. He is getting a fixed salary of ₹ 40,000 per month plus commission as a fixed percentage of sales.

(i) Identify which type of economic activity is highlighted in the case.

(ii) State some of the characteristics of economic activity identified in point (i). (4)

30. Describe various types of digital payments. (4)

Or Why is e-business referred to as the emerging mode of business? Discuss the factors responsible for growing importance of this trend.

31. Executions Limited is a leading company of India and is engaged in the business of event management. The board of directors of the company has recently got a proposal to manage the Miss World pageant. They are extremely excited about the proposal and have come to realise the importance of the global market.

They now plan to target it and have decided to raise the funds for the same through issue of debentures.

(i) Define the term debentures and explain any two features of debentures.

(ii) State any three points of difference between shares and debentures. (6)

Or

What is GST? Explain its key features.

32. Why does business need multiple objectives? Explain any five such objectives. (6)

Or

Distinguish between e-business and traditional business.

33. Describe the various types of insurance and examine the nature of risks protected by each type of insurance. (6)

34. Priya runs a small handicrafts business and wants to expand her market reach. She learns about a scheme that helps small businesses understand the importance of maintaining a good financial record to secure better credit ratings. To promote her products, she participates in both domestic and international exhibitions where she showcases her handicrafts to potential buyers.

Additionally, she attends a buyer-seller meet organised by a government body, where bulk buyers and large institutions are invited. Through these initiatives, she also gains insights into various government programmes supporting small businesses. Encouraged by the benefits, she utilises display centres and hoardings to effectively market her products.

Quoting lines from the case, identify and explain three schemes and support programmes launched by NSIC. (6)

Answers

1. (d)	2. (b)	3. (d)	4. (b)	5. (d)	6. (b)	7. (c)
8. (d)	9. (b)	10. (b)	11. (a)	12. (b)	13. (d)	14. (c)
15. (d)	16. (a)	17. (a)	18. (d)	19. (b)	20. (c)	

SAMPLE QUESTION PAPER 2

A Highly Simulated Sample Question Paper for CBSE Class XI Examination

BUSINESS STUDIES

Time : 3 Hours **Max. Marks : 80**

General Instructions

1. This question paper contains 34 questions. All questions are compulsory.
2. Marks are indicated against each question.
3. Answer should be brief and to the point.
4. Answer to questions carrying 3 marks may have about 50 to 75 words.
5. Answer to questions carrying 4 marks may have about 150 words.
6. Answer to questions carrying 6 marks may have about 200 words.

1. Which of the following level of management is required to follow ethics in a business enterprise? (1)

(a) Top level management
(b) Middle level management
(c) Bottom level management
(d) All of the above

2. **Assertion** (A) With the use of latest methodologies of production, the business remains in the good books of government.

Reason (R) Latest methodologies lead government to boast about its achievements. (1)

Alternatives

(a) Both Assertion (A) and Reason (R) are true and Reason (R) is the correct explanation of Assertion (A)
(b) Both Assertion (A) and Reason (R) are true, but Reason (R) is not the correct explanation of Assertion (A)
(c) Assertion (A) is true, but Reason (R) is false
(d) Assertion (A) is false, but Reason (R) is true

3. **Assertion** (A) Business represents exchange of goods and services.

Reason (R) Risk and uncertainties are always there with any form of business. (1)

Alternatives

(a) Both Assertion (A) and Reason (R) are true and Reason (R) is the correct explanation of Assertion (A)
(b) Both Assertion (A) and Reason (R) are true, but Reason (R) is not the correct explanation of Assertion (A)
(c) Assertion (A) is true, but Reason (R) is false
(d) Assertion (A) is false, but Reason (R) is true

4. Which of the following goods are exempted from GST? (1)

(i) Vegetables (ii) Fruits
(iii) Fire wood

Codes

(a) Both I and II (b) I, II and III
(c) Both II and III (d) Both I and III

5. **Statement I** Wholesalers purchase in bulk quantity and sell in small lots to the retailers.

Statement II The wholesalers perform several marketing functions. They provide considerable support to the consumers. (1)

Alternatives

(a) Statement I is correct and Statement II incorrect
(b) Statement II is correct and Statement I is incorrect
(c) Both the statements are correct
(d) Both the statements are incorrect

6. In the process of distribution of goods, retailers are at the (1)

(a) final stage
(b) intermediate stage
(c) initial stage
(d) None of the above

7. Which of the following is a part of trading profits that are not distributed in the form of dividend? (1)

(a) Share warrants
(b) Equity
(c) Retained earnings
(d) Provisions

8. "Inter-corporate deposits that are to be repaid at one day notice" are called **(1)**

(a) put-deposits
(b) call deposits
(c) commerical deposits
(d) bills of exchange

9. .... refers to legal rights granted with the aim to protect the creation of the intellect. **(1)**

(a) Intellectual capital rights
(b) Intellectual business rights
(c) Intellectual property rights
(d) Intellectual official rights

10. Intellectual property rights are used to protect **(1)**

(a) brand name (b) technology process
(c) design (d) All of these

11. A, B, C and D are partners in a partnership firm. A and B take active part in the management of the firm whereas C has contributed in capital but do not participate in management. D is a nominal partner. All four make partnership for a specified time period. Partnership between them is governed by a written agreement between them but the firm is still not registered.

Which kind of partnership is there between the partners in the case described above? **(1)**

(a) General partnership (b) Public partnership
(c) Limited partnership (d) None of these

12. With the help of picture given below, identify the document which is issued by commanding officer of the ship to the exporter after the cargo is loaded on the ship. **(1)**

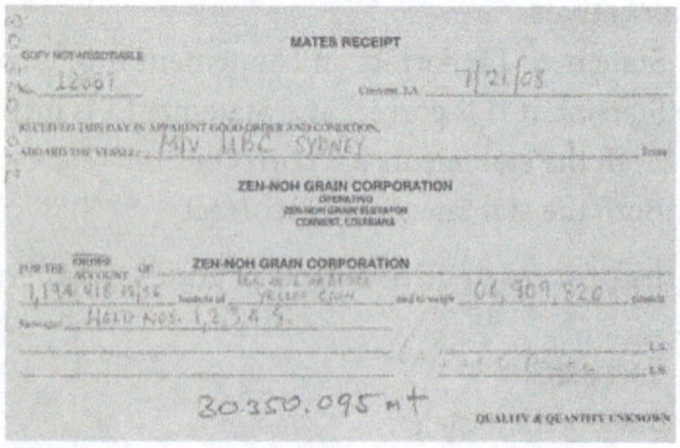

(a) Certificate of origin (b) Mate's receipt
(c) Letter of credit (d) None of these

13. **Statement I** LPG policy initiated by government in 1991 increased the benefits for small business enterprise.

Statement II National Small Industries Corporation has been accorded a Mini-ratna status by Government of India. **(1)**

Alternatives

(a) Statement I is correct and Statement II incorrect
(b) Statement II is correct and Statement I is incorrect
(c) Both the statements are correct
(d) Both the statements are incorrect

14. Paras started a manufacturing unit of electrical accessories. He is facing severe shortage of adequate finance to carry out the business activities. His manufacturing unit is also suffering from shortage of required inputs and he is unable to buy inputs in bulk due to lack of shortage facilities. Paras wants his product to be world class quality, but he is unable to hire professional experts due to shortage of funds. His manufacturing unit is operating below the full capacity level due to shortage of demand.

Identify the problems of small-scale business faced by Paras in his business by quoting lines from the given case. **(1)**

(a) Shortage of finance, raw material, managerial skills and idle capacity
(b) Shortage of finance, suppliers, managerial skills and idle capacity
(c) Shortage of finance, raw material, technical skills and idle capacity
(d) None of the above

15. Which of the following statement about SSIs are true? **(1)**

(a) It is generally owned by single entrepreneur or partnership
(b) There is a pre-dominance of labour
(c) The operations of a unit are localised
(d) All of the above

16. Which of the following communities managed the business in Northern reigon? **(1)**

(a) Chattis (b) Bhats
(c) Mahajans (d) Punjabi and Multani

17. Match the following **(1)**

Column I	Column II
A. Promotion of a company	(i) Article of Association
B. Issue of prospectus	(ii) Promotor
C. Compulsory document	(iii) Memorandum of Association
D. Secondary document	(iv) Public company

Codes

	A	B	C	D		A	B	C	D
(a)	(i)	(ii)	(iii)	(iv)	(b)	(iv)	(iii)	(ii)	(i)
(c)	(ii)	(iv)	(iii)	(i)	(d)	(iii)	(ii)	(i)	(iv)

18. Mahesh is a student pursuing B.Tech from IIT Mumbai. His father a general store owner in Jaipur had a heart attack and became completely paralysed. There was no other source of income for his family, so, Manish left his studies and decided to take charge of his father's general store.

While checking the books of accounts, he found that his father had taken a loan of ₹ 2 lakh from Bank of Baroda to be repaid this year only, but the business is running into losses due to his father's illness. His mother advised him to close the business and to look for a job outside.

The form of business organisation formed by his father is (1)

(a) joint stock company (b) partnership
(c) sole proprietorship (d) cooperative society

19. Neha has a property. She gets an insurance policy for ₹ 8 lakh from R & Co. and ₹ 4 lakh from S & Co. for her property. Because of fire, property is destroyed to the extent of ₹ 3 lakh. Neha cannot claim ₹ 3 lakh from R & Co. and ₹ 3 lakh from S & Co. as she cannot make profit by making full claim from both the companies. She can claim a total sum of ₹ 3 lakh from either of the companies or from both companies to the extent of their proportionate share. In case, she claim full loss amount of ₹ 3 lakh from R & Co. then S & Co. will pay its proportionate share to R & Co.

Which principle of insurance has been highlighted in the above case? (1)

(a) Principle of subrogation
(b) Principle of mitigation
(c) Principle of indemnity
(d) Principle of contribution

20. Sanjay wants to import machinery from Japan for manufacturing of automated cars. Identify the initial four stages in order to perform import machinery as per the correct sequence. (1)

(a) Obtaining registration-cum-membership certificate, opening a letter of credit, arrival of goods, obtaining I.E.C No.
(b) Opening a letter of credit, arrival of goods, obtaining I.E.C No., obtaining registration-cum-membership certificate
(c) Opening a letter of credit, obtaining registration-cum-membership certificate, arrival of goods, obtaining I.E.C No.
(d) Obtaining I.E.C No., obtaining registration-cum-membership certificate, opening a letter of credit, arrival of goods

21. Write three functions of indigenous banking. (3)

Or Kunal has opened a retail jewellery store. Since the cost of inventory is very high, therefore his financial advisor has adviced him to take a comprehensive insurance policy covering loss to property and stock. Kunal, however, is not convinced. Try to convince Kunal by stating advantages of insurance for a business.

22. Explain the main features of GST. (3)

23. Distinguish between preference shares and equity shares. (3)

Or Discuss the merits and demerits of preference shares as a source of finance.

24. Charu holds exhibitions of high-end imported goods. Her exhibitions are quite successful and popular among the elite class in Delhi. Recently, owing to ill health, she has been forced to take leave from her business.

Her daughter Kamakshi, who is studying fashion technology, has been forced to look after the business. Being new to the business, she is not aware how to get the goods cleared from the customs.

(i) Explain to Charu briefly the process of customs clearance of export goods.
(ii) State any objective of export trade. (3)

25. What is letter of credit? Why does an exporter need this document? (4)

26. Manmohan was the eldest son in his family. There were three younger brothers Jagdish, Subhash and Ramesh. Their father Mr. Kundan Lal Bhalla ran a successful jewellery shop and all the sons participated in the business in varying capacity. Manmohan and Jagdish looked after the sales aspect and Subhash and Ramesh were concerned with the production aspect. The business was flourishing under the guidance of Mr. Kundan Lal.

But, Mr. Kundan Lal met with a tragic accident and died. After his death, the sons decided to convert their business into joint hindu family business and Manmohan, being the eldest male member, became the Karta of the family. Explain the role of Karta in joint hindu family business to Manmohan. (4)

Or "Multinational Companies (MNCs) have great impact on international economy. A study has revealed that top 200 MNCs control over a quarter of the world economy." In the light of the above statement, explain the features of MNCs.

27. Jagdish runs a real estate brokerage firm. He believes that the only objective of business is to earn profits. To accomplish the above objective, he often defrauds his customers. Some of the common business practices followed by him include selling the same plot to more than one person, quoting exhorbitant prices for plots of land to increase his commission, selling land on the basis of fake papers, etc. All these practices, though profitable in the short-run, has now started to back fire. Jagdish is facing a number of litigations and his profits are also falling.

(i) Identify and state the concept which is violated by Jagdish in the case.

(ii) Advise Jagdish, why being socially responsible is important for a business by giving any three reasons. (4)

28. Why is there a need of entrepreneurship development in India? (4)

29. Subodh belongs to a middle class family. In order to increase his family income, he wants to start a provision store. As per your judgement, which form of organisation, would be best suited for him and why? (4)

Or You would like to start a business either as a partnership firm or a cooperative society but you are in a state of dilemma and would not be able to choose between them. Then in this case, what will you do?

30. Komalika wants to start her own business dealing in high-end crockery items. She decides to arrange for initial finance from her savings.

However, her savings are not enough to fulfil all the initial needs of the business. She seeks help of her husband, who works in government sector.

He advises her to start her business with limited finance and then use the revenues earned by the business to fulfil other financial requirements.

(i) Komalika's husband advocates the use of which source of finance?

(ii) Briefly explain any three merits of the source identified in (i) above. (4)

31. Briefly discuss limitations of multiple shops. (6)

Or What is WTO? State objectives of WTO in promoting international trade.

32. Arjun, Rohit and Karan started a business together without specifying any duration for their partnership. After a few years, Karan decided to exit and gave notice to dissolve the firm. Meanwhile, Neha and Pooja formed a partnership for a period of five years to run an event management company.

In another case, Vikram and Anil started a construction firm where both had unlimited liability and were actively managing the business.

On the other hand, Sanya joined a partnership firm but was not involved in decision-making as she had limited liability, while her partner bore unlimited liability.

Quoting lines from the case, identify and explain the various forms of partnership. (6)

33. Explain four modes of digital payments available to a consumer in India. (6)

34. Neelam is the owner of readymade garment factory. Her main motive is to earn maximum profits. For this, she has started to charge hefty price from her customers supplying them low quality products. She has also drastically falled in providing good working conditions to workers and pay them only minimum amount of wages.

She is completely ignorant about the amount of pollution her factory is generating. Due to all such reasons, the efficient workers of her factory are now leaving the job and joining the competition's business. The government has also put heavy penalty and customer's loyalty is completely missing.

(i) Which concept is lacking in Neelam's company?

(ii) How can the business gain back its position?

(iii) Explain the concept business ethics. (6)

Or Write a short note on role of business in environment protection.

Answers

1. (d)	2. (c)	3. (b)	4. (b)	5. (a)	6. (a)	7. (c)
8. (b)	9. (c)	10. (d)	11. (a)	12. (b)	13. (c)	14. (c)
15. (d)	16. (d)	17. (c)	18. (c)	19. (d)	20. (d)	

SAMPLE QUESTION PAPER 3

A Highly Simulated Sample Question Paper for CBSE Class XI Examination

BUSINESS STUDIES

Time : 3 Hours **Max. Marks : 80**

General Instructions

1. This question paper contains 34 questions. All questions are compulsory.
2. Marks are indicated against each question.
3. Answer should be brief and to the point.
4. Answer to questions carrying 3 marks may have about 50 to 75 words.
5. Answer to questions carrying 4 marks may have about 150 words.
6. Answer to questions carrying 6 marks may have about 200 words.

1. Which country is not a part of Indian sub-continent? **(1)**

(a) China (b) Bhutan
(c) Bangladesh (d) Nepal

2. Assertion (A) Earning livelihood is the main aim of economic activities.

Reason (R) It helps people in earning their bread and butter by performing several activities. **(1)**

Alternatives

(a) Both Assertion (A) and Reason (R) are true and Reason (R) is the correct explanation of Assertion (A)
(b) Both Assertion (A) and Reason (R) are true, but Reason (R) is not the correct explanation of Assertion (A)
(c) Assertion (A) is true, but Reason (R) is false
(d) Assertion (A) is false, but Reason (R) is true

3. The Karta of a HUF has absolute power related to all aspects of the business. This makes decision-making process faster and easier. However, this may also adversely affect the business because of **(1)**

(a) limited managerial skills of Karta
(b) limited resources of the business
(c) increased loyalty and business
(d) None of the above

4. Statutory corporations are financed by borrowings from government or by public and revenue generated by it. Therefore, it can be said that they are financially **(1)**

(a) dependent on State Government
(b) dependent on Central Government
(c) independent (d) None of the above

5. Which is the regulatory body for insurance sector in India? **(1)**

(a) IRBI (b) IIBI
(c) IRDA (d) RBI

6. A socially responsible business organisation needs to …… in order to fulfil its responsibility towards the society. **(1)**

(a) use cost effective techniques of production
(b) burn its waste products
(c) dispose of toxic chemicals in the sewerage
(d) use pollution control equipments

7. Public deposits are preferred by companies for a period upto 3 years. They are beneficial for depositors because **(1)**

(a) they are secured as they create a charge on companies' assets.
(b) depositors get a voting right in the company.
(c) depositors get a share in the profits of the company.
(d) depositors receive interest at a rate higher than the rate offered by banks.

8. Which institute provides credit guarantee fund for start-ups to banks and other lenders? **(1)**

(a) SEBI (b) RBI
(c) IMF (d) NCGTC

9. When start-ups need fund in initial stage, strength of IPRs of enterprise attract the **(1)**

(a) initial customers
(b) initial suppliers
(c) initial investors
(d) initial competitors

10. Which of the following statements is incorrect regarding small-scale industries? (1)

(a) Small-scale industries are generally owned by a single entrepreneur or a partnership.

(b) These industries have a complex managerial structure with multiple hierarchical levels.

(c) Small-scale industries primarily use labour-intensive techniques rather than mechanised production methods.

(d) Owners of small-scale industries can directly manage operations, ensuring flexibility and secrecy.

11. **Statement I** E-business is broader in scope than e-commerce.

Statement II E-commerce is a part of e-business. (1)

Alternatives

(a) Statement I is correct and Statement II incorrect

(b) Statement II is correct and Statement I is incorrect

(c) Both the statements are correct

(d) Both the statements are incorrect

12. Match the following (1)

Column I		Column II	
A.	Payment of taxes on time	(i)	Responsibility towards shareholders
B.	Providing good quality products	(ii)	Responsibility towards government
C.	Providing adequate return on investment	(iii)	Responsibility towards society
D.	Environmental protection	(iv)	Responsibility towards consumers

Codes

	A	B	C	D		A	B	C	D
(a)	(i)	(ii)	(iii)	(iv)	(b)	(iv)	(iii)	(ii)	(i)
(c)	(iii)	(i)	(iv)	(ii)	(d)	(ii)	(iii)	(iv)	(i)

13. With the help of picture given below, identify the document which is prepared by the importer and it show the details of goods imported and is used by custom authorities to determine import duty. (1)

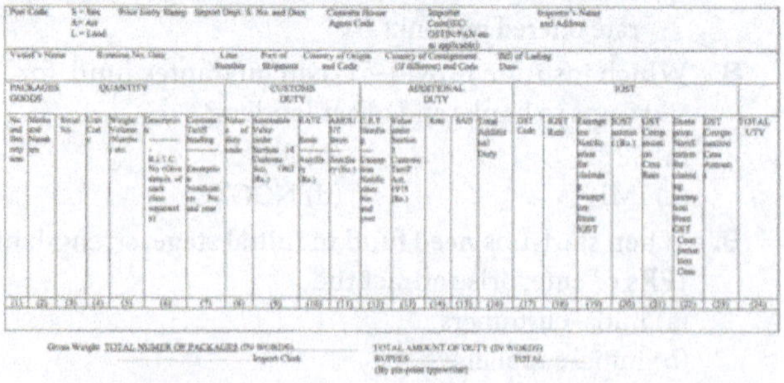

(a) Certificate of origin (b) Mate's receipt

(c) Bill of entry (d) None of these

14. Deep wants to export auto spare parts to Mr. Davidson in Paris. Mr. Davidson has asked for an enquiry to seek information about availability of goods, price, quality and terms and conditions for export of goods. In response to the enquiry, deep sends a reply in the form of Proforma Invoice. Mr. Davidson found the price and terms and conditions acceptable.

So, he placed the order for goods. After verifying the creditworthiness of Mr. Davidson, Deep obtains an export license and arranges the pre-shipment finance.

On the basis of given case study, state the next step to be followed by Pradeep related to the procedure of export trade. (1)

(a) Procurement of goods

(b) Pre-shipment inspection

(c) Excise clearance

(d) None of the above

15. **Assertion** (A) The difference in business systems and practices are much more amongst countries than within a country.

Reason (R) The degree of mobility of factors like labour and capital is generally less between countries than within a country. (1)

Alternatives

(a) Both Assertion (A) and Reason (R) are true and Reason (R) is the correct explanation of Assertion (A)

(b) Both Assertion (A) and Reason (R) are true, but Reason (R) is not the correct explanation of Assertion (A)

(c) Assertion (A) is true, but Reason (R) is false

(d) Assertion (A) is false, but Reason (R) is true

16. **Statement I** The Wildlife Protection Act was enacted in 1992.

Statement II Pollution causes danger to biological diversity. (1)

Alternatives

(a) Statement I is correct and Statement II incorrect

(b) Statement II is correct and Statement I is incorrect

(c) Both the statements are correct

(d) Both the statements are incorrect

17. Choose the correct statement from the following. (1)

(a) e-Business requires a huge investment to start operations.

(b) e-Business allows transactions to be conducted only during business hours.

(c) e-Business provides flexibility and convenience for both businesses and customers.

(d) e-Business is a slow mode of conducting transactions.

18. XYZ Ltd. is a readymade garment manufacturing company. It is selling its products on higher prices. It is not providing proper working conditions to its workers and employees. Activities of the company are causing pollution. What concept is lacking by XYZ Ltd.? (1)

(a) Concept of social responsibility
(b) Concept of ethics
(c) Both (a) and (b)
(d) None of the above

19. Mayank after completing his master's degree in management has decided to start his own enterprise with the name Mayank Food Industries in his village in Himachal Pradesh and opted for labour-intensive techniques to provide employment to local people. He took the help of DIC, government institution for promoting small-scale industries to get knowledge about incentives and schemes launched by the government for opening small-scale industries.

It was estimated that, the food and beverages plant to be set-up will require a fixed capital investment of ₹ 80 lakh. The working capital requirements is estimated to be ₹ 20 lakh. The directors of the company decided to raise the capital by issuing shares as well as taking loans from financial institutions.

Mayank has entrepreneurship skills as shown in above case. Which of the following indicates entrepreneurship? (1)

(a) Setting-up one's own business
(b) Pursuing employment
(c) Practising profession (d) All of the above

20. DIC stands for which of the following? (1)

(a) District Industrial Centre
(b) Development and Industrial Corporation
(c) Department of Infrastructure and Capital formation
(d) None of the above

21. "Profit plays an important role in the business." Give any three reasons to justify the statement. (3)

Or Why road transport is an important mode of transport in India?

22. (i) When was national renewal fund was established?
(ii) Why was national renewal fund established? (3)

23. Explain the main principles of insurance. (3)

Or "Economic activities are undertaken for earning a living." Do you agree? If yes, give reasons in support of your answer?

24. State the features of cottage industries. (3)

25. How does the wholesaler help the manufacturer in availing the economies of scale? (4)

26. Divij and Adhiraj are twin brothers. After completing their MBA from Symbiosis, Pune, they decided to start their own business, which will work as an ancillary unit of TATA motors. They decided to start their factory on a piece of land which is owned by their father.

Now, they are confused whether to start their business as a joint hindu family business or a partnership business. As an expert, enumerate the differences between these two forms of business organisations. (4)

Or Being a consumer, list certain responsibilities that you will expect from a businessman.

27. Which were the trading communities that existed in India during medieval period? (4)

28. Briefly explain any four characteristics of international trade. (4)

29. Mr. Krishan Lal Batra has retired from a government job and is now a pensioner. He is quite worried about his son Satpal Batra, who is not able to find a suitable job. Even if he finds a job, he is not able to hold on to it. Mr. Batra's nephew, Dinesh runs a successful business.

He advises his uncle to open a sole proprietorship firm for Satpal.

(i) Define sole proprietorship.
(ii) Explain briefly any three features of sole proprietorship. (4)

Or In the back drop of demonetisation, the importance of e-banking has increased tremendously. Explain briefly the services covered by e-banking.

30. Mr. Chandra Shekhar Bose has just retired from a government job. He wants to invest the money that he has received on account of provident fund and gratuity in the primary capital market by purchasing equity shares and preference shares.

But being new to the corporate world, he is not aware of the differences between the two and their benefits and limitations.

(i) Explain to him the meaning of equity shares.
(ii) Explain to him the meaning of preference shares and state one benefit and one limitation of the same. (4)

31. Differentiate between departmental stores and chain stores. (6)

Or What are the reasons for growing popularity of international trade in the modern times?

32. Rohit sells his playstation to his friend for ₹ 3,500. Is it a business activity? Explain any five characteristics of business. (6)

Or Distinguish between public company and private company.

33. Amit, a college student, prefers buying snacks and stationery from the nearby retail shop rather than going to a big supermarket. The shop owner ensures that essential products like chips, notebooks and pens are always available, allowing Amit to purchase them whenever required.

He also notices that new varieties of chocolates and beverages are displayed at the counter with details about their flavours and price.

Additionally, Amit finds it convenient to shop from this store as it is located near his hostel and remains open late at night. Quoting lines from the case, identify and explain the three services of retailers that are provided to customers. (6)

34. 'Fun Riders Automobile Company' is planning expansion after completing five successful years of operation. For funding their expansion plans, they have decided to approach commercial banks.

(i) Discuss the concept of commercial banks.

(ii) Give any two merits of availing finance from commercial banks.

(iii) Give any three limitations of availing finance from commercial banks. (6)

Answers

1. (a)	2. (a)	3. (a)	4. (c)	5. (c)	6. (d)	7. (d)
8. (d)	9. (c)	10. (b)	11. (d)	12. (c)	13. (c)	14. (a)
15. (b)	16. (d)	17. (c)	18. (c)	19. (a)	20. (a)	